S0-DTA-207

Special Edition

USING
Turbo C++ 4.5
for Windows

Written by

Edward B. Toupin

Mark Andrews

Bruce Copeland

Chris Corry

Mark Finlay

David Gunter

Oliver Lawrence

David Medinets

Sal Sanfilippo

Jack Tackett Jr.

K. Mitchell Thompson

Eric Uber

Clayton Walnum

Blake Watson

Charles Wood

que

Special Edition Using Turbo C++ 4.5 for Windows

Copyright© 1995 by Que® Corporation

Library of Congress Catalog Number: 95-68913

ISBN: 1-56529-837-3

98 97 96 95   6 5 4 3 2 1

Interpretation of the printing code: The rightmost double-digit number is the year of the book's printing; the rightmost single-digit number, the number of the book's printing. For example, a printing code of 95-1 shows that the first printing of the book occurred in 1995.

Screen Reproductions in this book were created by using Collage Complete from Inner Media, Inc., Hollis, New Hampshire.

Publisher: Roland Elgey

Associate Publisher: Joseph B. Wikert

Managing Editor: Sandy Doell

Director of Marketing: Lynn Zingraf

Credits

Acquisitions Editor
Lori A. Jordan

Product Directors
C. Kazim Haidri
Bryan Gambrel

Production Editor
Lori Cates

Editors
Susan Shaw Dunn
Thomas F. Hayes
Patrick Kanouse
Mike La Bonne
Susan Ross Moore
Jeff Riley
Caroline D. Roop

Technical Editors
Avram Grossman
Russell L. Jacobs
Bruce Copeland
Chris Corry
Eric Uber

Editorial Assistant
Michelle Newcomb

Acquisitions Coordinator
Angela C. Kozlowski

Cover Designer
Dan Armstrong

Production Team
Claudia Bell
Juli Cook
Amy Cornwell
Maxine Dillingham
Karen Gregor
Barry Jorden
Daryl Kessler
Bob LaRoche
Kris Simmons

Composed in *Stone Serif* and *MCPdigital* by Que Corporation

We'd Like to Hear from You!

As part of our continuing effort to produce books of the highest possible quality, Que would like to hear your comments. To stay competitive, we *really* want you, as a computer book reader and user, to let us know what you like or dislike most about this book or other Que products.

You can mail comments, ideas, or suggestions for improving future editions to the address below, or send us a fax at (317) 581-4663. For the on-line inclined, Macmillan Computer Publishing now has a forum on CompuServe (enter **GO QUEBOOKS** at any prompt) through which our staff and authors are available for questions and comments. In addition to exploring our forum, please feel free to contact me personally on CompuServe at 75230,1556 to discuss your opinions of this book.

Thanks in advance. Your comments will help us to continue publishing the best books available on computer topics in today's market.

Bryan Gambrel
Product Development Specialist
Que Corporation
201 W. 103rd Street
Indianapolis, Indiana 46290
USA

Trademarks

All terms mentioned in this book that are known to be trademarks or service marks have been appropriately capitalized. Que cannot attest to the accuracy of this information. Use of a term in this book should not be regarded as affecting the validity of any trademark or service mark.

Turbo C and Turbo C++ are registered trademarks of Borland International, Inc.

About the Authors

Degreed in mathematics, computer science, and electronics technology, **Edward B. Toupin** is an automation engineer for a Denver-based engineering firm. Edward designs and develops applications under various platforms for industrial control, expert system applications, database management, GIS, mobile satellite applications, integration solutions, and network management and communications. Some of his research is outlined in his 1993 book *Network Programming under VMS DECNet Phase IV*, published by QED/John Wiley & Sons. Edward's publications with Que include *Easy Programming with C*, *Easy Programming with Visual Basic*, *Visual Basic 4.0 Expert Solutions*, *Building OCXs*, and *Special Edition Using Turbo C++ for Windows*.

Mark Andrews is a well-known author, game designer, and computer consultant who lives in the heart of Silicon Valley and has written more than two dozen books about computers and computer programming. A former nationally syndicated electronics columnist for the New York Daily News, he has documented hardware and software products for companies including Apple, Borland, Microsoft, Hewlett-Packard, Amdahl, and many more. He has written five novels, including *Satan's Manor*, which was serialized in three weekly issues of the *National Examiner*.

Bruce Copeland is owner of CyberSym Technologies, a software development and consulting firm that specializes in scientific and engineering applications. Despite his Ph.D. in physical chemistry from Stanford University, he manages to make meaningful contributions to computational systems for real users. He has been developing software for more than 10 years in BASIC, Pascal, C, and C++. His interests include artificial intelligence, rational user interface design, and object-oriented approaches for hardware interfaces. When not driving a computer, Bruce can often be found on cross-country skis or a mountain bike in the Rocky Mountain backcountry.

Chris Corry is an OS/2 and Windows developer working in the Center for Advanced Technologies at American Management Systems of Fairfax, VA. His predominant professional interests include object-oriented programming, user interface design, and client/server technologies. He was a contributing author for *Killer Borland C++ 4*, published by Que, and *OS/2 Unleashed*, published by Sams Publishing.

Mark Finlay is president of Atlanta Innovation, Inc. His professional interests include applications of virtual reality, simulation, network communications, geographic information systems, and image processing. He has been involved in numerous projects developing real-time graphics applications for PCs, workstations, and custom embedded systems. He holds several patents for his work in the development of real-time visual systems. He is the author of *Real World Fractals* (M&T Books, 1994), *Getting Graphic* (M&T Books, 1993), and a co-author for *Photorealism and Ray Tracing in C* (M&T Books, 1992).

David Gunter holds a master of science degree in computer science and is currently working as a systems administrator at North Carolina State University. His areas of expertise include systems administration and systems programming for UNIX and VMS, TCP/IP network administration, and software development under Microsoft Windows. He lives in Cary, NC with his wonderfully supportive wife, Lola. Dave can be reached on the Internet at gunter@stat.ncsu.edu or on CompuServe at 73237,2551.

Oliver Lawrence is a systems programmer with more than 20 years of coding experience using many software development environments on hardware platforms ranging from mainframe to personal computers. His design experience includes working with compilers, decompilers, debuggers, and integrated systems. Oliver specializes in remote processing, diagnostics, and software automation solutions. He has developed applications in Borland's original Turbo Pascal and the original Turbo C, and is still a regular user of subsequent releases of these products, developing tools and applications.

David Medinets has been programming since 1980, when he started with a Radio Shack Model 1. He still fondly remembers the days when he could cross-wire the keyboard to create funny-looking characters on the display. Since those days, he has spent time debugging Emacs on UNIX machines, working on VAXen, and messing about with DOS microcomputers.

Sal Sanfilippo has over seven years of experience in the software industry. He has been programming Windows applications in C and C++ for three years and database applications for seven years. Most recently he has worked on the Borland C++/Turbo C++ 4.5 and dBASE 5 for Windows development teams. He has authored several shareware utilities for Windows. Sal also has expertise in the development of specialized technical training.

Jack Tackett Jr. is a systems analyst for the Duke University Medical Center in the Department of Pathology Informatics. He has published several books in the field of computer science. He lives with his wife, Peggy, and their two dogs and two cats in their new home in Cary, NC. Jack welcomes e-mail responses at tackett@cybernetics.net.

K. Mitchell Thompson has enjoyed more than 10 years as a software generalist in an age of specialization. His software development projects have included real-time embedded systems, operating system internals, computer graphics and distributed applications. His current interests are high-performance, distributed multimedia applications and software engineering techniques.

Eric Uber is a technical engineer at Borland International. He is currently a member of the Delphi team and has participated in the development cycle of the product. Eric was also on the dBASE for Windows team and participated in its development process. He has developed several shareware utilities and has knowledge of C and Pascal as well as Delphi's extended language and dBASE programming. Eric has provided sample programs and various other contributions including technical reviews for various publications and technical manuals. Eric has also developed applications used by in-house staff at Borland International. Eric is highly knowledgeable in data modeling and manipulation, object-oriented theory, and Windows development.

Clayton Walnum, who has a degree in computer science, has been writing about computers for almost 15 years and has published hundreds of articles in major computer publications. He is also the author of 20 books, which cover such diverse topics as programming, computer gaming, and application programs. His most recent book is *Dungeons of Discovery: Writing Dazzling Windows Games with WinG*, also published by Que. His other titles include *Turbo C++ for Rookies* (Que), *Object-Oriented Programming with Borland C++ 4* (Que), *PC Picasso: A Child's Computer Drawing Kit* (Sams), *Powermonger: The Official Strategy Guide* (Prima), *DataMania: A Child's Computer Organizer* (Alpha Kids), *Adventures in Artificial Life* (Que), and *C-manship Complete* (Taylor Ridge Books). Clayton lives in Connecticut with his wife, Lynn, and their three children, Christopher, Justin, and Stephen.

Blake Watson is a frequent contributor to magazines such as *PC Techniques* and *VBX/OCX Developer*, and the author of *Delphi By Example* (Que) and *OS/2 Warp Programming for Dummies* (IDG). You can reach Blake at 70303,373.

Charles Wood is a senior programmer analyst at Indiana Farm Bureau Insurance. He graduated with bachelors degrees in computer science and finance from Ball State University in 1986. Along with developing software in PowerBuilder, C++, COBOL, and QuickBasic, Charles has instructed in C and C++ at Indiana Vocational Technical College. He is currently pursuing his MBA at Butler University.

Contents at a Glance

Tools and Productivity

Learning C/C++

Designing User Interfaces

Customizing Code

Tools and Techniques

Appendixes

Contents

5 Operators   95

6 Expressions and Statements   115

10 Pointers   173

11 I/O   193

12 Classes and Objects   219

13 Object-Oriented Methods 267

V Advanced Tools and Techniques   521

24 Windows Programming Basics   523

29 Single and Multiple Document Interfaces   685

30 Object Linking and Embedding   729

31 Dynamic Data Exchange   785

VI Appendixes   817

A Help for the Turbo C++ for
Windows Developer   819

B Working with EasyWin   829

C Installing a Windows Application   837

Introduction

Before diving into this book, you should have a basic understanding of what application development with Turbo C++ is all about. You probably already have a pretty good idea of what programming is; otherwise, you would not be using Turbo C++ and your curiosity would not have been piqued enough to buy this book. There is one thing that you should know, though, before delving into the world of programming with Turbo C++. Most programmers would never admit to it, but—programming is easy!

If you are new to the programming racket, don't worry. This book will not only show you what you need to know for working with Turbo C++, but it also will step you through the intricacies of programming with C and C++. For those of you who already program until the crack of dawn, this book will step you through the capabilities of the tools and libraries of Turbo C++, as well as give you a feel for quick and easy 16-bit Windows application development.

Overview of Turbo C++ for Windows

As with many of the visual environments of today, you will see that the Turbo C++ Integrated Development Environment (IDE) provides you with a simple point-and-click method of accessing available tools and resources.

The IDE and associated tools provide you with a straightforward means of creating applications with minimal work. With all of the tools within easy reach, you can develop resources, write program code, debug, compile, browse objects, and access Help without leaving the Turbo C++ environment. This approach to application development allows you to focus on the inner workings of your application instead of worrying about the outer framework and the overhead of interfacing with Windows. This gives you a fast start into the world of Windows application development.

To ease the management of projects, the Project Manager—in conjunction with the TargetExpert—allows you to create and manage huge projects without a struggle. Once your project is created, AppExpert allows you to create the framework in which the specifics of your application will reside, whereas ClassExpert allows you to refine the application to suit your specifications. AppExpert works in conjunction with Resource Workshop, ObjectWindows, and the development environment's Project Manager to provide a complete visual approach to application generation.

To create a Windows user interface, you can use Resource Workshop to visually edit dialog boxes, window controls, and other such Windows controls that tie into your application. If you encounter an error in your code, simply use the Integrated Debugger to catch the bugs that reside in your application.

ClassExpert lets you create new classes, edit and refine the implementation of classes, and navigate through the source code for existing classes in your AppExpert applications. You can use ClassExpert with Resource Workshop to associate classes with resources. ClassExpert displays virtual functions and events for existing classes, and checks the ones implemented in your application. You can use ClassExpert also to instantiate and automate classes in your AppExpert project.

To ease development even more, Turbo C++ provides you with ObjectWindows and ObjectComponents. ObjectWindows *wraps,* or hides, the intricacies of Windows resources by providing an extensive class library for use by your applications. You have access to simple management of dialog boxes, scroll bars, bitmaps, buttons, edit controls, VBXs, and more with the ObjectWindows Library (OWL).

ObjectComponents hides the complexities of OLE 2.0 from you and allows you to incorporate OLE 2.0 technology into your application by way of a simple-to-use class library. With this library, you can create applications that support linking, embedding, in-place editing, drag-and-drop operations, OLE clipboard operations, compound document management, automation servers and controllers, localization, and registration. With ObjectComponents, you have an easy upgrade path to linking and embedding for existing C++ applications, as well as a simple path to the automation of existing C++ applications, whether or not they use ObjectWindows.

Finally, you can access standard C++ class libraries such as *container* classes that manage arrays, lists, and queues. The *I/O stream* classes handle input and output through streams, whereas *persistent stream* classes manage creation and manipulation of persistent objects. *Mathematical* classes handle complex mathematical operations. *Service* classes handle date, file, string, thread, and time information. *Run-time support* classes describe the classes for exception handling and run-time type information support.

With Turbo C++, you have access to a plethora of tools that you can use to easily create complex Windows-based applications. This book takes you through the intricacies of C, C++, and Windows application development, covering the information we have just discussed. By combining your current expertise and your knowledge acquired from *Special Edition Using Turbo C++ 4.5 for Windows,* you will be able to create powerful Windows-based applications using the tools of Turbo C++.

What This Book Contains

The following list is an overview of the contents of this book:

- The **"Tools and Productivity"** section overviews the Turbo C++ Integrated Development Environment as well as incorporated tools.

- **"Learning C/C++"** gives you a detailed look at programming in C and C++ from the ground up. The section covers a conceptual view of a C/C++ program, data types, variables, constants, operators, modular application development, pointers, input and output, object-oriented concepts, and compiling and linking.

- **"Designing User Interfaces"** describes the methods of creating a user interface for Windows applications using the tools of Turbo C++.

- **"Customizing Code"** details the specifics of using the Turbo C++ Experts, as well as how to develop an application with the available tools.

- **"Advanced Tools and Techniques"** is where this book takes what you have already learned and applies it to the specifics of Windows application development. Topics covered include Windows internals, document interfaces, OLE, DDE, ObjectWindows, ObjectComponents, and input and output.

- The **Appendixes** assist you in locating additional information concerning application development. Another appendix contains information on creating Windows applications using EasyWin.

Installation and Setup of Turbo C++

Okay, you've got your copy of Turbo C++ 4.5 and you're ready to jump in and start developing cool and exciting Windows applications. There's only one problem: the Turbo C++ box is sitting in your hands, unopened and wrapped in shiny cellophane. Well, don't waste any time—install it! Turbo C++'s installation procedure is a cinch, and you'll be ready to start programming in no time.

Types of Program Targets Supported

The Turbo C++ product is geared toward the non-professional programmer. It is a product that is quick to set up and easy to use. Within the Windows 3.x environment, you can use Turbo C++ to build executable programs, dynamic link libraries (DLLs), and even Visual Basic Controls (VBXs). Table I.1 gives a more detailed breakdown of the targets supported by Turbo C++ and Borland's higher-end C++ product.

Table I.1 Operating System Targets Supported by the Turbo C++ and Borland C++ Language Products		
Target	**Turbo C++ 4.5**	**Borland C++ 4.5**
DOS programs	No	Yes
16-bit Windows 3.x programs (Win16)	Yes	Yes
32-bit Windows 3.x programs (Win32s)	No	Yes
Windows 3.x DLLs (16-bit)	Yes	Yes
16-bit Visual Basic controls (VBXs)	Yes	Yes
Windows 95 and Windows NT-compatible programs (16-bit, Win16)	Yes	Yes
Native Windows 95 programs (32-bit, Win32)	No	Yes
Windows 95 DLLs (32-bit, Win32)	No	Yes
Native Windows NT programs (32-bit, Win32)	No	Yes
Windows NT DLLs (32-bit, Win32)	No	Yes
32-bit Visual Basic controls (VBXs)	No	Yes
OLE custom controls (OCXs) (32-bit)	No	Yes

As you can see, Turbo C++ is limited in the types of program targets that it can generate. Specifically, you can build 16-bit programs designed to run under the Windows 3.x operating environment—commonly called Win16 programs. Turbo C++ does not support the generation of plain-vanilla DOS programs. It also does not support the development of 32-bit programs designed to run natively under the Windows 95 or Windows NT operating systems (commonly called Win32 programs).

> **Note**
>
> Even though you cannot use Turbo C++ to write Win32 programs, the Win16 programs you build should run fine under both Windows 95 and Windows NT. In fact, the Turbo C++ development environment itself runs fine under these operating systems.

Borland C++, on the other hand, supports a wide range of targets and compiler optimization options that are not available to users of Turbo C++. Since compiler optimizations are usually of interest only to professional programmers, this might not apply to you. If, however, you do require compiler optimizations, or find yourself needing to build targets that the preceding table indicates are not supported by Turbo C++, consider purchasing Borland C++ 4.5, which fully supports the development of DOS and Win32 programs. Although virtually all of the information in this book can be successfully applied to the Borland C++ product, you might want to move over to Que's *Special Edition Using Borland C++ 4.5* if you do start using Borland C++.

Hardware Requirements

To install and effectively use Turbo C++, your hardware must have at least the following characteristics:

- An 80386-based processor

- DOS version 4.01 or higher

- Windows 3.1 or higher, running in Enhanced mode

- A hard disk with 65M of free disk space

- A 3.5-inch, high-density floppy disk drive or CD-ROM drive

- At least 4M of extended memory

- A Windows-compatible mouse

At least, that's the official word from Borland; however, this list does not tell the whole story. Some of these items have caveats that are worth some additional discussion.

Operating System

The Turbo C++ Integrated Development Environment (IDE) is a Windows 3.x application. Like any good 16-bit Windows application, if the developers have done their jobs right, the executable runs on a variety of operating systems other than Windows 3.x.

Fortunately, the programmers at Borland have done themselves proud. The Turbo C++ IDE can be run successfully on a wide variety of operating systems, including Windows 95, Windows NT, and OS/2 Warp. Of course, running Turbo C++ on an operating system other than Windows 3.x means that you will probably need more capable hardware than the minimum requirements endorsed by Borland. Under Windows 3.x, Turbo C++ performs adequately on the hardware in the preceding list, but you'll definitely want to add memory and probably use a more powerful CPU if you're running on an alternative platform.

Free Hard Disk Space

As mentioned previously, a full installation of Turbo C++ takes up approximately 65M of hard disk space. However, Borland's installation program gives you a number of options, each with varying disk space requirements. So, although a full installation might require 65M, a CD-ROM-based installation could require as few as 20M (of course, this is not an option if you are installing from floppy disks).

Caution

If you are installing Turbo C++ onto a hard disk that has been compressed (using DriveSpace, Stacker, or a similar product), make sure that you allow yourself 1M or 2M of extra free space. It's possible that the installation of Turbo C++ could alter your disk's overall average compression ratio, which would be reflected in an inflated disk space installation requirement.

Memory

Compilers and development products are notorious resource hogs. Even Borland confesses that, although the product will run fine with 4M of RAM, boosting your computer's memory up to 8M "greatly increases the performance of Turbo C++." This is certainly true, but you will find that Turbo C++ doesn't really start to scream until you install 12M or even 16M of RAM. If you think that sounds like a lot, remember that Windows programs are decidedly non-trivial. Windows application development is not a simple undertaking, no matter how easy-to-use your development tools are. Under the hood, Turbo C++ is performing a lot of grunt work on your behalf, which means that the more memory you have installed, the better. By the same token, a fast 486 (or even Pentium) processor will improve the performance of Turbo C++ dramatically.

Windows Installation

As demanding as developing sophisticated Windows applications can be, installing Turbo C++ really couldn't be much simpler. For the most part, you can run a complete install in half an hour with virtually no input needed from you except the obedient shuffling of floppy disks. If you're fortunate enough to be installing the CD-ROM version of the product, you can complete a fully functional install of Turbo C++ 4.5 in about five minutes!

A Typical Installation

Begin the installation process by placing the first disk into your floppy drive (Disk 1 is referred to as the Installation Disk), or by putting the Turbo C++ CD-ROM into your CD-ROM drive. The installation program for Turbo C++ is named INSTALL.EXE. If you are installing from floppy disks, INSTALL.EXE is in the root directory of the installation disk; if you are installing from CD-ROM, INSTALL.EXE is in the INSTALL directory.

Choose Run from Program Manager's File menu and enter the full path name of the install program. If you're using floppy disks, you type something like the following:

```
a:\install
```

A CD-ROM install, however, requires a command along the lines of the following:

```
d:\install\install
```

Of course, if you are installing from a floppy disk drive other than A, or from a CD-ROM drive other than D, you must substitute the appropriate drive letter. You can also use the Browse function to navigate to the install program, which is often easier if you are not sure whether you should type Install or Setup.

Saving Time by Using a Hard Disk Install

If you are planning to install Turbo C++ from floppy disks and you have a lot of free hard disk space, you might want to consider a *hard disk install*. Installing Turbo C++ from floppies can be a long and painfully slow process, but the hard disk install can cut installation time in half. It temporarily requires about an additional 40M of hard disk space, but you can easily reclaim this space after the installation process.

Create a new directory named TCINST and xcopy into it the contents of all the installation diskettes. Assuming that your floppy drive is A and your temporary installation directory is on C:, use the following command:

```
xcopy a:\*.* c:\TCINST /s /e
```

Now, run the installation program from the TCINST directory. INSTALL.EXE loads its compressed installation files out of TCINST on the hard disk, which is considerably faster than loading the same files from a floppy drive. Whatever you do, don't forget to delete the TCINST directory when the installation is complete. Nobody has that much disk space to waste!

The installation program displays a "splash screen" identifying itself, then maximizes itself to cover the entire screen. It displays a message indicating that it is performing some preparatory tasks, and then trundles along for a brief period of time before displaying the initial dialog box presented in figure I.1.

Fig. I.1
The Turbo C++
Installation/
Configuration
Notes dialog box.

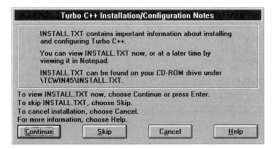

Note

The screen shots in this section are taken from a CD-ROM install. If you are installing from a floppy disk, you might notice slight differences.

Information about the installation process that Borland deems important enough to be read before you install the product has been placed in a file named INSTALL.TXT, and the installation program gives you the option of reading it now. Although you can bypass this step by clicking the Skip button, there is always the possibility that your installation will fail or encounter problems for reasons that might be explained in INSTALL.TXT. If you don't opt to read this file during installation, make a point of reading it at some point in the near future. The file is a normal, uncompressed text file residing on the first installation disk (or in the \TCWIN45 directory on the CD-ROM).

In some cases, the information in INSTALL.TXT is critical for performing a successful installation. Sections in this text file explain, for example, special procedures that you need to follow when installing Turbo C++ under Windows 95, Windows NT, and OS/2 Warp. Other pieces of information, such as how to install from a "clean configuration," are not critical but can help you avoid potential problems later.

Regardless of whether you have read or skipped INSTALL.EXE, the next dialog box presented by the install program is the one in figure I.2.

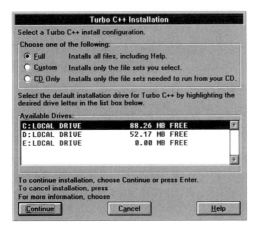

Fig. I.2
The main Turbo C++ Installation dialog box.

This dialog box presents a radio button group where you can indicate the type of installation to perform—Full, Custom, or CD-ROM-based—and a list of all the drives attached to your computer that are candidates for installation. The Available Drives list indicates what type of drive is assigned to each drive letter, and displays the amounts of free space available.

Typically, you will want to perform a full installation. This copies and uncompresses all of the product's files onto your local hard disk. If you are severely constrained by the amount of available hard disk space, you can opt for a CD-ROM-based installation (assuming, of course, that you have the CD-ROM version of Turbo C++). If you select this installation option, the install program copies only the minimal complement of files needed to run Turbo C++ directly off your CD-ROM drive. Although this results in a smaller portion of your hard drive being consumed, it also means that Turbo C++ will run quite slowly every time you use it. The remaining installation option, Custom, is discussed in more detail in the next section. You should select this option only if you want complete control over the files that will be installed on your hard disk.

When you elect to do a full or CD-ROM-based install, the next dialog box (see fig. I.3) presents you with a place to set the destination and configuration directories. This dialog box also contains two checkboxes for additional options.

Fig. I.3
The Installation directory selection dialog box.

The first checkbox, labeled Quick Tour, controls whether the Quick Tour help files are installed. Since the Quick Tour is a broad overview of the Turbo C++ product, it is of interest mostly to new users. Users of previous versions of Turbo C++, however, might want to explore the Quick Tour to get a feeling for product features that are new or have been enhanced.

The second checkbox, labeled Windows LAN Setup, should be checked only if the drive you are installing to is on a network and this installation will be shared by more than one programmer.

Performing a Customized Install

A customized installation gives you much more control over exactly which Turbo C++ components are placed onto your hard disk. This allows you to tailor your installation specifically to your programming priorities, or to reinstall specific components that have been accidentally damaged or deleted.

The customized installation breaks Turbo C++ components into the four categories shown in figure I.4. This is the dialog box you are presented with if you indicate that you want to perform a customized install.

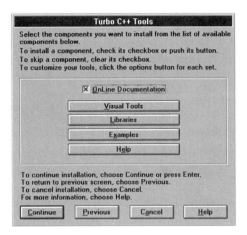

Fig. I.4
The Initial custom installation dialog box.

Each of these four categories—Visual Tools, Libraries, Examples, and Help—can be installed in its entirety (the default), or you can click the appropriate button and be taken to a dialog box that details the components contained within each category. These secondary dialog boxes are detailed in the next few sections.

Visual Tool Components

The first set of commonly grouped components are the Visual Tools listed in figure I.5.

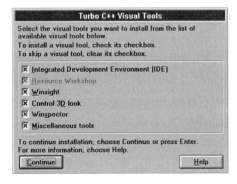

Fig. I.5
The Turbo C++ Visual Tools dialog box.

You should note that since the IDE option is selected by default, the Resource Workshop choice is grayed out. This is because the IDE is closely integrated with Resource Workshop, and you cannot install just the IDE alone. If you deselect the IDE option, however, you will see that you now have the option of deselecting the Resource Workshop as well. The Resource Workshop is *not* dependent on the IDE and can be installed by itself.

The other options in this dialog box are pretty straightforward. WinSight is a tool that allows you to track and record Windows messages, and WinSpector is a utility that tracks and records information about fatal Unrecoverable Application Errors (UAEs).

Library Components

The next group of installable components are the Libraries. The library install options are shown in figure I.6.

Fig. I.6
The Turbo C++
Libraries
dialog box.

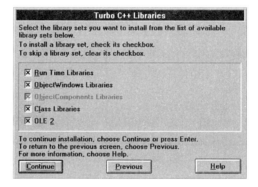

Select the libraries that you are interested in installing now. The Object Components Libraries—Borland's OLE support classes—are automatically installed with the ObjectWindows libraries (OWL). If you are not installing OWL, you still can install the Object Components classes separately. Also note that if you are installing Turbo C++ on an operating system that natively supports OLE 2 (such as Windows 95 or Windows NT), the OLE 2 option on this dialog box is grayed out. Under Windows 3.x, however, this is not the case. This happens because OLE 2 is not part of the Windows 3.x operating system, and is supplied as an operating system extension that needs to be installed.

Example Components

The third group of custom installable components is the example files. The examples are broken into the components shown in figure I.7. These example components provide source code, project files, resource definitions, and all the other Turbo C++ items needed to build the fully functional sample Windows applications.

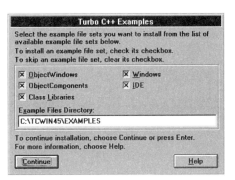

Fig. I.7
The Turbo C++
Examples
dialog box.

It is highly recommended that you install these example programs if you are unfamiliar with Turbo C++, or C++ in general. These samples provide a good place to start your Turbo C++ explorations. There is a wealth of solid, debugged code here that can be cut-and-pasted directly into your own applications. On the other hand, if you know that there is a specific type of Windows application you will not be building (OLE 2-compliant applications, for example), there is little reason to install the corresponding examples, and you should deselect the appropriate box.

Help Components
The final set of components is the Help files. The installation options for this group are shown in figure I.8.

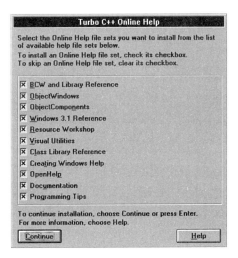

Fig. I.8
The Turbo C++
Online Help
dialog box.

Again, if you are new to Windows development with Borland products, it's probably a good idea to install as many of the Help files as you have room for. Although most of the information contained in the Help files is available in the written documentation (and in on-line documentation if you have installed from CD-ROM), installing this information in Help file form will allow you to quickly and easily access content from within the development environment. Although you may end up becoming very familiar with the Borland documentation, there's just no beating the simple process of highlighting something you don't understand and pressing F1 to get immediate help.

Finishing Up

After you have made all your choices, the installation program tells you how much total disk space will be required by your installation, and how much disk space you have available. If you do not have enough disk space, you will need to click the Previous button to return to the configuration dialog boxes and select different installation options. Otherwise, you're ready to go. Click the Install button to begin the actual Turbo C++ installation.

Once the main installation is underway, you don't have to do much except watch the "dashboard" installation screen and read the informational messages that cycle through the windshield notepad. If you're installing from diskettes, you will need to insert disks as they are requested.

Note

If necessary, you can cancel the installation at any time by clicking the Cancel button (no surprises there).

When the installation procedure has neared completion, you will be presented with the Turbo C++ Release Notes dialog box shown in figure I.9.

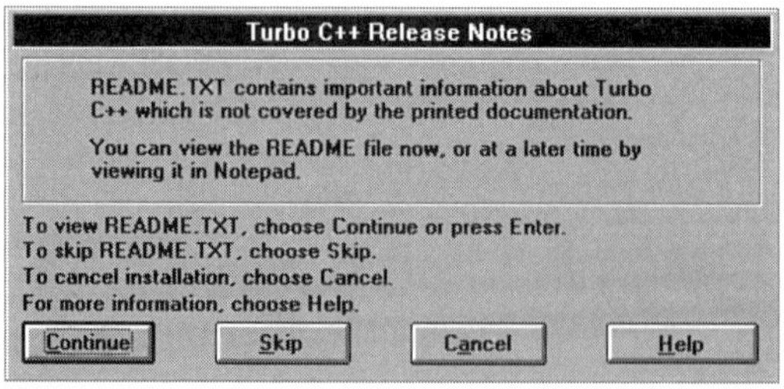

Fig. I.9
The Turbo C++
Release Notes
dialog box.

Borland places additional late-breaking news and information into the README.TXT file. For example, this file explains how to use Borland C++ project files (IDE files) from within Turbo C++. Make a point of reading README.TXT now! Since, by definition, the information in README.TXT does not appear in the hardcopy or softcopy versions of the documentation, reading this file early could save you a lot of trouble or calls to technical support.

The installation completes by creating the Turbo C++ program group, registering some Object Linking and Embedding (OLE) information, and reminding you that the PATH= statement in your AUTOEXEC.BAT file has been modified to include the Turbo C++ installation directory. It also mentions that the FILES= statement in AUTOEXEC.BAT must be set to 40 or higher. Before rebooting, use Windows Notepad or the DOS Editor to load AUTOEXEC.BAT and confirm that this is the case.

That's it! You need to shut down Windows and reboot your computer. As soon as that's done, you are all set to jump in and start writing Turbo C++ programs.

Part I

Tools and Productivity

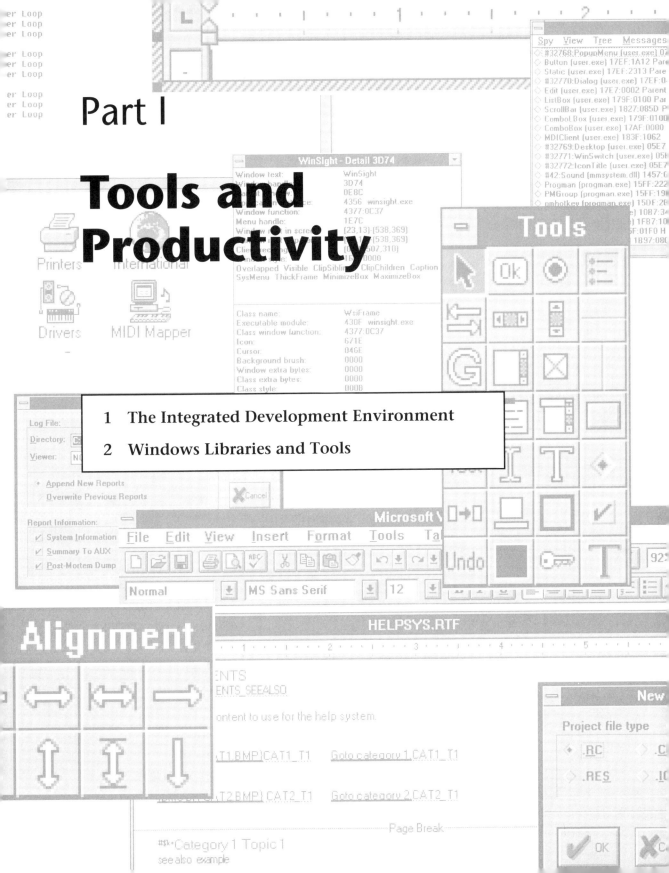

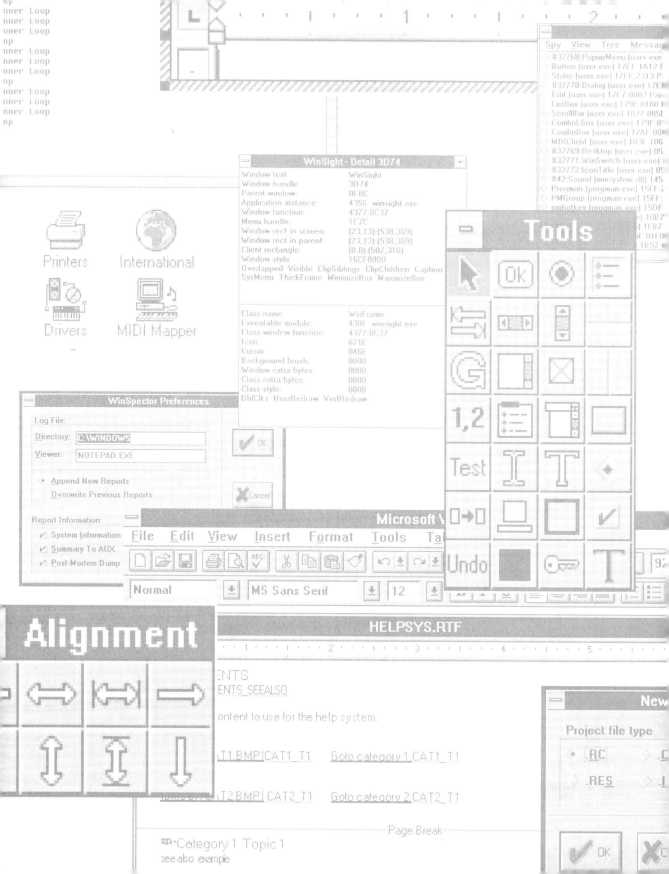

Chapter 1

The Integrated Development Environment

These days, application-development software is so complex that packages like Turbo C++ come with something called an *Integrated Development Environment*, or *IDE* for short. The IDE groups together all the programs (such as a text editor, a compiler, a linker, and a resource-construction program) you need to create an application. To this end, the IDE provides menus that give you access to these various development programs, making it seem as if you're using only one large development application, rather than a bunch of little ones.

In order to create a program with Turbo C++, you must complete a number of steps. All the major program-development steps are controlled from the IDE desktop. These processes are the following:

1. *Editing a source file.* In this step, which requires an editor that produces ASCII text files, you write your program's source code. The file extensions used for these text files are .c for C files and .cpp for object-oriented C++ source files, respectively.

2. *Compiling the source file.* At this point, a program called a *compiler* verifies the accuracy of the syntax used in the source file and converts the ASCII text source file into an intermediate binary form, called an *object file*. An object file has the file extension .obj.

3. *Linking libraries*. Next, the linker takes all the .obj files (and any required library files) and links them together to form an executable program file with an .EXE extension. This is the file that you run in order to use the application.

4. *Running the program*. Here, you load the .EXE file into memory, which executes the code. It is at this point that you check to see whether the program runs correctly.

5. *Debugging the program*. Chances are that, when you ran the program in step 4, you found a number of programming errors. To get rid of these, you *debug* the program, which means going back to step 1 and working your way back down the other steps in order to correct the source code and create a new .EXE file.

As you work through these steps, Turbo C++ reports any errors it finds in the program code. Some errors are detected only in later steps. For example, many coding problems are not detected by the compiler but can be uncovered only in the debugging stage. Similarly, a linker may fail after a successful compile if it can't find a required library or object file. You can learn more about the compiling and linking process in Chapter 15, "Compiling and Linking."

You must perform each of the preceding steps in sequence many times in order to create a fully functional program. (However, you'll soon see that Turbo C++ has some commands that perform several steps, one after the other, automatically.) Without an IDE, you would have to run a separate and independent program to perform each of the five processes in the programming development cycle. As you can see, the IDE offers a platform that runs these program-development functions as if they were all part of the same program-development application. To control the development functions, you use the IDE's menus and windows. In addition, the IDE's context-sensitive help gives quick answers to questions about the IDE.

Starting the Turbo C++ for Windows IDE

 Before you can write a program with Turbo C++, you must start the IDE. To do this, double-click the Turbo C++ program icon in the Turbo C++ group in your Windows Program Manager. The Turbo C++ IDE desktop then appears on the screen (see fig. 1.1). The IDE desktop contains many parts, most of which should be familiar to you if you've used Windows applications before. The menu bar, for example, enables you to select the commands that control the program-development process, whereas the main window's title bar shows the name of the currently open project.

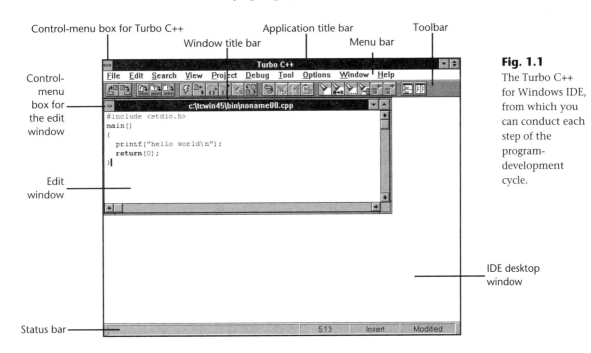

Fig. 1.1
The Turbo C++ for Windows IDE, from which you can conduct each step of the program-development cycle.

Other parts of the IDE include the edit windows, which hold the source code for a program; the toolbar, which gives you quick access to common commands; the status bar, which displays messages about the IDE; and the control menus, which enable you to manipulate each window in various ways. You learn more about the IDE's parts later in this chapter.

Editing, Compiling, and Running a Program in the IDE

Now that you have Turbo C++ up and chugging, you'd probably like to create and run your first Turbo C++ program. To do this, follow these steps:

1. In the edit window (refer to fig. 1.1), type the following six-line program:

```
#include <stdio.h>
main()
```

```
    {
      printf("Hello, world!\n");
      return(0);
    }
```

This step is equivalent to step 1 in the program-development cycle, which you learned about at the beginning of this chapter.

 2. Click the lightning icon on the toolbar. This command compiles, links, and runs the program.

This step is equivalent to steps 2, 3, and 4 in the program-development cycle. The Run command (represented by the lightning icon) automatically performs all three steps for you.

When you complete step 2, you see the window shown in figure 1.2, which displays the text string "Hello, world!". Close the program window by clicking on its control-menu box, which returns you to the IDE. (If this simple program had not run correctly, you would need to debug the program, which is step 5 of the program-development cycle.)

Fig. 1.2
The "Hello,
World!" program.

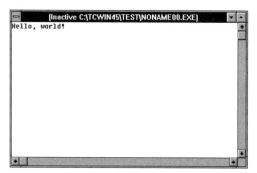

Now that you've had an introduction to program development with Turbo C++, it's time to take a closer look at Turbo C++'s many commands and options.

The Menu Bar

Turbo C++'s menu bar (see fig. 1.3) contains all the commands you need to control the IDE. To access a menu from the keyboard, press the Alt key and the underlined letter on the menu. For example, to access the File menu from the keyboard, hold down the Alt key and press the F key. To access the menu using the mouse, place the mouse pointer on the menu name and click. Whether you choose a menu from the keyboard or with your mouse, the commands that make up the menu appear on the screen (see fig. 1.4).

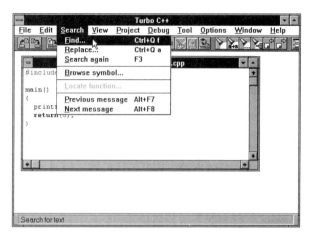

Fig. 1.3
The Turbo C++
menu bar.

Fig. 1.4
A selected menu in
Turbo C++'s IDE.

To select a command from a menu, simply click on the command with your
mouse. If you want to use your keyboard to select the command, press the
underlined letter in the command. For example, to select the File menu's
New command with the keyboard, first press Alt+F to display the File menu.
Then, press N to select the New command.

In addition to the menus on Turbo C++'s menu bar, each window has a control menu, which is located in the window's upper left corner. To display the
control menu, click on the window's control-menu box. To select the main
window's control menu with the keyboard, press Alt+Spacebar. To select the
edit window's control menu with the keyboard, press the Alt and hyphen (–)
keys.

The two windows in figure 1.5 show the commands available from the control menus of the IDE desktop window (left) and the edit window. The common items on these menus are the following:

Command	Purpose
Restore	Restores the active window to its previous size.
Move	Enables you to move the active window.
Size	Enables you to change the size of the active window.
Minimize	Reduces the active window to an icon.
Maximize	Expands the window to its maximum size.
Close	Removes the active window from the desktop.

Fig. 1.5
The control menus of the IDE desktop and the editor window.

The IDE's main window has one additional command:

Command	Purpose
Switch To	Opens the Windows Task Manager.

The editor window has one additional option:

Command	Purpose
Next	Activates the next edit window. The IDE supports multiple edit windows.

The File Menu

The File menu enables you to create, load, save, and print the source code files that make up a programming project. It also contains the Exit command, which quits Turbo C++ for Windows. The following table lists the File menu options and what they do.

Command	Purpose
New	Creates a new file.
Open	Opens an existing file.
Save	Saves the currently active file under the file name shown in the edit window's title bar.
Save As	Saves a file under a new file name.
Save All	Saves all open files, including desktop configuration files.
Print	Prints the contents of the currently active edit window.
Printer Setup	Enables you to set printer and paper options before printing.
Exit	Quits Turbo C++ for Windows.

Note

Menu commands appear as *enabled* or *disabled*. Enabled commands, shown in regular dark text, can be selected. Disabled commands, which are shown grayed out, cannot be selected. For example, if a window is maximized, the Maximize menu option is grayed out because you can't maximize a window that has already been maximized. On the File menu, if the Save option is grayed out, the text in the window hasn't been changed since the last time it was saved.

The Edit Menu

The Edit menu contains Turbo C++'s editing commands, including commands such as Cut and Paste, which access the Windows clipboard. The following table lists the commands and what they do.

Command	Purpose
Undo	Reverses the last edit operation.
Redo	Reverses the last undo operation.
Cut	Removes the highlighted text and stores it in the clipboard.
Copy	Moves a copy of the highlighted text into the clipboard.
Paste	Places the contents of the clipboard into the edit window, at the current cursor position.
Clear	Erases all text from the active window.
Select All	Highlights all text in the active edit window.
Buffer List	Displays a list of open files.

The Search Menu

The Search menu contains commands to locate and replace text strings in an edit window, as well as commands to browse for program symbols. The following table details the commands and their actions.

Command	Purpose
Find	Searches for a given text string.
Replace	Replaces a text string with any text string you specify.

(continues)

Command	Purpose
Search Again	Repeats the last search operation.
Browse Symbol	Reports details about any symbol used in the currently compiled and linked program.
Locate Function	Positions the cursor at any requested function.
Previous Message	Moves to the previous message in the message window. Also moves the edit cursor to the source code line referenced in the message.
Next Message	Moves to the next message in the message window. Also moves the edit cursor to the source code line referenced in the message.

Note

Whenever you see a key or key combination beside a menu choice, you can press those keys to activate the selection without using the menus. For example, pressing F3 from the IDE window is the same as opening the Search menu and choosing the Search Again command. This type of keystroke is often called a *hot key*.

The View Menu

The View menu contains commands that enable you to view data such as registers, variables, and the function-call stack. Such information helps you keep an eye on what your program is doing. The following table lists the options and their purposes.

Command	Purpose
ClassExpert	Starts ClassExpert, which enables you to modify a program's classes in various ways.
Project	Opens the Project window.
Message	Opens the Message window.
Classes	Displays a graphical view of the current program's classes.
Globals	Opens a selection list of all global variables.
Watch	Opens the Watch window.
Breakpoint	Opens the Breakpoints window.
Call Stack	Opens the Call Stack window.

Command	Purpose
Register	Shows all the processor registers and flags.
Event Log	Opens the Event Log window.
Information	Shows system information and resource utilization.

The Project Menu

The Project menu contains commands to create, edit, and build your project, which is a collection of files and attributes that tell Turbo C++ how to manage the current programming project. The following table lists the commands and their purposes.

Command	Purpose
AppExpert	Opens an AppExpert project to generate an OWL application.
New Project	Starts a new project.
Open Project	Opens an existing project.
Close Project	Closes the current project.
New Target	Adds a new target to an existing project.
Compile	Compiles the active file.
Make All	Updates all files by compiling and linking as necessary.
Build All	Rebuilds all files.

The Debug Menu

The Debug Menu is used to run or step through the program, to set breakpoints, and to inspect or modify variables. Using these handy commands makes it much easier to find errors in your programs because you can actually watch what your program is doing every step of the way. (For more information on debugging programs, check out Chapter 16, "Debugging.") The following table contains all the commands on the Debug menu and lists what they do.

Command	Purpose
Run	Compiles, links, and runs the current program. Similar to clicking on the lightning icon in the toolbar.
Step Over	Executes the current statement, without stepping into a called function.
Trace Into	Executes the current statement, stepping into any functions called within that statement.
Toggle Breakpoint	Sets or clears an unconditional breakpoint on the current line.
Find Execution Point	Shows the source line that is the next to be executed.
Pause Program	Pauses the currently running program and switches to the debugger.
Terminate Program	Stops the currently running program.
Add Watch	Enables you to add a new variable to those you're watching.
Add Breakpoint	Enables you to add a breakpoint to the current program.
Evaluate/Modify	Enables you to view or modify expressions in your program.
Inspect	Opens the Inspect Expression dialog box, in which you can view information about a given symbol, such as a function name or a variable.
Load Symbol Table	Loads a symbol table for any module that includes debugging information.

The Tool Menu

The Tool menu contains a set of additional utility programs used during the development of your application. Resource Workshop, for example, enables you to build dialog boxes, menus, and other resources for a Windows application, whereas WinSight displays the flow of messages through a Windows application. (For more information on the tools included with Turbo C++, see Chapter 2, "Windows Libraries and Tools.") Following is a list of commands in the Tool menu.

Command	Purpose
Resource Workshop	Loads the Resource Workshop utility, which is used to create and edit Windows resources.
Grep	Invokes the Grep utility, which searches for text in one or more files.
WinSight	Invokes the WinSight utility, which tracks window messages.
WinSpector	Intercepts Unrecoverable Application Errors (UAEs) and saves them in a log.
Key Map Compiler	Compiles the IDE key map file.

The Options Menu

The Options menu enables you to set system defaults and customize the way Turbo C++ handles your projects and tools. Every detail of the way the compiler, linker, IDE, and other tools work can be set using the dialog boxes that appear when you select one of these commands. The following table details the commands on the Options menu and what they do.

> **Caution**
>
> The Options menu has such a wide variety of options to choose from—and changing them is so easy—that you should carefully note the current settings before changing any options.

Command	Purpose
Project	Edits the project settings.
Target	Edits target settings for all available targets.
Environment	Edits environment settings.
Tools	Adds new tools.
Style Sheets	Edits style sheets.
Save	Saves all the options for the environment, desktop, and project.

Tools and Productivity

The Window Menu

The Window menu, which appears in most Windows applications, contains the commands that manipulate window arrangements in various ways, as well as maintains a list of open windows. The following table lists the commands and what they do.

Command	Purpose
Cascade	Arranges edit windows in a diagonal, overlapping order.
Tile Horizontal	Arranges edit windows as a vertical stack.
Tile Vertical	Arranges windows side-by-side.
Arrange Icons	Arranges icons at the bottom of the IDE window.
Close All	Closes all windows. Also can close all windows of a selected type (for example, all edit windows).
Minimize All	Minimizes all windows. Also can minimize all windows of a selected type.
Restore All	Restores all windows to their original size and position. Also can restore all windows of a selected type.

The Help Menu

Tip
If you want to have a hard-copy reference of all the functions in the Windows API, print the windows.h file, which also includes the constant and data type definitions used in Windows programming. You can find this file in the TCWIN45\INCLUDE directory.

The Help menu contains commands that access Turbo C++'s on-line help, which features extensive information on C and C++, the Windows API, Borland's ObjectWindows classes, and more. In addition, you can use the Quick Tour command to explore the Turbo C++ development system. (To learn how to create your own Help system, read Chapter 30, "Building a Help File.") The following table summarizes the Help menu's commands and what they do.

Command	Purpose
Contents	Displays Help's table of contents.
Quick Tour	Initiates a quick tour of the Turbo C++ for Windows IDE.
Keyword Search	Displays information about the word at the cursor position.
Keyboard	Displays information about the keyboard mapping.
Using Help	Displays information about using the Help system.

Command	Purpose
Windows API	Displays help for the Windows API.
OWL API	Displays help for the ObjectWindows Library API.
About	Displays version and copyright information for your copy of Turbo C++.

The IDE Toolbar

The IDE toolbar (see fig. 1.6) contains icons that, when selected, perform many of the commands described in the previous sections. By clicking on the icons in the toolbar, you can perform common commands quickly and easily, without having to dig through menus to find the command. You already know, for example, that you can click on the lightning icon in the toolbar to compile, link, and run the current program. That's a lot of performance from one quick mouse click!

Fig. 1.6
The IDE toolbar.

Moreover, you can configure the toolbar to suit your preferences. For example, you can move the toolbar from the top of the screen to the bottom. If you like, you can even hide the toolbar completely, giving you more room for edit windows. In addition, you can add or remove commands from the toolbar. You can perform these magical feats with the Speedbar commands found in the Environment Options dialog box. To display this dialog box, select the Environment command from the Options menu.

Context-Dependent Activities

Certain features of the IDE appear differently depending on what you're doing—or where your mouse pointer is located—at a given time. Specifically, you can access pop-up menus that contain commands specific to the current task. You can also access Help information specific to the current task.

Tip
If you place your mouse pointer on an item in the toolbar, a brief summary of the command appears in the status bar at the bottom of the IDE desktop window. Borland calls these command summaries *flyby hints*.

Tools and Productivity

I

Pop-Up Menus

In an edit window, clicking the right mouse button brings up a free-floating pop-up menu (see fig. 1.7). Some of the commands on this menu duplicate other commands that you read about in the previous sections. Still, this menu is a quick way to get at commands specific to the task at hand.

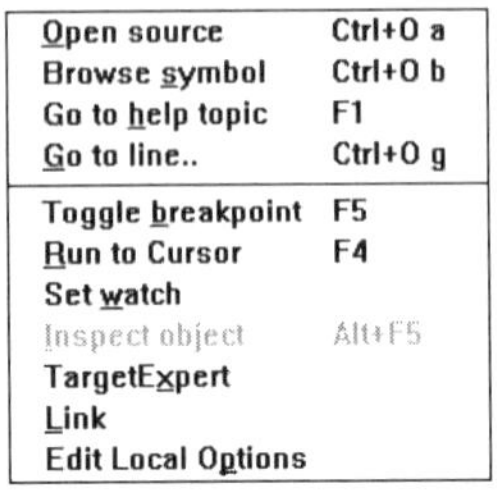

Fig. 1.7
The pop-up Edit menu.

```
Open source        Ctrl+O a
Browse symbol      Ctrl+O b
Go to help topic   F1
Go to line..       Ctrl+O g

Toggle breakpoint  F5
Run to Cursor      F4
Set watch
Inspect object     Alt+F5
TargetExpert
Link
Edit Local Options
```

Tip
Alt+F10 is the keyboard equivalent of clicking the right mouse button.

Other types of windows can display pop-up menus, too. Right-clicking in the Project window, for example, displays a pop-up menu containing commands that relate specifically to managing a project.

F1—Help

At any time while developing programs in Turbo C++ for Windows, you can press F1 to get context-sensitive help. For example, if you press F1 when the edit cursor is positioned on a word, the Help system searches for any references related to that word. On the other hand, if you press F1 with your cursor on a C++ function name that's part of a library included with Turbo C++, the function's on-line documentation is displayed. (If you press F1 for a word that the Help system doesn't recognize, a Search dialog box appears so that you can hunt for appropriate help.)

Other parts of Turbo C++'s IDE also support context-sensitive help. If you pull down a menu and highlight a menu command (without releasing the left mouse button), pressing F1 brings up information about the selected command. The Project window, too, has its own context-sensitive help. Just activate the Project window and press F1 to bring up information about project hierarchy. Buttons, list boxes, edit controls, and other objects also have context-sensitive help capabilities.

Getting Comfortable with the IDE

In the previous sections, you've explored just a few of the options and configurations over which Turbo C++ gives you control. Before you get too buried in your next programming project, though, it might be a good idea to take some time to explore all that Turbo C++ has to offer. Start by becoming familiar with the many commands in the menu bar. You'll quickly see that some commands lead to complex dialog boxes containing dozens of settings. Use your context-sensitive help and on-line Turbo C++ documentation to learn about these settings and what they do. A little time spent now will go a long way toward making your future program-development tasks easier and more pleasant to complete.

Building a Test Project

Now that you have some idea of how Turbo C++'s IDE works, you might want to create a test project that will give you hands-on experience with creating Turbo C++ applications. Because AppExpert provides the quickest and easiest way to start a new programming project, the following steps show you how to use this helpful tool.

1. Click on the Project menu's AppExpert command. The New AppExpert Project dialog box appears.

2. Type **FIRSTAPP** in the File Name edit box, set the Directories list box to TCWIN45, and click the OK button. The AppExpert Application Generation Options dialog box appears.

3. Click the Generate button. AppExpert creates the source code files for the new project. (This may take a little while.) These source code files are like a program "shell" in which you must type the source code specific to your application.

4. Click the toolbar's lightning icon to compile, link, and run the new project. The application's window then appears on the screen (see fig. 1.8).

Fig. 1.8
An AppExpert application.

When you created the preceding project, AppExpert generated a number of files, including a variety of .cpp files (source code), an .rc file (resources), a .def file (module definition), and an .EXE file (the executable application). You can view any of the source code files by double-clicking a file name in the Project window. Once you have a source code file in an edit window, you can add your own source code to create exactly the application you need. (Of course, that's the hard part! For more information, see Chapter 21, "Using AppExpert," and Chapter 28, "ObjectWindows Applications.")

Note that, in the preceding example, you used all the default settings for the AppExpert project. You can change the way the basic application looks by changing the various settings available in the AppExpert Application Generation Options dialog box. For example, you can tell AppExpert that you don't want a toolbar and that the application should allow only one document window at a time. Take some time now to experiment with AppExpert, choosing different settings in order to create different types of applications.

From Here...

As you've discovered, Turbo C++ for Windows includes a powerful IDE that you can use to manage the many files and settings that make up a programming project. In this chapter, you got a quick look at just some of the more important of the IDE's features, but you still have much to learn. For more information on using Turbo C++, see the following chapters:

- Chapter 15, "Compiling and Linking," contains more details on how your program source code becomes an executable application.

- Chapter 16, "Debugging," is a crash course on finding and squashing program bugs.

- Chapter 21, "Using AppExpert," shows how this powerful tool gets a programming project started quickly and easily.

- Chapter 22, "Using ClassExpert," discusses editing your program's classes with a few mouse clicks.

- Chapter 23, "Using Resource Workshop," shows you how to create attractive menus, dialog boxes, bitmaps, and other resources for your Windows applications.

Chapter 2
Windows Libraries and Tools

Turbo C++ for Windows is a complex development system, one that features more tools, libraries, and options than you can shake a menu bar at. Diving headfirst into a package of this complexity is a good way to drown. For that reason, this chapter gives you a quick introduction to the libraries and tools you need in order to create Windows applications with Turbo C++ for Windows. Once you get a general idea of how Turbo C++ expects you to use its development tools, you'll be armed with the knowledge you need to dive more deeply into the rest of this book.

In the sections that follow, then, you learn about

- Windows functions, constants, and data types

- The ObjectWindows library classes

- The WinSight Tool

- The WinSpector utility

- Resource Workshop

The Windows API

The Windows Application Programming Interface (API) is a set of functions that enables you to create applications that are compatible with Microsoft Windows. The hundreds of functions included in this library are in addition to the many other C++ library functions with which you may be familiar. But although you can use regular C++ library functions such as sprintf() in your Windows programs, you must use the Windows API to create a Windows program and to interact with any devices attached to the user's computer.

The truth is that creating a Windows program is very different from creating a DOS program. For example, a Windows program doesn't have a `main()` function like a DOS C++ program. Instead, a Windows application has a `WinMain()` function. A Windows program has many other differences, as well, including the necessity of creating, registering, and displaying a window.

Another difference is that a Windows program must never access devices directly. For example, although it is acceptable for a DOS program to draw graphics directly into screen memory, this technique is strictly forbidden under Windows. This is because Windows is *device independent*, which means Windows provides a uniform set of functions for handling all devices. You don't need to know, for example, what graphics modes the user's monitor supports. Instead, you call Windows functions to draw on the screen, and Windows takes care of all the details of displaying the requested image.

Windows Function, Constant, and Data Type Declarations

The Windows API functions are declared in the header file, WINDOWS.H. You must include the WINDOWS.H file in any source code module that calls Windows API functions, so that Turbo C++'s compiler will know about these functions when it comes across them in your source code.

In addition to function declarations, WINDOWS.H also defines a huge set of constants and data types that make Windows programming more convenient. *Symbolic constants* are written in uppercase to distinguish them from variable names. In C, the `#define` preprocessor statement creates symbolic constants. Here's a couple of examples of symbolic constants defined in windows.h:

```
#define FALSE    0
#define TRUE     1
```

After these lines are included in a program, `FALSE` will always represent the value 0, and `TRUE` will always represent the value 1 when you use either of these words in an assignment or expression. If you don't understand how constants work, check out Chapter 4, "Data Types, Variables, and Constants."

Data type definitions are convenient references to commonly used C types. In C, the `typedef` keyword is used for data type definitions. An example that appears in windows.h is

```
typedef char far * LPSTR;
```

The preceding line declares the data type LPSTR to be a far pointer to a string. (The LP stands for *long pointer*. You can learn more about pointers in Chapter 10, "Pointers.")

Function prototypes provide a means for the compiler to perform critical error checking on function call parameters. A prototype tells the C++ compiler how a function should be called. For example, the windows.h prototype for the WinMain() function is

```
int PASCAL WinMain(HINSTANCE, HINSTANCE, LPSTR, int);
```

The first int in the preceding line tells the compiler what type of data the function returns. The PASCAL keyword tells the compiler the order in which the function's parameters are placed on the stack. Finally, the two HINSTANCEs, the LPSTR, and the int, tell the compiler the data types of the function's parameters. Once the compiler has this information, it can determine whether you've called the function correctly in your source code.

Function Groups

Because there are so many functions in the Windows API, they are grouped in sets. For example, all the functions that work with Windows are organized in the Window Manager Interface group. The other major function groups are Graphics Device Interface functions, which enable you to display data in a window or on a printer, and System Services Interface functions, which handle things such as memory management, sound, and file input/output.

Each of these three major function groups is divided into even smaller groups. For example, the Window Manager Interface group is further divided into window-creation functions, painting functions, dialog-box functions, and many other groups. To see all the groups (there are more than 70 of them), flip through a good Windows programming reference, such as *Microsoft Windows Programmer Reference*, published by Microsoft Press. For the details of writing a Windows application, please read Chapter 24, "Windows Programming Basics."

ObjectWindows Classes

One of the class libraries that comes with Turbo C++ is the ObjectWindows library (known affectionately as OWL). OWL contains the Borland application framework for Windows 3.1, which helps you build full-featured Windows applications quickly and easily. Borland's ObjectWindows library goes a long way toward simplifying the process of writing Windows applications by hiding much of the details inside custom window classes. In fact, using OWL, you can create a fully operational window in about six lines of code!

The following list details just some of OWL's major features:

- *Window classes*. Using OWL's various window classes, you can create any type of window you like, including frame windows, client windows, dialog boxes, and more.

- *Message-response functions*. OWL features a complete set of functions that, when included in your program, automatically respond to Windows messages, which are sent to your application when an event—such as the user clicking a mouse button or typing on the keyboard—occurs.

- *Menu classes*. OWL's menu-handling functions make it a snap to create various types of menus, as well as to control menu-item actions such as checkmarking and enabling/disabling.

- *Control classes*. Most Windows programs must deal with many types of Windows controls, including buttons, list boxes, and edit boxes. OWL encapsulates all Windows controls in easy-to-use C++ classes.

- *GDI classes*. OWL includes classes that encapsulate Windows Graphics Device Interface, making it much easier to display data in your application's window.

- *Doc/View classes*. Using these classes, you can separate the contents of a document from the way it is viewed in a window.

- *Printer and print-preview classes*. OWL simplifies creating print-preview windows and sending data to a printer.

As you can see, OWL is a powerful library. Unfortunately, although OWL makes it easier to create Windows programs, OWL has its own learning curve. To learn the details of using OWL to create Windows applications, you should read Chapter 27, "The ObjectWindows Library," and Chapter 28, "ObjectWindows Applications."

The WinSight Tool

WinSight is a utility that provides debugging information about classes, windows, and messages. When you run WinSight, it sits in the background, intercepting and displaying information that is passed between Windows and running applications. By watching WinSight's display, you can see how your application interacts with the Windows system, information that is almost impossible to get using normal debugging techniques. The message-trace window, for example, shows Windows messages in the order in which they are sent and received, whereas the window-tree window lists information about all the windows currently registered with the system.

In the sections that follow, you learn to use WinSight to spy on Windows applications. But first you might like a quick, hands-on introduction to this valuable tool.

Tracing Windows Messages

When a Windows application is running, there is a constant flow of information between the application and Windows. This information is usually in the form of messages that pass commands back and forth, as well as keep applications and Windows aware of what each other is doing. One of the handiest features of WinSight is its ability to trace and display this message activity.

Figure 2.1 shows WinSight's Message Trace Options dialog box, which enables you to set which types of messages to watch. You can select all messages or any combination of the sets, such as mouse messages, clipboard messages, or DDE messages. You can also highlight selected messages by using the list box on the right side of the dialog box. Once WinSight gets started, it displays the messages it intercepts in a scrollable message window. In addition, if the Log File option is selected, WinSight copies the incoming message list to a text file.

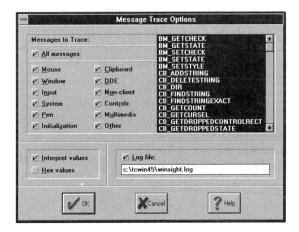

Fig. 2.1
The Message Trace Options dialog box.

To get an idea of how WinSight works, follow these steps to trace the Windows messages being passed between Windows and any running applications:

  1. Click the word Stop! in the menu bar. The word Stop! changes to Start!, and all message tracing stops.

2. In the View menu, set the menu items so that there is a checkmark only next to Message Trace. WinSight displays only the message-trace window.

3. Select the Clear command in the Messages menu. WinSight clears the message window.

4. Select the Options command from the Messages menu. The Message Trace Options dialog box appears.

5. Choose the messages you want to trace, by clicking on the option buttons.

6. Start any applications you want to trace.

7. Select the All Windows command from the Messages menu. WinSight is now set to trace all windows in the system.

8. Click the word Start! in WinSight's menu bar. Message tracing begins.

9. Watch the messages being traced. (If you want to see a ton of messages, move your mouse around the Windows desktop. Yikes!)

10. Click the word Stop! in the menu bar. All message tracing stops.

11. Use the message window scroll bars to view the messages passed between the running applications and Windows.

Now that you've traced the message activity flowing through your Windows system, you're probably a little confused about what all this information means. The sections that follow describe each of WinSight's windows and how information is displayed in them. If you'd like more information on Windows messages, you might want to read Chapter 24, "Windows Programming Basics." More importantly, you should probably have a good Windows programming manual by your side. Programming Windows applications is a complicated task. One good book you might want to add to your library is *Programming Windows 3.1* by Charles Petzold and published by Microsoft Press.

The Class-List View

The class-list view, shown in figure 2.2, provides information about all the window classes currently registered in the system. The information is presented in the following format:

```
Class (Module) Function Styles
```

Class is the name of the registered class. For example, in the first line in figure 2.2, the class name is `#32768:PopupMenu`. *Module*, on the other hand, is the name of the .EXE or .DLL module that registered the class. In the first line of figure 2.2, the module name is `user.exe`. *Function* is the address of the class's window function (which is the function that communicates with the Windows system). In the first line of figure 2.2, that address is `07FF:1587`. Finally, *Styles* is a list of the class styles with which the class was registered. In the first line of figure 2.2, the style list includes only `SaveBits`.

Fig. 2.2
The class-list view.

You can get a more organized and detailed view of the class's information by double-clicking the class. When you do, the WinSight-Detail window appears, as shown in figure 2.3.

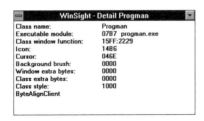

Fig. 2.3
The WinSight-Detail window showing class information.

The Window-Tree View

The window-tree view, shown in figure 2.4, displays a list of the windows on the desktop and organizes them into a hierarchy, based on which windows created child windows. (A *child window* is a window that was created by another window, which is then called the *parent window*.) The highlighted window in figure 2.4 is WinSight's main window. Listed below this window, and indented slightly to the right, are all five of WinSight's child windows (although four of these child windows are currently hidden, which means they don't appear on the screen).

Fig. 2.4

The window-
tree view.

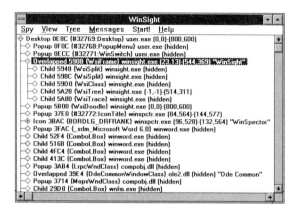

Notice that one of the windows in the figure has a plus sign (+) next to its
entry in the list. This means that the window has child windows. To display
the child windows in the list, click on the plus sign. When you do, not only
is information about the child windows displayed, but the plus sign becomes
a minus sign (–). Click on the minus sign to hide the list of child windows
again.

The information in the window-tree view is presented in this format:

```
Type Handle (Class) Module Position "Title"
```

Here, *Type* is the type of window, which, in the highlighted line in figure 1.4
is Overlapped. The second item, *Handle*, is the window's handle, a value that
identifies a specific window in the system. In the highlighted line, the
window's handle is 5908. *Class* is the window's class name, which is the
name under which you'd find the window in the class-list view. In the highlighted line, the class name is WsiFrame. *Module* is the name of the .EXE or
.DLL module that created the window. In the highlighted line, this name is
winsight.exe.

Position is where the window is located on-screen. These two sets of coordinates indicate the position of the window's upper left and lower right cor-
ners. In the highlighted line, *Position* is (23,13) - (544,369). (If the window is
hidden, the *Position* item appears as (hidden).) Finally, *Title* is the window
title that appears in the window's title bar. In the highlighted line, the title is
WinSight.

To get a more organized and complete look at the information about a certain window, double-click the window's line. The WinSight-Detail window
then appears, as shown in figure 2.5.

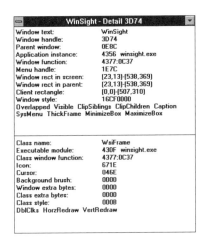

Fig. 2.5
The WinSight-
Detail window
showing window
information.

What good is the window-list view? Well, for one thing, you can use this
view to select the windows you want to trace. To do this, click on the window (you can select multiple windows by holding down your keyboard's
Ctrl key and clicking on the windows), and then choose the Selected
Windows command from the Messages menu.

Message Trace View

You've already had a little experience with this view. The message-trace
view, as shown in figure 2.6, shows the messages received by windows
you've selected. The messages are displayed in the following format:

        Handle ["Title" or {Class}] Message Status

Handle is the handle of the window that received the message. In the highlighted line in figure 2.6, *Handle* is 1984. The second item in the line is either
the window's title (inside quotes) or class name (inside curly braces). In the
highlighted line, the window's title, "ATIKey Hook", is shown. *Message* is the
Windows API constant that represents the received message. In the highlighted line, *Message* is WM_TIMER. Finally, *Status* can be several different things
depending on the message. Unless you understand Windows programming
well, the *Status* part of the message probably won't mean much to you.

You can find additional details about the messages and much more about
WinSight in your Turbo C++ on-line help. To do this, choose the Help
menu's Contents command, and then select Tools Reference from the help
window that appears.

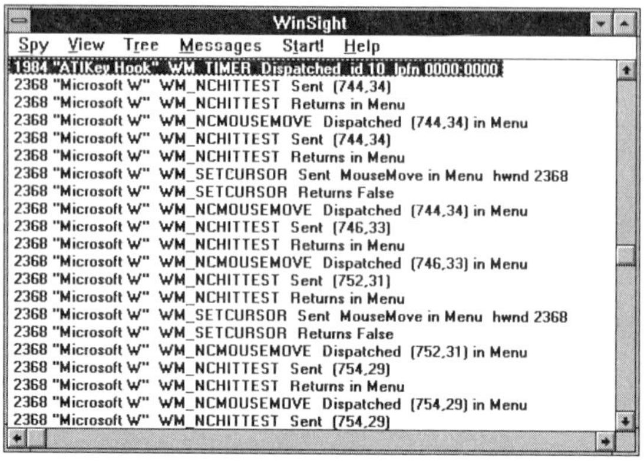

Fig. 2.6
The message-
trace view.

Fig. 2.6
The message-
trace view.

The WinSpector Tool

As every programmer knows, it's pretty hard to write a program without crashing the system a few times. Often, when a Windows application crashes, it produces an Unrecoverable Application Error (UAE) or General Protection Fault (GPF). Because these types of errors happen in the computer's memory, it's often very difficult to know what went wrong with your program. That's where WinSpector comes in. WinSpector creates a log file called WINSPCTR.LOG that provides helpful information about the UAE or GPF that just occurred. Just start up WinSpector, and it does its thing, safely tucked away in the background.

Configuring WinSpector

As with most tools, you can configure WinSpector in various ways, using a configuration dialog box. To bring up this dialog box, first double-click the WinSpector icon at the bottom of the screen, and then select the Set Prefs button. When you do, you see the WinSpector Preferences dialog box, as shown in figure 2.7.

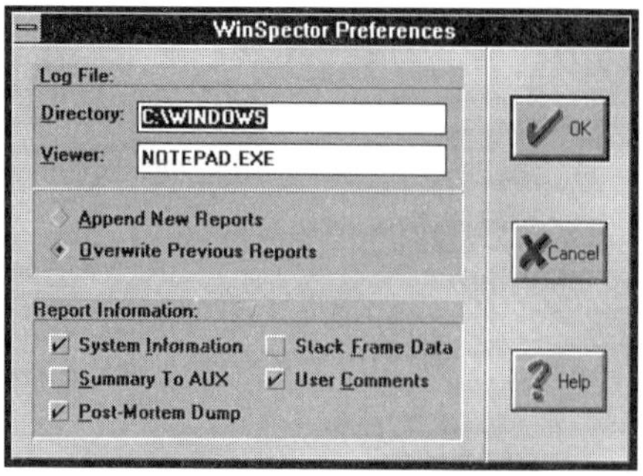

Fig. 2.7
The WinSpector
Preferences
dialog box.

The <u>D</u>irectory entry in the dialog box shows where WinSpector will store its log file. You can change this to whatever you want (the directory C:\TCWIN45 comes to mind), but the default is C:\WINDOWS. The <u>V</u>iewer edit box contains the location and name of the text editor that WinSpector will use to display its log file. The default is NOTEPAD.EXE, which is Windows' Notepad accessory. If you select a different text editor, be sure to include a complete path name.

The <u>A</u>ppend New Reports and <u>O</u>verwrite Previous Reports options determine whether WinSpector starts a brand new report each time it saves a log or whether it will add the new report to the end of the old one. The default is to start fresh and overwrite any old reports. Finally, the Report Information box enables you to select the type of information you want logged. System <u>I</u>nformation, <u>P</u>ost-Mortem Dump, and User <u>C</u>omments are the default selections.

WinSpector's Log File

The log file created by WinSpector starts with two lines of general information and then is divided into several sections. The first line in the report shows the time and date that the report was logged. The second line shows general information about the UAE or GPF, including the type of error, the name of the module that caused the error, and the address where the error occurred. Table 2.1 lists the sections in a WinSpector log file and the information contained in those sections.

Table 2.1   Sections in a WinSpector Log File

Section	Contents
Disassembly	Assembly language version of the code that caused the error.
Stack-Trace	Information about the function in which the error occurred.
Register	A list of the contents of the CPU's registers at the time of the error.
Message Queue	Status of the message queue, including the last message received.
Tasks	A list of the programs that were running at the time of the error.
Modules	A list of the modules that were running at the time of the error.

(continues)

Table 2.1 Continued	
Section	**Contents**
USER and GDI Heap	Remaining space in the USER and GDI heaps at the time of the error.
System Information	Lists information about the system, including the CPU type, amount of free memory, and the number of pages in the swap file.

As you can see, the information provided by WinSpector is highly technical. To use this information, you really need to understand programs at an assembly-language level. For this reason, the average programmer may find that only certain portions of the WinSpector log file provide useful information. If you want to learn more about WinSpector, you should consult your Turbo C++ on-line documentation. To do this, choose the Help menu's Contents command, and then select Tools Reference from the help window that appears.

The Resource Workshop Tool

Almost all Windows applications use a Windows resource file in one way or another. Such a file contains information about the application's menus, dialog boxes, string tables, controls, bitmaps, and more. In the old days, a programmer constructed a resource file by typing a special source code file known as a *resource script*. Because creating resource files this way is such a chore, compiler manufacturers such as Borland include resource editors that enable programmers to create resource files visually on the screen. For example, to create a dialog box with a resource editor, you select pictures of the controls that you want to include in the dialog box and drag those controls into place in the dialog box.

Turbo C++ comes with a resource editor called Resource Workshop (see fig. 2.8), which enables you to create menus, dialog boxes, string tables, bitmaps, icons, cursors, and more. After you've created these resources, Resource Workshop automatically creates the script file that the resource compiler uses to create the actual resources for your application. The best part is that, not only is Resource Workshop a time and grief saver, it's also a blast to use. To learn how to use this essential tool, please read Chapter 23, "Using Resource Workshop."

Fig. 2.8
Creating a dialog
box with Resource
Workshop.

From Here...

In this chapter, you got a quick look at the libraries used to create Windows applications. You also got an introduction to the tools that Turbo C++ provides, tools that make building and debugging your programs a more gratifying experience. You can find more information on these topics by consulting the following chapters:

■ Chapter 16, "Debugging," helps you get your program to work the way it's supposed to work.

■ Chapter 23, "Using Resource Workshop," teaches you how to create menus, dialog boxes, bitmaps, and other resources for your Windows applications.

■ Chapter 24, "Windows Programming Basics," discusses building a Windows application without using the ObjectWindows library.

■ Chapter 27, "The ObjectWindows Library," is a general overview of this powerful application framework.

■ Chapter 28, "ObjectWindows Applications," shows you the fast way to build Windows applications!

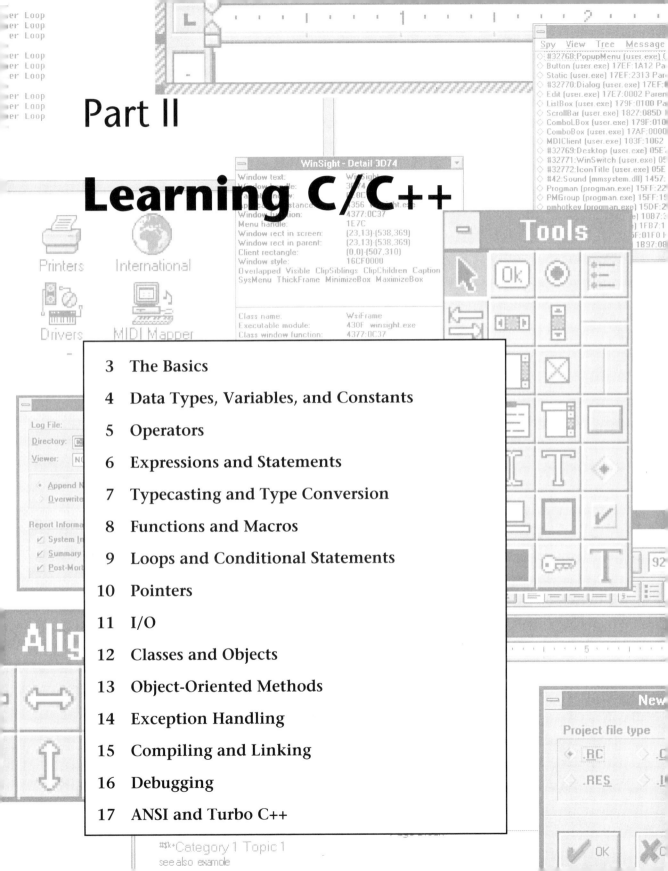

Part II

Learning C/C++

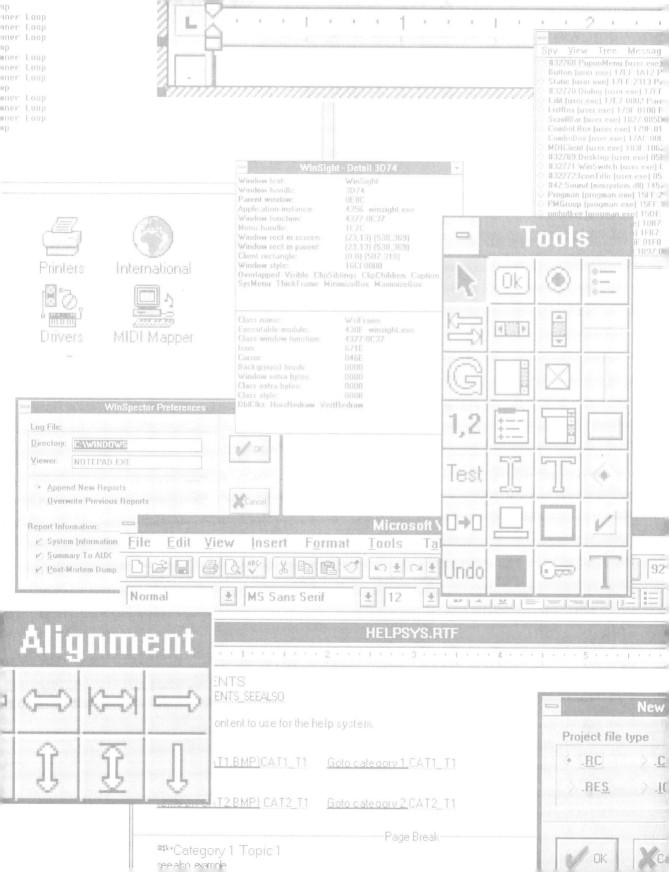

Chapter 3

The Basics

Today, C and C++ are the programming languages of choice for most commercial software applications, for a variety of reasons:

- They are extremely popular programming languages. There are many compilers, development tools, and books available to assist you in developing programs. You also can find a variety of on-line support on the Internet and all major on-line services (CompuServe, America Online, and so on).

- You can create very efficient code and still have the elegance and maintainability provided by a high-level language. As you will see in later chapters, you can manipulate data in a very efficient manner through the use of C structures and pointers, and even more flexibly with C++ classes and their associated methods.

- There are many example software packages and applications available for you to use once you have mastered the material presented in this book. Almost all commercial software is written in C and C++, so it's very likely that other people have developed code in C or C++ that you can use to create whatever application you have in mind.

This chapter is an introduction to the C and C++ languages. You will see the basic design philosophy behind C and C++ and learn how a program actually runs on your computer. You then will see some basic coding rules used throughout the book to keep your code readable, maintainable, and, above all, understandable. The benefits of structured programming and object-oriented design are presented, along with an overview of what a C++ class contains. Finally, an example of a prototype C++ header file is presented to illustrate the basic coding conventions used in the text. Subsequent chapters of this section of the book cover the syntactical and implementation details of C and C++.

What Is C?

The C programming language was developed in the early 1970s primarily as a language for coding operating systems. Previous computer languages, such as FORTRAN and PL/1, were primarily designed for implementing computational algorithms. They were not very adept at manipulating complex data structures or implementing non-sequential algorithms that you often encountered in low-level system programming. As such, a new, more suitable language was developed and ultimately became what is known now as C. C was designed to help bridge the gap between the need for the high-performance code you could get from assembly-level programming and the portability and clarity of higher-level languages.

Conceptually, a C program is basically just a series of function calls. A program is executed in sequential order, unless a statement is encountered that causes the program to execute a different section of code. Conditional statements such as `if` and `switch`, looping statements such as `for` and `while`, explicit `goto` statements, and function calls all cause your program to execute different portions of code at different times or under different conditions. When a function is called, the program branches to the function and executes the code defining the function. Each function performs some set of computations on its arguments and then returns to the calling function. The program then continues on to the next code statement or function call. In listing 3.1, for instance, the two functions together print the sum of the numbers 1 through 10 on your screen.

Listing 3.1   A Simple Program to Calculate the Sum of the Numbers from 1 to n

```
/*
  This function prints 10 lines:
  The sum of 1 to 1 is 1
  The sum of 1 to 2 is 3
  ...
  The sum of 1 to 10 is 45
*/

/* The void declaration means the function
   does not return a value */
void
print_sums()
{
  int i;

  /* Loop from 1 to 10 */
  for(i=1; i <= 10; i++) {
```

```
        /* The statement calc_sum(i) invokes the
           function calc_sum() to compute the
           result we need */
        printf("The sum of 1 to %d is %d\n",
               n, calc_sum(i));
    }
    return;
}

/* Calculates the sum from 1 to the passed
   number n */
int
calc_sum(int n)
{
    int i, sum;

    sum = 0;
    for(i=1; i <= n; i++)
        sum += i;

    return sum;
}
```

You define a function by declaring what type of value the function will return and what arguments the function takes. In this example, the function `print_sums()` is a function that does not actually return a value (this is what the declaration `void` means) but takes as an argument the single integer value n. You then declare the actions you want the function to take with code statements enclosed in braces. C uses the semicolon (;) to indicate the end of a single code statement. Thus, you can put a single statement on as many lines as you like (as shown by the call to the `printf()` function) for increased readability.

> **Note**
>
> Don't worry about anything in listing 3.1 other than the lines I specifically discuss. When you read the section "Source Files" later in this chapter, you'll learn about comments, line breaks, and other stylistic considerations, and then you'll be able to identify all the parts of this sample C code.

To write output to the screen, `print_sums()` uses the standard C function `printf()`. This function is described in greater detail in Chapter 11, "I/O." For this example, you just need to know what the arguments mean. The first argument to `printf()` is a string (specified in "") telling `printf()` what to print. Anything beginning with a % indicates something to be retrieved from the subsequent arguments to `printf()`. In this case, the %d means to print a

decimal number. The first %d refers to the argument n, whereas the second
argument refers to the function call calc_sum(n). To call a function, you must
specify the function name followed by the arguments to pass to the function.
If there is more than one argument, each argument is separated with a
comma. In this example, the function calc_sum() is passed the argument n,
the same argument passed to print_sums().

The function calc_sum() takes a single integer argument n and computes the
sum of the numbers from 1 to n. The sum is then returned as the value of
calc_sum(). In this example, the returned value of calc_sum() is then used
in the printf() statement of print_sums(). In general, a function call that
returns a value can be used anywhere a normal variable is appropriate.

Recursive Functions

As an example of the flexibility in C, let's examine another way to write the
function calc_sum(). Although the most common means of using functions
is to have them call other functions, you can even have functions call themselves. This is called *recursion,* and a function that calls itself is called a *recursive function.* We could present calc_sum() as a recursive function, as follows:

```
/* Calculates the sum from 1 to the passed
   number n, using recursion */
int
calc_sum(int n)
{
  int i, sum;

  if(n == 0)
    sum = 0;
  else
    sum = n + calc_sum(n-1);

  return sum;
}
```

Here we exploit the property that the sum of the numbers from 1 to n can
also be thought of as the sum of the numbers from 1 to n-1 added to n. Thus,
calc_sum() can call itself to find the sum of the numbers from 1 to n-1, and
add that sum to n to get the final desired answer. Recursion can be quite useful to compute complicated functions that cannot be easily expressed as a
simple iterative loop. Recursion is one example of how the flexibility of C
lets you express an algorithm in many different ways.

The *main( )* Attraction

Every C program must have at least one function named main(). This is the
first function that is called when your program begins execution. In effect,
the operating system is calling your main() function to start your program.

Once started, your program will execute each code statement in turn, calling any functions as they are encountered, until your program either uses the return keyword to exit from main() or calls the explicit exit() function to exit to the operating system. The following example of a main() function uses calc_sum() to print a user-specified sum on-screen:

```
void
main()
{
  int n;

  n = 0;
  /* This will loop until the user enters a 0 */
  while(n > 0) {
    /* Ask the user for what sum to compute */
    printf("Sum the numbers from 1 to ");
    /* Read the number from the screen */
    scanf("%d", &n);
    /* Print the result */
    printf("The sum of 1 to %d is %d\n",
            n, calc_sum(n));
  }

  /* We are done, return to the operating system */
  return;
  /* Can also use exit(); */
}
```

In this example of a main() function, the function scanf() is used to read input from the screen. The while() statement will keep executing the portion in the braces until the user enters a value of 0 (or a negative number). Notice that in this example main() has no arguments. You can specify optional arguments for main() that let you get arguments from the DOS command line if you like. You can find a detailed explanation of these arguments in Chapter 24, "Windows Programming Basics," which discusses both main() for DOS programs and WinMain() for Windows programs.

Source Files

Unlike previous programming languages, C was designed to format your source code in a very free-form manner. Single statements may use multiple lines, starting almost anywhere on a line. You can also separate items with as many spaces and tabs as you like. Despite the loose formatting requirements for C source code, there are some restrictions on where you can add extra spacing. You can't put extra spaces between the letters of C keywords or function names. Any spaces or tabs in a quoted string will be considered part of the string; thus, you should not continue a quoted string onto a second source line.

II

Learning C/C++

Generally, you should try to format your code to be as readable as possible. For instance, if you must pass many arguments to a function, you should use multiple lines to make it more readable, as in the following:

```
my_func("This is a very long string as the first argument to this function",
        argument3, argument4);
/* Line up successive arguments so they all start to the right of
   opening ( of the function name */
```

You'll see many other examples of how to format source code to make it more readable in the later chapters of the book. As you practice writing your own programs, you'll see that proper formatting can help tremendously in understanding the program's flow and operation.

In addition to free-format source lines, C and C++ also allow free-format comments within a program. You should liberally use source comments to remind yourself and guide others as to how the program works. In C, all comments begin with the character sequence /* and end with */. Thus, the following are valid comments:

```
/* This is a comment */
/*
   This is also a comment
*/
/************************
 * Another Comment      *
 ************************/

i++; /* Comment after a statement */
```

C++ provides an additional comment facility with the // sequence. All characters from the // to the end of the line are considered a comment and will be ignored by the compiler. The // sequence is useful for making single-line comments, for instance:

```
i++; // Comment after a statement
```

Headers and Modules

C source files are divided into two basic types, *header files* with an .h file extension and *modules* with a .c file extension. The modules represent the source code of your program. Although no general rules really exist for how to organize these files, you should try to keep each source module down to a reasonable size. Don't try to put each function in a separate module or put all of your functions in the same file, unless it is a very simple program. One useful rule of thumb is to try to keep all of your function definitions down to a single page in length. This makes them easy to catalog when printed and forces you to think about breaking complex functions into more manageable pieces.

The header file typically contains the definition of your structures, macros, and function prototypes. You should put any definition that you expect to use in multiple program modules into a header file that can be included by any number of program modules. In general, a single header file should contain definitions of related data types and functions. All of the standard C include files such as stdio.h and math.h are structured in this way.

Naming Conventions

To avoid conflicts with other code packages and your own routines, it is an excellent idea to adopt a common naming convention for your functions. For example, if you're writing graphics routines, you'll inevitably find that someone else has created a class called Circle or Point or a function called DrawCircle(). Unfortunately, any standardized naming convention always makes the names longer and sometimes less intuitive. But this is much better than having to change your source code later to avoid conflicts with the terrific new library you just purchased.

A straightforward naming convention for C++ classes and C structures (these are data types introduced in the next chapter and described completely in Chapter 12, "Classes and Objects") is

```
class TC<module>_<Name> {
  private:
  protected:
  public:
};
```

Each class name begins with an uppercase TC (for Turbo C++). As an alternative, you could use your initials, the initials of the project you're working on, or whatever you like as long as you can tell where the class came from. The <module> name should be the name of the module file in which the function is defined. For instance, a set of classes dealing with mathematical vectors, defined in a file called vec.hpp, would be called TCvec. The <Name> portion is a name you choose describing the particular class, such as TCvec_2DVector.

To distinguish function names from class names, all non-member functions begin with a lowercase prefix, such as tc_, as in tc_MoveMousePointer(). The rest of the function name is indicative of the purpose and operation of the function.

Structured Programming

One of the best features of C is the support for structured programming. Early programming languages tended to simply mimic how a computer actually worked. Thus, instructions were executed in a simple sequential manner, with the exception of the goto statement to jump to another line of code in the program and continue executing from that point. If you wanted to perform an iterative code loop, you had to specify a particular line of code you wanted to jump back to in a goto statement. Having to specify line numbers every time you want to reuse a certain portion of code becomes tedious and quite difficult to maintain, especially when you have several nested code loops. Instead, C uses a different approach, often referred to as *structured programming*.

In the previous example of main(), the while statement (described in detail in Chapter 9, "Loops and Conditional Statements") repeatedly executes a block of code until a particular condition is met. In this example, the block of code is repeated until the user enters a number equal to 0 or less. Notice that the block of code is enclosed in braces. In C, any block of code placed inside braces is considered a single statement. A keyword such as while can repetitively execute a single statement or any block of code enclosed in braces. Furthermore, you can nest blocks of code inside other code blocks as much as you like, so you can have as many nested levels of if or while statements as necessary.

With structured programs, it is much easier to tell how your program gets to a certain point than with an equivalent unstructured program. In general, goto statements are extremely difficult to trace through when you're trying to follow a program's logic, and the use of gotos can get out of hand very quickly.

ANSI Versus Non-ANSI

To help ensure the greatest compatibility and ease of implementation, the code provided in this book is ANSI (American National Standards Institute) compliant. This used to be a problem several years ago because many C compilers on the PC and other platforms were not necessarily fully compliant. This has changed in recent years to the degree that virtually every new compiler is ANSI-compliant. We strongly encourage you to program in an ANSI-compliant method by turning on the Turbo C++ option to have the compiler check your code for ANSI compatibility. This will aid in moving your application to other platforms and also encourages you to write cleaner code. A lot of the code "cheats" that older C and C++ compilers let you get away with—which ultimately cause trouble later—can be detected by the compiler and subsequently avoided. You'll see how to activate ANSI code checking by Turbo C++ in Chapter 17, "ANSI and Turbo C++."

Event-Driven Programming

C is an extremely powerful programming language. In addition to the facility for structured programming, C also provides the ability to create arbitrary data types called *structures* (described in detail in Chapter 4, "Data Types, Variables, and Constants"). However, with all of its flexibility, C still is not well designed for many applications. Traditionally, applications were treated as simply running from beginning to end. The user would enter whatever input the program required at the beginning, and then the program would run and produce a final result, perhaps printing the output on-screen or to a printer. This programming model works well for computationally based applications. Programming in Windows, however, requires a different approach altogether.

For Windows applications, a user usually needs to be allowed to dynamically change program input while a program is running, through the use of interactive dialog boxes. The program must be designed to take user input at virtually any time, not just at predefined points while the program is running. Generally, a Windows application is expected to respond immediately to changes the user makes, including moving the mouse, pressing buttons, selecting text, and so on. The application must then change the displayed output immediately to conform with the requested changes. An application such as a word processor or spreadsheet does not end until the user requests that it ends. Because a user of a Windows application can change many different parameters, in virtually any order, you do not have the luxury of simple sequential program execution.

A program that dynamically responds to external events is called *event-driven*. Almost all Windows programs are naturally event-driven and must be constructed with dynamic event handling in mind. Instead of operating in a sequential manner, your program receives notice of external events, such as clicking on the mouse, and responds to the user action appropriately. In C, you write functions to handle events. Thus, whenever the user left-clicks the mouse, one (or possibly several) of your functions will be called to perform whatever processing is needed to respond to the mouse click.

In addition, many Windows applications must work cooperatively with other applications to pass data from one program to another. The most obvious example in Windows is the clipboard. All Windows text-processing applications can write to (and retrieve text from) the clipboard. By using a common format for the data, many different applications can share data from the clipboard. Instead of writing a single massive utility to perform all functions of an application, you can break the application down into several separate modules, which each do a portion of the task. The modules can share whatever common data is needed, by adopting both a standard format for the data and a standard way of reading and writing the data. The need for event-driven programs and standardization of how data is shared among independent programs has led to the development of a different program paradigm known as *objects*.

Objects to the Rescue

The C++ programming language is an object-oriented extension to C. The term *object-oriented* refers to the notion that a program is made up of *objects* that possess two major attributes:

- The data that defines what they hold

- The functions associated with that object, which manipulate its data or interact with other objects

C has always possessed the first attribute with C structures. A structure lets you refer to a group of related data as a single entity. As stated previously, a C program is defined as a series of functions that take passed arguments and return a computed value. A function may access the data within a structure by manipulating the individual member elements.

However, the data in a structure is really only half of what you need to use the structure. In fact, you often don't really need to know exactly how the data is stored in a structure. You just want to know how to manipulate it. For instance, if you want to put a window on-screen, you want to be able to create a window of a specified size and place it at a specified location. You probably do not care how the size and position data is stored in the structure defining a window. You just need to know how to position it and change the size. So the other half of what you need with a structure are the functions to perform some action based on the data in the structure or to change the data of the structure.

Many programming problems in a C program come about when functions manipulate the data elements of a structure directly. For instance, you may have a structure that is stored as part of, say, a linked list of windows your application has on-screen. If another function corrupts the pointers defining the linked list, the list is destroyed. In effect, every function that uses the list structure must be coded with the method for processing the linked list; that is, it must know how to move elements around, delete elements, add new ones, and so on. If you later change from using a linked list to using an array or some more complicated list structure, you must change every function that uses the list structure to match this change. Changing all the functions is not only a lot of trouble but is likely to introduce some programming errors.

Defining an Object

The object-oriented approach to programming takes a different view of functions. The primary entity in an object-oriented program is, not surprisingly, an object. In C++, an object is defined using the `class` keyword. The object not only has the data stored in it, like the C structure, but also has functions defined as part of the object.

The functions associated with the object often are referred to as *methods*. The methods for an object define the interactions of other objects or functions with this object. In C++, the methods for an object are called *member functions* and are declared in the definition of each object class, just as the data elements in a C structure are. In general, your program will not directly access the data elements of the object but will manipulate them using the appropriate object methods. By explicitly controlling the methods for accessing the object data, you greatly reduce the chance that any part of your program can corrupt the internal data structure of the object.

An object-oriented approach makes programs considerably more modular in nature. Think of an object as a black box. The object's methods define the input and output to the black box. The data elements of the object define how it works internally and should generally be of no interest except to those internal functions. By accessing the object strictly via its methods, you can change the internal structure of the object without having to change any other programs. As long as the methods appear the same to the world outside the object, then even if the methods' implementation has completely changed, any outside programs using this object do not have to change.

Inheritance

In addition to providing controlled access to your data structures, objects have other tremendously useful features. There are many times where you must use the same kinds of structures repeatedly. For instance, linked lists are extremely useful ways to store dynamically allocated data of all types. Every time you want to store a series of structures as a linked list, you must put all of the extra data for the linked list into your data structure. Furthermore, you must create a set of functions to handle your specific linked list structure. If you have another structure you need to store in a linked list, you must define a whole new set of functions to handle the other structure's linked list. It would be extremely nice to be able to define a generic linked-list data type once and just declare your structure as having all of the features of a generic linked list in addition to having the specific features you need. C++ lets you do exactly that, using a property known as *inheritance*.

In C++, you would define a linked-list class that defines how the linked list operates; in other words, how to access a particular element of the list, how to add or delete an element, how to find out if the list is empty, and so on. To manipulate your data, you define a new class that is derived from this linked-list class. Your new class can now use all of the functions of the linked-list class without having to bother with any of the details of the linked-list class implementation. Your new class is said to *inherit* the properties of the linked-list class. The generic linked class is called a *base class*, and your new, derived structure is called a *derived class*.

There are numerous benefits to the object-oriented approach. For example, instead of using a simple forward-linked list, you may decide that a doubly linked-list would be an even better approach. But you have already developed many functions that use the structure you have currently defined. With C++, this poses no problem at all. You simply change the base class to use a doubly linked-list storage method. By redefining the methods of the base class (not the names of the methods, just how they work), you do not need to make any changes to your derived class. Thus, your application does not need to know how the linked list is actually implemented. It simply uses functions like getNext() and getPrevious() to get elements of the list, independent of the implementation.

You will see many examples of base classes being used in this way for derived classes throughout the software in this book and in virtually any C++ application. However, C++ also offers a number of additional enhancements to C that aid in programming and maintaining an application.

Running on Overload

Another useful feature in C++ is the ability to define functions with the same name but different arguments. For instance, you might want to create a function called draw(), with a different definition depending on whether you pass a Window, a dialog box, or some other type of object as the argument. This avoids the problem of having to come up with separate function names for each type of object you might want to draw.

In addition to overloading standard C-type functions, C++ lets you overload the *operator* functions such as +, *, -, and /. Almost every standard operator can be overloaded. (Function Overloading is described in detail in

Chapter 13, "Object-Oriented Methods.") In fact, you are already quite familiar with this facility within ordinary C, although it may not be obvious. C lets you add variables of different data types, such as a `float` and an `int`, performing the appropriate data type casting as needed. The compiler implicitly takes care of this for you. C++ simply gives you direct control to adapt the operators to any classes you like. Thus, you can create expressions such as `c = a + b;`, where a, b, and c are matrices or vectors.

Virtual Functions

In addition to letting classes inherit the properties of other classes, C++ lets you define generic function names, called *virtual functions*, that can be defined separately in each derived class. A virtual function is simply a placeholder for a function. A class derived from this base class may provide a new definition for any virtual function defined in the base class. So far, this is no different than ordinary function overloading. The difference comes in when you use pointers to a base class. A pointer to a base class may be used to point to any base class object or to an object derived from that base class. Consider the following two declarations:

```
/* Define a generic graphics object */
class base_object {
  private:
  protected:
  public:
  virtual void draw(void);
};

/* Define a circle as a publicly derived object */
class circle : public base_object {
  private:
  protected:
  public:
  void draw(void);
};

/* Declare pointers to objects */
base_object *obj;
circle      *circ;

/* The new statement creates a circle */
circ = new Circle;
obj = circ;

...

/* This calls the member function for the specific
   object, in this case the draw() method for circles */
obj->draw();
```

The `circle` class is derived from the `base_object` class. The pointer `obj` is assigned to point to a newly created `circle` object. When the call to draw the object is made with `obj->draw()`, the `draw()` function for the circle is called. This is very useful when you have a list of different kinds of objects all derived from one base class. For each `base_object` pointer, the appropriate function is called, depending on which specific object it points to. This basically eliminates the need for big `switch()` statements or function pointers to select the appropriate function to apply to a given object. The virtual function facility of C++ is covered in detail in Chapter 13, "Object-Oriented Methods."

C and C++

The C programming language has been in use for more than 20 years. As more and more people have developed ever more complex programs, the shortcomings of C have become more apparent. C++ is not only an attempt at adding object-oriented features to C, but also addresses some of the limitations of C. Among the many benefits of C++ are the following:

■ C++ provides strong type-checking of function arguments. The passed arguments to a function must have their type declared both in the definition of the function and in the header file defining the function. Although having to always make these argument declarations may seem painful, allowing the compiler to ensure that all functions are called with valid arguments can save a lot of time and grief.

■ As you have seen, a C++ class may be derived from other classes. Thus, you can create new classes that have all of the attributes of the base class. As in the linked-list example discussed previously, your program does not need to know how the base class is implemented, only how to access the methods of the base class.

■ A new type of passed value, the *reference*, lets you pass a pointer to an argument implicitly. This provides more natural-looking code for many types of functions. In addition, a function may return a reference as the return value. Referenced variables may be used as an `lvalue`; that is, the function call may appear on the left side of an expression. As you will see, this feature can be very useful when defining overloaded functions.

- The C operators such as +, -, *, /, and so on may be redefined to work with your data types. This feature can easily be overused, but it can greatly increase the readability of your code.

- A relatively new addition to C++, the *template*, provides an extension to the C macro capability. Instead of defining a C macro to perform a C function, you create a template that describes the function. The compiler then uses this template to create an appropriate function for the type of arguments you pass. In addition, templates may be used to define whole classes of objects that use different data types.

This list is by no means complete. C++ introduces many new programming features and unique abilities. As with any programming language, many of these new features must be used in practice before they can be appreciated.

The primary advantage of C++ over other object-oriented languages is that C++ is a superset of ANSI C. Thus, an ANSI C program can be compiled and executed with a C++ compiler. The compatibility of C++ with C is one of the primary reasons for the current success of C++. There are several other object-oriented languages that predate C++, but you must learn the new language to gain any benefit. By contrast, an experienced C programmer can use the new features of C++ in a gradual way, without having to learn an entirely new and unfamiliar language.

As previously stated, knowing the syntax and grammar of a programming language is only a part of learning how to create effective programs. Let's now look at some of the methods used in coding the software of this book to create readable, modular, and above all, working programs.

C++ Header Files

Just as in C, C++ source files are divided into two basic types, header files and module files. Since C++ is upwardly compatible with ANSI C, you can use standard C header files, which have a .h file extension, and C module files, with a .c file extension. To keep C and C++ files separate, you should keep C++ code in files with .cpp extensions and C++ headers in files with .hpp extensions. This will help to avoid confusing C and C++ code.

Note

The Turbo C++ Compiler will automatically do the extension naming for you. C++ source files will, by default, have a .cpp extension, while C++ header files will have an .hpp extension. Similarly, C source files will have a .c extension by default, and C header files have an .h extension.

In typical C programming, most of your coding effort goes into creating your functions. In C++, most of the effort is in creating your classes and their associated methods. You will find that once you properly structure your classes, creating and using the member functions is very straightforward. Many of the example programs in this book are surprisingly short because all of the work is done by the class member functions. Most of the source files are organized as a header file defining a particular class and an associated module file (same name, .cpp extension) that defines the non-inline member functions for those classes.

There is usually an .hpp header file corresponding to each C++ module file. Each header file provides definitions for the following:

- Class definitions

- Constant symbols and template definitions

- Function prototypes

The general structure of a standard header file is shown in listing 3.2. C++ class definitions (covered in detail in Chapter 12, "Classes and Objects") are an extension of C struct definitions (covered in Chapter 4, "Data Types, Variables, and Constants"). C++ provides the same macro capability as C with the #define directive. In addition, C++ provides the capability to create safer and more flexible inline function definitions with the *template* facility.

Unlike C, C++ requires prototypes for all functions. Instead of just declaring the return data type of a function, the function prototype also declares what the type of each argument should be. This gives the compiler the ability to check all of the uses of the functions throughout your program and report any argument mismatch errors (wrong number of arguments or wrong data type) at compile time. Function argument mismatch errors are a common cause of problems in many C applications. It may seem like a lot of extra work at first to do this, but the benefits are well worth the effort.

Listing 3.2   The Structure of a C++ Header File

```
#if !defined(HEADER_HPP)        // You can also use the
                                // equivalent #ifndef statement
// Use the name of the module, like MYLIB in place of the name
// header here

#define  HEADER_HPP      1

/****************************************************************/
/*
    header.hpp

    Programmer(s): Who gets blame if program doesn't work?

    Purpose: Why did you spend time on this?

    Revision History: Who changed it right before the demonstration?
*/

// A header file should be able to stand on its own, that is,
// it should include all of the other header files it needs
// to work all on its own.

#include <stdlib.h>      // Put all headers needed by this module
#include <windows.h>

/*************************************************************

    const statements that define module-wide constants.
    Using the keyword const for these symbols is preferred since
    the compiler can perform better type checking.

*************************************************************/

const  long MAXBUF       1024
const  long MAXSIZE      65536

/*************************************************************

    Typedef declarations

*************************************************************/

typedef    float         angle;

// A common use of typedef is to define symbolic names for
// template classes. This makes it very easy to change the
// storage method and type for a class.

typedef    TCvec_2DVector<float>    TCmodule_Vector;
```

(continues)

II

Learning C/C++

Listing 3.2 Continued

```
/*************************************************************

      Class Definitions

*************************************************************/

class TCmodule_Point {
     private:
     float x, y;
     protected:
     public:
     // Define the constructors and destructors
     TCmodule_Point(void)      {x = 0; y = 0;};
     // A constructor with different arguments
     TCmodule_Point(float xp, float yp) {x = xp; y = yp;};
     // Destructor
     ~TCmodule_Point(void)      {};
     // Copy constructor
     TCmodule_Point(TCmodule_Point &p) {x = p.x; y = p.y;};

     // Utility functions

     // Note that these are all defined as inline functions
     // since the function is defined immediately following
     // its declaration.

     void getXY(float &xp float &yp)     {xp = x; yp = y;};
     float getX(void)                    {return x;};
     float getY(void)                    {return y;};
     void setXY(float xp, float yp)      {x = xp; y = yp;};
     void setXY(TCmodule_Point &p)       {x = p.x; y = p.y;};
};

// Example of derived class
class TCmodule_Circle : public TCmodule_Point {
     private:
     float radius;
     protected:
     public:

     // Define the constructors and destructors
     TCmodule_Circle(void)      {radius = 1;};
     ~TCmodule_Circle(void)     {};
     // The copy constructor for the base class is
     // automatically called
     TCmodule_Circle(TCmodule_Circle &c)
       {c.radius = c.radius;};

     void move(TCmodule_Point &p);
};
```

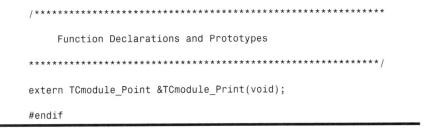

```
/***************************************************************

    Function Declarations and Prototypes

***************************************************************/

extern TCmodule_Point &TCmodule_Print(void);

#endif
```

From Here...

In this chapter, you have seen the overall design philosophy behind the development of C and C++. With its ability for structured programming and arbitrary data structures, C provides high-level control and great code efficiency. Using an object-oriented approach, C++ lets you tackle more complex, event-driven applications with greater ease. Using object methods and class inheritance, you can create reusable code modules to apply to a much wider range of applications than is readily available with C alone. You have also seen how adopting a few standard coding conventions can keep your programs more readable, portable, and compatible with other software packages.

In the following chapters, you'll learn about all the elements of the C and C++ languages:

- Chapter 4, "Data Types, Variables, and Constants," shows you the many different ways of representing data in a C program.

- Chapter 6, "Expressions and Statements," describes how to construct valid C code statements.

- Chapter 9, "Loops and Conditional Statements," shows you all of the basic C keywords for controlling the execution flow of your program.

- Chapter 10, "Pointers," discusses how dynamic memory allocation lets your program find whatever memory it needs as it needs it.

- Chapter 12, "Classes and Objects," shows you how to use C++ classes to create very modular, portable, and reusable code.

- Part V, "Advanced Tools and Techniques," talks about Windows programming and how to begin creating powerful Windows applications for yourself.

II

Learning C/C++

Chapter 4

Data Types, Variables, and Constants

Any program you create is essentially a recipe for taking one form of data as input and converting it into another form for output. Whether you are writing a database program to track employee records or creating the next great computer game, your program must manipulate data one way or another. The C and C++ programming languages give you tremendous flexibility in how you can process data of many different types. In this chapter, you learn how to do the following:

- Manipulate integers, floating-point numbers, and character strings using basic, built-in data types.

- Construct your own data types using C structures and unions.

- Understand the concept of variable scope so that you can determine when a variable may and may not be used.

Intrinsic Data Types

In a C/C++ program, you define variables using a type specifier in a variable declaration statement. The *type specifier* is simply a keyword that tells the compiler what kind of storage you want to use for the variable. For instance, you can declare a variable i to contain an integer with the following declaration:

```
int i;
```

C supports a variety of ready to use data types. These built-in data types are known as *intrinsic* data types because they are built directly into the C programming language. Later in this chapter, you will see how you can build more complex data structures from combinations of the intrinsic data types. For now, let's look at what's available to you. C supports three basic kinds of intrinsic data types:

- *Integers*, which contain ordinal numbers

- *Floating-point variables*, which contain limited-precision, floating-point values

- *Characters*, which contain an ASCII representation of a single character

Table 4.1 lists the available intrinsic data types.

Table 4.1   The ANSI C Intrinsic Data Types

Type Specifier	Description
char	Stores a single 8-bit character
int	Stores a single 16-bit integer (range –32768 to 32767)
short	Stores a single 16-bit integer (same as int)
long	Stores a single 32-bit integer (range –2147483648 to 2147483647)
float	Stores a single 32-bit floating-point value (roughly 6 significant digits)
double	Stores a single 64-bit floating-point value (about 13 significant digits)

For the integer and character data types (short, int, long, and char), C also provides another keyword: unsigned. The unsigned specifier tells the compiler to treat the variable of the declared type as having a positive value. Thus, the declaration unsigned int means that the variable will always be treated as a positive integer ranging from 0 to 65535, rather than the normal –32768 to 32767 range of int. You may use the unsigned qualifier with the short, int, long, and char type specifiers. An unsigned char variable can range from 0 to 255. Some examples of using type specifiers are the following:

```
int i;                  /* simple integer */
float data;             /* A floating-point variable */
unsigned int j;         /* Unsigned integer
                           (can be 0 to 65535) */
double d;               /* A double-precision variable */
unsigned char c;        /* c can hold a single character or
                           be treated as an integer ranging from
                           0 to 255 */
```

You can declare as many variables as you like with a single type specifier. Each new variable is separated by commas. For example, you can declare multiple variables with declarations such as:

```
float data1, data2, data3;  /* 3 floating point variables */
unsigned int I, j, k;       /* 3 unsigned integer variables */
long  d1, d2;               /* 2 32-bit integer variables */
```

As noted in table 4.1, the more digits you need, the more memory the variable requires. A `long` variable (4 bytes of storage) takes twice as much storage as a `short` or `int` (2 bytes of storage). Similarly, a `double` variable (8 bytes of storage) takes twice as much memory as a `float` to store.

Note

C provides the special function `sizeof()`, which returns the number of bytes of storage any variable uses. For instance, `sizeof(data)` would return 4 because `data` is a `float` variable. If your program ever needs to know how large something really is, you can use `sizeof()` to find out. `sizeof()` is even more useful in determining the size of programmer-defined data structures defined with the `struct` keyword described later in this chapter. You will also see more examples of how to use the `sizeof()` function in Chapter 10, "Pointers," when you need to dynamically allocate memory for a structure.

Until the advent of the 486 class PC with its internal 32-bit architecture, arithmetic operations on `long` variables was significantly slower than those with 16-bit `int` variables. However, processors are improving, especially with the built-in compiler support for the more advanced 32-bit instructions of the 486 and Pentium processors. Because of the internal memory architecture of the Intel PC, it is still advantageous to use `int` and `short` variables whenever you can. The less data your program has to move around, the more efficient your program will be. Use `long` variables only when you need the extra dynamic range they provide.

It is still the case that on almost all PCs, processing of double-precision floating-point variables (the double data type) takes much longer (often more than twice as long) than that of equivalent `float` variables, especially on machines with hardware floating-point capability. You should use `double` variables only in applications in which you really require the increased precision.

As you will see in Chapter 5, "Operators," in addition to the basic data types, C/C++ provides many of the normal mathematical operations such as addition, multiplication, division, and so on as built-in operators. Most of the common mathematical expressions like x + y, x * y, and x / y can be written just as you did in your math classes. C also provides a considerable library of standard mathematical functions such as sin(), sqrt(), and cos() for performing a wide variety of computations. As you will see in Chapter 13, "Object-Oriented Methods," with C++ you can even define how operators—such as + and *—and functions—like sin()—work on your own data types.

What Is a Variable?

A *variable* is simply a name you assign to a storage location of a certain type of data. In the declaration int i, you are declaring a variable i of the intrinsic type int. The compiler will assign a memory location for the variable i, with enough storage (2 bytes in this case) for the data type. As you will see later, not all declarations actually allocate storage, but simply act as definitions of a more complex data type.

Variable names may contain as many characters as you like, but in Turbo C++ only the first 32 characters are significant (which should be more than enough!). The name of a variable can contain letters, numbers, and the underscore character. By default, variable names are all case-sensitive, meaning that the variable i is different from the variable I. In general, it is good practice to devise a common naming convention for all of your variables. Use short, cryptic names such as i for local variables in small routines. Try to assign names that you will later recognize and know what they are for. Although it involves more typing, take advantage of the long names available to you; they can save a great deal of grief as your programs get bigger and more complicated.

Declaring Constants

C lets you specify constant values the way you would normally write them. For instance: 23, –1, 10.0, and 5000.0 are all valid constants. You can use an explicit numerical constant almost any place you would use a variable, as in the following examples:

```
int a, b, c;
float f1, f2;
float addData(float f);

a = 2;
b = a + 3 + 5;
f1 = 5.0;
f2 = f1 - 3.0;
```

```
/* Call the hypothetical function addData() using a constant
   for an argument */
addData(1.0);
```

Unlike variables, constants and constant expressions are resolved at compile time. For instance, the previous code example contains the expression b = a + 3 + 5. When you compile your program, the compiler will recognize (3 + 5) as a constant and will go ahead and replace the expression (3 + 5) with the result (8). The resulting object code will add 8 to the variable a and store the result in b. The resulting executable is more efficient, because no time is spent evaluating constant expressions. You should feel free to liberally use constants and constant expressions to make your programs more clear. Constants are even more useful when defined as macros, as you will see in Chapter 8, "Macros and Functions."

Things can get a little sticky when you pass constants of the wrong data type to functions. For instance, suppose the function addData() required a float variable as its argument, rather than an int variable. To implement the call addData(1), the compiler must be smart enough to pass the floating-point representation of 1 rather than the very different integer representation of 1. The correct format for the call is addData(1.0). In general, the compiler distinguishes floating-point constants from integer constants by looking for a decimal point. If your constant has a decimal point, it is treated as a floating-point constant. If there is no decimal point, it is treated as an integer constant.

Another commonly encountered situation occurs with passing integer arguments to functions. In some cases (especially when porting code between different operating systems), you may need to explicitly declare a constant as a long integer value (32 bits long), rather than the default int value (only 16 bits long). To deal with this problem, C/C++ provides a simple mechanism to explicitly declare the data type of a constant. By appending the constant with a special suffix character, you can control the exact data type of the constant. The available suffixes for constants are shown in table 4.2.

Table 4.2   ANSI Suffixes for Constants

Suffix	Data Type	Example
L	long	1000000L
U	unsigned int	32768U
UL	unsigned long	1000000UL
F	float	1.0f

II

Learning C/C++

The ANSI C standard states that if you use a floating-point value, such as 1.0, in an expression or pass it as an argument, the value is treated as a `double`, unless you explicitly declare the constant with an `f`, as in `1.0f`. However, in Turbo C++, if a function needs only a `float` type argument, then a passed constant is treated as a `float`. This is to avoid the relatively expensive overhead processing in converting a `float` to `double` and back again to `float` inside the function. In general, unless you have an explicit need, you will not need to use the `f` suffix.

In addition to specifying a data type, there are many occasions when you need to specify a `long` or `int` as an explicit binary value. You can do this using either an octal or hexadecimal representation for the number. In hexadecimal, you describe every 4 bits of the number using a hex digit, which can be 0 through 9 or A through F. A 4-bit binary number can have values from 0 to 15, so you need the extra A through F characters to represent the values 10 to 15. A hexadecimal number is specified by putting a leading 0x on the number. For instance, 0xA would correspond to the binary bit pattern 1010. The value 0xFFFF would correspond to the binary bit pattern 1111111111111111 (16 bits set to 1).

An `int` constant can have up to 4 hexadecimal digits, whereas a `long` can have up to 8 digits. You can also append an `L` suffix to indicate that a value should be treated as a `long`, just as with a normal representation. Ordinarily, you need to use a hexadecimal constant only when performing bit operations for special functions. For instance, many Windows functions generate special error codes as a single `int` or `long` value that is a combination of different bit fields. By performing various logical operations on the bit fields, you can extract the specific information your program needs.

Initializing Variables

A C/C++ declaration statement not only declares what data type a variable is, but also can initialize the variable to a specific value. The syntax is straightforward. The following are examples:

```
int i = 0;        /* Sets i to 0 */
float f = 3.0;    /* Sets f to 3.0 */
```

Just as you can specify multiple variables in a single declaration by separating each variable name with a comma, you can also optionally specify initial values for each of the variables, as in the following:

```
int i = 0, j = 2, k;   /* No initial value for k */
float f = 3.0, f2 = 5.0;
```

There is one important point to keep in mind about initialized variables. With the exception of `static` and global variables discussed later in this chapter in the section on static variables, initialized variables are reinitialized every time the function they are declared in is called. For instance, if you have a function called `compute()`, defined as

```
int compute(float a, float b)
{
  float result, f = 3.5;

  result = a + b + f;
  f = result;     /* f is now result */
  return result;
}
```

The variable `f` will be set equal to 3.5 every time `compute()` is called, even though `f` is set equal to `result` at the end of the computation. Unless a local variable is declared as `static`, the value of the variable will not retain the value from previous calls to the function. This topic is discussed in further detail in the section on static variables, later in this chapter.

Enumeration

In addition to the intrinsic data types already discussed, C provides a special type of `int` data type called the *enumerated type*. The enum keyword identifies a data type that has a finite number of possible discrete values. For instance, you might want a variable `command` that represents a number of different commands your program can process. You could represent the commands by simple integer values. However, this isn't very meaningful to look at in code. Instead, you might declare `command` to be an `enum` data type with several possible values:

```
enum command_types {
  COMMAND_NO_COMMAND,
  COMMAND_PROCESS_STRINGS,
  COMMAND_COMPUTE,
  COMMAND_FINISH
} command;
```

The variable `command` now can take on only one of the symbolic values specified in the comma-separated `enum` list. For instance, you can specify a command with a line such as

```
command = COMMAND_COMPUTE;
```

Internally, the `enum` data type is stored as an `int`. By default, the first symbolic value is assigned the value of 0, the second a value of 1, and so on. The enum data type is a simple way to assign multiple symbolic values to a variable.

In all respects, these symbolic values are treated by the compiler exactly the same way constants are. You will see enum data types commonly used in switch statements (described in Chapter 9, "Loops and Conditional Statements"). The advantage of using an enum is that you can very easily change it by adding new values to the enum list. You do not have to worry about the specific value (such as 1 indicating that your function should process all strings) in your program. By using the symbolic values, all of your existing code will work correctly even if you add many new commands or even change the sequential ordering of the commands. Furthermore, enum data types let the compiler check to make sure you are using a legal value for the variable.

The Syntax of *enum*

The enum declaration has two components. The optional identifier following enum identifies the specific enum declaration. The actual variable declaration, which allocates memory for a variable, follows the symbolic name definitions (bounded by { and }). With the declaration of command shown earlier, you can later declare other variables of the same type with a statement such as

```
enum command_types command2, command3;
```

This declaration declares two enum variables: command2 and command3, each of type command_types. In general, you should create only one definition of each enum type and put the definition into one of your header files. In your program modules, you can simply declare your enum variables as you need them, without having to recreate the definition each time.

Changing *enum* Assignments

One additional feature of enum in Turbo C++ is the ability to change the actual values stored for the symbolic values. This is useful for assigning symbolic names to commands or other data that come from other sources, such as routines written by other people. For example, the definition of command can be altered as follows:

```
enum command_types {
    COMMAND_NO_COMMAND = 0,
    COMMAND_PROCESS_STRINGS = 100,
    COMMAND_COMPUTE,
    COMMAND_FINISH
} command;
```

Here, COMMAND_NO_COMMAND is assigned the value 0, COMMAND_PROCESS_STRINGS is assigned the value 100, COMMAND_COMPUTE is assigned the value 101, and so on. Once you set one symbolic name to a specific value, subsequent entries are assigned sequential values (unless they are overridden by another specific assignment with =).

Data Arrays

Although the ability to declare individual variables is quite useful, it is not sufficient for most applications. Consider a simple spreadsheet in which you have one column for each month of the year. To produce a total for a row, it would be convenient to simply index from column 1 to column 12 and add the data from each column to get the final result. C provides the facility for declaring arrays of a data type to let you easily perform this sort of operation. An *array* is simply a set of sequential elements of a single data type. For instance, you could declare an array for your spreadsheet as follows:

```
float income[12];
```

This statement declares `income` as a 12-element array. In your program, you can use any element of the array by specifying the name of the array and the index, or array subscript, you want to use in brackets. In C, all arrays are *zero-indexed*, which means that the first element is at index 0. Thus, `income[0]` would be the first element; `income[11]` would be the last. In addition to accessing array elements with an explicit index, you can also use an integer variable (`int` or `long`) that contains the index you want to use. For instance, the following example code would produce the annual totals from the `income` array:

```
float total;           /* Total for the year */
float income[12];      /* Data for each month */
int i;                 /* Used as an array index */

/* Read in the data from the spreadsheet */

/* Ok, now sum up the results */
/* Initialize total to 0.0 */
total = 0.0;
for(i=0; i < 12; i++) /* Loop through all 12 months */
  total += income[i]; /* Add the income for the
                         month */
                      /* Note that the += operator does
                         a running sum */

/* total now contains the total we wanted */
```

In this example code, the variable `i` is an index into the array `income`. Note that the array is accessed in a straightforward, sequential manner with the `for` loop. You do not have to access the array sequentially. You can access any element you like by specifying the index you want. Furthermore, you can declare arrays of any data type you want, by using the appropriate type specifier (in this example, the `float` type was used). For more information on how to use the `for` statement to define a code loop, see Chapter 9, "Loops and Conditional Statements."

Two-Dimensional Arrays

In the spreadsheet example, you saw how to use an array to represent a row of the spreadsheet. But a spreadsheet is two-dimensional; it has both rows and columns. Suppose your spreadsheet had many rows representing the income of different people. One way to represent this in C/C++ is with multi-dimensional arrays. You can declare a two-dimensional array by adding another set of brackets, indicating how many rows you want to declare. For the spreadsheet example, this would be the following:

```
/* Declare an array for 100 rows of 12 columns each */
float income[100][12];
```

You can now access any particular element by specifying both a row and column index. For instance, you can find a total for the whole spreadsheet with the following code:

```
float total;          /* Total for the year */
float income[100][12]; /* Data for whole spreadsheet */
int i, j;             /* Used as an array index */

/* Read in the data from the spreadsheet */

/* Ok, now sum up the results */
/* Initialize total to 0.0 */
total = 0.0;
for(j=0; j < 100; j++) {   /* Loop through every row */
  for(i=0; i < 12; i++)    /* Loop through all 12
                              monthc */
    total += income[j][i]; /* Add to the total */
}

/* total now contains the total we wanted */
```

Multi-Dimensional Arrays

Arrays can have any number of dimensions. For instance, if you had a separate spreadsheet for several different companies, you might use a three-dimensional array, where the first index specifies the specific company the data is for. Note that if you declare a multi-dimensional array, you must always specify the correct number of indices when referencing an element of the array.

Although multi-dimensional arrays are quite useful, they are often not the most efficient, or even the best, way to store many types of large data sets. For instance, the preceding example assumes that every column of the spreadsheet is a single float value. A realistic spreadsheet has columns with floating-point values, characters, and integers, which must each be handled differently. Furthermore, when you declare an array as in the example, you automatically are assigning the number of rows and columns in the spreadsheet, which you may not know ahead of time. In Chapter 10, "Pointers," you will see how to solve both of these problems using array pointers and dynamic memory allocation.

Characters and Strings

There are numerous applications in which you need to manipulate nonnumeric data, such as characters in a text file. To handle this type of data, C provides the `char` data type. A `char` variable lets you store a single character (numerically stored by its ASCII value), such as A in a single byte of storage. Using an array declaration, you can store an entire string of characters in a character array. For instance, the following declaration defines an array named `string` with room for an 80-character string:

```
/* Declare a char array named string */
?* String has enough room for 80 characters plus the terminating
NULL,
    thus the array size of 81 */
char string[81];
```

It would be almost impossible for most applications to treat text strings as having a fixed number of characters. Instead, C defines a string as a sequence of ASCII characters terminated by the NULL character, which is simply the value 0. Thus, you can store strings of variable length and tell how many characters are in the string by looking for the first NULL character in the character array. You do not need to worry about what's stored in the character array beyond the terminating NULL. You can access any character of a string using a subscript, for instance `string[0]`. Using the NULL-terminated character convention for strings, C provides a number of useful functions for string manipulation. Some of the more basic ones are summarized in table 4.3. Note that to use any of these functions, you must include the header file string.h (`#include <string.h>`) in the modules calling these functions.

When you declare an array of characters, you should declare it to be large enough to hold the largest single string you expect to process, plus 1 more for the terminating NULL character If you are processing input from the command line or reading text from a file, an 81-character string, as shown in the example, is usually sufficient. To find the actual length of a particular string read from a file or input by the keyboard, you can use the `strlen()` function.

II

Learning C/C++

Table 4.3 Some Useful String-Manipulation Functions

Function Name	Description
`int strlen(char *s)`	Returns the length of the string, excluding the terminating NULL.
`char *strcpy(char *s1, char *s2)`	Copies the contents of string s2 over the contents of s1.
`char *strcat(char *s1, char *s2)`	This concatenates string s1 with string s2, so that s1 will contain s1 followed by s2.
`int sprintf(char *s, ...)`	This function works exactly like `printf()`, except it puts the output into the string s, rather than writing it to an output device. See Chapter 11, "I/O," for more information on `printf()`.

String and Character Constants

Just like numeric data constants, you can also declare and use character and string constants wherever you would use a character or string variable. A character constant is specified by putting the character you want to use between single quotation marks, such as `'a'` or `'1'`. A string constant is specified by a set of characters in double quotation marks, such as `"my string"`. For example, you can set a string to an initial value with code such as the following:

```
char string[80];
/* Initialize string to "This is a test" */
/* strcpy() copies the second string over
   the first string */
strcpy(string, "This is a test");
```

You can also initialize characters and strings in a declaration, just like you can for numeric variables. The following is an example:

```
char c = 'A';      /* Initializes c to 'A' */
/* An 80-character string, with an initial value */
char string[80] = "your name";
/* Create a string whose length is the same as the string */
char text_ext[] = ".txt";
```

Consider the constant `'A'` for a moment. It is not the same as the constant `"A"`, and they cannot be used interchangeably. `'A'` is a character constant that occupies one byte, whereas `"A"` is a two-byte character array, one byte for the character 'A' and one byte for a terminating NULL. You cannot use any of the string functions, such as `strlen()`, on a single-character variable or constant that isn't a string.

The last example for the string named `text` is one in which the length of the character array is not explicitly stated. Instead, the compiler uses the initial string to determine the array size for the string text. In this case, `text` will be five characters long (enough room for the four characters of `.txt` and the terminating NULL character). You must be careful when using this type of initialization. If you use a function such as `strcpy()` or `strcat()` to copy over the contents of `text`, you must make sure that the new string you are copying from contains no more than five characters. Otherwise, you will be writing into memory your program has not allocated, but may be used by another module. As a result, your program is likely to blow up or otherwise misbehave. In general, you should use the final method of initializing strings only for character arrays that will not be modified by your program (that is, treated as constant strings).

Although specifying a simple typed string is adequate in most cases, there are many non-printing characters such as carriage return, line feed (found in text files), and the NULL terminating character that you cannot simply type on your keyboard. One way to specify these characters is to use a leading backslash ('\') in the constant and specify the hexadecimal value of the character. For instance, '\x0' specifies the NULL character and '\x0D' specifies the carriage return character. In addition to specifying the hexadecimal value directly, C provides a number of special mnemonic sequences for several special characters used in printing and terminal interaction. For example, the newline character for terminating an output line is specified as '\n' and a horizontal tab is specified as '\t'. Chapter 11, "I/O," which covers file and terminal I/O, provides a complete list of these special mnemonic character sequences.

Manipulating Strings

In many instances, you can treat character variables (or equivalently, a subscript member of a string) as integers. As an example, to alphabetize a set of strings, you can compare two characters using the > operator to see which one is "greater" than the other. Another example is determining the digits in a decimal number:

```
int getdigit(char c)
{
  /* To be a digit, it must be 0 - 9 */
  if(c < '0' || c > '9')
    return -1;
```

```
        /* Must be a digit, subtract the ASCII character 0 */
        return (c - '0');
}
```

The function getdigit() returns –1 if the passed character is not a legal digit—if it isn't in the range extending from 0 through 9. If the character is a legal digit, the function returns the numeric value of the digit by subtracting the ASCII value of '0' from the digit. getdigit() is a simple example of how numeric operations can be mixed with character operations to perform special functions to parse strings.

> **Note**
>
> When performing string operations, remember that characters are naturally case-sensitive. The character a is not the same as A. Furthermore, strings read from files or other input can contain spaces, carriage returns, and other special characters which you must deal with properly for real applications, just as digits were checked in getdigit().

This section showed you the basics of string operations, but there are many other Turbo C string-processing functions to assist you in creating advanced text-processing applications. Chapter 11, "I/O," provides more detail about the functions available to you. You can find a complete list of string-manipulation functions in your Turbo C++ Library Reference (all of the ANSI C string functions start with the characters str).

Defining Your Own Data Types

One of the most useful features of the C and C++ languages is the ability to create your own data types. In Chapter 3, "The Basics," you saw a brief overview of how to define an application with objects and their associated methods. In this section, you will see how you can construct new data entities using the C structure. In Chapter 12, "Classes and Objects," you will see how C++ expands the definition of a structure to the more general class object, which not only includes data elements, but also lets you define functions for operating on those elements.

Declaring Structures

Most applications require that your program manipulate many different types of data. Consider the example of a spreadsheet program. A real spreadsheet application often has more than just single elements representing one number. For each row of the spreadsheet, you might need to store a person's name or employee ID, an address, a count of how many transactions have been processed, monthly data, or innumerable other combinations. A single array is not adequate to represent that many different data types as a single data entity.

In C, the `struct` keyword lets you define any collection of data types as a single entity. For instance, you could use the following definition for a row of the spreadsheet:

```
struct
{
  char name[40];      /* Name of person */
  int  id;            /* ID number */
  char address1[80];  /* First line of address */
  char address2[80];  /* Second line of address */
  char city[80];      /* Name of city */
  int  state;         /* Identifier for state (1-50) */
  long zipcode;       /* ZIP code */
  int numtrans;       /* Number of transactions */
  float month[12];    /* 12 months of numbers */
  float total;        /* Running total */
} row_data;
```

This declaration declares `row_data` to be a structure containing all of the data defined in the `struct` definition. Each entry in the definition of the `struct` is referred to as a structure *member*. To use any member element of `row_data`, you specify it with `row_data.<name>`, where `<name>` is one of the member items. For instance, `row_data.id` is the ID number for the row. You can use it wherever you would a normal `int` variable. Similarly, `row_data.name` is a character string containing the name of the person the data is for. You can access individual characters of the name with a reference such as `row_data.name[i]`, just as you can with any string variable.

All data associated with a `struct` is stored contiguously in memory. The total size of a structure is the sum of the sizes of each component of the structure and possibly some extra bytes used by the compiler to align the structure on even memory boundaries. As with any data type, you can use the `sizeof()` function to determine the exact number of bytes contained in a structure. See Chapter 5, "Operators," for more information on using `sizeof()`.

In addition to containing the intrinsic data types, the definition of a structure can contain other structures (except for declaring itself, that is, a structure cannot be recursively defined). For instance, you might modify the previous definition to a more hierarchical structure such as the following:

II

Learning C/C++

```
struct
{
  char name[40];      /* Name of person */
  int  id;            /* ID number */
  struct
  {
    char line1[80];   /* First line of address */
    char line2[80];   /* Second line of address */
    char city[80];    /* Name of city */
    int  state;       /* Identifier for state (1-50) */
    long zipcode;     /* ZIP code */
  } address;
  int numtrans;       /* Number of transactions */
  struct
  {
    float month[12];  /* 12 months of numbers */
    float total;      /* Running total */
  } financial;
} row_data;
```

In this example, if you wanted to access the city portion of the address, you would use the reference row_data.address.city (city is a member of the sub-structure address, which is a member of row_data). You may nest structure definitions as much as you like, although it can get quite cumbersome if the definition gets too many levels deep. To get around this situation, you can add an identifier to your structure definition (between the struct keyword and the first {), and then use it in subsequent definitions. For instance, you can redefine the previous row_data definition as follows:

```
/* Define an address structure, but don't actually
   declare a variable, just define it */
struct address_struct
{
  char line1[80];  /* First line of address */
  char line2[80];  /* Second line of address */
  char city[80];   /* Name of city */
  int  state;      /* Identifier for state (1-50) */
  long zipcode;    /* ZIP code */
};

/* Define the financial data structure */
struct financial_struct
{
  float month[12];  /* 12 months of numbers */
  float total;      /* Running total */
};

/* This is the only definition which actually
   declares anything, because we put row_data
   after the closing } */
struct row_data_struct
{
```

```
    char name[40];      /* Name of person */
    int  id;            /* ID number */
    struct address_struct address;
    struct financial_struct financial;
    int numtrans;       /* Number of transactions */
} row_data;

/* Equivalently, you could declare row_data as */
struct row_data_struct row_data;
```

Notice that the first two struct definitions only define a structure and give it a name; they do not actually declare any variables (no name appears after the closing } of the definition). The definition of row_data declares the variable address as a struct of address_struct type. Similarly, financial is a struct of type financial_struct. By providing a name in the structure definition, you can subsequently declare other variables of that structure type by simply using the declaration struct <struct_name> <variable>. This makes creating nested structures much easier, because you do not have to put all of the sub-structure definitions inside the structure definition every time you want to use it. In this example, you can now use the financial_struct and address_struct definitions in any other structures you might want to create. Even more importantly, if you decide to change the structure definition, the modified structure will automatically propagate everywhere the structure is used.

It is very important to distinguish between variable declarations and structure definitions. Just like the enum data type, the optional identifier following the struct keyword is simply a name reference for the structure definition (refer to the section "Enumeration" earlier in this chapter). It doesn't actually declare any variables. You specify the actual variables you want to declare after the keyword struct and either the identifier or the {} of the struct definition. As with any other declaration, you can declare multiple variables on one line if you want, such as the following:

```
/* Declare 2 struct variables */
struct row_data_struct row1, row2;
```

To keep from confusing the struct identifiers with variable names, it is a good idea to adopt a common naming convention for the identifiers. In this case, the name _struct has been appended to the identifier, and should also appear at the end of any other structure identifier in the program. As long as you are consistent with your naming convention, it is unlikely that you will confuse variables with definitions.

> **Note**
>
> As discussed in Chapter 3, "The Basics," it is always best to define all your structures in separate header source files (.h files). Each of your source code files should include (using the #include compiler directive) the appropriate header file defining the structures used in your code. By structuring your source files this way, you need only maintain each structure definition in one source file. If the definition needs to be changed, all the affected modules will automatically use the new structure definition whenever you rebuild your project (see Chapter 20, "Application Development in Turbo C++," for more details about how to do this). Nothing can cause more trouble than having the same structure defined in multiple source files, so avoid it at all cost—use header files!

Arrays of Structures

Just as with any variable declaration, you can use a struct declaration to generate an array of structures. Using the previous structure definitions, you could define a 100-row spreadsheet with the declaration

```
struct row_data_struct spread[100];
```

Each element of the array spread is now a row_data_struct structure. You can set the name and ID for the fifth row of the spreadsheet with code such as the following:

```
strcpy(spread[4].name,"Bob Farkel");
spread[4].id = 1;
```

Structure Initialization

When you declare a structure variable, all of the member elements are initially set to 0. You can override this behavior by defining the elements individually with a declaration similar to that of the intrinsic data types:

```
struct financial_struct finance =
  {0.0, 0.0, 0.0, 0.0, 0.0, 0.0,
   0.0, 0.0, 0.0, 0.0, 0.0, 0.0,
   0.0}
```

In this case, because the financial_struct contains a 12-element float array and a float total, you need 13 data values. In general, this type of initialization is worthwhile only for very simple structures with only a few data elements. Writing an initialization for row_data would take an entire page of code due to all of the character arrays (you need one entry for each array element!). However, there are cases in which this can be a handy way to initialize small structures.

It is important that you set the members of the structure to the correct initial values you want after the structure is declared. Normally, you do this by writing a separate function to create your structure variables dynamically. Chapter 12, "Classes and Objects," covers this topic in much greater detail. You will also see in Chapter 13, "Object-Oriented Methods," how to use class constructors to define exactly how you want to initialize a class or structure variable when it is declared, without having to have an explicit function call to initialize the structure.

Operations on Structures

There are actually only a few operations you can perform with a declared structure variable directly. You can, as you have already seen, access individual members of the structure using the . operator. You can also use a structure with the = operator to copy all of the data from one instance of the structure to another. For instance, you can set the fourth and fifth elements of the spreadsheet structure to the same values with the following statement:

```
/* Copy row 5 over row 4 */
spread[3] = spread[4];
```

The = operator performs a straight memory copy, without doing any interpretation of the data. For reasons that will become clear later (specifically in Chapter 10, "Pointers"), you will normally not want to copy the data between two structures this way if the structures contain pointers to other dynamically allocated data.

The only other operations you can perform on a structure are

- To take its address using the & operator

- To find out how much memory the structure occupies using the sizeof() function

You cannot operate on a structure directly other than with these basic operations. In Chapter 12, "Classes and Objects," you will see how the more advanced class data type lets you do everything a structure can do and allows you to define additional functions on the member elements of the structure.

Unions

A *union* is a special type of structure. There are times when you need to refer to the same data in a structure in several different ways. For instance, suppose you have a text file in which each line contains a fixed set of data, such as an

Learning C/C++

ID field, a name, and an address. You will need to access it two different ways, as either just whole lines of text for reading and writing, or as a collection of separate data entries that need to be individually processed. A very efficient way to do this is with a *union*. For this example, you could create the following definition:

```
/* Define the data on the line */
struct line_entries
{
  char id[2];           /* 2 character id */
  char space1;          /* Separating space */
  char name[30];        /* Max 30 character name */
  char space2;          /* Another space */
  char address[40];     /* Address entry */
};

/* Access the data as either a whole line,
   or as separate entries */
union line_union
{
  char linechars[80];
  struct line_entries line_data;
} line;
```

The variable `line` is a union of the 80-character array `linechars` and the structure `line_data`. `linechars` and `line_data` reference the same memory locations—they overlap in memory. Now with one data structure you can treat the same data two different ways. You access union members the same as you do structure members. For instance, you can read in the data from a text file with a call such as `fscanf(fp, "%s", line.linechars)`. Once the data is read in, you can access the `name` field by referencing `line.line_data.name`. Now you can modify the individual fields in `line` and easily write the whole record back out to another file. Without a union as defined here, you would have to create a separate function for writing out a `line_entries` type structure to a file.

Just as with the `struct` keyword, you normally declare unions in a header file with an associated identifier (`line_union` in this example). You declare individual variables using the `union` keyword and the appropriate identifier, just as shown for `struct`s.

Variable Scope

The scope of a variable is the section of a program that can legally reference the variable. In general, a declared variable can be used only inside the function in which it is declared. A variable declared inside a function definition is said to be *local* to that function, or just a *local variable*. In C, all your local variable declarations must follow the definition of the function parameters, right after the opening { that starts the function definition. In C++, you can define local functions inside any procedure body (inside any set of braces), not just at the beginning of a function definition. Local variables can be referenced only by code inside the braces in which they are defined. Thus, different functions can both have a local variable named i; each of these variables is completely separate from the other.

Although most variables are local in nature, you can create global variables that can be referenced by any function. If a variable is declared outside of any function definitions, that variable is considered a global variable. Any function within the entire source file can reference that variable. In fact, unless a global variable is declared static (described in the following section), any function in the entire program, even if the function is defined in a separate source file, can reference the global variable. However, for functions in other source files to recognize a global variable, they must declare the global variable as externally defined with the extern keyword. For instance, if you want to define the variable total_transactions, you would declare it as external with a declaration such as the following:

```
extern long total_transactions;
```

The extern keyword means that the variable is declared in one, and only one, source file. Typically, you would put a list of all global variables with extern declarations in a header file (with a .h extension). Then any program module that needs to access the global variables can do so simply by including the appropriate header file. The global variable must be defined in at least one source file, without the extern keyword, for the compiler to actually allocate space for it. In effect, extern is a cue to the compiler and linker to look for the actual variable definition in either the current program module, or in one of the other program modules.

Global variables are assigned fixed places in memory when the linker creates your program executable. Global variables let you easily pass data among different functions. For instance, if your program needs to know whether a particular event has occurred, one function can set a global variable to indicate that the event has (or has not) occurred, and any function can check the flag to determine if indeed the event has occurred. This is often much more convenient than having to pass a special event flag argument around to lots of different functions.

Global variables retain their value (unless altered by some routine) throughout the execution of your program. Local variables, on the other hand, do not retain their previous values once the function they are defined in exits. Furthermore, local variables are reinitialized every time the defining function is called. In effect, the memory locations for local variables are assigned at run time, when the function is called. Global variables are initialized only when the program first starts executing. Thus, if you have code such as

```
int i_global = 0;

int compute(float data)
{
  int result, i = 0;

  /* Do some computation */

  i_global++;      /* Keeps track of how many times
                      compute() has been called */
  return result;
}
```

then the variable i is set to 0 each time compute() is called. i_global is set to 0 only when the program starts. After that, i_global is incremented each time compute() is called, so you could report on how many times compute() was called.

Static Variables

There are many instances when you want local variables to retain their previous values. The most common occurrence is when you want a function to perform some special initialization the very first time it is called, but not for subsequent calls.

The keyword static is used to declare variables that are retained even after a function exits. If the static declaration is made inside a function definition, the variable will retain its value even after the function returns, just like a global variable. The static variable is still local to that function (still has local scope), and may be referenced only within that one function. If a static variable is declared at the beginning of a source module, outside of any function definition, the variable is available to every function in the one source module; unlike a global variable, however, it is not available to functions in other source modules. A static variable still refers to only one memory location; so if function foo1() changes it and then calls function foo2(), foo2() will see the changed value.

One common use for `static` variables within a function is to perform one-time initialization procedures. For instance, consider the following function:

```
int compute(float data)
{
  static int first_time = 1;

  if(first_time)
  {
    initialize_compute();
    first_time = 0;
  }

  <rest of function>
  return 1;
}
```

When `compute()` is called the first time, the static variable `first_time` is set equal to 1 (equivalent to TRUE in a conditional test). `compute()` will then call `initialize_compute()` and then set `first_time` to 0 (FALSE). In subsequent calls to `compute()`, `first_time` will retain its previous value of 0, and `initialize_compute()` will not be called again. Essentially, `static` variables are variables that are assigned fixed memory locations just as global variables are, but which can be referenced only locally. `static` variables defined in a source module, outside of any function definition, may be used by any function in the source file. With `static` variables, you can create function packages using global variables to pass information among all of the routines of the package; however, you can still avoid possible name collisions with global variables used by other source files.

In addition to declaring variables as static, you can also declare functions as static. A static function acts just like a static variable in a module. Only functions defined within the same source module as the static function can reference the static function. A function defined in one source module cannot reference a static function defined within a different source module. Static functions are useful when you need a specialized function and you want to make sure that no other modules can accidentally access it. Static functions provide a means of hiding specific implementation details from other source modules (and other programmers).

Although global variables can be useful, you should use them sparingly. Globals have their applications, such as keeping track of global state information to avoid having to pass extraneous arguments to all of your application functions. But you can avoid this problem by putting all the global information into a class definition and using appropriate member functions to get at the information needed by an application. Global variables should be treated

II

Learning C/C++

as variables that are modified only during program initialization or when a major change of program state has occurred that affects most of the modules. Otherwise, create an appropriate structure to contain your state information and pass it to the functions that need to use the information.

From Here...

In this chapter, you have seen how to declare constants and variables of all of the available C data types, including integers, floats, strings, and enumerated data. Using the `struct` and `union` keywords (and the `class` keyword), you can define arbitrary data structures of virtually unlimited complexity. Now that you have the variables, you need to be able to do something with them to create a useful program. For more information on how to manipulate variables and structures, please see the following chapters:

- Chapter 5, "Operators," covers all of the available C operators you can apply to variables.

- Chapter 6, "Expressions and Statements." You will see how to define C/C++ statements for implementing your algorithms.

- Chapter 10, "Pointers." Shows you how to dynamically allocate memory at run time for structures. You'll never have to hard-code array sizes again!

- Chapter 12, "Classes and Objects." C++ classes are the object-oriented extension to the C structure, providing you greater flexibility and portability in creating your data structures.

- Chapter 13, "Object-Oriented Methods," shows you how to use constructors and destructors to ensure that your structures are always created the way you want.

Chapter 5

Operators

Every computer language has its share of operators, and C++ is no different. The operators in a computer language serve to tell the computer how to connect or affect operands or expressions.

Chapter 6, "Expressions and Statements," is devoted to defining and demonstrating what an expression is. Suffice it to say that an expression usually consists of one or more operands affected by operators.

An *operand* is any quantity upon which you perform a math operation. In practical terms, operands in C++ boil down to some combination of integers and floating-point numbers. A particular operand might be a variable, structure, or class member or function call, but ultimately the type of the operand is either an integer or a floating-point number.

Operands are also recursive in nature. In the C++ language, the statement 3 + 5 can also be considered an operand with the value of 8. This chapter will consider all operands to be non-recursive, so when you see the notation op1 or op2, you can replace the notation with any integral number, and the C++ statement should compile and execute.

Of course, having said that, I will now tell you that in C++ everything might not be what it seems. C++ has a feature called *overloading*, which is discussed in Chapter 13, "Object-Oriented Methods." Overloading allows you to re-write the rules that govern how operators work. However, don't worry about overloading for now. This chapter proceeds with the assumption that no overloading is taking place.

In this chapter, you will learn the following:

- What operators are used by the C++ language.

- The various types of operators that are available.

- What precedence is and how to use it.

- Some code examples of operator use.

In this chapter, you will learn about operators and their order of precedence. Operators are usually simple instructions that you give to the computer so that it can perform some task or operation. The order of precedence indicates which operation should be done first.

I like to think about operators in the same way that I would give instructions to the driver of a car. I might say "turn left" or "turn right." These commands could be considered directional operators in the same way that + and − are mathematical operators that say "add this" or "subtract this." If I yell "stop" while the car is moving, on the other hand, it should supersede the other commands, which means that "stop" has precedence over "turn left" and "turn right."

Precedence is very important in the C++ language. Examples of how precedence can affect the order of operations are given in the section "Precedence" later in this chapter.

Operator Types

C++ supports many different types of operators. Table 5.1 shows all of the operator types in the C++ language. This section discusses the more commonly used types in detail. You can learn about any type not discussed in this chapter by looking in the chapter referenced in that type's description in table 5.1.

Table 5.1	The C++ Operator Types	
Operator Type	**Operator**	**Description**
Assignment	=, *=, /=, %= +=, -=, <<=, >>=, &=, ^=, ¦=	These operators are used to assign a value to a variable. Algebra uses assignment operators. For example, in the statement $X = 6$, the equal sign is the assignment operator.
Arithmetic	+, -, *, /, %	These operators mirror those that you learned in grade school. Addition, subtraction, multiplication, and division are the bread and butter of most mathematical statements.

Operator Type	Operator	Description
C++-specific	::, *, ->*	These operators are specific to the C++ language and mainly deal with classes. You can find more information in Chapter 12, "Classes and Objects."
Comma	,	The comma operator has two functions. It serves to separate parameters in function calls (see Chapter 8, "Functions and Macros") and it serves to separate expressions (see Chapter 9, "Loops and Conditional Statements").
Logical	&&, ¦¦, !	These operators implement Boolean logic. In the sentence "If John has a fever AND John has clogged sinuses OR an earache AND John is NOT over 60 years old, then John has a cold," the AND, OR, and NOT are acting as logical operators.
Bitwise	&, ^, ¦, ~, >>, <<	These operators affect the individual bits that make up a variable. For example, an unsigned char might consist of 8 bits. Using bitwise operators lets you affect each bit directly.
Conditional	?:	The conditional operator is shorthand that you can use instead of the IF..THEN..ELSE control statements.
Postfix	(), {}, [], ., ->	A member of this group of operators appears at the end of an affected object (usually a variable or function name).
Preprocessor	#, ##	The preprocessor operators are used to indicate when a preprocessor directive is started.
Reference/Dereference	&, *	These two operators reference (&) and dereference (*) are used to manipulate pointers. For more information, see Chapter 10, "Pointers."

II

Learning C/C++

(continues)

Table 5.1 Continued

Operator Type	Operator	Description
Relational	==, !=, <, >, <= >=	These operators allow you to test the relationship of one variable to another. For example, is the apple heavier THAN the orange?
sizeof	sizeof	The sizeof operator allows you to find out how many bytes a given variable takes up in the computer's memory. This operator is very useful when allocating memory or reading records from a file.

Assignment Operators

The assignment operators are the most basic type of operator. Almost everyone is familiar with the assignment (=) operator from studying algebra in school. This operator is used to set the value of a variable.

For example, to set the variable numDogs to 6, you use the following statement:

```
numDogs = 6
```

C++ also has an advanced or compound version of the assignment operator. The compound version combines an arithmetic operator with the assignment operator. The shorthand way to refer to the compound assignment operator is op=. Table 5.2 lists all of the possible op= operators and their descriptions.

Table 5.2 Examples of op= Compound Assignment Operators

op=	Expansion of op=	Description
x *= 4	x = x * 4	Multiplication
x /= 1	x = x / 5	Division
x %= 3	x = x % 3	Modulus
x += 5	x = x + 5	Addition
x -= 3	x = x - 3	Subtraction
x <<= 4	x = x << 4	Left shift
x >>= 4	x = x >> 4	Right shift

op=	Expansion of op=	Description
x &= 3	x = x & 3	Bitwise AND
x ^= 3	x = x ^ 3	Bitwise exclusive-OR
x ¦= 3	x = x ¦ 3	Bitwise inclusive-OR

All of the various arithmetic operands are described in the next section of this chapter.

In general, the op= statements have several advantages:

- The op= statements will be executed faster than the expanded statements because the variable x will be evaluated only once by the compiler.

- The op= statements are more clear and easier to understand when examining source code.

- The op= statements provide less chance to mistype variable names. This is a significant advantage with today's tendency to use long variable names.

Arithmetic Operators

Arithmetic operators should be familar to you from elementary school math class. Rather than repeat their definitions here, table 5.3 simply lists them.

There are five binary arithmetic operators: addition, subtraction, multiplication, division, and modulus. These operators act exactly as you expect them to. They are called *binary* because they act on two objects. In other words, the addition (+) operator can be used to add two numbers together like this: 4 + 5. The other binary operators act in similar fashion.

Table 5.3 The Five Binary Arithmetic Operators

Operator	Description
op1 + op2	Addition
op1 - op2	Subtraction
op1 * op2	Multiplication
op1 / op2	Division
op1 % op2	Modulus

The modulus operator is pretty much unused outside of computer programs (at least in my experience). It is used to find the remainder of the division between two integer operands. The following example shows how to use the modulus operator to display a message for every ten items that are processed:

Listing 5.1 How to Display a Message for Every Ten Items

```
#include <stdio.h>

int main(void)
{
    for (int i = 0; i <= 100; i++) {
        if (i % 10 == 0)
            printf("%d", i);
}
    return(0);
}
```

When this example is executed, the output should look like the following:

```
0 10 20 30 40 50 60 70 80 90 100
```

The statement

```
if (i % 10 == 0)
```

is where the work to determine every tenth item is done. You can use this type of programming to display a message as work is being done. For instance, if you are copying a large file, you might want to display what percentage of the file has been copied in 5 percent increments.

The statement

```
printf("%d", i);
```

prints the current value of i to the display. You can find more information about printf in Chapter 11, "I/O."

Table 5.4 The Unary Arithmetic Operators

Operator	Description
Changing the sign of *op1*	
+op1	Positive operand
-op1	Negative operand

Operator	Description
Changing the value of *op1* before usage	
++op1	Preincrement operand by one
--op1	Predecrement operand by one
Changing the value of *op1* after usage	
op1++	Postincrement operand by one
op1--	Postdecrement operand by one

Arithmetic operators start to get complicated when unary operators are discussed. Just between you and me, I didn't get the hang of negative numbers until someone said: "If you have five pieces of chocolate, and I add negative two pieces of chocolate..."

Now I know that you will never write a mathematics statement like the following: 345 + -23. However, you might use: 354 + iGasBill, where iGasBill represents a 23-dollar debit—in other words, a negative number.

The ++ and -- operators are examples of the shorthand notation that the C++ language is famous for. If the ++ or -- operators appear in front of the operand, the operand is affected before use in the statement. If the ++ or -- operators appear after the operand, the value of the operand is used in the statement and then incremented or decremented as required.

The following four examples demonstrate how these operators are used. Part A of each example shows the use of the ++ or -- statement. Part B shows how you can achieve the same effect using normal binary operators. Part C is commentary about the example.

Example 1:

Part A: `numPages = 5;`
         `++numPages;`   numPages is 6.

Part B: `numPages = 5;`
         `numPages = numPages + 1;`   Same result as Part A.

Part C: Please note that you can use the ++ and -- operators by themselves in a statement.

Example 2:

Part A: `numPages    = 5;`
          `totalPages = numPages++;`   totalPages is 5; numPages is 6.

Part B: `numPages    = 5;`
          `totalPages = numPages;`
          `numPages++;`   Same result as Part A.

Part C: It might help to note that postincrement and postdecrement operators do not affect the value of the variable on the left side of the assignment operator. If you see postincrement or post-decrement operators, evaluate the statement by ignoring the operators. Then, when done, apply the postincrement and postdecrement operators as required.

Example 3:

Part A: `numPages = 5;`
          `totalPages = --numPages + 5;`   totalPages is 9, numPages is 4.

Part B: `numPages = 5;`
          `numPages = numPages - 1;`
          `totalPages = numPages + 5;`   Same result as Part A.

Example 4:

Part A: `a = 5;`
          `b = 4;`
          `c = a-- + --b;`   a is 4, b is 3, and c is 8.

Part B: `a = 5;`
          `b = 4;`
          `b = b - 1;`
          `c = a + b;`
          `a = a - 1;`   Same result as Part A.

Part C: Part of the reputation that C++ has as a hard-to-understand language comes from the overuse of these two operators. If you look at Part A, you can see that it will take longer to decipher the shorthand than the expanded statements of Part B.

Tip

The C++ programming language has many ways of achieving the same objective. You will become a more efficient programmer if you decide on one approach to incrementing/decrementing and use it consistently.

Some note should be taken of what types of variables are being used with each operator. Of the arithmetic operators, only the modulus operator is restricted to integer variables. The other operators can use both floating-point and integer variables.

Logical Operators

Logical operators are mainly used to control program flow (see table 5.5). Usually you will find them as part of an IF..THEN..ELSE, a WHILE, or some other control statement. Control statements are discussed in Chapter 9, "Loops and Conditional Statements."

Table 5.5   The Logical Operators

Name	Operator	Description	Result Table		
AND	op1 && op2	Performs a logical AND of the two operands.	**op1** 0 1 0 1	**op2** 0 0 1 1	**op1 & op2** 0 0 0 1
OR	op1 ¦¦ op2	Performs a logical OR of the two operands.	**op1** 0 1 0 1	**op2** 0 0 1 1	**op1¦ op2** 0 1 1 1
NOT	! op1	Performs a logical NOT of the operand.	**op1** 0 1	**! op1** 1 0	

The concept of what logical operators do is simple. They allow a program to make a decision based on multiple conditions. The following examples demonstrate several different ways that logical conditions can be used. Part A is the English version, Part B is a C++ version, and Part C is commentary to point out the logical operand used.

Example 1:

Part A: If the number of files is equal to 10 AND the maximum number we can use is 9, THEN we have a problem and need to display an error message.

Part B: `if (numFiles == 10 && maxNum == 9) then displayError`

Part C: The logical operator used in this example is the AND (&&) operator. This operator will produce a TRUE or 1 value if both of the operands evaluate to TRUE.

Example 2:

Part A: If the caught fish is a striped bass OR the size is less than 4 inches, then throw it back.

Part B: `if (fish.type == STRIPED_BASS ¦¦ fish.size == SMALL)`
          `then tossFish`

Part C: The logical operator used in this example is the OR (¦¦) operator.
          This operator will produce a TRUE or 1 value if either of the
          operands evaluates to TRUE.

Caution

If the first operand of the OR (¦¦) operator evaluates to TRUE, the second operand
will not be evaluated. This could be a source of bugs if you are not careful. For example, in the following code fragment:

```
-- (a++) ¦¦ (b++) --
```

variable b will not be incremented if a++ evaluates to TRUE.

Example 3:

Part A: If the end of file is not reached, read in a new record.

Part B: `if (! endFile) then readRecord`

Part C: Assuming that the `endFile` variable gets set to FALSE when the file is
          opened, using the `!` operator will cause the expression to evaluate to
          TRUE until the `endFile` variable is changed when the last record is
          read.

Bitwise Operators

The bitwise operators, listed in table 5.6, are similar to the logical operators,
except that they work on a smaller scale. Bitwise operators are used to change
individual bits in a variable or operand. This can be useful when computer
memory is at a premium. An `unsigned char` variable, when treated as 8 individual bits instead of as a byte, can signify the ON/OFF status of 8 objects
because each bit can be used as a Boolean variable that can hold one of two
values: ON/OFF, TRUE/FALSE. As the programmer, you can decide what the
set of values will be.

Tip

The logical NOT
operator will re-
turn 0 (FALSE) if
given *any* non-zero
operand—for
example, `! 10 =`
`0`. This is useful to
know when you
are constructing
conditional expres-
sions. Chapter 9,
"Loops and Condi-
tional Statements,"
provides more
information.

Table 5.6   The Bitwise Operators

Name	Operator	Description	Result Table		
AND	op1 & op2	This operator compares two bits and generates a result of 1 if both bits are 1; otherwise, it returns 0.	**op1** 0 1 0 1	**op2** 0 0 1 1	**op1 & op2** 0 0 0 1
Exclusive-OR	op1 ^ op2	This operator compares two bits and generates a result of 1 if either or both bits are 1; otherwise, it returns 0.	**op1** 0 1 0 1	**op2** 0 0 1 1	**op1 ^ op2** 0 1 1 0
Inclusive-OR	op1 ¦ op2	This operator compares two bits and generates a result of 1 if the bits are complementary; otherwise, it returns 0.	**op1** 0 1 0 1	**op2** 0 0 1 1	**op1 ¦ op2** 0 1 1 1
Complement	~ op1	This operator is used to invert all of the bits of the operand.			
Shift right	op1 >> op2	This operator moves the bits to the right, discards the far right bit, and assigns the leftmost bit to 0. Each move to the right effectively divides op1 in half.			
Shift left	op1 << op2	This operator moves the bits to the left, discards the far left bit, and assigns the rightmost bit to 0. Each move to the left effectively multiplies op1 by 2.			

> **Note**
>
> Both operands associated with the bitwise operator must be integers.

> **Caution**
>
> The &, <<, and >> operators are context-sensitive. The & operator is used to reference variables and the << and >> symbols are used as input and output operators that work with the IOStream class. However, the IOStream class is beyond the scope of this book.

Now let's look at a more practical example of how to use bitwise operators. The first step is to define the meanings of the 8 bits that make up a byte variable. Figure 5.1 shows an example of a byte that could be used to control the attributes of text on display.

Fig. 5.1

The bit definition of a text attribute control byte.

Italic	Bold	Blinking	Underline	Dbl-Underline	Future Use	Future Use	Future Use	Attribute
7	6	5	4	3	2	1	0	Byte Position
128	64	32	16	8	4	2	1	Value

If you assume that the variable textAttr has been defined as a text attribute control byte, you can set the italic attribute by setting textAttr equal to 128 (textAttr = 128) because the bit pattern of 128 is 1000000. The bit that is turned on corresponds to the italic position in the control byte.

Now let's set both the italic and underline attributes on. The underline value is 16, which has a bit pattern of 00010000. You already found the italic value (128). Now we call on the inclusive-OR operator to combine the two values:

```
textAttr = 128 ¦ 16;
```

or using the bit patterns (this is just an example—you can't do this in C++):

```
textAttr = 10000000 ¦ 00010000;
```

If you look back at table 5.6 to see the results of the inclusive-OR of each pair of bits, you will see that textAttr will be set to 144, which has a bit value of 10010000. This will set both the italic and underline attributes on.

The next step would be to turn the italic attribute off. This is done with the exclusive-OR operator, like so:

```
textAttr ^= 128;
```

The resulting value of `textAttr` is 16, which leaves the underline attribute on and turns off the bold. Please note the use of the *op=* statement. It is much more concise than

```
textAttr = textAttr ^ 16.
```

Conditional Operators

The conditional (?:) operator is actually a sequence of operators. The syntax of the operator is as follows:

```
CONDITION-PART ? TRUE-PART : FALSE-PART
```

which is shorthand for the following C++ statement:

```
if (CONDITION-PART)
     TRUE-PART
else FALSE-PART
```

The value of the entire statement depends on the evaluation of the *CONDITION-PART* section of the statement. If the *CONDITION-PART* evaluates to TRUE, then the *TRUE-PART* is the value of the entire statement. If the *CONDITION-PART* evaluates to FALSE, then the *FALSE-PART* is the value of the entire statement.

I use this operator frequently to assign a value to a variable when it can take one of two values. This use of the operator is fairly straightforward. Here is an example:

```
fileSize = (! numFiles) ? 0 : files[i].size;
```

In this example, if the number of files is zero, the `fileSize` is 0. If the number of files is not zero, then `fileSize` is equal to the size of the file at location `i` in the `files` array.

The conditional operator can also be used to control which code sections are performed. The following examples show how this can be done.

Example 1:

Part A: `1 ? numFiles++ : numRecords++;`

Part B: In this example, the *CONDITION-PART* evaluates to TRUE, so the `numFiles` variable is incremented.

Example 2:

Part A: `0 ? numFiles++ : numRecords++;`

Part B: In this example, the `CONDITION-PART` evaluates to FALSE, so the `numRecords` variable is incremented.

Example 3:

Part A: `a == 0 ? numFiles++ : (a == 1 ? numRecords++ : (a == 3 ? numBytes++ : numErrors++));`

Part B: In this example, we get a little carried away. This example shows you that you don't always have only two actions to consider. Four different variables could be affected by the execution of this statement. Although this statement is legal, there are better ways of doing the same thing. Using the `switch` statement (described in Chapter 9, "Loops and Conditional Statements") will enable the compiler to create more efficient low-level assembly language.

Postfix Operators

The postfix operators fall into five categories:

- The (and) operators are used to group expressions, isolate conditional expressions, and indicate function calls and function parameters. See Chapter 8, "Functions and Macros," for more information.

- The { and } operators are used as the start and end of compound statements. See Chapter 9, "Loops and Conditional Statements," for more information.

- The [and] operators are used to indicate single- and multidimensional array subscripts. These are discussed in Chapter 4, "Data Types, Variables, and Constants."

- The . operator is used to access class, structure, and union members. This operator was also discussed in Chapter 4.

- The -> operator is used to access class, structure, and union members. This operator was also discussed in Chapter 4.

Each of these operators is used immediately after the affected variable or operand, and all are discussed in other chapters of this book.

Preprocessor Operator

The C++ language has a powerful feature called *preprocessing*. Before your program code is compiled, a preprocessor program is run. This program allows you to perform token replacement, macro definition, and conditional compilations. (See Chapter 8, "Functions and Macros," for additional information.) All of these activities are controlled by the *preprocessor operator*.

The preprocessor (#) operator is active only when it occurs as the first character on a line. It serves as a flag to the compiler that some special handling is required. Another way of saying this is that a compiler directive starts with a pound sign (#) as the first character on a line.

This section serves as an overview of the types of directives that can be used. Chapter 15, "Compiling and Linking," goes into more detail.

The compiler will recognize the directives at any point in your source file. In order to make programs more manageable, however, the compiler directives are typically located at the beginning of each source file. This makes it easier to find the information months or years later.

Turbo C++ for Windows supports the following preprocessor directives:

Directive	Explanation
#	This directive, called the *null directive*, consists of a line with a single pound sign and is always ignored.
#define	This directive provides a method of token replacement and macro creation. This does not sound very useful, but it is a very powerful tool. While reading the discussion about macros in Chapter 8, "Functions and Macros," keep in mind that you can apply the preprocessor as a separate program outside the Turbo C++ environment and use it in other projects.
#if, #elif, #else, #endif	These directives are used to conditionally compile parts of your program. Perhaps you have some source lines used to debug your program during testing. These directives could be used to isolate the debug code so that the final compile would not include the debug stuff. More information about these directives can be found in Chapter 15, "Compiling and Linking."
#error	This directive works in conjunction with the conditional compilation directives. It will produce an error message and stop the compilation process.

(continues)

II

Learning C/C++

Directive	Explanation
`#ifdef`, `#ifndef`	These directives allow you to test to see if an identifier or macro has been defined yet. I use this directive to see whether header files have been loaded. Additional information can be found in Chapter 8, "Functions and Macros."
`#include`	This directive tells the compiler to insert the contents of a given file into the source code at the point of the `#include` line. It is mainly used to incorporate header files into your source code. Header files are used to make sure that things that are common to multiple files stay the same (such as macros, structure definitions, and `#define` statements).
`#line`	This directive is used mainly by utilities that automatically generate C++ code so that error messages from the compiler can refer back to line numbers and the name of the original source file, which is typically not written in the C++ language. For example, if you had a BASIC-language-to-C++ translator, the line number and file name of the BASIC source code would be indicated by the `#line` directive.
`#pragma`	This directive is used for compiler options that fall outside the scope of the C++ language. There are 13 different versions of this directive, and each tells the compiler to do something different. For example, one variation `#pragma hdrfile` allows you to specify where to store precompiled header files.
`#undef`	This directive is used to remove a macro or token replacement set up by a `#define` statement. This might be used to override a macro created by a compiler header file.

Relational Operators

The relational operators, listed in table 5.7, are used to test the equality or inequality of operands. Like the logical operators, the value of the statement containing the relational operators can either be TRUE (non-zero) or FALSE (zero).

Table 5.7 The Relational Operators		
Name	**Operator**	**Description**
Equal	*op1* == *op2*	This operator returns TRUE if *op1* is equal to *op2*. For example, 6 == 6 is TRUE.
Not equal	*op1* != *op2*	This operator returns TRUE if *op1* is not equal to *op2*. For example, 6 != 5 is TRUE.
Less than	*op1* < *op2*	This operator returns TRUE if *op1* is less than *op2*. For example, 6 < 7 is TRUE.
Greater than	*op1* > *op2*	This operator returns TRUE if *op1* is greater than *op2*. For example, 6 > 5 is TRUE.
Less than or equal	*op1* <= *op2*	This operator returns TRUE if *op1* is less than or equal to *op2*. For example, 6 <= 6 is TRUE.
Greater than or equal	*op1* >= *op2*	This operator returns TRUE if *op1* is greater than or equal to *op2*. For example, 6 >= 5 is TRUE.

The relational operators are used a great deal with IF..THEN..ELSE, DO..WHILE, and all of the other control statements, which will be discussed in Chapter 9, "Loops and Conditional Statements."

The *sizeof* Operator

As you learned in Chapter 4, "Data Types, Variables, and Constants," the sizeof operator is used to determine how many bytes the operand uses in memory. The operand can be any variable type, either C++ or user-defined. The syntax is as follows:

```
sizeof(operand)
```

Listing 5.2 shows how the sizeof operator can be used to find out how many fixed-length records are in a file.

II

Learning C/C++

Listing 5.2   How to Determine the Number of Fixed-Length Records in a File

```
#include <dir.h>
#include <stdio.h>

struct nameSTRUCT {
    char surname[25];
    char first[20];
    unsigned char age;
} name;

int main(void)
{
int retValue;
struct ffblk ffblk;

    retValue = findfirst("names.dat", &ffblk, 0);
    if (retValue == 0)
        numRecords = ffblk.ff_fsize / sizeof(struct nameSTRUCT);
    else
        printf("File not found");
}
```

The first line of the `main()` function calls the `findfirst` function. If the file is found, the `ffblk` structure is filled with information about the file. The `ff_fsize` member is set equal to the size of the file.

The *true* portion of the `if` statement is where the `sizeof` operator is used. The statement divides the size of the file by the size of the record, resulting in the number of records in the file.

Precedence

We talked about precedence at the beginning of this chapter. Now that you are familiar with most of the C++ operators, it's time to look more closely at precedence. Table 5.8 shows all of the C++ operators and their precedence level. Operators at the same level have the same precedence. Otherwise, the higher precedence levels get evaluated first.

Table 5.8   The Precedence Level of C++ Operators

Precedence Level	Operators
16	() [] -> :: .
15	! ~ + - ++ -- & * sizeof new delete

Precedence Level	Operators
14	.* ->*
13	* / %
12	+ -
11	<< >>
10	< <= > >=
9	== !=
8	&
7	^
6	¦
5	&&
4	¦¦
3	?:
2	= *= /= %= += -= &= ^= ¦= <<= >>=
1	,

Let's look at some examples to clarify things.

Example 1:

Part A: numPages = 4
         endOfSection = TRUE
         totalPages = 34 + numPages-- + endOfSection ? 1 : 0

Part B: The evaluation of Part A leads to a value of 1 for totalPages. Because the conditional operator has a precedence level of 3, everything else has a higher precedence level and will be evaluated first.

Example 2:

Part A: numPages = 4
         endOfSection = TRUE
         totalPages = 34 + numPages-- + (endOfSection ? 1 : 0)

Part B: The evaluation of Part A leads to a value of 39 for totalPages because the parentheses operators have a precedence level of 16. They serve to isolate various regions of the statements and tell the compiler to evaluate the stuff inside before evaluating the rest of the statement.

Tip
In order to avoid worrying about precedence, I liberally sprinkle my code with parentheses operators to explicitly tell the compiler how I want statements to be evaluated. This has the side benefit of usually making the expression more readable.

II

Learning C/C++

From Here...

Now that you are familiar with the operators that are used by the C++ language, you can continue to explore the C++ language in many ways. You might want to go on to the following chapters:

- Chapter 4, "Data Types, Variables, and Constants," to review data types so that you can use the bitwise operators properly with integers.

- Chapter 6, "Expressions and Statements," to move to the next stage in your learning.

- Chapter 8, "Functions and Macros," to learn more about the preprocessor directives.

- Chapter 9, "Loops and Conditional Statements," to find out how to use the comma operator and more about how relational operators are used.

Chapter 6

Expressions and Statements

In the last chapter we discussed operators. In this chapter you will

- Learn what an expression is

- Learn what a statement is

- Find out how expressions and statements differ

- Look at examples of expressions and statements

Expressions are a sequence of constants, functions, variables, or literals, connected by one or more operators, which evaluates to a single value and may have one or more side effects (remember the ++ operator, which has the effect of incrementing a variable either before the expression is evaluated or after). It is important to note that although the expression is evaluated, nothing is done with the value unless the expression is being used inside of a statement. The second half of this chapter, "Understanding Statements," will show you how expressions are used in statements.

In a very real sense, the main reason for computer programs to exist is to manipulate data in some way. An expression, other than the side effects, does not change any data.

Statements, on the other hand, actually tell the computer to affect some data or to branch to a new line of program code. The statement is the building block of the C++ programming language. Whenever any action occurs, it occurs because a statement was executed.

You might note that I refer to expressions as being evaluated and statements as being executed. This difference gives a clue about how each affects your programming.

Of course, not every statement causes action. Later in this chapter, you'll see some statements that cause no action.

If you have read Chapter 5, "Operators," you have already seen many examples of expressions. The next section discusses simple expressions.

Understanding Expressions

The following sections will show both simple and complex types of expressions. Simple expressions consist of one variable, one literal, or two variables and an operator. Complex expressions can use many variables and multiple operators.

Simple Expressions

The simplest expressions consist of a single variable or literal. Some examples are shown in table 6.1. Not much can be said about these expressions because they are so basic.

Table 6.1   The Simplest C++ Expressions

Simple Expression	Description
1	Integer literal
"Chocolate is great!"	String literal
numPages	Variable

Simple Expressions with Side Effects

The next type of expression that we will look at is the simple expression that has side effects. Side effects are caused by the ++ and -- unary operators. These operators have the effects of changing the value of a variable just by the evaluation of the expression. No other C++ operator has this effect.

In addition, side effects may be caused when a function is used in an expression. The function may change the value of a variable. This is especially true when your program uses global variables. Table 6.2 gives some examples of expressions with side effects.

Table 6.2 Simple C++ Expressions with Side Effects	
Simple Expressions	**Description**
numPages--	Decrements a variable
--numPages	Decrements a variable
numPages++	Increments a variable

Please note that when the expressions numPages-- and --numPages are used, they have the same side effect even though they evaluate to different values. The first evaluates to numPages and the second to numPages-1. The side effect is to decrement numPages.

An expression such as numPages++ evaluates to the value of numPages. The expression has the side effect of incrementing the variable.

Simple Expressions with Operators

The next level of complexity is simple expressions with operators. Note that any arithmetic operators can be used in the expressions. Table 6.3 shows several examples.

Table 6.3 Simple C++ Expressions with Operators	
Simple Expressions	**Description**
10 + 20	Addition
20 - numPages	Subtraction
numPages / 10 + 5	Division and addition

Another way of viewing the expression 10 + 20 is as *simple expression +* *simple expression*. You will see in the next section that complex expressions are just simple expressions linked together.

Complex Expressions

A complex expression is one that incorporates several of the different variations discussed in the sections on simple expressions. The following are some examples of complex expressions:

```
(10 + 2) + 20 / (5 ^ 2)

20 - ((numPages - 1) * 2)

((numPages++ / numChapters) * (1.5 / 10) + 5)
```

There is a nearly infinite number of expressions that you can form with the C++ operator set and you can get extremely complex in your use of parentheses and conditional, postfix, and prefix operators if you are not careful. I prefer to keep the expressions short and easy to document.

Understanding Statements

Statements were briefly discussed at the beginning of the chapter. Statements are a complete unit of instruction for the computer to process. The computer executes each statement that it sees in sequence until a jump or branch is processed. Table 6.4 lists the C++ statement types and their associated keywords.

Table 6.4 Types of C++ Statements

Statement Type	Associated Keywords
No-action statements	none
Assignment statements	none
Exception statements	`__finally, try, throw, catch`
Decision statements	`switch..case..default, if..else`
Jump statements	`break, continue, goto, return`
Loop statements	`do, for, while`

The following sections briefly discuss each of these statement types.

No-Action Statements

Any valid expression can be made into a statement by adding a semicolon to the end of it.

Example 1:

```
numPages + 1                    Expression

numPages + 1;                   Statement
```

The statement `numPages + 1` in Example 1 will be executed by the computer, but no work will be accomplished because the statement has no side effects.

Example 2:

```
numpages++ / 2          Expression

numPages++ / 2;         Statement
```

The statement `numpages++ / 2` in Example 2 will be executed by the computer and the `numPages` variable will be incremented as a side effect, but no other work will be done.

Assignment Statements

The assignment statement is used to give a variable a value. Here are some examples of assignment statements:

```
numPages = 5;

largeBook = (numPages > 1000 ? TRUE : FALSE);

numChapters = (LargeBook == TRUE ? 10 : 5);
```

The second and third lines are examples of using the conditional operator to assign a value to a variable. Let's look at the second example in more detail. It says: If the number of pages is greater than 1,000, then assign the value of `TRUE` to `largeBook`, otherwise assign the value of `FALSE` to `largeBook`.

The assignment statement basically *changes* the value of a variable on the left side of the assignment operator to the value of the expression on the right side of the assignment operator.

> **Caution**
>
> Actually, in C++ it's a little more complicated because you can assign values to *lvalues,* or *object locators.* Whenever you reference a variable by name, the computer really sees the location, or address, of the variable. This becomes important when you deal with pointers, which are variables that hold as their value the memory location of another variable. Chapter 10, "Pointers," explains in detail how to handle pointers.

Exception Statements

Exception statements are used to tell the computer which program sections should be called when an unexpected error occurs. This error could range from a hard-disk error to not having a diskette in the drive when accessing drive A. Chapter 14, "Exception Handling," discusses how to use the exception statements.

II

Learning C/C++

Table 6.5	Types of Exception Statements
Keywords	**Description**
`try { }`	This keyword brackets a program section. While the program is executing the statements inside the section, program exceptions are handled by the error handlers defined in the `catch` statements.
`catch..throw`	`catch` tells the computer where the program can handle the unexpected error (called the error handler) and `throw` sends information about the error to the error handler.

Decision Statements

Decision statements are used when a choice needs to be made in your program. The choice could be to execute one block of statements instead of another or to change the value of a variable. Table 6.6 shows the two types of C++ decision statements. Both are discussed at length in Chapter 9, "Loops and Conditional Statements."

Table 6.6	Types of Decision Statements
Keyword	**Description**
`if`	This keyword is used to test a specific condition.
`switch`	This keyword is used to test a variable against a variety of values.

The *if* Statement

The `if` statement is used to test a single condition. For example:

```
if (numPages > 20) {
    // code block to execute if condition is true.
}
else {
    // code block to execute if condition is false.
}
```

The `else` section of the `if` statement is optional. If you have nothing to do when the condition is false, simply omit it, as in the following:

```
if (numPages > 20) {
    // code block to execute if condition is true.
}
```

Even though the `if` statement tests only one condition, you can use the logical operators (see Chapter 5, "Operators," for more information) to make complex conditions. For example:

```
if (numPages > 20 && (today == SATURDAY || today == SUNDAY)) {
    // read the book
}
```

This `if` statement has three comparisons to make as part of a single condition.

The *switch* Statement

The `switch` statement is used when you need to test a variable for many different values. For example:

```
switch (printerType) {
    case HPII:
        // do printer-specific stuff for Hewlett-Packard II.
        break;
    case HPIII:
    case HP4SI:
        // do printer-specific stuff for HP printers.
        break;
    case EPSON:
        // do printer-specific stuff for EPSON printers.
        break;
    default:
        // display error. unknown printer.
        break;
}
// Next C++ statement.
```

In this example, you can see that the variable `printerType` is tested three times. If the printer type is not recognized, the default section is entered and an error message is displayed. The `break` statement tells the compiler that the current `case` section is over and to jump to the statement after the `switch` statement, where the `Next C++ statement` comment is.

If no `break` statement is used as in the section on HPIII printers, the code will fall through to the next section. In the example, the code falls through to the section on HP4SI printers.

Jump Statements

Jump statements are used to unambiguously change the execution order of the statements in your program. Most of the jump statements are used as part of loop or condition statements. Only the `goto` and `return` keywords stand alone.

Because this chapter is really an overview chapter, most of the statements are fully described in other chapters as indicated in table 6.7. Only the goto statement is described here.

Table 6.7 Types of Jump Statements

Keyword	Description
break	This keyword is used to jump out of loops, case statements, and code sections bracketed by braces. You can find further details in Chapter 9, "Loops and Conditional Statements."
continue	This keyword is used within loops to jump out of the code section. It is usually used to force reevaluation of the loop condition. You can find further details in Chapter 9, "Loops and Conditional Statements."
goto	This keyword is used to jump directly to a local label. goto statements are rarely used in C++ programming. In fact, most computer texts frown on their use because they usually make programming more difficult to understand.
return	This keyword is used to jump back to the calling routine. It can be used anywhere in a subroutine. A return value can optionally be passed back to the calling routine. More information about how the return statement is used can be found in Chapter 8, "Functions and Macros."

The goto statement can be used anywhere to redirect program execution to a local label. For example:

```
loop:
    // statement1
    // statement2
    goto loop;
```

Please note that the example results in an infinite loop. A more complete example would be the following:

```
loop:
    // statement1
    // statement2
    if (counter == 100)
        goto afterLoop;
    goto loop;
afterLoop:
    // the rest of the program.
```

The do..while loop statement described in the next section, "Loop Statements," provides an alternative, and perhaps better, way of performing this task. I recommend using the goto statement infrequently. Its best use might be to jump from inside of loops nested several levels deep.

Loop Statements

Loop statements are very powerful programming tools. The `for` statement is probably the most-used loop statement in the C++ language. Since these statements are discussed at length in Chapter 9, "Loops and Conditional Statements," only a brief introduction is provided here.

Table 6.8	Types of Loop Statements
Keyword	**Description**
for	This statement is used to loop through a given set of values; when a specified condition is met, the loop is exited. This is the only loop construct that allows you to initialize variables, check a continuation condition, and change variables after each loop all in one statement.
do..while	This statement is used to execute a specific block of program code until a specified condition is met. The block of program code will *always* be executed at least once.
while	This statement is used to execute a specific block of program code if the specified condition is true.

The `for` statement allows you to loop through a range of values. For example:

```
for (index = 0; index < 200; index = index + 3) {
    // index starts a 0, and each loop increments it by 3
    // until index is greater than 200.
}
```

The `for` statement uses three expressions to control the parameters of the looping. The first expression usually values loop variable. The loop variable is the variable that changes each time the loop is executed. The second expression is the condition that causes the loop to exit when true. And the third expression is used to change the loop variable after the condition is evaluated to false.

`do...while` statements are used when you need to execute a block of code at least once. For example:

```
do {
    // block of code that may set endFile equal to true.
} while (endFile == false);
```

In the preceding example, a file was opened and we know that at least one record can be read from it. If the file contained only one record, the `endFile` flag would be set to true and the `do..while` statement would end because the condition statement would evaluate to false.

II

Learning C/C++

The `while` statement is used when you might execute a block of statements depending on a given condition. When using the `while` statement, it is important to remember that the code block might never be executed. For example:

```
while (numPages > 0) {
    // print a page.
    numPages--;
}
```

In the preceding example, if `numPages` is zero (0) before the `while` statement, no pages will print. Otherwise, a page will be printed and the variable decremented. Eventually, `numPages` will be zero and the loop will be exited.

From Here...

Ok, you've come a long way to get to this point. You are now familiar with some of the building blocks of C++ in the form of expressions and statements. In essence, you can now form a complete thought in the C++ language.

The rest of this book teaches you how to refine your thinking:

- Chapter 9, "Loops and Conditional Statements," talks about how to think iteratively using several different C++ language constructs such as the `for` and `do..while` statements.

- Chapter 11, "I/O," shows how to communicate with users by displaying messages and how to interact with files to save and read information.

- Chapter 14, "Exception Handling," discusses how to handle the unexpected.

- Chapter 24, "Windows Programming Basics," shows you how to think about the Windows environment, which requires whole new thought patterns.

Chapter 7

Typecasting and Type Conversion

When I was little, my parents gave me a set of building blocks that linked together to form structures. Some of the blocks were round and some were square. Round blocks attached to round blocks and square blocks attached to square blocks. Only blocks of the same type would attach to each other unless a special connector was used.

I faced a similar situation when I first started to program in the C++ language. Part of a program that I was creating did not produce the result that I expected. After some examination, I found the problem in the code, which looked like the following:

```
#include <stdio.h>

int main(void)
{
int numApples = 10;
int numBins = 3;

    printf("%d", numApples / numBins);

    return(0);
}
```

This code displayed a value of 3 instead of 3.33333 as I expected. After investigation, I discovered that the problem was that I was using integer variables (round blocks) instead of floating-point variables (square blocks). Floating-point variables should be used when fractions are needed.

In order to tell the compiler that fractions were needed, I had to *cast* the variables as the variable type `float` for the duration of the expression. The cast operator was similar to the special connector that I had used as a child to overcome incompatibility. The next code fragment shows the cast operation:

```
#include <stdio.h>

int main(void)
{
int numApples = 10;
int numBins = 3;

    printf("%f", (float)numApples / (float)numBins);

    return(0);
}
```

The printf statement shows how to cast one variable type into another. You might ask: Why not simply declare the variables as float to begin with? The answer is that floating-point variables take longer to process than integer variables, and most of the time I needed those variables only in integer expressions.

This chapter will discuss the following:

■ The definition of typecasting

■ The definition of type conversion

■ How to use the cast operation to interpret your variables and expressions in different ways

What Is Typecasting?

Typecasting allows you to temporarily change the variable type of a given expression. The syntax for the cast operator is

```
(variable type) (expression)
```

This ability is valuable in different ways. The following examples demonstrate various situations in which typecasting is useful. You might never use typecasting in the ways demonstrated, but you might find another application for the general principles being used.

This first program shows how to cast the char variable type as an integer so that you can use arithmetic operators to manipulate each member of the character array. When the program is run, the string "BCD" is displayed, which is the value of tempString after the for loop is finished.

```
#include <stdio.h>

int main(void)
```

```
{
char *tempString = "ABC";

    for (char *p = tempString; *p; p++) {
        *p = (int)*p + 1;
    }
    printf("%s", tempString)
return(0);
}
```

Before we go further, let's quickly run through the example to explain a few of the concepts used. I'll overview only the stuff that has not been discussed yet in this book.

- The #include line tells the compiler to load information about standard input/output routines. This is needed for the printf routine to work properly.

- The char *tempString line tells the compiler to allocate 3 bytes of memory (a buffer), set each byte to A, B, and C respectively, then use the tag of tempString to refer to the buffer in future lines of the program.

- The line containing for starts a loop statement, which are explained in Chapter 9, "Loops and Conditional Statements." The loop statement starts at the beginning of the buffer, tempString, and looks at each byte (a null byte indicates the end of the buffer).

- The next line has the cast expression. For each byte of the buffer, the compiler will increment the value of the byte. Byte one, which was valued A, will be incremented to B. Byte two, which was valued B, will be incremented to C, and so on.

- The printf() function, discussed in Chapter 11, "I/O," is used to display information. In this case, it will display the contents of the buffer tempString.

You can also use the cast operator to make a block of memory mean different things. For example, you can define a buffer like this:

```
char buffer[20];
```

You can refer to it in several ways. The simplest possibility is to view it as 20 characters, as in the following code:

```
char *p;
int    index;

    for (p = buffer, index = 0; index < 20; index++, p++) {
        *p = 100;
    }
```

This code sets each byte of the buffer to the value of 100. You should also note that I used the comma operator to cause two statements to be executed in the condition section of the for loop. You can use the comma operator to group statements for execution wherever a single statement can be used.

Another way of looking at the buffer is as a series of integers. You can do this by using the following code fragment:

```
int   *p;
int    index;

    for (p = (int *)buffer, index = 0; index < 10; index++, p++) {
        *p = 100;
    }
```

This code has three differences from the preceding code:

- The declaration section defines p as a integer pointer. You many recall that a pointer is a variable that holds the location of another variable or position in memory. In this case, the compiler needs to know that you want to view the buffer as integers so that it can increment the p variable properly. In the second example in this section, the variable p is incremented once by the statement p++ to account for the size of a char variable. In the previous example, the statement p++ causes the variable to be incremented *twice* to account for the size of an integer variable, which is two bytes long.

- In the assignment expression of the for loop (the first section), a cast operation is used to tell the compiler to view the buffer as if it refers to integers. The first difference created an integer *pointer,* and now we are essentially creating an integer *buffer.*

- The last change was to change the continuation expression of the for loop (the second section) so that the program loops only 10 times because each pass through the loop processes two bytes, and 2 * 10 = 20, which is the size of the buffer we are using.

What Is Type Conversion?

Sometimes, the C++ compiler automatically does some typecasting. This is called *type conversion*. Type conversion is done only during the evaluation of an arithmetic expression in order to promote more accurate and consistent results.

C++ has rigidly defined rules to determine when to perform type conversion. Here are the steps that are followed:

1. All small integral types (char, unsigned char, signed char, short, unsigned short, and enum) are converted to int. The char variable type has the extra byte either zero-filled or sign-extended, depending on whether the original type was unsigned or signed.

2. Otherwise, if either operand is of type *long double*, the other operand is converted to long double.

3. Otherwise, if either operand is of type *double*, the other operand is converted to double.

4. Otherwise, if either operand is of type *float*, the other operand is converted to float.

5. Otherwise, if either operand is of type *unsigned long*, the other operand is converted to unsigned long.

6. Otherwise, if either operand is of type *long*, the other operand is converted to long.

7. Otherwise, if either operand is of type *unsigned*, the other operand is converted to unsigned.

8. Otherwise, both operands are already of type *int*.

9. The result of the expression is the same as that of the operands being evaluated, because their types are now identical.

> **Note**
>
> Automatic conversion goes only from smaller integral types to larger types, which use larger blocks of memory. This avoids the possibility of truncating a variable. For example, a `long` variable with a value of `40000` will successfully convert to a `signed int` value of `-25536`.

The preceding steps are performed automatically by the compiler. Although you should be aware of them, you will not need to worry about them. Very rarely are your expressions impacted by the type conversion rules. In fact, the only instance that I'm aware of is when the compiler promotes an integer variable to a floating-point variable for the duration of the expression. This type of action is always a good spot to check for problems if you suspect rounding errors in the evaluation of your expressions.

II

Learning C/C++

Look once again at the first example in this section, in which the cast operation was used to convert a char variable type to an integer variable type in order to increment the values of the bytes in a string. If you look at step 1 of the type conversion rules, you can see that the compiler automatically makes the conversion, saving you the trouble of explicitly typecasting.

More Typecasting

One of the biggest uses for typecasting is to change the variable type of a parameter to a function. Functions are discussed in depth in Chapter 8, "Functions and Macros," but a working definition of a function could be a small block of code, optionally with its own declaration of local variables. The block of code can be programmed in such a way that outside information is needed. The outside information is given to the code block through parameters. If a function is defined as using parameters, usually a specific type of variable is specified. You can use typecasting to change your variable type to the variable type required by the function.

For example, your program could use the fseek() function to find a specific location in a file. The fseek() function is defined as follows:

```
int fseek(FILE *stream, long offset, int whence);
```

This function can be used to move past a fixed-length record in a file. If you are using an int variable as the length of your record, your code is in conflict with the definition of the offset parameter. To get around this problem, you would do the following:

```
returnValue = fseek(fp, (long) recordLength, SEEK_CUR);
```

Another common use of typecasting is to change the way a pointer is used. You have already seen pointers used in this chapter as a way to hold the address of a variable or buffer. Sometimes you have a pointer defined as *void*, which means that it can refer to the address of any type of variable. When the pointer is used to refer to a structure member, it must be cast to the appropriate structure before use. This example will need some setup; the structure memberInfo and a void pointer (vPtr) are declared this way:

```
struct memberInfo {
    char name[20];
    char surname[20];
    char gender[1];
}

void *vPtr;
```

If, sometime later in a problem, you need to check the gender of a member whose information is pointed to by vPtr, you could check the gender with the following if statement:

```
if (((struct memberInfo *)vPtr)->gender == 'F') {
    // gender is female.
}
```

The cast operation tells the compiler how to handle the offsets to address the structure members correctly.

From Here...

Typecasting, although important, is not often used. Most programmers work to minimize the conflicts between the variable types that they use. In general, typecasting should be used as a last resort, and only when you have a solid reason why the original variable declaration should not be changed.

We have talked about many topics in this chapter besides typecasting and type conversion. For more information about these topics, you can turn to the following chapters:

■ Chapter 4, "Data Types, Variables, and Constants," to read about the basic data types.

■ Chapter 8, "Functions and Macros," for more information about parameters and how they are used.

■ Chapter 9, "Loops and Conditional Statements," for more information about the for loop and how it is defined.

■ Chapter 11, "I/O," for more information about the printf statement and how to display output.

Chapter 8

Functions and Macros

This chapter takes a look at C++ functions and macros, focusing closely on how they are created and used in Turbo C++. You will see the reasoning behind the use of functions and macros in a C++ application and see how the planning of functions and macros affects application development. In particular, this chapter covers the following topics:

- What functions and macros are

- How to create functions and macros in a C++ application

- Specific ways to use functions and macros in a C++ application

- Functions and macros that are available in the Turbo C++ run-time library

Differentiating between Functions and Macros

Thus far, you have been introduced to a few simple topics and have an idea how simple Turbo C++ programs are written and operate. In a simple application, you essentially have only a main() function containing code that is executed by the computer when the application is run. One simple main() function is fine for small applications, but what happens if you want to write something relatively complex? Are you going to simply place hundreds of lines of code between the braces of the main() function?

In C++ there is a better way to handle the development of large programs: you can take a *modular approach*. The first advantage to this method is that it gives you a chance to verify that each discrete operation of the program executes properly. For each function that you develop, you can test its operation, thus debugging your application at each step of the development. A second advantage to the modular approach is readability—if *you* can't read the code and follow it, how is anyone else supposed to maintain it? Functions are the answer! When you develop an application, you should break it into parts. Each part, or function, has a certain operation that it can perform. When a lot of different but related functions are placed together, much like a puzzle, you have a fully functional application (see fig. 8.1).

Fig. 8.1

Functions are building blocks that you fit together to create a full application.

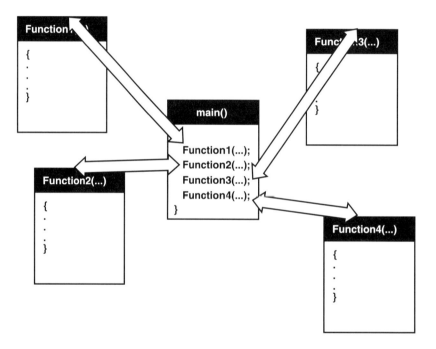

Another important point introduced with the development of modular applications is *information hiding*. This sounds like a bit of an odd term involved in programming principles, but it is very important to the development of reusable code and complex application development. Information hiding deals with the fact that discrete components of operations are hidden from the main operational components of the application.

For example, you can write a small function that adds two numbers together and returns the result of the addition. When you use this function in an application, all you really need to know is how to call this function, not how to add two numbers. The actual addition operation is internal to that function; it stays hidden and is essentially unimportant to the rest of the program. The only visible aspects of the function are the calling mechanism, the parameters, and the value the function returns.

> **Note**
>
> A *parameter* accepts arguments containing values or variables passed to a function or macro. Parameters are located between parentheses after a function or macro name and are a means of sending information between the `main()` function and the called functions or macros of a program.

A *macro* is more or less a cousin of the function because it, too, is an encapsulated block of code. The difference lies in how the macro is handled within a program. A function establishes a specific place in memory when the computer runs your program. To access the function, the program simply jumps to the address of the function to execute the code of the function and returns to the prior segment of code when the function completes.

A macro is handled a bit differently. Instead of jumping to an address to execute the macro, the operational code of the macro is placed *inline* at compile time. The compiler literally places the code for the macro wherever a call to the macro exists within your program. By making the code inline with the program's code, the execution is actually more efficient because the computer doesn't have to jump around in memory in order to execute operations.

Tip

An *inline statement* is inline with the primary code of the program. All inline code, such as a macro, is written to encapsulate certain discrete operations such as adding two numbers or getting a character from the screen.

So how do you know when you should favor a macro over a function? This decision is more or less up to you when you develop your application. If a particular code segment is nothing more than a single line that contains no function calls, it might be good to use a macro. If the code segment is large or you make function calls within it, create a function. One thing to remember is that the code for a macro is literally copied and placed throughout your program wherever the macro is referenced, so you don't want to duplicate a 200-line macro several times throughout your program. A macro this length can make your compiled and linked code larger than necessary and may be a bit overbearing for the computer. In such a case, use a function whose code exists once and is called each time its segment of code is needed.

II

Learning C/C++

Now, let's detail the use and creation of functions and macros as well as how they work. Functions and macros are very important parts of the C++ language. Mastering the information in this chapter will establish an excellent base of understanding for the remainder of this book as well as the C++ programming language. One thing to remember is that every call you make in C++ is either a function call or a macro call.

Functions

A function is a callable module of code and looks much like the `main()` function to which you have been introduced. The difference between `main()` and a regular function is that regular functions are called from within the `main()` function. Modularity comes into play when you encapsulate certain operations within a function where each function performs a specific task but, in conjunction with other functions, adds to the features and functions of the overall program.

> **Note**
>
> An *encapsulated* piece of code performs only one operation within your program. For example, if you are creating a small database manager for a music CD database, the code that controls the entry screen for the database would be specific to data entry and should be isolated from code that saves the CD information to the CD database. The data entry code is said to be encapsulated—placed into specific functions that handle only data entry.

Functions must have a function definition and should have a prototype, although a function definition can serve as a prototype if the definition appears before the function is called within your application. The function definition includes the function body—the code that executes when the function is called. A prototype establishes the name, return type, and attributes of a function that is defined elsewhere in the program but maintains no code.

The compiler uses the prototype to compare the types of arguments in subsequent calls to the function with the function's parameters and to convert the types of the arguments to the types of the parameters whenever necessary. A prototype or function definition must precede the calls to the function. This is why the header files containing the declarations for the run-time library functions are included in your code before a call to any of the run-time functions.

Function Prototypes

A function prototype precedes the function definition and specifies the name, return type, storage class, and other attributes of a function. To be a prototype, the function declaration must also establish types and identifiers for the function's arguments.

The prototype has the same form as the function definition, except that it is terminated by a semicolon immediately following the closing parenthesis; therefore, it has no body. In both cases, the return type of the prototype must agree with the return type specified in the function definition.

Function prototypes have the following important uses:

- They establish the return type for functions that return types other than int. Although functions that return int values do not require prototypes, prototypes are recommended.

- Without complete prototypes, standard type conversions are made by the compiler, but no attempt is made to check the type or number of arguments with the number of parameters.

- Prototypes are used to initialize pointers to functions before those functions are defined.

- The parameter list is used for checking the correspondence of arguments in the function call with the parameters in the function definition.

The type of each parameter determines the interpretation of the arguments that the function call places on the stack. A type mismatch between an argument and a parameter may cause the arguments on the stack to be misinterpreted. For example, on a 16-bit computer, assume that a 16-bit pointer variable is passed as an argument to a function that declares that pointer to be a long parameter. The computer will see that pointer parameter and the first 32 bits on the stack will be interpreted as a long parameter. This error creates problems not only with the long parameter but with any parameters that follow it. Errors such as this can be eliminated by declaring complete function prototypes for all functions.

Complete parameter declarations (int a) can be mixed with abstract declarators (int) in the same declaration. Such function declarations are legal because prototypes are concerned only about the data types and not the parameter names. The parameter names are assigned in the actual function definition. For example, the following declarations are legal:

II

Learning C/C++

```
int add( int a, int );
int add( int, int );
int add( int, int a );
```

The warning `"argument not used"` is issued, within a called function, when an argument is not used within the called function (including `main()`). Abstract declarators in a function prototype do not remedy the warning because abstract declarators are used for prototyping—not function declarations. In this section, the discussion focused on function prototypes (function declarations) rather than function definitions.

In the function declarations, we are declaring two integer parameters for a function to be defined later in the code of a program. In the actual function definition, the abstract declarators are provided variable names in the parameters of the function definition. In some cases, those parameters' assigned names are given other variable names; therefore, the parameters in a prototype are specifically for declaring parameter types for compilation purposes.

The prototype can include both the type of and an identifier for each expression that is passed as an argument; however, such identifiers have scope only until the end of the declaration. The prototype can also reflect the fact that the number of arguments is variable or that no arguments are passed. Without such a list, mismatches may not be evident at compile time, so the compiler will not be able to generate diagnostic messages associated with the arguments.

ANSI-compliant prototype scope means that, for instance, if you declare a `struct` or `union` tag within a prototype, the tag is entered at that scope rather than at global scope. For example, you can never call the following function without getting a type mismatch error:

```
void func1(struct S *);
```

To correct your code, define or declare the `struct` or `union` at global scope before the function prototype:

```
struct S;
void func1(struct S *);
```

Function Arguments

In a function call, an *expression list* is a list of parameters separated by commas. The values of these parameters are the arguments passed to the function. If the function takes no arguments, the expression list should either contain the keyword `void` or should be empty. The following examples demonstrate void parameter lists.

```
void func1()
{
.
.
.
};

void func1(void)
{
.
.
.
};
```

Note

Placing void in an empty parameter list is the ANSI standard method of declaring an
empty parameter list.

An argument can be any value of an intrinsic, structure, union, or pointer
type. Arguments are usually *passed by value*, meaning that a copy of the argument is assigned to the corresponding parameter. The function does not
know the actual memory location of the argument passed but instead uses
this copy without affecting the variable from which it was originally derived.
The following examples demonstrate pass by value function parameter
definitions.

```
void func1(int a, float b)
{
.
.
.
};

void func2(struct S)
{
;

void func3(char c)
{
};
```

Although you cannot pass arrays or functions as arguments, you can pass
pointers to these items. Pointers provide a way for a function to access a
value by reference. Because a pointer to a variable holds the address of the
variable, the function can use this address to access the value of the variable.
Pointer arguments allow a function to access arrays and functions, even
though arrays and functions cannot be passed as arguments.

```
void func1(int *a)
{
  .
  .
  .
};

void func2(char b[])
{
  .
  .
  .
};

void func3(int (*(funcparam))(void))
{
  .
  .
  .
};
```

The expression list in a function call is evaluated applying standard arithmetic conversions on each argument in the function call. If a prototype is available, the resulting argument type is compared to the prototype's corresponding parameter. If the arguments and parameters do not match, either a conversion is performed or a diagnostic message is issued.

The number of arguments in an expression list must match the number of parameters, unless the function's prototype or definition explicitly specifies a variable number of arguments. In this case, the compiler checks as many arguments as there are type names in the list of parameters and converts them as required.

If the prototype's parameter list contains only the keyword void, the compiler expects zero arguments in the function call and zero parameters in the definition. A warning message is issued if the compiler finds any arguments.

This following example uses pointers as arguments:

```
void main()
{
    /* Function prototype */

    void swap( int *num1, int *num2 );
    int x, y;
      .
      .
      .
    swap( &x, &y );  /* Function call */
}

/* Function definition */
```

```
void swap( int *num1, int *num2 )
{
    int t;

    t = *num1;
    *num1 = *num2;
    *num2 = t;
}
```

In this example, the swap() function is declared in main() to have two arguments, represented by identifiers num1 and num2. The parameters num1 and num2 in the prototype definition are also declared as pointers to int type values.

In the function call swap(&x, &y), the address of x is stored in num1 and the address of y is stored in num2. Now two names, or *aliases*, exist for the same location. Pointers to *num1 and *num2 in swap() are essentially pointers to x and y in main(). The assignments within swap() actually exchange the contents of x and y.

The compiler performs type checking on the arguments to swap() because the prototype of swap() includes argument types for each parameter. The identifiers within the parentheses of the prototype and definition can be the same or different. What is important is that the types of the arguments match those of the parameter lists in both the prototype and the definition.

Variable Argument Lists

To establish a function definition and prototype for a function that accepts a variable number of arguments, the function's parameter list can be terminated with ellipses (...). The ellipses indicate that there will be an undefined number of additional undefined arguments passed to the function. At least one parameter must precede the ellipses, and the ellipses must be the last item in the parameter list.

To call a function with a variable number of arguments, simply specify any number of arguments in the function call. An example is the printf() function, which must include one argument for each type name declared in the parameter list or the list of argument types.

The number of parameters declared for the function determines how many of the arguments are taken from the stack and assigned to the parameters. You are responsible for retrieving any arguments of the variable argument list from the stack and for determining how many arguments are present.

The code in listing 8.1 demonstrates the use of variable argument lists, which provide a means of handling an indefinite number of arguments passed to a function.

Listing 8.1   Using Variable Argument Lists

```c
#include <stdio.h>
#include <stdarg.h>       // Contains prototypes and macros for
                          // variable argument lists
#include <string.h>

void my_vararg_func(char*, ...);

void main()
{
    my_vararg_func("Add",22,1,3,4,0);
    my_vararg_func("Subtract",22,1,3,4,0);
}

void my_vararg_func(char *msg, ...)
{
    int total = 0;
    va_list ap;
    int iarg;

    va_start(ap, msg);

    if(!stricmp(msg,"Add"))
    {
        while ((iarg = va_arg(ap,int)) != 0)
        {
            printf("%d\n",iarg);
            total += iarg;
        }
    }

    if(!stricmp(msg,"Subtract"))
    {
        while ((iarg = va_arg(ap,int)) != 0)
        {
            printf("%d\n",iarg);
            total -= iarg;
        }
    }

    printf("%s : %d\n",msg, total);

    va_end(ap);
}
```

Three important macros involved in handling variable argument lists are
va_start(va_list ap, lastfix), va_arg(va_list ap, type), and
va_end(va_list ap). The va_arg(), va_end(), and va_start() macros provide a
simple and portable means of accessing the arguments in the variable argument list. Primarily, these macros are used for stepping through a list of arguments when the called function does not know the number and types of the
arguments being passed.

The va_list is an array that holds information needed by va_arg() and va_end(). When the function my_vararg_func() is called, it takes a variable argument list and declares a variable ap of type va_list.

The va_start() macro sets ap to point to the first argument being passed to the function in the variable argument list. va_start() must be called before any calls to va_arg() or va_end(). va_start() takes a variable argument list and a parameter reference as arguments. The variable argument list, ap in this example, points to the va_list, variable argument list, of the function. The parameter reference is the identifier of the last fixed parameter being passed to the function immediately preceding the variable argument list.

The va_arg() macro expands to an expression that has the same type and value as the variable argument being passed to the function. The va_list argument, ap, must be the same va_list variable that va_start() initialized. The first time va_arg() is used, it returns the first argument in the list. Each successive call to va_arg() returns the next argument in the list. This operation is performed by first dereferencing the va_list variable, ap, and then incrementing the variable to point to the next item in the list. va_arg() uses the data type passed as the second parameter to perform the dereferencing operation and to locate the next item in the list.

The va_end() macro deallocates any variables allocated for use in extracting elements from the variable argument list and allows the called function, my_vararg_func(), to perform a normal return to its caller. The call to va_end() modifies the va_list argument so that it cannot be used unless va_start() is recalled. va_end() should be called after va_arg() has read all the arguments; otherwise, undefined program behavior might result.

Function Attributes

The following function attributes are the more commonly used keywords that precede function definitions. These function attributes define how the function is to be treated within the application. These optional attributes enable you to select a calling convention on a per-function basis.

inline

```
inline <datatype> <class>_<function> (<parameters>) { <statements>; }
```

Use the inline keyword to define C++ functions as inline functions. Inline expansion, or *inlining*, replaces the function reference within the application code with the body of the function's code. It is best to use inline functions with small, frequently used functions because the body of the function is duplicated throughout the application. The following code demonstrates the use of inline with a function definition.

```
inline int function(int a)
{
      return a + 1;
};
```

cdecl

```
cdecl <datatype> <class>_<function> (<parameters>)
  { <statements>; }
```

The cdecl modifier is used to declare a variable or a function with the C-style naming conventions—case-sensitive with leading underscore appended. When you use a cdecl modifier in front of a function, it affects how the parameters are passed—the last parameter is pushed on the stack first, and the caller of the function cleans up the stack. The following code block uses the cdecl modifier.

```
cdecl int function(int a, in b)
{
      return a + b + 1;
};
```

pascal

```
pascal <datatype> <class>_<function> (<parameters>) { <statements>; }
```

The pascal keyword declares a variable or a function using a Pascal-style naming convention, in which the name is in uppercase. In addition, the pascal modifier declares Pascal-style parameter passing when applied to a function where the first parameter is pushed on the stack first and the called function cleans up the stack. The following code demonstrates the use of the pascal modifier with a function definition.

```
pascal int function(int a, in b)
{
      return a + b + 1;
};
```

far

```
<type> far <datatype> <class>_<function> (<parameters>)
  { <statements>; }
```

The far modifier generates function code for calls and returns using variables that are outside the current data segment—pointers will be two words with a range of 1M. You should use the far keyword when compiling small or compact models to force pointers to be far. The following code demonstrates the use of the far modifier.

```
int far function(int a, in b)
{
      return a + b + 1;
};
```

near

```
<type> near <datatype> <class>_<function> (<parameters>)
  { <statements>; }
```

The near type modifiers force pointers to be within a range of 64K and to generate function code for a near call and a near return. This modifier is used when compiling in the medium, large, or huge memory models to force pointers to be near. The following code demonstrates the use of the near modifier.

```
int near function(int a, in b)
{
     return a + b + 1;
};
```

fastcall

```
_fastcall <function-name>
```

The fastcall modifier declares functions that expect parameters to be passed in registers. The compiler treats this calling convention as a new language specifier similar to cdecl and pascal.

Functions declared using cdecl or pascal cannot have the fastcall modifier because they use the stack to pass parameters. Likewise, the fastcall modifier cannot be used together with export or loadds.

_export

```
return_type _export <function-name>
```

This modifier is used to export functions to make them accessible to other modules. In Microsoft Windows, by declaring a function as _extern, you are allowing access to the function by calls from other programs or libraries. The linker enters functions, modified as far, flagged with _export into an export table for the module. Functions that are not flagged with _export receive abbreviated prolog and epilog code, resulting in a smaller object file and slightly faster execution.

_stdcall

```
_stdcall <function-name>
```

The _stdcall keyword forces the compiler to generate function calls using the standard calling convention. The resulting function calls are smaller and faster, and the functions must pass the correct number and type of arguments.

II

Learning C/C++

Recursive Functions

Any function in a C++ program can be called recursively—essentially, this means that it calls itself. The number of recursive calls is limited to the size of the stack. Each time the function is called, new storage is allocated for the parameters and local variables so that their values in previous, unfinished calls are not overwritten. Parameters are only directly accessible to the instance of the function in which they are created, and previous parameters are not directly accessible to ensuing instances of the function.

> **Note**
>
> Variables declared with static storage do not require new storage with each recursive call. Their storage exists for the lifetime of the program and each reference to such a variable accesses the same storage area.

Listing 8.2 illustrates recursive function calls in a simple program, which call themselves repeatedly internal to the function's block of code.

Listing 8.2   Using Recursive Functions

```
int factorial( int num );        /* Function prototype */

void main()
{
    int result, number;
    .
    .
    .
    result = factorial( number );
}

int factorial( int num )         /* Function definition */
{
    .
    .
    .
    if ( ( num > 0 ) || ( num <= 10 ) )
        return( num * factorial( num - 1 ) );
}
```

The `main()` function calls the `factorial()` function, passing the `number` variable as the argument. When the `factorial()` function runs, it checks that the value of the parameter `num` is greater than 0 or less than 10. If the value is within the bounds, the `factorial()` function is called again with the `num` parameter of the previous function decremented and passed as an argument to the next call. Each successive call places the new instance of `factorial()` on the stack.

If at any time the value of num exceeds the bounds of the Boolean expression, the function will begin to *unwind*. No more calls to the function are made, and each of the previously made calls is taken from the stack. Since the recursive call occurred in the middle of a multiplication expression, each time an instance of factorial() is taken from the stack, its return value is multiplied by the value of num in the then-current version of the factorial() function (see fig. 8.2).

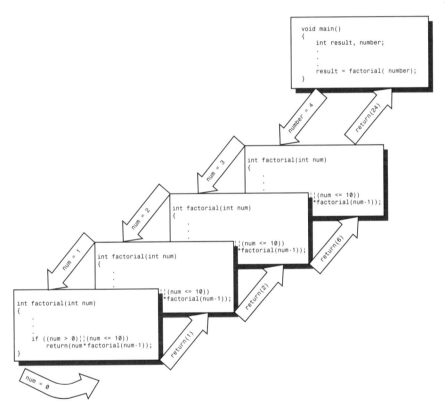

Fig. 8.2
The factorial function here has been called four times, once by some other part of the program and three times recursively.

Seeing the Impact of Function Prototypes

In the following example, the function prototype provides a definition for the function print_word(). Without the prototype, the compiler sees the function call in main() before the definition of the function itself. This causes the compiler to generate an error because it does not know of any function named print_word(). The prototype tells the compiler that the function does indeed exist, as well as the parameters to be passed to the function. Prototyping allows the compiler to continue compilation and place all code for the prototyped function into the block of memory reserved by the prototype. Listing 8.3 demonstrates the use of prototypes, which allow you to provide a definition of how a function is to be called by program statements.

Listing 8.3 Using Prototypes

```
#include <stdio.h>

//Function prototype
void     print_word(char *c_string);

void main()
{
     char     WordString[20];

     printf("Enter a word to print : ");
     scanf("%s",WordString);

     print_word(WordString);
}

//Function definition
void     print_word(char *c_string)
{
     printf("The word is : '%s'\n",c_string);
}
```

The one parameter to be passed to the function, as defined by the prototype, is an array of characters. The char * is a pointer to a string of characters that is passed to the function. In this program, the pointer contains the address of the string contained in the variable WordString. When the function receives the pointer, it is able to read the information at WordString's address in memory by going to the address referenced in the pointer c_string located in the function's parameter.

Notice the void reference preceding the function name. This tells the compiler that the function does not return any values after it has completed its execution.

The main() function of the program prints the message Enter a word to print : to the screen using the printf() function. The program then waits for the user to enter a string and press the Enter key. The scanf() function accepts your input and stores the entered string into the variable WordString.

Once the data is entered, the program calls the function print_word(), passing the variable WordString as shown in parentheses following the function call. This is how parameters are passed to a function so that the function can receive data.

The function definition is the actual block of code that contains the function name, parameter definitions, and functional code. When the function is called, it reads the information passed to it in the `char *c_string` parameter. The pointer itself references the variable `WordString` from the `main()` function. The function calls `printf()` to print the message `The word is :` followed by the string that was entered in `main()`.

Function Return Values

Some of the function definitions thus far had a return type of `void`—meaning that they do not return anything to the caller. Functions can, however, return values to the caller by way of a return type. Listing 8.4 defines a function called `CalcSum()` that takes two numbers (`Val1` and `Val2`), adds them, and returns the sum. Notice for this prototype that there is an `int` instead of a `void` preceding the function name. The `int` data type tells the compiler that the function returns an integer value to the caller.

Listing 8.4   A Function that Adds Two Numbers

```
#include <stdio.h>

int     CalcSum(int Val1, int Val2);

void main()
{
    int     IntVal1;
    int     IntVal2;
    int     RetVal;

    printf("Enter the first number to add  : ");
    scanf("%d",&IntVal1);
    printf("Enter the second number to add : ");
    scanf("%d",&IntVal2);

    RetVal = CalcSum(IntVal1,IntVal2);
    printf("The sum of %d and %d is %d\n",
        IntVal1,IntVal2,RetVal);
}

int     CalcSum(int Val1, int Val2)
{
    int     Val;

    Val = Val1 + Val2;
    return(Val);
}
```

The program requests two values be entered using the `scanf()` function. The `scanf()` function reads the values you enter and stores them in the variables `IntVal1` and `IntVal2`. The program makes a call to the function `CalcSum()`, passing the numeric values of the two variables just entered at the `scanf()` functions.

The function definition for this function contains two `int` parameters. The `main()` function calls this `CalcSum()` function and passes to it `IntVal1` and `IntVal2`. The values are read by the function out of its parameters `Val1` and `Val2`. The function then adds the two values and stores the result in the local variable `Val`. The sum is then returned to `main()` using the `return()` statement to return the value stored in the `Val` variable. The `return()` statement must be called with the value that you want to return located in the parentheses. With `return()`, you can return pointer, intrinsic, and user-defined data types to the caller.

Warning

If you define a return type for a function, other than void, and you do not call `return()` within the function body, the compiler will generate the following warning:

```
Warning FILENAME.CPP XX: Function should return a value
                         in function main()
```

Parameter Passing by Value

Pass by value is a method of parameter passing that copies the value of an argument into a function parameter. When variables are passed by value to a function, the value of the variable can be used by the function but cannot be changed by the function. Passing a value to a function is a common method of transferring data to a function so that the function can operate on that data. Listing 8.5 demonstrates the action of passing data to a function by copying the value of the arguments to the parameters of the function.

Listing 8.5 Passing Data to a Function

```c
#include <stdio.h>

void    SetValue(int Val);

main()
{
    int     IntVal;
```

```
    int      TempVal;

    printf("Enter a number : ");
    scanf("%d",&IntVal);

    TempVal = IntVal;

    SetValue(IntVal);
    printf("Original value is %d.   Set value is %d.",
        TempVal, IntVal);
}

void     SetValue(int Val)
{
    Val = 100;
    printf("Inside the function the value is %d\n",Val);
}
```

The function prototype defines a function called SetValue() that takes a
number (Val), attempts to change its value, then prints the result. The program requests the entry of a value and accepts that entry using the scanf()
function. The function read in is stored in the variable IntVal, which is then
assigned to the variable TempVal.

The program makes a call to the function SetValue(), passing IntVal as the
parameter. This pass by value operation copies the value of IntVal to the
function's parameter line. The value then becomes local to that function by
way of its parameter.

The function definition takes the value copied into its parameter variable
(Val) and sets it equal to 100. The function then prints the variable's value
to show that it was indeed changed. The variable Val is local to the function
and any changes to that variable are local. This means that the change of
the variable's value to 100 is not seen back in the caller (the main() function,
in this case).

Parameter Passing by Reference

Pass by reference is a method of parameter passing that copies the address of
a variable into a function parameter, rather than the value of the variable.
A variable is passed by reference to a function whenever the variable is to be
changed by the function. The address of the changed variable is then sent
back to the calling code for use in the rest of the program. Listing 8.6 demonstrates passing values by reference.

Listing 8.6 Passing Values by Reference

```
#include <stdio.h>

void     SetValue(int *Val);

main()
{
    int     IntVal;
    int     TempVal;

    printf("Enter a number : ");
    scanf("%d",&IntVal);

    TempVal = IntVal;

    SetValue(&IntVal);
    printf("Original value is %d.  Set value is %d.",
        TempVal, IntVal);
}

void     SetValue(int *Val)
{
    Val = 100;
    printf("Inside the function the value is %d\n",*Val);
}
```

As in the previous section covering passing by value, the function prototype defines a function called SetValue() that takes a number, changes its value, then prints the result. The primary difference is in the method in which the arguments are passed. The asterisk, made part of the parameter for the prototype, tells the program that a pointer to an integer is to be passed to the function. By passing a pointer to an integer, you are telling the function the address of the integer variable IntVal. This passing by reference allows the function SetValue() to change the value of IntVal and allow main(), the caller of SetValue(), to receive the new value of IntVal.

The scanf() function reads the value you enter and stores it in the variable IntVal. The value in IntVal is then assigned to the variable TempVal for comparison after the function is called.

The program makes a call to the function SetValue(), passing IntVal as the argument. Notice the ampersand (&) preceding the variable. This operator tells the application that it is to pass the address of the variable and not the value. This pass by reference operation passes the address of the variable to the function's parameter, thus referencing the variable in memory.

The function definition here looks much like the ones you saw in the previous section except for the asterisk (*) preceding the variable name. The asterisk operator tells the application that any information passed to the function by way of this parameter is an address pointing to a variable located in the calling function.

The function SetValue() then *dereferences* the pointer. The dereferencing operation, symbolized by the asterisk operator again, tells the computer to set to 100 the memory block pointed to by Val.

Note

Dereferencing is the method of accessing the block of memory pointed to by a pointer. When you dereference a pointer, you are telling the computer to get the information located at the address contained in the pointer for your use.

Macros

As you have seen, a function is a block of code that performs a certain operation. You may find that a function is overkill in some instances in which it may be easier to simply replicate small portions of code throughout a program. For example, why write a function to add the values of two variables when you can simply enter an equation such as C = A + B into the code to add the variables together. The solution to this dilemma is a macro. Listing 8.7 demonstrates a small macro to add two numbers in a small program.

Listing 8.7   A Macro that Adds Two Numbers

```c
#include <stdio.h>

#define    VADD(X,Y) (X+Y)

main()
{
    int     IntVal1;
    int     IntVal2;

    printf("Enter the first number   : ");
    scanf("%d",&IntVal1);
    printf("Enter the second number  : ");
    scanf("%d",&IntVal2);

    printf("The sum of %d and %d is %d\n", IntVal1, IntVal2,
           VADD(IntVal1,IntVal2));
}
```

The VADD() macro allows you to pass two values (X and Y) to it; they are added together, and a sum is returned. Notice that the definition itself is similar to that of a function, but the code associated with the macro is a bit different. All you see is the small operation that occurs on the two values to be passed.

The program prints a message to the screen containing the two values entered at the scanf() functions and the sum of the values calculated by the macro. The macro is entered into the printf() statement to allow the results of the addition to be printed. When you compile the program, the C++ compiler takes the macro definition VADD(X,Y) and literally replaces it with (X+Y). In this program, VADD(IntVal1,IntVal2) is replaced by (IntVal1 + IntVal2).

One advantage to using a macro is that of efficiency. The code becomes inline, allowing all operations to be directly incorporated into the code. Another advantage is that of maintainability. Instead of going through your code and entering numerous calculations, you can replace these calculations with a macro. You can enter the equation into the code if you want; however, if you had this same equation in the code many times, maintainability would become cumbersome. With only one instance of the equation as a macro, all you have to do is change that one definition of the equation and let the compiler distribute updated equations throughout your code.

The following syntax is used to define a macro within a C++ program:

```
#define macro_identifier(<arg_list>) token_sequence
```

Any comma within parentheses in an argument list is treated as part of the argument, not as an argument delimiter, and there can be no whitespace between the macro identifier and the opening parenthesis. The optional arg_list is a sequence of identifiers separated by commas, not unlike the argument list of a C function. Each comma-delimited identifier plays the role of a parameter. Such macros are called by writing the following in the subsequent source code:

```
macro_identifier (<actual_arg_list>)
```

The syntax is identical to that of a function call; however, there are some important semantic differences, side effects, and potential pitfalls. A macro call has no built-in typechecking, so a mismatch between formal and actual argument data types can produce unusual results with no immediate warning. Macro calls can also give rise to unwanted side effects, especially when an actual argument is evaluated more than once.

Note

Many standard run-time library functions are implemented as macros. See the following section for details.

The `actual_arg_list` must contain the same number of token sequences, known as *actual arguments*, as found in the `arg_list` of the macro definition. An error will be reported if the number of arguments differs between the macro usage and the definition.

A call to a macro within an application results in two sets of replacements. First, the macro identifier and the parentheses-enclosed arguments are replaced by the token sequence. Next, any formal arguments occurring in the token sequence are replaced by the corresponding real arguments appearing in the argument list of the macro call.

Library Functions and Macros

Now that you understand functions and macros in Turbo C++, you will be able to use any of the run-time library functions and macros available with the environment. Turbo C++ provides numerous functions and macros, loosely grouped as follows:

- *Classification routines* classify ASCII characters as letters, control characters, punctuation, uppercase, and so on. These routines are declared in ctype.h.

- *Console I/O routines* output text to the screen or read from the keyboard. They are declared in conio.h.

- *Conversion routines* convert characters and strings from alphabetic to different numeric representations (floating-point, integers, longs), numeric to alphabetic representations, and uppercase to lowercase (and vice versa). They are declared in stdlib.h and ctype.h.

- *Diagnostic routines* provide built-in troubleshooting capability. These routines are declared in assert.h, math.h, and errno.h.

- *Directory control routines* manipulate directories and path names. They are declared in dir.h, direct.h, dos.h, and stdlib.h.

■ *EasyWin routines* are not available in Windows 16-bit programs, but they are provided to help you port DOS programs into Windows 16-bit applications. They are declared in stdio.h, conio.h, and errno.h.

■ *Inline routines.* The compiler will generate code for the inline versions when you use #pragma intrinsic or if you specify program optimization. These routines are declared in math.h, stdlib.h, string.h, and mem.h.

■ *Input/output routines* provide stream- and operating-system-level I/O capability. They are declared in io.h, stdio.h, dos.h, conio.h, and file.h.

■ *Interface routines* provide operating system, BIOS, and machine-specific capabilities. They are declared in bios.h, dos.h, and conio.h.

■ *Manipulation routines* handle strings and blocks of memory with copying, comparing, converting, and searching operations. They are declared in stdlib.h, string.h, and mem.h.

■ *Math routines* perform mathematical calculations and conversion. They are declared in complex.h, stdlib.h, math.h, and float.h.

■ *Memory routines* provide dynamic memory allocation in the small and large memory models. They are declared in alloc.h, malloc.h, and stdlib.h.

■ *Process control routines* invoke and terminate new processes from within another routine. They are declared in process.h, signal.h, and stdio.h.

■ *Time and date routines* are time-conversion and time-manipulation routines. These routines are declared in time.h, bios.h, and dos.h.

■ *Variable argument list routines* are for use when accessing variable argument lists. They are declared in stdarg.h.

To use any of the run-time functions available with Turbo C++, you must include the header file associated with the desired functions and macros with the #include directive. To assist you when writing your applications, the names of the header files associated with the functions you require are found in Turbo C++ Help. The prototypes in the header files allow the compiler to compile the application code to incorporate the macros and provide type checking for the desired functions. During the link operation, the function definition is linked from the run-time library modules into the application to create the executable file.

From Here...

In this chapter, you learned how to use and create functions and macros in Turbo C++. The chapter discussed many different forms of functions, as well as how to pass arguments by value and by reference to a function. Macros, you learned, are similar to functions in many ways, with the notable exception of how they are compiled into an application. For further information, see the following:

- Chapter 10, "Pointers," discusses the pointer variables and how pointers are used within an application for arrays, dynamic memory management, and passed by reference to functions.

- Chapter 12, "Classes and Objects," details classes and class hierarchy for application development.

- Chapter 13, "Object-Oriented Methods," uses the concepts from Chapter 12 and discusses the specifics of object-oriented application development.

- Chapter 17, "ANSI and Turbo C++," overviews the similarities and differences between ANSI standards and Turbo C++.

- Chapter 24, "Windows Programming Basics," walks you through Windows application development and the tools available to assist you.

II

Learning C/C++

Chapter 9

Loops and Conditional Statements

Up to this point, you have read about discrete elements of the C++ language. You have read about data types, operators, expressions, statements, and functions. In this chapter, you start to tie some elements together.

Back in Chapter 6, "Expressions and Statements," we discussed decision, jump, and loop statements in basic terms. This chapter describes the same language elements from a different point of view. You will learn to combine individual statements into language units called *loops* and *conditional statements*.

This chapter discusses the following topics:

- The fundamentals of loops

- The fundamentals of conditional statements

- How these language units are used

- Various examples of these types of language units

Using Loops

A loop is used to repeat the execution of a block of statements or computer code until a certain condition is reached. A loop can be used to iterate through an array looking for a certain value. Loops also can be used to count quantities. Actually, the number of uses for loops is pretty much unlimited.

There are three types of loops in the C++ language: for loops, do..while loops, and while loops. We will look at the statements that represent each of these kinds of loops, starting with the for statement.

A Simple *for* Loop

Let's start with one of the simpler for statements. Listing 9.1 shows a loop that runs through its code section 100 times.

Listing 9.1   A Simple *for* Loop

```
#include <stdio.h>

int main(void)
{
int i;

    for (i = 0; i < 100; i++)
        printf("%d\n", i);

    return(0);
}
```

The output from the program in listing 9.1 is a list of numbers from 0 to 99. When the loop is over, the value of the variable i will be 100.

Because you are familiar with most of the elements in the program by now, we will look only at the for statement. The syntax for a for statement is

```
for (assignment expr; continuation expr; increment/decrement expr)
```

The *assignment expression* can be used to initialize any variables that are used inside the loop. This, of course, could have been done on the line before the for statement. However, including the assignment statement aids in identifying the loop variables.

Be sure not to confuse the equality operator == with the assignment operator = in the assignment expression of the for loop. The following is an example of what this error could look like:

```
for (i == 0; i < 100; I++)
```

One of the two equals signs should be removed. If you think you are having a problem with programming the for statement, be sure to check out the operators.

The *continuation expression* is used to determine whether the loop should continue or be ended. When the condition evaluates to FALSE, the loop will end. In listing 9.1, the continuation expression is false when i is equal to 100.

Caution

Choose your continuation expression carefully. If the continuation expression can never evaluate to FALSE, the computer will loop endlessly. This is sometimes referred to as "hanging" the computer.

The *increment/decrement expression* is used to modify the loop variables in some way each time the code block has been executed. In listing 9.1, the loop variable i is incremented by 1 after the code section is executed.

The code block that is being executed consists of the line containing the printf statement. In this case, the value of i is displayed using the printf function. You can find more information about the printf function in Chapter 11, "I/O."

Note

You should note that the value of i at the end of the loop is 100, not 99, even though the program displayed only from 0 to 99. If you plan to use the loop variable after the loop is done, be sure that you know what its value will be. If the *continuation* expression had used the greater-than-or-equals operator (>=), the value of i after the loop is done would be 101.

An Advanced *for* Loop

For statements can be nested inside one another to increase their usefulness. Nested for loops are often used to deal with the complexity of multidimensional math. Quite frequently, statistical analysis needs to deal with more than one variable, and each variable is a new dimension in the statistical equation.

Nested loops are also used when working with graphics. Typically, the horizontal axis is related to one variable that I usually name col for columns, and the vertical axis is related to another variable that I name row for rows.

Listing 9.2 shows two loops: an inner loop and an outer loop.

Listing 9.2 An Advanced Loop

```c
#include <stdio.h>

int main(void)
{
int i,j;

    for (i = 0; i < 4; i++) {
        for (j = 3; j > 0; j--) {
            printf("[%d,%d]  Inner Loop\n", i, j);

        }
        printf("Outer Loop\n");

    }
    printf("%d\n", i);
    printf("%d\n", j);

    return(0);
}
```

Listing 9.2 shows you how to nest two loops. The loop with the variable j is called the inner loop. It logically follows that the loop with the variable i is called the outer loop.

You should note that the inner loop counts backward from 3 to 0. Most programmers choose not to use backward-counting loops, but sometimes you can't avoid it. An example of this would be going from Z to A with an array that has already been alphabetically sorted. In this case, you would need to start at the end of the array and work backward to the beginning.

If you run the program in listing 9.2, your output should look like figure 9.1.

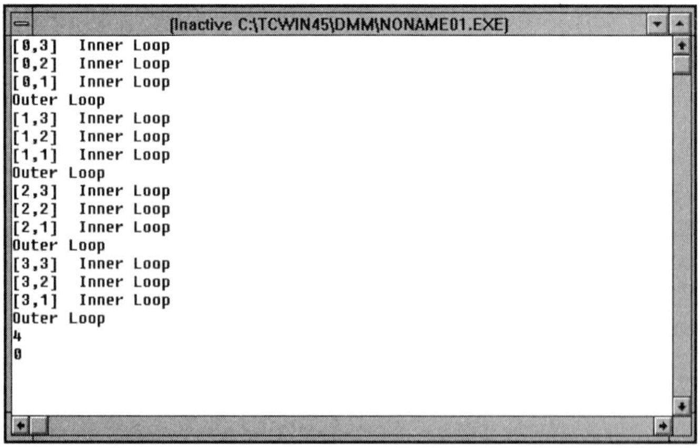

Fig. 9.1

The output from listing 9.2.

```
[0,3]  Inner Loop
[0,2]  Inner Loop
[0,1]  Inner Loop
Outer Loop
[1,3]  Inner Loop
[1,2]  Inner Loop
[1,1]  Inner Loop
Outer Loop
[2,3]  Inner Loop
[2,2]  Inner Loop
[2,1]  Inner Loop
Outer Loop
[3,3]  Inner Loop
[3,2]  Inner Loop
[3,1]  Inner Loop
Outer Loop
4
0
```

Using the Comma Operator in *for* Statements

Back in Chapter 5, "Operators," you read about C++ operators. The *comma* operator was mentioned briefly, but not fully explained. Now, we can discuss the *comma* operator in the context of how it is actually used.

The comma operator allows one statement to contain two or more sub-statements in the same way that a comma indicates subordinate clauses in the English language. This ability is frequently used in the assignment expression of the for statement to set the value of more than one variable. The following is an example:

```
for (endOfFile = FALSE, j = 0; j < 100; j += 2) {
    // code block
}
```

This example initializes both the endOfFile flag variable and the j loop variable.

We will look again at the comma operator when we talk about if statements in the "Using the Comma Operator in *if* Statements" section later in this chapter.

The *Do..While* Loop Statement

The second type of loop statement that C++ supports is the do..while statement. The syntax for do..while is the following:

```
do {
    // code block
} while (continuation expression);
```

This type of loop ensures that the code block always executes at least once. The loop will end when the *continuation expression* evaluates to FALSE. This is the same behavior as the for statement, which also loops until the *continuation expression* evaluates to FALSE.

If you run the program in listing 9.3, you will see that it is functionally the same as the program in listing 9.1. However, the various expressions that are integral to the for statement need to be explicitly added to the code inside and above the do..while loop statement. The comments in listing 9.3 show you where the analogs of the for statement's expression are located.

Listing 9.3   A Simple *do..while* Loop

```
#include <stdio.h>

int main(void)
{
int i;

    i = 0;                          // assignment expression
    do {
        printf("%d\n", i);
        i++;                        // increment/decrement expression
    } while (i < 100);              // continuation expression
    printf("Outside of Loop and i is equal to %d\n", i);
    return(0);
}
```

You can see that the continuation expression of the do..while loop is evalu-ated after the code section is executed. If the continuation expression evalu-ates to FALSE, the loop statement is done.

I rarely use a do..while loop when a for loop will do the job because the expressions of the for statement are in known locations and seem easier to interpret.

The do..while loop comes in handy when a program needs to count down to zero. This is because zero and FALSE have the same value to the C++ com-piler. The following example shows how to decrement a variable to zero:

```
// The variable, numPages, is valued here as an example. Normally
// it would be set through some function call or in another section
// of code.
//
numPages = 10;
do {
    // display the current page.
} while (--numPages);
```

When this loop is done, all of the pages will have been displayed. This type of loop would be used when you know that there will always be pages to pro-cess. Notice that because the prefix decrement operator is used, the numPages variable is decremented before the continuation expression is evaluated.

Also note that the continuation expressions --numPages and --numPages != 0 are the same. The C++ language automatically equates all continuation ex-pressions with FALSE to see if a loop should continue. Even an expression that uses "not-equal to zero" will evaluate to either TRUE or FALSE. If the continuation expression evaluates to FALSE, the loop will end.

The *while* Statement

The while statement has the following syntax:

```
while (continuation expression) {
    // code block
};
```

The main difference between the while statement and the do..while statement is that when you use the while statement, the code section may never be entered if the *continuation expression* evaluates to FALSE.

Listing 9.4 shows how to use a while loop to read and display the contents of a file, character by character.

Listing 9.4   A *while* Loop

```
#include <stdio.h>

int main(void)
{
FILE *fp;
int   c;

    fp = fopen("c:\\config.sys", "r");
    while ((c = fgetc(fp)) != EOF) {
        printf("%c", c);
    }
    return(0);
}
```

The line that contains the fopen routine also specifies the name of the file that will be opened and read from. Almost all IBM and IBM-clone microcomputers have the c:\config.sys file, so if you run the program, it should work for you. On the other hand, if you change the file name parameter to the fopen routine to be "qwaklk.txt," you should get no output, because the code block is not entered (of course, if your directory happens to have a file named qwaklk.txt, it will be displayed—but you get the picture).

Note

Listing 9.4 does not check the fopen routine for an error. This is not good programming practice, and it is done here only to shorten the examples for clarity's sake.

Refining Your Control of Loops

Sometimes simply controlling the continuation expression is not enough. What if you want to terminate the loop in the middle of its execution? Another situation might be that you want to skip the rest of the code block and loop immediately. C++ has mechanisms to handle each of these conditions: the break and continue statements.

The *break* Statement

The break statement is used to jump to the statement following the current code section. Listing 9.5 shows how to use the break statement to exit from a while loop. The first time that a lowercase s is read, the loop will exit and the printf statement will be executed.

Listing 9.5 An Example of the *break* Statement

```
#include <stdio.h>

int main(void)
{
FILE *fp;
int   c;

    fp = fopen("c:\\config.sys", "r");
    while ((c = fgetc(fp)) != EOF) {
        if (c == 's')
            break;
        printf("%c", c);
    }
    printf("\nThe last character read was %c\n", c);
    return(0);
}
```

The break statement is also used in the switch statement. This use is shown in the section "The *switch* Statement" later in this chapter. The break statement that is used in the switch statement has the same effect as when it is used anywhere else. The program jumps to the statement after the current code section.

The *continue* Statement

The continue statement is used to jump back to the beginning of the loop. If there are nested loops, the program jumps to the beginning of the innermost loop. Listing 9.6 shows how to use the continue statement. The program will display every character of the file being read except for the lowercase s.

Listing 9.6   An Example of the *continue* Statement

```
#include <stdio.h>

int main(void)
{
FILE *fp;
int   c;

    fp = fopen("c:\\config.sys", "r");
    while ((c = fgetc(fp)) != EOF) {
        if (c == 's')
            continue;
        printf("%c", c);
    }
    return(0);
}
```

Using Conditional Statements

Sometimes a loop is not the statement type that you need. Instead of looping, you might need to execute one of two code sections depending on the value of an expression. At another time, the value of a variable (sometimes called the *state* of a variable) might kick off more than two alternative code sections.

Conditional statements are used quite often. For example, a program might need to run one code section if a customer's gender is female and another code section if the customer is a male. On the other hand, a tax program might need to run a different code section for each of the 50 states.

The situation with two alternatives is handled by the if statement. You have already seen the if statement used in this book. In the next section, "The *if* Statement," it is discussed in detail.

When you need to choose from multiple code blocks, you can use the switch statement. For example, you can test the value of a variable called monthNumber and select a different code block for each month. The switch statement is discussed later in this chapter, in the section "The *switch* Statement."

The *if* Statement

The syntax for the if statement is the following:

```
if (conditional expression) {
    // code block if expression is true
} else {
```

```
                    // code block if expression is false
    }
```

The conditional expression can use any of the operators discussed in Chapter 5, "Operators." The else part of the if statement is optional. Let's run through some examples.

Example 1:

```
    if (numPages > 0)
        printBook();
```

This example simply checks to see whether the number of pages is greater than zero; if so, the book is printed. Notice that the else clause was not used, nor were the braces ({}). If you need to execute only a single statement, you don't need to use the braces.

> **Note**
>
> If you always use braces to indicate the code blocks to be executed, you will save time when modifying and testing your code. An easy way to test the execution of a condition statement is to add print statements saying "inside true section" or "inside false section." Using the braces all of the time helps you avoid forgetting to add them while debugging, which causes bad results.

Example 2:

```
    if (numPages == 0) {
        displayErrorMessage();
    }
    else {
        printBook();
    }
```

This example shows the use of the else clause of the if statement. If the number of pages is zero, an error message is displayed; otherwise, the book is printed.

Example 3:

```
    if ((numPages = readBook()) == 0) {
        displayErrorMessage();
        updateLogFile();
    }
    else if (numPages < 11) {
        printSmallBook();
        updateLogFile();
    }
    else {
        printLargeBook();
```

```
            UpdateLogFile();
    }
```

This example shows how to use nested `if` statements. In this case, if there are zero pages, the program will display the same error message as does Example 2. However, I added the test to see whether the program is printing a small book (less than 11 pages) or a large book.

Using the Comma Operator in *if* Statements

There is an alternative to using braces to indicate blocks of code. If you have only a few small statements to execute, you can use the comma operator in the following manner:

```
    if (numItems > 100)
        largeOrder = TRUE, rushDelivery = FALSE, handlingCharge =
        FALSE;
```

In this case, both variables will be set if the number of items is greater than 100.

For a further example, let's rework Example 3 from the previous section:

```
    if ((numPages = readBook()) == 0)
        displayErrorMessage(), updateLogFile();
    else if (numPages < 11)
        printSmallBook(), printMessage(), updateLogFile();
    }
    else printLargeBook(), updateLogFile();
```

> **Caution**
>
> Please note that using the comma operator in this fashion makes the code more difficult to interpret. I've included this usage simply to let you know that it exists. I don't recommend that you use it too often.

The *switch* Statement

The `switch` statement is used when you need to select from more than one code block based on the value of a single variable. This ability can be useful in a number of situations. If you are writing a program to support printers, you could execute a different code block depending on a variable that holds the printer type. Another example would be executing a different code block depending on what type of video controller your program is using.

The syntax for the `switch` statement is the following:

```
    switch (variable) {
        case constant 1:
```

```
                    // code block
                    break;
            case constant 2:
                    // code block
                    break;
            default:
                    // code to execute if variable is not
                    // equal to any constant in one of the
                    // case clauses of the switch statement.
                    break;
    }
```

Listing 9.7 is an example of how to use the switch statement. The output of the program changes depending on what value you assign to the curDay variable. Assigning tue to curDay, as is done here, results in an output of "It is Tuesday!"

Listing 9.7   An Example of the *switch* Statement

```
#include <stdio.h>

enum days { sun, mon, tue, wed, thu, fri, sat };

int main(void)
{
enum days curDay;

    // Please note that this assignment statement is here only for the
    // purpose of this example. Normally, the switch variable, curDay,
    // would be set by another code section or a routine that is called.
    //
    curDay = tue;

    switch (curDay) {
        case mon:
            printf("It is Monday!\n");
            break;
        case tue:
            printf("It is Tuesday!\n");
            break;
        case wed:
            printf("It is Wednesday!\n");
            break;
        case thu:
            printf("It is Thursday!\n");
            break;
        case fri:
            printf("It is Friday!\n");
            break;
        case sun:
        case sat:
            printf("It is the weekend!\n");
            break;
        default:
```

```
                printf("curDay has a bad value.\n");
                break;
        }
        return(0);
    }
```

Please note that the `break` statement is used to stop the processing of each `case` clause of the `switch` statement. If more than one case uses the same code block, you can group them together. The Sunday and Saturday clauses demonstrate this.

The `default` clause is used to catch any stray values of the condition variable. This is a good place to put code that detects error conditions.

The `default` clause can also be used for code that handles the generic values of the `switch` variable. If this is the situation, the `case` clauses would be used to handle the exceptions. The next example illustrates this:

```
switch (shipToState) {
    case ALASKA:
        cost = 14.50;
        break;
    case HAWAII:
        cost = 18.00;
        break;
    default:
        cost = 4.00;
        break;
}
```

This code example treats 48 of the states identically. Only Alaska and Hawaii have individual code sections.

You do not need to use `enum` variable types in the `case` clauses. Instead, you could use `#define` definitions like this:

```
#define TRUE    1
#define FALSE   0

    switch (largeBook) {
        case TRUE:
            printf("Large Book\n");
            break;
        case FALSE:
            printf("Small Book\n");
    }
```

Or you could use regular numbers like this:

```
        switch (largeBook) {
            case 1:
```

```
                    printf("Large Book\n");
                    break;
            case 0:
                    printf("Small Book\n");
    }
```

From Here...

In this chapter, you learned about loops that use the `for`, `do..while`, and `while` statements, and how to implement conditional statements with `if` and `switch`. In addition, you saw how to use the comma operator, and why you should use it sparingly.

At this point, you are ready to tackle more advanced notions of the C++ programming language. You might want to look at the following chapters:

- Chapter 10, "Pointers," to read about pointers.

- Chapter 11, "I/O," to read about the `cout` and `printf` statements used throughout the examples.

- Chapter 15, "Compiling and Linking," to read about how to compile the examples.

- Chapter 16, "Debugging," to get some debugging advice if your examples aren't working properly.

Chapter 10

Pointers

Pointers are a crucial element in most computer languages—and especially so in C and C++. Despite this, novice programmers (and even some advanced programmers, for that matter) often cringe at the thought of using them, or treat them as an arcane subject from which no good can come. This is probably because the most spectacular and devastating crashes that computer programmers experience—as well as the most pernicious and undetectable bugs that they have to correct—usually stem from a misuse of pointers.

However, there's no need for you to fear, because if you follow a few simple rules when using pointers, you can eliminate most of the problems that give pointers a bad name.

In this chapter, you'll learn the basics of pointers and how to use them without injuring yourself. You'll also get a taste of the rich variety of techniques used by programmers to take advantage of pointers. In addition, you'll learn about the following:

- What a pointer is

- How to declare a pointer variable

- How to access pointer variables

- Working with pointers and structured types

- Pointer math

- Dynamic memory allocation

- Function pointers

- Far and near pointers

Getting a Grasp on Pointers

First, you need to understand what a pointer is and why you would use one. As you know, a *variable* describes a location in RAM that you've set aside for a specific purpose. For example, if you code the declaration

```
int c;
```

you're telling the compiler to set aside an int-sized space of RAM that you can refer to as c and use to hold some integer value. You generally don't care what part of RAM, you just want someplace to store a number. When you subsequently perform operations on c, you're manipulating the integer value that c contains. You have *direct access* to the integer value stored by c.

Pointers involve one more level of abstraction. A pointer variable contains the *address* of some data. You aren't primarily interested in the pointer—you're interested in the value that it points to. Figure 10.1 illustrates this. When you get to a value based on a pointer, you're indirectly accessing it.

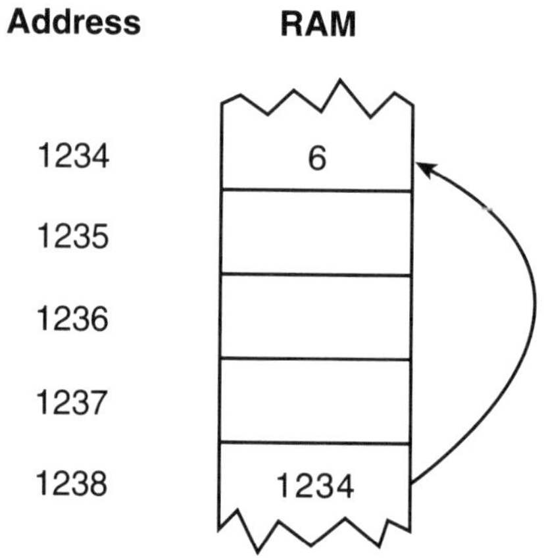

Fig. 10.1
A pointer is an area of RAM that "points" to another area of RAM by containing the other area's address.

Using Simple Pointer Types and Declarations

Using Simple Pointer Types and Declarations

Pointers have types beyond just "it's a pointer." If you want the compiler to be able to type-check the pointer variable, you need to tell it what type of variable it's supposed to point to. Declaring a pointer of a specific type is as simple as putting an asterisk (*) in front of the variable:

```
int *c;
```

The c variable is now declared as pointing to an integer.

Where Do You Put the Asterisk?

A lot of programmers like to put the asterisk immediately after the data type instead of immediately before the variable, like this:

```
int* c;
```

I confess, I used to be one of those programmers. I don't know why others do it, but for me, it was because every other language I had used actually considered the pointer operator to be attached to the data type. In other words, the preceding code line would have been read, "Declare c to be of a type that points to an integer." In C, however, the code line should be read, "Declare c to be a pointer to an integer."

Even though the compiler will take either one, it's an important distinction when declaring more than one variable on a line.

```
int* c, d; /* Warning: ONLY c is a pointer; d is an integer */
```

If you associate the asterisk with the integer, you might get confused and think that you had just declared two pointers when you haven't. This is correctly declared:

```
int *c, *d; /*Now BOTH c and d are pointers.
```

As you'll see later, any confusion can be completely resolved by declaring a pointer type.

One philosophy many C++ programmers live by is to never declare more than one variable on a line, which removes any chance of ambiguity.

Having declared a pointer to an integer, you may wonder what integer it points to. The answer to that brings up the first rule of using a pointer safely:

Pointers, like any other variables, must be initialized before being used, or the results are undefined and often spectacularly disastrous.

This is a very important point (pardon the pun) and one of the primary reasons for pointers' bad reputation. If you try to access data reference by a pointer that hasn't been properly initialized, it could be pointing anywhere, and you could end up writing over the operating system code, sending stuff out the printer port—*anywhere!* So aim your pointers before you fire them!

Preparing and Using Simple Pointer Variables

To "aim" your pointer, you must give it the address of a valid integer variable. This is done through the ampersand operator (&). The ampersand or "address of" operator was first covered in Chapter 8, "Functions and Macros," when you learned how to pass a variable by value to a function, so that changes made to the variable within the function persisted after the function was over.

This is really no different: The pointer needs the address of a valid data object to be safely used. So, if you had two variables declared,

```
int *c;
int d;
```

you could then give the pointer c a legitimate value in this fashion:

```
c = &d;
```

Referencing the value that a simple pointer points to is done through the asterisk.

```
*c = 1;
```

Look at the following short program:

```
#include <stdio.h>
main()
{
    int *c = &d;
    int d;

    d = 7;
    printf("%d",*c);
    *c = 6;
    printf("%d",d);
}
```

Note

Some examples in this chapter use the printf() function, which is covered in detail in Chapter 11, "I/O." For these examples, all you need to know about it is that it formats and displays a string.

If you change the value that c points to, d's value changes. If you change d's value directly, the value that c points to changes. That's because they both refer to the same location in memory. They're essentially both names for the same area of RAM, and c is referred to as a *pointer alias* for d. Although giving a variable a pointer alias can be useful, it's not the most common use of pointers. (The section "Allocating Dynamic Memory" later in this chapter discusses their most popular—and arguably most important—use.)

Manipulating Arrays and Strings

If you've programmed in other languages, you may be surprised to discover that C and C++ provide no direct access to strings or arrays. Think of C as a kind of high-level, portable assembler—and, of course, the CPU has no concept of strings and arrays either. (C++ is a kind of assembler with object extensions!)

The fact that all string variable names are just pointers to character arrays creates one of the most common idioms in C and C++: String manipulations are often done by adjusting pointers to the string instead of by creating copies of the string or altering the string.

Of course, there are functions to copy and alter strings; but say you were writing a function to output a string, and you wanted the function to print out only as much of the string as would fit in a certain length and break at the word (word wrap). You also wanted clients of the function to be able to call it consecutively so that they could easily output an entire word-wrapped string on multiple lines.

In some languages, you would output as much of the string as you could and return a number telling how many characters you had output. In C, however, you would do something like this:

```
char *strwrap(char *str, int width);
```

The strwrap function would return not a pointer to a new string, but a pointer to the *same* string, which would be set to point right after the last character you printed. The programmers who used your function could then write code like this:

```
p = str;
while (*p!='/0')
{
    p = strwrap(p, width);
    /* other code here as necessary */
}
```

This association of pointers with arrays makes it possible to write very compact code to perform certain tasks, as you can see. To understand how this is possible, you need to understand the concept of *pointer math*.

Performing Pointer Math

From figure 10.1, you can see that the pointer does, in fact, hold a value, and C and C++ allow you to actually perform math on a pointer value—a no-no in many languages.

One of the most important things to remember is that doing math on the pointer is *not* the same as doing math on the object pointed to. To carry on with a previous example, if you have the code

```
int *c;
int d;

d = 0;
c = &d;
d++;
```

you can see that d has a value of 1 at the end of the code and c points to the value of 1. If you have the following, on the other hand,

```
int *c;
int d;

d = 0;
c = &d;
c++;
```

that's something else entirely, and leads to the second big rule for not getting into trouble when using pointers:

> *Always dereference the pointer when you want to act on the value that the pointer references.*

This is a really obvious statement, of course, but it isn't uncommon for programmers to forget that they're dealing with a pointer and not a directly accessible variable. This is one of the reasons that many languages don't allow pointer math.

Pointer math has a place, however. If you have a pointer that doesn't point to a simple variable but points to an array, all of a sudden pointer math becomes an appealing way to traverse that array:

```
#include <stdlib.h>
#include <stdio.h>            //Required by printf function
#include <string.h>          //Required by strcpy function

char *strwrap(char *str, int width)
{
   char *q, *r;
   int  number;

   while (*str == ' ') str++;
   if (*str == '\0') return str; /* blanks to the end */

   q = str;                    /* q points to first word */
   r = str;                    /* initialize r */
   while ((str-q)<width)   {
      if ((*str++!=' ') && (*str==' ')) r = str;
```

```
            /*r will point to end of the last word */
            if (*str=='\0') break;
            }

        number = r-q;
        if (number <= 0) {
            number = width;
            str = q+width;
            }
        else if (*str != '\0') str = r;
        printf("%0.*s\n", number,q);

        return str;
        }
void main()
{
        char str[1000];
        char *p;

        strcpy(str, "Some long string.");
        p = str;

        while (*p!='\0') p=strwrap(p,20);
}
```

As you can see, you can have your functions return a pointer to a type—in fact, you *are* doing that anytime you return a string.

This is the strwrap function and a simple program using it. Replace "Some long string." with some (really) long string and try it out.

Notice that this program is one place where an alias comes in handy. The pointer p starts out as an alias for the str variable but quickly proves useful as a way to index the rest of the string. (Right now, you might try rewriting this code without using a pointer and discover that it's a bit more work.) Try this function out with various widths and messages.

The trick to writing code like this is knowing when to dereference the pointer and when not to. Take a look at the strwrap function and see if you can understand it. For example, do you understand this line?

```
    while (*str == ' ') str++;
```

As long as str *points to* a space, the *pointer* is incremented. That's pretty straightforward, and it makes sure that all the text strwrap prints is left-justified. Notice that here—and everywhere else you dereference a char* variable—you're pointing to a *character*! That's why, for example, the next line is

```
    if (*str == '\0') return str; /* blanks to the end */
```

and not

```
if (*str == "\0") return str; /* no! not a string! */
```

When dereferencing, you can access only single characters. Functions, on the other hand, take the pointer and assume that you have a string of characters terminated by a null:

```
printf("%0.*s\n", number,q);
. . .
strcpy(str, "Some long string.");
```

This is why C functions fail so completely when you forget to end strings with a null—the pointers end up referencing all kinds of unauthorized memory.

It's also why you must make sure that there's plenty of memory for copies and concatenation. In those cases, the functions (such as strcpy) will actually write over memory that might have anything in it. In fact, if you want to prove this to yourself, define str in the preceding program as

```
char str[10];
```

and try the strcpy line as

```
strcpy(str, "This is going to cause big problems.");
```

Among the lines that I would consider most difficult to understand is

```
if ((*str++!=' ') && (*str==' ')) r = str;
```

And, in fact, I would never write this in one of my programs. It's here primarily because I've seen things like this in a lot of code, and you should get used to reading code like this. It's also here because the nature of the language and the ease of pointer math is going to make you inclined to write code like this, too.

This expression in particular is difficult:

```
(*str++!=' ')
```

It mixes the postfix operator ++ with dereferencing. If you have to write something like this, keep the table of operator precedence on hand (you'll find this in Chapter 5, "Operators") and remember that the postfix operator applies only after the expression is evaluated. That's why the second evaluation, which might seem to compare the same value with two contradictory comparisons, works.

Here's the actual process that goes on:

*str++!=' ' is actually two statements combined into one. Let's assume the pointer starts at the beginning of a string:

```
A very long string
```
↑

When `*str++!=' '` is encountered, two things happen: first, the `str!=' '`
checks for blanks, and then the `str++` increments the pointer:

```
A very long string
```
↑

Notice also that, as long as you're manipulating pointers mathematically, you
can do tricks such as

```
number = r-q;
```

and

```
str = q+width;
```

which are used in `strwrap` to determine how many characters to print out.

You can perform other forms of math on a pointer, but addition (and subtraction) are by far the most common.

Using Pointers with Structures

Pointers can, of course, be used with structures, and this is probably their
most important use. (The next section will explore this in depth.) As explained in Chapter 4, "Data Types, Variables, and Constants," you can build
your own structures like this:

```
struct month
    {char *name;
     int  days;
     };
```

And then you can declare variables of that type and reference them like so:

```
month m;
. . .
m.days = 31;
```

Pointers to user-defined types, including structures, are declared the same
way as any other type of pointer, by prefixing the asterisk:

```
month *m;
```

And you can still reference the entire structure—say, to pass it to a function—by prefixing the * to it in your code:

```
printCalendar(*m);
```

You can even reference the structure members in the same way, except that the . (period) operator normally used to reference members is a higher-order operator than the *. So this won't work:

```
*m.days = 31;   /* nope! */
```

The compiler will try to connect the . to the m pointer, not the value referenced by m. Fortunately, although you can fix this with parentheses,

```
(*m).days = 31; /* will work, but uncommon */
```

you don't have to. Instead, the structure members can be indicated with the character description of a pointer, ->, as in

```
m->days = 31;
```

More on Pointer Math

The strwrap function has a number of lines like

```
while (*str == ' ') str++;
```

which increments the pointer variable. You might wonder whether you can do this same trick with an array of something larger than a byte. For example, would the following code have the desired effect of displaying the months of the year?

```
#include <stdio.h>

struct month
    {char *name;
     int  days;
     };

main()
{
   int i;

   month year[12] = {{ "January", 31},
        {"February", 28}, {"March", 31},
        {"April", 30}, {"May", 31},
        {"June", 30}, {"July", 31},
        {"August", 31}, {"September", 30},
        {"October", 31}, {"November", 30},
        {"December", 31}};

   month *p;
```

```
    p = &year[0];
    for (i=1;i<=12;i++) {
        printf("%s\n", p->name);
        p++;
        }
}
```

The answer is—perhaps surprisingly—yes! When you increment a pointer to an array, it changes to point to the next element of the array.

Pointer Types

An incredibly common practice these days is to eliminate the free-floating declaration of pointers wherever possible by declaring each new type to have a pointer type as well. For example, the month structure in the preceding section might have been declared as

```
struct month
     {char *name;
      int  days;
      };
typedef month *pMonth;
```

Then the p variable would have been declared as

```
pMonth p;
```

Note that the * part of the definition has now been integrated into the type. The rest of the program remains the same, however, so you may wonder whether there's much point to this.

This is a matter of opinion. Some feel that any pointer type that might be used over and over again should have its own type definition, and that's what should be used in function parameter lists and so on. Others feel this is overkill. I like the theory of having a type for every pointer, but there does seem to be a potential danger of the programmer *forgetting* that the type is a pointer.

Allocating Dynamic Memory

You may have any number of opinions about pointers, based on the material covered so far in this chapter: You can use them for cute tricks, and you can get in trouble using them. But are they really necessary?

Well, maybe not with what I've covered up to this point. But the primary use of pointers isn't for aliases, or so that you can do math with them. Pointers exist so that you can access as much memory as the system has available, but only as much as you need. This is called *dynamic memory allocation*, and object-oriented programming (covered in Chapter 13) depends heavily on dynamic memory allocation.

Now go back to the simple pointer examples used earlier in this chapter.

```
main()
{
    int *c = &d;
    int d;

    d = 7;
    *c = 6;
}
```

The obvious question when looking at this is why a programmer wouldn't just use d. Why bother with a pointer to it at all? Well, suppose that you don't know whether you need d. You know you *might* need an integer, but you aren't sure you will, and the amount of memory you allocate is significant. You'll want to allocate memory for the integer only when and if you need it:

```
main()
{
    int *c;

    . . .
    if (someCondition) allocate(d) /*allocate is hypothetical fn*/
    . . .
    if (!allocated(d)) doSomething;
    else doSomethingElse(d);
```

Maybe you're still not sold on the idea. After all, it's only an integer—why not just go ahead and allocate it? Well, suppose that it wasn't a single integer, but an *array* of integers. You know you're going to need the array, but you don't know how big it's going to be.

```
main()
{
    int x, y;
    int *pArray;

    printf("Dimensions for maze? (x y)");
    scanf("%d%d",&x,&y);

    pArray = allocate(x, y); /* allocate is hypothetical fn*/
    . . .
    /* build maze */
```

This surely has some value. If you can dynamically allocate the memory, then if the allocation fails, you can inform the user so that he can scale down his request. By contrast, you could allocate the maximum amount of space that your program will allow, as in

```
int array[200,200];
```

but then if the user didn't have that much memory on his machine, your program would simply fail.

Functions for Allocating Memory

To realize the benefits of dynamically allocating an array, you have to know how to request memory and dispose of it when you're done with it. You also have to know whether a given request for memory has been granted.

Allocating an array of variable dimensions is done differently between C and C++. Look at the C approach first, which is to use `malloc` or `calloc`. The `malloc` function is the simpler of the two:

```
array = malloc(x*y);
```

It allocates the amount of memory specified as its only parameter. In this case, it will return a pointer to an area of memory that's x times y bytes long.

C++ is a bit more restrictive regarding `malloc` and `calloc`, and requires the return of these functions to be typecast as a type appropriate to the target:

```
array = (int *)malloc(x*y);
```

If the memory is unavailable to the requesting application, `malloc` returns `NULL`. In pointer terms, `NULL` is nowhere, as in no data is referenced. This brings us to another safety rule when using pointers:

Always check to make sure that your pointers are pointing somewhere before trying to use them.

In other words, you wouldn't want to do this:

```
char *array;
. . .
array = (char *)malloc(x*y);
*array = 10; /* No! Array could be NULL! */
```

Instead, check to see whether the allocation was successful first:

```
char *array;
. . .
array = (char *)malloc(x*y);
if (array == NULL) break;
*array = 10; /* We're okay now! */
```

NULL is usually defined as zero, so this kind of compaction is allowed:

```
if (!array) break;
```

However, at least in theory, NULL may not be 0—that's one of the reasons the NULL define is used instead of the literal 0. In practice, I've seen a lot of code that depended on NULL being 0, and I've never known it to fail—but can you imagine how difficult it would be to track down this bug if it did fail? (This doesn't make it into the category of common pointer errors, but it should be a sobering thought.)

One error you might make with malloc is this:

```
int *array;
. . .
array = (int *)malloc(x*y);
*array = 1000; /* big trouble here—array is only half size */
```

malloc doesn't know you want an array of x*y integers. It thinks you're asking for x*y *bytes*. (Theoretically, it's possible for a C implementation to have a byte-sized integer, but that's not so under DOS and Windows.) A common response to this is to restructure the malloc call:

```
array = (int *)malloc(x*y*2);
```

And this works as long as an integer is two bytes (true for current versions of DOS and Windows).

The calloc function is often used to increase portability. Its functionality is the same as malloc, but it has two parameters: the number of memory objects you want to allocate and the size of those objects.

```
array = (int *)calloc(x*y, sizeof(int));
```

This code will always return the proper amount of memory—if it's available. (Check for NULL, as always.) As a side effect, calloc also clears all the memory allocated to zero, which can be handy sometimes.

Memory is a finite resource: You can use it all up. You can reduce the chances of running out by letting the system know you're done with it. This is done with the free function:

```
free(array);
```

Failing to free memory allocations is a common, often subtle error that happens with pointers. The phenomenon of losing memory and not knowing where it went or how to get it back is called a *memory leak*. Because most programs rely heavily on memory allocation, this has wide-ranging effects.

In DOS, for example, it tends to make programs gradually less useful, as the program is less and less capable of allocating the memory it needs to function. The traditional user cure for a DOS program that leaks is to leave the program and rerun it.

Under Windows, on the other hand, you can bring the entire system to its knees as you use up precious resources that no other program can have. It's even possible to consume memory that can't be regained without shutting Windows down completely. So the obvious rule here is:

Always free up memory you've allocated as soon as you're done with it.

You can save yourself a lot of grief by deciding where allocated memory is going to be freed in your program, and writing that code *immediately* after writing the code to allocate it.

Note that it doesn't matter whether array was allocated with malloc or calloc; free returns it to the system. And that brings us to yet another rule for safely handling pointers:

After freeing the memory that a pointer references, set that pointer to NULL.

This rule works especially well if you followed the rule about checking to see whether the pointer is NULL before using it. Here are two very common errors:

```
char *array;
. . .
array = (char *)malloc(x*y);
if (array == NULL) break;
*array = 10;
. . .
free(array);
. . .
*array = 99; /* Bad news! */
```

You freed it, but then you tried to use it again. This is just as bad and potentially just as devastating as never having allocated it in the first place. But maybe you can't always tell whether the flow of the program has caused the memory to be allocated or freed, so you start the pointer as NULL and check it every time:

```
char *array = NULL;
. . .
array = (char *)malloc(x*y);
if (array == NULL) break;
*array = 10;
. . .
free(array);
. . .
if (array == NULL) break;
*array = 99; /* More bad news! */
```

If array is never allocated, you're fine. If the allocation of array fails, you're still fine. But if the allocation succeeds and array is subsequently freed, you're in trouble again. The free function does *not* set the pointer to NULL. So after freeing a pointer, be sure to set it to NULL!

```
free(array);
array = NULL;
. . .
if (array == NULL) break;
*array = 99; /* Safe at last! */
```

The Impenetrable Void

Not to be confused with a NULL pointer, which is a pointer that references nothing, is a pointer with a *void* type. Void pointers are basically a programmer's way of saying, "Hey, it's a pointer, and it's none of your business as to what kind of pointer it is."

This is vastly useful because a void pointer is compatible with every other pointer type. Under C, every pointer type is compatible with void, too, so that if you use malloc and calloc to return a void pointer, you don't need the typecast.

```
pArray = malloc(x*y); /* OK no matter what kind of pointer */
                      /* array is */
```

C++, as mentioned, is more restrictive. Given the following code,

```
void *v;
char *p

v = p;          /* OK in C and C++ */
p = v;          /* OK in C, C++ chokes */
p = (char *)v   /* OK in both */
```

C and C++ compilers will react differently. C++ has a different and better approach to allocating memory. (The malloc and calloc calls are still widely used, however, so it's good to be aware of them.)

New and Delete

With C, restricted to using malloc and calloc, a programmer often ended up writing an allocation function for each structure he created. In other words, if you had a structure called fish that you used a lot, you'd have a function that looked like this:

```
fish *newfish;
{
   return malloc(sizeof(fish));
   }
```

C++ adds missing functionality to the C language with the new feature. new automatically allocates the right amount of memory for a structure.

```
f = new fish;
```

A common error is to use the variable name instead of the type name, as in

```
f = new f; /* Don't do this! */
```

Freeing the fish, or any variable, is as simple as typing **delete** before it.

```
delete f; /* frees the f fish variable */
```

> **Note**
>
> Don't try to use delete with memory allocated using malloc or calloc, and don't try to use free with memory allocated using new.

Using Function Pointers

Now that you've got a good handle on pointers, it's time to throw one more mind-bending concept at you: A pointer doesn't have to point to data—it can also point to *code*.

At the CPU level, of course, nothing is especially dramatic about this. Code is just data that's interpreted differently. On the practical programming level, this can have a wide-ranging impact. Pointers to functions can be said to be the basis on which object-oriented programming is implemented.

The simplest way to declare a pointer to a function is to specify the type, followed by parentheses containing the variable name preceded by an asterisk, followed by another set of parentheses containing the formal parameter list.

```
mytype (* myfuncptr)(t1 p1, t2 p2, t3 p3);
```

This line declares a pointer called myfuncptr to a function that returns mytype and that has three parameters p1, p2, and p3 of types t1, t2, and t3. Of course, an actual declaration could use any number of parameters and return any type.

And since the main point of using a pointer to a function would be to change what function it pointed to, you'd probably start any project that was going to use a pointer to a function with a type for that function.

```
typedef mytype (* myfuncptrtype)(t1 p1, t2 p2, t3 p3);
```

Then later, you would declare variables of the `myfuncptrtype` type:

```
myfunctptrtype func1, func2, func3;
```

Assigning a function type to a pointer simply requires that you use the assignment operator:

```
func1 = somecompatiblefunction;
```

You may also use the ampersand operator to emphasize the fact that the address of the function is being assigned, *not* the result:

```
func1 = &somecompatiblefunction;
```

To call the function requires only that you dereference the pointer and, naturally, supply the correct actual parameters.

Designating Pointers as Far and Near

Pointers on the PC may be categorized as *near* or *far*. Although that sounds like a designation of location, it is, in fact, a designation of *reach*. A near pointer is a two-byte pointer, which, therefore, is capable of a maximum reach of 64K.

A far pointer, on the other hand, is a four-byte pointer, which can reach anywhere in the system. This whole near/far scheme is directly tied to the PC and Intel's x86 family of CPUs, which began their existence as segmented architectures. (*Segmented* means that the memory has to be dealt with in blocks of a certain size. In the PC's case, under DOS and Windows, that's 64K.) The operating systems built on the early 8086 and 80286 chips (DOS and Windows and even early versions of OS/2) have the concept hard-wired into their makeup.

As a result, the concepts of far and near as used on the PC aren't portable, and you should try to avoid them. This isn't always possible, unfortunately, but the areas where it's not possible are usually system-specific anyway, so you lose little when you use them in these circumstances.

For example, the keyboard is located at a specific memory location (0040:0017), and you could use a far pointer to access it. The memory for the video screen is located at a higher address in the system (a location that varies based on the type of screen), and you could use a far pointer to access the screen directly.

A far pointer is declared by using the keyword far after the type of the pointer and before the asterisk.

```
void far *ptr;
```

By default, pointers are near. The main thing to remember about near and far is that if they *are* specified in a function or declaration, it's probably because they're necessary. In other words, if you see a function defined as

```
systemfunc(void far *ptr);
```

you'll need to know how to declare a far pointer to pass to that function. (The compiler will warn you if you pass a near pointer when far is specified, fortunately.)

From Here...

As you have read, pointers are not especially mysterious or dangerous if you use them properly. In object-oriented programming, pointers are indispensable because most objects are created at run time—you'll see that in later chapters. In fact, you'll see pointers in action throughout this book, but you might be interested particularly in the following:

- Chapter 4, "Data Types, Variables, and Constants." It's a good idea to look at strings and arrays with your new understanding of pointers and the true nature of strings and arrays.

- Chapter 12, "Classes and Objects." Here you'll learn that pointers are indispensable to object-oriented programming in C++.

- Chapter 29, "Single and Multiple Document Interfaces." A solid understanding of pointers is necessary to smoothly implement a multiple-document interface application. This chapter shows you how to handle pointers to windows and to objects that appear on windows in order to facilitate programs working well with more than one open document window.

II

Learning C/C++

Chapter 11

I/O

At some point, almost every computer program must communicate with either a person sitting at a monitor or a file to which it can read or save information. Even programs that require no input or output (for example, some hardware driver programs) use output statements at least temporarily during the debugging stages of development.

You can use the routines found in this chapter to make your program aware of its environment so that it can make intelligent choices about what functions the user needs. For example, a program that is aware of its environment is one that monitors the names of users who invoke the program in a file on their local hard drive. The next time a user launches the program, the program can look for that file and greet the user by name.

Good communication with your programs' users is an art form. Part III, "Designing User Interfaces," deals with the mechanics of a user interface. There also are entire books that deal with the design of user interfaces. You should consult one of these books if your program requires a lot of user interaction.

This chapter discusses the various types of interactions and the input/output (I/O) routines that facilitate them. You will see some examples of how to use the routines.

The topics in this chapter include the following:

- User interaction—reading from the keyboard and displaying information on the monitor

- Basic file interaction—reading and writing to a file

- Advanced file interaction—looking at log files to store messages

- Device interaction—learning how to access the printer and modem for debugging purposes

Many books address input and output separately. This book, however, focuses on *program interaction*—all the points at which a program interacts with users, files, or devices. All other types of program interaction are simply variations on these themes.

User Interaction

There are two basic ways your program interacts with a user:

- It gets keyboard input through a means such as a dialog box.

- It displays information to the user via the monitor.

Getting Keyboard Input

In the Windows operating system, applications accept input from their users in many different ways. One particularly interesting method is through the use of dialog boxes. Dialog boxes are usually used when information about a specific topic is needed. For example, when a program needs information about how many copies of a document to print, a Printer Setup dialog box might be used.

> **Note**
>
> The C++ run-time library still contains functions, inherited from DOS, that get information directly from the keyboard. With the widespread adoption of Windows, however, these are now archaic and beyond the scope of this book.

Another example is when you need to stop the execution of a program at a given point for debugging reasons—for example, to display a message about the currently executing code block and then wait for the user to press Enter before continuing. Listing 11.1 shows an example of how to use the MessageBox routine to handle this situation.

Listing 11.1 Using the *MessageBox* Routine

```
#include <windows.h>

int main(void)
{
    MessageBox(NULL, "Entering the EndPage function.",
              "DEBUG", MB_OK);
    return(0);
}
```

This function, which needs the windows.h header file, displays the dialog box shown in figure 11.1. More information about the MessageBox routine is in the next section, in Chapter 18, "A User Interface," and in Chapter 19, "Developing Windows Resources for a User Interface." However, it also belongs here as a tool to temporarily halt your program and wait for a user action.

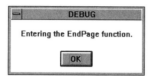

Fig. 11.1
The MessageBox dialog box.

Displaying Information

This section discusses routines that display information on the monitor for the user to read. These two routines are the printf and MessageBox routines.

The *printf* Routine

The C++ language has inherited an entire library of routines from its predecessor, C. This allows older programs written in C to be compiled with the newer C++ compilers. One of the I/O functions that was inherited is called printf, which can be used to display formatted information. You can use it to display any of the following basic variable types:

- Integer

- Floating-point

- Character

- String

- Pointer

You can also display the members of a structure or union if they're one of the basic variable types.

The printf routine generates TTY, or TeleType-style, output. TTY is characterized by output that is created one line at a time. Once a line has been printed, there is no mechanism for moving backward to delete or change the previous output. You can contrast this with the Windows paradigm of a graphical screen where a program can address any point on the screen, and therefore can write or rewrite anywhere on the display.

> **Note**
>
> For Turbo C++ to correctly understand how to process the TTY output of the `printf` routine when creating a Windows program, you need to use the `_InitEasyWin()` routine. The `_InitEasyWin` routine creates a window where the TTY output will be displayed. EasyWin is a feature of the Turbo C++ compiler that makes it easy to compile DOS-based programs so that they will run in Windows.

Here is the syntax of the `printf` function:

```
int printf(const char *format[, argument, ...]);
```

> **Note**
>
> The `printf` routine—like most of the input/output routines from the C language—needs the header file `stdio.h` to be included.

This function can take a variable number of arguments. For example, you can display a single string variable or the floating-point values of variables in a mathematical calculation.

The *format* parameter controls how the rest of the arguments are displayed. Each variable to be printed should have a corresponding format specifier to define how it should be printed. The following two short examples illustrate this:

```
printf("Book Title: %s\n", bookName);

printf("Book Title: %s\tNumber of Pages: %d\n", bookName, numPages);
```

The first example shows the `printf` routine displaying a string literal (`Book Title:`) and then displaying the variable as a string (`%s`). The percent sign (`%`) is used as an escape character the same way the backslash (`\`) is used as an escape character in string literals. Notice that the escape character is used to display a new line (`\n`) and a tab (`t`). These are useful when displaying information.

The second example displays two variables; `bookName` is a string and `numPages` is an integer (`%d`).

Table 11.1 shows the five most popular format specifiers. These specifiers also have modifiers to allow fine control of how to display a variable. For example, to display a zero-filled four-digit number you would use "%04d". This would display the value of 10 as "0010". However, because this book is mainly about Windows and C++, you should—at least in theory—need to use only `printf` for debugging reasons. For debugging, the basic formatting options should be enough.

You should note that the program in listing 11.2 uses the `WinMain` routine instead of the `main` routine of the C language. The `WinMain` routine is used when you write a Windows program.

Table 11.1   The Five Most Popular Format Specifiers Used by *printf*

Type Char	Expected Input	Format of Output
%d	Integer	Signed decimal integer.
%x	Integer	Unsigned hexadecimal int (with a, b, c, d, e, f).
%f	Floating-point	Signed value of the form [-]dddd.dddd.
%s	String pointer	Displays characters until a NULL character is found or precision is reached.
%p	Pointer	Prints the input argument as a pointer; format depends on which memory model was used. It will be either XXXX:YYYY or YYYY (offset only).

Listing 11.2 demonstrates each of the five format specifiers in table 11.1.

Listing 11.2   Various *printf* Examples

```c
#include <stdio.h>
#include <windows.h>

int PASCAL WinMain( HANDLE hInstance, HANDLE hPrevInstance,
                    LPSTR lpszCmdParam, int nCmdShow )
{
int gridCoordinate = 10;
unsigned int tempValue = 34;
float amountOwed = 123.32;
char *bookName = "Hound of the Baskervilles";

    _InitEasyWin();
    printf("The grid coordinate is %d.\n", gridCoordinate);
    printf("The value of 34 in base 16 is %x.\n", tempValue);
    printf("John Doe owes $%f dollars to Elizabeth.\n", amountOwed);
    printf("I am reading a book called \"%s\".\n", bookName);
    printf("The address of the variable bookName is %p.\n", bookName);
    return(0);
}
```

II

Learning C/C++

Tip
You can use double percent signs (%%) to display a single percent sign on the monitor.

The next section discusses the C++ cout routine, which has superseded the printf routine for displaying variables and text. However, your new knowledge of the printf function is still useful in the C++ world. This is because a function called sprintf uses the same format parameters and variable number of arguments. The sprintf function basically directs the output of the printf function to a buffer instead of to a display. Listing 11.7 in the "File Stream Routines" section shows an example of using the sprintf function.

The *cout* Routine

The cout routine is part of the iostream library of the C++ language. This routine also produces TTY output like the printf routine. Because of this, the InitEasyWin() routine also needs to be used in programs that include the cout routine.

The syntax of cout is generally considered more simple and elegant than that of the printf routine. It makes extensive use of *overloading* to allow you to display the standard variable types as well as new variable types you might define in your program. (Overloading, which is described in Chapter 13, "Object-Oriented Methods," allows an operator to act on many different variable types.)

When the cout routine is used to display information, the insertion operator (<<) is used. This operator essentially sends literals and variables to the cout routine. No special formatting flags are needed to handle simply displaying standard literal and variable types. This contrasts with the format specifier needed by the printf routine.

When special formatting is needed, such as displaying a hexadecimal value, a manipulator is used. The necessary manipulator is inserted into the I/O stream using the << operator exactly like a variable. Table 11.2 shows seven of the most-used manipulators.

Table 11.2 The Seven Most-Used *cout* Manipulators

Manipulator	Description
dec, oct, hex	Sets the conversion base. For example, if oct is used, the variable will be displayed as an octal value.
endl	Inserts a new-line into the iostream.
setw(n)	Sets the width of the field in which to display the variable.
setfill(n)	Sets the fill character.
setprecision(n)	Sets the precision at which to display the variable.

Listing 11.3 shows how each manipulator is used. The lines that display grid coordinates show how to use the setw and setfill manipulators. The lines that display the value of 34 show how to set the conversion base. The lines that display the temperature value show how to use the setprecision manipulator. If you use the iostream manipulators, you must include the iomanip header file.

Listing 11.3 Various *cout* Examples

```
#include <iomanip.h>
#include <iostream.h>
#include <windows.h>

int PASCAL WinMain( HANDLE hInstance, HANDLE hPrevInstance,
                    LPSTR lpszCmdParam, int nCmdShow )
{
int gridCoordinate = 10;
unsigned int tempValue = 34;
float temperature = 23.12345;
char *bookName = "Hound of the Baskervilles";

        _InitEasyWin();
        cout << "The grid coordinate is " << gridCoordinate << ".\n";
        cout << "The grid coordinate is " << setw(4)
                << setfill('0') << gridCoordinate << ".\n";
        cout << endl;
        cout << "The value of 34 in base  8 is "
                << oct << tempValue << ".\n";
        cout << "The value of 34 in base 10 is "
                << dec << tempValue << ".\n";
        cout << "The value of 34 in base 16 is "
                << hex << tempValue << ".\n";
        cout << endl;
        cout << "The temperature is " << temperature << " degrees.\n";
        cout << "The temperature is " << setprecision(5)
                << temperature << " degrees.\n";
        return(0);
}
```

Although the cout statements are sometimes longer than their printf counterparts, it is more intuitively obvious what the programmer intends to do in the cout statements. In addition, the implementation of the cout routine, according to Borland, is faster and more efficient.

The output from listing 11.3 is shown in figure 11.2.

Fig. 11.2

The Output from the program in listing 11.3.

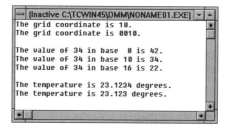

As mentioned previously, one of the main advantages of the `cout` routine is that the `<<` operator can be overloaded. This means that you can tell the compiler how to use the `<<` operator to display a user-defined variable type. Listing 11.4 shows how to overload the `<<` operator.

Listing 11.4   Overloading the `<<` Operator

```
#include <iomanip.h>
#include <iostream.h>
#include <windows.h>

struct member {
      char *firstName;
      char *lastName;
};

ostream& operator << (ostream &stream, member& temp)
{
      stream << temp.lastName << "," << temp.firstName;
      return stream;
}

int PASCAL WinMain( HANDLE hInstance, HANDLE hPrevInstance,
                    LPSTR lpszCmdParam, int nCmdShow )
{
member list[2] = {{"Harold", "Jackson"}, { "Janet", "Jones"}};

      _InitEasyWin();
      cout << "The first member is " << list[0] << "." << endl;
      cout << "The second member is " << list[1] << "." << endl;

      return(0);
}
```

The line beginning with `ostream&` begins the routine that actually overloads the `<<` operator. This routine accepts an output stream and a variable type as its parameters. Then you simply need to use the `<<` operator to send the appropriate structure members to the `stream` parameter. In this case, both the first name and last name members were used. However, you do not need to output all members if you don't want to.

Caution

The overload routine must return the output stream parameter. This is done so that << operators which follow the overloaded instance will know where to send their output. If this is not done, unpredictable behavior may arise.

The *MessageBox* Routine

Some of the information that you display in Windows will be in some type of dialog box. Dialog boxes in general are discussed in Chapter 19, "Developing Windows Resources for a User Interface;" however, I would like to mention the MessageBox routine in more detail here.

The MessageBox routine is very handy. It's most commonly used to display short error messages or informational messages, or to display debugging information. It can also be used to ask the user questions that can be answered with a simple yes or no.

The declaration of MessageBox is the following:

```
int MessageBox(HWND hwndParent, LPCSTR lpszText, LPCSTR lpszTitle,
               UINT fuStyle)
```

- The hwndParent parameter is the hWnd of the calling window (or you can use NULL).

- The lpszText parameter is a string that contains whatever you want the dialog box to say.

- The lpszTitle parameter is the title of the dialog box.

- The fuStyle parameter is more complicated. You can use more than 18 styles. The simplest style is MB_OK, which simply shows an OK button (refer to fig. 11.1). The most complex style might be MB_YESNOCANCEL or MB_ABORTRETRYIGNORE, which can be used to question the user.

Unlike the printf routine, MessageBox can't accommodate a varying number of parameters; you can pass only a string or LPCSTR to it. You can get around this by using the sprintf routine. The sprintf routine works exactly like printf, but rather than display the output to the monitor, it stores the result in a buffer that you specify. However, it takes several steps (each is shown in listing 11.5).

Listing 11.5 A Message and *sprintf* Example

```
#include <iostream.h>
#include <stdio.h>
#include <windows.h>

int main(void)
{
int index = 32;

    // This printf statement and the one at the end of the program
    // are used for debugging so that you can see if things go
    // wrong.
    cout << "Before MessageBox routine.\n";

    // Here we use a curly brace to define a self-contained code
    // section. Three steps are the following:
    //      1. Declare a local buffer.
    //      2. Use sprintf to load the buffer with information.
    //      3. Use MessageBox to display the buffer.
    {
    char localBuf[100];

        sprintf(localBuf, "Inside loop 3: index = %d", index);
        MessageBox(NULL, localBuf, "DEBUG", MB_OK);
    }
    cout << "After MessageBox routine.\n";
}
```

This technique of using functionality already present in prewritten routines can be very useful and time-saving. In this instance, you did not need to write and debug a routine that takes a variable number of arguments and essentially displays their values to a buffer. The `sprintf` routine takes care of this for you.

The technique of the self-contained code section was shown to emphasize that the curly braces of the C++ language start a new code section. Any variables defined inside the curly braces are valid only inside that code section. Just as a reminder, these are local variables and their scope is the code section.

If you plan on using the functionality contained in a code section more than once, consider using an inline function. Inline functions are discussed in Chapter 12, "Classes and Objects."

Other *MessageBox* Options

Thus far, you have looked only at `MessageBox` dialog boxes that display an OK button. Now you will look at the rest of the possibilities. First, you can add some icons to the dialog box by using the following flags:

- MB_ICONEXCLAMATION—an icon of an exclamation point appears in the message box.

- MB_ICONINFORMATION—an icon of a lowercase letter i enclosed within a circle appears in the message box.

- MB_ICONQUESTION—an icon of a question mark appears in the message box.

- MB_ICONSTOP—an icon of a stop sign appears in the message box.

You can use only one of these flags at a time, to add meaning to your dialog boxes. For example, all questions that you present to the user can use the MB_ICONQUESTION flag and all critical error messages can use the MB_ICONEXCLAMATION flag.

In addition to controlling which icon is displayed, the MessageBox routine also has flags that allow you to control which push buttons are displayed:

- MB_ABORTRETRYIGNORE—the message box contains three push buttons: Abort, Retry, and Ignore.

- MB_OK—the message box contains one push button: OK.

- MB_OKCANCEL—the message box contains two push buttons: OK and Cancel.

- MB_RETRYCANCEL—the message box contains two push buttons: Retry and Cancel.

- MB_YESNO—the message box contains two push buttons: Yes and No.

- MB_YESNOCANCEL—the message box contains three push buttons: Yes, No, and Cancel.

If you have push buttons for the user to select, you also need to be able to interpret the return value of the MessageBox routine. The following values can be returned (corresponding to the selected push button):

- IDABORT—Abort button was selected.

- IDCANCEL—Cancel button was selected.

- IDIGNORE—Ignore button was selected.

- IDNO—No button was selected.

- IDOK—OK button was selected.

Learning C/C++

- IDRETRY—Retry button was selected.

- IDYES—Yes button was selected.

> **Note**
>
> When the dialog box has a Cancel push button, IDCANCEL is returned if the Esc key is pressed.

As you can see, there are several possibilities when using the MessageBox routine. Listing 11.6 shows a few of the possibilities in an effort to help you understand how to combine the flags using the bitwise exclusive-OR operator that you read about in Chapter 5, "Operators."

Listing 11.6 Examples of the *MessageBox* Routine

```c
#include <windows.h>

int main(void)
{
int retValue;

    // Present the error and if the user selects abort, exit the
    // program.
    retValue = MessageBox(NULL, "No Input File.", "ERROR",
            MB_ICONEXCLAMATION ¦ MB_ABORTRETRYIGNORE);
    if (retValue == IDABORT)
        return(1);

    // Present the message; the return value can be ignored.
    MessageBox(NULL, "Today is Tuesday.", "MESSAGE",
            MB_ICONINFORMATION ¦ MB_OK);

    // Present the question and if the user selects cancel,
    // exit the program.
    // If yes is selected, print the document.
    retValue = MessageBox(NULL, "Do you want to print?",
                    "QUESTION", MB_ICONQUESTION ¦ MB_YESNOCANCEL);
    switch (retValue) {
        case IDYES:
            MessageBox(NULL, "Printing document.", "MESSAGE",
                    MB_OK);
            break;
        case IDNO:
            MessageBox(NULL, "Not Printing.", "MESSAGE", MB_OK);
            break;
        case IDCANCEL:
            MessageBox(NULL, "Exiting Program", "MESSAGE", MB_OK);
            return(1);

    }
```

```
            // Critical Error! Present the message and then exit.
            MessageBox(NULL, "No Fixed Disk Found!", "CRITICAL ERROR",
                    MB_ICONSTOP | MB_OK);
            return(0);
        }
```

The program in listing 11.6 starts by displaying an error message, No Input File, and waiting for the user to select the Abort, Retry, or Ignore button. If the Abort button is selected, the program ends with an exit value of 1.

> **Note**
>
> Exit values are sometimes used inside batch files to determine whether a program ended successfully. Typically, an exit value of zero is considered successful. Anything other than zero is considered unsuccessful.

The program next displays a message that Today is Tuesday and waits for the user to click the OK button.

The third use of the MessageBox routine displays a question and waits for a yes or no response from the user. An appropriate message is displayed depending on which button is clicked.

The last example in listing 11.6 shows a critical error. When the user clicks the OK button to acknowledge reading the message, the program ends.

As you can see, the MessageBox routine is very flexible and easy to use.

File Interaction

The C++ language has several ways to read data from a file and write data to a file. There are the *DOS-level routines* (open, read, write, and close) and the *file stream routines* (fopen, fread, fwrite, and fclose).

> **Note**
>
> Rather than access a normal file, you might want to access a database. Database access is normally achieved through a *dynamic link library* (DLL), which is a set of routines grouped around a common interest. If you need to access multiple databases on more than one platform, you might consider using the Open Database Connectivity (ODBC) standard; that subject is beyond the scope of this book. See Que's *Special Edition Using ODBC 2.0* for information about how to interact with databases using C++ and the ODBC standard.

II

Learning C/C++

DOS-Level Routines

I call this class of routines *DOS-level routines* because they closely track the routines available through the DOS interrupts. These functions (open, read, write, close, and others) are not ANSI-compatible and therefore shouldn't be used when programming for the Windows operating system. We won't discuss these in this book; I merely mentioned them for completeness.

File Stream Routines

File stream routines (see table 11.3) originated in the C language and are very simple to use. They're ANSI-compliant; therefore, you can use them if you're concerned about supporting different operating system platforms.

Table 11.3	The Most-Used File Stream Routines
Routine	**Description**
fclose	Closes the file stream.
fopen	Opens a file stream using a file name and a mode flag. The mode flag determines whether the file is open for reading, writing, or appending.
fread	Reads from the file stream.
fseek	Positions the file pointer to a specified location. Subsequent reads and writes start from the new location.
fwrite	Writes to the file stream.

To give you a feel for how these routines are used, listing 11.7 shows a program that can be used for duplicating a file. The comments in the listing describe the action as it happens. After the listing, you will take a detailed look at the routines and the parameters that they accept.

Listing 11.7 File Stream Routines

```
// First thing to do is load the appropriate header files for the
// routines that we will be using.
#include <dos.h>        // for the _dos_findfirst routine.
#include <stdio.h>      // for the file stream and sprintf routine.
#include <stdlib.h>     // for the calloc routine.
#include <windows.h>    // for the MessageBox routine.

int main(void)
{
// Declare two variables to handle the file I/O. The FILE structure
// holds information about where in the file we are looking (the
```

```
// file pointer), among other things.
FILE                    *inpFp;
FILE                    *outFp;

// This variable will hold the size of the file to be read.
size_t                  fileSize;

// The pointer will hold the address of a buffer where we can store
// the contents of a file.
char                    *fileBuf;
int r;
// If we store the file names here, they're easy to change and
// you don't have to worry about misspelling them later.
char                    *srcFile = "c:\\config.sys";
char                    *destFile = "c:\\config.bak";

// This structure will be used to find the file size of the file to
// be copied.
struct find_t       ffblk;

    // First, we find the file. If it exists, a zero is returned
    // and the ffblk structure is filled with information.

    if (_dos_findfirst(srcFile, _A_NORMAL, &ffblk) == 0) {

    // Next, we allocate some memory to hold the data from the
    // file. Please notice that I have declared a variable of
    // size_t tohold the size of the file. This avoids using the
    // cast operator later on so that the code is easier to read.

        fileSize = (size_t)ffblk.size;
        fileBuf = (char *) calloc(fileSize, sizeof(char));
        if (fileBuf == NULL)
            MessageBox(NULL, "Not enough memory!", "CRITICAL ERROR",
                    MB_ICONSTOP | MB_OK);
        else {

    // Here we open the input file in read mode and then open
    // the destination file in write mode. Be careful here! If
    // the destination file already exists, it will be overwritten
    // with no warning. If needed, you could do another
    // dos_findfirst call to double-check that you aren't
    // overwriting a file.

            inpFp = fopen(srcFile, "r");
            if (inpFp == NULL)
                MessageBox(NULL, "Unable to open source file!",
                "CRITICAL ERROR", MB_ICONSTOP | MB_OK);
            else {
                outFp = fopen(destFile, "w");
                if (outFp == NULL)
                    MessageBox(NULL,
                        "Unable to create destination file!",
                        "CRITICAL ERROR", MB_ICONSTOP | MB_OK);
```

(continues)

Listing 11.7   Continued

```
                        else {
// The next line reads in the file in one fell swoop.
// Immediately after reading, we close the input file.

                            fread(fileBuf, fileSize, 1, inpFp);
                            fclose(inpFp);

// Here, write it back out and close the destination file.
                            fwrite(fileBuf, fileSize, 1, outFp);
                            fclose(outFp);
                            MessageBox(NULL, "File copy completed.",
                            "Message", MB_ICONINFORMATION ¦ MB_OK);
                        }
                    }
                }
                free(fileBuf);
            }
            else {
                char localBuf[100];

                // Here is another example of using a local buffer to
                // customize the MessageBox text.
                sprintf(localBuf, "Unable to open %s.", srcFile);
                MessageBox(NULL, localBuf, "CRITICAL ERROR",
                        MB_ICONSTOP ¦ MB_OK);
            }
            return(0);
        }
```

The program in listing 11.7 uses the _dos_findfirst routine to accomplish two things: first, to find out whether the file you are trying to copy exists; and second, to find out how big the file is. Once the program knows how big the file is, a buffer is allocated using the calloc routine. Then the input file is opened and its contents are read into the buffer and then it is closed using the fopen, fread, and fclose routines. Note that the destination file is created using another fopen statement and the contents of the buffer are written to the new file using the fwrite routine. Finally, the destination file is closed using the fclose routine, the buffer memory is released using the free routine, and the program is finished.

It is a good practice to close files and release allocated memory immediately after the program is finished with them. In a multitasking environment such as Windows, programs should close files and release allocated memory as quickly as possible. There might be another program running in the system that is waiting for the resource that your program is using.

Note

The _dos_findfirst routine is part of the Borland runtime library extensions and is not one of the ANSI standard routines. This means that the function will probably not be available on a UNIX or Macintosh machine. If you intend to run your program on multiple computer platforms, you need to be cautious when using a non-ANSI routine.

The *fopen* Routine

The fopen routine is discussed first because it's the routine that starts the I/O ball rolling. The syntax for fopen is as follows:

```
FILE *fopen(const char *filename, const char *mode);
```

The filename parameter is self-explanatory. The mode parameter, however, is more complex. It can take the following values:

Value	Meaning
r	Open for reading only.
w	Create for writing. If a file by that name already exists, it will be overwritten.
a	Append. This will add information to the end of an existing file (good for error or message logs) or create the file if it doesn't exist.
r+	Open an existing file for update (reading and writing).
w+	Create a new file for update (reading and writing). If a file by that name already exists, it will be overwritten.
a+	Open for append. Open (or create, if the file doesn't exist) for update at the end of the file.
b	Opens the file in binary mode. Add a b to the r, w, or a in the mode parameter string. For example, using rb as the mode parameter opens a file for reading in binary mode.

There are two main differences between text mode and binary mode. The first difference relates only to DOS machines. DOS recognizes the character 0x26 as an end-of-file marker. Reading a file in binary mode ignores the end-of-file marker, which enables you to have it as part of the data in a file. The other difference relates to end-of-line characters. In text mode, the code \n is the end-of-line character. Usually this maps to two characters—a carriage return (0x10) and a line feed (0x13)—in the physical file on the hard disk.

Tip
If you try to read a file and seem to be reading only part of the information, check to see if the data has an end-of-file marker (0x26). If so, you might be using text mode when you need binary mode.

The fopen routine returns a NULL if the open doesn't succeed; otherwise, it returns a variable of type FILE *.

The *fread* and *fwrite* Routines

After opening a file, you usually want to read or write to it. Since fread and fwrite each use the same parameter, I will present them together. The syntaxes are as follows:

```
size_t fread(void *ptr, size_t size, size_t n, FILE *stream);

size_t fwrite(const void *ptr, size_t size, size_t n, FILE *stream);
```

The first parameter, ptr, is the location of a buffer to hold the information that is read in. In listing 11.5, this was fileBuf.

Caution

Be sure the buffer is at least the size of the data to be read. If not, unpredictable results might occur. C++ will happily overwrite memory to accommodate the extra information. This can result in severe problems.

The second parameter, size, is the size of the information block to read. This could be the size of a structure or the entire file.

The third parameter, n, is the number of information blocks to read. If you're reading more than one block (whose length is size), you need to account for this when calculating the buffer size that is needed.

The last parameter, stream, is the FILE * that was returned from the fopen routine.

Each routine also returns the same value. If the routine is successful, the number of units read or written is returned.

The *fseek* Routine

Sometimes it is necessary to reposition the file pointer to a new position in the file. This is especially true if the file has fixed-length records that are accessed in a random manner. The fseek routine is used to accomplish this task. The syntax is as follows:

```
int fseek(FILE *stream, long offset, int whence);
```

The first parameter, stream, is the FILE * that was returned from the fopen routine.

The second parameter, offset, is the amount to move the file pointer.

The last parameter, whence, tells the computer how to interpret the offset parameter. If whence is equal to SEEK_SET, the file pointer is moved offset bytes from the start of the file. If whence is equal to SEEK_CUR, the file pointer is moved offset bytes from the current location. If whence is equal to SEEK_END, the file pointer is moved offset bytes from the end of the file.

The header file stdio.h, when included, defines the SEEK_SET, SEEK_CUR, and SEEK_END values.

If the routine is successful, a value of 0 is returned. Actually, the fseek routine might return a 0 indicating success, when in fact the file pointer was not moved correctly. This is because DOS, which really does the moving of the pointer, does not verify its action.

Using fseek on a file opened in text mode is an uncertain operation. This is because the text mode causes pairs of carriage return/new-line characters to be seen as one character, which makes it difficult to determine where to position the file pointer.

The *fclose* Routine

After the I/O operations have been performed, it's time to close down the file stream. This is done with the fclose routine. Its syntax is as follows:

```
int fclose(FILE *stream);
```

The parameter, stream, is the FILE * that was returned from the fopen routine. If the close is successful, the routine returns 0.

Using a Log File

This section takes a look at an advanced example of file interaction: how to use a file for logging messages. It's very handy to keep some routines around to handle these chores. If you're writing code to install your program, logging the installation steps can aid you in debugging any problems your new users encounter.

The program in listing 11.8 shows you how to use a log file to store messages and to read the log file to find messages of a specific type.

Listing 11.8   Using a Log File

```cpp
#include <iostream.h>   // for the cout routine.
#include <dos.h>        // for the _dos_findfirst routine.
#include <stdio.h>      // for file i/o, sprintf routines.
#include <string.h>     // for strlen routine.
#include <time.h>       // for time,localtime routines.

// Let the compiler know what routines we will call.
void dspMessage(struct STRUCTmsg *msg);
int  getMessage(int recNum, struct STRUCTmsg *msg);
void logMessage(enum msgType msgType, char *message);
int  main(void);

// Here is the name of the log file that we will maintain.
char *logFile = "log.dat";

// This is a list of the message types that we will support.
enum msgType { inform = 0x30, critical, question };

// Now we define the structure of the message.
struct STRUCTmsg {
    char            date[10+1];
    char        fill1;
    char            time[8+1];
    char        fill2;
    enum msgType msgType;
    char        fill3;
    char            msg[100];
    char            cr;             // carriage return
    char            lf;             // linefeed
};

// This routine overloads the << operator for later use
// by the cout routine.
ostream& operator << (ostream &stream, STRUCTmsg& m)
{
    stream << m.date << "*" << m.time << "*" << m.msg;
    return stream;
}

int main(void)
{
// Declare a variable so that we have somewhere to store
// messages that we read back in from the data file.
struct STRUCTmsg tempMsg;

// We'll use this variable to look through the log file
// at the end of the program.
int recNum;


    remove(logFile);
```

```
// Here the program runs and, as messages are generated and
// errors are encountered, they're written to a log file.
logMessage(inform, "Today is Monday.");
logMessage(critical, "File not found!");
logMessage(question, "Want to print?");
logMessage(critical, "Printer not connected!");

// The program has finished running; now we can look into the
// log file and print a report of critical messages.
for (recNum = 0; getMessage(recNum, &tempMsg) == 0; recNum++) {
    cout << "looking at record: " << recNum;
    if (tempMsg.msgType == critical) {
        cout << " Critical! " << tempMsg;
    }
    cout << endl;

}
return(0);
}

// This routine will append a record to the log file.
// It is responsible for correctly filling the STRUCTmsg
// structure before writing to the log file.
void logMessage(enum msgType msgType, char *message)
{
FILE                    *outFp;
time_t                  timer;
struct tm               *tblock;
struct STRUCTmsg    msg;

    timer = time(NULL);             // get current time.
    tblock = localtime(&timer);     // convert time/date to structure.
    // The date is stored in year-month-day format so that it will
    // sort correctly if needed.
    sprintf(msg.date, "%04d-%02d-%02d", tblock->tm_year+1900,
            tblock->tm_mon+1, tblock->tm_mday);
    // Store the time the record was written.
    sprintf(msg.time, "%02d:%02d:%02d", tblock->tm_hour,
            tblock->tm_min, tblock->tm_sec);
    sprintf(msg.msg, "%-100.100s", message);
    // The next line will add zeroes to end each of the strings in
    // the structure. This is another measure to aid in viewing the
    // file from DOS.
    msg.date[10] = msg.time[8] = msg.msg[strlen(message)] = '\0';
    msg.fill1 = msg.fill2 = msg.fill3 = '¦';
    msg.msgType = msgType;
    msg.cr = 0x0d;
    msg.lf = 0x0a;

    // The structure has been filled and you can finally write
    // the record to the log file.
    outFp = fopen(logFile, "ab");
    fwrite(&msg, sizeof(struct STRUCTmsg), 1, outFp);
    fclose(outFp);
```

(continues)

Learning C/C++

Listing 11.8 Continued

```
    }

    // This routine will read a specific record from the log file.
    int getMessage(int recNum, struct STRUCTmsg *msg)
    {
    FILE              *inpFp;
    struct find_t     ffblk;

        // First, see if the log file exists. If not, you need
        // to return a '1' to indicate an error.
        if (_dos_findfirst(logFile, _A_NORMAL, &ffblk) != 0)
            return(1);

        // The last statement had a side effect of getting the file
        // size while checking for the existence of the file. Here you
        // take advantage of this to see if the recNum is valid. If
        // the recNum is greater than the number of records in the log
        // file, we need to return a '1' to indicate an error.
        if (recNum * sizeof(struct STRUCTmsg) >= ffblk.size)
            return(1);

        // Now we can open the file in read mode.
        inpFp = fopen(logFile, "rb");
        if (fseek(inpFp, recNum * sizeof(struct STRUCTmsg),
            SEEK_SET) != 0)
            return(1);
        fread(msg, sizeof(struct STRUCTmsg), 1, inpFp);
        fclose(inpFp);

        // return a '0' to indicate success.
        return(0);
    }
```

Figure 11.3 shows you what the output of the program looks like.

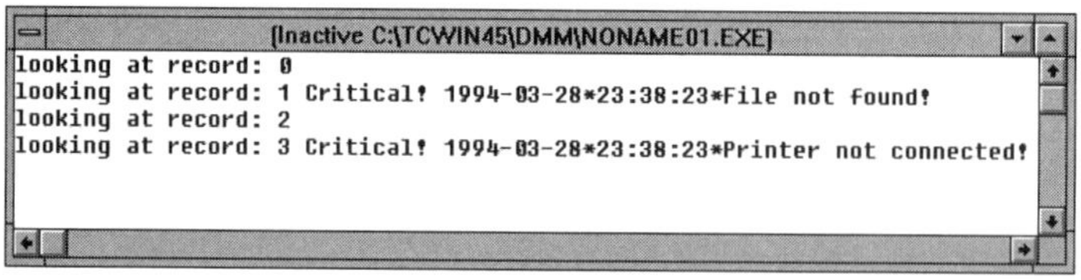

Fig. 11.3
The output of the
log file program.

The listing is too long to describe in detail. However, it is important that you understand how the program defines the structure of a message. This is the structure called STRUCTmsg. It is reproduced here for easy reference:

```
struct STRUCTmsg {
    char        date[10+1];
    char        fill1;
```

```
        char        time[8+1];
        char        fill2;
        enum msgType msgType;
        char        fill3;
        char        msg[100];
        char        cr;              // carriage return
        char        lf;              // linefeed
    };
```

The structure has members to store the date, time, message type, and the message itself. The `logMessage` routine fills in this information before saving the record to the log file.

The rest of the members in `STRUCTmsg` are there to make it easy to look at the log file using a regular editor, such as the Windows Notepad. Figure 11.4 shows you what the log file will look like after the program is done. Note that each filler member was set equal to a ¦ to delimit the fields. Also, the `cr` and `lf` fields were set equal to carriage-return and line-field ASCII values so that an editor program (Notepad in this case) knows where the lines end.

Keeping the log file in a format that you can read has a couple of advantages. One, you can easily import the file into a word processor to incorporate parts of the log into a report. Two, you can use DOS commands to display the file for reading. You might not need to write a special display program.

Despite the length of the program in listing 11.8, all of the routines needed to use a log file are not shown. In particular, a cleanup routine is needed to ensure that the log file doesn't grow beyond a given size. If you're using the log file in an application that will be heavily used, the log file may become quite large. You must use some mechanism to keep the size under control.

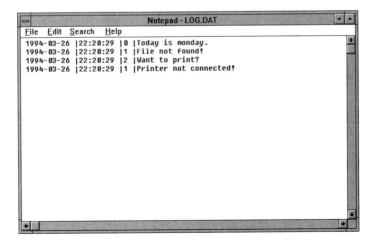

Fig. 11.4
The log file.

The program gets around this problem by simply deleting the old log file every time it is run. This is done by using the `remove` routine. It takes the name of the file to be deleted as its parameter.

Another useful routine might be a reporting mechanism. You could use the report routine to print the messages in order of severity to highlight problems quickly. The report could also supply the total number of each type of error and how many errors occurred per day.

Device Interaction

You can use the file stream routines to interact with various DOS devices. Each device has a special file name that is used to address it.

For example, the device (usually a printer) on the parallel port can be addressed as `LPT1`. This makes it simple to send debugging information directly to the printer. Simply open the printer for writing, send your information, and then close the file stream. The following is an example of the `fopen` statement to use to open the printer:

```
fp = fopen("LPT1", "wb");
```

In similar fashion, you can open the serial port (where the modem is attached) using the file name `COM1`.

However, in the Windows environment, special API functions are provided to handle printing and serial communications. Using the file stream routines for application use (as opposed to debugging) isn't recommended because of the following:

■ The Windows Printing API allows you to print graphics as well as all the fonts that Windows supports.

■ Using the API will allow your program to support all the printers that Windows itself supports.

■ The file stream routines were designed for a DOS world, not the multitasking, graphical world in which Windows works.

In addition to printer and modem control, you can use the device `NULL` to ignore any output. This actually is more useful than it sounds. If you're debugging and want to stop the program from generating a large file, simply change the file name to `NULL:` rather than comment out the code involved. Of course, you need to remember to change the `NULL` to a real file name before finishing your program.

From Here...

You now know how to interact with users, files, and printers. That's enough information to create some very useful programs. In fact, you can probably handle a large portion of your programming needs at this point.

But the world of C++ object-oriented programming lies ahead. So far, we have looked mostly at things that the C language could do because your programs need to walk before they can run (pun intended).

Using the objects that C++ enables you to create, you soon will be able to quickly reuse code and modify programs with ease. Consider turning to one or more of the following topics next:

- Chapter 13, "Object-Oriented Methods," starts you on the road to using objects.

- Chapter 16, "Debugging," helps you get the examples running if you're having problems.

- Chapter 25, "File I/O," talks about file I/O using the Windows API.

- Appendix B, "Working with EasyWin," further describes EasyWin, which is used by the examples in this chapter.

Chapter 12

Classes and Objects

All the object-oriented features of C++ spring from a common source—a humble C-language data structure called a struct. This chapter shows how the struct used in C has been promoted to a class in C++, and explains how classes provide the foundation for the object-oriented features of C++. The sample programs presented in this chapter show how classes are used in C++ programs, and you are introduced to the most important features of C++ classes.

This chapter explores the following topics:

- Structs and classes in C++

- What is a class?

- Member variables and member functions

- What is an object?

- Constructing and destroying objects

- Copy constructors

- Class hierarchies

- Function overloading and operator overloading

- The Turbo C++ for Windows container class library

The chapter ends with an example program that shows how classes defined in the Turbo C++ class libraries can be used in a C++ program.

Using Structs in C++

A struct, as C programmers know, is a simple construct that can group related variables of different data types together so they can be accessed conveniently from other parts of a program. To illustrate, the following is a definition of a struct that stores data about employees in a company:

```
struct EmpData {
    char *name;
    char *dept;
    char *position;
    long salary;
};
```

In C++, as in C, a struct definition such as the one just shown does not allocate any memory for the struct being defined. It announces an intention to use such a struct in a program.

To make use of a struct you have defined, you must declare a physical structure that occupies memory and can therefore be used to store data. Then you must supply code that can fill the structure with data and access data from the structure.

This is how you might declare the struct that was defined in the preceding example:

```
/* declaring a struct */
struct empData empInfo;
```

The preceding statement declares an empData struct named empInfo.

Placing Data in a Struct

When you have declared a struct, as the empInfo struct is declared in the preceding example, you can write code that populates the struct with data. For example, this code places information in the four fields of the empInfo struct:

```
/* Populate the empInfo struct with data. */
empInfo.name = "Jared Lopez";
empInfo.dept = "Admin";
empInfo.position = "CEO";
empInfo.salary = 22000;
```

Accessing Data in a Struct

Once you have declared a struct and have populated it with data, you can write code to access the data stored in the struct. Listing 12.1, titled EMPDATA.C, is a simple text-based application that does the following:

- Defines and declares the empInfo struct

- Populates the empInfo struct with data

- Displays the data on your computer monitor

Listing 12.1   Using a Struct in C++

```c
/* empdata.c */
#include <windows.h>
#include <stdio.h>

struct EmpData {
    char *name;
    char *dept;
    char *position;
    long salary;
};

/* declaring a struct */
struct EmpData empInfo;

void PrintData()
{
    printf("\nName: %s\n", empInfo.name);
    printf("Department: %s\n", empInfo.dept);
    printf("Position: %s\n", empInfo.position);
    printf("Salary: $%d\n", empInfo.salary);
}

int main()
{
    /* Populate the empInfo struct with data. */
    empInfo.name = "Jared Lopez";
    empInfo.dept = "Admin";
    empInfo.position = "CEO";
    empInfo.salary = 22000;

    PrintData();

    return 0;
}
```

The EMPDATA.C program was written in C, but it works in both C and C++.
Later in this chapter, under the heading "Using Access Specifiers," there's a
C++ version of the program named EMPDATA.CPP. A number of code
samples based on the EMPDATA.C and EMPDATA.CPP programs appear in
the rest of this chapter and in Chapter 13, "Object-Oriented Methods."

> **Note**
>
> The EMPDATA program is a text-based Turbo C++ application, so you should compile and execute it as an EasyWin program (see Appendix B). The other example programs in this chapter and Chapter 13, "Object-Oriented Methods," are also EasyWin applications.

In listing 12.1, the `main()` function fills in the four fields of the `empInfo` struct. Then the `PrintData()` function prints the data on your screen.

Figure 12.1 shows the output of the EMPDATA program.

Fig. 12.1
The EMPDATA program is compiled and executed as an EasyWin application.

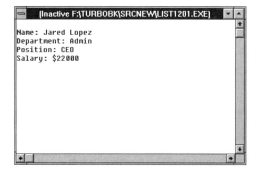

```
[Inactive F:\TURBOBK\SRCNEW\LIST1201.EXE]
Name: Jared Lopez
Department: Admin
Position: CEO
Salary: $22000
```

From Struct to Class

Once you know how a struct works in a C (or C++) program, you've come a long way toward understanding how classes work in C++. In essence, a C++ class is nothing but a C-style struct with a few simple, but far-reaching, enhancements. In the following paragraphs, you see how structs have been enhanced in C++. Later in this chapter, under the heading "Class Hierarchies" you'll see how a new kind of data structure (called a *class*) has evolved from the struct to provide even more power to C++ programs.

Member Variables and Member Functions

There is a major difference between the way structs work in C and the way they work in C++. In C++, a struct can contain fields that declare functions as well as fields that declare data. Variables that are declared inside a struct definition are called *data members* or *member variables*. Functions declared inside a struct definition are called *member functions*. As explained later in this chapter, C++ classes also have member variables and member functions.

You can define a class in a C++ program in the same way you define a struct. To define a simple class, you can simply write a struct definition and substitute the keyword class for the keyword struct. For example, in the two code fragments that follow, a change of one word promotes the EmpData struct to a class. In the second code fragment, the word struct is changed to the word class, and that's all it takes to make a class out of EmpData:

```
struct EmpData {
    char *m_name;
    char *m_dept;
    char *m_position;
    long m_salary;
    void PrintData(EmpData empData);
};
```

```
class EmpData {
    char *m_name;
    char *m_dept;
    char *m_position;
    long m_salary;
    void PrintData(EmpData empData);
};
```

Each of the preceding code fragments has four member variables: m_name, m_dept, m_position, and m_salary. Each code fragment is also a member function named PrintData().

Instantiating Objects

The similarity between structs and classes is more than skin-deep. There is also a similarity between the way memory is allocated for a struct and the way memory is allocated for a class.

When you define a struct in C++, your compiler does not immediately allocate any memory for the struct's member variables or member functions. Later, when you define the *contents* of the struct's member variables and member functions, memory space is allocated for the struct and all its members.

The same principle applies to C++ classes. When you define a class in C++, no memory for the class is allocated. Later, when you define the contents of the class's member variables and member functions, memory space is allocated for each member variable and member function you define.

In C++, when a class's member variables and member functions have been defined and the compiler has allocated the memory needed to store each member function, you can create an *object* that contains your class's member variables and member functions. C++ also stores them in memory by using the architecture you have defined for your class.

An object that is created from a class is often referred to as an *instance* of that class. The act of creating an object is referred to as *instantiating* an object.

Listing 12.2 shows how you can define and then instantiate an object in a C++ program.

Listing 12.2   A Class with Member Functions

```c
/* empdata.c */
#include <stdio.h>

class EmpData {
private:
    char *m_name;
    char *m_dept;
    char *m_position;
    long m_salary;
public:
    void PrintData();
};

void EmpData::PrintData()
{
    printf("\nName: %s\n", m_name);
    printf("Department: %s\n", m_dept);
    printf("Position: %s\n", m_position);
    printf("Salary: $%d\n", m_salary);
}

int main()
{
    // Instantiate an object.
    EmpData empInfo;

    // Populate the empInfo object with data.
    empInfo.m_name = "Jared Lopez";
    empInfo.m_dept = "Admin";
    empInfo.m_position = "CEO";
    empInfo.m_salary = 22000;
    empInfo.PrintData();
    return 0;

    // Print the contents of the member variables.
    empInfo.PrintData();
}
```

As you can see, the program in listing 12.2 is divided into three parts. The first part, which begins with the line

```
class EmpData {
```

is a definition of a class named `EmpData`. The second part of the program, which starts with the line

```
void EmpData::PrintData()
```

defines a member function named `EmpData::PrintData()`. Notice that the name of the `EmpData` function, followed by a pair of colons (`::`), precedes the name of the `PrintData()` function. That's the standard C++ convention for defining a member function of a class.

The third part of the program in listing 12.2 is the program's `main()` function. In the `main()` function, it takes just one line of code to instantiate an object:

```
EmpData empInfo;
```

The preceding statement instantiates an object of the `EmpData` class. The object is named `empInfo`.

When the object named `empInfo` has been created, the object's member variables are populated with data. Then the member function named `EmpData::PrintData()` is called. The `EmpData::PrintData()` function prints the contents of the `empInfo` object's member variables.

Data Encapsulation and Data Abstraction

If you have looked closely at listing 12.2, you may have noticed the words `private` and `public` in the definition of the `EmpData` class. Those words are *access specifiers* that provide the `main()` function with access to members of the `EmpData` class.

Access specifiers can permit access to specific members of a class while restricting access to others. This capability can prevent private data members from being changed inadvertently by functions that access them—a problem often caused by the sloppy use of global variables in C programs.

Access specifiers are the key to a C++ feature called *data encapsulation.* By using access specifiers, a class can control access to member variables and member functions. When data is protected by encapsulation, calling functions can access the data and request actions involving the data without knowing specific details about how the data is manipulated or how the actions are performed.

The data-encapsulation feature of C++ is closely related to another feature of the language, called *data abstraction*. Data abstraction is a C++ feature that lets functions do their jobs without knowing the specifics of how hidden data is manipulated.

Access Specifiers

There are three access specifiers in C++: `private`, `protected`, and `public`. The following class definition shows how the `private` and `public` keywords can be used in a C++ program. The `protected` keyword doesn't appear in this particular definition, but as you see in later examples, the `protected` keyword is used in exactly the same way as the `private` and `public` keywords:

```
class EmpData {
private:
    char *m_name;
    char *m_dept;
    char *m_position;
    long m_salary;
public:
    void SetName(char *name) { m_name = name; }
    void SetDept(char *dept) { m_dept = dept; }
    void SetPosition(char *position)
        { m_position = position; }
    void SetSalary(long salary)
        { m_salary = salary; }
    void PrintData();
};
```

When you declare a member of a class to be `private`, the only functions that can access the member are functions that are defined in the same class. Thus, in the preceding example, the only functions that can access the m_name, m_dept, m_position, and m_salary members are the five functions that are members of the same class—that is, the `SetName`, `SetDept`, `SetPosition`, `SetSalary`, and `PrintData` functions.

Class members declared as `public` can be freely accessed inside *and* outside their class.

When a member of a class is declared to be `protected`, it is accessible not only from member functions of its own class, but also from derived classes. Class derivations are described in the "Class Hierarchies" section later in this chapter.

Notice that the five functions in the `EmpData` class are declared as `public`. That means they are freely accessible outside the `EmpData` class. Also, because these functions are members of the EmpData class, they have access to the class's four private member variables. That means there is a way for functions outside the EmpData class to access the class's four private data members. They can access the private members of the EmpData class indirectly—through the class's five public member functions. Even though m_name is a private member variable, any function defined outside the EmpData class can set the m_name variable by simply calling the SetName member function.

So how does this precaution protect the m_name variable? Well, it doesn't mean that the m_name variable is totally inaccessible to functions declared outside the EmpData class; if that were true, the variable would work like just another local variable. But the precaution does make you do a little work to access the m_name variable—and that is what it is supposed to do.

If you decide to assign a value to m_name by going to the trouble of calling SetName, chances are pretty good that you're doing something you intended to do—and, when you debug your program, you can find out what function has set the value of m_name without too much trouble. On the other hand, if m_name were to implement a global variable that any function could use to modify m_name directly with an assignment statement, there would be a much greater chance that sooner or later, it would inadvertently get changed.

> **Note**
>
> Actually, you can use access specifiers in C++ structs as well as in classes. But C++ programmers rarely make use of that capability. The general feeling is that once you start using features such as access specifiers in a struct, you might as well turn the struct into a class, so you can equip it with other kinds of features that are available to classes but not to structs. You see what those features are as you make your way through the rest of this chapter and Chapter 13, "Object-Oriented Methods."

Using Access Specifiers

Listing 12.3 shows how access specifiers can be used in a C++ program.

Listing 12.3   Using Access Specifiers in a C++ Program

```
/* empdata.cpp */
#include <windows.h>
#include <stdio.h>
class EmpData {
private:
```

(continues)

Learning C/C++

Listing 12.3   Continued

```
        char *m_name;
        char *m_dept;
        char *m_position;
        long m_salary;
public:
        void SetName(char *name) { m_name = name; }
        void SetDept(char *dept) { m_dept = dept; }
        void SetPosition(char *position)
            { m_position = position; }
        void SetSalary(long salary)
            { m_salary = salary; }
        void PrintData();
};
void EmpData::PrintData()
{
        printf("\nName: %s\n", m_name);
        printf("Department: %s\n", m_dept);
        printf("Position: %s\n", m_position);
        printf("Salary: $%d\n", m_salary);
}
int main()
{
        // Declaration of an instance of class EmpData
        EmpData empInfo;
        // Populate the empInfo class object with data.
        empInfo.SetName("Jared Lopez");
        empInfo.SetDept("Admin");
        empInfo.SetPosition("CEO");
        empInfo.SetSalary(22000);
        empInfo.PrintData();
        return 0;
}
```

Note

Because EMPDATA.CPP is a short program, all its modules appear in the same source file. In a full-size C++ program, customarily the definition of the EmpData class would appear in a header (.H) file and the implementation of the class would appear in a separate (.CPP) file. When this convention is followed in the design of a program, the names of each class's member functions are all grouped together, so it's easy to determine whether a class contains a particular member. You simply scan the class definition in the header file to find the declaration of the member you want to use.

What Is an Object?

In C++, an *object* is what you get when you instantiate an instance of a class. When you define a class, no memory is allocated until you instantiate an object of the class. Once you instantiate an object, you have a physical object in which data can be stored.

In listing 12.3, the `main` function instantiates an object of the `EmpData` class with the statement:

```
EmpData empInfo;
```

Next, the `main` function sets the values of the `EmpData` class's `private` member variables by calling `public` member functions:

```
empInfo.SetName("Jared Lopez");
empInfo.SetDept("Admin");
empInfo.SetPosition("CEO");
empInfo.SetSalary(22000);
```

When the values of `EmpData`'s member variables are set, the `main` function prints the program's output by calling another `public` member function: `PrintData`.

```
empInfo.PrintData();
```

Although `PrintData` is declared inside the definition of the `EmpData` class, it is defined outside the `EmpData` definition, as follows:

```
void EmpData::PrintData(EmpData empInfo)
{
    printf("\nName: %s\n", m_name);
    printf("Department: %s\n", m_dept);
    printf("Position: %s\n", m_position);
    printf("Salary: $%d\n", m_salary);
}
```

The Scope Resolution Operator

Notice the use of the `::` operator in the heading of the `PrintData` function's definition. In C++, the `::` operator is called the *scope resolution operator*. The scope resolution operator, as used in C++ programs, is described in detail in the following section.

Often you define a class member function outside the class definition itself. To do this, you need a way to indicate that the member function belongs to the class. The syntax to use is the class name followed by the scope resolution operator and then the function name. For the `PrintData()` function in the `EmpData` class of listing 12.3, this looks like the following:

```
void EmpData::PrintData()
{
    // . . .
}
```

II

Learning C/C++

This syntax simply says that the `PrintData()` function defined here is a member (in the scope) of `EmpData`.

> **Note**
>
> When a member function of a class has the same name as a function declared outside the class, you can call the externally defined function instead of the member function by using the scope resolution operator. For example, if an API you were using supplied a global function named `PrintData`, you could call the global `PrintData` function from inside an `EmpData` object by using the scope resolution operator in this fashion:
>
> ```
> ::PrintData();
> ```

Inline Member Functions

The `PrintData` function is defined outside the definition of the `EmpData` class because it is too long to be embedded conveniently inside the `EmpData` class's definition. But shorter member functions of a class can be (and often should be) declared and defined at the same time, inside the definition of their class. Member functions defined inside a class definition are called *inline functions*.

In listing 12.3, four member functions of the `EmpData` class are inline functions, defined inside the definition of the `EmpData` class using this syntax:

```
void SetName(char *name) { m_name = name; }
```

The differences between ordinary member functions and inline member functions are more than cosmetic. The two kinds of functions are stored in memory in different ways, and are accessed differently at run time. For more details about inline member functions, see the section "Inline Member Functions" in Chapter 13, "Object-Oriented Methods."

Constructors and Destructors

As you have seen, the act of creating an object from a class is called *instantiation*. In the examples you have encountered up to now, objects have been instantiated in the same way structs are created in C programs—that is, with a statement such as

```
EmpData empInfo;
```

In real-world programming, that is one way to instantiate an object, but it is not the only way—and it is not the whole story.

In this section, you learn more about how C++ objects are instantiated and destroyed.

In C++, there are special kinds of functions for instantiating and destroying objects. A function that initializes an object of a class when the object is instantiated is called a *constructor*. A function that cleans up after an object of a class when the object is destroyed is called a *destructor*. When an object performs memory-allocation operations, a destructor can ensure that any memory that the object has allocated is deallocated.

Constructors make it easier—and safer—to create objects and to destroy them when they are no longer needed. Constructors can also perform special kinds of operations, such as converting data from one type to another and making copies of objects. Constructors are often used, for example, to make copies of strings that are implemented as objects of the Turbo C++ string class (for more about the string class, see "The Turbo C++ Class Library" later in this chapter).

Creating Constructors

When you write a constructor for a class, your constructor is invoked automatically whenever you instantiate an object of that class. A constructor function is easy to recognize because it always has the same name as the class in which it is declared. In a class definition, a constructor can be declared using this format:

```
class MyClass {
public
        MyClass();
...
```

The `MyClass` constructor declared in the preceding code fragment can be defined this way in the implementation section of a program:

```
MyClass:: MyClass()
{
        // . . .
}
```

A constructor never returns a value, so C++ does not allow you to specify a return type—not even `void`—when you define a constructor class.

A constructor can take arguments, however. This is an example of a class that takes parameters:

```
class AClass {
public
        AClass(int paramA, int paramB);
...
```

The constructor declared in the preceding example could be defined as follows:

```
AClass:: AClass(int ParamA, int ParamB)
{
     // . . .
}
```

When you write a constructor that takes parameters, as in the preceding example, the constructor often uses the values of those parameters to perform any special kinds of initialization procedures that the object requires. For example, a constructor's parameters can be used to specify initialization values for member functions of the object being initialized. Of course, if you are the one who writes the constructor, you are responsible for providing the code that carries out any specialized operations that you want performed.

To create a constructor, you must declare it inside the definition of a class. Then you must define the constructor, either inline (inside the class definition) or outside the class definition after the class has been defined.

When a constructor is declared inside a class definition and is defined in the same place and at the same time, it is called an *inline constructor*. When a constructor is declared and defined inline, it does not have to appear in its class's implementation file. In this respect, a constructor is like any other member function.

These are two examples of inline function definitions:

```
AClass(char *nm) { m_memVar = nm; }


BClass() {}
```

In these two inline function definitions, notice that all the elements of a function definition are present. In the second example, the braces that customarily enclose a function's executable code are empty because the constructor does not have a function body. A constructor does not necessarily have any executable code, so the second example is a complete constructor, even though the curly braces that follow it do not contain any executable code.

A constructor does not have to be declared and defined inline. A constructor, like any other member function, can also be declared inside a class definition and defined outside the class definition, in the class's implementation file. The following two lines show examples of the constructor declarations that might appear in the class definition when the constructor is defined outside the class definition:

```
AfterClass(char *nm);


InClass();
```

The definitions for these constructors might look like:

```
AfterClass::AfterClass(char *nm)
{
    m_memVar = nm;
}
InClass::InClass()
{
}
```

When a constructor for a class is declared inside the class definition but is defined outside the class's definition—that is, when the constructor is not an inline constructor—the constructor's definition uses the name of its class and the scope resolution operator (::) just like any other class member function defined outside the class definition.

For more information about inline and non-inline functions, see Chapter 13, "Object-Oriented Methods."

Creating Objects without Constructors

When you instantiate an object in C++, the compiler always calls a constructor. If you don't provide a constructor in your program, the compiler creates a simple constructor when you declare the object. Then the compiler uses the constructor that it has created to initialize the object.

Because the compiler automatically creates a constructor when an object is declared, you can define and use a class without explicitly writing a constructor for the class.

But constructors that are created by the compiler are often too primitive to be very useful, and good C++ programs rarely, if ever, trust the compiler to provide a constructor by default. The safest way to initialize an object is to write an explicit constructor. That doesn't cost anything, so most experienced C++ programmers write explicit constructors for the classes they use in their programs.

Using Destructors

A destructor, like a constructor, has the same name as the object with which it is associated. However, the name of a destructor is always preceded by the tilde symbol (~), as in this example:

```
~AClass() {}
```

II

Learning C/C++

A destructor takes no arguments and, like a constructor, never returns a value.

When an object that has a destructor goes out of scope or is otherwise about to be destroyed, the object's destructor is automatically invoked. So you never have to make an explicit call to an object's destructor when the object is no longer needed.

Two Ways to Call a Constructor

There are two techniques for invoking a constructor to instantiate an object. You can allocate memory for the object on the stack simply by declaring the object, or you can allocate memory for the object on the heap (often called dynamic memory allocation) and invoke it using a pointer. In either case, if you want the object to be created using a particular constructor, then you must supply appropriate parameters in parentheses immediately after the object name (allocation on the stack) or after the class name following the new operator (allocation on the heap). If you don't want to pass parameters, then parentheses are not required following the object name or class name.

When you allocate memory for an object on the stack, memory for the function is allocated on the stack frame of the function that invokes the object's constructor (a stack frame is a block of memory that is set up when a function is called; the stack frame contains the function's local variables and any data structures that have been allocated to the function). When an object is created on the stack, the object is destroyed when the function that calls its constructor terminates.

Stack allocation usually is used for objects that are designed to pass out of existence as soon as they are no longer needed. For example, stack allocation is often used for objects such as modal dialog boxes, which are around for only as long as they are needed, and then disappear as soon as the user clicks an OK button.

Objects with longer persistence are usually allocated space on the heap. They then can be accessed as often as required, from any function that is allowed access to them.

Creating an Object on the Stack

To allocate memory for an object on the stack, you declare it in the same way you would define an ordinary variable, as illustrated in listing 12.4.

Listing 12.4   Creating an Object on the Stack

```
#include <cstring.h>
class AClass {
public:
    string m_nm;
    string m_addr;
    string GetName() { return m_nm; }
    string GetAddr() { return m_addr; }
};
main()
{
    AClass seniorClass;
    string nm = "Danny White";
    string addr("27 Wistful Vista");
    return 0;
}
```

In listing 12.4, the following statement instantiates an object of a class named AClass:

```
AClass seniorClass;
```

The object that is created is named seniorClass.

When you instantiate an object by allocating space on the stack, you access its members using the dot operator (.). The following statements then could be used to access the members of the seniorClass object created in listing 12.4:

```
string guysName = seniorClass.GetName();
string galsAddress = seniorClass.m_addr;
```

You may have noticed that this is the same technique used to access members of a struct when memory space for the struct is allocated directly rather than with a pointer.

One advantage of using stack-frame allocation is that objects stored in stack frames don't have to be explicitly deallocated when they are no longer needed. When a function that contains a stack-frame object terminates, the memory that has been allocated for the object is deallocated automatically.

The main disadvantage of stack-frame allocation is that allocating and deallocating frame objects can slow a program down. Another potential problem is that stack-frame storage requires memory space on the stack, which may be in short supply.

II

Learning C/C++

Creating an Object on the Heap

To create an object on the heap, you declare a pointer to the object and then call the object's constructor by invoking the C++ new operator. The new operator, covered in more detail in Chapter 13, "Object-Oriented Methods," is a C++ operator that allocates memory space. Another operator, called delete, is provided to deallocate memory that the new operator has allocated.

To allocate memory for an object on the heap, you can declare a pointer to the object using this syntax:

```
AClass *seniorClass;
```

The preceding statement declares a pointer to an object of a class named AClass. The pointer to the object is named seniorClass.

You often will find pointers to objects declared in this way inside the definitions of classes.

Once you have declared a pointer to an object, you can use the new operator to create an instance of the object, as shown in listing 12.5.

Listing 12.5 Creating an Object on the Heap

```
#include <cstring.h>
class AClass {
public:
    string m_nm;
    string m_addr;
    string GetName() { return m_nm; }
    string GetAddr() { return m_addr; }
};
main()
{
    AClass *seniorClass = new AClass;
    string nm = "Danny White";
    string addr("27 Wistful Vista");
    string guysName = seniorClass->GetName();
    string galsAddress = seniorClass->m_addr;
    delete seniorClass;
    return 0;
}
```

In listing 12.5, the following statement instantiates an object from the class named AClass:

```
AClass *seniorClass = new AClass;
```

> **Note**
>
> Although a pointer to a base-class object can point to a derived-class object, a pointer to a derived-class object can't be set to point to a base-class object. That's logical because there's no way for a base class to be aware of the member functions and member variables that are added to its derived classes.

The *this* Pointer

You often see the word this in C++ programs. That's because every object in a C++ program is equipped with a pointer to itself, and that pointer is always named this. Whenever a program calls a non-static member function (most member functions are non-static; static member functions are described in Chapter 13), a hidden pointer to the current object is passed to the member function that is called. The member function can then use that unseen pointer—named this— to access any other member of its class.

In C++ programs, member functions of classes often use the this pointer as a parameter when they call other functions. The called function can then use the this pointer to access the calling function.

The following example shows how the this pointer works:

```
#include <iostream.h>

class TestClass {
public:
        TestClass() {}          // default constructor
        ~TestClass() {}         // destructor
        void *IAm() { return this; }
};

int main()
{
        void *pClass;
        TestClass anObject;
        pClass = anObject.IAm();
        cout << "pClass's pointer is "
            << pClass << '\n.';
        return 0;
}
```

In the preceding example, the class named TestClass has a member function named IAm() that returns the this pointer of a TestClass object:

```
void *IAm() { return this; }
```

When you execute the program, its `main()` function instantiates a `TestClass` object and then calls the `IAm()` member function. The program then stores the `this` pointer returned by `IAm()` in a pointer variable named `pClass`. This is the statement that calls `IAm()`:

```
pClass = anObject.IAm();
```

When the `TestClass` object's `this` pointer has been stowed away, the `main()` function prints out the pointer it has stored in the `pClass` variable. The output of the program looks something like this:

```
pClass's pointer is 0x603f223011786
```

Copy Constructors

A *copy constructor*, as its name suggests, is a special kind of constructor specifically designed to copy objects. Copy constructors are often used in C++ programs because they provide a means of copying a complex structure such as an object in a single step.

Unfortunately, C++ does not provide a powerful generic copy constructor that can automatically make a copy of any object. Your C++ compiler can copy very simple objects without the need for a copy constructor. But when you need a copy constructor that will make a copy of a more complex object, you must write your own (or use one that someone else has written and provided in a class library).

In practice, the default kind of object-copying that C++ is capable of is almost never used in real-world programming. In other words, when you want to copy an object, you'll almost always need an explicit copy constructor.

How Copy Constructors Work

A copy constructor always takes one *argument*—a reference to a class—and, being a constructor, a copy constructor never returns a result.

When you have declared a copy constructor, you can define it in the same way you define any constructor—for example:

```
TestClass::TestClass(TestClass& anObject);
{
    // body of copy constructor
}
```

You can invoke a copy constructor by executing a statement that uses this syntax:

```
TestClass& anObject(anObject&);
```

The challenge in writing a copy constructor is, of course, what you substitute for the comment `// body of copy constructor` in the preceding example. You get to that in a moment.

When you have declared and defined a copy constructor, you can invoke it by executing a statement that has this syntax:

```
TestClass objectA;            // initialize an object
TestClass objectB = objectA   // copy objectA
```

When the two statements in the preceding example are executed, an object named `objectA` already exists. The first statement instantiates an object of the same class named `objectB`. The second statement copies `objectA` to `objectB`.

Invoking a Copy Constructor

As noted previously, there are two ways to invoke a copy constructor. One way is to write your own copy constructor and use it to initialize an object. Or, if you have a very simple object to copy, there may be times when you can let the compiler write a copy constructor for you.

Before you decide which way to go, you must determine whether the object you are copying requires a *shallow copy* or a *deep copy*. These are the differences:

- A shallow copy, sometimes called a *memberwise copy*, is the object-copying technique that your C++ compiler uses if you don't explicitly provide a copy constructor. In a shallow copy, every data member of an object is copied, but there is no provision for copying strings or pointers. If the object being copied contains a pointer, the pointer is copied verbatim to the destination object, but the information pointed to by the pointer is not copied. Shallow copying does not work if the object being copied is any more complex than a pointerless struct. So, in most situations, forget about shallow copying—the kind of default-style object copying that C++ provides.

- When you make a deep copy of an object, you copy not only the object, but also any data that is pointed to by any pointers that the source object contains. Then you reset the pointers in the destination object to point to the data that has been copied, not to the data pointed to by pointers in the source object. In other words, when you make a deep copy, you copy everything. A deep copy is the only safe kind of copy, so in virtually every situation it is the kind of copy you should use.

Writing a Copy Constructor

The program in listing 12.6 shows how a copy constructor can be used in a C++ program. The `main` segment of the program initializes an object named `myCash` and then uses a copy constructor to make a copy of `myCash`. The copy of `myCash` is named `moreCash`.

Listing 12.6   Demonstrating a Copy Constructor

```
// Demonstrating a copy constructor

#include <iostream.h>
class Money {
     int dl, pn;
public:
     Money() {}          // null constructor
     Money(Money&);      // copy constructor
     Money(int dol, int pen):dl(dol), pn(pen) {}
     int GetDol() { return dl; }
     int GetPen() { return pn; }
};

Money::Money(Money& cash)
{
     dl = cash.dl;
     pn = cash.pn;
};

int main()
{
     Money myCash(29, 95);
     Money moreCash = myCash;
     int d = moreCash.GetDol();
     int p = moreCash.GetPen();
     cout << '$' << d << '.' << p << '\n';
     return 0;
}
```

Because the program in listing 12.6 copies an object that contains no pointers, the copy constructor the program uses is quite straightforward:

```
Money::Money(Money& cash)
{
     m_dl = cash.m_dl;
     m_pn = cash.m_pn;
};
```

When you call the preceding copy constructor, it copies the `Money` class's `m_dl` member variable into a new member variable that has the same name but belongs to the new class being created. The `m_pn` member variable is also copied into a member variable of the same name in the new class. The Money class has only two member variables, so that completes the copying operation.

Initializer Lists

In the course of demonstrating the use of copy constructors, listing 12.6 introduces another useful feature of C++: *initializer lists* in calls to constructors. In listing 12.6, an initializer list appears in the following constructor definition:

```
Money(int dol, int pen):dl(dol), pn(pen) {}
```

In the preceding constructor definition, notice that the argument list of the Money class's constructor is followed by a colon, and then by a pair of constructs that look like calls to C functions. In this case, those two constructs are not functions, but serve as an *initializer list* for the Money class's constructor.

In the preceding example, the initializer list that is supplied for the Money class initializes a pair of member functions named dl and pn. The operation of the initializer list is quite straightforward; when the constructor is called, the dl member function is initialized to the value of the dol argument that is passed to the constructor, and the pn member function is initialized to the value of the constructor's pen argument. Thus, the constructor works in exactly the same way it would work if it were defined this way:

```
Money::Money(int dol, int pen) {
        dl = dol;
        pn = pen;
}
```

As you can see, initializer lists are optional. Many C++ programmers like them because they take up a little less space than conventional member-variable initializations and because they keep the initialization of member functions separate from the rest of the code in a constructor. Initializer lists are optional, though; whether you want to use them in your own code or not is entirely up to you.

Using Default Argument Values in Function Calls

Initializer lists are used only with constructors—never in calls to ordinary member functions. But there is a similar C++ feature that can be used with ordinary functions and member functions, as well as with constructors.

When you write a function definition in C++, you can supply the function with *default arguments* in its argument list. Then, when the function is called, the caller of the function does not have to supply values for arguments that have default values. If the calling function fails to supply a value for an argument that has a default value, the default value is used.

To supply default values for a function's arguments, you simply write a function definition that has this kind of format:

```
void AFunction(int paramA = 6, int paramB = 32,
               float paramC = 29.95)
{
      // ...
}
```

In the preceding example, default values are supplied for all three arguments required by the function named AFunction: paramA, paramB, and paramC.

When a C++ function has been supplied with default values for its arguments, you don't have to use them if you don't want to. If you specify an explicit value for a function argument that has a default value, the value that you supply overrides the argument's default value. If you wanted to override all the default arguments specified for the function shown in the preceding example, you could do that by simply calling the function and supplying your own argument values, as follows:

```
AFunction(95, 14, 42.78);
```

If you want to override some of the default arguments of a function, but not all of them, you can do that. However, if you omit one of a function's default arguments, you must also omit any default arguments that follow the first one you omitted. That means if you want to use any of the default argument values supplied for a function, the first explicit argument you must drop is the one at the end of the function's argument list. Then you can drop the second explicit argument from the end, and so on. So you could call the function shown in the preceding example using this format:

```
AFunction(95, 14);
```

If you called AFunction in this way, the default value of 29.95 would be assigned to the function's last argument, the argument named paramC. If you wanted to use the default values assigned to the function's second and third arguments, you could issue this kind of function call:

```
AFunction(95);
```

To use default values for all three of the function's arguments, you could execute this statement:

```
AFunction();
```

Class Hierarchies

You have seen how member functions and member variables can be declared inside C++ classes, so that outside functions can make use of member functions and member variables using the principle of *data abstraction.*

You also have seen how the `private`, `protected`, and `public` access specifiers can isolate member variables of classes from unwanted access from outside their classes—the principle known as *data encapsulation.*

In this section, you learn the fundamentals of a third important feature of C++: the inheritance of class features and class behaviors through *class hierarchies.*

How Class Hierarchies Work

To illustrate how class hierarchies work, suppose the company using the EMPDATA.CPP program opens branch offices abroad and hires employees in other countries. Assume that the company then decides to add the names of countries to the information printed out by the EMPDATA.CPP program.

In a C++ program, one easy way to carry out such a task is to create a new class that is derived from the `EmpData` class. In C++, a derived class inherits all the `public` and `protected` member functions and member variables of its parent class. A derived class also can be equipped with its own members— that is, member variables and member functions that are not present in its parent class.

> **Note**
>
> Derived classes do not inherit `private` member functions from their parents. Members that are declared `private` inside a class definition are inaccessible to all other classes—even to derived classes.

Using Derived Classes

Figure 12.2 shows how a derived class works in a C++ program. As you can see, the derived class named `OffshoreEmpData` inherits all member functions and member variables of the `EmpData` class, and has one additional member member variable named `m_country`.

Fig. 12.2

Derived classes inherit all the public and protected members of their parent classes.

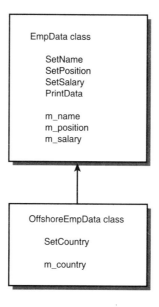

EmpData class

SetName
SetPosition
SetSalary
PrintData

m_name
m_position
m_salary

OffshoreEmpData class

SetCountry

m_country

Note

In figure 12.2, notice that the arrow connecting the EmpData class to the OffshoreEmpData class points upward—not downward as you might expect. This odd convention is used in C++ class diagrams because members of parent classes are visible to derived classes, but members of derived classes are not visible to their parents.

Listing 12.7 is a version of the EMPDATA.CPP program that has been expanded to include the derived OffshoreEmpData class. The OffshoreEmpData class inherits all public and protected member variables and member functions of the EmpData class, and is also equipped with some extra member variables and member functions of its own.

Listing 12.7   Using a Derived Class

```
// empdata.cpp
#include <windows.h>
#include <stdio.h>

// Parent class
class EmpData {
public:
    // 'structors
    EmpData() {}
    ~EmpData() {}
private:
```

```cpp
        char *m_name;
        char *m_dept;
        char *m_position;
        long m_salary;
public:
        void SetName(char *name) { m_name = name; }
        void SetDept(char *dept) { m_dept = dept; }
        void SetPosition(char *position)
            { m_position = position; }
        void SetSalary(long salary)
            { m_salary = salary; }
        virtual void PrintData();
};

// Derived class
class OffshoreEmpData : public EmpData{
public:
        // 'structors
        OffshoreEmpData() {}
        ~OffshoreEmpData() {}
private:
        char *m_country;
public:
void SetCountry(char *country)
        { m_country = country; }
        void PrintData();
};

void EmpData::PrintData()
{
        printf("\nName: %s\n", m_name);
        printf("Department: %s\n", m_dept);
        printf("Position: %s\n", m_position);
        printf("Salary: $%d\n", m_salary);
}

void OffshoreEmpData::PrintData()
{
        EmpData::PrintData();
        printf("Country: %s\n", m_country);
}

int main()
{
        /* Class object instance declaration*/
        OffshoreEmpData empInfo;
        /* Populate the empInfo class with data. */
        empInfo.SetName("Toni Kinoshita");
        empInfo.SetDept("Admin");
        empInfo.SetPosition("Receptionist");
        empInfo.SetSalary(24000);
        empInfo.SetCountry("Japan");
        empInfo.PrintData();
        return 0;
}
```

Learning C/C++

Inheritance

Listing 12.7 shows how derived classes can be used in C++ programs. The program contains this definition of a derived class:

```
// Derived class
class OffshoreEmpData : public EmpData {
public:
    // 'structors
    OffshoreEmpData() {}
    ~OffshoreEmpData() {}
private:
    char *m_country;
public:
void SetCountry(char *country)
    { m_country = country; }
    void PrintData();
};
```

In the preceding class definition, notice that the OffshoreEmpData class is derived from EmpData using the public keyword:

```
class OffshoreEmpData : public EmpData {
```

In C++ programs, derived classes are almost always publicly derived from their parent classes. You can hide derived classes from the rest of a program by declaring them using the private keyword, but this feature of C++ is rarely used.

A feature of the OffshoreEmpData class that you are likely to find more useful is the use of the keywords public and protected *inside* the class definition. When a C++ program defines a derived class, the definition of the derived class does not have to redeclare the member functions and member variables of that class that are declared by the parent of the derived class.

That is because the derived class *inherits* all public and protected members that are declared inside the definition of its parent class. This convention saves unnecessary typing and shortens source files. Because derived classes always inherit their parents' public and protected member variables and member functions, it is not necessary to repeat the definitions of those members in the definitions of derived classes.

Adding New Member Variables to a Derived Class

Derived classes declare member variables in the same way that other classes do. In listing 12.7, the OffshoreEmpData class declares one new private member variable, named m_country:

```
private:
    char *m_country;
```

This member variable is used later in the OffshoreEmpData class's PrintData() function.

Overriding Member Functions

A derived classes can modify, or *override*, member functions it inherits from a parent. In listing 12.7, there are two different PrintData() member functions: one named EmpData::PrintData() and the other named OffshoreEmpData::PrintData(). The OffshoreEmpData::PrintData() member function overrides the EmpData::PrintData() member function. This is the definition of the OffshoreEmpData::PrintData() member function:

```
void OffshoreEmpData::PrintData()
{
    EmpData::PrintData();
    printf("Country: %s\n", m_country);
}
```

In the OffshoreEmpData::PrintData() function, the OffshoreEmpData class uses the scope resolution operator :: to call its parent class's EmpData::PrintData() member function. The EmpData::PrintData() function prints four lines of text, and then the OffshoreEmpData::PrintData() function prints one more line. Figure 12.3 shows the output of the modified EMPDATA program.

Fig. 12.3
This is the output of the modified EMPDATA program.

When you write a C++ member function that you expect to be overridden, you should use the virtual keyword in the function definition that may be overridden. When you declare a member function of a class to be virtual, you can provide descendants of the class with member functions that have the same name as the overridden function but have different effects. In listing 12.8, the PrintData() function is identified as a virtual function in the EmpData class definition because the function is designed to be overridden in the definition of the OffshoreEmpData class.

Listing 12.8 Overriding Member Functions in a C++ Program

```cpp
// empdata.cpp
#include <windows.h>
#include <stdio.h>

// Parent class
class EmpData {
public:
    // 'structors
    EmpData() {}
    ~EmpData() {}
private:
    char *m_name;
    char *m_dept;
    char *m_position;
    long m_salary;
public:
    void SetName(char *name) { m_name = name; }
    void SetDept(char *dept) { m_dept = dept; }
    void SetPosition(char *position)
        { m_position = position; }
    void SetSalary(long salary)
        { m_salary = salary; }
    virtual void PrintData();
};

// Derived class
class OffshoreEmpData : public EmpData{
public:
    // 'structors
    OffshoreEmpData() {}
    ~OffshoreEmpData() {}
private:
    char *m_country;
public:
void SetCountry(char *country)
    { m_country = country; }
    void PrintData();
};

void EmpData::PrintData()
{
    printf("\nName: %s\n", m_name);
    printf("Department: %s\n", m_dept);
    printf("Position: %s\n", m_position);
    printf("Salary: $%d\n", m_salary);
}

void OffshoreEmpData::PrintData()
{
    EmpData::PrintData();
    printf("Country: %s\n", m_country);
}

int main()
```

```
{
    // Class object declarations
    EmpData empInfo1;
    OffshoreEmpData empInfo2;
    OffshoreEmpData empInfo3;

    // Populate the empInfo classes with data.
    empInfo1.SetName("Jared Lopez");
    empInfo1.SetDept("Admin");
    empInfo1.SetPosition("CEO");
    empInfo1.SetSalary(22000);
    empInfo1.PrintData();

    empInfo2.SetName("Toni Kinoshita");
    empInfo2.SetDept("Admin");
    empInfo2.SetPosition("Receptionist");
    empInfo2.SetSalary(24000);
    empInfo2.SetCountry("Japan");
    empInfo2.PrintData();

    empInfo3.SetName("Muriel Giraud");
    empInfo3.SetDept("Sales");
    empInfo3.SetPosition("Clerk");
    empInfo3.SetSalary(17000);
    empInfo3.SetCountry("France");
    empInfo3.PrintData();

    return 0;
}
```

In listing 12.8, in the `main()` function of the EMPDATA program, these three statements define three separate objects: one `EmpData` object and two `OffshoreEmpData` objects:

```
EmpData empInfo1;
OffshoreEmpData empInfo2;
OffshoreEmpData empInfo3;
```

In the following block of code, these three objects are populated with data and a printout is generated:

```
    // Populate the empInfo structs with data.
    empInfo1.SetName("Jared Lopez");
    empInfo1.SetDept("Admin");
    empInfo1.SetPosition("CEO");
    empInfo1.SetSalary(22000);
    empInfo1.PrintData();

    empInfo2.SetName("Toni Kinoshita");
    empInfo2.SetDept("Admin");
    empInfo2.SetPosition("Receptionist");
    empInfo2.SetSalary(24000);
    empInfo2.SetCountry("Japan");
    empInfo2.PrintData();
```

```
empInfo3.SetName("Muriel Giraud");
empInfo3.SetDept("Sales");
empInfo3.SetPosition("Clerk");
empInfo3.SetSalary(17000);
empInfo3.SetCountry("France");
empInfo3.PrintData();
```

The output of the program is the following:

```
Name: Jared Lopez
Department: Admin
Position: CEO
Salary: $22000

Name: Toni Kinoshita
Department: Admin
Position: Receptionist
Salary: $24000
Country: Japan

Name: Muriel Giraud
Department: Sales
Position: Clerk
Salary: $17000
Country: France
```

> **Note**
>
> If you think this is an unwieldy way to handle data, you're right. Obviously, the three discrete objects defined in listing 12.8 would be easier to manage if they were defined as members of an array. That technique is not used in listing 12.8 because there are special ways to create arrays of objects that you haven't been introduced to yet. Later in the chapter, "The Turbo C++ Class Library" shows how class-library arrays can be used in a Turbo C++ program.

Function and Operator Overloading

To anyone but a C++ programmer, the word *overload* generally has a pretty bad connotation. In the sometimes strange lexicon of C++, though, overloading is generally thought of as being quite a good thing. There are two kinds of overloading in C++—function overloading and operator overloading—and both these kinds of overloading are major features of the C++ language.

Function Overloading

Function overloading is a feature that adds flexibility to C++ programs. To implement function overloading in a C++ application, all you have to do is supply a class with two member functions that share the same name but have different argument lists.

When you provide a C++ class with two or more overloaded functions, you can tell your compiler which overloaded function you want to call by simply calling the function using the appropriate set of arguments. If the class you are using has another member function with the same name but with a different kind of argument list, that function is not called.

The main benefit of function overloading is that it lets you give the same name to member functions that perform different, but similar, operations in a program. Function overloading is often used in C++ because it imposes almost no run-time penalty and requires practically no overhead.

Listing 12.9 shows how you can use function overloading in a C++ program.

Listing 12.9   Demonstrating Overloaded Member Functions

```cpp
#include <iostream.h>

void PrintMsg(char *name, char *weapon, int ability)
{
     cout << name << '\n';
     cout << weapon << '\n';
     cout << ability << "\n\n";
}

void PrintMsg(char *message)
{
     cout << message << "\n\n";
}

void PrintMsg(int n)
{
     cout << n << "\n\n";
}

int main()
{
     // calling overloaded functions
     PrintMsg("apples", "oranges", 6);
     PrintMsg(5000);
     PrintMsg("Lo, the lightning has struck the postilion.\n");

     return 0;
}
```

In listing 12.9, there are three overloaded versions of the member function named `PrintMsg()`. The first version takes three arguments, the second takes one integer argument, and the third takes one string argument.

Each of these member functions performs a similar task; each prints a message on the screen. But in C++, because of operator overloading, each `PrintMsg()` member function is recognized as a different function. So when you run the program, it has this output:

```
apples
oranges
6

5000

Lo, the lightning has struck the postilion.
```

Constructor Overloading

In C++, you can overload constructors as well as ordinary member functions. In fact, *constructor overloading* is used extensively in C++. It's very common to see a constructor that has two constructors: one that has arguments and one that doesn't. Many constructors have even more overloaded versions. Here's an example of what a pair of overloaded constructs might look like in the definition of a class:

```
AClass {
    AClass();
    AClass(int paramA, int paramB);
```

Argument Matching

When a constructor (or a member function) is overloaded, the compiler decides which constructor to call by using *argument matching*; that is, by comparing the numbers and types of the arguments that are passed to the base class with the numbers and types of the arguments in the argument list of each constructor defined for the base class. Chapter 8, "Functions and Macros," describes argument matching in more detail.

Operator Overloading

Operators as well as member functions can be overloaded in C++. And *operator overloading*, like function overloading, is a common feature of C++ programs.

Operator overloading is a C++ feature you can use to customize operator symbols such as +, -, =, and ++. With operator overloading, you can make an operator symbol behave differently when it is used with objects of different classes.

As an illustration of how operator overloading works, consider the addition operator (+). Ordinarily, you use the addition operator simply to add numbers together, like this:

```
1 + 1 = 2
```

There may be times, though, when you want the addition operator to serve different functions—for example, you might decide that you want to use the + operator to concatenate a pair of strings, like this:

```
StringClass myString, string1, string2;
myString = string1 + string2;
```

With operator overloading, you can customize the + operator to concatenate a pair of string objects, as illustrated in the preceding example. In fact, the + operator is often overloaded to work as a concatenation operator when used with string objects in C++.

You can also overload the + operator to add other kinds of objects in other ways. One common practice is to overload the + operator in such a way that it adds C++ objects together in other ways. Listing 12.10, presented later in this section, shows how you can use an overloaded + operator to convert a pair of floating-point numbers to two member functions of a class.

Writing Operator-Overloading Functions

To overload an operator in C++, you must declare and define an operator-overloading function (usually a member function). A function that overloads an operator always contains the keyword operator. For example, this is a declaration of a member function that overloads the + operator:

```
Money operator+(int);
```

In the declaration of an operator-overloading member function, you follow the operator keyword with the operator you want to overload. Then, inside a pair of parentheses, you place the name of the data type that you want your overloaded operator to affect.

When you have declared an operator-overloading member function inside a class definition, you can define your operator-overloading member function operator in any way you like. Then, whenever you use your overloaded operator to perform whatever task you like, it is used with the data type you have specified.

The Scope of Operator-Overloading Functions

When you overload an operator, normal scope rules apply; if you overload the operator inside a class definition—which is usually the case—the operator is overloaded only within the scope of its class.

An Example of Operator Overloading

Listing 12.10 shows how you can overload the + operator to convert a pair of floating-point numbers to two member functions of a class. One member variable is used to store dollars and the other is used to store cents.

When you execute the program, you pass it a floating-point number that represents a monetary value expressed in dollars and cents. The program converts the decimal number passed to it into two separate numbers, one representing dollars and the other representing cents. The program then stores the dollar amount passed to it in one member variable in one member variable, and stores the cents amount passed to it in the other member variable.

Listing 12.10   Operator Overloading

```cpp
// Overloading the + operator

#include <iostream.h>
#include <math.h>
#include <stdlib.h>

class Money {
public:
      double dollars;
      double cents;
public:
      Money() {}                    // default constructor
      ~Money() {}                   // destructor
      Money(double);                // conversion from double
      Money operator+(Money m);     // operator overloading
};

Money Money::operator+(Money m)
{
      ldiv_t result;

      cents += m.cents;
      dollars += m.dollars;

      if (cents > 99) {
          result = ldiv((long)cents, 100);
          dollars = dollars + result.quot;
          cents = (double)result.rem;
      }
```

```
        return *this;
}

Money::Money(double cash)      // conversion constructor--
{                              // converts fp to Money
        double      frac, n;
        frac = modf(cash, &n);  // a math.h function
        cents = frac * 100;
        dollars = n;            // n comes back as a double
}

int main()
{
        double c, d;
        float deposit1 = 3.50;
        float deposit2 = 4.63;

        Money totalCash = deposit1 + deposit2;

        d = totalCash.dollars;
        c = totalCash.cents;

        cout << "You now have " << d << " dollars.\n";
        cout << "You also have " << c << " cents.\n";

        return 0;
}
```

When you execute the program in listing 12.10, it tells you what value is stored in each member variable of a Money object named totalCash.

The output of the program looks like this:

```
You now have 8 dollars.
You also have 13 cents.
```

The Turbo C++ Class Library

In any object-oriented language—including Turbo C++—one of the most important advantages of using classes is the advantage of inheritance. When derived classes inherit members and behaviors from their parents, software development designers can create libraries of functions with specific relationships built in.

To meet this challenge, Borland has developed an enormous class library called the Turbo C++ class library. A copy of the Turbo C++ class is an integral part of the Borland C++ development environment.

The Turbo C++ class library works like any other professionally designed C++ class library. It offers a generous supply of predesigned C++ classes that you can use in your programs instead of having to create your own classes and write your own member functions.

The Turbo C++ for Windows class library contains classes that implement data structures, such as arrays, lists, iterators, stacks, and queues. These classes can be divided into categories:

- *Container classes*—create and manipulate common data structures, such as arrays, lists, and queues

- *I/O stream classes*—create and manipulate stream I/O

- *Persistent stream classes*—describe the classes for creating and manipulating persistent objects

- *Mathematical classes*—include the BCD (binary coded decimal) and complex mathematical classes that Turbo C++ provides

- *Run-time support classes*—used for exception handling and run-time type information support

- *Class diagnostic macros*—used for debugging your C++ code

- *Service classes*—used for handling date, file, string, thread, and time information

For details about the most important classes in the preceding list, see "Categories of Turbo C++ Class Libraries" later in this chapter.

How the Turbo C++ Class Library Works

The Turbo C++ for Windows container class library works like any other C++ class library. With the Turbo C++ class library, you don't have to write all your code from scratch; you can call on a professionally designed, thoroughly debugged set of classes and class hierarchies to manage data objects you frequently use in your program.

The libraries of functions that compiler designers develop are vital to the success of an object-oriented language such as C++. Without a well-designed class library such as the Turbo C++ for Windows class library, a language like Turbo C++ would not be much more useful than straight C. The Borland container class library is what gives Turbo C++ most of its power.

The classes in Turbo C++ are quite flexible; to a large degree, they let you decide how you implement particular data structures. For example, by just changing a type definition, you can switch your stack implementation from a vector-based stack to a list-based stack. All member functions of the stack template class remain the same, regardless of the implementation.

Features of C++ Class Libraries

There are several important features that any well-designed C++ class library should have. For example, every good class library should offer:

- Support of code reusability

- A well-designed set of class hierarchies

Some class libraries come with valuable extras, such as support for multiple inheritance, support for C++ templates, and built-in exception-handling capabilities (Turbo C++ exception handling is the topic of Chapter 14, "Exception Handling.")

The Turbo C++ for Windows container class library scores high in all these departments, as you will see in the sections that follow.

Class Libraries and Code Reusability

A good C++ class library should make it easy for software developers to write reusable code. (Ease of code reusability is one of the most widely praised benefits of writing programs in C++; by reusing the code written for one application in other applications, you can save enormous amounts of development time.)

You can't write good reusable code with the classes in a library unless that library is built around a set of class hierarchies that are themselves reusable. Armed with a library of well-written reusable classes, software developers can easily write reusable code by simply using the classes the library provides.

To permit code reusability, a well-designed class hierarchy should keep code and data duplication to a minimum. Derived classes should be equipped with extra variables and functions only when those variables or functions are missing from their parent classes or when different behaviors (that is, overridden functions) are required.

Class Hierarchies in Class Libraries

Another requirement of a good class library is a well-defined set of class hierarchies, each one designed to implement a well-designed set of functionalities. The classes in each hierarchy should be arranged into levels of ever-increasing specialization. This kind of arrangement makes it easier for software

II

Learning C/C++

developers to browse through the various class hierarchies that are available to find the exact classes that meet their needs.

In a well-crafted class hierarchy, classes near the bottom generally represent more specialized ideas than the classes near the root. Attributes shared by different classes are abstracted and placed higher in the hierarchy. Removing commonalities is an iterative procedure that results in many class attributes being positioned high in the inheritance tree. Typically, hierarchies in a class library have one or more levels of abstract classes at the top, where each class might be considered to contain attributes for lower classes.

Another requirement of a good C++ class library is a fixed relationship among the members of the class hierarchies that are provided. This relationship should be provided in advance, not determined at run time. When the structure of a class hierarchy is well thought out, it often parallels the conceptual structure of real-world systems, making it easier for program designers to comprehend complex programming tasks. Furthermore, maintenance and debugging are easier when class libraries are well structured because each class adds only limited code to the classes from which it is descended.

The Question of Overhead

One interesting feature of C++ is that using classes that are several levels down from their root class can increase your programming power significantly—through inheritance—without requiring any significant amount of increased overhead. That's because the instantiation of a class many levels down from its root class in an inheritance tree does not necessarily require more storage space than the root class would require. Because of the way C++ classes use memory, the memory space required to store a class is determined by the storage requirement of all the class's base classes, not by the number of base classes used.

How Class Libraries Simplify Debugging

Still another feature of a good class library is that it simplifies debugging. Debugging code in a class hierarchy is easy if you follow a rational order, starting at the class root and proceeding downward. If you fully debug a class before you use it as a base class, any problems that crop up in a derived class are usually caused by misuse of the base class or by bugs in the derived class. The encapsulation of private data and functions makes it more difficult for bugs to propagate from one class to another.

Competition in the Class-Library Market

One major problem that C++ programmers face is the lack of a generic, all-purpose class library that runs on any platform. That restriction limits the benefit of C++ code reusability to programs written especially for a particular vendor's compilers. It would be terrific if vendors of C++ development systems agreed on a set of generic class hierarchies and incorporated those into all class libraries.

Unfortunately, that hasn't happened yet, and doesn't seem be likely to happen in the foreseeable future. At the moment, in the world of Windows, most software designers seem to have two alternatives: the Borland container class library or the Microsoft Foundation Class (MFC) library. You pay your money and take your chance. If you're interested in the Microsoft MFC classes, sorry, that's another book. For more about the Borland container class library, read on.

Multiple Inheritance

Multiple inheritance, described in Chapter 13, "Object-Oriented Methods," can increase the usefulness of a class library. Multiple inheritance lets classes in a library inherit from more than one parent, increasing the number of features that are available to a derived class. Multiple inheritance has long been a feature of the Borland collection class library, but at this writing was still missing from the Borland library's major competitor, the Microsoft Foundation Class (MFC) library used by Microsoft Visual C++. Every class library has its pluses and minuses, and multiple inheritance is a plus for the class libraries supplied with Turbo C++.

Chapter 13, "Object-Oriented Methods," describes multiple inheritance in more detail.

Support for Templates

The Turbo C++ class library is based on *templates*: a feature of C++ that allows a special kind of class called a container to hold virtually any data type.

In C++, templates are often used as wrappers, or containers, for collections of data. With a template, you can use the same C++ class to store collections of different kinds of data. For example, the Turbo C++ class library provides a template-based class named TArrayAsVector that is designed for the storage of arrays. When you instantiate an object of the TArrayAsVector class, you can store any kind of array you like: an array of strings, an array of integers, or even an array of your own classes.

And why would you want to store data or objects in a TArrayAsVector array instead of in a standard, C-style array? Because objects derived from Turbo C++-supplied classes are equipped with many kinds of features that ordinary data structures do not have. For example, objects instantiated from Turbo C++ library classes are automatically *streamable*—that is, they can be easily written to disk or read from disk using streaming capabilities that are built into Turbo C++.

The data stored in a template class can have almost any user-specified data type. When you declare a template in a C++, you specify the kind of data you want to store in objects that belong to your template-derived class.

For more information about C++ templates and the template-based classes in the Turbo C++ class library, see "Class Library Example: The AGES Program," later in this chapter.

Categories of Turbo C++ Class Libraries

The classes in the Turbo C++ for Windows container class library can be broken down into seven categories (listed under the heading "The Turbo C++ Class Library" earlier in this chapter). Of these seven categories, the most important four groups in your day-to-day programming will probably be the container class category, the iostream category, the persistent stream category, and the service classes. These four categories of classes are described under separate headings in the following paragraphs.

Container Classes

Container classes are used for creating and manipulating common data structures such as arrays, lists, and queues. There are 14 container classes in the Turbo C++ class library.

One important group of container classes is the category of *array containers*, which store and manage arrays of objects. This category of classes includes nine container classes and nine corresponding iterator classes. Containers in the array containers family manage objects and pointers to objects, and can sort objects. This category of classes includes the TArrayAsVector class, which can store and manage arrays of objects. The container class category also includes classes that can manage groups of objects stored in linked lists, hashed lists, "bags" (collections of undefined structure), and various other kinds of collections.

For an example of a program that uses the TArrayAsVector class, see "Class Library Example: The AGES Program" later in this chapter.

I/O Stream Classes

The `iostream` library is the only class library that is specified in the ANSI C++ standard and works in the same way in all implementations of C++. The `iostream` classes work much like the `printf` and `scanf` family of functions supplied in the C-language STDIO.H library. They are used to print program output and to retrieve user input, and also to input and output, or *stream*, file data.

In C++, both output and input are handled as streams of bytes. Output is regarded as a C++ object called `cout`, and input is regarded as an object called `cin`.

The `iostream` library provides two special operators that are often used for I/O operations in C++ programs. The *extraction operator* (>>), an overloaded version of the >> bitwise operator, is used with the `cin` stream to retrieve input from the user, and also to retrieve input from files. The *insertion operator* (<<), an overloaded version of the bitwise << operator, is used with the `cout` stream. It can print streams of output to output devices such as monitors and printers, as well as to files.

One of the handiest features of the << and >> operators is that they can be used with either strings or numeric variables, without the need for any formatting characters. For example, consider the following short program:

```
#include <iostream.h>
int main()
{
    int price = 5;
    cout << "The price is $" << price << ".\n";
    return 0;
}
```

The output of the preceding `main()` function is the following:

```
The price is $5.
```

Once you get accustomed to using the >> and << operators, you may find that they are easier to use than the `printf` and `scanf` family of functions because they do not require the use of the formatting character % or the contorted syntax it often requires.

The EMPDATA sample program at the end of this chapter provides a more comprehensive example of how the cout << operator can be used in a C++ program. Chapter 11, "I/O," covers Turbo C++ I/O in much more detail.

The Persistent Stream Classes

The *persistent stream classes* in the Turbo C++ class library are closely related to the `iostream` classes described under the preceding heading. With the persistent stream classes, your application can automatically read data from a disk and save data to a disk at the appropriate times—for instance, when your program starts up or shuts down, or when the user chooses a Load or Save command from a File menu.

You can also use the persistent stream classes to load and save persistent objects—that is, objects that remain in memory even when they are not in use. With the persistent stream classes, you can make persistent objects streamable so they can be streamed into and out of memory to provide interprocess communication. For example, you can stream data from memory to a modem for transmission at the same time other processes are running.

To make a class streamable, you must derive it either directly or indirectly from the `TStreamableBase` class. You must also use certain member functions, member variables, and operators that are designed to support streaming.

The easiest way to create a streamable class is to use an existing streamable class as a base class. If your class must also fit into an existing class hierarchy, you can use multiple inheritance to derive a class from the `TStreamableBase` class.

To make a class streamable, you must place the `DECLARE_STREAMABLE` macro in the definition of the class, and place the `IMPLEMENT_STREAMABLE` macro in the file that implements the class. Then you must execute the `TStreamableBase::Write()` function to write data to a stream, or the function `TStreamableBase::Read()` to read stream data.

The `Write()` member function is a pure virtual function (see Chapter 13, "Object-Oriented Methods") that you must redefine for every streamable class. The `Write()` member function can write any streamable data members you specify to a specified output stream object, or `opstream` object.

The `Read()` member function is a pure virtual function that must also be redefined for every streamable class. It reads streamable data members of any specified streamable class from a specified input stream, or `ipstream`.

Service Classes

The Turbo C++ service class category is a group of classes used for handling date, file, string, thread, and time information. The Turbo C++ string class—one of the most often-used classes in the Turbo C++ container class library—is one of the Turbo C++ service classes.

Every known implementation of C++ has some kind of string class, but the ANSI C++ standard does not lay down any rules for string classes, so every implementation of a string class is different.

The string class supplied with Turbo C++ is one of the most robust string classes available anywhere. Like most string classes, the Turbo C++ string class has functions that create, compare, copy, and append (or concatenate) strings. The Turbo C++ string class also supplies overridden operators (see Chapter 13, "Object-Oriented Methods") that let you concatenate strings using the + operator, test strings for equality by using the operator ==, and perform other operator-based string operations.

The purpose of a string class is to make string manipulation easy, and the Turbo C++ string class achieves that goal with admirable results. For example, executing the following statements has exactly the result you might expect:

```
#include <cstring.h>
#include <iostream.h>

main()
{
        string lastName, firstName, fullName;
        firstName = "Wolfgang ";
        lastName = "Mozart";
        fullName = firstName + lastName;
        cout << fullName;
        return 0;
}
```

Execute the preceding statements in a text-based Turbo C++ program, and you'll see this output:

```
Wolfgang Mozart
```

Class Library Example: The AGES Program

Listing 12.11, a sample program named AGES, contains a potpourri of features that illustrate topics covered in this chapter. It uses two container classes: the TDDAssociation class, which associates an object with a specific location in a list, and the TDictionaryAsHashTable class, which implements a dictionary of objects. In the AGES program, TDDAssociation objects are used to hold the names and ages of a group of people, and the a TDictionaryAsHashTable object is used to build up a dictionary of the TDDAssociation objects used in the program.

The program also makes use of a user-defined class named EmpData. In the program's main() function, the following code uses the EmpData object to add association objects to a dictionary container:

```
EmpData *empInfo = new EmpData;
empInfo->SetName("Tanya");
empInfo->SetAge(23);
// One way to add association objects to a
// dictionary container.
assocType Assoc1(empInfo->GetName(), empInfo->GetAge());
dict.Add(Assoc1);
assocType Assoc2("Jackie", 28);
dict.Add(Assoc2);
```

The AGES program illustrates how you can retrieve information from a dictionary object. And, while it is doing these tricks, it demonstrates the use of the string class and the cout << iostream operator.

Listing 12.11   The AGES Program

```
#include <string.h>
#include <iostream.h>
#include <classlib\assoc.h>
#include <classlib\dict.h>
#include <cstring.h>

class EmpData {
public:
    EmpData() {}
    ~EmpData() {}
private:
    char *m_name;
    int m_age;
public:
    char *GetName() { return m_name; }
    int GetAge() { return m_age; }
    void SetName(char *name) { m_name = name; }
    void SetAge(int age) { m_age = age; }
};

typedef TDDAssociation < string, int > assocType;
typedef TDictionaryAsHashTable < assocType > dicType;
typedef TDictionaryAsHashTableIterator < assocType >
    dicIterType;

unsigned HashValue( const string& t )
{
  return t.hash( );
}

void main( )
{
    dicType dict;
```

```
assocType assoc;
EmpData *empInfo = new EmpData;
empInfo->SetName("Tanya");
empInfo->SetAge(23);

// One way to add association objects to a
// dictionary container.
assocType Assoc1(empInfo->GetName(), empInfo->GetAge());
dict.Add(Assoc1);
assocType Assoc2("Jackie", 28);
dict.Add(Assoc2);

    // Another way to add association objects to a dictionary.
    // These are unnamed association objects of type
    // assocType.
    dict.Add ( assocType( "Pebbles", 19 ) );
dict.Add ( assocType( "Steve", 14 ) );
dict.Add ( assocType( "Martin", 44 ) );

// This code finds and prints out value data in a
// dictionary container.
assocType* Res = dict.Find(Assoc1);

  if (Res != 0) {
          cout << "Tanya's age is:   ";
          cout << Res->Value( ) << "\n "<< endl;
  }

// This code displays all dictionary container contents
// on your screen. Note that Current( ) is an
// iterator function that returns an association object.
// Key( ) and Value( ) are association object functions
// that return key and value data, respectively.

  dicIterType dicIter (dict);
cout << "These are the dictionary contents:\n" <<
    endl;
    while ( dicIter != 0 ) {
          cout << dicIter.Current( ).Key( ) << ":   " ;
    cout << dicIter.Current( ).Value( ) << endl;
    dicIter++;
      }
      delete empInfo;
  }
```

The "Templates" section of Chapter 13, "Object-Oriented Methods," describes and demonstrates the use of templates in greater detail.

From Here...

It's only a short leap from a struct to a class. In this chapter, you made that leap and kept going. You learned how to create a class, how to instantiate an object from a class, and how to create and use member variables and member functions. You also learned how to use such special features of C++ as class hierarchies, function overloading, and operator overloading.

To learn how to use still more of the features of C++, see the following chapters:

- The "Function Overloading" section of this chapter introduced the topic of argument matching. Chapter 8, "Functions and Macros," describes argument matching in more detail.

- Chapter 11, "I/O," describes and demonstrates I/O streams, the cin and cout objects, the << and >> operators, and other aspects of Turbo C++ input and output.

- Chapter 13, "Object-Oriented Methods," shows you how to use C++ features including derived classes, polymorphism, multiple inheritance, static member variables, and the new and delete memory-allocation operators.

- Chapter 14, "Exception Handling," shows how you can implement state-of-the-art error handling by mastering the exception-handling features of Turbo C++.

Chapter 13

Object-Oriented Methods

Chapter 12 introduced the topic of object-oriented programming by showing what classes and objects are and how they are used in Turbo C++. This chapter takes you deeper into the territory of object-oriented programming by revisiting some of the most important features of C++ and introducing a few more.

This chapter covers the following topics:

■ How derived classes let you create customized objects with low over-head and high efficiency

■ How polymorphism makes it possible to change the behavior of a member function without changing its name

■ How you can use multiple inheritance to create objects that inherit characteristics from more than one class

■ How static member variables provide the benefits of global variables without many of the risks

■ How to allocate memory easily with `new` and `delete`

■ How to use templates to create type-safe lists

Inheritance and Polymorphism

As noted in Chapter 12, you can derive new classes from existing C++ classes by using the mechanism of *inheritance*. A class from which another class is derived is called a *base class*.

When a class is derived from a base class, the derived class inherits characteristics from the base class; specifically, a derived class inherits all public and protected member variables and member functions of its base class. However, a derived class does not inherit members of its base class that are labeled `private`.

Along with the member variables and member functions that it inherits from its base class, a derived class can, of course, define its own member variables and member functions. If it couldn't do that, there would be no reason for it to exist.

When a class is derived from another class, more classes can be derived from the derived class. Thus, a derived class can also be a base class. Multiple levels of classes that are derived from each other form a *class hierarchy*. In a class hierarchy, classes at the bottom of the hierarchy inherit all the public and protected (but not the private) member variables and member functions of their base classes.

Reasons for Using Derived Classes

C++ programmers use inheritance to create derived classes for a number of reasons:

- When you use a base class to derive a new class, the new class is a new data type that inherits all the qualities of the base class without disturbing the relationships the base class may have with other parts of the program. If you are already using the base class in your program, its behavior remains intact for objects that already use it but can be modified for use by objects that require different behaviors.

- You don't need access to the source code for the base class when you want to derive a class from a base class. If you have access to a header file (a .H file) that defines a base class, you have all you need to derive classes from that base class.

- You can use *abstract classes* in a class hierarchy. Abstract classes are general-purpose classes that do nothing by themselves, but are specifically designed to be used as base classes. The only purpose of an abstract class is to define the behavior of a generic data structure.

Derived classes can then add implementation details. For example, you could define an abstract class to manage objects in a list. Then you could provide it with member functions that insert, change, delete, reorder, and search entries in the list without having to know any details about objects in the list. You would probably implement such a class as an abstract class because it would have no usefulness unless it were associated with an actual list. Abstract classes are described in more detail later in this section.

■ When you set up a class hierarchy on a foundation of base classes and derived classes, you can make use of other properties of the object-oriented languages, such as *polymorphism*. Polymorphism is also described in some detail later in this chapter, in the section titled "Polymorphism."

Benefits of Using Derived Classes

There are two major benefits of using derived classes in C++ programs. One advantage is that derived classes provide a means for building a well-organized object-oriented class hierarchy in which user-defined data types descend from a common root class. Also, derived classes let you use the C++ property of inheritance; by deriving classes that inherit behaviors from other classes, you can create new classes that are similar to—but not identical to—other classes. Thus, inheritance provides a systematic, logical, easy-to-use mechanism for creating new classes with new behaviors.

Listing 13.1, a new version of the EMPDATA.CPP program used in several of the examples in Chapter 12, illustrates some new details about how derived classes can be used in C++ programs.

Listing 13.1   The EMPDATA.CPP Program with a Pure Virtual Member Function

```
// empdata.cpp
#include <stdio.h>
#include <cstring.h>
#include <iostream.h>
#include <strstrea.h>
#include <classlib\arrays.h>

// Parent class
class Employee {
public:
    // constructors and destructors
    Employee() {}
```

Listing 13.1 Continued

```
  ~Employee() {}
     virtual void PrintData() = 0;
     void SetName(char *name) { m_name = name; }
     void SetDept(char *dept) { m_dept = dept; }
     void SetPosition(char *position)
           { m_position = position; }
     void SetSalary(long salary)
           { m_salary = salary; }

protected:
     char *m_name;
     char *m_dept;
     char *m_position;
     long m_salary;
};

class ExemptEmp : public Employee {
// class description
public:
       // Constructor and destructor
       ExemptEmp(char *name, char *dept, char *position,
             long salary);
       ~ExemptEmp() {}

       void PrintData();
};

class SalesEmp : public Employee {
// class description
public:
       // Constructor and destructor
       SalesEmp(char *name, char *dept, char *position,
             long salary, long sales, float commissionPerCent);
       ~SalesEmp() {}

       void PrintData();

private:
       char *m_country;
       long m_sales;
       long m_commission;
       float m_commissionPerCent;
       long m_totalPay;
};

class OffshoreEmp : public Employee {
// class description
private:
       char *m_country;
public:
```

```
        // Constructor and destructor
        OffshoreEmp(char *m_name, char *m_country, char *m_dept,
            char *m_position, long m_salary);
        ~OffshoreEmp() {}

        void PrintData();
};

ExemptEmp::ExemptEmp(char *name, char *dept, char *position,
        long salary)
{
    m_name = name;
    m_dept = dept;
    m_position = position;
    m_salary = salary;
}

OffshoreEmp::OffshoreEmp(char *name, char *country, char *dept,
        char *position, long salary)
{
    m_name = name;
    m_country = country;
    m_dept = dept;
    m_position = position;
    m_salary = salary;
}

SalesEmp::SalesEmp(char *name, char *dept, char *position,
        long salary, long sales, float commissionPerCent)
{
    m_name = name;
    m_dept = dept;
    m_position = position;
    m_salary = salary;
    m_sales = sales;
    m_commissionPerCent = commissionPerCent;
    m_commission = m_sales  * commissionPerCent;
    m_totalPay = m_salary + m_commission;
}

void ExemptEmp::PrintData()
{
        printf("\nName: %s\n", m_name);
        printf("Department: %s\n", m_dept);
        printf("Position: %s\n", m_position);
        printf("Salary: $%d\n", m_salary);
}

void OffshoreEmp::PrintData()
{
        printf("\nName: %s\n", m_name);
        printf("Department: %s\n", m_dept);
        printf("Country: %s\n", m_country);
        printf("Position: %s\n", m_position);
        printf("Salary: $%d\n", m_salary);
}
```

II

Learning C/C++

(continues)

Listing 13.1 Continued

```
void SalesEmp::PrintData()
{
        printf("\nName: %s\n", m_name);
        printf("Department: %s\n", m_dept);
        printf("Position: %s\n", m_position);
        printf("Salary: $%d\n", m_salary);
        printf("Sales: $%d\n", m_sales);
        printf("Commission level: %f\n", m_commissionPerCent);
        printf("Commission: $%d\n", m_commission);
        printf("Total Pay: $%d\n", m_totalPay);
}

int main()
{
        Employee *emp[3];

        emp[0] = new ExemptEmp("Jorge Washington", "Admin",
                "CEO", 22000);

        emp[1] = new OffshoreEmp("Toni Kinoshita", "Japan", "Admin",
                "Receptionist", 24000);

        emp[2] = new SalesEmp("Muriel Burnett", "Sales", "Salesperson",
                17000, 2200, .15);

        for (int c = 0; c < 3; c++)
                emp[c]->PrintData();

        for (c = 0; c < 3; c++)
                delete emp[c];

        return 0;
}
```

Abstract Classes and Pure Virtual Functions

There are some important differences between the EMPDATA program presented in listing 13.1 and the earlier versions of the program presented in Chapter 12.

For example, in listing 13.1, the Employee class is an *abstract class*—that is, a class that does nothing by itself but is designed to be used only as a base class. The reason an abstract class can do nothing by itself is that objects cannot be created from an abstract class.

You can tell that the `Employee` class is a virtual class because the definition of the employee class contains a declaration of a *pure virtual member function*. In C++, a pure virtual function is a function that is assigned a value of 0 in its declaration. This is the pure virtual member function that appears in the definition of the `Employee` class:

```
virtual void PrintData() = 0;
```

In the definition of the `Employee` class, the preceding statement is all it takes to make `Employee` an abstract class. In C++, you can declare a class to be an abstract class by simply placing at least one pure virtual member function declaration inside the definition of a class.

The main characteristic of a pure virtual member function is that it must be overridden by at least one derived class. In the EMPDATA program in listing 13.1, the `PrintData()` function is overridden by three derived classes: `ExemptEmp`, `OffshoreEmp`, and `SalesEmp`.

Polymorphism

In listing 13.1, the `PrintData()` function shows how *polymorphism* works in C++. Polymorphism is a C++ capability that lets descendants of a class override a member function of that class with member functions that have the same name but have different effects.

How Polymorphism Works

Here's how polymorphism works in the EMPDATA program: When you run the program, each of the three classes derived from the `Employee` class executes a function named `PrintData()`. But each derived class has its own version of the `PrintData()` function. When you execute the EMPDATA program, the program's main function makes three identical calls to a member function named `PrintData()`—and each call has a different result:

```
for (int c = 0; c < 3; c++)
    emp[c]->PrintData();
```

In the preceding statement, which appears in the EMPDATA program's `main()` function, each call to `PrintData()` has an identical syntax—in fact, all three calls to `PrintData()` are made inside the same `for` loop. Nonetheless, each call produces a different result! The `ExemptEmp::PrintData()` function prints out basic employee information, the `OffshoreEmp::PrintData()` function prints out a block of employee data that includes the name of a country, and the `SalesEmp::PrintData()` function computes and prints out a block of employee data that includes information about sales commissions.

II

Learning C/C++

In the EMPDATA program, all that is accomplished through the magic of polymorphism. Figure 13.1 shows the output of the new, polymorphically correct version of the EMPDATA.CPP program.

Fig. 13.1
The magic of polymorphism.

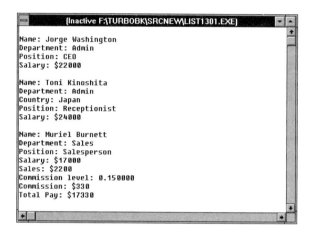

```
[Inactive F:\TURBOBK\SRCNEW\LIST1301.EXE]

Name: Jorge Washington
Department: Admin
Position: CEO
Salary: $22000

Name: Toni Kinoshita
Department: Admin
Country: Japan
Position: Receptionist
Salary: $24000

Name: Muriel Burnett
Department: Sales
Position: Salesperson
Salary: $17000
Sales: $2200
Commission level: 0.150000
Commission: $330
Total Pay: $17330
```

Benefits of Polymorphism

What makes polymorphism special is that it makes your computer do what you meant, not what you said. When a member function is defined by a parent class and is then overridden by a derived class, both functions have the same name but the appropriate function executes automatically at the appropriate time.

When you call an overridden function from a parent class, the version of the function defined by the parent class is the version that executes. But when you call the function from a derived class, the derived class's version of the function executes instead.

This feature has profound effects in C++ programs. You can write a block of code that calls a function with a specified name, and you can give that name to as many different functions as you like, as long as each overridden function you write appears in a different class definition. Then you can trust polymorphism to ensure that the right function is called each time the calling function executes.

> **Note**
>
> With polymorphism, you can implement the functionality of a `switch` statement without doing any switching. Instead of using a `case` clause to determine how your `switch` statement should behave when different kinds of conditions exist, you can create a class for each potential target of your `switch` statement. Then you make use of the polymorphic capabilities of C++ to make sure that the right function is executed at the right time. So, if you're looking for ways to use polymorphism in your programs, one way to start experimenting is to look for a `switch` statement and replace it with a set of derived classes with overridden member functions.
>
> This technique may require an overhaul in your programming techniques, but it will be worth it in the long run. You'll quickly see how much sense it makes to use overridden member functions instead of monster case statements in your C++ programs.

Access Specifiers and Class Derivation

As you may recall from Chapter 12, classes can be *publicly* or *privately* derived from other classes. When a class is privately derived from a base class, members of the base class that are declared to be `public` and `protected` become private members of the derived class. When a class is publicly derived from a base class, members of the base class that are designated `protected` are also protected members of the derived class, and members of the base class that are designated `public` are also public members of the derived class.

In this chapter's version of the EMPDATA program, three classes are publicly derived from virtual base class named `Employee`: `ExemptEmp`, `OffshoreEmp`, and `SalesEmp`. This is the first line of the definition of the `ExemptEmp` class:

```
class ExemptEmp : public Employee {
```

Similarly, this is the first line of the definition of the `OffshoreEmp`:

```
class OffshoreEmp: public Employee {
```

Finally, the `SalesEmp` class is defined this way:

```
class SalesEmp: public Employee {
```

Because the `ExemptEmp`, `OffshoreEmp`, and `SalesEmp` classes are all publicly derived from the `Employee` class, objects of the `EmpData` class inherit all the member functions of the `Employee` class. That's because public member functions of a C++ class remain public when inherited by derived classes.

In this chapter's version of the EMPDATA program, all member functions of the EmpData class are designated protected. That means they can be accessed by the PrintData function of the OffshoreEmpData class.

Writing Constructors for Derived Classes

In listing 13.1, each of the three classes derived from the Employee class has a different constructor. The constructor for the ExemptEmp class initializes a set of member variables that contain basic employee data. The constructor for the OffshoreEmp class initializes an identical set of member variables, plus a string-type member variable that holds the name of a country. The constructor for the SalesEmp class does not initialize a country-name variable, but does calculate commissions and fill in a set of member variables that deal with commissions and salaries.

These are the definitions of the three derived-class constructors that appear in listing 13.1:

```
ExemptEmp::ExemptEmp(char *name, char *dept, char *position,
      long salary)
{
      m_name = name;
      m_dept = dept;
      m_position = position;
      m_salary = salary;
}

OffshoreEmp::OffshoreEmp(char *name, char *country, char *dept,
      char *position, long salary)
{
      m_name = name;
      m_country = country;
      m_dept = dept;
      m_position = position;
      m_salary = salary;
}

SalesEmp::SalesEmp(char *name, char *dept, char *position,
      long salary, long sales, float commissionPerCent)
{
      m_name = name;
      m_dept = dept;
      m_position = position;
      m_salary = salary;
      m_sales = sales;
      m_commissionPerCent = commissionPerCent;
      m_commission = m_sales  * commissionPerCent;
      m_totalPay = m_salary + m_commission;
}
```

As you can see, the constructors of the three derived classes in the EMPDATA program initialize the member variables that each class uses to execute its version of the `PrintData()` member function.

How Virtual Functions Work

To understand how polymorphism works, it helps to know something about *virtual functions*. In a nutshell, this is how virtual functions work:

Ordinarily, when a base class has a member function with the same name and argument list as a member function of a derived class, you can't execute the version of the function that is defined for the derived class by calling the function through a pointer to the base class. Instead, when you call the derived class's function through a pointer, the compiler executes the base-class version of the function.

You can reverse this behavior by declaring the base class's version of the member function to be `virtual`. When a derived class has a member function that exactly matches a public or protected member function of a base class, and the base-class member function is designated `virtual`, the derived class's version of the function is executed when the function is called. (Of course the objects themselves still have to be created as objects of their derived classes, even though the pointer is a pointer of the base class type.)

The EMPDATA program has several new features that help it make use of virtual functions. First, the `m_country` member variable and the `SetCountry` member function appear only in the definition of the `OffshoreEmp` class; they do not appear in the definitions of the `ExemptEmp` class or the `SalesEmp` class. Similarly, member variables that deal with commissions appear only in the definition of the `SalesEmp` class; they do not appear in the definitions of the other two classes.

When you execute the EMPDATA program, its `main()` function appears to instantiate an array of three objects of the `Employee` class. But of course that is not possible; as you have seen, the `Employee` class in the EMPDATA program is an abstract class, and you can't instantiate objects of an abstract class. But you can instantiate objects of classes that are *derived* from an abstract class— and that is exactly what the EMPDATA program does in its `main()` function:

```
int main()
{
        Employee *emp[3];

        emp[0] = new ExemptEmp("Jorge Washington", "Admin",
                "CEO", 22000);
```

```
                    emp[1] = new OffshoreEmp("Toni Kinoshita", "Japan", "Admin",
                    "Receptionist", 24000);

                    emp[2] = new SalesEmp("Muriel Burnett", "Sales", "Salesperson",
                        17000, 2200, .15);

                    for (int c = 0; c < 3; c++)
                        emp[c]->PrintData();

                    for (c = 0; c < 3; c++)
                        delete emp[c];

                    return 0;
        }
```

As you can see by examining the three constructors that follow the initialization of the Employee object array, the three objects that are actually constructed in the EMPDATA program's main() function are not really Employee objects at all. Instead, they are instantiations of three different kinds of objects that are *derived* from the abstract Employee class: one ExemptEmp object, one OffshoreEmp object, and one SalesEmp object.

This feature of the EMPDATA program illustrates an important fact about polymorphism in C++: When you derive one class from another, you can instantiate an object of the derived class just as if it were an object of its parent class. That's because C++ allows you to use an abstract class pointer to point to a derived object. This capability is very important in C++ because it facilitates use of polymorphism. Without this capability, there wouldn't be much use for abstract base classes.

The PrintData() function in the EMPDATA program also makes use of the C++ feature that lets you use an abstract class pointer to point to a derived object. In the program's main() function, the PrintData() function is called using a pointer to the abstract Employee class. However, each call that is made to PrintData() has a different result. That's because PrintData() is a virtual function that is defined in a different way by each object that is derived from the Employee class. So, even though the program calls PrintData() using a pointer to an abstract parent class, the Turbo C++ compiler tracks down the appropriate PrintData() member function and executes that member function each time PrintData() is called.

This is the rule to remember: When a C++ statement calls a member function of an object that is a member of a hierarchy, the target of the action can be either an object of the specified class or an object of a class that lies lower in the object's class hierarchy. You can see how that works by studying the PrintData() loop in the preceding code fragment.

Pure Virtual Functions

A member function that not only *can* be overridden, but *must* be overridden, is called a *pure virtual function*. When you declare a pure virtual function in a base class, you are specifying not only that the member function must be overridden before it can be used, but also that the base class does not contain a definition of the function.

To turn a virtual member function into a pure virtual member function, all you have to do is assign the function a value of zero (effectively, a NULL pointer). For example, in listing 13.1, the `Employee::PrintData()` function is a pure virtual function. It is defined this way in the definition of the base class `Employee`:

```
virtual void PrintData() = 0;
```

When a function is defined in a class definition using the preceding format, the compiler treats the function as a pure virtual function. A pure virtual function can appear only in the definition of a base class, and must be overridden in a derived class.

When a class contains at least one pure virtual function, the class is known as an *abstract class*. An abstract class, as noted earlier in this chapter, is a class from which objects cannot be created. In the EMPDATA program, the `Employee` class is the abstract class in which the pure virtual `PrintData()` function is declared.

Notice that there are no `Employee` objects in the program; you couldn't create any if you wanted to, because you can't create objects from an abstract class. But `ExemptEmp`, `OffshoreEmp`, and `SalesEmp` are all derived from the `Employee` class. That's allowed; in fact, that's what abstract classes are there for. The only purpose of an abstract class is to serve as a root for derived classes.

Similarly, the only purpose of a pure virtual function is to serve as a root function for other functions. You cannot instantiate an object that belongs to an abstract class, and you cannot directly call a pure virtual function; you can, however, call an overridden version of a virtual function when the override is provided in the definition of a derived class.

II

Learning C/C++

> **Note**
>
> Although you can't instantiate an abstract class, you can declare a pointer to a base class, and that base class can be an abstract class. That opens the door to indirect manipulation of an abstract class, which can cause problems. If you access an abstract class through a pointer and then try to invoke a member function of that class that is a pure virtual function, the result is an error that might remain undetected until run time.
>
> Consequently, when you access a function in an abstract base class through a pointer to the base class, you should always check to see if the function is a virtual function. If it is, you should make sure that the function is overridden in the derived class from which it is called. If it isn't, you can encounter run-time problems.

Classes That Inherit Pure Virtual Functions

If a class inherits a pure virtual function but does not override that function, the class is considered an abstract class. That means that a class can be considered an abstract class even if the definition of the class does not contain a definition of a pure virtual function. In C++, if a class does not explicitly provide an implementation for a virtual function that it inherits, the class is considered an abstract class, and no objects that belong to the class can be created.

If a class inherits a pure virtual function and you try to create an object of the derived class, your compiler returns an error informing you that you are trying to instantiate a member of an abstract class. If you aren't familiar with the rules that govern the implementation of pure virtual functions, you may not understand why an error is being returned. You can prevent such errors from occurring by making sure that every virtual function that is defined in a base class is overridden by every class that is derived from that base class.

Pure Virtual Functions in Class Hierarchies

When you build a hierarchy of classes, it is particularly important to remember the rules that govern the inheritance of pure virtual functions. In C++, when a class that is a member of a hierarchy defines a pure virtual function, every concrete class that appears in the lower hierarchy must override the function. If a derived class fails to override the pure virtual function, that class becomes an abstract class from which objects cannot be created.

If a pure virtual function is defined in a base class and is then passed down through a hierarchy of classes, there may be classes in the hierarchy that have no particular need for the virtual function they have inherited.

If a class inherits a pure virtual function, but must provide an implementation of the function anyway so that it won't be considered an abstract class, the class can implement the pure virtual function by defining it as a *null virtual function*. A null virtual function is a virtual function with an empty function body. This is a definition of a null virtual function:

```
virtual void PrintSomeStuff() {}
```

It's not the same as a pure virtual function. A null virtual function is simply a virtual function that does nothing. When you declare a pure virtual function in the base class of a class hierarchy, you can use null virtual functions as placeholders in intermediate classes in the hierarchy. The null virtual functions implemented in the hierarchy serve no purpose except to make the pure virtual function accessible to lower classes in the chain.

How Virtual Functions Work

As mentioned at the beginning of this chapter, virtual functions are the key to polymorphism. When you define a virtual member function in a base class, the function's declaration notifies the compiler that the function might be overridden in base classes. Therefore, when you write a base-class function that you think you might override, it's a good idea to make the function a virtual function.

Except for the ironclad rules that govern the use of pure virtual functions, C++ is fairly forgiving about how you use virtual functions in your programs. When you write a base-class function and declare it to be a virtual function, C++ does not force you to override the function in derived classes; if you don't override the function, it still works fine using the function in the base class in which it is defined.

Conversely, if you write a base-class function and don't make it virtual, C++ does not force you to override the function in a derived class. However, it's a good idea to designate a base-class function virtual when you think it might be overridden in a derived class. That's because C++ compiles virtual functions and non-virtual functions in very different ways. Virtual functions work more efficiently than non-virtual functions when they're overridden. More important, because of the way they're compiled, virtual functions are the key to polymorphism in the C++ language.

V-Tables

Until object-oriented languages came along, programs called functions in a very straightforward way. When a procedural program called a function, the compiler knew exactly what function was being called, and knew exactly where in memory the function resided. Therefore, when an application called a function, the call to the function was simply built into the program when the program was compiled. Today, that technique is known as *early binding*, or *static binding*.

When a C++ program calls a non-virtual function, the function is called using static binding, in the same way that it would be called in a C program. However, when a C++ program calls a virtual function through a pointer to a class, the compiler calls the function using a different technique. That technique is called *late binding*, or *dynamic binding*.

When a program calls a virtual function through a pointer to a base class—that is, when a function calls a virtual function using dynamic binding—the compiler doesn't know at link time which version of the function will be called when the program is executed. That's because the program doesn't call the function through a pointer to a specific derived class, but rather through a pointer to a base class that can (and usually does) have multiple derived classes.

Because the compiler doesn't know which version of the function to access when the program is linked, the program itself must evaluate the calling statement at run time, when it can determine which version of the function to call. Thus, when a program uses dynamic binding to call a function through a pointer to an object, the calling statement is evaluated at run time.

One important advantage of dynamic binding is that it lets your application call functions that are individually tailored for individual objects, even when functions have the same names. That capability, as demonstrated in listing 13.1, is what polymorphism is all about. Another advantage of dynamic binding is that it lets you modify the behavior of code that has already been compiled. That means you can use dynamic binding to provide extensible class libraries to other programmers.

By calling functions using dynamic binding, you can let other programmers derive new classes from classes that you have defined. They can also redefine the virtual functions in your classes, even if you don't give them access to your source code. You can keep your source code private and distribute only your header files (.H files), along with the compiled object code (.OBJ or .LIB files) for the hierarchy of classes you've written and the functions that use those classes. Other programmers can then derive new classes from your classes, and can redefine virtual functions that you have declared. And you don't have to hand out copies of your implementation code (your .CPP files) to make that possible.

Dynamic binding wouldn't be very useful in commercial-quality applications if it were an inefficient mechanism requiring a lot of overhead. Fortunately, virtual functions are very efficient; calling a virtual function takes only slightly more overhead than calling a normal function.

To implement dynamic binding, C++ uses *virtual function tables*, or *v-tables*. A v-table is an array of function pointers that the compiler constructs for every class that uses virtual functions. For example, in this chapter's version of the EMPDATA program, the compiler sets up separate v-tables for the EmpData class and the OffshoreEmpData class.

When you compile a C++ program, the compiler stores the program's v-tables in a location that is accessible to all of the objects in the program. When you create a class that accesses virtual functions in a parent class, the code for each instance of the class contains a hidden pointer to the v-table of the class. The v-table for each object is built at run time so that references can be resolved when the program that contains the object is executed.

Figure 13.2 shows how a v-table works in C++. Suppose that while a program is running, it encounters a reference to a virtual function. When the reference is encountered, the object on the left is in scope, and the object's v-table pointer contains the address of an entry in the object's v-table.

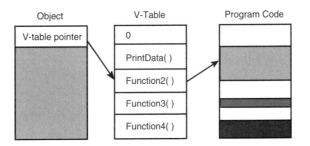

Fig. 13.2
Using a V-table.

Now assume that when a reference to a virtual function is encountered, the object's v-table pointer points to the second entry in the object's v-table. In figure 13.2, the second entry in the object's v-table is the PrintData() function. So the PrintData function, which resides in the code segment of the program, is called.

Because the call to a virtual function is indirect—through a pointer to an object—the code for the implementation of a virtual function does not have to be in the same code segment as the caller of the virtual function.

A v-table that is set up for a class contains one function pointer for each virtual function in the class. For example, in this chapter's version of the EMPDATA program, the `EmpData` class and the `OffshorePrintData` class have separate v-tables for the `PrintData()` function. The v-table for the `EmpData` class contains a pointer to the `EmpData::PrintData()` function, while the v-table for the `OffshoreEmpData` class contains a pointer to the `OffshoreEmpData::PrintData()`. But, as you have seen, both functions can be called through a pointer to an `EmpData` class.

When a program that is being executed calls the `PrintData()` function, the pointer to the function points to the version of the function that is appropriate to the class that is currently in scope. Thus, the correct function is called.

Virtual Functions: Pros and Cons

Although dynamic binding is a powerful feature of C++, it doesn't mean that all functions in a program should be designated virtual functions. Because virtual functions are called indirectly, they do add some overhead (though not very much) to an application, and therefore slightly slow down the program's execution speed. So, when you design a class, you really should use the `virtual` keyword only for virtual functions that you expect to be overridden.

If you make a function virtual and discover later that there is little chance of it being overridden, you can remove the `virtual` keyword from the declaration of the function and save a little overhead. But nothing terrible will happen if you fail to notice that the function isn't overridden and forget to remove its `virtual` designation.

Multiple Inheritance

In Chapter 12, you saw how a C++ object can inherit behaviors from more than one class. The derivation of a class from multiple base classes is known as *multiple inheritance*.

Some implementations of C++, including Turbo C++, support multiple inheritance. Other C++ implementations, such as Microsoft Visual C++, do not. Vendors whose C++ compilers do not support multiple inheritance say that multiple inheritance adds needless complexity to programs—along with potential problems—without doing anybody much good. Companies whose compilers do support multiple inheritance say it's a valuable programming tool.

As a Turbo C++ programmer, you are in an ideal position to do some experimenting and decide where you stand in this raging controversy.

Single Inheritance and Multiple Inheritance

Multiple inheritance isn't just a feature of object-oriented languages; you find it in nature all the time. Figure 13.3 shows how multiple inheritance occurs in the animal kingdom.

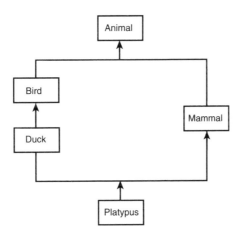

Fig. 13.3
Multiple
inheritance.

In figure 13.3, there is one root class, named Animal, from which every other class is derived. Every derived class except the Platypus class has a single base class. The Mammal and Bird classes are derived from the Animal class, and the Duck class is derived from the Bird class. So each of those classes is created in a simple way, using single inheritance.

The Platypus class is created differently. It has two base classes: the Mammal and Duck classes. Because the Platypus class has two parent classes instead of one, you can say that it is derived using multiple inheritance.

Using More than Two Base Classes

When you derive a class using multiple inheritance, the derived class is not limited to having two base classes. In figure 13.4, which shows how rock music evolved in the 1950s, three classes are derived from a base class named Music. Those classes are named Pop, R&B (rhythm and blues), and Country. Finally, another derived class, named Rock, is derived from the Pop, R&B, and Country classes.

Fig. 13.4
Multiple inheritance in the music business.

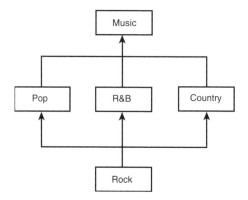

Multiple Inheritance in the Animal Kingdom

When you define a class in a C++ program and you want the new class to inherit member variables or member functions from more than one base class, you can create the new class by using multiple inheritance. To create a class that inherits data or behaviors using multiple inheritancy, all you have to do is specify the base classes of the new class in the heading of its definition, as shown in this example:

```
class Platypus: public Mammal, public Duck {
public:
      void What()
            { cout << "What am I?\n"; }
      void Conclusion()
            { cout << "I'm a duckbilled platypus.\n"; }
};
```

The preceding code fragment, taken from the PLATYPUS program shown in listing 13.2, defines an object named Platypus. The PLATYPUS program corresponds with the class diagram shown earlier in figure 13.2. The program uses multiple inheritance to identify some characteristics of the duckbilled platypus.

Listing 13.2 Multiple Inheritance

```
// Demonstrating Multiple Inheritance

#include <iostream.h>

class Animal {
public:
      void General()
            { cout << "I'm a sentient creature.\n"; }
};
```

```
class Bird: virtual public Animal {
public:
     void Mouth()
          { cout << "I have a beak.\n"; }
     void BirthMethod()
          { cout << "I lay eggs.\n"; }
};

class Duck: public Bird {
public:
     void Mouth()
          { cout << "I have a bill.\n"; }
};

class Mammal: virtual public Animal {
public:
     void Coat()
          { cout << "I have fur.\n"; }
};

class Platypus: public Mammal, public Duck {
public:
     void What()
          { cout << "What am I?\n"; }
     void Conclusion()
          { cout << "I'm a duckbilled platypus.\n"; }
};

int main()
{
     Platypus mysteryBeast;

     mysteryBeast.What();
     mysteryBeast.General();
     mysteryBeast.Coat();
     mysteryBeast.Mouth();
     mysteryBeast.BirthMethod();
     mysteryBeast.Conclusion();

     return 0;
}
```

The PLATYPUS program in listing 13.2 corresponds exactly to the class diagram shown earlier in figure 13.3. Every class defined in the program except the Platypus class inherits from a single base class named Animal. The Mammal and Bird classes are derived from the Animal class, and the Duck class is derived from the Bird class. So each of those classes is created using single inheritance.

In listing 13.2, just as in figure 13.3, the Platypus class has two base classes: Mammal and Duck. So the Platypus class is defined using multiple inheritance.

When you execute the program, this is its output:

```
What am I?
I am a sentient creature.
I have fur.
I have a bill.
I lay eggs.
I'm a duckbilled platypus.
```

Virtual Base Classes

Because computers do what you say, not what you mean (except when you use polymorphism), there are some precautions that you have to take when you use multiple inheritance. For example, when a derived class inherits member functions from multiple base classes, you must make sure that there are no ambiguities in the names of the functions.

One common technique for avoiding ambiguities in function names is to create virtual base classes. In the definition of a derived class, as you learned earlier in this chapter, you can declare a base class to be a virtual base class by preceding the name of the base class with the keyword `virtual`.

In the PLATYPUS program, for example, the definitions of the `Bird` and `Mammal` classes declare the `Animal` class to be a virtual base class. These are the lines in the program in which the `Animal` class is declared to be virtual:

```
class Bird: virtual public Animal {
// ...
class Mammal: virtual public Animal {
// ...
```

When a derived class declares a base class to be virtual, the `virtual` keyword instructs the compiler to construct only one subobject of the base class. In the PLATYPUS program, if the `Animal` class were not declared to be virtual, the program's class hierarchy would not be constructed as shown back in figure 13.3. Instead, it would look like the hierarchy shown in figure 13.5.

In figure 13.5, because the `Animal` class is not designated virtual, there are two subobjects of the `Animal` class. One is created when the `Bird` class is instantiated, and another is created when the `Mammal` class is instantiated.

When two subobjects of the `Animal` class exist, an ambiguity arises when the program's `main()` function calls the `General()` function, which is a member function of the `Animal` class. In the program architecture shown in figure 13.5, because there are two `Animal` derived objects, there also are two copies of the `Animal::General()` function. The two copies are identical, but the compiler has no way of knowing that. It simply detects an ambiguity and returns an error message.

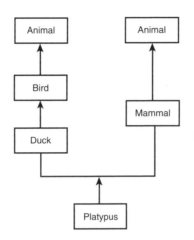

Fig. 13.5
Multiple inherit-
ance without
virtual base
classes.

You can resolve this ambiguity by simply declaring the Animal class to be a virtual base class. When you make the Animal class a virtual base class, the compiler creates only one copy of Animal subobjects, no matter how many objects of the class are instantiated. Then the compiler accesses the class object through a table of addresses, in much the same way that virtual member functions are accessed through v-tables.

Static Member Variables

Every C programmer uses global variables, but should remember how danger-ous they can be. The problem is that global variables are too vulnerable. Any function can change the value of a global variable; all too often a global variable is inadvertently modified, from somewhere out in left field, by a function you may not even remember writing. Unexpected changes in global variables can wreak havoc on C programs, and can be enormously difficult to track down.

You can use global variables in C++, but you are strongly encouraged not to. The recommended alternative is to use a different kind of variable that C++ provides: a *static member variable*. Static member variables are used in much the same way that global variables are often used in C++. But static member variables have built-in safety features that make them safer from being inad-vertently changed than ordinary global variables are.

A static member variable is a special kind of variable shared by all objects in a class. When a class has a static member variable, only one copy of the vari-able exists, and that single copy of the variable is shared by all objects that belong to the class. Thus, a static member variable can provide a class with all the benefits of a global variable, but without many of the risks.

In programming situations that would call for a global variable in C, the C++ programmer can often substitute a static member variable. One typical use of a static member variable is to keep track of the number of objects in a list. Each time a program creates an object in the list, you can increment the value of the static member variable, and each time an object is destroyed, you can decrement the variable. In this way, a static member variable can always provide any object in a class with the number of currently active objects in the list.

Creating a Static Member Variable

When you define a class, you can create a static member variable that belongs to the class by preceding the variable's declaration with the static keyword. For example, this statement declares a static member variable named count:

```
static int count;  // declare static member variable
```

If you do not declare a member variable to be static, it is non-static by default.

When you declare a static member variable, a fixed memory location is allocated for the variable at link time; that location doesn't change for the lifetime of the program. In this sense, a static member variable works just like a global variable.

However, access to a static member variable is more limited than access to a global variable. After you have initialized a static member variable, functions outside its class can access it only by using the scope resolution operator (::), preceded by the name of the class in which the variable is declared. To make this technique work, of course, you must make the static variable a public member of the class. And that act removes much of the protection against misuse that is enjoyed by static member variables. So if you want to make a static member accessible outside a class, you should take other precautions, such as keeping the static member variable private, allowing it to be changed from outside the class only through a public static member function (static member functions are described later in this section).

For example, this statement assigns a value of 0 to a static member variable named count that is declared inside the definition of a class named MonteCristo:

```
MonteCristo::count = 0;
```

Declaring and Defining Static Member Variables

Listing 13.3 shows how a static member variable can be used in a C++ program.

Listing 13.3   A Static Member Variable

```
#include <iostream.h>

class SampleClass {
public:
    static int staticVar;       // declare static member variable
    SampleClass() {}
    void SetStaticVar(int a) { staticVar = a; }
};

int SampleClass::staticVar;     // define static member variable

int main()
{
    SampleClass myObject;        // define local object
    myObject.SetStaticVar(100); // initialize static data member
    cout << SampleClass::staticVar << '\n';
    SampleClass::staticVar = 200;
    cout << SampleClass::staticVar << '\n';
    myObject.staticVar = 300;
    cout << SampleClass::staticVar << '\n';
    return 0;
}
```

Using Static Member Variables

In listing 13.3, a static member variable named staticVar is defined inside the definition of a class named SampleClass:

```
class SampleClass {
public:
    static int staticVar;       // declare static member variable
    SampleClass() {}
    void SetStaticVar(int a) { staticVar = a; }
};
```

Next, between the SampleClass definition and the application's main function, staticVar is defined:

```
int SampleClass::staticVar;     // define static member variable
```

Because static member variables can be shared by multiple functions, they must be defined and declared in this peculiar way. You must *declare* a static member inside a class definition, but you must *define* it outside the definition of its class.

When a static member variable has been declared and defined, it is accessible from any member function of its class. If it is a public or a protected member variable, you also can access it from other classes—or from outside any class—in accordance with normal rules of accessibility.

Accessing a Static Member Variable

In listing 13.3, a class named `SampleClass` has a member variable named `SetStaticVar()` that can be called to set the value of the static member variable named `staticVar`:

```
void SetStaticVar(int a) { staticVar = a; }
```

The following statement in the `main()` segment of the program sets the value of `staticVar` by calling the member function `SetStaticVar()`:

```
myObject.SetStaticVar(100);
```

Because access to `staticVar` is public, the `main()` segment also can set the value of `staticVar` by accessing the variable directly:

```
SampleClass::staticVar = 200;
```

Notice that in this statement, the scope resolution operator (`::`)— preceded by the name of `SampleClass`—is used to access `staticVar`.

Another statement in the `main()` segment of listing 13.3 accesses `staticVar` with the dot operator (`.`) preceded by the name of the object `myObject`. This construct is possible because a static member variable that has public access is from anywhere in its module:

```
myObject.staticVar = 300;
```

In the `main()` segment of listing 13.3, all three of the techniques shown in the three preceding examples are used to assign values to `staticVar`:

```
main()
      SampleClass myObject;          // define local object
      myObject.SetStaticVar(100);   // initialize static data
                                    // members
      cout << SampleClass::staticVar << '\n';
      SampleClass::staticVar = 200;
      cout << SampleClass::staticVar << '\n';
      myObject.staticVar = 300;
      cout << SampleClass::staticVar << '\n';
      return 0;
}
```

In the preceding code fragment, it's important to remember that because `staticVar` is a static member variable, only one copy of the variable exists. That means that each assignment statement shown in the preceding code fragment assigns a value to the same memory location, overwriting the previous value of `staticVar`.

Private Static Member Variables

A static member variable, like any other member variable, can be public, protected, or private. If a static member variable is private, it cannot be accessed from a function outside its class unless access to it is specifically granted—for example, through friendship status or through a public member function.

Listing 13.4 shows how a program can use a private static member variable to keep track of objects that belong to a class.

Listing 13.4   A Private Static Member Variable

```
#include <iostream.h>

class LittleList {
private:
    static int ct;       // declare static member variable
public:
    LittleList() { ct++; }
    ~LittleList() { ct--; }
    static int GetCount() { return ct; }  // static member
                                          // function
};

int LittleList::ct = 0;    // initialize static member variable

int main()
{
    LittleList obj1, obj2, obj3;    // define local objects
    cout << "Number of objects: " << LittleList::GetCount() << '\n';
    return 0;
}
```

The name of the static member variable used in listing 13.4 is ct. Although access to ct is private, the variable is initialized using the same technique that would be used to define any other static member. That isn't surprising because there is only one way to define a static member variable: from outside the variable's class in a statement that accesses the variable using the scope resolution operator (::):

```
int LittleList::ct = 0;
// initialize static member variable
```

With one exception, the format of this statement is the same as the format of the statement that initialized the static member variable staticVar back in listing 13.3. The exception is that in the preceding definition, the value of the variable being defined is initialized with a specified value.

Of course this difference has nothing to do with whether the variable is public or private; any static member variable can be initialized when it is defined.

In listing 13.4, the static member variable ct is used to keep a running count of three objects in a class named LittleList. The objects are named obj1, obj2, and obj3.

In the program, each time an object of the LittleList class is initialized, the object's constructor increments the ct variable:

```
LittleList() { ct++; }
```

Similarly, each time an object's destructor is called, ct is decremented:

```
~LittleList() { ct--; }
```

Because ct is a private variable and because no friends of the LittleList class are declared, the only way to access ct from outside its class is through a member function. In listing 13.4, ct is accessed through a public member variable named GetCount():

```
cout << "Number of objects: " << LittleList::GetCount() << '\n';
```

The preceding statement, which appears in the program's main() section, accesses the GetCount() member function using the scope resolution operator (::).

Static Member Functions

Now that you know about static member variables, you will probably not be surprised to find out that C++ programs also have *static member functions*. As you learned in Chapter 12, an ordinary, non-static member function can access any member of the class in which the function is declared. A static member function, by contrast, can access only the static member variables. So, when you create a class that includes a static member variable, you can access that variable with a static member function.

When you declare a member function inside a class definition, you can declare it to be a static member function by preceding its definition with the static keyword. If you do not declare a member function to be static, it is non-static by default. For example, inside the definition of a class named ObjectCount, you can declare a static member function named Count() using this syntax:

```
class Ob;
ectcount
{
```

```
private:
     int x;
protected:
     static int ct;
public:
     static int Count(); // declaring static member function }
```

In the preceding class definition, the static member function `Count()` can access the static member variable `ct`, but it cannot access the non-static member variable `x`. That's because a static member function can access static member variables and other static member functions. A static member function cannot access non-static member variables or non-static member functions.

Another feature of a static member function is that it has no `this` pointer. As noted in Chapter 12, the `this` pointer is a hidden pointer to the current object. The `this` pointer is secretly passed to the member function. The member function can then use that unseen pointer to access any other member of its class. Because a static member function is not associated with any particular object of a class, a static member function has no `this` pointer. So a static member function can't access any non-static member variables or member functions of a class.

Inline Member Functions

In Chapter 12, you learned that constructors and destructors can be implemented as *inline* functions—that is, functions that are declared and defined at the same time, inside the declaration of a class.

Other kinds of functions can also be declared and defined inline. Listing 13.1, at the beginning of this chapter, contains a number of inline member functions. These member functions of the `Employee` class are all declared and defined inline:

```
void SetName(char *name) { m_name = name; }
void SetDept(char *dept) { m_dept = dept; }
void SetPosition(char *position)
     { m_position = position; }
void SetSalary(long salary)
     { m_salary = salary; }
```

The *inline* Keyword

All the inline member functions in the preceding example are declared and defined in the same step. That is the most common way to implement inline member functions. But it is also possible to declare an inline function in one place and define it in another. To do that, you use the `inline` keyword. For example, the `SetName()` function in the preceding example could just as easily be declared this way inside the definition of the `Employee` class:

```
void SetName(char *name);
```

If the `SetName()` function is declared as shown in the preceding statement, it subsequently would have to be defined as follows to be compiled as an inline member function:

```
inline void Employee::SetName(char *name)
{
    m_name = name;
}
```

Because the `inline` keyword is used in the preceding function definition, the effect is the same as the effect of the one-step declaration and definition of `Employee::SetName()` that actually occurs in the EMPDATA program: When the `Employee::SetName()` member function is compiled as shown in the preceding example, it is compiled as an inline member function.

Characteristics of Inline Member Functions

You can implement any function as an inline function, but that does not necessarily mean that your compiler will implement the function inline. That depends on a complicated set of rules used by the compiler, and different compilers implement inline functions different ways. Nonetheless, conventional wisdom is that inline functions work best when they are short, fast, and efficient. These are roughly the same characteristics that macros in C programs should have.

When you want to write a short routine that a program can call without the stack-manipulation overhead that functions require, you can implement the routine as an inline function. Inline functions run much faster than ordinary functions do, usually at the cost of a slight increase in program size.

How Inline Member Functions Work

The difference between an inline member function and an ordinary member function is that your compiler does not call an inline function using the standard C++ calling convention. That means that the compiler does not call an inline member function by placing local variables on the stack. Instead, each time an inline member function is called, the compiler attempts to make a verbatim copy of the function body and to place that copy at the point in the source code at which the function is called. Then, if this attempt is successful, your program executes the function inline, without touching the stack.

If an inline member function is too long to be pasted into a program at each point where it's called—or if a compiler decides for some other reason that the function should not be implemented as an inline function—the compiler doesn't expand the function at the point where it is called. Instead, the compiler makes just one copy of the function. Then your program calls this copy of the function each time the function appears, using a stack-based calling method similar to the standard C++ calling convention.

Friend Classes and Friend Functions

In at least one respect, C++ is a friendly language. In a C++ program, you can declare classes and functions to be friends of each other—and in C++, as in life, there are special bonds between friends.

In C++, an object can grant friendship status to any function in a program by simply identifying the function to be a friend by using the `friend` keyword. Then the friend function that has been granted friend status can access all private and protected members of the object that has befriended it.

An object can also grant friend status to another object. In this case, too, the object that has been named a friend is granted access to the other object's private and protected members.

Friend functions and friend objects can be useful when you want to relax the access rules that ordinarily apply to private and protected member variables. For example, suppose you write a program that has to execute a public member function of a class repeatedly because it needs access to a certain private data member of a class. In such a situation—which arises often in C++ programming—each read or write of the desired data member requires the overhead that normally results from a call to a function. To eliminate this overhead, you can specify that the accessing function is a friend of the class that owns the desired member variable.

You can also use friend classes to prevent class descriptions from growing to unwieldy lengths. If there is a particular set of variables and functions that a class refers to only rarely, you can place them in a class and then make that class a friend of the class that refers to them from time to time. That way, the variables and functions that are accessed only from time to time can be kept separate from the class that sometimes accesses them.

> **Caution**
>
> In C++, as in life, friendships can be abused. If you find that you're using friends all over the place in your applications to circumvent the data- and code-protection mechanisms built into C++, you should take a close look at your programming habits. The truth is that friends, while useful at times, should not appear very often in your C++ programs.

The *friend* Keyword

To declare friend classes and friend functions, you use the `friend` keyword. The `friend` keyword is usually used inside a class definition. You can use it in three ways:

- When you declare that a class is a friend of another class, the class that is granted friendship status has access to all private and protected members of the class that contains the `friend` declaration.

- A class can also grant friendship status to a member function of another class. The class that is granted friendship status becomes a friend of the class that is being defined. By preceding the declaration of the member function with the keyword `friend`, you can declare that the specified nonmember function is a friend of the class being defined.

- Finally, a class can grant friendship status to a function that is not a member of another class—that is, to a standalone function that appears anywhere in a program.

You can declare a class to be a friend of a member function of another class. To do that, you simply precede the declaration of the friend class with the keyword `friend`, using this kind of syntax:

```
void HighClass::Befriend()
{
    friend OtherClass;
    // ...
}
```

In the preceding function definition, a class named `OtherClass` is declared to be a friend of a member function of another class, named `HighClass`. From that point on, functions in the `HighClass::Befriend()` member function can access private variables of the class named `OtherClass`, even though `Befriend()` is not a member function of the class named `OtherClass`.

Another way to use the `friend` keyword is to declare that a member function of one class is a friend of another class:

```
class HighClass {
private:
     void Befriend();
protected:
     friend int OtherClass::FriendMembFunc();
};
```

Friend Declarations and Access Specifiers

In the preceding class definition, the member function `OtherClass::FriendMembFunc()` is declared to be a friend of a class named `HighClass`.

One-Way Friendships

One important fact about friend labels is that they are effective in only one direction. In the preceding definition of the class named `HighClass`, the member function named `OtherClass::FriendMembFunc()` is declared to be a friend of `HighClass`, so it has access to all the `private` and `protected` members of `HighClass`. But nothing in the definition of `HighClass` grants `HighClass` any access to private and protected members of the class named `OtherClass`. If such access were granted, it would have to be granted inside the class definition of `OtherClass`.

Friend Classes and Friend Functions in a C++ Program

Listing 13.5 shows how friend classes and friend functions can be used in a C++ program. In this program, a class named `FriendlyClass` is granted friendship access to another class and to two functions. `FriendlyClass` then exercises its friendship rights by printing some privileged information to standard output, normally the screen.

Listing 13.5   Using Friends

```
// Using friends

#include <iostream.h>
class FriendlyClass {
private:
     friend class FriendlyClass2;
     friend main();
     int privateVar;
     FriendlyClass():privateVar(500) {}   // private constructor
public:
```

(continues)

Listing 13.5 Continued

```
            int GetPrivateVar() { return privateVar; }
    };

    FriendlyClass *GlobalFriendlyClass;

    class FriendlyClass2 {
    private:
            int privateVar2;
    public:
            FriendlyClass2(FriendlyClass *x) :
                    privateVar2(x->privateVar) {} // constructor
            int GetPrivateVar2() { return privateVar2; }
    };

    int main()
    {
            int x, y;
            FriendlyClass *myFriendlyClass = new FriendlyClass;
            FriendlyClass2 myFriendlyClass2(myFriendlyClass);
            x = myFriendlyClass->GetPrivateVar();
            cout << x << '\n';

            y = myFriendlyClass2.GetPrivateVar2();
            cout << y << '\n';

            return 0;
    }
```

In listing 13.5, an object named FriendlyClass grants friendship status to a class named FriendlyClass2. FriendlyClass also grants friendship status to two functions: the program's main() function and a private member function named MakeAnObject.

Because FriendlyClass2 and MakeAnObject are declared as friends, both FriendlyClass2 and MakeAnObject have access to a private member variable of FriendlyClass named privateVar. The privateVar variable is declared in the definition of FriendlyClass.

Listing 13.5 contains an interesting precaution that helps prevent misuse of its friend mechanisms. The safeguard is that the constructor of the class named FriendlyClass is designated private. That means only friends of FriendlyClass can instantiate FriendlyClass objects. Another special feature of the program is that its main() function is declared to be a friend of the class named FriendlyClass. This feature permits the main() function to create FriendlyClass objects.

```
int x, y;
FriendlyClass *myFriendlyClass = new FriendlyClass;
FriendlyClass2 myFriendlyClass2(myFriendlyClass);
x = myFriendlyClass->privateVar;
cout << x << '\n';

y = myFriendlyClass2.GetPrivateVar2();
cout << y << '\n';
```

When you execute the program in listing 13.5, the main() function constructs two objects: one named FriendlyClass and one named FriendlyClass2. FriendlyClass is constructed on the heap, and FriendlyClass2 is constructed on the stack.

Notice that the FriendlyClass function has a constructor that is declared private. But main() is permitted to construct a FriendlyClass object anyway because the class definition of FriendlyClass declares main() to be a friend of FriendlyClass.

When the FriendlyClass function is constructed, the FriendlyClass constructor uses an initializer list (see "Initializer Lists" in Chapter 12) to set the value of a private integer variable named privateVar to 500. When FriendlyClass2 is initialized, FriendlyClass2 obtains the value of FriendlyClass's privateVar and stores that value in a private variable of its own named privateVar2. This is permitted because FriendlyClass2 is a friend of FriendlyClass.

When the main() function has constructed a FriendlyClass object and a FriendlyClass2 object, main() obtains the values of the FriendlyClass::privateVar and FriendlyClass::privateVar2 variables and prints them out. The main() function is able to obtain the value of FriendlyClass::privateVar directly, without any difficulty, because main() is a friend of FriendlyClass. However, main() is not a friend of FriendlyClass2. Therefore, main() has to obtain the value of FriendlyClasss::privateVar2 in a more conventional way: by calling a member function that retrieves the value of the variable.

Because each variable retrieved by main() contains the value 500, the program's output is the following:

```
500
500
```

The *new* and *delete* Operators

In many ways, C++ is a higher-level language than C. One area in which this is most evident is memory management. In C, you're pretty much on your own when it comes to allocating and deallocating memory. C does allocate memory space for data when you declare a pointer. So you must allocate the memory you need yourself by calling `malloc` or performing some other action to allocate memory manually.

C++ is a little kinder than that. In C++, instead of calling a function to allocate or deallocate memory, you invoke an operator. C++ provides two memory-management operators—new and `delete`—that allocate and deallocate memory from a memory supply called the *free store*.

The new and `delete` operators are more versatile than `malloc` and `free` because they can associate the allocation of memory with the way you use it. They are also more reliable because the compiler performs type-checking each time a program allocates memory with new. Another advantage stems from the fact that C++ implements new and `delete` as operators, not functions. That means new and `delete` are built into the C++ language itself, so programs can use new and `delete` without including any header files.

Still another important feature of the new and `delete` operators is that they never require typecasting—and that makes new and `delete` easier to use than `malloc` and `free`.

The *new* Operator

When you call the `malloc` function in a C program, you pass a size to `malloc` and the function returns a `void` pointer, which you must cast to whatever data type you want. For example, suppose you want to allocate memory for a `struct` in a C program. Suppose the `struct` is of a type named `Memory`, and suppose you want to call the `struct` `memBlock`. In a C program, you might write these statements:

```
struct Memory *memBlock;
memBlock = (struct Memory*)
    malloc(sizeof(struct Memory));
```

The preceding statement returns a void pointer, which you must then cast to a pointer to a `Memory` structure.

Using the new operator is similar but simpler. The new operator also returns a pointer, but it isn't a `void` pointer, so you don't have to cast the pointer to the data type for which you are obtaining memory. Instead, the new operator returns the kind of pointer you have requested. To illustrate, you can obtain memory for an object named `memBlock` by writing the following pair of statements:

```
Memory *memblock;
memblock = new Memory;
```

If you want to be more concise, you can write:

```
Memory *memBlock = new Memory;
```

The `new` operator can allocate memory for data structures that are not objects of classes. For example, this code fragment allocates memory for an array of integers:

```
int *intArray;
intArray = new int[1000];
```

This more concise statement has the same effect:

```
int *intArray = new int[1000];
```

Both of the preceding examples declare a pointer named `intArray` and initialize it to the address returned by `new`. If a pointer of the requested size is available, `new` returns a pointer to the beginning of a block of memory of the specified size. If there is not enough dynamic storage available to satisfy a request, `new` returns a zero.

Each time you compile an expression that invokes the `new` operator, the compiler performs a type check to make sure that the type of the pointer specified on the left side of the operator is the correct type for the memory being allocated on the right. If the types don't match, the compiler issues an error message.

When you have invoked the `new` operator, you can find out whether `new` has succeeded in fulfilling your request for memory by simply checking the value that the `new` operator returns. The `new` operator returns a pointer value. If a zero value is returned, memory allocation has failed.

The *delete* Operator

When you allocate memory with the `new` operator, you can delete it with the `delete` operator. The `delete` operator is easy to use, but it can be dangerous if you don't use it wisely. In fact, the `delete` operator can crash programs if you aren't careful. But by exercising some common-sense precautions, you can keep that from happening.

The delete operator is safe if the pointer to the object being deleted is NULL or if the pointer correctly addresses allocated memory. But problems can arise if a nonzero pointer does not actually have memory allocated for an object at its address, and a program attempts to delete at that pointer's address.

This problem can occur two ways: if a program inadvertently neglects to allocate memory and associate it with a pointer, or if a program inadvertently deletes memory associated with a pointer more than once.

The safe way to avoid these two situations is to always initialize pointers to NULL and always set all pointers to NULL immediately after their associated memory is deleted.

For example, suppose a program contains an object of type Memory. Also suppose the object is pointed to by a pointer named m_pMemBlock, which is declared in a header file. To allocate memory for the object pointed to by m_pMemBlock, you can initialize the m_pMemblock pointer to a NULL value before allocating memory with the new operator:

```
Initialize()
{
      m_pMemBlock = NULL;
};
```

Once the preceding function is executed, it is safe to allocate memory for m_pMemBlock using this statement:

```
m_pMemblock = new Memory;
```

Templates

As you may recall from Chapter 12, the Turbo C++ for Windows class library is based on *templates,* a feature of C++ that allows a special kind of class called a *container* to hold virtually any data type.

In C++, templates are often used as containers, or wrappers, for collections of data. With a template, you can use the same C++ class to store collections of different kinds of data. For example, the Turbo C++ class library provides a template-based class named TArrayAsVector that is designed for the storage of arrays. When you instantiate an object of the TArrayAsVector class, you can declare the array type to be anything you desire: string, integer, or one of your own classes.

When you encounter a template in a C++ program, you can always identify it
as a template by the angle brackets in the header of its definition. For example, you might see the TArrayAsVector template instantiated this way in a
Turbo C++ program:

```
TArrayAsVector<float>FloatArray;
```

In the preceding statement, FloatArray is the name of the object instance
being created, and the word float appears between a pair of angle brackets.
Why is this construct used? Because in this case, the TArrayAsVector template
being initialized will hold an array of values of the float data type.

What makes templates so useful is that they are not restricted to holding
information of specific data types. A TArrayAsVector template, for example,
can also be declared as a template that will hold an array of string objects:

```
TArrayAsVector<string>StringArray;
```

In fact, a TArrayAsVector template can even hold an array of user-declared
objects:

```
TArrayAsVector<MyClass> MyClassArray;
```

Furthermore, TArrayAsVector is not the only kind of template provided in the
Turbo C++ class library. Turbo C++ provides many kinds of templates, which
can be used not only to store arrays of objects, but also to store linked lists,
doubly linked lists, hashed lists, and even "bags"—collections of data that fall
into no readily definable structure.

The sample program named AGES, presented at the end of Chapter 12 in
listing 12.11, shows how two kinds of templates can be used in Turbo C++
programs. The AGES program demonstrates the use of the TDDAssociation
class, which binds a direct key with a direct value, and the
TDictionaryAsHashTable class, which implements a dictionary of objects.

In the AGES application, TDDAssociation objects are used to hold the names
and ages of a group of people, and the TDictionaryAsHashTable object is used
to build up a dictionary of the TDDAssociation objects used in the program.
Figure 13.6 shows the output of the program.

Fig. 13.6
The output of the
AGES program.

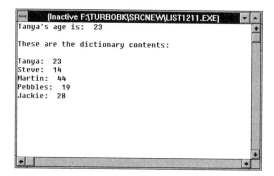

```
     [Inactive F:\TURBOBK\SRCNEW\LIST1211.EXE]
Tanya's age is:  23

These are the dictionary contents:

Tanya:  23
Steve:  14
Martin:  44
Pebbles:  19
Jackie:  28
```

From Here...

This chapter covered the fundamental techniques of object-oriented
programming with Turbo C++—techniques such as polymorphism, multiple
inheritance, static member variables, and the use of the `new` and `delete` operators. For a closer look at some of the topics introduced in this chapter, see:

■ Chapter 8, "Functions and Macros," shows how argument matching is
used in overloaded member functions.

■ Chapter 11, "I/O," demonstrates the use of the the `cin` and `cout` objects,
the << and >> operators, and other aspects of Turbo C++ streams.

■ Chapter 12, "Classes and Objects," shows how to create a class, how to
instantiate an object from a class, and how to create and use member
variables and member functions. It also shows how to use such special
features of C++ as class hierarchies, function overloading, and operator
overloading.

■ Chapter 14, "Exception Handling," shows how exception handling
provides Turbo C++ with state-of-the-art error management.

Chapter 14

Exception Handling

This chapter focuses on handling errors that occur at run time. In Turbo C++, such errors take the form of exceptions. Turbo C++ has implemented exception handling in accordance with the specifications of the American National Standards Institute (ANSI). Turbo C++ supports only synchronous exceptions; that is, exceptions that occur from within your program (for example, memory errors, math errors, and so on). The following is a list of topics covered in this chapter:

- The uses and benefits of exception handling in general

- The implementation of exception handling in C++

- An overview of the exception classes provided with the Runtime Library (RTL) and an explanation of creating custom exception classes

- What to do when there is no handler for the current exception

- A discussion of the IDE settings that deal with exception handling

- Implementation of exception handling in a common application

Understanding Exceptions

Turbo C++ offers exception handling as a more structured way of handling errors that occur during the execution of a program. The exception handling mechanism empowers the programmer to trap such errors and take action accordingly. Such action may take the form of correcting the problem and continuing on, or simply terminating the program gracefully.

What Are Exceptions?

An *exception* is an event that causes a program to stop executing and transfer control to a special routine designed to handle the exception. Turbo C++ provides only a mechanism for exception handling. Implementation of such a routine is the programmer's responsibility. If no routine is provided, the program will terminate.

There is only one predefined exception class, xmsg, provided with Turbo C++. This exception class is part of the Runtime Library (RTL), and is defined in except.h. xalloc is derived from the xmsg class. Please refer to the xmsg class and xalloc class sections later in this chapter.

What Are the Benefits of Exception Handling?

Exception handling offers a more structured approach to error handling. Consider the following code, which demonstrates a very common method of detecting memory-allocation errors:

```
...
if ((buf = (char *) malloc(1024) == NULL)
{
    cout << "Allocation has failed!" << endl;
    exit(EXIT_FAILURE);
}
...
```

The problem with this method of error handling is that you need to repeat the same code for each buffer you want to create. This can result in much redundant code. Another problem is that the error-handling code becomes integrated with the actual working code of the program. This decreases the readability of the code. Both of these problems increase the risk that you'll make errors when modifying the code.

Exception handling has the following major benefits:

- It allows you to handle related errors in one centralized location. Overall, this central location reduces the size of the error-handling code, because you don't have to repeat the error-handling code if there are other places in the program where the same errors might occur. This also makes the overall program more readable and reduces the risk of errors when you make changes to the program.

- You can gather information about the error at the point where the error occurred, then pass this information to the handler. The handler can use this information to determine the appropriate course of action.

Using Exception Handling

In a perfect world, programs would work without a glitch. However, you do not live in a perfect world and the likelihood of errors manifesting themselves while a program is executing is great. Use exception handling to make an application more robust. With exception handling, it is possible to keep problems from occurring, or to recover when they do happen.

Exception Handling Syntax

Exception handling is a complex topic; however, the syntax involved in its implementation is not. There are three important keywords: try, throw, and catch.

try

Use the try keyword to delimit blocks of code that may raise exceptions. For example

```
try {
    char *name = new char[100];
    int  *age = new int();
}
```

In the preceding example, the new operator may raise an xalloc exception if it is unable to allocate the requested memory.

throw

Use the throw keyword to raise an exception. For example

```
if ((buf = malloc(1000)) == NULL)
{
    throw xalloc(string("Out of Memory"));
}
else
    return buf;
```

In the preceding example, if the memory allocation fails, an xalloc exception is raised. For more information about raising exceptions, please refer to the "Raising an Exception" section later in the chapter.

catch

Use catch to handle exceptions thrown in a try block. More than one catch block may exist for each try block, but they always must follow a try block. For example

```
try {
    char *name = new char[100];
}
catch (xalloc &Error) {
    cout << Error.why() << endl;
}
```

In the preceding example, it is possible for the new operator to raise an exception. If this happens, the catch block executes and you see a message indicating the failure.

Raising an Exception

The throw keyword is used to raise an exception. When an exception is raised, execution of the current routine stops, and control is passed to a handling routine, called a *handler*. If the compiler cannot find a handler, the exception becomes unhandled, and the program simply terminates. Please refer to the "Handling an Exception" section for an explanation of handling exceptions. For more information about unhandled exceptions, please refer to the "Unhandled Exceptions" section.

Raising an exception occurs in two ways. The most common way is to specify an expression after the throw keyword. For example

```
throw "Error";
throw ExceptionObject;
```

Both statements raise an exception; however, they raise different types of exceptions. This is important when trying to handle these exceptions. Since these are different types of exceptions, a handler must be specified for each type.

The second way to raise an exception is to use the throw keyword by itself. When an exception is raised, control is passed to a handler. At this point, the exception exists. If the throw keyword is used by itself in this handler, the exception is raised again. For example

```
try {

    throw xmsg (string("Exception"));

}

catch (xmsg &msg) {

    // xmsg exception currently exists, and is being handled.

    // Use throw to re-raise the xmsg exception.

    throw;

}
```

Copy Constructor

When throwing objects, a temporary object is created at the point at which
the exception was thrown. In this case, the *copy constructor* is called. That's
why it is important to provide a copy constructor for your exception classes.
However, this is not a requirement; implement one only if your class needs it.
For example

```
class ExceptOne {
    public:
        ExceptOne() {}
        ~ExceptOne() {};
        void Message()
        {
            cout << "An exception has occurred!" << endl;
        }
};

class ExceptTwo {
    public:
        // Copy constructor is needed to initialize
        // private member.
        ExceptTwo(ExceptTwo &Src)
        {
            ErrMsg = new string(Src.Message());
        }
        ExceptTwo(string &Msg)
        {
            ErrMsg = new string(Msg);
        }
        ~ExceptTwo()
        {
            delete ErrMsg;
        }
        string & Message()
        {
            return *ErrMsg;
        }
    private:
        string *ErrMsg;
};
```

Because the first class has no members to initialize, you do not need a copy
constructor. However, the second class does have a member that requires
initialization, so a copy constructor is needed.

Exception Specifications

When creating functions, you can specify the types of exceptions allowed to propagate out of the function. When specifying such a list, you are creating exception specifications for the function. Consider the following function declarations:

```
// Only DivideByZero exceptions can propagate from this function.
int Div(int x, int y) throw(DivideByZero)
{
    ...some program statements
}

// Only NegativeSqRoot exceptions can propagate from this function.
int SqRt(int x) throw(NegativeSqRoot)
{
    ...some program statements
}

// Only xalloc exceptions can propagate from this function.
void * AllocMem(size_t x) throw(xalloc)
{
    ...some program statements
}

// EObjOne and EObjTwo exceptions can propagate from this function.
int MyFunc1() throw (EObjOne, EObjTwo)
{
    ...some program statements
}

// No exceptions can propagate from this function.
int MyFunc2() throw()
{
    ...some program statements
}

// Any type of exception can propagate from this function.
int MyFunc3()
{
    ...some program statements
}
```

Only the exceptions listed in the exception specification can propagate from a function. The function must handle all other exceptions. If it fails to do so, the unexpected() function is called.

unexpected()

When an exception that is not specified in the exception specification propagates from a function, the unexpected() function executes. The default behavior for unexpected() is to call abort(), terminating the program. You may use the set_unexpected() function to specify your own behavior. This is described on the following page.

set_unexpected()

Since the default behavior of the unexpected() function is to call the abort()
function and end the program, it is likely that the remaining environment
may be unfit for other applications to execute properly. For example,
Windows applications usually load cursors, icons, bitmaps, and other resources into memory when they execute. In order for these resources to be
available to other programs, the application must free its resources before
quitting. If an unhandled exception occurs and the program simply terminates, these resources will not be available until Windows is restarted. This
poses a serious problem, and you can't ignore it.

However, there is a solution. It is possible for an application to register its
own function, which will be called instead of unexpected(). This function
could perform the proper cleanup, then call the abort() function. The function used to register the replacement function is set_unexpected() and is
defined in the except.h header file. See listing 14.1 for an example of registering the replacement function.

**Listing 14.1   setunexp.cpp—A Program that Registers the
Replacement Function**

```cpp
#include <windows.h>
#include <except.h>
#include <cstring.h>

void My_Unexpected()
{
   // Cleanup code goes here...
   MessageBox(NULL, "Function successfully called!",
                    "My_Unexpected()", MB_OK | MB_SYSTEMMODAL);
   abort();
}

void MyFunc(int ExceptionType) throw (xmsg)
{
   // If the parameter is 1, throw the allowed exception
   if (ExceptionType == 1)
      throw xmsg(string("This exception is okay to throw!"));
   else
      throw "Exception!";
}

int PASCAL WinMain(HINSTANCE, HINSTANCE, LPSTR, int)
{
   // Register the replacement function
   set_unexpected(My_Unexpected);
   try {
```

(continues)

Listing 14.1 Continued

```
            // This will cause MyFunc() to throw an xmsg exception.
            // Since xmsg is listed in the exception specification,
            // the handler below will execute.
            MyFunc(1);
        }
        catch (xmsg &Error) {
            MessageBox(NULL, Error.why().c_str(),
                        "xmsg Exception", MB_OK ¦ MB_ICONINFORMATION);
        }

        try {
            // This will cause MyFunc() to throw an char * exception.
            // Since char * is not listed in the exception
            // specification, unexpected() is called.
            MyFunc(2);
        }
        catch (xmsg &Error) {
            MessageBox(NULL, Error.why().c_str(),
                        "xmsg Exception", MB_OK ¦ MB_ICONINFORMATION);
        }
        return 1;
    }
```

The preceding example demonstrates two things: the steps needed to register a user-defined unexpected function, and implementation of exception specification.

Handling an Exception

Use catch to handle exceptions thrown in a try block. The catch block must immediately follow a try block. There can be more than one catch block for one try block. Each catch block specifies the type of exception it handles. You must specify a catch block for each exception that the preceding try block might raise. Otherwise, an unhandled exception will occur and terminate() is called. For example

```
    try {
        // Code may cause exceptions
        ... program statements
    }
    catch (int ErrNum) {
        // catches int exceptions
        ... program statements
    }
    catch (const char * Error) {
        // catches const char * exceptions
        ... program statements
    }
    catch (xmsg &Error) {
        // catches xmsg exceptions
```

```
    ... program statements
}
```

To specify a default handler for any exception type, use the ellipses (...) in place of the exception type. For example

```
try {
    // Code may cause exceptions
    ... program statements
}
catch (...) {
    // catches all exceptions
    ... program statements
}
```

When you are specifying an exception type, you can catch derived class types when specifying a base type. For example

```
try {
    // Code may cause exceptions
    ... program statements
}
catch (xmsg &Error) {
    // catches xmsg and xalloc exceptions
    ... program statements
}
```

Because xalloc is derived from xmsg, an xmsg exception can also be handled by this handler. If you want to handle these separately, specify a handler for the derived class first. For example

```
try {
    // Code may cause exceptions
    ... program statements
}
catch (xalloc &Error) {
    // catches xalloc exceptions.
    ... program statements
}
catch (xmsg &Error) {
    // catches xmsg and xalloc exceptions, however
    // xmsg exceptions will always be caught by the
    // preceding handler.
    ... program statements
}
```

Note

Placing the xmsg handler first results in a warning message:

```
Handler for 'xalloc &' hidden by previous handler for 'xmsg &'
    in function ...
```

II

Learning C/C++

Stack Unwinding

When an exception is raised, destructors are called for all automatic objects that were fully created since the beginning of the try block. Destructors are called before control is passed to the handler. This is known as *stack unwinding*. Without stack unwinding, the stack remains polluted after an exception is raised.

To show this concept, start by creating a new class that outputs a message when the destructor executes. Listing 14.2 shows the definition of this class, which is called TestClass.

Listing 14.2 unwind.h—The Definition of the *TestClass* Class

```
#include <iostream.h>
#include <cstring.h>

class TestClass {
   public:
      TestClass(string &msg)
      {
         str = new string(msg);
      }
      ~TestClass()
      {
         cout << "Destructor Called for " << *str << "!" << endl;
         delete str;
      }
   private:
      string *str;
};
```

Now that the TestClass class has been defined, use it to demonstrate the unwinding process. Listing 14.3 implements the class, and the output that is generated shows stack unwinding occurring. Figure 14.1 shows the output generated by this program.

Listing 14.3 unwind01.cpp—The Implementation of the *TestClass* Class

```
#include <iostream.h>
#include <cstring.h>
#include "unwind.h"

void main()
{
   try {
      TestClass var1(string("Var1")), var2(string("Var2"));
```

```
        throw "Exception thrown!";
    }
    catch (const char *ErrMsg) {
        cout << ErrMsg << endl;
    }
}
```

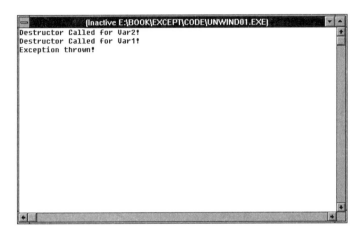

Fig. 14.1
The output
generated by
unwind01.cpp
shows how
automatic objects
are destroyed
during stack
unwinding.

The previous example demonstrated stack unwinding in action. Remember
that stack unwinding occurs only for automatic objects. Objects created dynamically will not be destroyed. Listing 14.4 creates the objects dynamically.
When the exception is thrown, the destructors don't execute and control
is passed to the handler. Figure 14.2 shows the output generated by this
program.

Listing 14.4   unwind02.cpp—Creating Objects Dynamically

```
#include <iostream.h>
#include <cstring.h>
#include "unwind.h"

#pragma warn -aus
void main()
{
    try {
        TestClass *var3, *var4;

        var3 = new TestClass(string("Var3"));
        var4 = new TestClass(string("Var4"));

        throw "Exception thrown!";
    }
```

(continues)

Listing 14.4 Continued

```
        catch (const char *ErrMsg) {
            cout << ErrMsg << endl;
        }
    }
```

Fig. 14.2
The output generated by unwind02.cpp shows how dynamic objects don't get destroyed during stack unwinding.

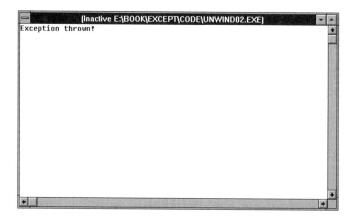

Destructors are called automatically by default. Settings in the Project Options dialog box allow you to disable this behavior. You'll read more about these settings in the "Exception Handling Settings in the IDE" section later in this chapter.

Exception Classes

Turbo C++ comes with a couple of predefined exception classes, xmsg and xalloc. Applications can use these classes directly, or use them as a foundation for new exception classes.

The *xmsg* Class

xmsg is one of the predefined exception classes. xmsg is a very simple class. Its main use is to report a message related to an exception. xmsg is the base class for xalloc. You'll read more about this in "The xalloc Class" section later in the chapter.

Constructors for *xmsg*

There are two constructors for the xmsg class. The first constructor takes a string as a parameter. The string is the error message stored with this exception. The second constructor is the copy constructor and takes an xmsg object as a parameter. The string class is defined in the cstring.h header file. There is no default constructor for the xmsg class. For example

```
// Instantiate an object using xmsg::xmsg(string &)
x = new xmsg(string("Divide by Zero"));

// Instantiate an object using xmsg::xmsg(xmsg &) (copy constructor)
y = new xmsg(x);
```

Public Member Functions for *xmsg*

Use the raise() member function to raise an xmsg exception. For example

```
xmsg(string("Out of Memory")).raise();
```

Use the why() member function to retrieve the message passed to the constructor. For example

```
x = xmsg(string("Out of Memory"));
cout << "An error, " << x.why() << ", has occurred!" << endl;
```

The *xalloc* Class

xalloc is derived from the xmsg class. xalloc has added an additional member to store the requested size and an additional member function, requested(), to retrieve the request size. The requested size must be passed to the constructor when instantiating the exception object. The raise() method has also been modified to throw the xalloc exception.

Constructors for *xalloc*

There are two constructors for the xalloc class. The first constructor takes a string and a size_t as parameters. The string is the error message and the size_t is the requested size stored with this exception. The second constructor is the copy constructor, which takes an xalloc object as a parameter. The string class is defined in the cstring.h header file. There is no default constructor for the xalloc class. For example

```
// Instantiate an object using xalloc:: xalloc(string &, size_t)
x = new xalloc(string("Divide by Zero"), 25);
```

Public Member Functions for *xalloc*

Use the raise() member function to raise a xalloc exception. For example

```
xalloc(string("Out of Memory"), 25).raise();
```

Use the why() member function to retrieve the message passed to the constructor. For example

```
x = xalloc(string("Out of Memory"), 25);
cout << "An error, " << x.why() << ", has occurred!" << endl;
```

Use the `requested()` member function to retrieve the requested size passed to the constructor. For example

```
x = xalloc(string("Out of Memory"), 25);
cout << "Requested: " << x.requested() << endl;
```

Creating Exception Classes

In Turbo C++, exceptions can take the form of almost any data type. However, it is good practice to create specific exception classes. This will allow you to include information about the error in the exception object. Consider the following code:

```
#define OUTOFMEMORY    1
#define DIVIDEBYZERO   2

void MyFunc(void)
{
    // Throw the exception
    throw (OUTOFMEMORY);
}

try {
    // Call the function.
    MyFunc();
}
catch (int ErrNum) {
    // Determine which type of exception was thrown.
    switch (ErrNum) {
        case OUTOFMEMORY:
            cout << "An Out of Memory error has occurred! " << endl;
        case DIVIDEBYZERO:
            cout << "A Divide by Zero error has occurred! " << endl;
        default:
            cout << "An unknown error has occurred! " << endl;
    }
}
```

The preceding code is functional; however, the `switch` statement can become very confusing. This is similar to the use of the `errno` constant used by the RTL functions to report various errors.

Now, consider creating special exception classes. By creating specialized exception classes, it is possible to make exception handling much more clear. Consider the previous example. Start by creating the custom exception classes. Listing 14.5 defines the exception classes.

Listing 14.5 math.h—Defining the Exception Classes

```
#include <iostream.h>

class MathError {
    public:
        MathError() {}
        ~MathError() {}
        virtual void Message() = 0;
};

class DivideByZero : public MathError {
    public:
        DivideByZero() : MathError() {}
        void Message() { cout << "Divide by Zero!" << endl; }
};

class NegativeSqRoot : public MathError {
    public:
        NegativeSqRoot(double Val) : MathError(), Value(Val) {}
        void Message() { cout << "Negative Square Root!" << endl; }
        double Value;
};
```

Errors often arise when you are performing mathematical functions—errors such as division by zero or an attempt to determine the square root of a negative number. To handle such errors, create a hierarchy of math exception classes.

Start with an abstract base class called MathError. MathError has one member function, Message(). Message() will print the error message associated with the class. As classes are derived from MathError, the implementation of Message() will change to print the appropriate message for each class. Polymorphism is used to implement this method in the derived classes. *Polymorphism* is the ability to redefine a method in a derived class. For more information about polymorphism, see Chapter 13, "Object-Oriented Methods."

Now that you have created a base class, derive two types of math exceptions, DivideByZero and NegativeSqRoot. The implementation of Message() for DivideByZero prints "Divide by Zero!". The implementation of Message() for NegativeSqRoot prints "Negative Square Root!". The NegativeSqRoot class also adds a new member, Value. When throwing a NegativeSqRoot exception, pass the offending value in the call to the constructor. For example

```
throw NegativeSqRoot(-4);
```

Now that the definition of the classes is complete, they are ready for implementation. Listing 14.6 demonstrates the implementation of these classes in two user-defined functions.

II

Learning C/C++

Listing 14.6   mathfunc.cpp—Implementing *DivideByZero* and *NegativeSqRoot*

```cpp
#include <math.h>
#include "matherr.h"

int Div(int x, int y)
{
    if (y == 0)
        throw DivideByZero();
    return x/y;
}

double SqRt(double x)
{
    if (x < 0)
        throw NegativeSqRoot(x);

    return sqrt(x);
}
```

Two functions are declared, `Div()` and `SqRt()`. `Div()` returns the result of the integer division of the two given parameters. If the second parameter is zero, a `DivideByZero` exception is thrown. `SqRt()` returns the square root of a given number. If the parameter is negative, a `NegativeSqRoot` exception is thrown.

Listing 14.7 demonstrates the implementation of the custom exception classes.

Listing 14.7   matherr.cpp—Implementing the Custom Exception Classes

```cpp
#include "matherr.h"

int Div(int, int);
double SqRt(double);

void main()
{
    try
    {
        int    var1, var2;

        cout << "Enter a positive integer for SqRt(): ";
        cin  >> var1;
        cout << "Square Root of " << var1 << " = ";
        cout << SqRt(var1) << endl;
```

```
            cout << "Enter two integers for Div(): ";
            cin  >> var1 >> var2;
            cout << var1 << " divided by " << var2 << " = ";
            cout << Div(var1, var2) << endl;
        }
        catch (NegativeSqRoot &Error)
        {
            Error.Message();
            cout << "Converting value to a positive value...";
            cout << "new result = " << SqRt(-Error.Value) << endl;
        }
        catch (DivideByZero &Error)
        {
            Error.Message();
        }
    }
```

The preceding program requires the user to input an integer value, then calculates and displays the square root of the value. A NegativeSqRoot exception is thrown if the user enters a negative value. If no exceptions are thrown, the program continues. The program requires the user to input two integer values, then calculates and displays the result of the division of the two values. A DivideByZero exception is thrown if the user enters a zero for the second value.

If the SqRt() function throws an exception, control is transferred to the catch block for NegativeSqRoot exceptions. Then, an error message is displayed by calling the Message() member function of the exception object. The offending value is converted and the SqRt() function is called again. This time the result displays.

If the Div() function throws an exception, control is transferred to the catch block for DivideByZero exceptions. Then, an error message is displayed by calling the Message() member function of the exception object.

If any other exceptions are thrown, control is transferred to the default catch block. An error message indicating that an unknown exception occurred is displayed.

Compile the preceding example as an EasyWin target. The program is also included in the MathErr IDE file on the sample disk.

Fig. 14.3
Sample output
generated by
matherr.cpp when
a negative value is
entered for the
SqRt( ) function.

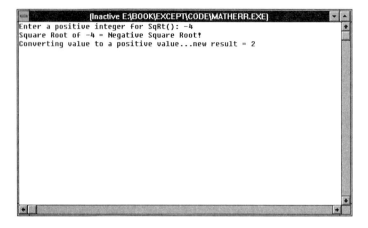

Fig. 14.4
Sample output
generated by
matherr.cpp
when a zero
value is entered
for the *Div( )*
function.

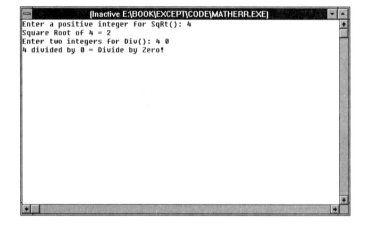

Unhandled Exceptions

Unhandled exceptions occur when no corresponding handler for the given exception is found following the try block in which it was raised. For example

```
try {
    char * Buf = new char[100];
    delete[] Buf;
}
catch (char * Error) {
    cout << "An error, " << Error << ", has occurred!" << endl;
}
```

In the preceding code, if an exception is thrown by the new operator, an unhandled exception will occur and the program will terminate. This is because new throws an xalloc exception if memory allocation fails. As you can see, we have not specified a handler for an `xalloc` exception. To avoid the unhandled exception, the code should be as follows:

```
try {
   char * Buf = new char[100];
   delete[] Buf;
}
catch (xalloc &Error) {
   cout << "An error, " << Error.why() << ", has occurred!" << endl;
}
```

Another way an unhandled exception occurs is if the `throw` keyword is used by itself, and no exceptions currently exist. For example

```
...other program lines
throw;
...other program lines
```

A robust application will take into account most errors that may occur during its execution. However, since programmers are only human, complete error handling is not likely to happen. This makes it possible that some exceptions may be overlooked, causing unhandled exceptions.

What Happens When an Unhandled Exception Occurs?

Default behavior for an unhandled exception is straightforward: the application terminates. When such an exception occurs, the `terminate()` function is called, which in turn calls `abort()`, and the program ends.

set_terminate()

Since the default behavior of the `terminate()` function is to call the `abort()` function and end the program, it is likely that the remaining environment may be unfit for other applications to execute properly. An application can register its own function, which will be called instead of `terminate()` when an unhandled exception occurs. This function could perform the proper cleanup, then call the `abort()` function. The function used to register the replacement function is `set_terminate()` and is defined in the except.h header file. See listing 14.8 for an example of registering the replacement function.

Listing 14.8   setterm.cpp—Registering the *set_terminate* Function

```
#include <windows.h>
#include <except.h>
```

(continues)

Listing 14.8   Continued

```
void My_Terminate()
{
   // Cleanup code goes here...
   MessageBox(NULL, "Function successfully called!",
                     "My_Terminate()", MB_OK | MB_SYSTEMMODAL);
   abort();
}

int PASCAL WinMain(HINSTANCE, HINSTANCE, LPSTR, int)
{
   // Register the replacement function
   set_terminate(My_Terminate);
   // Create an unhandled exception.
   throw;
}
```

Exception Handling Settings in the IDE

The Project Options dialog box contains settings for exception handling (see fig. 14.5). To invoke this dialog box, do the following:

1. Select Project from the Options menu.

2. Expand the C++ Options item in the Topics list box.

3. Select the Exception Handling/RTTI item under the C++ Options.

Fig. 14.5
The Project Options dialog box.

Table 14.1 contains a list of the name, defaults, and descriptions for each of the exception handling settings.

Table 14.1 Project Options Settings		
Setting Name	**Default Setting**	**Description**
Enable exceptions	Off	Turn this setting on to enable exception handling. The compiler generates errors if this setting is off and exception handling code is present.
Enable exception location information	Off	Turn this setting on to enable run-time identification of exceptions.
Enable destructor cleanup	On	Turn this setting on to enable automatic calling of destructors for automatic objects (stack unwinding).
Enable fast exception prologs	Off	Turn this setting on to enable inline code expansion for exception handling functions.
Enable compatible exceptions	Off	Turn this setting on to make Turbo C++ targets compatible with programs compiled with other compilers.
Enable runtime type information	On	Turn this setting on to allow generation of run-time type identification.

Sample Program

The following sample program allows the user to copy files. The heart of this program is a file input/output class. This class encapsulates file input/output using Runtime Library functions. Since file I/O operations are prone to errors, it is a great place to implement exception handling. This program will demonstrate creating exception classes, using exception specifications, handling exceptions, and stack unwinding. For more on file I/O, please refer to Chapter 25, "File I/O."

Start by defining the exception and the file I/O classes. The class definitions can be found in sample.h, which is shown in listing 14.9.

Listing 14.9   sample.h—The Header File for the Sample Program

```
#include <dos.h>
#include <fcntl.h>
#include <io.h>

// Base Exception Class
class EFile {
    public:
        // Copy Constructor
        EFile(EFile &Src);
        EFile(const string &Filename);
        ~EFile();
        const string & File() const;

    private:
        string *filename;
};

class EFInvalidAccess : public EFile {
    public:
        EFInvalidAccess(const string &Filename) : EFile(Filename) {}
};

class EFTooManyFiles : public EFile {
    public:
        EFTooManyFiles(const string &Filename) : EFile(Filename) {}
};

class EFNotFound : public EFile {
    public:
        EFNotFound(const string &Filename) : EFile(Filename) {}
};

class EFAccessDenied : public EFile {
    public:
        EFAccessDenied(const string &Filename) : EFile(Filename) {}
};

class EFBadFile: public EFile {
    public:
        EFBadFile(const string &Filename) : EFile(Filename) {}
};

class EFNoFileOpen: public EFile {
    public:
        EFNoFileOpen(const string &Filename) : EFile(Filename) {}
};

class EFEof: public EFile {
    public:
        EFEof(const string &Filename) : EFile(Filename) {}
};

class File {
    public:
```

```
                enum Attributes {
                    FANORMAL    = 0,
                    FAREADONLY  = FA_RDONLY,
                    FAHIDDEN    = FA_HIDDEN,
                    FASYSTEM    = FA_SYSTEM,
                };

                enum Access {
                    READONLY    = O_RDONLY,
                    WRITEONLY   = O_WRONLY,
                    READWRITE   = O_RDWR
                };

                enum Offset {
                    CURRENT = SEEK_CUR,
                    END     = SEEK_END,
                    BEGIN   = SEEK_SET
                };

                const string & Name() const;
                int Create(int AccessFlag) throw(EFTooManyFiles, EFNotFound,
                        EFAccessDenied);
                int Open(int AccessFlag) throw(EFInvalidAccess,
                        EFTooManyFiles, EFNotFound, EFAccessDenied);
                int Close() throw (EFNoFileOpen, EFBadFile);
                int EoF() throw(EFNoFileOpen, EFBadFile);
                int Read(int NumBytes) throw (EFNoFileOpen, EFAccessDenied,
                        EFBadFile, EFEof, xalloc);
                int Write(unsigned char * Buf, int NumBytes)
                        throw (EFNoFileOpen, EFAccessDenied, EFBadFile);
                long int CurPos() throw (EFNoFileOpen, EFBadFile);
                long int SetCurPos(int offset, int relpos) throw (EFNoFileOpen,
                            EFBadFile);
                unsigned char* GetBuffer();
                File(const string &file);
                ~File();

            private:
                string          *_filename;
                int             _FHandle;
                unsigned char   *_Buf;
        };
```

The EFile exception is defined; the specific exception classes will be derived from EFile. The constructor for EFile takes a file name as a parameter. Also notice that a copy constructor is also defined. This will be used to create temporary objects when an exception is thrown. EFile also has a member function File(). Use this function to retrieve the file name associated with this exception.

As stated previously, EFile is the base class from which all other exception classes are derived. There are seven possible errors that may occur when implementing the file I/O class. The following is a description of the different exception classes created to handle these possible errors:

- EFInvalidAccess—throw this type when an Invalid Access error occurs.

- EFTooManyFiles—throw this type when a Too Many Files Open error occurs.

- EFNotFound—throw this type when a File Not Found error occurs.

- EFAccessDenied—throw this type when an Access Denied error occurs.

- EFBadFile—throw this type when a Bad File Handle error occurs.

- EFNoFileOpen—throw this type when the file has not been opened and a file operation is requested.

- EFEof—throw this type when an End of File error occurs.

The next step is to define the file I/O class, File. File has only one constructor. The constructor takes a file name as a parameter. The constructor initializes the private members. The destructor performs cleanup. It is responsible for closing the file if it is still open when the associated object is destroyed. This is very useful if an exception occurs (stack unwinding). This class also has several member functions. The functions are described in the following list:

- **Open()**

   Use this function to open the file. This function requires one integer parameter. This parameter is the mode in which the file is opened and may be one of the following enumerated values: File::READONLY, File::WRITEONLY, or File::READWRITE. If too many files are open, an EFTooManyFiles exception is thrown. If the file name cannot be located, an EFNotFound exception is thrown. If an invalid access is specified, an EFInvalidAccess exception is thrown. If access to the file is denied by the operating system, an EFAccessDenied exception is thrown.

- **Create()**

   Use this function to create the file. This function requires one integer parameter. This parameter represents the DOS file attributes to assign to this file (for example, read-only, hidden, or system). It may be one of the following enumerated values: File::FANORMAL, File::FAREADONLY, File::FAHIDDEN, or File::FASYSTEM. The file is always opened in read/write mode. If too many files are open, an EFTooManyFiles exception is thrown. If the file name cannot be located, an `EFNotFound` exception is thrown. If access to the file is denied by the operating system, an `EFAccessDenied` exception is thrown.

■ **Close()**

Use this function to close the open file. If the file associated with the current object is not open, an `EFNoFileOpen` exception occurs. If the file handle is bad, an `EFBadFile` exception occurs. Since the file handle is maintained behind the scenes, it is unlikely that this exception will occur.

■ **Eof()**

Use this function to see whether the file pointer is at the end of the file. The return value is 1 if the pointer is at the end of the file. Otherwise, the function returns 0. If the file associated with the current object is not open, an `EFNoFileOpen` exception occurs. If the file handle is bad, an `EFBadFile` exception occurs. Since the file handle is maintained behind the scenes, it is unlikely that this exception will occur.

■ **Read()**

Use this function to read from the file. This function requires one integer parameter. Use this parameter to specify the number of bytes to read from the file. The data read from the file is stored in a buffer. A pointer to this buffer may be retrieved using the `GetBuffer()` method. The return value is the number of bytes read from the open file. If access to the file is denied by the operating system, an `EFAccessDenied` exception is thrown. If the end of the file is encountered, an `EFEof` exception is thrown. If there is not enough memory available to allocate the read buffer, an `xalloc` exception is thrown. If the file handle is bad, an `EFBadFile` exception occurs. Since the file handle is maintained behind the scenes, it is unlikely that this exception will occur.

■ **Write()**

Use this function to write to the file. This function requires two parameters. The first parameter is a pointer, `unsigned char *`, to the buffer to be written. The second parameter is an integer that specifies the number of bytes to be written. The return value is the number of bytes written to the file. If access to the file is denied by the operating system, an `EFAccessDenied` exception is thrown. If the file handle is bad, an `EFBadFile` exception occurs. Since the file handle is maintained behind the scenes, it is unlikely that this exception will occur.

■ **CurPos()**

Use this function to retrieve the current position of the file pointer. If the file associated with the current object is not open, an `EFNoFileOpen` exception occurs. If the file handle is bad, an `EFBadFile` exception occurs. Since the file handle is maintained behind the scenes, it is unlikely that this exception will occur.

■ **SetCurPos()**

Use this function to move the file pointer to a given position. This function requires two integer parameters. The first, `offset`, is the number of bytes to move. The second parameter, `relpos`, should be one of the enumerated offset values defined in the `File` class. This indicates how the offset should be applied. The return value is the new position in the file. If the file associated with the current object is not opened, an `EFNoFileOpen` exception occurs. If the file handle is bad, an `EFBadFile` exception occurs. Since the file handle is maintained behind the scenes, it is unlikely that an `EFBadFile` exception will occur.

■ **GetBuffer()**

Use this function to retrieve a pointer to the contents read from the open file stream.

The sample.cpp file shown in listing 14.10 contains the implementation of the exception classes. It also contains the program's `main()` function, which is where everything comes together.

Listing 14.10   sample.cpp—The Implementation of the Exception Classes

```
#include <iostream.h>
#include <cstring.h>
#include <io.h>
#include <errno.h>
#include <except.h>
#include "sample.h"

EFile::EFile(EFile &Src)
{
    filename = new string(Src.File());
}

EFile::EFile(const string &Filename)
{
    filename = new string(Filename);
```

```
}

EFile::~EFile()
{
   delete filename;
}

const string & EFile::File() const
{
   return *filename;
}

const string & File::Name() const
{
   return *_filename;
}

int File::Create(int AccessFlags) throw(EFTooManyFiles, EFNotFound,
                                         EFAccessDenied)
{
   if ((_FHandle = _rtl_creat(Name().c_str(), AccessFlags)) == -1) {
      switch (errno) {
         case EACCES:
            throw EFAccessDenied(Name());
         case EMFILE:
            throw EFTooManyFiles(Name());
         case ENOENT:
            throw EFNotFound(Name());
      }
   }
   cout << "Creating file: " << Name() << endl;
   return 1;
}

int File::Open(int Flags) throw(EFInvalidAccess, EFTooManyFiles,
                                EFNotFound, EFAccessDenied)
{
   if ((_FHandle = _rtl_open(Name().c_str(), Flags)) == -1) {
      switch (errno) {
         case EACCES:
            throw EFAccessDenied(Name());
         case EINVACC:
            throw EFInvalidAccess(Name());
         case EMFILE:
            throw EFTooManyFiles(Name());
         case ENOENT:
            throw EFNotFound(Name());
      }
   }

   cout << "Opening file: " << Name() << endl;
   return 1;
}
```

(continues)

Listing 14.10 Continued

```cpp
int File::Close() throw (EFNoFileOpen, EFBadFile)
{
    int iRetVal;

    if (_FHandle < 1)
        throw EFNoFileOpen(Name());

    if ((iRetVal = _rtl_close(_FHandle)) == -1)
        throw EFBadFile(Name());

    // Reset the file handle
    _FHandle = 0;

    cout << "Closing file: " << Name() << endl;
    return iRetVal;
}

int File::EoF() throw(EFNoFileOpen, EFBadFile)
{
    int iRetVal;

    if (_FHandle < 1)
        throw EFNoFileOpen(Name());
    if ((iRetVal = eof(_FHandle)) == -1)
        throw EFBadFile(Name());

    return iRetVal;
}

int File::Read(int NumBytes) throw (EFNoFileOpen, EFAccessDenied,
                                    EFBadFile, EFEof, xalloc)
{
    int retval;

    // If no file open, throw exception
    if (_FHandle < 1)
        throw EFNoFileOpen(Name());

    // If a buffer currently exists, destroy it.
    if (_Buf)
        delete [] _Buf;

    // Allocate a new buffer.
    _Buf = new unsigned char[NumBytes];

    // Read the data from the file stream.
    retval = _rtl_read(_FHandle, _Buf, NumBytes);

    // Check for EOF.
    if (retval == 0)
        throw EFEof(Name());

    // Check for other errors.
    if (retval == -1) {
```

```
      switch (errno) {
         case EACCES:
            throw EFAccessDenied(Name());
         case EBADF:
            throw EFBadFile(Name());
      }
   }

   // Return number of bytes read.
   return retval;
}

int File::Write(unsigned char * Buf, int NumBytes) throw
            (EFNoFileOpen, EFAccessDenied, EFBadFile)
{
   int retval;

   // If no file open, throw exception
   if (_FHandle < 1)
      throw EFNoFileOpen(Name());

   // Write the data to the file stream.
   retval = _rtl_write(_FHandle, Buf, NumBytes);

   // Check for errors.
   if (retval == -1) {
      switch (errno) {
         case EACCES:
            throw EFAccessDenied(Name());
         case EBADF:
            throw EFBadFile(Name());
      }
   }

   // Return number of bytes written.
   return retval;
}

long int File::CurPos() throw (EFNoFileOpen, EFBadFile)
{
   long int retval;

   // If no file open, throw exception
   if (_FHandle < 1)
      throw EFNoFileOpen(Name());

   // Get the current file position.
   retval = tell(_FHandle);

   // Check for error.
   if (retval == -1)
      throw EFBadFile(Name());

   return retval;
}
```

(continues)

Listing 14.10   Continued

```
long int File::SetCurPos(int offset, int relpos) throw
                          (EFNoFileOpen, EFBadFile)
{
   long int retval;

   // If no file open, throw exception
   if (_FHandle < 1)
      throw EFNoFileOpen(Name());

   // Set the file position.
   retval = lseek(_FHandle, offset, relpos);

   // Check for error.
   if (retval == -1)
      throw EFBadFile(Name());

   return retval;
}

unsigned char* File::GetBuffer()
{
   return _Buf;
}

File::File(const string &file)
{
   _filename = new string(file);
   _FHandle  = 0;
   _Buf      = 0;
}

File::~File()
{
   // Delete the file name string
   delete _filename;

   // Delete the Read Buffer if it exists
   if (_Buf)
      delete [] _Buf;

   // Close file if it is still open
   if (_FHandle > 0) {
      cout << "Closing file: " << Name() << endl;
      _rtl_close(_FHandle);
   }
}

void main()
{
   try {
      char   szIn[128], szOut[128];
      int bytesread;

      cout << "Enter the source name: ";
```

```
        cin >> szIn;

        cout << "Enter the destination name: ";
        cin >> szOut;

        // Instantiate the File objects.
        File InFile(string((const char far *) szIn));
        File OutFile(string((const char far*) szOut));

        // Open the source file...
        InFile.Open(File::READONLY);
        // Create the destination file...
        OutFile.Create(File::FANORMAL);

      // Copy the file.
      while (!InFile.EoF()) {
          // Retrieve a block of 100 bytes from the source file.
          bytesread = InFile.Read(100);
          // Write the block to the destination file.
          OutFile.Write(InFile.GetBuffer(), bytesread);
      }

      // Close the files
      InFile.Close();
      OutFile.Close();
    }
  catch (EFAccessDenied &Error) {
      cout << "Error: Access Denied, " << Error.File() << endl;
  }
  catch (EFInvalidAccess &Error) {
      cout << "Error: Invalid access, " << Error.File() << endl;
  }
  catch (EFTooManyFiles &Error) {
      cout << "Error: Too many files open, " << Error.File() << endl;
  }
  catch (EFNotFound &Error) {
      cout << "Error: File not found, " << Error.File() << endl;
  }
  catch (EFNoFileOpen &Error) {
      cout << "Error: No file open, " << Error.File() << endl;
  }
  catch (EFBadFile &Error) {
      cout << "Error: Bad file handle, " << Error.File() << endl;
  }
  catch (EFEof &Error) {
      cout << "Error: EOF encountered, " << Error.File() << endl;
  }
  catch (xalloc &Error) {
      cout << "Error: Unable to allocate buffer." << endl;
  }
  catch (...) {
      cout << "Error: an unexpected exception has occurred." << endl;
  }
}
```

The implementation of main() is quite simple. Since there is a possible chance an exception will be raised, the commands responsible for copying the file will reside within a try block. The following steps describe the actions taken in the try block.

1. Prompt the user for the source file name.

2. Read the input from the user.

3. Prompt the user for the destination file name.

4. Read the input from the user.

5. Create a File object for the source file using the file name entered by the user.

6. Create a File object for the destination file using the file name entered by the user.

7. Open the source file.

8. Create the destination file.

9. Repeat step 10 while not at the end of the source file.

10. Read 100 byte blocks of data from the source file and write the blocks to the destination file.

11. Close the source file.

12. Close the destination file.

That accounts for the meat of the program. The remaining code, the exception handlers, make up the rest of the program. If no exceptions occur in the try block, the handlers will never execute. There is a handler for every possible exception, including a handler for unexpected exceptions.

Notice that none of the handlers close the open files. There is no need. Remember stack unwinding? All automatic objects created prior to the exception will be destroyed automatically before transferring control to the matching handler. The destructor for the File class checks for an open file and closes it. See figure 14.6 for sample output of SAMPLE.EXE.

Both source files and an IDE project file are available on the disk that comes with this book.

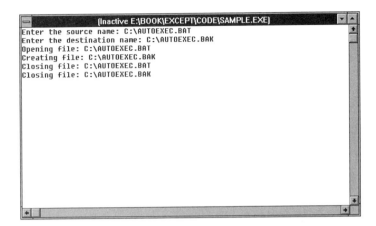

Fig. 14.6
Sample output of
SAMPLE.EXE.

From Here...

In this chapter, you've learned what exceptions are, how they are handled, and the benefits of exception handling in an application. You've seen how exception handling works in normal tasks such as file copying. You've also learned the importance of creating custom exception classes. The following list of chapters will aid in the implementation of your own exception classes.

- Chapter 10, "Pointers," has more information about pointers and references to variables.

- Chapter 12, "Classes and Objects," contains more information about creating C++ classes. This can help to create more robust exception-handling objects.

- Chapter 25, "File I/O," has more information about reading and writing files using the Runtime Library (RTL) and Windows API functions.

- Chapter 27, "The ObjectWindows Library," contains more information about the ObjectWindows library and the implementation of exception handling.

II

Learning C/C++

Chapter 15
Compiling and Linking

Computers don't understand English. In fact, they can't even understand the C++ programming language. Computers understand only one thing: machine language, which is composed entirely of numeric values. Unfortunately, human minds don't deal well with numbers; therefore, C++ program code uses words and symbols so that people can understand the program. How, then, can the computer understand and run the program? The truth is, before you can run a C++ program, you must compile and link it to convert it to something that the computer can understand.

The first of two steps involved in this conversion is to compile the C++ code into what is known as object code. *Object code* is the binary representation of the code that you entered into your program. This binary representation informs the computer of the commands it is to execute from the code that you entered; however, the object code is not capable of being executed on a computer. To ready your object code for execution, the object code must be linked to the C++ run-time libraries. When you link your object code, you are providing information to the object code that tells the computer how it is supposed to load and run the object code. In addition, the linker information provides references to the additional libraries to be loaded to provide functionality for the object code (OWL, OCF, VBX, and so on).

Topics covered in this chapter include:

- Memory Models
- Projects and TargetExpert
- Compiling
- Linking

Memory Models

The 286, 386, and 486 processors implement a *segmented memory model,* in which the system's memory is separated into segments containing up to 64K—or 65,535 bytes (see fig. 15.1). When the processor is in real mode, the address of any byte consists of two 16-bit values—a segment address and an offset. In the protected mode (see fig. 15.2), the processor replaces the segment address with a selector value that the processor uses to access the 64K segment. In either mode, a memory object larger than 64K occupies all or part of several segments. An application cannot access such an object as though it consisted of a single contiguous block simply by incrementing a pointer to the memory. Instead, the application can increment only the offset portion of the address, taking care not to exceed the 64K boundary of the segment.

Fig. 15.1
Segmented memory is separated into 64K segments and is accessible via *segment:offset* in real mode.

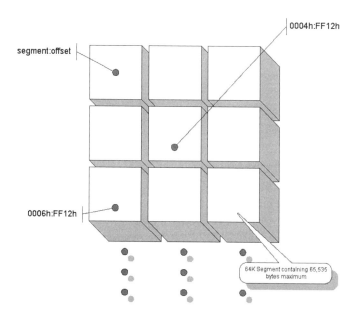

With the advent of the 386 processor came 32-bit registers that replaced the 16-bit registers of previous processors. The 32-bit register makes it possible to access memory in segments larger than 64K. In fact, the maximum segment size is so large that a flat memory model in a single segment is now possible. In this flat memory model, an application's code, data, or both occupy a single segment. An application can use a 32-bit offset as though it were a simple pointer to memory, and it can increment or decrement the pointer throughout the entire address space without dealing with multiple segment boundaries.

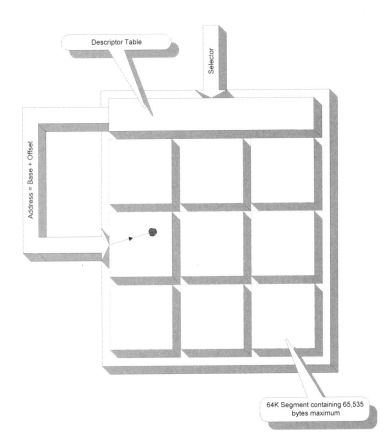

Fig. 15.2
Segmented
memory is
accessible via
selectors in
protected mode.

The flat memory model is a memory model in which both code and data occupy a single segment; however, the segment is much larger than the 64K limit imposed by the segmented memory model. As in the tiny memory model, the beginning of the segment of the flat memory model can appear anywhere in memory. In other words, the segment-descriptor portion of the address can refer to virtually any location in memory. As the application moves through memory, the segment descriptor never changes. Only the offset is incremented and decremented to point to different locations in memory.

When developing applications, you have to be aware of the memory model required for your application. If you are developing a 32-bit application, the memory model is not selectable—instead, it is strictly a flat memory model. In 16-bit applications, you have to select the memory model that will be used for your application—small, medium, compact, or large. The memory model you choose will affect how efficiently your application will run within the Windows operating system.

The Small Memory Model

The small model, also the default memory model, provides one code segment and one data segment, with each segment limited to 64K (see fig. 15.3). The total size of a program using the small model can never exceed 128K.

Fig. 15.3
The small memory model for 16-bit applications can have only one code segment and one data segment.

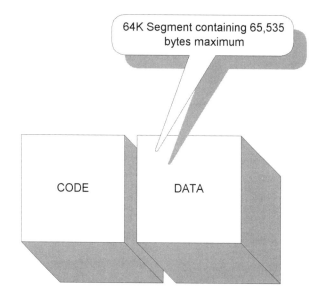

By default, both code and data items in small-model programs are accessed with near addresses, which makes a small-model program run faster than one that uses far addresses.

The Medium Memory Model

The medium memory model provides a single segment for data and multiple segments for code, with each segment limited to 64K (see fig. 15.4). Medium-model programs typically contain more than 64K of code in multiple segments but less than 64K of data.

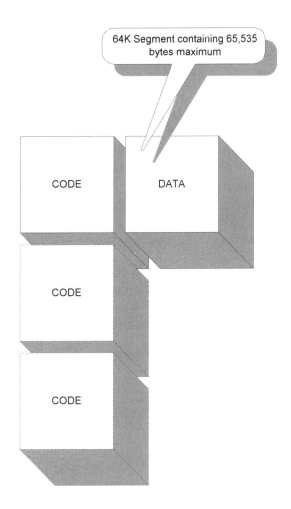

II

Learning C/C++

Fig. 15.4
The medium
memory model for
16-bit applications
can have only one
data segment, but
it can have
multiple code
segments.

The Compact Memory Model

The compact memory model allows multiple segments for data but only
one segment for the code (see fig. 15.5). Each segment is limited to 64K.
Compact-model programs typically have a large amount of data but a relatively small number of program statements. Program data can occupy any
amount of space and is given as many segments as needed.

Fig. 15.5
The compact
memory model for
16-bit applications
can have only one
code segment but
can have multiple
data segments.

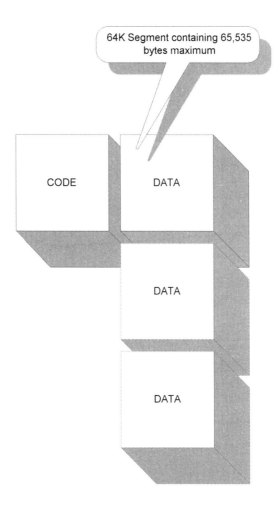

The Large Memory Model

The large memory model provides multiple segments for code and data (see fig. 15.6). Each segment is limited to a maximum of 64K.

Large-model programs are typically very large and use a large amount of data storage during normal processing. By default, both code and data items in large-model programs are accessed with far pointers.

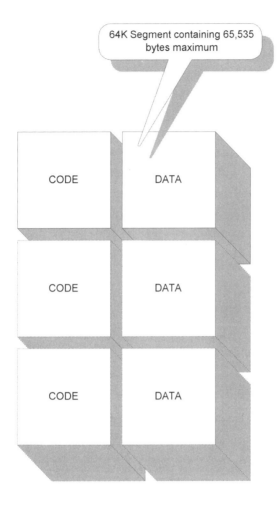

Fig. 15.6
The large memory
model for 16-bit
applications can
have multiple code
and data segments.

II

Learning C/C++

Note

A far pointer is one that consists of a segment value and an offset value and references data outside of the current data segment. A near pointer, on the other hand, has only an offset value and points to data within the current 64K segment. Refer to Chapter 10 for more information on pointers.

Projects

A project contains references to files that are part of your application, as well as options that are specific to the compiling and linking of your application. Turbo C++ uses the project approach so that you can merely load the project into the IDE and have all compiler and linker options and files readily accessible without having to reconfigure the IDE manually.

To create a project in Turbo C++, you select the Project, New Project menu option. The TargetExpert New Target dialog box appears, which enables you to configure your project (see fig. 15.7).

Fig. 15.7
TargetExpert
allows you to
configure your
project for work
in Turbo C++.

> **Note**
>
> A target type is the type of output application or library you want to create. Target types include Windows applications, Windows DLLs, EasyWin applications, static libraries, import libraries, and Windows Help projects.

TargetExpert lets you specify a target type for a node in the active project or the program loaded in the active edit window. You can change existing target attributes by selecting the desired node and editing the attributes using TargetExpert. New targets are created with a default project skeleton; however, you can change the default project skeleton for a specific project type with the Advanced button in the New Target dialog box.

Note

A *node* is an entry in a project tree. Node types include the following:

Type	Description
Project	Represents the entire project
Target	Created when its dependent nodes are built
Source	Used to build a target
Run-time modules	Used during the linking stage of your project (in other words, startup code and .LIB files)

The options on the New Target dialog box are the following:

- The Project Path and Name contain the directory for the new project as well as the name of the file, or project, in which the project information will be saved.

- The Target Type is the type of output file. The selected target type affects the resulting project skeleton that is created for your project. The selected node's extension changes to reflect the new target type. Target types include standard application (EXE), dynamic link library (DLL), EasyWin character-oriented Windows-based application (EXE), static library (LIB) file for use by a standard application, static library (LIB) file for a use by a dynamic link library, import library (LIB) file, or Windows Help project (HPJ) file.

- The Standard Libraries options determine which standard libraries or defines to use in your application. Choose which libraries should be added to your project or which standard defines should be used if you are building a static library.

- Platform allows you to select the desired platform for your project, whether it be Windows 3.0 or Windows 3.1.

- Target Model allows you to select the memory model for your program: small, medium, compact, or large.

- The Advanced button in the dialog box brings up the Advanced Options dialog box, in which you specify deviations to the default project skeleton generated for a selected target type (see fig. 15.8).

II

Learning C/C++

Fig. 15.8
The Advanced
Options dialog
box for
TargetExpert.

When you are done setting project options, click OK. Turbo C++ generates a
project with the options you selected (see fig. 15.9).

Fig. 15.9
Generated project
information is
displayed in the
Project window of
the Turbo C++
environment.

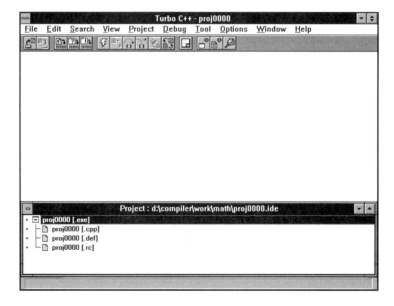

> **Note**
>
> If you choose to use the diagnostic versions of the OWL or Class libraries for built-in troubleshooting and debugging purposes, you must first build them using the Turbo C++ compiler and linker.

Compiling

From the developer's point of view, the entire operation of compiling and linking occurs at the press of a button. The compiler takes the C++ code and compiles and links it for you.

Figure 15.10 shows a sample program in the edit window of the Turbo C++ environment.

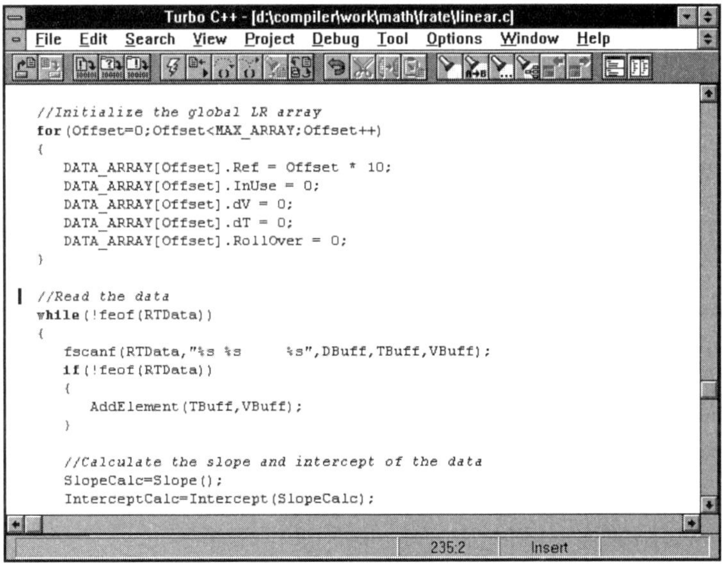

Fig. 15.10
Program code in the edit window of the Turbo C++ environment.

To compile the application, you use the Project menu. The pull-down menu that appears contains several compile methods (see fig. 15.11). The Compile selection (Alt+F9) compiles the currently active code window. When you select Make All, the project manager checks all the files in a project, compiles all of the files that have been updated since the last recompile, and links the object files to create an executable file. The Build All selection is similar to

Make All except that it compiles all of the files in the project, regardless of their update time, and links the object files to create an executable. For this program, we will merely select Build All to compile and link this code.

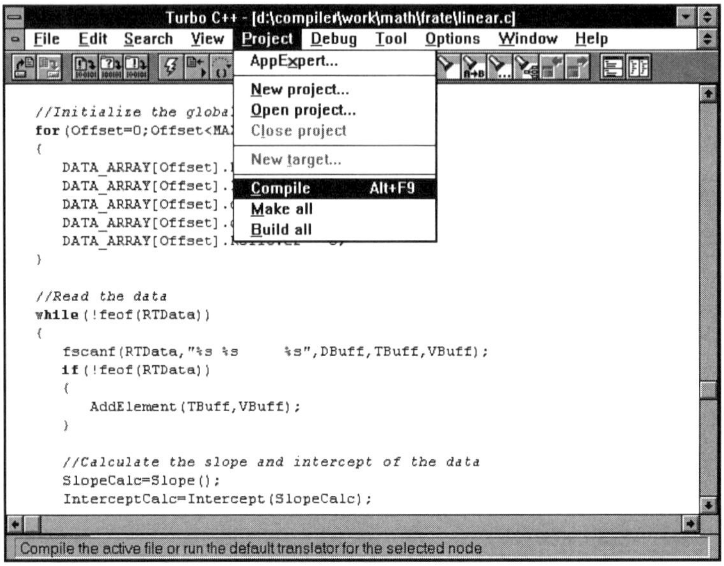

Fig. 15.11

The Turbo C++ environment allows you to select one of three options to compile and link your application.

While compiling, as shown in figure 15.12, Turbo C++ displays a status window to report the progress and status of the compile and link operation. Notice how, during the compile stage, Turbo C++ shows you the file names it is compiling, as well as the current line numbers on which it is working. At the bottom of the small window, the compiler tells you the number of warnings and errors it has encountered. These errors and warnings are the discrepancies that you have to fix to make the program fully operational.

When the compiler compiles your code, it performs a couple of different operations. Each operation converts your code to bring it closer to being machine-readable object code.

The first operation, called *preprocessing*, involves the incorporation of all include files. To do this, your main source file is placed into memory first. The compiler then looks at each #include directive and brings the file that is named in that directive into memory with your code. The compiler then goes through your code and replaces #defined values, macros, and inline functions with the literals and operational code.

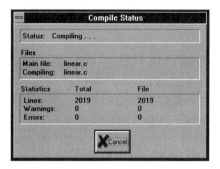

Fig. 15.12
Turbo C++ informs you of the status of the build operation on your application.

Once all of the code for each file listed in your project is prepared, the compiler makes another pass through the code to make sure that the syntax of all of the statements is correct and that all variables and functions referenced within the code exist.

If, after the compiler has finished, it encounters any errors or problems in your code, the compiler provides a list of the errors and warnings in the Message window (see fig. 15.13). To jump to the lines of code that caused any of the errors or warnings listed in the window, you can double-click on the desired information line. Once the edit window displays the code in question, you can simply correct the code as required.

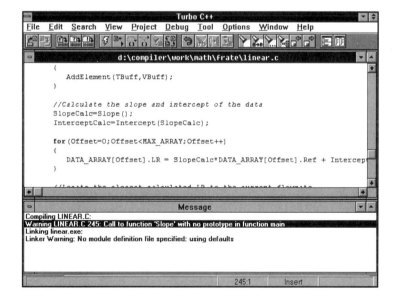

Fig. 15.13
Turbo C++ generates a list of warnings and errors to inform you of problems in the code.

II

Learning C/C++

Name Mangling

When the compiler compiles your code into object files, function names are *mangled*. Mangling means the compiler provides a way of using the same function reference for several different functions. This is also known as *function overloading*.

For instance, if you compile a function defined as follows:

```
int foobar(int);
```

a C++ compiler may produce this:

```
i?foobar?i
```

whereas a function defined as

```
char *foobar(char *);
```

may look like this:

```
c@?foobar?c@
```

The C++ compiler encodes the data types and arguments passed to a function as part of the function name. C++ compiler vendors can support name mangling in any way they desire; therefore, object modules produced by different C++ compilers cannot be mixed together into one application.

There are two major benefits provided by function name mangling. First, it provides a means by which a C++ compiler can ensure type-safe linkage. When you use a function in one module that has been defined in another, the compiler forces you to pass the correct number and type of parameters as long as you use the same function prototype when each is compiled.

Second, because name mangling creates a new means by which a function is identified (with the mangled name), you can create more than one function in the same scope with the same base name, as long as the number or type of the arguments differs—again referring to function overloading.

Linking

Once compiled, the object code can now be linked. This operation is initiated immediately after a compile, as long as there are no errors generated during the compile, and if you selected to Build All or Make All. During the link operation, the *linker* reads the object code and associates all function calls to functions that exist in the C++ run-time libraries.

For example, in the following line of code, the linker encounters a function called `i?printf?c@v,` for the `printf()` function, in your program's object code. The linker then goes to the C++ run-time library and attempts to locate the function in the library. If found, the linker tells the object code where in the library the actual code for the `printf()` call exists.

```
printf("MA: %f     %f\n",TestVal2,TestVal2*3600);
```

After the linker provides all functions and symbols in your program's object code references to the run-time library functions, the linker attaches a header to the beginning of the file. This header contains loading information and a table of references—a symbol table, pointing to all symbols within your program. At this point you have an executable application that can be run on your computer.

Development Options

Numerous options are available for the compile and link operation of the Turbo C++ environment. Each of the options is accessible by selecting Project from the Options menu (see fig. 15.14).

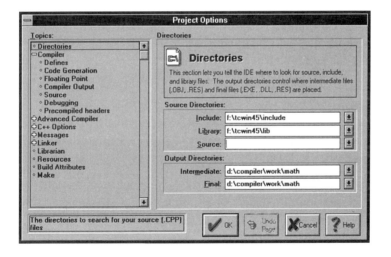

Fig. 15.14
User-modifiable options for compiling and linking.

The options that you can modify to customize the compilation and linking of your project are the following:

- Directories options tell the compiler where to find or where to put header files, library files, source code, output files, and other program elements.

■ Compiler options are common to all C++ programs and affect how the compiler generates code. Modifiable options include `defines` for compiler directives, string and numeric code generation, floating-point optimization, location of compiler output (object files), source code interpretation standards, debugging information generation, and whether precompiled headers should be used.

■ Advanced compiler options affect the compilation of all 16-bit Windows 3.x applications. Options available include selection of the type of processor on which your application will run, the calling convention for the application (C, Pascal, or Register), the memory model (small, medium, compact, or large), segment names for data and code, and entry/exit code options to determine what type of Windows application (EXE or DLL) the compiler is to create.

■ C++ options affect compilation of all C and C++ programs to adapt for older C++ implementations or to take into account newer C++ technology. Options include how member pointers and casts are treated, handling of C++ compatibility issues, how virtual tables and inline functions are handled when debugging, how the compiler generates template instances, and how to handle run-time exceptions.

■ Messages options control the types of messages output by the compiler. Compiler messages are indicators of potential trouble spots in your program and inform you of problems that may occur. Such problems include variables and parameters that are declared but never used, type mismatches, and so on.

■ Linker options affect how an application is linked and let you control how intermediate files (OBJ, LIB, and RES) are combined into executables (EXE) and dynamic-link libraries (DLL).

■ Librarian options affect the behavior of the built-in Librarian, which combines OBJ files in your project into LIB files. Options in this section control that process.

■ Resources options control how resources from applications such as Resource Workshop are compiled and bound to your application by the Resource Compiler and Resource Linker.

■ Make options control the building of a project and how the project manager uses dependency information.

Note

Precompiled header files can increase compilation speed by storing a symbol table on disk in a file and then later reloading that file from disk, as opposed to parsing all the header files during each consecutive compile.

From Here...

In this chapter you learned how to create projects using TargetExpert and how to select options for the project. You learned how applications are compiled and linked with the Turbo C++ IDE. We discussed memory models and how these models apply to linking an application with the Turbo C++ IDE. For further information see the following:

- Chapter 2, "Windows Libraries and Tools," reviews some specifics of the Turbo C++ IDE.

- Chapter 10, "Pointers," contains more information about near and far pointers.

- Chapter 19, "Developing Windows Resources for a User Interface," gives you more information on integrating resources into Windows-based applications.

- Chapter 23, "Using Resource Workshop," explains how resources are created for Windows-based applications.

- Chapter 24, "Windows Programming Basics," contains more information about Windows programming.

II

Learning C/C++

Chapter 16

Debugging

Debugging refers to the process of finding and correcting bugs in a program. A *bug* is a program error, and ultimately bugs prevent your programs from doing what they are supposed to do. Since bugs need to be ferreted out with maniacal fervor, it's not surprising that Turbo C++ provides an arsenal of tools to help you with this task. The primary tool for debugging your C++ programs is the integrated debugger.

This chapter explains how the debugger that's built into the Turbo C++ IDE helps you verify your program's logic and ensure the integrity of your program's data. You will closely follow the debugging of a sample program. By the end of this debugging session, you should feel comfortable debugging your own Turbo C++ programs.

Different Aspects of Debugging

When we talk about debugging a program, we're actually talking about two different investigative acts.

In the first case, the programmer is interested in following the flow of execution within the program. The primary purpose of this type of debugging is to ensure that the program logic is sound and that the appropriate code is being executed given a certain set of inputs or preconditions.

In the second case, the logic of a program may appear to be sound, but the programmer is interested in the values of program data at a particular time. Since the logic of a program is often driven by the state of data, these two debugging tasks are hardly unrelated, but they do imply two separate approaches to tracking down bugs and using a program debugger.

Debugging a Sample Program

Think for a second about what functions you might find useful for tracing through your programs. You would probably like the ability to walk through your program a line at a time, drilling down into function and method calls as you think appropriate. You might also want the ability to run your program up to a particular point and then stop so that you can examine data or step through the program logic that immediately follows. Turbo C++'s integrated debugger can do all of this and more.

We'll start exploring the different features of the Turbo C++ debugger by examining the execution of a program called PRIME.CPP. PRIME.CPP, as you will soon see, is quite a troubled piece of code. The worst part is that as it initially stands, PRIME looks like a reasonable piece of programming. However, as you may already know, just because a program *looks* like it should work doesn't guarantee that it will even compile, let alone function correctly.

PRIME.CPP is an EasyWin program that has a minimalist text-based user interface. EasyWin is a Turbo C++ feature that allows you to use the standard C/C++ run-time library console-based input and output routines from a Windows program. PRIME.CPP is a good example of the sort of quick-and-dirty Windows programs that you might use the EasyWin subsystem to build. Obviously, the program takes no advantage of those user-interface elements that generally make Windows programs so easy to use, but it does help to demonstrate how—in a pinch—you might not need all those fancy accoutrements. For more information on building EasyWin programs, jump ahead and give Appendix B a quick once-over.

> **Note**
>
> There are some types of "bugs" that Turbo C++ cannot help you find. For example, the PRIME.CPP program in this chapter suffers from a very inefficient algorithm. Although the program does what it's supposed to (at least once it's debugged), it doesn't do it very quickly. If program performance is important to you, be sure to pick and choose your algorithms carefully.

Stepping through the Program

Take a close look at the initial version of PRIME.CPP. The program is shown in its entirely in listing 16.1, but future listings will show only those parts of the program that have changed from version to version.

Listing 16.1   The Initial Version of PRIME.CPP

```cpp
// Get needed include files
#include <stdio.h>
#include <stdlib.h>
#include <iostream.h>

// Boolean type
typedef unsigned int bool;
const bool TRUE = 1;
const bool FALSE = 0;

// Gets a single integer from the keyboard
int InputInt()
{
    char* buffer;
    return atoi(gets(buffer));
}

// Given an integer, returns a bool indicating whether it's prime
bool IsPrime(int CheckNum)
{
    bool StillPrime = TRUE;
    int  CountDown = CheckNum;
    while (StillPrime) {
        if (!(CheckNum % --CountDown))
            StillPrime = FALSE;
    }
    return (CountDown == 0 ? TRUE : FALSE);
}

void main()
{
    // Get the number of primes to calculate
    cout << "How many prime numbers do you want to see? ";
    int NumPrimes = InputInt();

    // Show the primes
    cout << "\nHere are the first "
        << NumPrimes << " prime numbers...\n";
    int CurrCandidate, NumFoundPrimes = 0;
    while (NumFoundPrimes < NumPrimes) {
        if (IsPrime(CurrCandidate))
            cout << CurrCandidate << "   ";
        CurrCandidate++;
    }
}
```

Learning C/C++

As you skimmed through the program, it should have become pretty clear that the purpose of this code is to calculate prime numbers. A prime number is a number that is evenly divisible by only two numbers: 1 and itself.

On the face of it, PRIME.CPP seems pretty straightforward. The program prompts the user for the number of prime numbers to find and then, starting at 1 and working upwards, starts to test numbers to see whether they are prime. If the current candidate number is prime, it is printed to the screen. If it is not prime, the current candidate variable is incremented and the program tries again. What could be simpler? Unfortunately, all is not well in Number Land.

If you type the program in listing 16.1, place it into a project, and click the Make toolbar button, you will gratified to see that the program compiles without errors. When you run the program, you see the initial prompt asking you to input the number of prime numbers to calculate. So far so good.

Unfortunately, your luck is about to run out. Type the number **10** and press Enter. Boom! Much to your dismay, you get one of those dreaded UAEs—an Unrecoverable Application Error. Figure 16.1 shows the aftermath of your program's gruesome death.

Fig. 16.1
A sad end for
PRIME.CPP.

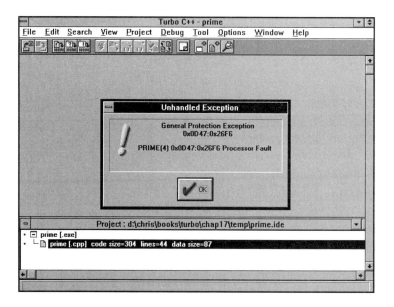

Roll up your shirt sleeves; it's time to get to work. With PRIME's project loaded into the Turbo C++ environment, press the F8 key or select the Step Over option from the Debug menu. Turbo C++ checks to make sure that the project is in a consistent state, recompiles if it isn't, and then shows you the code with a blue bar over the first line of main(). Welcome to debug mode.

When Turbo C++ is debugging a program, the blue bar highlights the current statement of execution. Table 16.1 shows you the execution commands, along with any keyboard equivalents and their toolbar counterparts.

Table 16.1 Execution Control Commands

	Command	Key	Action
	Run	Ctrl+F9	Runs the program until termination or until a breakpoint is encountered.
	Run to cursor	F4	Runs until the debugger encounters the line of source code that the cursor is on.
	Step over	F8	Executes the current statement. Doesn't move into functions or methods.
	Step into	F7	Executes the current statement. Moves into the function or method if the current statement is a call.
	Show execution point	None	Switches the source code view to emphasize the current statement.
	Pause	Ctrl+Alt+SysRq	Stops the currently executing program.
	Terminate	Ctrl+F2	Ends the program.

Note

Although Windows programs often don't require or use command-line arguments, there is no rule that says they can't. If your program uses command-line arguments and you need to specify them for a particular debugging session, you can enter them in the Debugger section of the Environment settings (which is reached by choosing Environment from the Options menu).

Press the F8 key to step over the next couple of lines. It shouldn't take too long to realize that the program is blowing up inside the call to InputInt(). Restart the program. This time, when the current line of execution is

```
int NumPrimes = InputInt();
```

press the F7 key to step into the function. Once inside InputInt(), keep pressing F8 until you encounter the line of code that is causing the protection violation.

Tip
To avoid the annoying screen flicker caused by jumping between your program and Turbo C++, you can tile the program's window alongside Turbo C++.

It should now be quite obvious what the problem is. The programmer didn't actually reserve any storage for the input buffer, so the program was storing the user input at a random memory location. You can fix this by making buffer a fixed-length character array. Listing 16.2 shows the corrected InputInt() function.

Listing 16.2   The Corrected *InputInt()* that Reserves Memory for User Input

```
int InputInt()
{
    char buffer[80];
    return atoi(gets(buffer));
}
```

Congratulations! You've just fixed your first Turbo C++ bug. Pretty easy, wasn't it? Rebuild the project and it's on to the next bug.

Using Breakpoints

The program has stopped blowing up. Unfortunately, now it does something just as bad. When you run PRIME, the program accepts your input and displays the message that it is about to start spitting out prime numbers. But nothing happens after that. In fact, not only do you not get a single prime number, but it appears as if your entire Windows desktop has frozen up.

Don't panic. Remember from the table in the previous section that as long as you are running the program in the debugger, you can press Ctrl+Alt+SysRq to stop the program while it's running. Once you do this, Turbo C++ springs back to life and the blue execution bar highlights the currently executing statement. As you can see from figure 16.2, it appears as though the program is stuck in an infinite loop. It's hard to tell by just looking at the code, however, whether the infinite loop is inside IsPrime() or main().

Since PRIME is a short program, there's no real problem with pressing F8 until you enter the main program loop. All the same, there is a better way that can save you a lot of time, especially when you're working with larger programs. It's called a *breakpoint*.

Setting a Breakpoint

When you set a breakpoint on a line of code, you're telling the debugger that you want to stop there the next time you run your program. You can set a breakpoint by placing the cursor on the appropriate line and pressing the F5 key. Figure 16.3 shows the PRIME program with a breakpoint set right before

the main program loop. The debugger denotes breakpoints by highlighting
the line in red.

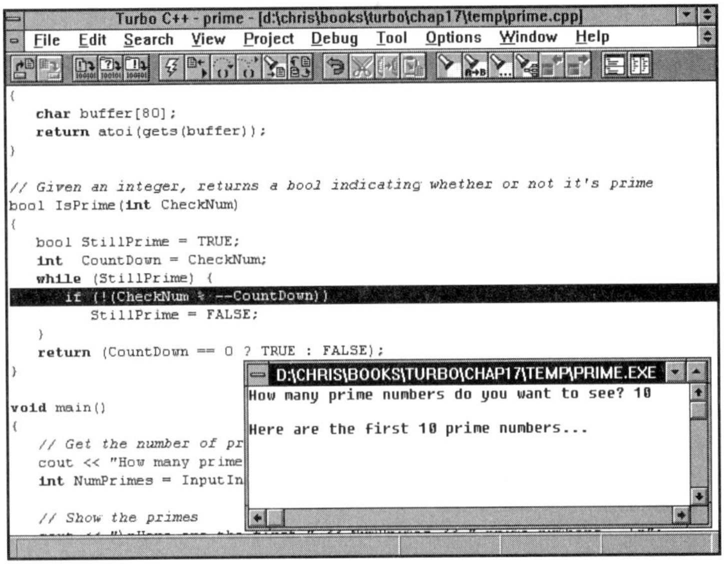

Fig. 16.2
Breaking out of
PRIME's infinite
loop.

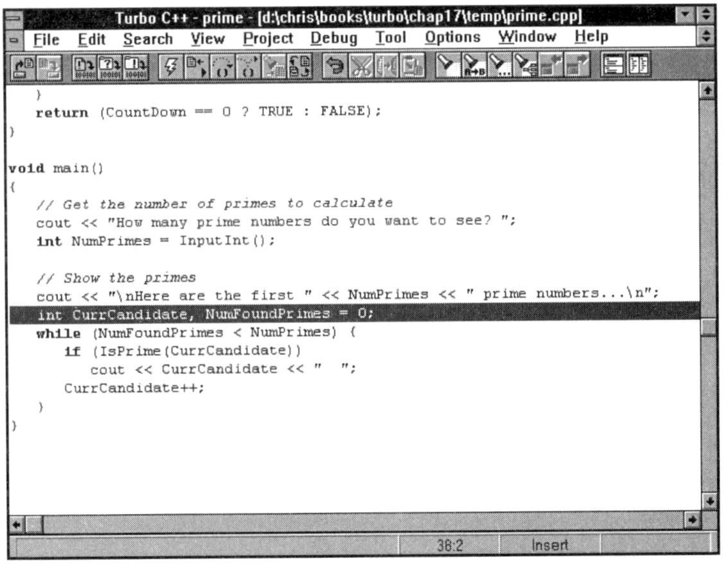

Fig. 16.3
Setting a
breakpoint.

There are a couple of other ways you can set a breakpoint. You can click on a
line of code with the right mouse button and select the Toggle Breakpoint

option from the editor's SpeedMenu. You can also choose the Toggle Breakpoint option from the <u>D</u>ebug menu.

> **Note**
>
> As you start to experiment with breakpoints, you might come to the realization that there are some lines of code that Turbo C++ probably shouldn't let you set a breakpoint on. For example, it doesn't make a whole lot of sense to place a breakpoint on a line that contains only a comment, on a blank line, or on a line that contains just a variable declaration. After all, these are lines that have no logical counterpart at the object code level.
>
> Actually, although the debugger will let you create a breakpoint virtually anywhere, breakpoints that fall on lines such as these are ignored. The breakpoint is still created, however, and you can examine it in the breakpoint list (select <u>B</u>reakpoint from the <u>V</u>iew menu).

Using figure 16.3 as a model, set a breakpoint on the line right before the main program loop and then run the program by pressing Ctrl+F9 (or by selecting <u>R</u>un from the <u>D</u>ebug menu). PRIME starts up, asks for your input, and then gives Turbo C++ the focus as your breakpoint is hit.

If you press F8 a dozen or so times, you can see that the loop processes without ever finding a prime number. It's probably a little frivolous, but let's make sure that the loop really is just spinning its wheels and that the "freeze-up" that we experienced earlier wasn't the result of some crazy system anomaly. One way we could probably convince ourselves of this is to let the loop run until the CurrCandidate variable was some large value (say 5000) and then trigger the breakpoint. Since we know that there are a good number of prime numbers less than 5000, if we get to 5000 and haven't seen a prime number yet, it proves two things. First, the program is not dead. It is simply running itself ragged in an apparently endless loop. Second, and perhaps most obvious, getting CurrCandidate to 5000 without finding a prime number proves that we do indeed have a bug.

Of course, one big disadvantage to this plan is that it's going to take an awful lot of presses of the F8 key to get the CurrCandidate variable up to 5000. Again, however, Turbo C++ has a solution that makes this task a cinch. But first you need to bring up the breakpoint list.

The Breakpoint List

When you select the <u>B</u>reakpoint option from the <u>V</u>iew menu, Turbo C++ presents you with a list of all the currently defined breakpoints. This list tells you what source file the breakpoint is in, the line number that the breakpoint falls on, and the breakpoint's state. Breakpoints usually have a state of *Verified*, which indicates that the breakpoint is legal and has been successfully compiled into the program. However, under certain conditions the breakpoint could be *Unverified*, indicating that the program has not been recompiled since the breakpoint was added. Finally, the list might indicate that the breakpoint is *Invalid*. An invalid breakpoint means that the line on which you set the breakpoint does not contain executable code. Invalid breakpoints are ignored.

You might be wondering what the checkbox next to each breakpoint represents. Breakpoints can be disabled, which is different than deleting them. For all practical purposes, a disabled breakpoint is ignored by the debugger and will not be triggered. The breakpoint still exists, and you can easily reinstate it by simply re-enabling it. Unchecking a breakpoint on this list disables it; checking it again reactivates it. Figure 16.4 shows the breakpoint list. A disabled breakpoint appears in the source window as a green bar instead of the red. You can also see that the breakpoint defined in PRIME.CPP has been disabled.

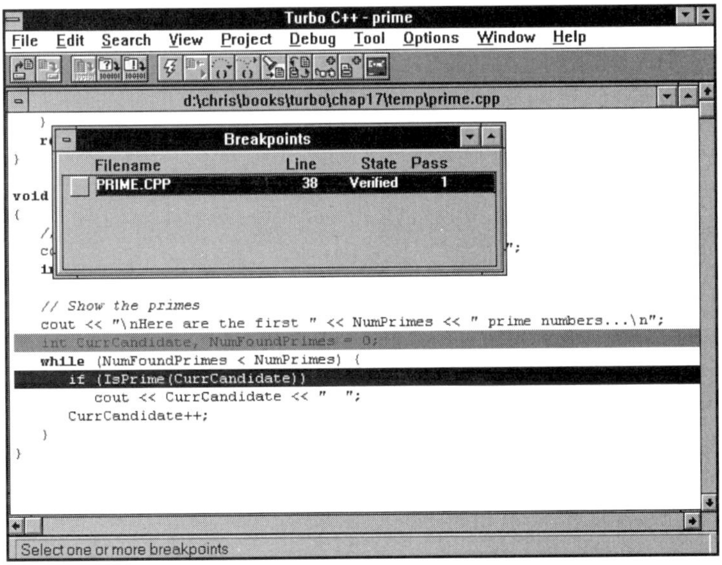

Tip
You can click the right mouse button in the Breakpoint list and use the SpeedMenu to quickly perform many breakpoint management tasks.

Fig. 16.4
The breakpoint settings list.

This is all well and good, but how does the breakpoint list help you trigger a breakpoint when `CurrCandidate` equals 5000? If you double-click on a breakpoint, Turbo C++ displays the Breakpoint Properties dialog box. In this dialog box, the full power of conditional breakpoints can be unleashed.

Setting Conditional Breakpoints

Figure 16.5 shows the Breakpoint Properties dialog box. Some of the items in this dialog box are straightforward. The source file name, line number, and state information are all the same as displayed in the breakpoint list. However, the Conditional Expression and Pass Count portions of this dialog box are a little more interesting.

Fig. 16.5

The Breakpoint Properties dialog box.

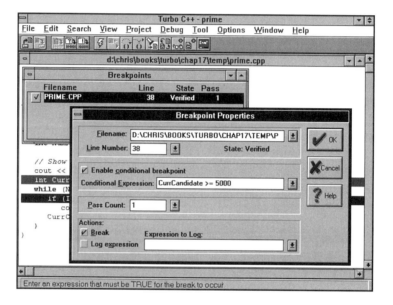

A conditional breakpoint is triggered only when its corresponding condition evaluates to TRUE (in other words, a non-zero value). Since the breakpoint condition can use any in-scope variable values and can be composed of any valid C++ expression, you have a tremendous amount of flexibility and control over your breakpoint activation criteria. Take another look at figure 16.5. The depicted breakpoint has a conditional expression of CurrCandidate >= 5000. This means that the breakpoint will be triggered only when the CurrCandidate variable is greater than or equal to 5000; in all other cases, the debugger will act as though the breakpoint doesn't exist.

> **Caution**
>
> Turbo C++'s conditional breakpoints suffer from a small problem: They really slow things down. Since the debugger is essentially interpreting and recalculating the breakpoint condition every time the breakpoint line is encountered, there is a lot of overhead associated with a conditional breakpoint that is not present with a normal breakpoint. This is especially apparent when you are dealing with tight loops such as the one in the PRIME.CPP example. If you try this example yourself, be patient. Depending on the speed of the machine you're using, you may have to wait a couple of minutes for the breakpoint to trigger.

If you create the breakpoint as described previously and as shown in the figure, you should be able to recompile the program and run it. PRIME will trundle away for a bit and the breakpoint will be activated when CurrCandidate is incremented up to 5000.

In this case, there is another way to achieve the same result using a pass count. For breakpoints that have a pass count, the debugger keeps track of how many times the breakpoint line has been "passed over." When the pass count value is reached, the debugger triggers the breakpoint. In the PRIME example, you can ensure that CurrCandidate is at least 5000 by setting the breakpoint's pass count equal to 5000. Because comparing a pass count is more efficient than evaluating a conditional expression, code executing with pass count breakpoints performs better than code executing with an equivalent conditional breakpoint. Of course, a pass count doesn't have the flexibility that a conditional expression does, and in some cases you won't have the luxury of using pass counts.

Investigating Program Data

The previous discussion of conditional breakpoints asks you to take a lot of information at face value. Yes, the debugger appears to work for a moment before triggering your breakpoint, but how do you really know that the value of CurrCandidate is 5000?

The Turbo C++ debugger provides several different ways for you to investigate the values of your program's data. Specifically, you can view your data in the Watch window, or by using the Inspector or Evaluator.

Setting Watches

The Watch window allows you to display the value of an expression. Whenever the debugger stops or pauses execution of your program, the values of the expressions in the Watch window are recalculated and updated.

You can place a new expression into the Watch window by choosing the Add Watch option from the Debug menu. You can also add a watch expression by pressing Ctrl+F5 or by displaying the watch view (choose Watch from the View menu) and using the SpeedMenu. You can also choose Set Watch from the source view's SpeedMenu. This displays the watch view and creates a new watch expression, but you will have to double-click the new item to see the Watch Properties dialog box shown in figure 16.6.

Fig. 16.6

The Watch Properties dialog box.

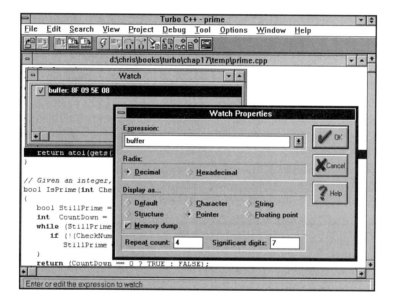

Virtually any legal C++ expression can be used as a watch expression. Most of the options in this dialog box pertain to specifics about how the expression is displayed in the Watch window. Numeric values, for example, can be displayed in decimal or hexadecimal form as indicated by the Radix radio button selection.

When deciding which type you should display your data as, keep in mind that the default case will probably be appropriate for the vast majority of cases. When displaying certain structures, memory buffers, or strings, however, it may be more appropriate to display the expression as a simple address, string, or memory dump. Since the watch view is dynamic, you can adjust these properties and they will be immediately reflected in the Watch window. Sometimes it takes a little bit of experimenting to get the intended result.

If you are displaying an array variable, it might help to use the *repeat count*. The repeat count dictates how many elements of the array to show. For example, if you wanted to see the first four bytes of the buffer variable used in PRIME's InputInt() function, you might select a Pointer display type with memory dump enabled and a repeat count of 4. The debugger might display this expression like so:

```
buffer: 8F 09 5E 08
```

You can also override the display options by including a *format specifier* directly in the expression field. Format specifiers are offset from the expression by a comma and are composed of one or more of the specifiers described in table 16.2. Using the buffer variable again as an example, and assuming that the display was already configured to display the first four bytes in a memory dump format, you could elect to display the first six bytes of the buffer as a string by entering the following expression:

```
buffer, 6MS
```

Tip

Just as in the breakpoint list, you can click the right mouse button in the Watch window and use the SpeedMenu to quickly perform many watch expression management tasks.

Table 16.2   Watch Expression Format Specifiers

Specifier	Effect
H or X	Displays the value in hexadecimal format
C	Displays the ASCII characters from 0-31 as special C-style escape sequences
D	Displays the value in decimal form
Fn	Displays the value in floating-point form with *n* significant digits
nM	Displays the value as an *n*-byte memory dump
P	Displays the value as a pointer (*segment:offset* format)
R	Displays the value as a structure or union
S	Displays the value as a string (used only to modify the memory dump specifier)

If you enter CurrCandidate into the Watch window, you'll see something very similar to figure 16.7 when the conditional breakpoint is triggered. Clearly, the breakpoint is performing as advertised.

Fig. 16.7

The *CurrCandidate* variable in the Watch window after the conditional breakpoint.

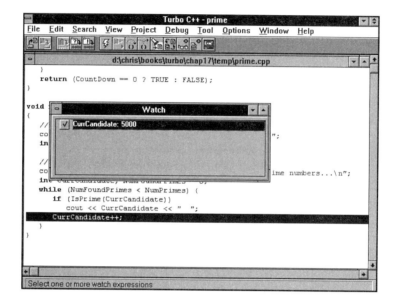

Since the watch window is continuously updated as you step through your code a line at a time (using F7 and F8), you might be surprised at what you see when you single-step through PRIME.CPP with the CurrCandidate watch still defined. Since the programmer neglected to initialize CurrCandidate, the variable initially contains a garbage value. Bug number 2! Listing 16.3 shows how to correct this oversight.

Listing 16.3   The Main Loop with a Correctly Initialized *CurrCandidate*

```
// Show the primes
cout << "\nHere are the first "
     << NumPrimes << " prime numbers...\n";
int CurrCandidate = 1, NumFoundPrimes = 0;
while (NumFoundPrimes < NumPrimes) {
    if (IsPrime(CurrCandidate))
        cout << CurrCandidate << "   ";
    CurrCandidate++;
}
```

Don't get too excited, though. We're not done yet. If you rebuild the program and run it again, you'll find that all of a sudden it has started blowing up again! Only this time, instead of a memory protection violation, PRIME appears to be generating a divide-by-zero exception. Back to the drawing board.

Inspecting

When a program generates an exception and it's running in the debugger, Turbo C++ shows the programmer a notification dialog box and then displays the line of source code that was responsible for the dirty deed. In this case, the debugger is telling us that the problem is in IsPrime(), and that the following line is the culprit:

```
if (!(CheckNum % --CountDown))
```

At this point, it would make sense to check out the current values of CheckNum and CountDown. Now you could add both of them to the Watch window, but that certainly seems like a lot of work just to get a quick peek at their current values. Unlike the CurrCandidate variable, which you wanted to track for an extended period of time, you really just want to see their values right now and be done with it. Why add an expression to the Watch window unless you're sure you have to?

Luckily, there's a very simple way to display the current value of variables using the debugger's Inspect command. You can highlight any expression in the source code and then select Inspect Object from the source view's SpeedMenu (you can also press Alt+F5). Alternatively, you can choose Inspect from the Debug menu. However, if you inspect expressions in this manner, you'll have to enter the expression into an input box first; the former methods are incrementally quicker.

The nice thing about the debugger's Inspector windows is that they are smart enough to discern the type of data that you are viewing, and they tailor the view as appropriate. There are different views for integral types, arrays, structures, classes, and functions. Turbo C++ takes care of selecting the appropriate one. For data types such as structures, unions, and classes that are composite entities, you can inspect member values by double-clicking the member name, selecting the member and pressing Enter, or selecting the member and then choosing Inspect Object from the SpeedMenu.

Turbo C++ even allows you to change the value of variables loaded into the Inspector. The SpeedMenu contains the Change Value option, which presents you with an input dialog box for entering a new value.

Tip
Sometimes when you are inspecting arrays, you might be interested in only a particular part of the array. By using the Set Range option (Ctrl+R) on the Inspector SpeedMenu, you can limit what part of the array is displayed.

Right now, however, all you really want to do is see the current value of CountDown. Highlight the variable name and press Alt+F5; you should see something similar to figure 16.8.

Fig. 16.8
Inspecting the
CountDown and
CheckNum
variables.

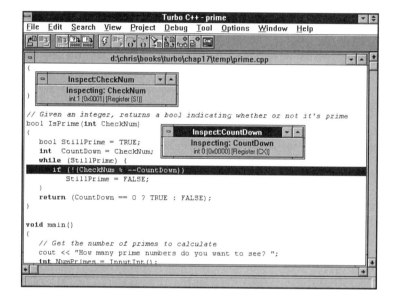

Well, no surprises here. CountDown is zero, and since the modulus operator performs an implicit division operation, there is every reason in the world to expect a divide-by-zero exception. Now inspect CheckNum to get a feel for how far PRIME made it before it blew up. As also shown in figure 16.8, CheckNum is 1, so apparently the program died on its very first call to IsPrime().

A thoughtful analysis of the function reveals that although the logic appears to be fine, it's the placement of the CountDown decrement operation that is at fault here. By moving the place where CountDown is decremented, the logic of the function is retained but the messy exception is avoided. Listing 16.4 shows the corrected IsPrime() function.

Listing 16.4 The Corrected *IsPrime()* Function

```
bool IsPrime(int CheckNum)
{
    bool StillPrime = TRUE;
    int  CountDown = CheckNum;
    while (--CountDown && StillPrime) {
        if (!(CheckNum % CountDown))
            StillPrime = FALSE;
    }
    return (CountDown == 0 ? TRUE : FALSE);
}
```

Evaluating

There's yet a third way for you to investigate program data, and now that you're familiar with setting breakpoints and controlling execution, you might feel inspired to practice some of your new debugging skills before moving onto PRIME's last bug. The Expression Evaluator dialog box, activated through the Debug, Evaluate/Modify menu option, is sort of a combination of the Inspector and the Watch window. Figure 16.9 shows the Evaluator in action.

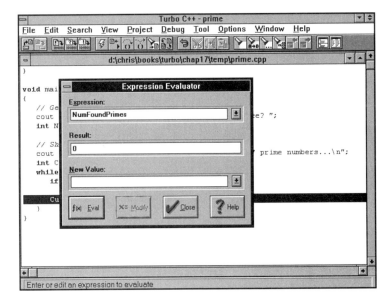

Fig. 16.9
Using the Evaluator.

There's really nothing that you can do in the Evaluator that you can't do with watches or inspectors, but the Evaluator is a little more efficient at certain operations. In particular, the Evaluator is an excellent mechanism for not only displaying program data but also modifying it. The Watch window doesn't allow you to modify data at all, and the procedure for modifying data in the Inspector is rather cumbersome. On the other hand, the Evaluator always has a field immediately available for directly manipulating the variable's data.

The expression field of the Evaluator understands the same format specifiers used in the Watch window. You cannot, however, evaluate expressions that contain function or method invocations, source code symbols that rely on the C++ preprocessor (such as #define), or data that is currently out of scope.

Finishing Up with PRIME.CPP

It appears that we're getting pretty close to finishing the prime number program. When you run the program now, you should finally be rewarded by the outputting of a list of prime numbers. Ironically, though, the program is stuck in another infinite loop. This time, the program won't stop giving right answers.

You know enough about the debugger to figure this problem out by yourself—it's quite really simple. If you're having problems, here's a hint: put the NumFoundPrimes variable into the Watch window and then experiment with a variety of conditional and pass count breakpoints. Listing 16.5 shows the fully debugged source code for PRIME.CPP.

Listing 16.5 The Fully Debugged Version of PRIME.CPP

```cpp
// Get needed include files
#include <stdio.h>
#include <stdlib.h>
#include <iostream.h>

// Boolean type
typedef unsigned int bool;
const bool TRUE = 1;
const bool FALSE = 0;

// Gets a single integer from the keyboard
int InputInt()
{
    char buffer[80];
    return atoi(gets(buffer));
}

// Given an integer, returns a bool indicating whether or not
// it's prime
bool IsPrime(int CheckNum)
{
    bool StillPrime = TRUE;
    int  CountDown = CheckNum;
    while (--CountDown && StillPrime) {
        if (!(CheckNum % CountDown))
            StillPrime = FALSE;
    }
    return (CountDown == 0 ? TRUE : FALSE);
}

void main()
{
    // Get the number of primes to calculate
    cout << "How many prime numbers do you want to see? ";
    int NumPrimes = InputInt();
```

```
        // Show the primes
        cout << "\nHere are the first "
             << NumPrimes << " prime numbers...\n";
        int CurrCandidate = 1, NumFoundPrimes = 0;
        while (NumFoundPrimes < NumPrimes) {
            if (IsPrime(CurrCandidate)) {
                cout << CurrCandidate << "  ";
                NumFoundPrimes++;
            }
            CurrCandidate++;
        }
    }
```

From Here...

In addition to an overview of the Turbo C++ integrated debugger and basic debugging techniques, this chapter has touched on a number of other programming issues. For more information on application design in the IDE and using EasyWin, see the following chapters:

- Chapter 1, "The Integrated Development Environment," provides information on using facets of the IDE that are not necessarily debugger-related.

- Appendix B, "Working with EasyWin," gives detailed information on how you can use EasyWin to quickly develop Windows applications such as the prime-number example used throughout this chapter.

II

Learning C/C++

Chapter 17

ANSI and Turbo C++

Unlike many other popular programming languages (such as C, COBOL, FORTRAN, and so on), the C++ language has not been officially standardized. For this reason, compiler vendors such as Borland rely on a variety of mechanisms that help dictate a *de facto* standard. Although this state of affairs may appear on the surface to be rather chaotic, in reality the language is evolving toward a stable and consistent implementation.

This is due in large part to the efforts of the joint ANSI/ISO committee that has been working to standardize the language for the last five or six years. Although compiler vendors have been free to implement their compilers in any fashion that they want, most follow the work of the ANSI effort very closely (indeed, most of the major vendors have representatives serving on the committee). The result is that although a final standard has not been ratified, most compiler vendors have been making every effort to keep in sync with the current working draft of this committee.

Borland is certainly no exception. In this chapter you'll learn how closely Turbo C++ complies with the still-evolving standard and you'll read about some of the features that still have to be incorporated into Borland's C++ implementation.

A Brief History of the C++ Standard

C++ was a product of Bjarne Stroustrup's interest in building an efficient simulation language at AT&T's Bell Labs during the early 1980s. However, it wasn't until 1989 that C++ had achieved enough of a critical mass to inspire the American National Standards Institute (ANSI) to create a standardization committee, X3J16. The International Organization for Standardization (ISO), which addresses concerns similar to ANSI's but on an international scale, embarked on a similar project with its own committee, WG21. In 1991, the two organizations put their efforts together and formed a single committee tasked with creating a unified ANSI/ISO C++ standard.

So what did this really mean? At the time, not much. Standardizing a computer language is a notoriously difficult task—it took ANSI about ten years to finish the C standard—and C++ is a notoriously complex language. As is typical of the standardization process, things initially moved ahead rather slowly.

For the last few years, however, the ANSI/ISO effort has been a very powerful and influential force in the C++ compiler industry. Vendors feel that keeping their compilers up to date with the current work of the standards committee is a competitive advantage. This has had the practical result of allowing X3J16 to control and shape the evolution of the language, without allowing a single vendor's implementation to become a *de facto* standard that might jeopardize or distract the standardization effort.

At the time of this writing, in early 1995, the committee has released its long-awaited public draft and the committee draft registration process has begun. This has a number of profound implications. The most important is that the standard is now feature-complete. The committee will no longer accept new feature proposals and will instead be concentrating on refining and polishing the current feature set in preparation for ratification. Although ratification is still a while off, there is a light at the end of the tunnel. Observers can at least feel confident that they know what features will be present in the final standard.

An Overview of Turbo C++'s Support for Standard C++

Despite the flurry of activity coming out of the ANSI/ISO committee, there is currently no such thing as an ANSI-compliant C++ compiler. Even if the standard were to be ratified tomorrow, there is still a certain amount of inherent lag time needed for vendors to incorporate features into their existing compiler products. Borland is no different from anyone else in this respect; Turbo C++ has a way to go before it satisfies the requirements of the current working draft.

The good news is that the Borland C++ products are some of the most up-to-date incarnations in the industry. Not only does Turbo C++ sport a number of cutting-edge features such as templates and exception handling, but some of these features have been in the product for years. For example, Turbo C++ has supported templates since 1991. Microsoft's Visual C++, on the other hand, did not get template support until late 1994. Clearly, Borland is one of the pioneers in the field of advanced C++ compiler design.

Table 17.1 will help give you a good idea of the major features you can expect to find in the final standard. The table also indicates whether the feature is currently supported by Turbo C++ 4.5. Note that by the time you read this, some of the specific names used within a feature may have been changed by the committee (for example, changing the name of the `xruntime` exception class to `runtime_error`). The features themselves, however, are expected to remain fairly constant. Also note that the table includes only the largest or most profoundly significant features. More minor features are not listed individually. Features such as enumeration overloading and template member functions fall into this category and do not appear in table 17.1.

Table 17.1 Language Extensions Expected To Appear in the Final ANSI/ISO Standard	
Extension	**Supported by Turbo C++ 4.5**
Type `bool`	No
operator `new[]()` and operator `delete[]()`	Yes
Specialty casts (for example, `const_cast`, `static_cast`, and `reinterpret_cast`)	Yes
Wide-characters (`wchar_t`)	Yes
Complex number class	Yes
`string` class	Yes
Wide-character `string` class	No
`iostreams`	Yes
Wide-character streams (template-based streams)	No
Templates	Yes
Exception handling	Yes

(continues)

Table 17.1 Continued	
Extension	**Supported by Turbo C++ 4.5**
Exception classes (for example, exception, logic_error, and runtime_error)	Some
Run-Time Type Identification (RTTI)	Yes
Namespaces	No
Standard Template Library (STL)	No

Many of these features are relatively new to the standard and it will be some time before you will see compilers supporting them. The Standard Template Library (STL), for example, is a large and very sophisticated piece of code. It will take a while for vendors to incorporate STL support into their products.

Other features are not as difficult to implement but still haven't "settled down" enough for compiler vendors to start incorporating them into their products. Although Borland may be able to integrate a feature such as namespaces into Turbo C++ quite quickly, there is little incentive to do so if the ANSI committee is changing the namespace specification often enough to make any released product immediately out of date.

ANSI Extensions That Turbo C++ 4.5 *Does* Support

In this section, you'll learn about some of the significant features of the draft standard that Turbo C++ currently supports in the 4.5 release. The following sections are overviews; other chapters cover many of these topics in more detail.

Operator *new[ ]()* and Operator *delete[ ]()*

Until recently, there was no simple and compiler-independent way for a program to dictate how memory for arrays was to be dynamically allocated. As discussed in Chapter 13, "Object-Oriented Methods," if you want to allocate memory for an object off the program's heap, you use operator new().

```
MyObj* pMyObj = new MyClass(arg1, arg2);
```

This simple implementation of memory management has been with C++ since the language's inception. It does not, however, explicitly address what to do about allocating arrays of items. An array of objects may have special concerns regarding memory requirements, multiple-dimensionality, and constructor/destructor invocation. With this in mind, it seems unfair to ask a user to address the question of array allocation within an overridden `new()` or `delete()` operator. After all, an array of `MyClass` is not the same as a single instance of `MyClass`. They are two separate cases with separate implementation concerns.

The solution that the ANSI committee decided on is to simply have two operators for allocating and deallocating objects: one set for single object instances (in other words, the traditional operators `new()` and `delete()`) and one set for the special case of arrays (in other words, operators `new[]()` and `delete[]()`). This allows the programmer who is providing his own versions of `new` and `delete` to ignore the issue of arrays if he knows it's not relevant.

The *string* Class

C++ is historically grounded in the C programming language designed by Brian Kernighan and Dennis Ritchie in the early 1970s. In C, and in C++ if the programmer so decides, character strings are represented by runs of character memory terminated with a NULL (ASCII character code zero). The problem with this technique is that it is error-prone because, among other things, the programmer has to constantly be aware of whether there is enough memory available to hold a particular string. For example, what do you think would happen if you allocated space for a ten-character string and then executed the following line of code?

```
strcpy(pMyString, "Here is a string longer than 10 characters.");
```

The compiler will not find fault with this code because it is syntactically correct. However, this string overrun will likely cause a Windows memory protection fault if it finds its way into your code.

In standard C++, you'll be able to take advantage of a `string` class that encapsulates the programmer's interaction with character strings. Errors such as the one described previously can't happen with a string object because the object would first check to see whether it has internally allocated enough memory before copying over the new string. If there is not enough memory allocated, the string can transparently extend or reallocate its internal memory buffer so that it can accommodate the new string. The following code compiles and executes without error:

Learning C/C++

```
string MyString("Ten chars");  // Including the NULL
cout << "The string is ->" << MyString << "<-" << endl;
MyString = "Here is a string longer than 10 characters.";
cout << "Now the string is ->" << MyString << "<-" << endl;
```

The string class also provides a wide variety of other services such as copy-on-write memory optimization, overloading of common operators, and encapsulated support for virtually all of the common functions that programmers need to perform with strings.

Templates

Templates were briefly discussed in Chapter 13, "Object-Oriented Methods," but we'll review them here for the sake of completeness. A template provides a function or class "skeleton" that leaves certain typing details unspecified. At compile time, complete classes are generated "under the covers" that satisfy the typing requirements made by your program.

Take as an example the case of the Middle() function in listing 17.1. Middle() takes three integers as arguments and returns the integer in the middle of the sort order.

Listing 17.1   A Version of the *Middle* () Function for Integers

```
int Middle(int a, int b, int c)
{
return (a <= b ? (b <= c ? b : Middle(a,c,b))) : Middle(b,a,c));
}
```

The problem with this approach is that you would have to provide a separate Middle() function for every different type with which you wanted to use Middle(). You would need a different Middle() function to process floats and yet another one for characters, but each of these function implementations would look identical. Now look at listing 17.2, which shows how to solve this problem using a template.

Listing 17.2   A Template-Based Version of *Middle* ()

```
template <class Type>
Type Middle(Type a, Type b, Type c)
{
    return (a <= b ? (b <= c ? b : Middle(a,c,b))) : Middle(b,a,c));
}
```

This template says to the compiler, "Here is the description of a function `Middle()` that takes three arguments of the same type and then performs these operations on them. Use this as an example to generate actual functions as they're needed." If the compiler then encountered a line of code that called `Middle()` with floating point numbers, like the following:

```
cout << "The middle valued item is "
     << Middle(21.34, 22.234, 99.234) << endl;
```

it would use the template description to generate a function that looks exactly like listing 17.2 but with the generic `Type` argument replaced by floating-point qualifiers. Although this example uses a simple function definition, templates can be used with classes as well.

As it turns out, templates are extremely useful for building *container classes*. A container class is a class that is responsible for maintaining collections of other object instances. Templates fit this bill quite nicely because the programmer can design and build a template-based container class without having any clue as to what will be stored inside it. These are exactly the sort of techniques used in the design and implementation of the Standard Template Library described later in this chapter.

Exception Handling

Nobody writes perfect programs, not even you. It is a fact of life that many (if not most) programs have bugs. It is also a fact of life that even those programs that don't have bugs need to deal with a wide range of error conditions, some of which were not anticipated by the programmer who wrote the program. Exception handling is an extension to C++ that provides a formalized mechanism for trapping and dealing with exceptional events.

Before exception handling, C++ programmers typically relied on codes returned from functions and methods to track error conditions. This led to code that often looked like that found in listing 17.3.

Listing 17.3   Error Handling before Exception Handling

```
// Declare our objects
Address    MyAddress("John Doe", "123 Park St.", "Anywhere", 61523);
Letter     MyLetter;

// Make sure that this is a correctly formatted address
int Error = MyAddress.Validate();
if (Error == BAD_FORMAT)
    cout << "Bad address format." <<endl;
```

(continues)

Listing 17.3 Continued

```
// The address is OK, so send off our letter
else
      MyLetter.Send(MyAddress);
```

There are a couple of problems associated with writing code such as this. First of all, the programmer has to know about the magic value BAD_FORMAT. What other error codes could be returned by the Validate() method? You can't tell. There's not even a clue as to what is returned when no error occurs. But the worst part of this code is found on the last line. The Send() method may return an error code, but since the programmer opted to not check, the letter may not get sent and the program would never realize it. One of the biggest problems with traditional error-reporting techniques is that most of them are optional. A lazy or uninformed programmer can potentially let serious errors slip by unnoticed.

With exception handling, however, it is possible to write code that signals serious errors in a manner that the programmer cannot ignore. Look at listing 17.4, which is the same piece of code but with some rudimentary exception handling added.

Listing 17.4 Catching Errors Using Exception Handling

```
// Activate exception handling for this piece of code
try {
    // Declare our objects
    Address    MyAddress( "John Doe", "123 Park St.",
                    "Anywhere", 61523);
    Letter     MyLetter;

    // Check for a valid address and send off the letter
    MyAddress.Validate();
    MyLetter.Send(MyAddress);
}
catch (string ErrorMsg) {
    cout << "An error occurred.\n" << ErrorMsg << endl;
}
catch (...) {
    cout << "An unanticipated error occurred." << endl;
}
```

Listing 17.4 is a big improvement over the first piece of code. You'll immediately notice that there are no more secret error numbers that you need to remember and that the execution path of a problem-free run is immediately self-apparent. If something goes wrong in Validate() or Send(), these methods can "throw" an exception. Exceptions are caught by handlers—those parts of the code in listing 17.4 that are denoted by the `catch` keyword. Because control reverts immediately to a handler when an exception is thrown, there's no way that a programmer can ignore an error condition that is serious enough to merit throwing an exception. To learn more about exception handling, you can refer back to Chapter 14, "Exception Handling."

Run-Time Type Identification

Here's an easy question: given a pointer with this definition,

```
Food *pMyFood;
```

what is the type of the object pointed to by `pMyFood`? If you stop to think about it for a second, you'll start to realize that maybe the question isn't quite as obvious as it first appears. The pointer could be uninitialized and point to garbage. The pointer could be initialized but unassigned (that is, it could be NULL). The pointer could, of course, be pointing to an object instance of type `Food`. However, the pointer could also be pointing to an object of a class *derived* from `Food`. `pMyFood` could actually be pointing to an object of type `Apple` or `ReesesPeanutButterCup`, but you can't tell if all you're given is a pointer to a `Food`.

Now what happens if you're pretty sure that `pMyFood` points to an `Apple` object and you want to call the `Peel()` method? Assume that `Apple` objects have a `Peel()` method and `ReesesPeanutButterCups` don't (Have you ever tried to peel a peanut butter cup?). Calling `Peel()` on a peanut butter cup would be disastrous. Your program would almost certainly cause a Windows protection exception when you tried to call the nonexistent method.

Run-time type identification provides a variety of mechanisms for determining the types of objects at run time. Using the preceding example, you could use the new `dynamic_cast` operator to check for the appropriate type, as in the following:

```
Apple *pMyApple = dynamic_cast<Apple*>(pMyFruit);
if (pMyApple)
    cout << "This fruit is an apple." << endl;
else
    cout << "This fruit is not an apple." << endl;
```

This casting operation will succeed only if `pMyFruit` really does point to an `Apple`. If it doesn't, `pMyApple` will be assigned a NULL value.

You can also use run-time type identification to get information about a class through its `Type_info` object. The `Type_info` class provides ways to get the name of a particular object class and to do simple comparisons. You can extract the appropriate class `Type_info` object using the `typeid()` operator:

```
if (typeid(*pMyFruit) == typeid(Apple))
    cout << "This fruit is an "
        << typeid(*p1).name() << "." << endl;
else
    cout << "This fruit is not an apple." << endl;
```

ANSI Extensions That Turbo C++ 4.5 *Does Not* Support

As good as Turbo C++'s coverage of the standard is, there are a number of key features that are not included in the currently shipping product. This does not reflect poorly on Borland; as previously mentioned, the Borland C++ products are some of the most ANSI-compliant on the market. It is probably safe to say that you can expect many—if not all—of the following language features to appear in the *next* version of Turbo C++ and Borland C++.

Namespaces

As C++ has gained popularity, more and more programmers have been developing their own class libraries for fun and profit. The popularity of the language has caused a number of unanticipated problems to arise that are related to pollution of the global namespace. Say, for example, that you want to use your friend Walter's cool `Gizmo` class. Walter gives you his library and header file, and you proceed to develop some classes that use `Gizmo`. Unfortunately, when it comes time to compile your code, the Turbo C++ compiler burps out an error message. It turns out that his `Gizmo` class is dependent on his definition of a Boolean type:

```
// Walter's Boolean
typedef enum { true, false } bool;
```

but your code uses a different definition for Booleans:

```
// Your Boolean
typedef unsigned char bool;
```

Just because you and Walter both happened to name your Boolean types exactly the same thing, you can't use the cool `Gizmo` class. Your program ends up being substandard, no one buys it, you declare bankruptcy, and you die lonely and embittered.

Don't worry. The ANSI committee has just saved your life and your friendship with Walter. Namespaces allow you to declare named areas of logical scope. Name collisions at the global level of scope can be solved by wrapping one of the definitions in a namespace. In the case of our `Gizmo` class, you can elect to create a `Walter` namespace.

```
// Create Walter namespace
namespace Walter {
    #include "Gizmo.h>
}
```

Classes, functions, definitions, and other symbols that appear within a namespace are accessed using a namespace prefix. To declare an instance of a `Gizmo`, you would write something similar to the following (assuming, of course, that the `Gizmo` class had a default constructor):

```
// Declare an instance of a Gizmo
Walter::Gizmo      MyGizmo;
```

Now you can use any of Walter's classes without fear of collisions. Your classes can continue to use your own definition of `bool` and his classes will end up using `Walter::bool`. Of course, prefixing your use of Walter's classes with the `Walter::` syntax is a little cumbersome, but the ANSI standard provides mechanisms for "hoisting" definitions from a namespace into the current scope. Since hoisted definitions do not require the namespace prefix, you can hoist all of Walter's definitions that don't collide with any of yours. In the worst case you may have to occasionally use the prefixes, but at least you gain access to the code.

The Standard Template Library

One of the largest and most dramatic additions to the ANSI standard occurred in the summer of 1994 with the acceptance of the *Standard Template Library* (usually referred to as *STL*). The STL is a container class library designed using generic programming techniques devised by Alexander Stepanov, Meng Lee, David Musser, and others. It tackles the problem of creating collection classes from an algorithmic vantage point. As a result, the STL classes perform efficiently but are very flexible and extendible.

Before you can start using STL, you need to have a firm grasp of three simple concepts: algorithms, iterators, and containers. A program uses containers to hold type instances, iterators to access and refer to items held by a container, and algorithms to process and manipulate container contents. As an example, this code fragment depicts how you might code a search through an array of integers:

```
// Declare the array
vector<int>  MyVector(100, 0);

... Do some things ...

// Now see if the number 7 is in the array
int found = binary_search(MyVector.begin(), MyVector.end(), 7);
```

In this code, `MyVector` is the container. It holds integers, as indicated by its template argument. The algorithm is encapsulated in the `binary_search()` function. Algorithms know nothing about the containers on which they work. Instead, they interact only with iterators, which know how to move about in containers and provide a consistent interface to item insertion and extraction. In the preceding example, `MyVector.begin()` and `MyVector.end()` are two container methods that return iterators.

The STL is a large class library, made up of many different container and algorithm types. Although it is efficient and sophisticated, it is surprisingly approachable and easy to learn.

From Here...

Now that you've learned the basics about Turbo C++'s ANSI-compliant features, you'll probably want to jump right in and give them a whirl. The following chapters give detailed advice and instructions on how to incorporate some of the programming features discussed in this chapter into your own programs:

- Chapter 13, "Object-Oriented Methods," contains information on a number of relevant C++ topics, including templates and the `new[]()` and `delete[]()` operators.

- Chapter 14, "Exception Handling," gives in-depth instructions on how to use exception handling in your programs.

Part III

Designing User Interfaces

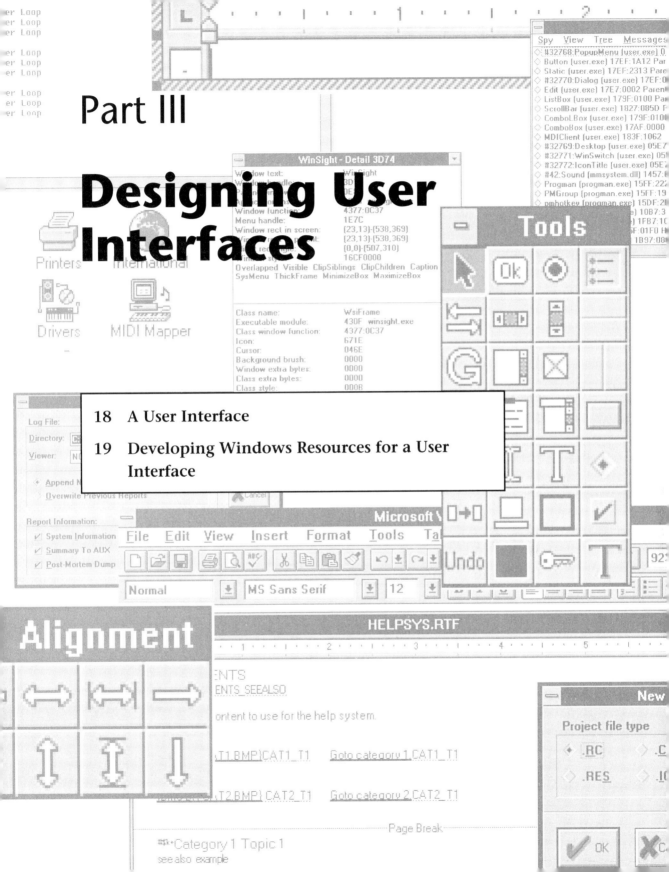

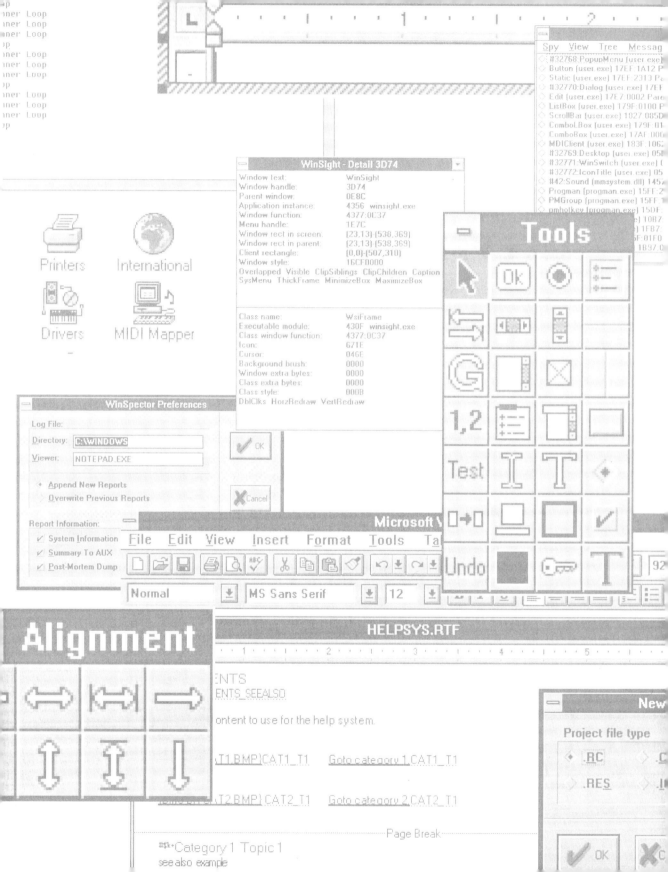

Chapter 18
A User Interface

Have you ever wondered what makes Microsoft Windows so overwhelmingly popular? There are probably lots of factors, but a major one has to be user interface features that behave similarly in different applications. This includes the Windows Clipboard, Windows Help, and Windows menus. These ingredients make it easy to use different Windows applications. In a nutshell, once you learn how to use one Windows application, you know the basics of most other Windows applications. As a Windows application developer, you can take advantage of this by making sure your applications contain the important things everyone expects in a Windows user interface.

This chapter covers the following topics:

- Features of a user interface

- Menu standards and guidelines

- Control and dialog box standards and guidelines

- Mouse and keyboard input guidelines

- Using color

- Designing effective user interfaces

- The relationship between a user interface and program code

The Components of a User Interface

A user interface consists of all the ways in which a program permits a user to provide input, along with all the mechanisms by which the program communicates information to the user. This includes the obvious things such as menus, dialog boxes, control buttons, and status bars. But it includes a lot more, too. The different activities an application allows a user to carry out with the mouse are part of the user interface. The Clipboard capabilities offered in an application are part of the user interface. A user interface also includes the ways in which a program changes colors or shapes of objects when they are selected or moved. An application's on-line Help is part of the user interface. Even the colors used in a program are a feature of the user interface. Finally, the manner in which program data is formatted for presentation on the display or for printing is part of the user interface. Basically, anything that conveys or receives information has to be considered part of the user interface.

When thinking about features in a user interface, avoid the temptation to categorize each as either user interface input or output. User interfaces are rarely that simple. For example, it might seem as though menus are just a mechanism for user input. However, well-crafted menus also provide important direction to the user. In effect they train the user to make best use of an application.

Some User Interface Standards and Guidelines

Certain things have become standard in a Windows interface. You can save yourself or your organization or business lots of time and money in software support if you ensure that software you produce follows most of these standards.

Menus

Menus are not a requirement in Windows applications, but nearly all applications have them. We usually think of menus in terms of the menu bar, the pull-down menus that are available from the menu bar, and toolbars that offer actions equivalent to those available on the pull-down menus. In addition to these menus, many applications have begun offering pop-up menus that are opened with the secondary mouse button (usually the right button).

Menu Bars

The menu bar is where the titles of all the pull-down menus appear. Figure 18.1 shows an example of a menu bar in a typical Windows application—in this case, Turbo C++ for Windows. Several features of this menu bar are common to nearly all Windows applications. All the menu titles on the menu bar are single-word nouns or verbs with the first letter capitalized. Each menu title also has a unique underlined letter that is the hot key for that menu. (The *hot key* is the letter that, when you type it while you press Alt, allows you to select the option.)

Tip
If you want your application to make a really positive impression on your users, try using verbs for menu titles whenever possible.

Fig. 18.1
A typical Windows application menu bar and toolbar from Turbo C++.

Several specific pull-down menus are found on the menu bar in nearly all applications. A number of other menus are common, but not universal. Table 18.1 summarizes the different menus frequently found on menu bars.

Table 18.1	Common Menu Bar Menus	
Menu	**Menu Bar Position**	**Comment**
File	Far left	Found in almost all applications except games, databases, and hardware utilities
Edit	Second from left	Expected in all applications that have editable objects or that use the Clipboard
Search	Third or fourth from left	Found in most text applications
View	Third or fourth from left	Found in many applications where different ways of visualizing data can be selected
Format	Fourth or fifth from left	Found in complex applications where there is extensive need to configure different data objects
Options	Varies	Often present if there are many configurable features in an application

(continues)

III

Designing User Interfaces

Menu	Menu Bar Position	Comment
Table 18.1 Continued		
Tools	Varies	Often present when there are utility type actions that provide additional analysis of application data without altering the data
Window	Second from right	Found in all applications with more than one window open at a time
Help	Far right	Expected in all applications

Even though menus such as View, Search, Format, Options, and Tools are not universal, it is easier for users of your applications whenever you can use these same menu titles.

Pull-Down Menus

A pull-down menu is what you see when you select a menu title from the menu bar. Figure 18.2 shows an example of a typical pull-down menu from Turbo C++. Pull-down menu commands can consist of more than one word, but only rarely is it a good idea to use more than three words. Main words are capitalized, and the access key for the command is underlined. Commands that require additional information from the user are followed by ellipses (...). Such commands usually produce a dialog box. If a command has an accelerator key or combination, it is always listed to the far right of the command. When the accelerator is a key combination, a plus sign separates the keys. Menu commands can also be represented by a small bitmap in addition to the text command. It is even acceptable to use a bitmap by itself, but this is not very common.

Related menu commands are always grouped together in a pull-down menu, and groups are separated by separator bars. The order and organization of commands in a pull-down menu are important. This is especially true for menus that are fairly universal in different applications. Figure 18.2 shows the standard organization of commands for the File menu. You may find applications in which there are additional options, or some commands may be absent because they don't apply. You will not, however, find good applications in which the ordering or grouping is substantially different. Examine the Edit, Window, and Help menus in Turbo C++, and you will see typical organization for these standard menus.

Fig. 18.2
A typical File pull-
down menu—this
one from Turbo
C++.

Toolbars

A toolbar is a row or column of buttons on the top, left, right, or bottom of
an application. Often these buttons duplicate the action of some pull-down
menu option. Toolbars have become very common in Windows applications.
They can save the user some effort with the mouse or keyboard, but only if
the functions of the buttons are obvious. Usually the only clue to a button's
function is a small bitmap image. Some applications use larger buttons. This
has the advantage that the function of each button is more obvious, or that
text can be added to indicate the button's function. This approach makes
sense if the application (and the user) can afford the extra space for larger
buttons.

> **Note**
>
> In designing an image for a toolbar button, it is natural to try to depict the computer
> activity actually initiated by the button. Sometimes, however, the name of the button
> has a meaning in everyday life that is easier to show than the actual computer activi-
> ty. A button image of this everyday meaning is often more memorable for users.
> Examples of this are the scissors and paste jar that are sometimes used to represent
> the electronic Clipboard activities cut and paste.

Many users only take the time to learn the location and function of buttons
in a few applications they use all the time. Therefore, unless the function of
the toolbar is always necessary in applications you produce (certain games,
for example), you should give your users the option to make the toolbar visible or invisible.

Pop-Up Menus

Pop-up menus are organized similar to pull-down menus, but they are not
attached to the menu bar. They typically appear when the secondary mouse
button (usually the right one) is clicked on some object in the main part of
an application. Figure 18.3 shows an example of a pop-up menu often seen in
Turbo C++. Pop-up menus depend on the particular context in an application. The pop-up menu shown in figure 18.3 is what you see after clicking the

secondary mouse button on a target node in the Project window. If you click this same mouse button from somewhere else in Turbo C++, you will see a menu with different options.

Fig. 18.3
A typical pop-up menu—the Turbo C++ SpeedMenu for a target node in the Project window.

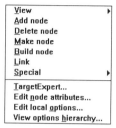

Controls and Dialog Boxes

Controls and dialog boxes offer important parts of Windows user interface functionality. Probably nothing distinguishes a great user interface from an average one more than effective choice of controls and dialog box layout.

Controls

Controls can be used in various parts of a user interface, but we usually think of them in the context of dialog boxes. Table 18.2 lists the major Windows controls and their main functions in a user interface. Figure 18.4 shows examples of some of these controls in the Turbo C++ Watch Properties dialog box.

Table 18.2	**The Major Windows Controls and Their Uses**
Control	**Use**
Push (command) button	User choice of commands (OK, Cancel, and so on). May have text, bitmap, or both on button face.
Check box	User selection of on/off setting.
Radio (option) button	User selection from among a series of mutually exclusive options.
Static	Program display of text or graphic.
Edit control	User text entry and editing.
List box	User selection from a list of text items.
Combo box	User entry of text or selection from a list.

Control	Use
Group box	Visual way to group related controls.
Scroll bar	User control of position in a window.

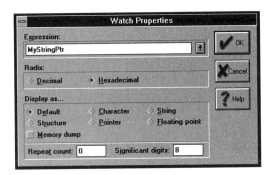

Fig. 18.4
A typical dialog box and controls—the Turbo C++ Watch Properties dialog box.

Edit controls, list boxes, and combo boxes deserve a few extra comments. Edit controls are very easy to program compared to list boxes and combo boxes. However, list boxes and combo boxes help reduce the amount of typing a user has to do. Further, even when a user needs to type a new selection in a combo box, the available list of other selections often helps the user overcome uncertainty about what to type.

In addition to the standard Windows controls described in table 18.2, there are a variety of custom controls available. The Borland controls (provided with Turbo C++) are a good example. Many custom controls simply give your interface a fancier appearance. But some, such as Borland's bitmapped OK, Cancel, and Help buttons, make your interface more clear for users.

Dialog Boxes
Dialog boxes have fewer standards than other parts of a windows user interface. This lends great flexibility and power to dialog boxes. Still, there are some guidelines it is wise to follow.

Always try to group related controls together (preferably in a group box). Don't, for example, put all the checkboxes together unless they are actually related. Optimal layout and grouping often require considerable trial and error, but this pays off in the long run. Refer to figure 18.4 as an example of layout and grouping of controls in a dialog box.

III

Designing User Interfaces

Don't put too much into any single dialog box. If the user really needs to make that many choices, usually you can organize the material into two or more different dialog boxes. You can nest dialog boxes by having a second dialog box appear when the user selects an appropriately labeled button in the first dialog box. This works well when there are satisfactory default selections in the second dialog box. In this way, selections in the second dialog box are strictly optional for the user. If it is really necessary for the user to make some kind of selection, do not put that item in a dialog box nested inside another dialog box. Also, it is generally unwise to nest dialog boxes more than two deep.

Learn to use *modal* versus *modeless* dialog boxes in appropriate situations. Modal dialog boxes force the user to exit the dialog box (by pressing OK, Cancel, Close, and so on) before the user can do anything else in the application. This is the most common and simplest type of dialog box. Modeless dialog boxes require more programming on your part. However, they help the user tremendously in any situation where the user may need to access another part of the application while a dialog box is open.

Caution

Users and developers seem to get confused by the different buttons that can be used to exit from a dialog box. OK should be used whenever the dialog requires the user to confirm selections or information before exiting. Cancel should always be available in addition to OK if the dialog box permits selections or entry of information. Close or Exit is appropriate whenever the dialog is constructed so that the user's selections take effect before leaving the dialog. In this latter case, it doesn't really matter how the user exits the dialog box.

Windows Common Dialogs

Windows provides default dialog boxes for file opening, file saving, printer selection, printing, font selection, color selection, and text searching. Using these dialog boxes generally saves you some programming. More importantly, these dialog boxes give your users standard interfaces they regularly see for these operations in other applications.

Mouse and Keyboard Input

The keyboard and mouse are standard vehicles for interface input in a Windows program. Other types of input such as pen and voice are becoming more common, but are beyond the scope of this discussion.

You can get a good idea how to use mouse and keyboard input by looking at different Windows applications. But if you are charting new territory, do not hesitate to develop new methods to use keyboard or mouse input in your application. Simply make sure your methods are as intuitive as possible for the user. Also, make sure your mouse and keyboard input methods do not conflict severely with methods used in other kinds of Windows applications. In addition to the usual types of mouse and keyboard input for menus and controls, you will want to carefully consider the following categories of mouse and keyboard input.

Creating Objects

Frequently the mouse and keyboard are used to create data objects within an application. For example, the keyboard is used to "create" text data objects in a word processor, and the mouse is used to create graphical objects such as lines, circles, and so on in drawing applications. If the user can select which type of object to create, it is necessary to implement different types of mouse pointers or keyboard cursors to indicate the type of activity permitted.

Selecting Objects

Selecting objects is an important input activity. It's best to make selection possible with either the mouse or keyboard. However, in some heavily graphical applications, it may not be practical to implement all types of selection with the keyboard. Usually, it should be possible to select either single or multiple objects (for example, a single character or a whole paragraph in a text editor).

Mechanisms for selection of single and multiple objects vary with the application. However, it is common to carry out multiple selection by dragging a rectangle around a region or group of objects with the mouse. Regardless of the types and mechanisms of selection, it is important to clearly indicate what is selected both during the selection process and after selection has occurred. Usually this means reversing or inverting the colors of the selected region or objects.

Moving Selections

In many cases, it is necessary to move a selection. We often think of moving a selection by grabbing and dragging the selection with the mouse, but sometimes the user can better control the move with cursor keys.

Moving a selection often requires the same mouse actions as making the selection. For this reason, it is essential to use different mouse pointers to initiate these two types of mouse activity. Because it is common to show a standard arrow pointer whenever the mouse pointer passes over a selection, it is usually necessary to show some other type of mouse pointer (a text or crosshair cursor, for example) for input the rest of the time. Make sure to give your users graphical cues when a selection is being moved. This usually means showing either the whole selection or an outline of the selection (or its objects) moving.

Executing Object Actions

You can often make things easy for users if you enable them to initiate important actions by double-clicking an appropriate object with the mouse. The action needs to be obvious and intuitive. It also should be equivalent to an action initiated with a menu command or toolbar button. If your application uses or displays different types of objects, it is very common to initiate different kinds of actions by double-clicking on different objects.

Colors

Tip

The Windows common Color dialog box is an easy way for you to let your users select the color(s) they prefer in your application.

Color can help make your application both functional and impressive. However, be cautious about using colors that are not defined to be the same as some Windows interface feature, such as window text. You don't, for example, want to use some specific drawing color if there's a chance one of your users has a window background color that's the same. Not everyone necessarily likes the same colors you do. Also, a fair number of users still have monitors or video cards that produce flicker. For these users, sometimes the only way to minimize flicker is through use of dark background colors. If your application must use colors other than those selected through Control Panel, make sure you provide a menu option and dialog box so that users can select the colors they prefer.

Creating Effective User Interfaces

Even with user interface standards, some user interfaces are much more effective than others. Here are four things you can do to create a really great Windows user interface:

1. Identify the most important tasks your users must do; then make those tasks easy. This usually requires thoughtful interface design as well as lots of behind-the-scenes programming. But your users won't soon forget your application.

2. Make sure your application behaves predictably. Menu commands should appear where the user expects them and do what their names

suggest. Controls should carry out whatever tasks the user expects. In short, you want a new user to know how to use the application on the first try.

3. Use visual cues liberally. User uncertainty is a big barrier in many software applications. You can do much to give users confidence by putting appropriate messages and information on a status bar. If a menu option or a control button isn't relevant in some situation, gray it out or remove it entirely.

4. Design good Help from the start. Today, most computer users expect good on-line Help. Unfortunately, you usually do not produce good on-line Help if it's the last phase of application development. Planning the Help system should be part of your program design process.

Connecting Program Function with the User Interface

By now you should have a good idea about the relationship between the user and a user interface. However, you probably wonder how user interface components connect to underlying program function. The following is a very brief overview of the relationship between a user interface and program code.

Handling User Input

Each user input operation has a corresponding function located in the program code. These functions are named *event handlers*. There is an event handler for each menu command. There also is an event handler for each kind of mouse action. When a user selects a menu command, Windows sends a message that causes the corresponding event handler to execute. Windows also takes responsibility for any immediate change in the user interface, such as closing the menu.

You write your program so that its functionality is called from within appropriate event handlers. Fortunately, you don't have to write code for every event handler. The ObjectWindows library already contains suitable code for many standard menu commands and interface activities. You don't need to modify this if you want standard behavior. This is yet another reason to use standard user interface features as much as possible.

III

Designing User Interfaces

Communicating from Your Program to the User

Methods used to convey information from a program to the user differ a bit from methods for user input. Most user interface controls have corresponding objects in the program code. You can send information to a control or alter its state by calling an appropriate function for the control's object. For example, using OWL you can display a text message on a status bar by calling the status bar object's SetText() function with the text string as an argument.

Displaying data in the main (client) region of an application window is a bit more complicated. In an OWL application, you write code in a Paint() function to display the data appropriately. Windows causes this function to be called whenever the display needs to be updated. You also can force the Paint() function to be called from within your program.

From Here...

This chapter has provided an overview of user interfaces. Included have been some standards and guidelines for Windows interface components and some strategies for building good user interfaces into Windows applications you develop. The coverage of many of these topics has been necessarily brief. Before you can actually put this information to work, you need to get some additional information about the specifics of creating Windows applications.

- Chapter 19, "Developing Windows Resources for a User Interface," shows you how to begin building some of the essential user interface features in Resource Workshop.

- In Chapter 21, "Using AppExpert," you can find out how to quickly produce user interface shells.

- Chapter 23, "Using Resource Workshop," demonstrates how to link resources to code to produce user interfaces.

- Chapter 24, "Windows Programming Basics," helps you grasp the finer points of incorporating graphics, resources, and mouse and keyboard input into your applications.

■ Chapter 27, "The ObjectWindows Library," lets you see the ObjectWindows library features you can use to build better user interfaces.

■ Chapter 28, "ObjectWindows Applications," gives concrete examples that implement user interface features, such as menus and mouse input, through ObjectWindows library code.

Chapter 19

Developing Windows Resources for a User Interface

It might surprise you if I said it's possible to create a Klingon-language version of the standard Windows 3.1 NOTEPAD.EXE file without having any of the code for the application, and without recompiling the executable. Of course you *would* have to know the Klingon language. Along the way, I suspect you also might encounter some ugly problems associated with the Windows Cyrillic alphabet code page and keyboard. Oh, and you would need something called a resource editor.

I really don't recommend you try this experiment. The copyright restrictions alone should stop you dead in your tracks. Nevertheless, the possibility points out some interesting things about Windows programs. Those menus, icons, dialog boxes, and other user interface features we associate with Windows software are really not all that tightly embedded in the programs themselves. These features are called *Windows resources*, and this chapter is all about how you can create them for your own Windows applications.

The chapter covers the following topics:

- Windows resources
- Using Resource Workshop
- Creating and editing menus
- Building and configuring dialog boxes
- Laying out dialog box controls

- Editing bitmaps

- Constructing icons and cursors

- Implementing string resources

Windows Resources

Resources are data objects you can include separately from your main code in a Windows development project. The most common resources are menus, dialog boxes, controls, icons, cursors, bitmaps, and strings. Even though resources are really just static data objects, we think of most of them as user interface features that we can lay out visually.

Resources offer a number of advantages. They reduce some of the complexity of developing a Windows application, because you can often design and create them without thinking in detail about the code to incorporate them into your applications. Storing user interface features as resources usually also improves memory management and efficiency in Windows programs. This occurs because resources are stored in memory separate from main program code, and resources usually aren't loaded into memory until they are actually needed. Resources are especially valuable in 16-bit Windows programs because they provide a way to have static data that doesn't take up precious space in main data segments but also doesn't need to be loaded from a separate file.

Using Resource Workshop

Resource Workshop is a graphical environment for creating and editing resources visually. It stores all the necessary information about your resources for a project in a text-based resource script file. Resource Workshop has special editors for menus, dialog boxes, graphics, strings, accelerators, and text. This chapter covers the menu editor, dialog editor, graphic editor, and string editor.

Starting Resource Workshop

To start Resource Workshop, double-click the Resource Workshop icon found in the Turbo C++ 4.5 group in Program Manager. Initially, the Resource Workshop window appears, along with the Borland Resource Workshop logo. When the logo disappears after a few seconds, you are ready to get your hands dirty with resources.

First, you need a resource project. To create a new resource project, choose
File, New Project. When the New Project dialog box appears, select .RC
(resource script) for the Project file type, and then choose OK. A resource
project window with the caption untitled.rc appears in Resource Workshop,
immediately followed by an Add File to Project dialog box. You can close this
dialog box by clicking the Cancel button. At this point, Resource Workshop
looks something like figure 19.1. Before you go much further, you probably
want to use File, Save File As to rename and save your project.

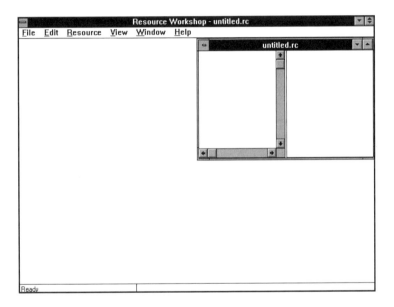

Fig. 19.1
An initial resource
project window
in Resource
Workshop.

To work on an existing resource project rather than a new project, use File,
Open Project to select the resource file you want. Resource Workshop can
open a variety of different kinds of files. Here you are interested only in .RC
resource script project files.

Adding New Resources

In Resource Workshop, you often need to add new resources to your resource
project. To add a new resource, do the following:

1. Choose Resource, New.

   The New Resource dialog box appears, as shown in figure 19.2.

2. Select the desired type of resource from the Resource Type list box in
   the New Resource dialog box. The available resource types are ACCEL-
   ERATORS, BITMAP, CURSOR, DIALOG, DLGINIT, FONT, ICON, MENU,

RCDATA, STRINGTABLE, and VERSIONINFO. Many of these are discussed in greater detail later in this chapter.

3. Make any necessary changes in the Place Resource In combo box and the Place Identifiers In combo box.

4. Click OK to close the New Resource dialog box.

Fig. 19.2
Using the New
Resource dialog
box to select a
new resource.

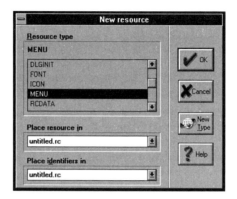

Resource Workshop immediately prompts you for any additional essential information. It then adds your new resource to the resource project window using a default identifier name. Finally, Resource Workshop opens the appropriate editor for the resource.

Resource Identifiers

Individual resources (and often parts of resources) in a resource project are usually associated with numerical identifier values. There are usually also associated identifier names to make resources more easily recognizable. Commonly, you put the identifier names and their associated values in an included file (.H or .RH). For simplicity, I haven't done this for the examples in this chapter. It is always advisable to avoid duplicate names that have the same identifier values. Very often, therefore, you need to change the identifier value or name assigned to a resource. To change the identifier name or value for a resource, do the following:

1. Choose Resource, Identifiers from the Resource Workshop menu.

An Identifiers dialog box similar to figure 19.3 appears.

2. You can use the radio buttons in the Sort group to list identifiers in alphabetical order by name, or in numerical order by value.

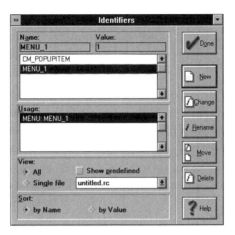

Fig. 19.3
The Identifiers
dialog box allows
you to change
identifier names
and values for a
resource.

3. Click the Rename button if you want to change the identifier name
associated with a particular identifier value. Alternatively, click the
Change button if you want to change the identifier value associated
with an identifier name.

4. Click the Done button when you are finished.

Developing Resources for a User Interface

You generally use Resource Workshop to develop all the user interface resources for a Windows application. Typical steps in developing a complete
resource project are the following:

■ Use Resource Workshop to add new MENU resources for each main menu
and pop-up menu your application needs. Add pull-down menus and
menu items to each menu using the menu editor. Usually an application needs one or more main menus and possibly one or two pop-up
menus.

■ Add as many new ICON resources as you need, and use the graphic editor to draw the images for the icons. An application nearly always has
one application icon—with possibly two or more images. You may need
additional icons for other purposes such as different types of windows
in a Multiple Document Interface (MDI) application.

■ Add new CURSOR resources for any custom cursors in your application.
For each cursor, use the graphics editor to draw the image and set the
cursor hot spot (the image pixel used by Windows as the cursor location). Many applications don't use custom cursors.

III

Designing User Interfaces

- Add new BITMAP resources for each toolbar button in your application. Draw the images in the graphic editor.

- Add new BITMAP resources and use the graphic editor to produce any additional bitmaps your application needs.

- For each dialog box needed by your application, add a new DIALOG resource and use the dialog editor to add controls and configure and organize the dialog box.

- Add new STRINGTABLE resources to your project. Use the string editor to add or edit the string text and group the different strings appropriately.

- Name and organize the identifiers for different resources in Resource Workshop.

It is not necessary to do these steps in any particular order, nor is it necessary to do them in a single Resource Workshop session. It is very common to develop the menu(s), icon(s), and perhaps only one or two dialog boxes early in a Windows software development project. You then add more dialog boxes as your project progresses.

The RCDEMO.RC resource project is an example of a typical resource project for a simple application. Figure 19.4 shows what the resource project window looks like for RCDEMO.RC. In a minute, you'll use these resources to examine some of the different editors in Resource Workshop.

Fig. 19.4
The resource project window for RCDEMO.RC in Resource Workshop.

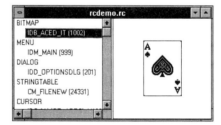

Editing Resources

To edit any resource in the resource project window, you either double-click the resource identifier or you select the resource identifier and choose Resource, Edit. For most resources, this immediately invokes the appropriate editor. However, ICON and CURSOR resources can have different images as part of the resource. When you select one of these resources to edit, Resource Workshop opens another text window showing the available image types. To visually edit one of these images, you need to choose Images, Edit Image for the desired image.

The Menu Editor: Menus and Accelerators

Almost all Windows programs contain one or more menus. Resource Workshop provides a convenient visual facility for working with menus. If you open the menu editor for the IDM_MAIN menu in RCDEMO.RC, you should see something like figure 19.5.

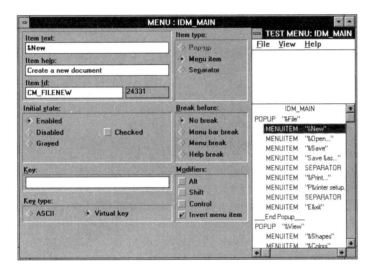

Fig. 19.5
The Resource Workshop menu editor with the *IDM_MAIN* menu.

The menu editor window has three main window panes. On the left is an attribute dialog box for entering and selecting menu item information, accelerator key information, and other related menu attributes. In the upper right of the menu editor is a test pane showing what the resulting menu will look like. You can pull down menus and generally examine the look and feel of your menu in this pane. In the lower right pane of the menu editor is an outline text representation of the menu resource script.

In the menu editor, you can add pull-down menus, menu items, or even entire preconstructed pull-down menus to a MENU resource. You do this with commands from the Resource Workshop Menu menu, shown in figure 19.6.

Tip
If you prefer to see the test menu spread out over the entire top of the menu editor, you can select this layout from the Resource Workshop View menu.

III

Designing User Interfaces

Fig. 19.6

Use Resource Workshop's Menu menu to add items to a *MENU* resource.

Menu	
New pop-up	Ctrl+P
New menu item	Ins
New separator	Ctrl+S
New file pop-up	
New edit pop-up	
New help pop-up	
Check duplicates	
Accelerator key value	
Change identifier prefix...	
√ Track test menu	

Caution

Resource Workshop uses the term "pop-up" in several confusing and contradictory ways. When you add a new MENU resource to your project, Resource Workshop puts *Pop-up* as the default pull-down menu name on your menu bar. This name is merely a placeholder, and you should replace it with a name that is appropriate for your particular menu. On the Resource Workshop pull-down Menu menu, pop-up also is used in several commands that actually add a pull-down menu to your menu bar. You can use the New Pop-up menu item to add either a pull-down menu or a true pop-up menu. If you intend to add a true pop-up menu, you should select View, View as Pop-up to see the menu as a pop-up. In this case, Pop-up has its true meaning.

Tip

Once you are comfortable with the menu editor in Resource Workshop, the accelerator combinations Ctrl+P, Ins, and Ctrl+S provide the fastest way to add new pull-down menus, menu items, and separators to your menu resources.

To add a new pull-down menu, menu item, or separator to a MENU resource in the menu editor, follow these steps:

1. Select the line in the outline pane of the menu editor immediately preceding where you want to insert the pull-down menu, menu item, or separator.

2. Choose New Pop-up from Resource Workshop's Menu menu for a pull-down menu, or choose New Menu Item or New Separator for a menu item or separator.

As soon as you make an addition, you see it on the menu in the test pane. New pull-down or pop-up menus have the default name Popup. New menu items have the default name Item. In each case, the corresponding text appears in the outline pane of the menu editor.

The menu editor also provides very convenient facilities for editing existing menus or menu items. To edit an existing menu or item, follow these steps:

1. In the outline pane of the menu editor, select the POPUP line for any pull-down menu you want to edit, or the MENUITEM line for any menu item you want to edit.

2. Change the Item Text to whatever you want in the attribute dialog pane of the menu editor.

3. For menu items, the Item Help box will be enabled. Type whatever description of the command you want the user to see on the status bar in your application. This is an important clue to help your users navigate the menu(s) in your application.

4. The Item Id box will be enabled only when you are editing menu items. Type whatever identifier name you want for the menu item.

5. Make any desired selections in the Initial State and the Break Before parts of the dialog box. (Experiment with these options if you are uncertain what they do.)

6. Press Enter to put your changes into effect.

If you want an accelerator key associated with a menu item command, select the item in the outline pane. Then choose Menu, Accelerator Key Value and follow the indicated instructions. (Make sure to add \t and a text abbreviation for the accelerator combination to the right of the menu item in the Item Text box.)

In addition to the various options described previously, you also can cut, copy, or delete menu items or entire pull-down menus in the menu editor. First, select the desired MENUITEM line or POPUP line in the menu editor outline pane, and then choose the desired operation from the Resource Workshop Edit menu.

Using the Dialog Editor: Dialog Boxes and Controls

Dialog boxes and controls are essential parts of nearly every Windows application. The Resource Workshop dialog editor allows you to add, position, group, and otherwise configure radio buttons, check boxes, static controls, edit controls, list boxes, combo boxes, icons, push buttons, and even custom controls in your dialog box resources. In addition, the editor provides tools for ordering and grouping controls, for setting tab stops, and for testing the overall behavior of your dialog boxes.

III

Designing User Interfaces

Dialog Resources

If you open the dialog editor for the IDD_OPTIONSDLG resource in RCDEMO.RC, you should see something like figure 19.7.

Fig. 19.7

The Resource Workshop dialog editor showing the *IDD_OPTIONSDLG* dialog box.

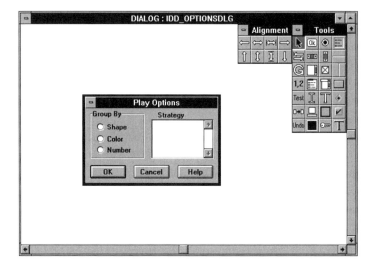

The dialog editor always shows the approximate location and appearance of the dialog box resource. The location is relative to the dialog editor window. You can move a dialog box into a different location by grabbing its caption box and dragging with the mouse. Likewise, you can change the shape or size of the dialog box by grabbing and dragging a side or a corner with the mouse (just as you would for a regular window).

If you double-click anywhere on the main part of a dialog box, you see a Window Style dialog box that is similar to figure 19.8.

■ You can type whatever default caption you want for the dialog box in the Caption box.

■ The Class list box refers to different dialog appearances that are available. The list box lets you select bordlg, BorDlg_Gray, or none.

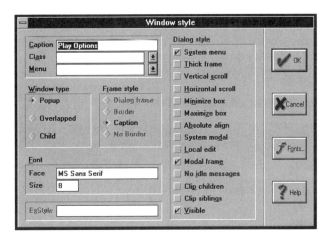

Fig. 19.8
Set characteristics
for your dialog
box in the
Window Style
dialog box.

Fig. 19.8
Set characteristics
for your dialog
box in the
Window Style
dialog box.

> **Note**
>
> Resource Workshop allows you to select from among three different classes of
> dialog box appearance: none (the standard Windows dialog appearance), the
> bordlg appearance with a stippled, aluminum gray background, and the
> BorDlg_Gray appearance with a smooth, aluminum gray background. Ex-
> amples of the latter two classes can be found in different dialog boxes in
> Turbo C++ and in Resource Workshop. If you choose either of these classes,
> you also need to enable the BWCC library in your application code. In addition
> to these options, you can enable the Windows 3D Control Library in your
> application code to give your dialog boxes and controls the modern Windows
> 3-D look. If you want this appearance, you should use none for the dialog class
> in Resource Workshop. With this appearance, you also may want to select Use
> Ctl3dv2.dll under Options, Preferences to make your dialog boxes in Resource
> Workshop appear more like they will in the actual application.

- Menu is seldom used, but it permits you to select a menu resource to attach to your dialog box.

- Window Type is usually popup, but you can experiment with other choices.

■ Frame Style is usually Caption. In fact, Caption is the only option if you already have a caption in the Caption box. You may want to try other options after removing any text from the Caption box.

■ Font is usually MS Sans Serif for the Face and 8 for the Size. You can change these by clicking the Fonts button.

■ There are many options for Dialog Style. The usual selections are System Menu, Modal Frame, and Visible. You can play with other alternatives, but some of these affect only your actual application.

Your selections in the Window style dialog box take effect when you click OK.

The Dialog Editor Floating Palettes

The dialog editor has two floating palettes. You can drag either of these palettes anywhere you like in the dialog editor.

The Alignment palette contains different buttons that make it easy to align or move groups of controls in a dialog box. To use these buttons, you must first group two or more controls in the dialog box by drawing a rectangle around or through them with the mouse. Then choose one of the alignment buttons from the palette to center or align the selected controls as indicated on the button.

The Tools palette is the most useful part of the dialog editor. Some of the tools in the Tools palette have equivalent Resource Workshop menu commands. In most cases, however, the tools are much easier to use than the menu options. All the tools in the left column of the palette are used to accomplish general editing and configuration tasks for your dialog box. The tools in the second and third columns allow you to add different standard Windows controls to your dialog box. The tools in the fourth column allow you to add different Borland-style controls to your dialog box, and are the only easy way to do so.

Dialog Controls

To add a control to a dialog box, select the tool palette button for the control you want to add. The cursor immediately changes to the image for that control tool with a plus sign in the upper left corner. Position the plus sign at the location where you want the top left of the control. Click the mouse, and the control appears in the dialog box. You can adjust the position and size of a

Tip
When positioning a control in a dialog box, you can make finer movements by selecting the control with the mouse and then moving the control with the cursor keys.

control by grabbing and dragging either the entire control or a corner or side of the control with the mouse. You also can double-click a control to access a configuration dialog box for that control. Double-clicking the Shape radio button in the IDD_OPTIONSDLG dialog box produces the Button Style dialog box shown in figure 19.9.

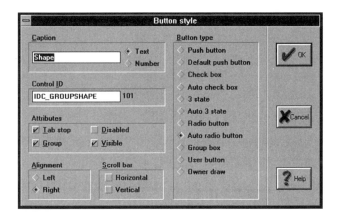

Fig. 19.9
The Button Style dialog box for configuring a radio button.

Ordering, Grouping, and Setting Tab Stops

For a dialog box to function properly, it is important to properly set the order, grouping, and tab stops for all the controls in the dialog box. If you don't do this, a user without a mouse (or with a disabled mouse) cannot navigate around your dialog box. There are three steps:

1. Set the proper order for all controls. You want controls to be ordered in the same way you expect a user to progress through the controls with the Tab key. If any controls are to be grouped, you want those controls to be in sequential order appropriate for the group.

2. Group controls. You do this by giving group designation to the *first* control in each group. You also have to give group designation to *all* controls that are *not* part of any group.

3. Set tab stops for each control or group that you want the user to be able to access with the Tab key.

Once you have carried out these steps, your users should be able to use the cursor keys to move between controls within any group. They also should be able to use the Tab key to move among different groups and individual controls.

III

Designing User Interfaces

Using the Graphic Editor: Bitmaps, Icons, and Cursors

Nearly all Windows applications have one or more icons, and many applications also have bitmaps or cursors. Resource Workshop provides a really good graphic editor for working on image resources such as these. The graphic editor has many features in common with Windows Paintbrush, but it offers broader control over image attributes, it has color palettes up to 256 colors, and it has greater capacity to zoom in on images.

Bitmap Resources

Figure 19.10 shows what the Resource Workshop graphic editor looks like for the IDB_ACED_IT bitmap resource in RCDEMO.RC after zooming in on the image twice.

Fig. 19.10

The graphic editor showing the *IDB_ACED_IT* bitmap.

Tip

Split views in the graphic editor are very useful for small images. To see more of large images, you probably want to move the split divider all the way to the side.

The Resource Workshop View menu provides options to zoom in on or out from your image. It also allows you to control how the graphic editor image screen is split. The Text menu gives you control over fonts and positioning of any text you add to your image. You can use the Options menu to select pen, brush, airbrush, and region fill patterns and shapes. The Bitmap menu permits you to edit palette colors and change your image attributes, such as image size and number of colors.

Much of the power in the graphic editor lies in the floating palettes of image tools and colors. You can move these palettes anywhere you want in the graphic editor. From the Colors palette, you can select the foreground color with the primary (left) mouse button and the background color with the secondary mouse button. The background color is mostly important only when you cut or move regions of your image. The Tools palette provides a variety of different drawing and painting tools.

Icon and Cursor Resources

When the graphic editor opens for an icon or cursor image, things appear much the same as for a bitmap image. Figure 19.11 shows what the IDC_MAJOR_ARROW cursor from the RCDEMO.RC project looks like in the graphic editor.

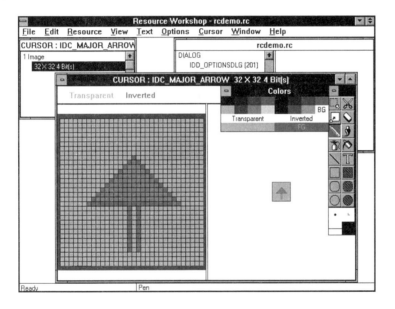

Fig. 19.11
The graphic editor showing the *IDC_MAJOR_ARROW* cursor.

The Colors palette for ICON and CURSOR resources does differ a bit from that for BITMAP resources. There are two additional boxes labeled Transparent and Inverted. Icons and cursors frequently use a transparent background. The graphic editor has to have some color to represent these transparent regions of the icon image. Likewise, you sometimes want to use a color guaranteed to contrast against whatever transparent background appears behind the icon. The Inverted color achieves this.

ICON and CURSOR resources also have a Test command on the Icon and Cursor menus. CURSOR resources have an additional command to set the cursor hot spot. The hot spot is the exact cursor pixel used as the cursor position when you click on something with the cursor. Always make sure the cursor hot spot is obvious to the user from the shape of your cursor. To set the hot spot for a cursor, follow these steps:

Tip
It is easier to edit small images such as icons and cursors with a grid present. To get a grid, choose Options, Editor Options and check the Grid on Zoomed Windows checkbox.

III

Designing User Interfaces

1. With your cursor visible in the graphic editor, position the mouse cursor over the pixel you want for the cursor's hot spot.

2. Read the x and y coordinates of this pixel from the Resource Workshop status bar.

3. Choose <u>C</u>ursor, Set <u>H</u>ot Spot.

4. Type the coordinates for the cursor hot spot in the Set Hot Spot dialog box and click OK.

The hot spot for the IDC_MAJOR_ARROW cursor is located at position x = 16 and y = 8, just at the upper tip of the arrow.

Using the String Editor: Strings and String Tables

Strings are a powerful but much underutilized resource in Windows programs. By putting your application's text strings in a resource project, you achieve several things. You free up valuable space in the program data segment for your application. You may also reduce the memory used by your application if your string resources are organized so that only certain groups of strings are used in your application at any time. Finally, if you put all your application text into your resource project, you make it much easier to adapt your application for different foreign languages without having to completely recode your application. Now that software is becoming more international in flavor and distribution, this last feature is especially important.

String Table Resources

String resources are organized in string tables. When you add a new STRINGTABLE to your resource project, Resource Workshop names your STRINGTABLE with the identifier of the first string in the table. Figure 19.12 shows what the string editor looks like when it starts up in Resource Workshop.

The string editor shows three fields for every string in a STRINGTABLE. The ID Source is simply the identifier name or number for the string. You can edit this as a text field in the string editor. The ID Value is the number of the identifier. You cannot edit the ID Value for a string directly in the string editor, but you can change the number associated with the identifier by choosing <u>R</u>esource, I<u>d</u>entifiers from the menu and editing the selected identifier in the resulting Identifiers dialog box. The String field is simply the text for your string. You can edit this at will in the string editor. To add new strings to your STRINGTABLE resource, choose <u>S</u>tringtable, <u>N</u>ew Item from the Resource Workshop menu.

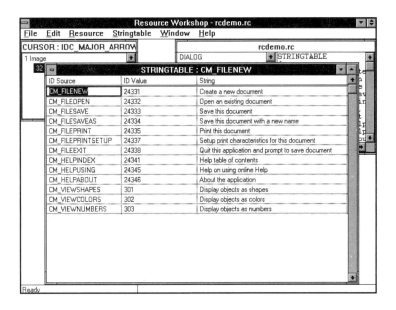

Fig. 19.12
The string editor.

Considerations for Using String Resources

There are a few practical things you should know about string resources. Individual strings are limited in length to 255 bytes. Also, you cannot use the usual C language syntax for linefeeds and carriage returns. Instead, you should use octal notation: \012 for a linefeed and \015 for a carriage return.

Windows loads resource strings for your application in groups of up to 16 strings. You might think Windows loads groups of strings as they are organized in the STRINGTABLE resource. This can be true, but it doesn't have to be. Windows actually organizes your string resources according to their identifier numbers. So, Windows treats all strings with identifiers between 0 and 15 as one group, all strings with identifiers between 16 and 31 as a second group, and so on. The group doesn't have to have strings for every identifier in the range. You can use this feature to optimize the performance of resource strings in your application. For strings that all need to be used at the same time, you want to choose identifiers in the same group of 16. Strings that don't need to be used at that same time should have identifiers in a different range(s). If you want, you can choose identifiers for different strings to optimize the string loading performance, but group those strings in STRINGTABLES on some other logical basis.

Editing Resource Scripts as Text

The .RC file for your resource project is really a text resource script. Even though Resource Workshop provides a convenient visual environment for

III

Designing User Interfaces

working with resources, there are times when it is more useful to view or edit a resource script as text. You can do this several ways. To view or edit the text for any specific resource, select that resource in the resource project window, and then choose Resource, Edit as Text. Resource Workshop then opens a text window for the selected resource. You also can open the entire resource script file as text in Windows Notepad or in Turbo C++ by choosing File, Open and then selecting the desired .RC file.

From Here...

You should now have a basic understanding of the fundamental Windows resources and how to create and edit them using Resource Workshop. You're probably still unclear exactly how resources relate to your application code. You can find more information about this in the following places:

- Chapter 22, "Using ClassExpert," explains how to connect resource identifiers to program code.

- The application of Resource Workshop to actual software projects is covered in Chapter 23, "Using Resource Workshop."

- Chapter 24, "Windows Programming Basics," addresses resource loading and communication with resources through Windows messages.

- A number of examples that implement resources can be found in Chapter 28, "ObjectWindows Applications."

Part IV

Customizing
Code

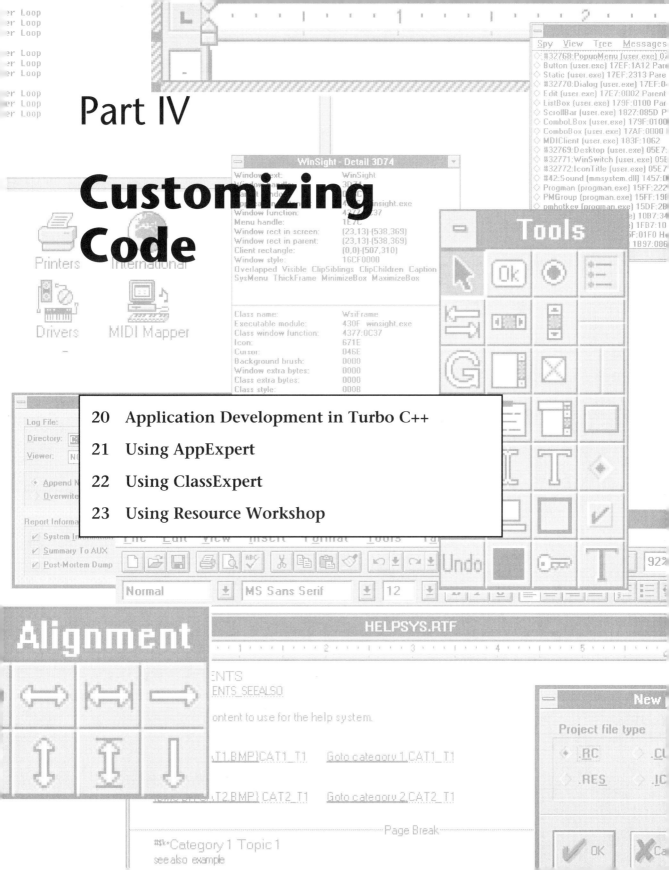

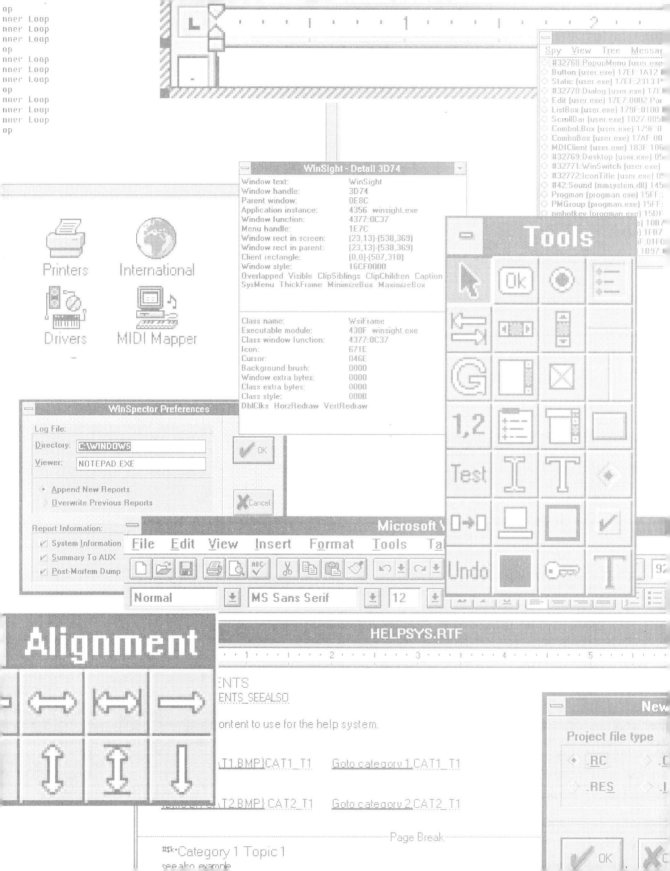

Chapter 20

Application Development in Turbo C++

Whether you are a new or experienced Windows programmer, Turbo C++ provides two tools that will increase your application development productivity and enjoyment: AppExpert and ClassExpert.

These tools automate the mundane-but-required programming tasks necessary for developing Windows applications by creating a code foundation to support applications and allow you to build your application by modifying and extending this code base. These tools are an integral part of the Turbo C++ development environment, working in conjunction with the IDE, TargetExpert, Resource Workshop, and the ObjectWindows Library.

These tools free you from Windows programming details, allowing you to concentrate on your application. In minutes or hours, rather than days or weeks, you can create a professional-caliber, custom Windows application. Windows applications are now within reach of even the casual programmer for programs of all ranges of complexity.

In this chapter, you learn

- The basics of Windows application design.

- How to use the Turbo C++ AppExpert to create the source code for a Windows application.

- How to modify a Windows application using ClassExpert.

- How to incorporate code from other projects using Rescan.

Doing Windows Is Work

This was once universally true, but as you are about to see, Borland has made Windows easy. What makes Windows so hard? While Windows application development is not intellectually challenging, it is laborious. A lot of programming effort, in a lot of files, containing a lot of lines of code, is involved in creating a basic Windows application that does very little. Even a minimal Windows application has an icon, a window, a toolbar and some basic drop-down menus. Figure 20.1 shows what such a Windows application looks like.

Fig. 20.1
A basic Windows application interface.

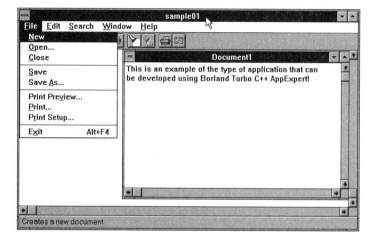

This application can be resized, minimized, and maximized. Menus can be dropped down from the toolbar, and many of the toolbar functions produce reasonable results.

Each of the elements and operations in this application represents some amount of code—often a great deal—that you have to write. This effort has often discouraged programmers from writing a simple application for Windows.

A competent Windows programmer might spend hours or even days creating this basic program foundation, and this is time that would be better spent developing the application. A more experienced programmer would save much of this time by copying code created for a previous application to use as the starting point for the new application. The programmer would then modify this code by modifying the classes and objects to create the new application and might incorporate application code from other projects.

This Windows development expert would have a tool chest filled with basic applications of all varieties to use as a starting point for new development. For each minor variation, the programmer would either create a new application foundation or try to remember what changes are necessary. This process is expensive in time and money and prone to error. Fortunately, it is also a process that can be automated.

While there are more similarities than differences between windows applications, there are a few common variations (covered in detail in Chapter 29, "Single and Multiple Document Interfaces"):

■ Single Document Interface (SDI). This application model supports child windows outside the application main window. The child windows may be positioned and sized independent of the main window.

■ Multiple Document Interface (MDI). In this model, the child windows are constrained within the application main window. Child windows exceeding the main window in size will be clipped to the edge of the main window.

■ Dialog Client. This model restricts your application to a single dialog window. The client area of the application is a dialog box in this window.

Borland has captured the techniques and trade secrets of Windows development experts (Borland has a lot of them) in the AppExpert and ClassExpert tools. Unlike some human experts, the Borland Experts listen: You can specify application options and have the Borland Experts create a code foundation tailored to meet your needs. You can now develop Windows applications like a pro, using a foundation of error-free code produced by the Borland Experts.

You can even incorporate code from other projects using Rescan. Rescan is a project maintenance tool used to update, rebuild and repair the project database (the .APX file) based on the contents of the source code. This allows you to add to the source code listed in your AppExpert project file (.IDE) and use Rescan to rebuild the AppExpert project database.

Borland's AppExpert and ClassExpert are more than simply convenient labor-saving utilities. When you use these tools you get a great deal of functionality including drop-down menus, file operations, and help, print, and print preview features. You also get consistency in the appearance and operation of your Windows applications, both with your other applications and with applications developed by others. This provides your application with a professional appearance and reduces the learning curve associated with using your application. You will reap the benefits of code reuse, and you will move your starting point forward to the point where Borland's professional team of developers left off. Also, you will be in position to take advantage of the other tools and libraries in the Turbo C++ suite to make your task even easier.

In the following sections you will see exactly how easy it is to use these tools in your next development effort.

Generating Windows Code Foundations with AppExpert

AppExpert generates the basic files you need for any Windows program, completing the first step in creating a Windows application: The code foundation. Based on your input, AppExpert creates all files needed for a complete, working Windows program. All that is left is to add the parts that make your application unique.

With AppExpert, you can create full-featured Windows programs that conform in appearance and operation to other Windows programs on your system. As you save the time and effort of mundane Windows programming tasks, you simultaneously benefit from a code base created by professionals for commercial applications. This well-tested and optimized code foundation helps you produce robust, high-performance applications.

Accessing AppExpert from the IDE

To start AppExpert from the Borland Turbo C++ IDE, choose Project, AppExpert. The New AppExpert Project dialog box appears (see fig. 20.2).

Fig. 20.2
The New
AppExpert Project
dialog box.

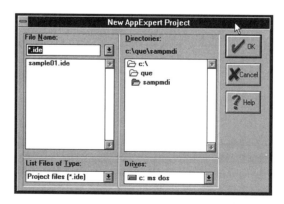

The AppExpert defaults shown in figure 20.2 are probably not what you want to use. If you would like your projects on another disk, click on the Dri<u>v</u>es combo box (drop-down list) and select the appropriate drive. Use the mouse to navigate through the <u>D</u>irectories icons until you have your desired directory folder open. Type in the desired new project name in the <u>F</u>ile Name text box. When satisfied with your selections, click the OK icon. The AppExpert Application Generation Options dialog box appears (see fig. 20.3).

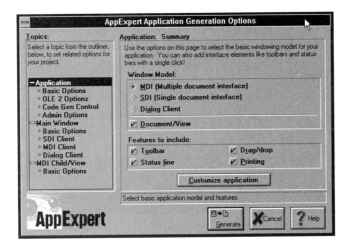

Fig. 20.3
The AppExpert Application Generation Options dialog box.

This screen is the focal point for defining your application.

Application Generation Options

The AppExpert Application Generation Options dialog box is divided into three regions:

- <u>T</u>opics, with an outline of application options. This provides a road map through the various options you will select to control the generation of your application foundation.

- The options region, to the immediate right of the <u>T</u>opics region. The contents of the options region change based on the selection made in the outline area of the <u>T</u>opics region. Each options region page contains several options for code-generation control.

- The control buttons immediately below the options region let you <u>G</u>enerate the application, Cancel, returning to the Borland IDE, or access on-line help.

You will notice a minus sign beside each of the main topics in the outline of the Topics region in figure 20.3. The subtopics, which are normally hidden, are shown in figure 20.3 for clarity. Normally, when the subtopics are not displayed, the main topics are preceded by a plus sign (not shown in fig 20.3). Clicking the plus sign expands the subtopics, while clicking the minus sign hides the subtopics.

You configure your application by selecting a topic from the outliner, which brings up a page of application-generation options. This will appear in the Options region of the AppExpert Application Generation screen. You can then set the options on these pages. Use the Application topic to select the basic windowing model for your application: MDI, SDI, or Dialog Client. You can also add or delete these features: Toolbar, drag-and-drop, status line, and printing. Use the Basic Options subtopic (or click Customize Application) to include help, control application startup state (Normal, Minimized, or Maximized) and to select a Windows style (Standard Windows, Borland BWCC, or MS Control 3D).

Use the Main Window topic to set the name and color of your application's main window. Use the Basic Options subtopic (or click Customize Main Window) to select window styles and control interaction of the window with sibling and children windows.

Use the MDI Child/View topic to set the class and source names for the default MDI child class. Use the Basic Options subtopic (or click Customize Child and View) to set document and view options. This section affects MDI applications only.

As you can see, there are many options for your use in controlling the generation of your application foundation. Once you have set all the options for your application, click the Generate button to automatically create the Windows code foundation for your application.

> **Note**
>
> If you leave something out or change your mind about a selection after you have generated your code foundation, you must either modify the code by hand or regenerate the code with your new selections. Regenerating the code wipes out any code from your previous selections. For this reason, you should build and test your foundation code before you leave AppExpert.

Files Generated by AppExpert

AppExpert creates all the source files for a complete Turbo C++ Windows program. In addition to the application files shown in figure 20.4, AppExpert creates the necessary project files, and icon and bitmap files used in your application. You have a complete, working code base from which to begin your application!

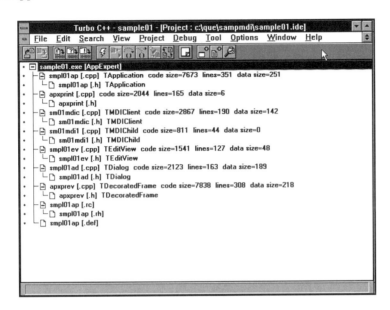

Fig. 20.4
Application files generated by AppExpert.

Once AppExpert has created your application code foundation, you return to the Borland Turbo C++ IDE screen. To test your code foundation, you choose Project, Build All and Debug, Run (or Ctrl+F9). If you selected the default AppExpert options, your application appears as shown in figure 20.5.

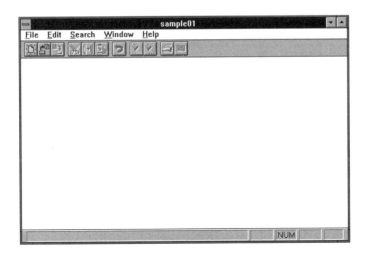

Fig. 20.5
The default application generated by AppExpert.

Now that you have your application code foundation, let's see how you use ClassExpert to complete your application.

Using ClassExpert to Build on AppExpert Foundations

Once you have built an application with AppExpert, you are ready to build on this code foundation. ClassExpert is the Turbo C++ tool for this job. ClassExpert lets you add classes, event handlers, and member functions to an AppExpert-generated application. You can browse your code to locate and modify the implementation of your existing classes, and you can customize the classes generated by AppExpert. Also, ClassExpert works with Resource Workshop to associate resources with your classes. You are never isolated from the full capabilities of the Turbo C++ environment.

You start ClassExpert by first opening a project created by AppExpert. Do this by choosing Project, Open Project and selecting the appropriate project. Then you choose View, ClassExpert or simply double-click the target node (the .ide file) of the AppExpert project. A ClassExpert window appears (see fig. 20.6).

Fig. 20.6
The ClassExpert window with three panes.

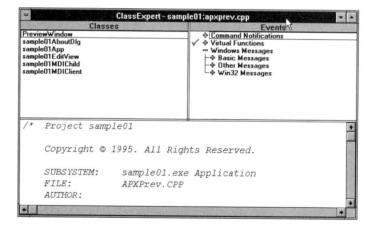

The ClassExpert Interface

Look at the basic controls you have when you use ClassExpert. The ClassExpert window is divided into three panes: the Classes pane, the Events pane, and the Edit pane at the bottom. These three panes provide a comprehensive view of your application code.

The Classes pane lists the classes managed by ClassExpert for the current project. This includes all classes generated by AppExpert as well as any classes you have added with ClassExpert. Your selection in the Classes pane controls the contents of the other two ClassExpert panes.

The Classes pane has a SpeedMenu that is accessed by right-clicking in the Classes pane (or pressing Alt+F10). SpeedMenus are a feature of Turbo C++ that offers quick access to frequently used functions. You can use the Classes SpeedMenu to add classes, view class options, examine and modify source code, and associate document classes with view classes.

The Events pane lists command notifications, virtual functions, and Windows messages of the class selected in the Classes pane. The contents of each of these lists depends on the base class of the class selected in the Classes pane.

You may notice checkmarks to the right of the entries in the Events pane. A light gray checkmark indicates that some of the events in that category are handled. You can view which specific events are handled by expanding the list. The handled events will have a dark checkmark beside them.

The Events pane SpeedMenu is accessed by right-clicking in the Events window (or pressing Alt+F10). You use this menu to add or modify event handlers, virtual functions and instance variables of the selected class. You have access to the capabilities of the Resource Workshop with the Edit Menu and Edit Dialog commands.

The Edit pane displays the source code associated with your selected class. For the most part, the Edit pane is the same as your IDE editor—it even uses customizations you have made to the IDE editor. However, the Edit pane cannot be split to view multiple files, and you cannot view other files from this pane.

The Edit pane SpeedMenu provides access to the most frequently used ClassExpert commands associated with source code. These include opening source files, browsing objects, and setting breakpoints and watchpoints. The Use Class selection creates code to instantiate a new class you have added.

With these controls you can complete a Windows application. From this interface you can do the following:

- Add a new class
- Create document types

IV

Customizing Code

■ Add and delete event handlers

■ Add and delete instance variables

■ Add classes from another project

Let's look at how these actions are accomplished with ClassExpert.

Adding a New Class

With ClassExpert you can add new ObjectWindows-based classes to any application you generated with AppExpert.

> **Note**
>
> ClassExpert supports single inheritance only. If your application requires a new class that must have multiple inheritance, you can create a simple, single inheritance class with ClassExpert and then manually modify this new class for the other derivations. See Chapter 13, "Object-Oriented Methods," for detailed information about multiple inheritance.

To add a new class, select the Add New Class option from the Classes SpeedMenu. The Add New Class dialog box appears (see fig. 20.7).

Fig. 20.7
The Add New
Class dialog box.

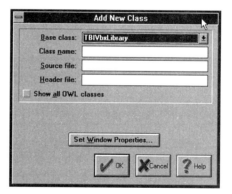

Select the base class for your new class using the Base Class drop-down menu. Selecting Show All OWL Classes allows you to select from all available ObjectWindows Library classes, rather than just the GUI subset.

You should then provide the class name and source and header file names for your class. The source and header files should be located in the source directory for your application.

Depending on your base class selection, you will have additional options. If your base class is TDialog, you must specify a Resource ID. You will be presented with a Resource ID combo box with all the IDs for dialog box resources in your application. The Resource ID combo box appears as a new entry in the current dialog screen. If you specify an identifier that does not exist, ClassExpert will create an empty dialog box template with your specifier and load Resource Workshop. Resource Workshop will allow you to define the dialog box.

If your class is TWindow, TFrameWindow, or a derivative of either, you will be presented with a Set Window Properties button in the current dialog screen, associated with the Window Styles dialog box (see fig. 20.8).

Fig. 20.8
The Window Styles dialog box.

If your Base Class selection is TFrameWindow or a derivative, you will be presented a Client Class combo box in addition to the Set Window Properties button. You can choose an existing class to represent the client area of the new frame window.

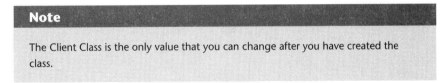

Note

The Client Class is the only value that you can change after you have created the class.

After you have selected all your options, click OK to add the new class to your application and have ClassExpert create the source files and add them to your project.

Creating Document Types

If your application supports Document/View, you can use ClassExpert to create document types. The Document/View model breaks data handling into two parts based on classes: Data storage and control in the document class, and data display and manipulation in the view class.

To use the Document/View model, choose View Document Types from the Classes SpeedMenu. The Document Types dialog box appears (see fig. 20.9).

Fig. 20.9

The Document Types dialog box.

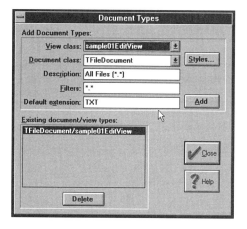

From this dialog box, you select a View Class, either one of your own or one of the default classes provided by Borland. Then you use the Description Class text box to describe the class of files associated with the Files of Type lists that appear in Windows common File dialog boxes. Your entry here should describe the type of files your application operates on and that are selected by the filters. The actual files to list in the dialog box are selected based on wild-card file specifications in the Filters text box. If your new document type is for text files, you should have a filter for *.TXT. You should also set your default file extension to be consistent with your filters.

The Styles button displays the Document Styles dialog box (see fig. 20.10).

Document Styles selections allow you to control the behavior of the view or document type. This includes how the application searches for and deals with files, and how the user interacts with the data in the file.

Fig. 20.10
The Document
Styles dialog box.

IV

Customizing Code

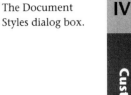

Adding and Deleting Event Handlers

ClassExpert provides a simple and fast means for adding and deleting event
handlers in your application. To add a handler, you must first select the class
that will handle the event in the Classes pane of ClassExpert. Then in the
Events pane you select the event to be handled and right-click to display the
Event pane SpeedMenu. Select Add Handler, and the appropriate default code
is generated and appears in the Edit pane. When you add a handler for either
command or control notifications, you are prompted for a function name
before the code is generated.

> **Note**
>
> Add Handler applies only to those events that are not already handled by a member
> function of the selected class. These are identified by the checkmarks to the left of
> the event.

You can delete a handler just as easily. Simply select the appropriate class in
the Classes pane, then select the event in the Event pane. From the Event
pane SpeedMenu, select Delete Handler. The handler is removed from the
Events pane.

> **Note**
>
> Delete Handler will not remove the function that handles the event from your source
> code. You must remove this manually and remember to remove the function defini-
> tion from the header file.

Adding and Deleting Instance Variables

Instance variables simplify the handling of controls and are used in conjunction with transfer buffers that are added to your code when you use ClassExpert to add an instance variable. If your application used a dialog box with checkbox controls, then you want to add an instance variable for each control and use transfer buffer data in your code. This technique supports applications that change action based on which specific boxes are checked.

ClassExpert makes it easy to add instance variables to your code. In the Class pane, select a class associated with control notifications. In the Events pane select a specific control notification and display the Events SpeedMenu by right-clicking the control notification. You may have to expand the list of control notifications to locate the particular control. Select Add Instance Variable from the SpeedMenu, and the Add Instance Variable Dialog box appears (see fig. 20.11).

Fig. 20.11
The Add Instance
Variable dialog
box.

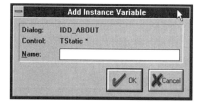

Choose a name for the instance variable and click OK. ClassExpert then updates your source files for the instance variable and the transfer structure.

Instance variables can be deleted as easily as they are added. From the Events pane, right-click the control with the instance variable you want to delete. Select Delete Instance Variable from the SpeedMenu; ClassExpert modifies your source code to remove the variable.

Adding Classes from Other Projects

Borland provides a special project tool called Rescan for managing the project database. Rescan examines the sources listed in the IDE file of your AppExpert project and uses information from these files to update or rebuild the project database.

Rescan has several uses, but one of the most important to the developer of a new application is that you can use Rescan to import a class from another project. This allows you to easily share code between several different applications.

To reuse a class from another application, you must first copy all source code files (the .cpp extension) into the current source directory and all header files (the .h extension) into the header include directory. These directories were set up for you when you ran AppExpert.

You then add the class source file as a dependent node under the target in the IDE project, using Add Node from the Project Window SpeedMenu. Then add the header file associated with the class as a dependent node under the class source file in the AppExpert project.

Finally, in the Project window, right-click the AppExpert target and choose Special, Rescan. This properly updates your project database to reflect the addition of the new class.

From Here...

In this chapter, you learned about Borland Turbo C++ tools for Windows application development: AppExpert and ClassExpert. You learned how easy it is to operate these tools to support professional, robust application development. You now can appreciate the benefits of AppExpert and ClassExpert and are prepared to examine these tools in detail and develop a real application step by step, with the help of the following chapters:

- Chapter 21, "Using AppExpert," discusses the intricacies of using AppExpert to create your application code foundation.

- Chapter 22, "Using ClassExpert," tells you how to use ClassExpert to modify the code foundation to create a final application.

Chapter 21

Using AppExpert

In the old days (that is, two or three years ago), developing even a fairly basic Windows application meant writing many lines of code. Since then, Windows class libraries such as ObjectWindows library have greatly reduced the amount of interface code a developer actually has to write. More importantly, a whole new generation of tools has come along that eliminates much of the drudgery of getting a basic Windows interface up and running. AppExpert is one of those tools.

In this chapter, you learn the following:

- What to select in AppExpert to get the basic features you want in a Windows application

- How to use AppExpert to generate code for a project

- How to build an AppExpert application

- What the files and code generated by AppExpert do

- Ways in which you can most effectively use AppExpert

What Is AppExpert?

AppExpert is a *smart tool* you can use to create the code for a basic Windows application. Using AppExpert's dialog boxes, you specify the basic characteristics you desire in your application. AppExpert then generates the appropriate code for you. The code generated by AppExpert ultimately produces only an application shell. You still need to use Resource Workshop and ClassExpert to generate additional specific user-interface features. Naturally, you also have to write the code to give your application its specific function.

The interface shell produced by AppExpert has a default menu and toolbar, a default icon, and a default About dialog box. If you so choose, AppExpert produces basic code for file opening and saving and for printing and print preview. You can also have AppExpert generate basic context-sensitive Windows Help for your application.

AppExpert uses the ObjectWindows library (OWL) and ObjectComponents library (OCF) as the basis for the code it generates. The classes AppExpert produces are therefore derived from OWL and OCF. But don't worry, you can still choose the names for most of the derived classes, and in some cases you can also choose the base OWL classes.

Running AppExpert

AppExpert provides a dialog box interface where you configure a large number of options to specify how you want AppExpert to create your application. You'll get a careful description of many of these options.

The File Example Project

If you have AppExpert generate a real project, it will make your tour through AppExpert more concrete. The example you're going to create is a multi-file text editor application named FILE. This same example is used in Chapters 22, "Using ClassExpert," and 23, "Using Resource Workshop."

Starting AppExpert

Tip

If you haven't already created a new directory for your project, just add a new directory path in front of your project file name. AppExpert creates the directory for you.

To start AppExpert, choose Project, AppExpert. You see the New AppExpert Project dialog box (see fig. 21.1). Select the directory path you want from the Directories list box, and enter the File Name you want for your IDE project. Putting each of your projects in a different directory is a good idea.

Choose OK to proceed when you are ready.

Selecting Options in AppExpert

The next thing you see is the AppExpert Application Generation Options dialog box (see fig. 21.2).

On the left side of the AppExpert Application Generation Options dialog box is the Topics section, showing an outline of the different categories of options you can set. The outline actually has two levels. The main level topics are Application, Main Window, and MDI Child/View. When you first start AppExpert, you see only these three topics with a plus sign at the left of each. The plus sign indicates there are subtopics beneath a main topic. To expand

IV

Customizing Code

the outline view so that you see the subtopics under any main topic, click the plus sign for that main topic. Figure 21.3 shows the full outline after expanding all three main topics. Notice that when a main topic is expanded, the symbol to the left of the main topic changes from a plus sign to a minus sign. This outline is present at all times in AppExpert.

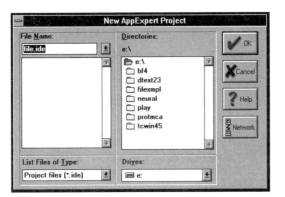

Fig. 21.1
Set the IDE project file name in the New AppExpert Project dialog box after starting AppExpert.

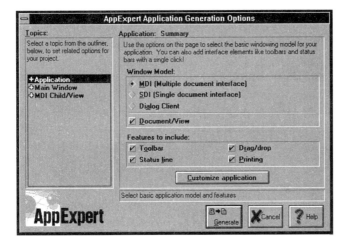

Fig. 21.2
The initial AppExpert Application Generation Options dialog box.

Each different topic or subtopic consists of a variety of options you can select or configure. You navigate between different topics and subtopics by selecting a different topic or subtopic from the outline at the left of the AppExpert Application Generation Options dialog box.

The Generate, Cancel, and Help buttons are always present at the lower right corner of the AppExpert Application Generation Options dialog box. The Generate button is what you choose when you are ready to have AppExpert actually produce the code for your project. You don't want to choose

Generate until you have configured all the necessary options under the relevant topics and subtopics in AppExpert. The Cancel button allows you to exit AppExpert at any time without generating any code or a project file. The Help button provides additional information about any screen you are on in AppExpert.

Fig. 21.3
The AppExpert Application Generation Options dialog box with the expanded topic outline.

The Application Topic

The most important topic in AppExpert is Application. This is the topic you see when the AppExpert Application Generation Options dialog box first appears. You can return to this topic from anywhere in AppExpert by selecting the Application topic in the outline at the left. Many of the choices you make under Application determine what you can do or need to do under other topics.

The Window Model section allows you to select one of three interface styles: MDI (Multiple Document Interface), SDI (Single Document Interface), and Dialog Client. SDI allows you to have only one window or document open in your application at any time. MDI allows you to have open multiple windows. These may be windows of the same type or of different types. MDI gives you the capability to maximize or minimize individual windows and view multiple windows cascaded or tiled. (See Chapter 29, "Single and Multiple Document Interfaces," for a more complete description of SDI and MDI.) Both MDI and SDI give you standard window styles, although you can change these styles to something else once AppExpert is finished. Dialog Client refers to a model in which the main window has a dialog box style—typically created by using Resource Workshop. Windows Calculator is an example of a dialog client model.

Note

AppExpert places certain restrictions on the dialog client model. In this model, AppExpert does not produce code required for printing (even if you mark the printing option). Nor does AppExpert produce code for file handling unless you select Document/View. These restrictions are probably appropriate for many applications that use a dialog box style main window. However, if you need either printing or file handling in your application, you may want to select SDI instead of Dialog Client as your model. After AppExpert has generated your application code, you can then change your client window class so that it is derived from the OWL TDialog class. You then have printing and file handling in addition to a dialog client style.

The Document/View option at the bottom of the Window Model section allows you to select the document/view method of application programming. Document/view offers more than one way of viewing data associated with a particular document. In many cases, document/view also offers a very organized way to separate actual data from its presentation. Nevertheless, many programmers find the document/view style difficult to learn. For this reason, document/view is not covered in detail in this book. You can find a demonstration of document/view in steps 12 through 17 of the TUTORIAL example provided with Turbo C++.

In the Features To Include section, the Application topic allows you to select a number of features to include in your application. Selecting Toolbar places a toolbar just below your application menu. Selecting Status Line gives your application a status bar at the bottom of your main window. Drag/Drop adds code so that your application can open files (MDI) or a file (SDI) when they are dragged from File Manager and dropped on your main window. Selecting this feature has no effect for a dialog client window model without document/view. Finally, selecting Printing adds support for printing and print preview in your application. This option does nothing if your window model is dialog client.

All these features are worth including. They provide important functionality that improves your user interface. The AppExpert implementations of the toolbar, status bar, and drag/drop are all quite good. You will probably need to modify the toolbar for your particular application. But it's easy to see how to add or delete buttons on the toolbar generated by AppExpert. AppExpert also saves you from having to write a lot of printing support code, although you do often need to make modifications to get proper print output scaling.

There is also a Customize Application button. Choosing this button selects the Basic Options subtopic under Application.

The Application topic in figure 21.3 shows the selections that are appropriate for the File example project.

The Basic Options Subtopic. When the Basic Options subtopic under Application is selected, the AppExpert Application Generation Options dialog box looks like figure 21.4. This subtopic offers several options in addition to those selected under the Application topic itself. Target Name is the name to be used for your application's executable file. Base Directory is the directory for your application project. Once again, if you specify a directory that doesn't already exist, AppExpert creates the directory for you when it generates your code.

Fig. 21.4
Application: Basic Options subtopic for the project.

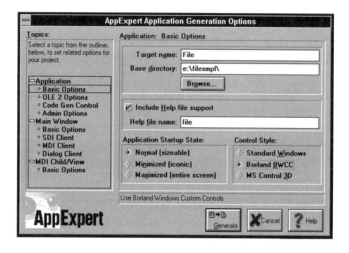

Tip
AppExpert uses your Target Name text as the basis for several class names under other topics. You can avoid the need to edit those class names by entering a Target Name complete with upper- and lower-case letters.

You can select Include Help File Support to have AppExpert generate a basic Windows Help file for your application. You can also specify the name for the Help file. Users expect Help in all Windows applications, so letting AppExpert generate a basic help file can save you a lot of time. AppExpert creates the Help source text files and provides the code to integrate Help into your application. Of course, once you begin customizing your application, you will need to modify and add source text to keep your Help file in tune with your application's commands and capabilities.

You can select three states under the Application Startup State section: Normal, Minimized, or Maximized. In most cases, you should select Normal.

Minimized might be appropriate if you are producing an application that always (or almost always) runs in the background.

Control Style offers three choices that affect the appearance of dialog boxes (and message boxes). Standard <u>W</u>indows produces dialog boxes with a standard window background. Borland <u>B</u>WCC provides support for Borland's controls and either the smooth or stippled Borland aluminum gray dialog box background. MS Control <u>3</u>D provides support for the newer Microsoft three-dimensional dialog box and control appearance. Chapter 19, "Developing Windows Resources for a User Interface," provides some additional discussion of the different control styles.

The Basic Options shown in figure 21.4 are for the FILE project.

The OLE 2 Options Subtopic. OLE 2 is a highly complex subject. Until recently, many developers avoided it. Borland's OWL and OCF implementations now hide most of the nasty OLE 2 complexities. Unfortunately, the AppExpert OLE 2 support is rather inflexible and also requires document/view. Usually it's easier to add OLE 2 support after AppExpert. If you want to find out more about OLE 2, see Chapter 30, "Object Linking and Embedding." Chapter 28, "ObjectWindows Applications," also contains an example of an OLE 2 container application implemented with OWL.

The FILE project doesn't use OLE 2.

Tip
Avoid selecting maximized as the default application startup state, except for your own personal applications. Many Windows power users despise fully maximized windows.

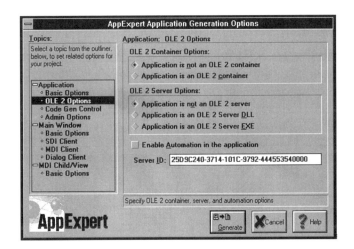

Fig. 21.5
Use the Application: OLE 2 Options subtopic to add OLE 2 capability to your application.

The Code Generation Control Subtopic. The Code Generation Control subtopic (see fig. 21.6) allows you to set a variety of useful options for the code AppExpert generates. The first two edit boxes under this topic allow you to specify subdirectories for your source code and header files. If the subdirectories you specify in these edit boxes don't already exist, AppExpert creates them when it generates your code.

Fig. 21.6

The Application: Code Generation Control subtopic for the FILE project.

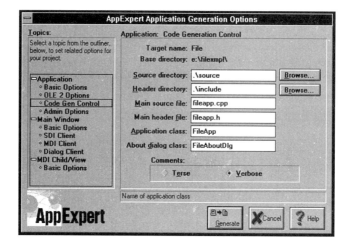

It's a good idea to put source code and header code files in different subdirectories for all but the very simplest C++ development projects. This is especially true when using AppExpert and ClassExpert because these experts tend to generate separate source and header files for nearly every class you use. That can amount to a lot of files. You'll find your life as a programmer easier if those files are organized in subdirectories.

Using the text you chose for Target Name, AppExpert generates default names for your Main Source File, Main Header File, Application Class, and About Dialog Class. The About Dialog Class refers to the class AppExpert builds for the dialog box that appears when a user selects Help, About in your application.

Caution

Unfortunately, the default names provided by AppExpert for Main Source File, Main Header File, Application Class, and About Dialog Class sometimes look like gibberish. These are the names that will appear in the Project window and in your project files. It's worth spending a minute at this stage to edit these names so that they make sense. It's a lot more trouble to change them later.

Also be aware that if you change your Target Name after editing these class and file names, you will need to edit the class and file names again.

Under Comments, you can choose to have AppExpert add either T**e**rse or **V**erbose comments to the code it generates for your project. Comments provide important documentation in code and make it more readable. The AppExpert Verbose comments are more abundant and more descriptive than the Terse comments. They may not win any technical writing awards, but they document most features adequately, and they will save you lots of time writing comments yourself.

Figure 21.6 shows the Application Code Generation subtopic settings for the FILE project.

The Administrative Options Subtopic. Figure 21.7 shows what the Administrative Options subtopic looks like. This topic allows you to specify **V**ersion Number, **C**opyright, **D**escription, **A**uthor, and C**o**mpany information for your project. Do take the time to fill out or correct the information under this topic. AppExpert incorporates this information into every file it generates for you and also uses this information in your About dialog box. This feature alone is probably sufficient reason for using AppExpert to generate the initial shell of all your Windows projects.

Tip
To have AppExpert use your preferred administrative information every time, you can edit the default AppExpert administrative information under the category [Annotation] in the file EXPERT.INI (probably in your WINDOWS directory).

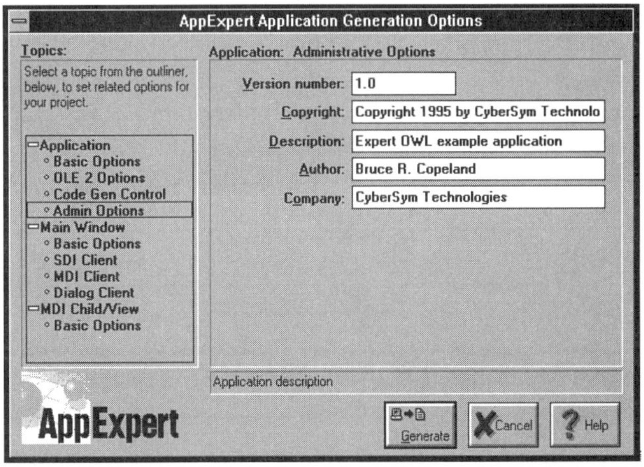

Fig. 21.7
Use the Application: Administrative Options subtopic to add administrative information to all the files in your project.

The Main Window Topic

The Main Window category allows you to configure a variety of options regarding the look and nature of your application's main window. The Main Window topic, shown in figure 21.8, allows you to define the caption or title for your main window, as well as the background window color. In most cases, using a Windows default color for your window background rather than specifying a color here is better. You might, however, want to select a background color in a test project just to see how to actually set the background color in your code. The Customize Main Window button takes you to the Main Window Basic Options subtopic.

Fig. 21.8
The Main Window topic lets you set the title and background color for your application main window.

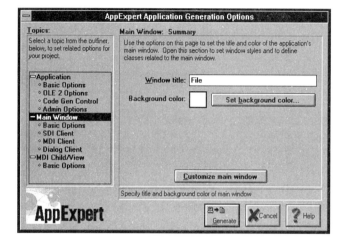

The Basic Options Subtopic. This subtopic presents you with a variety of window style options (see fig. 21.9). In most cases, you want everything marked except Disabled and Clip Siblings and possibly also Vertical and Horizontal scroll. The window styles here all correspond to standard Windows style attributes. Under OWL, you can also set these by using the `TWindowAttr::Style` member of the `TWindow` class. You may want to experiment with different selections here to see what code AppExpert generates for the different options. You can also find additional discussion about using the `TWindowAttr::Style` member in Chapter 28, "ObjectWindows Applications."

Fig. 21.9
Use the Main Window: Basic Options subtopic to select the window styles for your main window.

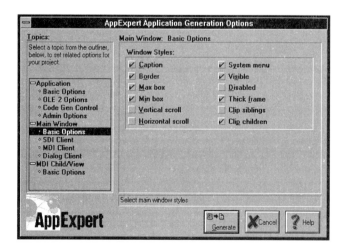

The SDI Client Subtopic. The SDI Client subtopic is relevant only if you selected SDI as the window model under the Application topic. When you select the SDI Client subtopic, you see something similar to figure 21.10.

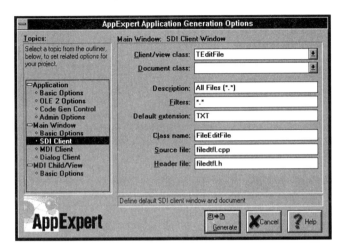

Fig. 21.10
The SDI Client subtopic in AppExpert.

Note

Client is one of the more overused words in computing today. The term is especially confusing in the context of Windows application development. In a window, the client region is the main part of the window inside the frame and any other decorations, menu bars, or caption. Often this region is managed by another specific window called a *client window*. In the case of an SDI application, this concept is fairly straightforward. However, things get complex quickly in MDI applications. An MDI application always has an MDI client window to manage the client region of the main MDI window frame. Very often, MDI children also have their own, different client window to manage their client region. Such a window is usually called an *MDI child client*.

The Client/View Class drop-down list box allows you to select the base class for your client window (or view). If you marked Document/View under the Application topic, then your choices for the client base class are TEditView, TListView, or TWindowView. Otherwise, your choices for the client base class are TEditFile, TListBox, and TWindow.

You may want to read more about these classes in the Turbo C++ OWL documentation. The TEditView and TEditFile classes give your client window all the functionality of a basic text window, including the capability to cut, copy, delete, paste, and search text. The TListView and TListBox classes give your client window the basic capabilities of a list box. TWindowView and TWindow offer basic window characteristics. If you need to draw or paint graphics in your client window, TWindow or TWindowView is the logical choice.

The Document Class drop-down list box is relevant only for document/view. Your only option here is TFileDocument.

In the middle of the SDI Client subtopic are three edit boxes labeled Description, Filters, and Default Extension. You use these edit boxes to configure the default characteristics of files your application opens or saves. For an SDI window model, AppExpert generates code so that your application can open and save files by using the Windows common file dialog boxes. The text you enter into the Description edit box ultimately appears in the List Files Of Type box at the lower left of the common file dialog box. The string you enter into the Filters edit box is ultimately used in the File Name box and the list box immediately beneath. The Default Extension is appended if a user enters a file name without an extension.

The last three boxes in the SDI Client subtopic allow you to specify the class name and source and header file names for your client class. You may want to change these if the default names chosen by AppExpert are not meaningful.

The MDI Client Subtopic. If you selected MDI for the Application window model, then the MDI Client subtopic is where you configure options for the MDI main window client. Figure 21.11 shows the basic options under this topic. AppExpert fills in default names for your client class and the client source and header files. Make sure these names are what you really want to use. Making changes now is a lot easier than later. The names shown in figure 21.11 have been changed to suit the AppExpert FILE example.

The Dialog Client Subtopic. The Dialog Client subtopic allows you to configure several options for the client window in an application by using the dialog client window model. You can ignore this subtopic for other window models. Figure 21.12 shows typical default settings for these options that AppExpert might provide for a project with a target name of FILE.

In line with the earlier discussion about AppExpert default names, you should edit, as needed, the names chosen here by AppExpert for Client Class, Source File, and Header File. Dialog ID is the identifier for the dialog box resource that is going to appear in your application's client window. AppExpert creates a default dialog box resource with this identifier when it generates your project.

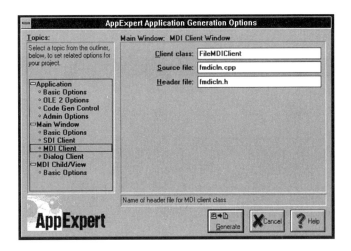

Fig. 21.11
An example of the
Main Window:
MDI Client
subtopic in
AppExpert.

IV

Customizing Code

Mark the Include A Menu Bar check box if your dialog client application is
going to need a menu in addition to buttons. Generally, you do not need a
menu bar for a simple application with only a few self-explanatory buttons.
However, if there are going to be many buttons, you should offer a menu in
addition to the buttons. You may also need a menu for options that you
don't intend to implement with buttons.

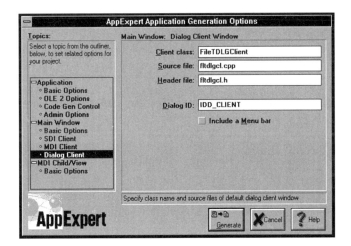

Fig. 21.12
A typical view of
the Main Window:
Dialog Client
subtopic in
AppExpert.

The MDI Child/View Topic

The MDI Child/View topic and its Basic Options subtopic are meaningful
only if you are producing an application with the MDI window model. One
of the unfortunate complexities in MDI applications is the number of

different kinds of windows usually required. In addition to the main window frame and main window client, there is always at least one kind of MDI child window. Frequently the MDI child is itself really a frame window, meaning that there is at least one kind of MDI child client window as well. Keeping all this straight can be a mind bender when you are starting out with MDI.

The MDI Child/View topic (see fig. 21.13) allows you to specify the class and source and header file names for the MDI child. AppExpert fills these fields for you by default, but as with other AppExpert topics, you want to make sure AppExpert's choices are satisfactory for your purposes and style. The fields shown in figure 21.13 have been edited for the FILE project.

The MDI Child/View topic has a Customize Child and View button. This button takes you to the Basic Options subtopic under MDI Child/View.

Fig. 21.13
The MDI Child/
View topic in
AppExpert.

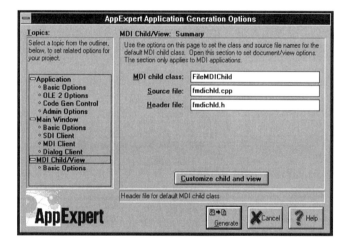

The Basic Options Subtopic. The MDI Child/View topic has one subtopic, Basic Options (see fig. 21.14). The options under this subtopic are nearly identical to those available under the Main Window: SDI Client subtopic. This reflects the fundamental relationship between MDI and SDI applications. In an MDI application, the child client is generally equivalent to the main window client in an SDI application. Make sure the fields under this topic contain what you want. (Refer to the "The SDI Client Subtopic" section for a more detailed description of what each field does.) Figure 21.14 shows the names chosen for the FILE project.

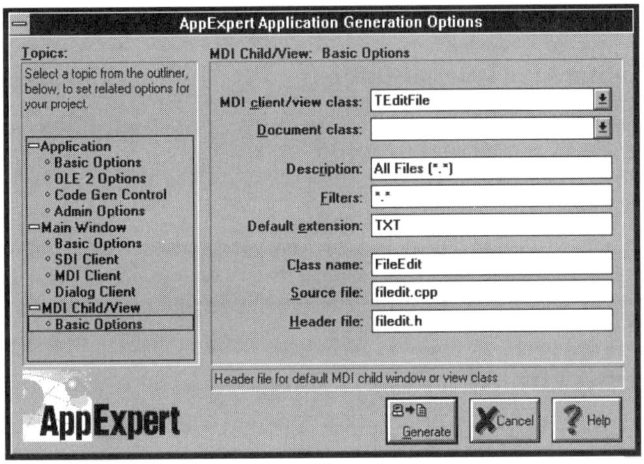

Fig. 21.14
The MDI Child/
View: Basic
Options subtopic
in AppExpert.

IV

Customizing Code

AppExpert Topics Summary

All the different topics and subtopics under AppExpert are a lot to keep straight. By now, your mind may be spinning. It's unfortunate that AppExpert doesn't indicate what things you can ignore by disabling options when they aren't relevant. To make things a little easier, table 21.1 summarizes the different AppExpert topics and subtopics. The second column in the table describes the types of options available under each topic. The third column shows the Window model(s) (SDI model, MDI model, SDI dialog, or All models) for which the topic is applicable.

Table 21.1 Summary of AppExpert Topics and Subtopics		
Topic/Subtopic	**Types of Options**	**Applicability**
Application	Window model and application features such as toolbar, status bar, printing	All models
Basic Options	Target name, help support, startup state, dialog box control style	All models
OLE 2 Options	OLE (client, server, automation) status	All models
Code Generation Control	Directories, file names, class names	All models
Administrative Options	Author, company, copyright, version information	All models
Main Window Basic Options SDI Client	Main window title, background color Main window style features SDI client class, file names, file filter information	All models All models SDI model

(continues)

Topic/Subtopic	Types of Options	Applicability
Table 21.1 Continued		
MDI Client Dialog Client	MDI client class, file names Dialog client class, file names, resource ID	MDI model SDI dialog box
MDI Child/View Basic Options	MDI child class, file names MDI child client class, file names, file filter information	MDI model MDI model

Generating the AppExpert Code

Once you've completed the necessary AppExpert topics and subtopics, you're ready to have AppExpert generate the code for your application. You might want to make one last quick pass through some of the more important AppExpert topics to make sure everything really is as you desire. Then choose the <u>G</u>enerate button at the bottom of AppExpert, and you're off and running. AppExpert prompts you with a message box to make sure you really want to generate the application. Choose <u>Y</u>es. (<u>N</u>o returns you to where you were in AppExpert.)

Depending on how fast your computer is and how much RAM you have, AppExpert takes anywhere from a few seconds to several minutes to generate your application. When AppExpert is finished, you should see a project window at the bottom of the Turbo C++ IDE. If you maximize the project window, it looks something like figure 21.15 for the FILE project.

Fig. 21.15

The project window for the FILE project produced by AppExpert.

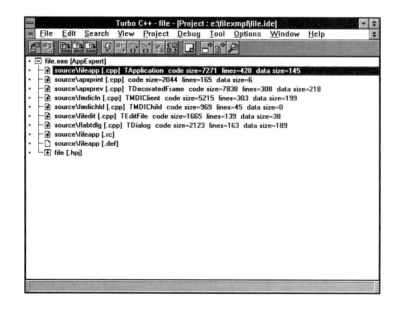

Building an AppExpert Application

Usually there's still plenty to do before you have a fully functioning application, but at this stage most developers go ahead and build the application just to see what it's like. Before doing that, it may be a good idea to examine the Project Options dialog box under Options, Project to make sure you have everything set up the way you want for a project build. See Chapter 15, "Compiling and Linking," for a description of how different project options affect building an application.

> **Note**
>
> The default options under Options, Project are satisfactory for most purposes. However, there are a few specific things you may want to double-check.
>
> Make sure your directories are correct. Also, Under Compiler, Precompiled Headers, make sure you have the settings and Precompiled Header Name you desire. Precompiled header files can be huge (3–10M). If you have only one or two projects at any time, the default precompiled header name probably gives best performance. However, if you have many projects, you probably want to specify some common precompiled header file for all your projects.
>
> Make sure you have the right Mixed model Override for Memory Model under Advanced Compiler. Usually this is Large. Generally you also want to make sure that Cache & Display is selected for Autodependencies under Linker, Make.

To build your application, choose Project and either Make All or Build All. While Turbo C++ is building your project, you should see something that looks like figure 21.16. Building is likely to take a while—even on a powerful computer.

Once your project is built, you can execute it by choosing Debug, Run. Figure 21.17 shows what the FILE program looks like when running.

The FILE program is basically a multi-file text editor. Unlike many applications you may build with AppExpert, the FILE program has much of its required functionality as soon as you build it. This is a good example of the power inherent in OWL. The demonstration in figure 21.18 shows the FILE program after it was used to open the header file fileapp.h. You can cruise around the menu bar and test the different buttons and menu items in this example. You can even open Help for the FILE example.

Fig. 21.16
Building the
AppExpert FILE
project in Turbo
C++.

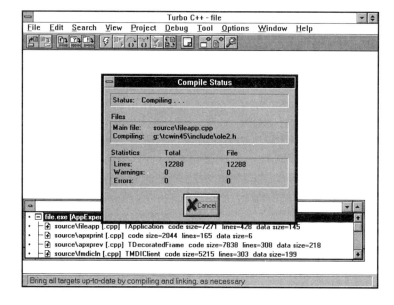

Fig. 21.17
The FILE applica-
tion showing
fileapp.h in an
MDI child
window.

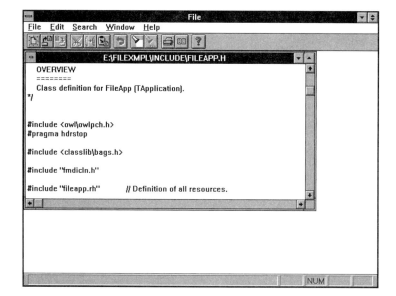

The Code Produced by AppExpert

It is instructive to look at some of the files and code produced by AppExpert.
You can learn quite a bit about the design and organization of OWL applications this way. You can also gain some insight about how AppExpert marks
code to permit future modification or expansion in ClassExpert.

Files and Classes Generated by AppExpert

AppExpert generates a variety of files. Many of these are for the different C++ classes generated by AppExpert. Other files serve several additional purposes. Table 21.2 summarizes the files and their purposes and classes for the FILE project generated by AppExpert. AppExpert always generates help source file names and class names and file names for printing and print preview as shown in this table. Most of the remaining names are those we configured in AppExpert for this particular example. You may get somewhat different names, depending on what you select in AppExpert.

Table 21.2 The Files and Classes Generated by AppExpert for the FILE Project

File Name	Purpose	Classes
fileapp.cpp	Main source file—provides OwlMain, drag/drop support, and application class code	FileApp TFileDrop
fileapp.h	Header for FileApp application class and TFileDrop drag/drop class	FileApp TFileDrop
apxprint.cpp	Printing support source code	APXPrintOut
apxprint.h	Header for APXPrintOut printing class	APXPrintOut
apxprev.cpp	Print preview support source code	PreviewWindow
apxprev.h	Header for PreviewWindow class	PreviewWindow
fmdicln.cpp	Source code for main client window	FileMDIClient
fmdicln.h	Main client window FileMDIClient header	FileMDIClient
fmdichld.cpp	MDI child window source code	FileMDIChild
fmdichld.h	FileMDIChild window class header	FileMDIChild
filedit.cpp	MDI child client window source code	FileEditView
filedit.h	FileEdit header for MDI child client	FileEditView
flabtdlg.cpp	Source code for the About dialog box	FileAboutDlg
flabtdlg.h	FileAboutDlg header for About dialog box	FileAboutDlg
fileapp.rc	Resource script file for the FILE project	

(continues)

Table 21.2 Continued

File Name	Purpose	Classes
fileapp.rh	Header for the FILE project resource identifiers	
fileapp.def	Module definition file for the FILE project	
file.hpj	Help project file for the FILE project	
mainhelp.rtf	Primary help source file (menus and options)	
toolbar.rtf	Source file for toolbar help	
keys.rtf	Source file for accelerator key help	
fileapp.ide	Main project file	
fileapp.apx	AppExpert/ClassExpert database for project	

Understanding the AppExpert Code

A complete explanation of all the code produced by AppExpert is well beyond the scope of this chapter. You can, however, get a fair understanding of much of what is going on by looking at some of the code for the header and main source files in the FILE project. Listings 21.1 and 21.2 show the code in these files.

Listing 21.1 fileapp.h—The Main Application Header File for the FILE Example

```
#if !defined(_ _fileapp_h)   // Sentry, use file only if it's not
                             // already included.
#define _ _fileapp_h

/*  Project File
    CyberSym Technologies
    Copyright 1995 by CyberSym Technologies. All Rights Reserved.

    SUBSYSTEM:    file.exe Application
    FILE:         fileapp.h
    AUTHOR:       Bruce R. Copeland
```

```
    OVERVIEW
    ========
    Class definition for FileApp (TApplication).
*/


#include <owl\owlpch.h>
#pragma hdrstop

#include <classlib\bags.h>

#include "fmdicln.h"

#include "fileapp.rh"              // Definition of all resources.


// TFileDrop class Maintains information about a dropped file,
// its name, where it was dropped, and whether or not it was in
// the client area
class TFileDrop {
public:
    operator == (const TFileDrop& other) const
      {return this == &other;}

    char*   FileName;
    TPoint  Point;
    bool    InClientArea;

    TFileDrop (char*, TPoint&, bool, TModule*);
    ~TFileDrop ();

    const char* WhoAmI ();
private:
    //
    // hidden to prevent accidental copying or assignment
    //
    TFileDrop (const TFileDrop&);
    TFileDrop & operator = (const TFileDrop&);
};

typedef TIBagAsVector<TFileDrop> TFileList;
typedef TIBagAsVectorIterator<TFileDrop> TFileListIter;


//{{TApplication = FileApp}}
class FileApp : public TApplication {
private:
    bool      HelpState;      // Has the help engine been used.
    bool      ContextHelp;    // SHIFT-F1 state (context sensitive
                              // HELP)
    HCURSOR   HelpCursor;     // Context sensitive help cursor

    void SetupSpeedBar (TDecoratedMDIFrame *frame);
    void AddFiles (TFileList* files);
```

(continues)

Listing 21.1   Continued

```
public:
    FileApp ();
    virtual ~FileApp ();

    TOpenSaveDialog::TData  FileData;  // Data to control open/
                                       // saveas standard dialog

    FileMDIClient  *mdiClient;

    // Public data members used by the print menu commands and
    // Paint routine in MDIChild.
    TPrinter        *Printer;  // Printer support.
    int             Printing;  // Printing in progress.

//{{FileAppVIRTUAL_BEGIN}}
public:
    virtual void InitMainWindow();
    virtual void InitInstance();
    virtual bool CanClose ();
    virtual bool ProcessAppMsg (MSG& msg);
//{{FileAppVIRTUAL_END}}

//{{FileAppRSP_TBL_BEGIN}}
protected:
    void CmHelpContents ();
    void CmHelpUsing ();
    void CmHelpAbout ();
    void EvDropFiles (TDropInfo drop);
    void EvWinIniChange (char far* section);
//{{FileAppRSP_TBL_END}}
DECLARE_RESPONSE_TABLE(FileApp);
};    //{{FileApp}}


#endif                    // _ _fileapp_h sentry.
```

Listing 21.2   fileapp.h—The Main Application Source File for the FILE Example

```
/*  Project File
  CyberSym Technologies
  Copyright 1995 by CyberSym Technologies.  All Rights Reserved.

  SUBSYSTEM:  file.exe Application
  FILE:      fileapp.cpp
  AUTHOR:     Bruce R. Copeland


  OVERVIEW
  ========
  Source file for implementation of FileApp (TApplication).
*/
```

```
#include <owl\owlpch.h>
#pragma hdrstop

#include <dir.h>

#include "fileapp.h"
#include "fmdicln.h"
#include "flabtdlg.h"              // Definition of about dialog.


//
// Generated help file.
//
const char HelpFileName[] = "file.hlp";


// Drag / Drop support:
TFileDrop::TFileDrop (char* fileName, TPoint& p, bool inClient,
  TModule*)
{
  char  exePath[MAXPATH];

  exePath[0] = 0;
  FileName = strcpy(new char[strlen(fileName) + 1], fileName);
  Point = p;
  InClientArea = inClient;
}

TFileDrop::~TFileDrop ()
{
  delete FileName;
}

const char *TFileDrop::WhoAmI ()
{
  return FileName;
}


//{{FileApp Implementation}}


//
// Build a response table for all messages/commands handled
// by the application.
//
DEFINE_RESPONSE_TABLE1(FileApp, TApplication)
//{{FileAppRSP_TBL_BEGIN}}
  EV_COMMAND(CM_HELPCONTENTS, CmHelpContents),
  EV_COMMAND(CM_HELPUSING, CmHelpUsing),
  EV_COMMAND(CM_HELPABOUT, CmHelpAbout),
  EV_WM_DROPFILES,
  EV_WM_WININICHANGE,
//{{FileAppRSP_TBL_END}}
END_RESPONSE_TABLE;
```

(continues)

Listing 21.2 Continued

```cpp
//////////////////////////////////////////////////////////
// FileApp
// =====
//
FileApp::FileApp () : TApplication("File")
{
  HelpState = false;
  ContextHelp = false;
  HelpCursor = 0;

  Printer = 0;
  Printing = 0;

  // INSERT>> Your constructor code here.
}


FileApp::~FileApp ()
{
  if (Printer)
    delete Printer;

  // INSERT>> Your destructor code here.
}


bool FileApp::CanClose ()
{
  bool result = TApplication::CanClose();

  //
  // Close the help engine if we used it.
  //
  if (result && HelpState)
    GetMainWindow()->WinHelp(HelpFileName, HELP_QUIT, 0L);

  return result;
}


void FileApp::SetupSpeedBar (TDecoratedMDIFrame *frame)
{
  //
  // Create default toolbar New and associate toolbar buttons
  // with commands.
  //
  TControlBar* cb = new TControlBar(frame);
  cb->Insert(*new TButtonGadget(CM_MDIFILENEW, CM_MDIFILENEW));
  cb->Insert(*new TButtonGadget(CM_MDIFILEOPEN, CM_MDIFILEOPEN));
  cb->Insert(*new TButtonGadget(CM_FILESAVE, CM_FILESAVE));
  cb->Insert(*new TSeparatorGadget(6));
  cb->Insert(*new TButtonGadget(CM_EDITCUT, CM_EDITCUT));
  cb->Insert(*new TButtonGadget(CM_EDITCOPY, CM_EDITCOPY));
  cb->Insert(*new TButtonGadget(CM_EDITPASTE, CM_EDITPASTE));
```

```
    cb->Insert(*new TSeparatorGadget(6));
    cb->Insert(*new TButtonGadget(CM_EDITUNDO, CM_EDITUNDO));
    cb->Insert(*new TSeparatorGadget(6));
    cb->Insert(*new TButtonGadget(CM_EDITFIND, CM_EDITFIND));
    cb->Insert(*new TButtonGadget(CM_EDITFINDNEXT,
                                  CM_EDITFINDNEXT));
    cb->Insert(*new TSeparatorGadget(6));
    cb->Insert(*new TButtonGadget(CM_FILEPRINT, CM_FILEPRINT));
    cb->Insert(*new TButtonGadget(CM_FILEPRINTPREVIEW,
                                  CM_FILEPRINTPREVIEW));
    cb->Insert(*new TSeparatorGadget(6));
    cb->Insert(*new TButtonGadget(CM_HELPCONTENTS,
                                  CM_HELPCONTENTS));

    // Add fly-over help hints.
    cb->SetHintMode(TGadgetWindow::EnterHints);

    frame->Insert(*cb, TDecoratedFrame::Top);
}


//////////////////////////////////////////////////////////////
// FileApp
// =====
// Application intialization.
//
void FileApp::InitMainWindow ()
{
  if (nCmdShow != SW_HIDE)
    nCmdShow = (nCmdShow != SW_SHOWMINNOACTIVE)
                           ? SW_SHOWNORMAL : nCmdShow;

  mdiClient = new FileMDIClient;
  TDecoratedMDIFrame* frame = new TDecoratedMDIFrame(Name,
                          MDI_MENU, *mdiClient, true);

  // Set the client area to the application workspace color.
  frame->SetBkgndColor(::GetSysColor(COLOR_APPWORKSPACE));

  //
  // Assign ICON w/ this application.
  //
  frame->SetIcon(this, IDI_MDIAPPLICATION);

  //
  // Menu associated with window and accelerator table associated
  // with table.
  //
  frame->AssignMenu(MDI_MENU);

  //
  // Associate with the accelerator table.
  //
  frame->Attr.AccelTable = MDI_MENU;

  SetupSpeedBar(frame);
```

(continues)

Listing 21.2 Continued

```
        TStatusBar *sb = new TStatusBar(frame, TGadget::Recessed,
                        TStatusBar::CapsLock    |
                        TStatusBar::NumLock      |
                        TStatusBar::ScrollLock  |
                        TStatusBar::Overtype);
    frame->Insert(*sb, TDecoratedFrame::Bottom);

    SetMainWindow(frame);

    frame->SetMenuDescr(TMenuDescr(MDI_MENU));

    //
    // Borland Windows custom controls.
    //
    EnableBWCC();
}


//////////////////////////////////////////////////////////
// FileApp
// =====
// Menu Help Contents command
void FileApp::CmHelpContents ()
{
  //
  // Show the help table of contents.
  //
  HelpState = GetMainWindow()->WinHelp(HelpFileName,
            HELP_CONTENTS, 0L);
}


//////////////////////////////////////////////////////////
// FileApp
// =====
// Menu Help Using Help command
void FileApp::CmHelpUsing ()
{
  //
  // Display the contents of the Windows help file.
  //
  HelpState = GetMainWindow()->WinHelp(HelpFileName,
            HELP_HELPONHELP, 0L);
}


//////////////////////////////////////////////////////////
// FileApp
// ===========
// Menu Help About file.exe command
void FileApp::CmHelpAbout ()
{
```

```
  //
  // Show the modal dialog.
  //
  FileAboutDlg(MainWindow).Execute();
}


void FileApp::InitInstance ()
{
  TApplication::InitInstance();

  // Accept files via drag/drop in the frame window.
  GetMainWindow()->DragAcceptFiles(true);
}


void FileApp::EvDropFiles (TDropInfo drop)
{
  // Number of files dropped.
  int totalNumberOfFiles = drop.DragQueryFileCount();

  TFileList* files = new TFileList;

  for (int i = 0; i < totalNumberOfFiles; i++) {
    // Tell DragQueryFile the file interested in (i) and the
    // length of your buffer.
    int    fileLength = drop.DragQueryFileNameLen(i) + 1;
    char   *fileName = new char[fileLength];

    drop.DragQueryFile(i, fileName, fileLength);

    // Getting the file dropped. The location is relative to
    // your client coordinates, and will have negative values if
    // dropped in the non-client parts of the window.
    //
    // DragQueryPoint copies that point where the file was
    // dropped and returns whether or not the point is in the
    // client area.  Regardless of whether or not the file
    // is dropped in the client or non-client area of the window,
    // you will still receive the file name.
    TPoint  point;
    bool  inClientArea = drop.DragQueryPoint(point);
    files->Add(new TFileDrop(fileName, point, inClientArea, this));
  }

  // Open the files that were dropped.
  AddFiles(files);

  // Release the memory allocated for this handle with DragFinish.
  drop.DragFinish();
}


void FileApp::AddFiles (TFileList* files)
{
```

(continues)

Listing 21.2   Continued

```
    // Open all files dragged in.
    TFileListIter fileIter(*files);

    TFrameWindow *tfw = TYPESAFE_DOWNCAST(GetMainWindow(),
                        TFrameWindow);
    if (tfw) {
      FileMDIClient *theClient = TYPESAFE_DOWNCAST(tfw->
                                 GetClientWindow(), FileMDIClient);

      if (theClient)
        while (fileIter) {
          theClient->OpenFile(fileIter.Current()->WhoAmI());
          fileIter++;
        }
    }
}


bool FileApp::ProcessAppMsg (MSG& msg)
{
  if (msg.message == WM_COMMAND) {
    if (ContextHelp || (::GetKeyState(VK_F1) < 0)) {
      ContextHelp = false;
      GetMainWindow()->WinHelp(HelpFileName,
                       HELP_CONTEXT, msg.wParam);
      return true;
    }
  } else
    switch (msg.message) {
    case WM_KEYDOWN:
      if (msg.wParam == VK_F1) {
        // If the Shift/F1 then set the help cursor and turn on
        // the modal help state.
        if (::GetKeyState(VK_SHIFT) < 0) {
          ContextHelp = true;
          HelpCursor = ::LoadCursor(GetMainWindow()->GetModule()
            ->GetInstance(), MAKEINTRESOURCE(IDC_HELPCURSOR));
          ::SetCursor(HelpCursor);
          return true;     // Gobble up the message.
        } else {
          // If F1 w/o the Shift key then bring up help's main
          // index.
          GetMainWindow()->WinHelp(HelpFileName, HELP_INDEX, 0L);
          return true;     // Gobble up the message.
        }
      } else {
        if (ContextHelp && (msg.wParam == VK_ESCAPE)) {
          if (HelpCursor)
            ::DestroyCursor(HelpCursor);
          ContextHelp = false;
          HelpCursor = 0;
          GetMainWindow()->SetCursor(0, IDC_ARROW);
          return true;  // Gobble up the message.
        }
      }
```

```
        break;

      case WM_MOUSEMOVE:
      case WM_NCMOUSEMOVE:
        if (ContextHelp) {
          ::SetCursor(HelpCursor);
          return true;    // Gobble up the message.
        }
        break;

      case WM_INITMENU:
        if (ContextHelp) {
          ::SetCursor(HelpCursor);
          return true;    // Gobble up the message.
        }
        break;

      case WM_ENTERIDLE:
        if (msg.wParam == MSGF_MENU)
          if (GetKeyState(VK_F1) < 0) {
            ContextHelp = true;
            GetMainWindow()->PostMessage(WM_KEYDOWN, VK_RETURN, 0L);
            return true;     // Gobble up the message.
          }
        break;

      default:
        ;
    };  // End of switch

  // Continue normal processing.

  return TApplication::ProcessAppMsg(msg);
}


void FileApp::EvWinIniChange (char far* section)
{
  if (strcmp(section, "windows") == 0) {
    // If the device changed in the WIN.INI file then the printer
    // might have changed.  If we have a TPrinter (Printer) then
    // check and make sure it's identical to the current device
    // entry in WIN.INI.
    if (Printer) {
      char printDBuffer[255];
      LPSTR printDevice = printDBuffer;
      LPSTR devName;
      LPSTR driverName = 0;
      LPSTR outputName = 0;

      if (::GetProfileString("windows", "device", "",
          printDevice, sizeof(printDevice))) {
        // The string which should come back is something like:
        //
        //     HP LaserJet III,hppcl5a,LPT1:
        //
```

(continues)

Listing 21.2 Continued

```
            // Where the format is:
            //
            //    devName,driverName,outputName
            //
            devName = printDevice;
            while (*printDevice) {
              if (*printDevice == ',') {
                *printDevice++ = 0;
                if (!driverName)
                  driverName = printDevice;
                else
                  outputName = printDevice;
              } else
                printDevice = ::AnsiNext(printDevice);
            }

            if ((Printer->GetSetup().Error != 0) ¦¦ (strcmp(devName,
                Printer->GetSetup().GetDeviceName()) != 0) ¦¦
                (strcmp(driverName, Printer->GetSetup().
                GetDriverName()) != 0) ¦¦ (strcmp(outputName,
                Printer->GetSetup().GetOutputName()) != 0)) {

              // New printer installed so get the new printer device
              // now.
              delete Printer;
              Printer = new TPrinter(this);
            }
          } else {
            // No printer installed (GetProfileString failed).
            delete Printer;
            Printer = new TPrinter(this);
          }
        }
      }
    }


    int OwlMain (int , char* [])
    {
      try {
        FileApp  app;
        return app.Run();
      }
      catch (xmsg& x) {
        ::MessageBox(0, x.why().c_str(), "Exception", MB_OK);
      }

      return -1;
    }
```

You can ignore the first two lines of code. The first really important step in `InitMainWindow()` is the creation of `mdiClient` as an instance of the `FileMDIClient` class. Once this is done, `InitMainWindow()` next uses that instance to construct `frame` as an instance of the OWL class `TDecoratedMDIFrame`. So `frame` is going to be the main window frame, and `mdiClient` is its main window client.

A couple of lines later, `InitMainWindow()` calls `frame->SetIcon()` to make the resource `IDI_MDIAPPLICATION` the icon for the application. Next `InitMainWindow()` calls `frame->SetMenu()` to make the resource `MDI_MENU` the menu for the frame window. `InitMainWindow()` also sets `MDI_MENU` as the accelerator table for `frame`. The next lines set up the tool bar and status bar for the frame window. After this, `InitMainWindow()` calls `SetMainWindow()` to officially make `frame` the main window for the application. The remainder of the `InitMainWindow()` function we can ignore for now.

Event Handlers and Event Handler Macros

In listings 21.1 and 21.2, you can see several functions that begin with either the letters `Cm` or `Ev`—for example `CmHelpAbout()` and `EvDropFiles()`. Functions like these play a special role and are collectively called *event handlers*. In Windows, nearly all communication between applications and Windows (and therefore between the user and applications) is accomplished through messages. Every time some event occurs, a message is sent. So event handlers are really just functions that respond to or "handle" messages. Some glue is necessary to connect an event handler to the message it's supposed to handle. This is what event handler macros do. In listing 21.2, you can see examples of event handler macro in the lines:

```
DEFINE_RESPONSE_TABLE1(FileApp, TApplication)
//{{FileAppRSP_TBL_BEGIN}}
    EV_COMMAND(CM_HELPCONTENTS, CmHelpContents),
    EV_COMMAND(CM_HELPUSING, CmHelpUsing),
    EV_COMMAND(CM_HELPABOUT, CmHelpAbout),
    EV_WM_DROPFILES,
    EV_WM_WININICHANGE,
//{{FileAppRSP_TBL_END}}
END_RESPONSE_TABLE;
```

AppExpert Syntax

By now you may have noticed some seemingly strange comment lines in listings 21.1 and 21.2. An example is the line

```
//{{TApplication = FileApp}}
```

just before the `FileApp` class declaration in listing 21.1. These are not really comments at all. Instead, they are lines that enable AppExpert and ClassExpert to interpret the code in your project whenever you use the Experts to make changes and additions. These lines always begin with a comment marker so as not to confuse the compiler. The text and positioning of these expert syntax lines are important. After you work with AppExpert projects for a while, you will eventually understand enough about them to move or edit them. Even then, you want to be careful. Removing or garbling these lines won't cause problems for the compiler or linker, but it might make it impossible for you to use ClassExpert to edit your project further.

Making the Best Use of AppExpert

AppExpert and the related experts ClassExpert and Resource Workshop are very powerful tools for rapid application development. Many professional developers routinely use these tools even though they already know how to write all the underlying code. It doesn't make sense to spend a lot of time writing and editing code if tools such as AppExpert and ClassExpert can do it in a fraction of the time. That's not to say everything about AppExpert and ClassExpert is perfect. In practice, many users have a short list of things that they always change. But a lot of that is personal preference. As you use AppExpert, you will undoubtedly develop your own list.

If you're just starting out with OWL, AppExpert can play another useful role. Most of the code generated by AppExpert is quite good. You can learn a lot about how to use OWL simply by using AppExpert to generate a particular kind of application and then looking at the code to see how it works. Even experienced developers do this. I routinely keep a directory named PLAY on my hard disk for just this purpose.

From Here...

You've covered a lot of territory in this chapter. By now you should have a basic understanding of how to make AppExpert build a Windows project for you. In most applications, however, you need to make other additions and modifications before your application really does what you intend. Typically you need to modify the menu(s) AppExpert provides for you. You almost always need to add dialog boxes for specific purposes. And who wants to use the default icons that AppExpert provides? Probably, you also need to add or modify other interface features. The following chapters can all help you move beyond what AppExpert has created to a robust application that really suits your needs:

■ Chapter 15, "Compiling and Linking," gives you a better understanding of Project Options and how you can efficiently use Turbo C++ to manage and build your application code.

■ Chapter 22, "Using ClassExpert," describes how to make many application modifications at the coding level.

■ Chapter 23, "Using Resource Workshop," tells how to integrate Resource Workshop with an AppExpert/ClassExpert project so that you can add and modify resources.

■ Chapter 28, "ObjectWindows Applications," teaches you the specifics about coding and working with OWL applications.

■ Chapter 29, "Single and Multiple Document Interfaces," helps get you up to speed on MDI and SDI applications and their differences.

■ Chapter 30, "Object Linking and Embedding," covers OLE in case you are wondering how or why you should incorporate OLE into your applications.

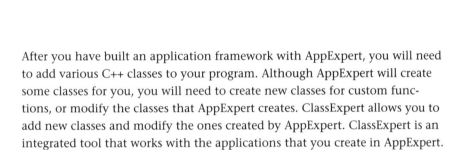

Chapter 22

Using ClassExpert

After you have built an application framework with AppExpert, you will need to add various C++ classes to your program. Although AppExpert will create some classes for you, you will need to create new classes for custom functions, or modify the classes that AppExpert creates. ClassExpert allows you to add new classes and modify the ones created by AppExpert. ClassExpert is an integrated tool that works with the applications that you create in AppExpert.

With ClassExpert, you can easily view and modify the class hierarchies in your program. You can view and edit the classes in your application, add new classes, and add and modify event handlers and virtual functions.

In this chapter, you learn how to use ClassExpert to effectively manage your application's classes, including the following:

- Starting ClassExpert

- Navigating the ClassExpert interface

- Viewing, editing, and adding classes

- Adding and deleting instance variables and event handlers

- Working with virtual functions

Getting Started with ClassExpert

To use ClassExpert, you must have a project that was generated by AppExpert open within the Integrated Development Environment (IDE). Open the project by choosing the Open Project option from the Project menu. You can then start ClassExpert by choosing ClassExpert from the View menu, or by double-clicking the target name of your application target in the graphical project viewer. Figure 22.1 shows an example of the ClassExpert screen.

Fig. 22.1
The ClassExpert window.

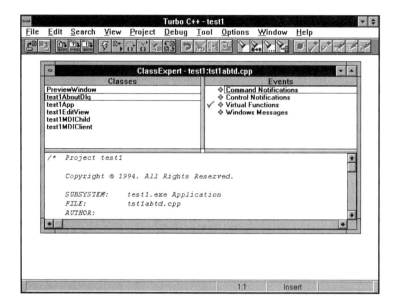

You see that the ClassExpert screen is divided into three panes. The upper left pane is the *Classes* pane. This pane displays all the classes that ClassExpert manages in your application.

The pane to the right of the Classes pane is the *Events* pane. Here, ClassExpert lists the different events that the class handles.

The third pane in the ClassExpert display is the *Edit* pane. ClassExpert uses the Edit pane to display the source file associated with the class that you have selected in the Classes pane. The Edit pane has most of the features of the IDE editor. You can edit, add, and delete code in this pane.

The Classes Pane

The Classes pane displays all classes in your application that are managed by ClassExpert. It includes classes that were created by AppExpert or added with ClassExpert. This window gives you an easy way to see all of your application's classes in one place.

Note

ClassExpert manages classes generated only by AppExpert or classes that you have added in ClassExpert. If you add classes to your project's source code outside of ClassExpert, they will not show up in the Classes pane.

Within the Classes pane, as with the other ClassExpert panes, the left and right mouse buttons perform different functions. A single click on a class with the left mouse button brings the source file for that class into the Edit pane. Double-clicking a class with the left mouse button brings the source for the class into the Edit pane and displays the constructor for the class. A single click with the right mouse button while in the Classes pane brings up a speed menu that allows you to perform several operations on the class. You can also display this menu by pressing Alt+F10 when the cursor is in the Classes pane. Figure 22.2 shows the speed menu for the Classes pane.

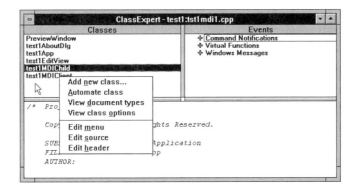

Fig. 22.2
Clicking the right mouse button in the Classes pane brings up the speed menu.

Adding a Class

You can use ClassExpert to add classes to your application. ClassExpert allows you to add ObjectWindows-based classes, and allows one level of inheritance. If you want to add a class that is more than one level of inheritance from an ObjectWindows base class, you will need to add the class manually.

To add a class, click the right mouse button in the Classes pane to bring up the Classes speed menu. From the speed menu, select the Add New Class option. This option displays a dialog box that allows you to fill in the various options for your new class. Figure 22.3 shows the Add New Class dialog box.

Fig. 22.3

The Add New
Class dialog box.

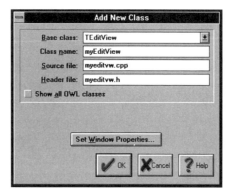

The Add New Class dialog box allows you to specify several options for your class. You will need to provide the name of the base class that you are deriving from, the class name for the new class, and the names of the source and header files for the class.

Depending on the base class of your new class, you can specify additional information. The Add New Class dialog box will change its appearance depending on the base class that you select. For example, for some base classes, a Client Class combo box appears that allows you to select an existing class to represent the client area. Clicking the Set Window Properties button displays classes derived from TWindow and allows you to set various window properties. If your new class is derived from TDialog, the Resource ID combo box displays all the resource IDs for the dialog resources in your application. If you specify a new ID, ClassExpert creates an empty dialog template and loads Resource Workshop.

After you have filled in all the information for your new class, click OK. ClassExpert adds an entry to the project outline display for the source file for your new class.

Viewing Class Information

Choosing the View class options option from the speed menu allows you to see information about the currently selected class. This option displays the Class Options dialog box that displays the base class of the selected class, the name of the selected class, and the source and header files associated with the selected class.

The Class Options dialog box displays additional information depending on the derivation of the selected class. If the base class of the selected class is TDialog, the resource ID of the associated dialog template also appears. If the selected class is a TWindow or is derived from TWindow, the current background color of the window and a scroll box listing the various properties of the window are shown. If the selected class is a TFrameWindow or is derived from TFrameWindow, the name of the class that represents the client area also appears.

Other Speed Menu Options

Several additional options are available from the Classes pane speed menu. When you select the View Document types, ClassExpert displays the Document Types dialog box, which allows you to define different document types for your application. The Edit Source and Edit Header menu selections start a text editor window that modifies either the class source file or header definition. The Edit Menu option starts Resource Workshop so that you can edit the menu resources in the application.

The Events Pane

The Events pane lists the various Windows messages, virtual functions, command and control notifications, and automations of the class that are selected in the Classes pane. These events are listed in an outline format. The actual contents of the outline depend on how the selected class was derived.

> **Note**
>
> The particular events listed in the Events pane depend on the class selected in the Classes pane.

As in the Classes pane, the left and right mouse buttons perform different functions. Single-clicking an event category with the left mouse button selects that event category. A single click on the outline symbol expands the elements under the selected category. Double-clicking the category name also expands the category. Clicking the right mouse button while in the Events pane brings up a speed menu that allows you to perform several operations. You can also display this menu by pressing Alt+F10 when the cursor is in the Events pane. Figure 22.4 shows the speed menu for the Events pane.

Fig. 22.4
Pressing the right
mouse button in
the Events pane
brings up the
speed menu.

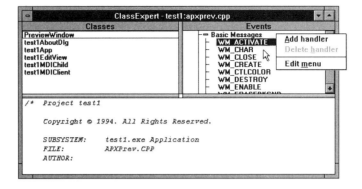

Event Handlers and Virtual Functions

The Events pane displays the different types of events that your application
can process. These events appear in an outline form. A light gray check mark
next to an event category shows that some events under the indicated category have handler functions already associated with them. Figure 22.5
shows the Events pane with some of the event categories expanded.

Fig. 22.5
The Events pane
showing different
levels of expan-
sion in the event
categories outline.

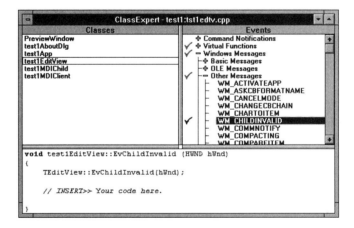

The Events pane in ClassExpert makes it easy to add and delete event-
handling routines from your C++ classes. To add an event handler, select
the class that contains the handler routine from the Classes pane. The event
categories in the Events pane are updated to reflect the types of events
relevant for the selected class.

After you have chosen a class, select the event that you want to handle. You
may need to expand the event category outline to get to the desired event.

Select the particular event you want, and choose Add Handler from the Events pane speed menu. A member function for handling the selected event will be inserted into your code and will be displayed in the Edit pane.

> **Note**
>
> Events that have handlers associated with them are shown with a dark check mark beside them. A lighter check mark on an event outline category means that some events under the category have associated handlers.

When you add a handler for a Windows message, ClassExpert adds an entry into the response table. For both Windows message handlers and virtual functions, default handler code is added to the handler routine displayed in the Edit pane.

Deleting a handler is only slightly more complicated. To delete a handler routine, select the associated event in the Events pane. Bring up the Events pane speed menu and choose Delete Handler. ClassExpert displays a warning box, which tells you that the handler code associated with the selected event will not be deleted. If you choose OK, ClassExpert deletes the event entry from the appropriate response table and displays the code for the handler in the Edit pane. You need to delete the handler code manually in the Edit pane. Also, you need to delete the handler function definition from the class header file.

Instance Variables

You can use the Events pane to add instance variables to your classes to access the status of controls. To add an instance variable, select a class in the Classes pane that has controls associated with it. In the Events pane, expand the Control Notifications outline item and select the ID of the control that you want. Then, choose the Add Instance Variable option from the Events pane speed menu. A dialog box appears and prompts you for the name of the variable. Click OK and ClassExpert adds the instance variable declaration, allocation, and initialization code to the selected class. ClassExpert also adds a transfer buffer that collects run-time information about the control.

Deleting an instance variable is similar to deleting an event handler. Select the control ID in the Events pane and choose the Delete Instance Variable option from the speed menu. ClassExpert deletes the variable from your class source code.

The Edit Pane

The Edit pane provides an editor for the various class members and event handlers displayed as a result of selecting classes and events in the other ClassExpert panes. In addition to being an editor, the Edit pane also allows you to perform additional operations on your application via its speed menu. You can open source files, browse symbols and inspect objects, get context-sensitive help, set breakpoints and watches, and start execution of your application.

As in the other panes in ClassExpert, the left and right mouse buttons perform different functions. A single click in the Edit pane with the left mouse button positions the editing cursor at the selected point. A single click with the right mouse button brings up the Edit pane speed menu. You also can display this menu by pressing Alt+F10 when the cursor is in the Edit pane. Figure 22.6 shows the speed menu for the Edit pane.

Fig. 22.6

Pressing the right mouse button in the Edit pane brings up the speed menu.

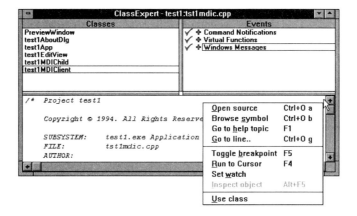

Working with the Edit Pane

As you would expect, the Edit pane supports basic editing operations similar to the IDE editor. The speed menu gives you access to several operations that are useful when editing your class source code. The Open Source Menu option allows you to choose and open a source file in another edit window. The Go To Line menu option allows you to set the editing cursor on a specific line in the Edit pane; ClassExpert shows the current line number in the status bar. The Browse Symbol option opens the Symbol Inspection window for the selected text in the Edit pane. A dialog box prompts you for a symbol if there is no text at the cursor position.

Creating Class Instances

An instance of a class is a particular object that has a class definition as its type. Creating an instance of a class is known as *instantiation*. The Edit pane provides a facility for creating instances of classes in your application.

To create an instance of a class, choose the Use Class menu option from the Edit pane speed menu. The Use Class dialog box appears and prompts you to select a class to instantiate. Figure 22.7 shows the Use Class dialog box.

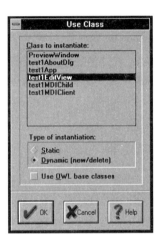

Fig. 22.7

The Use Class dialog box.

By default, the Use Class dialog box displays only the application classes managed by ClassExpert. When you select the Use OWL Base Classes check box, the class list is updated to show all the ObjectWindows base classes.

After you have selected the class to instantiate, you must choose whether to have the instance created statically or dynamically. Dynamic creation uses the new and delete operators to create and destroy the object, where static instances are local or global variables created on the heap.

After selecting static or dynamic instantiation, click the OK button. The code to create an instance of the class is automatically added to the code in the Edit pane. The code is generated as a comment. You will have to change the name of the class instance to be unique and uncomment the code segment before it can be compiled into your application.

Run-time Operation

In addition to various editing and class instantiation functions, the Edit pane also gives you the ability to perform some run-time operations with your application. The Edit pane speed menu allows you to set breakpoints and watches, start execution of the application, and inspect objects in the debugger.

Two menu choices allow you to control execution of your application during debugging. The Toggle Breakpoint menu option sets a breakpoint at the current source line, or clears a breakpoint if one already exists. The Run to Cursor option starts execution of your application normally, and stops execution at the current source line in the Edit pane.

The speed menu also provides three options for examining data and symbols in your application. The Browse Symbol menu option allows you to inspect a symbol on the current line in the Edit pane. You can set watch points in the debugger by choosing the Set Watch menu option. This enables you to see changes to a symbol via the watch window as the program executes. The Inspect Object menu item displays the contents of the data element at the current cursor position in the Edit pane.

Getting Help

One very useful feature of the Edit pane is the ability to get context-sensitive help on keywords. This feature is invoked from the Go to Help Topic menu option on the Edit pane speed menu. This option is also available by pressing F1. When you position the cursor on a word in the Edit pane, this option performs a keyword search in the on-line help system for entries related to the selected word.

By using the Go to Help Topic feature, you can get help on almost any aspect of the Borland C++ programming language. You can access help information for reserved words, global variables, library functions, ObjectWindows library functions, and Windows API functions.

ClassExpert and Resource Workshop

ClassExpert and the Resource Workshop provide an integrated system for creating and managing resources and the C++ classes that operate with them. The Resource Workshop is a tool for creating and modifying program resources, such as dialog boxes and menus. Depending on the class that you have selected in the Classes pane, the Edit Dialog and Edit Menu options appear in the Classes pane speed menu. If you choose one of these options, the Resource Workshop tool is activated so that you can perform the edit function.

ClassExpert and Resource Workshop work together to maintain the classes associated with your application resources. If you are using the Resource Workshop with code generated by AppExpert, always start Resource Workshop from ClassExpert. Resource Workshop notifies ClassExpert of any event or control changes in your application resources, and ClassExpert updates its listing of application events accordingly.

From Here...

ClassExpert is an extremely useful tool for creating and managing classes for your application. It allows you to easily add classes and handler routines for many different types of events. It also provides integrated editing capabilities, keyword help searching, and run-time support.

You can learn more about classes and the other IDE tools in the following chapters:

- Chapter 12, "Classes and Objects," introduces the various concepts of classes, objects, and class hierarchies.

- Chapter 13, "Object-Oriented Methods," discusses the basic concepts of object-oriented design.

- Chapter 21, "Using AppExpert," shows you how to use the AppExpert application generation tool to create application framework code.

- Chapter 23, "Using Resource Workshop," discusses the Resource Workshop tool used to create and manage application resources.

Chapter 23

Using Resource Workshop

Every Windows application has myriad visual components, such as menus, icons, bitmaps, and dialog boxes. These components are designed, compiled, and bound to the application through a series of operations. In this chapter you learn about the following:

- Windows resources

- How to create Windows resources and attach them to your application

- How Borland's Resource Workshop greatly improves this process

- How to use Resource Workshop to create and modify many different types of Windows resources

Explaining Windows Resources

Windows resources compose most of the visual aspects of the application, such as menus and dialog box controls. These resources are first defined in a text file that has the .rc extension. This file is the source code that defines the various resources. The Resource Compiler, a program Borland licenses from Microsoft, uses this source file to create a binary representation of the various resources. The Resource Compiler then takes this binary file and binds it to the end of the application's executable file. Thus, the Resource Compiler performs two tasks: compiling the .rc file into a .res file and then binding the .res file to the application. A .res file is the binary form of the resource script contained in the .rc file.

In the early days of Windows programming, the .rc file was created by hand, just as any other source code file. Later, graphical editors were created to help developers design the various components visually rather than with text. These tools then took the graphical representation and produced the text file automatically. Some tools can even take the already compiled resource file, the .res file, and modify it rather than requiring the developer to edit the .rc file and then recompile the resources. Fortunately, Borland's Resource Workshop is such a tool.

A General Overview of Resource Workshop

Borland's Resource Workshop allows you to graphically design the various elements of the application. These representations are then saved as source code in the application's .rc file. Resource Workshop also allows you to modify pre-existing resource files, even those already bound to an executable. And if need be, you can modify the .rc file by hand, using the text-based commands, rather than graphically. Basically, each type of resource has its own editor and Resource Workshop provides an integrated editor for each item. Table 23.1 indicates the various resource types that Resource Workshop supports with a graphical editor. Only version information, DLGINIT, and RCDATA resources are not supported graphically; they can be created and edited only via a text editor. Version information provides various facts about an application such as the operating system under which it runs and what languages it supports. DLGINIT resources provide initialization data for Visual Basic Controls (VBXs) within the resource script file. RCDATA resources are used to provide user-defined resources consisting of one or more lines of data in standard C language format. RCDATA can consist of a combination of numeric values and strings. Numeric values can be represented in hex, octal, or decimal, while strings are surrounded by quotation marks and terminated by a null terminator, \0, at the end of the string.

Table 23.1 Resources Supported by a Graphical Editor in Resource Workshop	
Resource	**Description**
ACCELERATOR	Quickly selects a menu item from the keyboard
BITMAP	Contains graphical images for inclusion into an application

Resource	Description
CURSOR	Indicates various conditions, such as an hourglass
DIALOG	Defines a dialog box and its associated controls
FONT	Contains the fonts used to display text in the application
ICON	Small bitmapped images used to represent minimized applications in the Windows desktop
MENU	Provides the menu selections for the main window and other windows
String Table	Provides string resources that can be modified to aid in internationalization of applications

Invoking Resource Workshop

Resource Workshop can be started in one of three ways: from the Tools menu on the IDE, double-clicking the Resource Workshop icon in the Turbo C++ 4.5 group, or typically by double-clicking the resource file entry in the project window of an open project. The latter method is demonstrated in figure 23.1.

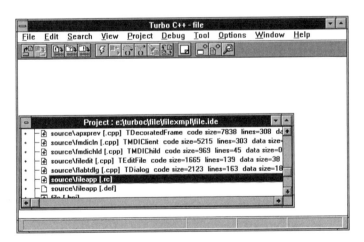

Fig. 23.1

Invoking Resource Workshop from the project file.

When you run Resource Workshop, the application initializes and displays an empty workspace in the main window, as shown in figure 23.2. In this figure, you can see that you have access to the main menu from which you can choose to create or edit resources for your application.

Fig. 23.2
Resource
Workshop's main
window.

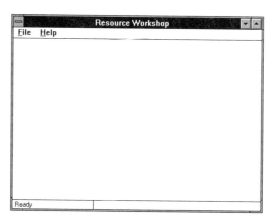

Once the application is initialized, you can open a project that you wish to edit by selecting the File, Open menu option. You have access to several editors within Resource Workshop to edit the resources types listed in table 23.2.

Table 23.2	The Resource Types Editable with Resource Workshop
Extension	**Type**
RC	Resource script
DLG	Resource script for dialog box resources
CUR	Cursor image
ICO	Icon image
BMP	Bitmap image
FNT	Fonts
RES	Resource object file
EXE	Application
DLL, VBX, CPL	Library files
FON	Font library
DRV	Windows device driver

Once the specified file is opened, Resource Workshop displays the resource file in an MDI child window, as shown in figure 23.3.

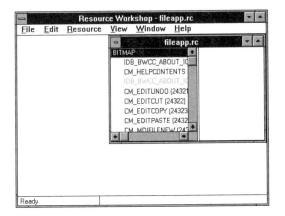

Fig. 23.3
The resource
file, as shown
in Resource
Workshop's
project window,
contains a list of
resources available
for a Windows
application.

IV

Customizing Code

Navigating through Resource Workshop

Resource Workshop supports the standard Windows movement commands
using both the keyboard and the mouse. Resource Workshop edits most resources graphically; however, the only exceptions are version info and string
table resources, which can be edited only with a text editor (which Resource
Workshop provides). Choosing the Resource, Edit and Edit as Text menu
options allows you to choose how to edit a resource. The Resource, Edit selection allows you to graphically edit a resource, whereas selecting Edit as Text
accesses the resource script for the resource.

Using the Menus

The following sections indicate the primary menus displayed by Resource
Workshop when a project is first opened. As different resource editors are
activated, additional menu items appear. These additional menu items are
covered in the appropriate sections throughout this chapter.

The File Menu

Table 23.3 provides a list of the primary file operations allowed by Resource
Workshop. This menu also allows you to set preferences and to install controls such as the VBXs supplied in the Borland Visual Solutions Pack.

Table 23.3	The File Menu
Menu Item	**Description**
New Project	Creates a new project

(continues)

Table 23.3 Continued

Menu Item	Description
Open Project	Opens an existing project
Save Project	Saves the current project
Save File As	Saves the current project with a different name
Close All	Closes the current project
Add to Project	Adds a file to the project
Remove from Project	Removes a file from the project
Preferences	Specifies resource editor options to manage how resources are edited within Resource Workshop
Install Control Library	Installs a custom control DLL (VBXs)
Remove Control Library	Removes a custom control library
Exit	Exits Resource Workshop

The Edit Menu

The Edit menu contains the standard Windows editing features plus a few specific to working with resources, in particular, the Delete Item option. The Delete Item menu option allows you to delete an item from the resource file or a control from a dialog box. Table 23.4 provides a listing of the Edit menu selections.

Table 23.4 The Edit Menu

Menu Item	Description	Accelerator Keys
Undo	Undoes the previous editing action. The number of undos is specified in File, Preferences.	^Z
Redo	Reapplies the previous undo.	Shift+^Z
Cut	Cuts selected item.	^C
Copy	Copies the selected item to the clipboard.	^X

Menu Item	Description	Accelerator Keys
Paste	Pastes the contents of the clipboard to the current area.	^V
Delete	Deletes the current selection.	Del
Delete Item	Deletes the current item.	^Del
Duplicate	Makes a copy of the current selected controls and places them in rows/columns.	none
Select All	Select all items.	none

The Resource Menu

The Resource menu provides the workhorse functions for Resource Workshop. Here is where resources are created and edited. To create a new resource you should choose the Resource, New menu option, which displays the dialog box shown in figure 23.4.

Fig. 23.4
The New Resource dialog box.

Resource Workshop then invokes the appropriate editor to create the new resource. You can choose to edit the resource as text to be placed directly in the script file, by selecting the Edit As Text menu option.

Table 23.5 The Resource Menu	
Menu Item	**Description**
New	Creates a new resource
Edit	Modifies selected resource
Edit As Text	Edits current resource item as text in the .rc file
View	Displays the current selected resource in its editor
Save Resource As	Saves the current resource to a file
Rename	Renames the current selected resource
Memory Options	Specifies memory options for selected resource, such as LOADONCALL
Language	Specifies the language to use with the selected resource when more than one language is specified in VERSIONINFO
Move	Moves the current resource from this file to another resource file
Identifiers	Manages the identifiers for the various resource items

The View Menu

The View menu specifies how the resources are displayed in the resource window shown in figure 23.3. They can be displayed in order by file type (for example, bitmap, icon, and so on) or in order by the identifier used to represent the resource. The View menu also controls where the graphical representation, or preview, of the resource appears in the window—left, bottom, or not shown at all. The Preview and Show By X menu options are mutually exclusive, meaning that only one selection among these items can be selected at one time. Active menu items are shown with check marks to the left of the item. Table 23.6 shows the View menu items.

Table 23.6 The View Menu	
Menu Item	**Description**
By Type	Views resources in type order—toggled with By File

Menu Item	Description
By File	Views resources in file order—toggled with By Type
Show Identifiers	Shows or hides the identifiers for a resource
Show Resources	Shows or hides resources
Show Items	Shows or hides items
Show Unused Types	Shows or hides unused resource types
Show Vertical Preview	Displays resources to the right of the .rc window
Show Horizontal Preview	Displays resources underneath the .rc window
Hide Preview	Does not display the resource

The View menu changes items depending on what resource editor, if any, is currently active.

The Window Menu

The Window menu contains commands for manipulating and opening windows within Resource Workshop. The Window menu also displays a list of open windows. Table 23.7 lists the Window menu commands.

Table 23.7   The Window Menu

Menu Item	Description
Tile	Tiles the open windows so that all are visible (Alt+W+T)
Cascade	Cascades the windows so that the active window is on top of the pile (Alt+W+C)

The Help Menu

The Help menu provides the standard help on using the Microsoft WinHelp engine and Borland's extensions to it. The menu also provides detailed help on several Resource-Workshop-specific topics, such as the source code used to create resources and how to use Resource Workshop in general. Table 23.8 lists the options in the Resource Workshop Help menu.

Table 23.8 The Help Menu	
Menu Item	**Description**
Contents	Displays the contents page for the help file
Using Help	Contains information on using the help system
Getting Started	Contains information for first-time Resource Workshop users
Projects	Contains help on managing resource projects
Resources	Provides an overview of working with resources
Using The Menus	Provides a detailed description of each menu option
Error Messages	Provides an alphabetical listing of all warning and error messages
Resource Script	Provides detailed information on the language used to build resources
About Resource Workshop	Displays the application's About dialog box

Working with Dialog Boxes

Dialog boxes are resource items that are easily created and maintained for Windows-based applications. Resource Workshop provides an easy-to-use toolkit for operations associated with dialog boxes. Dialog boxes provide an easy way to get input from the user. They send messages to the user, such as when an error condition is encountered during the normal flow of your program. Essentially, dialog boxes are child windows that have designated styles and window controls. It is the availability and functionality of these controls that make dialog boxes so useful.

Explaining Dialog Box Components

As stated above, dialog boxes are windows containing Windows controls. Table 23.9 contains a list of window controls. You can also create custom controls or use controls created by others. These controls are typically used to gather or report information to users. Dialog boxes make up a significant portion of the input and output done within Windows applications.

Table 23.9   Dialog Box Controls

Control	Description
Push button	A control that produces an action. A dialog box has one default push button that can be activated by the Enter key. ClassExpert is used to associate events with class members. For instance, clicking a button will cause an event that can execute a class' member method.
Radio button	A button control in the shape of a circle. Several controls are typically arranged in a mutually exclusive group—only one button can be selected at a time. This is a great control for selections such as baud rates.
Check box	A rectangle, when selected, is marked with an X. Check boxes are typically used when more than one option can be selected at a time.
List box	Provides a list of choices, typically strings, although graphics can be displayed in a list box. Users can scroll through list boxes to make a selection. The Fileapp example of this chapter uses a list box to select a file on which to operate.
Combo box	A combo box comes in different flavors, but basically it is the merging of an edit box and a list box. A combo box displays the currently selected item from the list in the edit box. Some combo boxes also allow the user to enter a selection in the list box and search for the entry in the list.
Edit box	Allows the user to enter a text string. An edit box can be marked as multiline and thus provide a simple text editor.
Static text	Provides a text string that the user cannot modify. Useful for prompts, etc.
Group box	Groups a series of controls together so that all controls work together as part of a group.
Scroll bars	Provides horizontal and vertical scroll bar controls to move around a window.
Bitmap	Provides graphics to the dialog box.
Icon	Gives the dialog box the capability to display an icon.
Custom	Uses custom controls, such as VBXs or those supplied by the Borland custom windows controls (for example, 3-D buttons, text boxes, and so on).

IV

Customizing Code

You can determine how controls appear and behave by setting the styles of the controls. These styles dictate what type of messages a control sends or receives to do its job. The styles are set within the dialog editor of Resource

Workshop through the style or properties dialog boxes. Listing 23.1 contains a resource script demonstrating how styles are set for controls.

Listing 23.1   The File Dialog Box .rc File Entry

```
DIALOG_1 DIALOG 11, 26, 198, 124
STYLE DS_MODALFRAME ¦ WS_POPUP ¦ WS_VISIBLE ¦ WS_CAPTION ¦ WS_SYSMENU
CLASS "bordlg"
CAPTION "File Handler"
FONT 8, "MS Sans Serif"
{
 CONTROL "", -1, "BorShade",
   BSS_VDIP ¦ BSS_LEFT ¦ WS_CHILD ¦ WS_VISIBLE,
   136, 1, 1, 124
 CONTROL "", IDOK, "BorBtn",
   BS_DEFPUSHBUTTON ¦ WS_CHILD ¦ WS_VISIBLE ¦ WS_TABSTOP,
   144, 14, 37, 25
 CONTROL "", IDCANCEL, "BorBtn",
   BS_PUSHBUTTON ¦ WS_CHILD ¦ WS_VISIBLE ¦ WS_TABSTOP,
   144, 49, 37, 25
 CONTROL "", IDHELP, "BorBtn",
   BS_PUSHBUTTON ¦ WS_CHILD ¦ WS_VISIBLE ¦ WS_TABSTOP,
   144, 84, 37, 25
 CONTROL "Files", IDC_LISTBOX1, "LISTBOX",
   LBS_STANDARD ¦ LBS_MULTIPLESEL ¦ LBS_HASSTRINGS,
   15, 13, 63, 85
 PUSHBUTTON "Delete", IDC_PUSHBUTTON1, 84, 17, 45, 14
 PUSHBUTTON "Rename", IDC_PUSHBUTTON2, 84, 38, 45, 14
 PUSHBUTTON "Copy", IDC_PUSHBUTTON3, 84, 62, 45, 14
}
```

Creating Dialog Boxes

Resource Workshop provides the DialogExpert to help create dialog box resources. Figure 23.5 shows DialogExpert.

DialogExpert provides the basic groundwork for the dialog box. DialogExpert mostly decides if the dialog box will appear as a traditional Windows dialog box, or if it will use the aesthetic 3-D appearance provided by Borland's Custom Control Library BCWW.DLL. This library provides the trademark OK, Cancel, and Help buttons shown in figure 23.6.

Using DialogExpert to create a dialog box with controls down the right side of the dialog produces the dialog box shown in figure 23.6. The dialog editor, in which the dialog of the figure is contained, provides a series of alignment tools as well as a floating tool palette of dialog box controls. This palette allows you to select from and drag controls to the dialog box for placement in a dialog box.

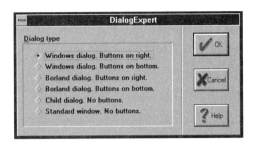

Fig. 23.5
The DialogExpert
dialog box.

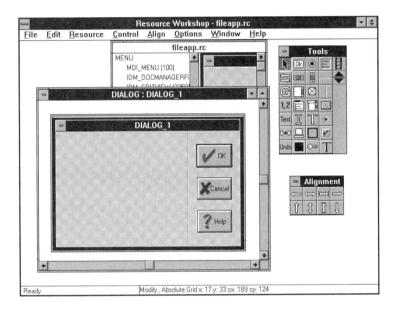

Fig. 23.6
The initial dialog
box created by
DialogExpert.

Once activated, the dialog editor also provides new menu items to create and modify dialog boxes. The new menus are Control, Align, and Options, shown in tables 23.10 through 23.12.

Table 23.10 The Control Menu Items	
Menu Item	**Description**
ClassExpert	Invokes ClassExpert to attach code to the dialog box controls to respond to the messages generated for and by the control
Style	Sets the styles for the selected control or for the dialog box

(continues)

Table 23.10   Continued

Menu item	Description
Check for Duplicate IDs	Checks for duplicate command IDs within the dialog box's controls
Push Button	Creates a push button control
Radio Button	Creates a radio button control
Horizontal Scroll Bars	Creates a horizontal scroll bar control
Vertical Scroll Bars	Creates a vertical scroll bar control
List Box	Creates a list box control
Check Box	Creates a check box control
Group Box	Creates a group box to place around controls
Combo Box	Creates a combo box control
Edit Text	Creates an edit control
Static Text	Creates a static text control
Icon	Creates an icon
Black Frame	Creates a static black frame border control
Black Rectangle	Creates solid black rectangle control
Custom	Creates a new custom control

Table 23.11   The Align Menu Items

Menu Item	Description
Align	Aligns the selected controls to the desired positions.
Size	Sizes the selected controls.
Array	Formats controls and numbers each control as a member of the array group.
Grid	Sets grid properties that help align controls.

Table 23.12 The Options Menu Items	
Menu Item	**Description**
Hide Tools	Toggles to show or hide the tools palette.
Hide Alignment	Toggles to show or hide the alignment palette.
Show Properties	Displays the property dialog box that allows editing of a control's properties. VBXs can only be edited with the Properties dialog box.
Modify Control	Places Resource Workshop in edit mode.
Set Tabs	Sets a tab stop for selected controls.
Set Group	Defines a selection of controls as a group.
Set Order	Sets the order of controls within the dialog box.
Test Dialog	Allows you to test the control.
Preferences	Sets preferences for such items as how units of measure are displayed.
Change Identifier Prefix	Changes the prefix assigned to controls within the resource file. The default values are IDS_ for string tables, CM_ for menus and accelerators, and IDS__ for dialogs.
Redraw Now	Updates the dialog box's display in the dialog editor.

The FileApp Dialog Box

The following sections, "The List Box," and "The Command Buttons," quickly illustrate how to design the file modification dialog box for the FileApp example application. Figure 23.9 shows the completed dialog box. The dialog box sports the unique Borland command buttons for OK, Cancel, and Help. DialogExpert created the initial dialog box (refer to fig. 23.6). To this dialog box you will add a list box control along with three command buttons. The list box control will contain a list of files to act upon. The three command buttons will allow users to Delete, Rename, and Copy the selected files from the list box.

The List Box

First select a list box control from either the control menu or the floating control palette located to the right of the dialog box editor window. Selecting a control will change the cursor to reflect the type of control selected. Next, move the cursor to the general area within the dialog box where the list box should go. Click the mouse and the dialog editor will "drop" the list box control onto the dialog box. Using the mouse you can size the control using the sizing borders that surround the control.

Tip
To make sizing and aligning the controls easier, don't forget to turn on the grid from the Align, Grid menu command. This command places a grid in the dialog editor that is used to *snap and glue* the controls into place. This snapping action automatically aligns the controls with respect to the lines of the grid and glues them down onto the grid.

Once the control is placed and sized, you must set the control's properties using the style editor, as shown in figure 23.7. The properties, also known as styles, of the control allow you to establish how the control will operate within a Windows application. To activate the List box style dialog box, simply double-click on the list box control in the dialog box. Because this list box will contain a list of files composed of simple strings, you need to set the Has strings property. If you want to operate on several files at once you might also want to check the Multiple Select property. The following list describes the selectable styles for the list box control:

- The Caption input box allows you to enter the caption to be displayed with the control. The radio buttons for the Caption allow you to choose how the caption is displayed.

- The Control ID allows you to enter the control's identifier.

- The Attributes check boxes allow you to select the control's attributes. These attrbutes describe how the list box operates within a Windows application.

- The Scroll Bar check boxes position scroll bars in the list box control.

- The Owner Drawing radio buttons determine whether the list contained within the control should be drawn automatically by the control or by the application.

- The List Box check boxes define the specific characteristics of the list box.

Resource Workshop and ClassExpert use default resource IDs to identify the control within the application. These IDs are passed to the application using the list box as part of a message for information processing of list box events. Many times these default IDs do not make much sense within the application. Therefore, you should change the IDs to something more maintainable, such as `IDC_FILELIST` rather than the default `IDC_LISTBOX1`.

The Command Buttons

We now wish to place a button control in the dialog box, so you will need to select the button control and drag it to the dialog box. Once the button is placed onto the dialog, you can copy and paste three versions of the control, using the Edit, Copy and Edit, Paste menu commands, to create the required three buttons. To perform this copy, select the original button and then select the Edit, Copy menu selection. To create the three buttons, select the Edit, Paste selection three times.

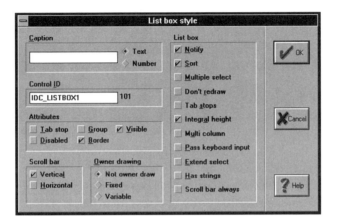

Fig. 23.7
The List box style dialog box.

Do not worry about getting them in proper position. To place the controls in the proper position, all aligned with each other, you must use the alignment palette (or menu commands). First select all three buttons by dragging the mouse cursor across them. Once all the buttons are selected, as evidenced by the highlighted border around them, click the appropriate alignment tool. In this case you want the buttons left edge-aligned with the list box.

Next, double-click on the button control with the mouse to activate the Button style dialog box. Using this dialog box, you can change the default text appearing within the button. For instance, you would want the first button's text to say "Delete" rather than "Button."

You need to also change the ID for this button to something more appropriate, such as IDC_FILEDELETE. This identifier will be sent back to the application as a message when the button control is clicked by a user. The identifier is used by the application to execute certain operations based on the button click. You can use the Control, Check For Duplicate IDs menu option to make sure you don't have duplicate identifiers created for any of the controls. These IDs are important because this is how ClassExpert can distinguish which control handler should be called when a button is clicked. Figure 23.8 shows the Button Style dialog box.

Fig. 23.8

The Button style dialog box.

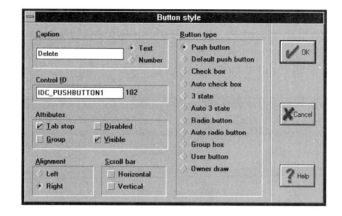

You should now set the names of the buttons and the IDs as shown in figure 23.9 for each of the other button controls you created with the Edit, Copy and Edit, Paste menu selections. You do not have to worry about the pre-defined buttons (OK, and so on) since Turbo C++ already maintains a list of IDs for them which ClassWizard can access.

Once the list box and command buttons are placed and their styles set, the finished dialog box appears like the one in figure 23.9.

Fig. 23.9

The completed file handler dialog box.

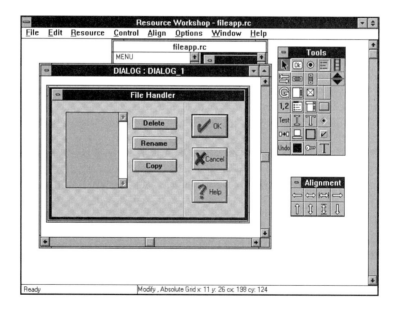

Using ClassExpert with Dialog Boxes

One of the productivity enhancements possible in the Turbo C++ visual programming environment is found when you use Resource Workshop and
ClassExpert together to map dialog box controls to various class member
functions. The two tools are tightly integrated and allow you to move quickly
from designing a dialog box to making it fully functional. Chapter 22, "Using
ClassExpert," provides detailed coverage of using this remarkable tool, but
this section provides a brief overview of using ClassExpert with Resource
Workshop.

First, you need to add a new class derived from TDialog. Open ClassExpert
from the Control menu. Then click the right mouse button within the
Classes pane in ClassExpert and select Add a New Class from the Classes pane
speedmenu. Make sure to derive the class from TDialog and select the proper
resource ID.

Next, ClassExpert creates the class and its associated files (the implementation .cpp file and header .h file). Then you can add handler functions for
messages and member variables for the various controls within the dialog
box. ClassExpert displays all the controls within the dialog box to make
selection easy. After defining member variables for the controls and message
handlers, you can use ClassExpert to edit the source files and fill in the implementation code that responds to the various messages. Figure 23.10 illustrates
adding a handler function to the list box using ClassExpert. This handler
responds to a user double-clicking within the list box.

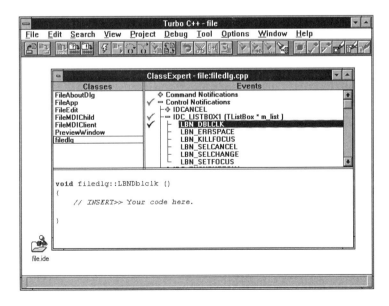

Fig. 23.10

Adding a message
handler for the list
box.

Working with Menu Resources

Menus define the available options, and the direction in which a user can proceed, at any given point in a Windows application. While the mouse is the most expedient way to invoke a menu option, you must provide a mechanism to allow the user to access a menu item via the keyboard; the familiar accelerator key and the direction arrow keys accomplish this task. Menus come in three flavors:

- *Drop-down*, or *pull-down*, *menus*. An example is the standard menu bar defined by the *Windows Application Design Guide*. This menu contains the standard items such as File, Edit, and so on.

- *Pop-up menus*. Pop-up menus are the rectangular boxes displayed when you select a menu name from the window's menu bar. These pop-up menus can either be drop-down menus or floating menus that contain a list of menu items. A drop-down menu is displayed from the menu bar or from within a menu, whereas floating menus can appear anywhere in the application window.

- *Cascading menus*. These are menu options that display other menus. These menus have a right-pointing triangle after the menu item text.

If a menu choice requires the user to supply additional information via a dialog box, an ellipsis (...) follows the menu option.

Creating Menus

To create a new menu, simply choose Resource, New from the main menu. Then select MENU from the New Resource dialog box. Clicking OK then displays the MENU editor dialog box shown in figure 23.11.

From this dialog box you can add menu items as well as view the menu as a resource script or graphically as it will appear. To specify the hot key for the menu item, use the & character. The editor also allows you to indicate hot keys for the menu item. Finally the editor allows you to specify the menu item's identifier value by name and number. Listing 23.2 illustrates an example menu entry from the FileApp example. We will detail adding and editing menu options later in this chapter.

The Menu Editor is separated into three different panes. The first pane, the Attribute pane, allows you to edit the attributes for pop-up commands and menu items. The components of the Attribute pane are described in the list following figure 23.11.

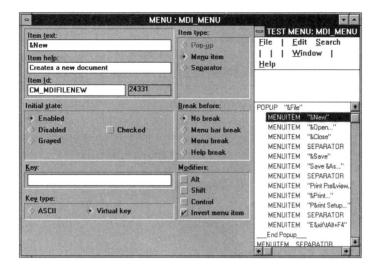

Fig. 23.11
The MENU editor
dialog box.

- Item Text (Alt+T) specifies the name of a menu item or pop-up menu.

- Item Help (Alt+L) specifies help text that appears in the status line of the application window when you select the menu item.

- Item ID (Alt+I) specifies the identifier for the menu item. This identifier is assembled for you by the Menu Editor as you enter the Item Text and is equivalent to the identifier we discussed earlier in this chapter for the dialog box controls.

- The Initial State radio buttons (Alt+S) determine the current menu item's initial state. Enabled menu items can be used by the user; however, Disabled or Grayed menu items are not accessible. The EnableMenuItem() function enables a Disabled or Grayed menu item from within the application.

  If you wish to toggle a menu item on and off, select the Checked check box to place a checkmark next to the menu item. The CheckMenuItem() function allows you to change the state of the menu item from within the application.

- Key (Alt+K) specifies a key to assign to the current menu command.

- The Key Type radio buttons specify the type of key assignment whether it be an ASCII or virtual key. ASCII keys follow standard conventions for representing ASCII characters and are surrounded by quotation marks. Typically, ASCII keys are combined with Alt or Ctrl, such as Alt+R or Ctrl+L.

Virtual keys are usually function keys, arrow keys, or the Home or End keys. Virtual keys do not use the Ctrl, Shift, and Alt combinations and are typically associated with accelerator keys, which are discussed in the next section of this chapter.

■ The Item Type radio buttons determine the type of menu being added. Pop-up (Alt+U) menus appear on the main menu bar of an application while Menu Items (Alt+N) appear in the pop-up window for a pop-up menu. A Separator (Alt+P) is merely a line that appears in a pop-up menu to separate the menu items.

■ The Break Before radio buttons (Alt+B) specify the format of the menu bar and pop-up menus. The No Break radio button places no line breaks before the current menu item, whereas the Menu Bar Break radio button starts a new line in the menu bar or a new column in a pop-up menu. The Menu Break radio button starts a new line in the menu bar, but in a pop-up menu this option starts a new column and draws a vertical line to separate the columns.

The Help Break radio button applies to a Help menu bar selection, if one is provided in your application, and places the menu item to the far right of the menu bar.

■ The Modifiers check boxes (Alt+O) specify what additional keys are used for the Key you assigned to this menu command. The selection made here determines the operation of the accelerators for a given menu selection.

The Outline pane of the Menu Editor displays the new menu's pop-up commands, menu items, and separators in the resource's script language. The top line shown in the pane is the name of the menu, with each successive line containing statements defining pop-up menus and menu items.

The Test Menu pane displays your menu as you develop it and allows you test the pop-up menus and menu items. The Menu Editor automatically updates the menu, allowing you to test each step of your menu's development.

Listing 23.2   The Main Menu for FileApp

```
MDI_MENU MENU
BEGIN
    POPUP "&File"
    BEGIN
        MENUITEM "&New", CM_MDIFILENEW
```

```
            MENUITEM "&Open...", CM_MDIFILEOPEN
            MENUITEM "&Close", CM_FILECLOSE
            MENUITEM SEPARATOR
            MENUITEM "&Save", CM_FILESAVE, GRAYED
            MENUITEM "Save &As...", CM_FILESAVEAS, GRAYED
            MENUITEM SEPARATOR
            MENUITEM "Print Pre&view...", CM_FILEPRINTPREVIEW, GRAYED
            MENUITEM "&Print...", CM_FILEPRINT, GRAYED
            MENUITEM "P&rint Setup...", CM_FILEPRINTERSETUP, GRAYED
            MENUITEM SEPARATOR
            MENUITEM "E&xit\tAlt+F4", CM_EXIT
        END
        MENUITEM SEPARATOR
        POPUP "&Edit"
        BEGIN
            MENUITEM "&Undo\tAlt+BkSp", CM_EDITUNDO, GRAYED
            MENUITEM SEPARATOR
            MENUITEM "Cu&t\tShift+Del", CM_EDITCUT, GRAYED
            MENUITEM "&Copy\tCtrl+Ins", CM_EDITCOPY, GRAYED
            MENUITEM "&Paste\tShift+Ins", CM_EDITPASTE, GRAYED
            MENUITEM SEPARATOR
            MENUITEM "Clear &All\tCtrl+Del", CM_EDITCLEAR, GRAYED
            MENUITEM "&Delete\tDel", CM_EDITDELETE, GRAYED
        END
        POPUP "&Search"
        BEGIN
            MENUITEM "&Find...", CM_EDITFIND, GRAYED
            MENUITEM "&Replace...", CM_EDITREPLACE, GRAYED
            MENUITEM "&Next\aF3", CM_EDITFINDNEXT, GRAYED
        END
        MENUITEM SEPARATOR
        MENUITEM SEPARATOR
        MENUITEM SEPARATOR
        POPUP "&Window"
        BEGIN
            MENUITEM "&Cascade", CM_CASCADECHILDREN
            MENUITEM "&Tile", CM_TILECHILDREN
            MENUITEM "Arrange &Icons", CM_ARRANGEICONS
            MENUITEM "C&lose All", CM_CLOSECHILDREN
        END
        MENUITEM SEPARATOR
        POPUP "&Help"
        BEGIN
            MENUITEM "&Contents", CM_HELPCONTENTS
            MENUITEM "&Using help", CM_HELPUSING
            MENUITEM SEPARATOR
            MENUITEM "&About...", CM_HELPABOUT
        END
    END
```

Notice the TEST MENU window on the right of the MENU dialog box (refer to fig. 23.11). This displays the current menu item as both a functioning menu and as a resource script. To edit a specific menu item, simply scroll to the desired item.

Adding a New Pop-up Menu

Tip

If your cursor is within another pop-up menu of the Outline pane, the new pop-up will be added as a sub-pop-up of the pop-up in which the cursor is located. To add the pop-up as a top-level pop-up, make sure that the cursor is at the bottom of the Outline pane's menu option list.

Tip

When choosing hot keys for menu selections, make sure that for each pop-up or top-level menu you have only one menu item that uses a given hot key. If you have multiple selections with the same hot key, the menu items containing the hot key will not execute immediately upon selecting the hot key.

To add a menu to your application you must first add pop-up menus to your menu bar. To add a pop-up menu you select the Menu, New Pop-up (Ctrl+P) Resource Workshop menu option. Resource Workshop will add a new entry in the Outline pane and clear the Attribute pane for the new entry.

The Attributes pane has been cleared and contains &Popup in the Item Text for the new pop-up menu. The ampersand (&) preceding the text informs Resource Workshop that the P is to be the hot key for the menu selection. For instance, when you wish to select this option you only have to press the P key in order to execute the menu option. You can place the ampersand anywhere within the item text to make another character of the text become the hot key for the menu item.

You can see from the figure that the Key, Key Type, and Modifiers sections of the Attributes pane are grayed, or disabled. For pop-up menu items you cannot assign a virtual key since these menu selections do not directly execute functions for the application. The primary purpose of virtual keys, accelerators, is to speed up the process of executing menu selections within an application; therefore, only menu items can be assigned a virtual key. We will discuss accelerators and accelerator tables in more detail in the next section.

For this menu we will need to change the &Popup menu Item Text to represent a meaningful menu selection. In this instance we will change the text to &Edit. Once the text has been changed, press the Enter key to accept the new text and update the Test Menu pane as well as in the Outline pane. When we add menu items to this pop-up, we will add items such as Cut, Copy, and Paste, which are all elements of Windows' edit and clipboard operations.

Adding a New Menu Item

Once you have added pop-up menus, you can add menu items to these pop-up menus or to the menu bar for the menu. To add a menu item, simply select the Menu, New Menu Item (Ins) selection from the Resource Workshop menu. When selected, a new item is added to the pop-up listed in the Outline in which the cursor resides.

The identifier for a new menu item contains its parent pop-up menu's name and the text ITEM. By changing the Item Text for the new menu item to &Cut, the identifier will automatically be changed to suit the new item's text— CM_EDITCUT. The attributes are set so that this menu item will be a standard menu item Item Type and it will be enabled. There will be no breaks, whether it be column or line break, preceding the item in the pop-up menu's list.

Once these attributes are set, pressing the Enter key tells the Menu Editor to accept the changes and update the Test Menu and Outline panes.

Modifying Menus

When the Menu editor is invoked, it adds a new menu item called, appropriately enough, Menu, to Resource Workshop's main menu. Table 23.13 lists the menu options available with the editor. From this menu you can add new menu items and menu types, change how the menu resource identifiers are distinguished from other types of resources, and check to make sure menu items are uniquely identified.

Table 23.13   Menu Editor Items

Menu Item	Description	Accelerator
ClassExpert	Invokes ClassExpert to attach member functions to the selected resource.	
New Popup	Inserts a new popup menu at the current location.	^P
New Menu Item	Inserts a new menu item at the current location.	Ins
New Separator	Inserts a menu separator bar at the current location.	^S
New File Popup	Inserts a pop-up menu containing the standard File menu items New, Open, Save, Save As, Print, Page Setup, Printer Setup, and Exit at the current location.	
New Edit Popup	Inserts a pop-up menu containing the standard edit menu items Cut, Copy, and Paste at the current location.	
New Help Popup	Inserts a pop-up menu containing the standard help menu items Index, Keyboard, Commands, Procedures, Using Help, and About at the current location.	
Check Duplicates	Checks the designed menu for duplication command identifiers.	
Accelerator Key Value	Assigns an accelerator key to the current menu item.	

Tip

As a shortcut to manually adding the File, Edit, and Help pop-up menus you can select the Menu, New File Pop-up, the Menu, New Edit Pop-up, and the Menu, New Help Pop-up menu selections. These selections will build the selected menu pop-ups for you in your menu.

Tip

To add menu items to the menu bar, make sure that the cursor is located at the end of the list in the Outline pane.

IV

Customizing Code

(continues)

Table 23.13 Continued		
Menu Item	**Description**	**Accelerator**
Change Identifier Prefix	Changes the prefix used to identify menu resources. The default value is CM_.	
Track Test Menu	Toggles test menu tracking in the Resource View window.	

Working with Accelerators

Accelerators are shortcut keys that allow a user to quickly select a menu option without using the mouse. These keys are shown to the right of a menu item and can consist of a series of keystrokes. These keys are stored in a resource called an *accelerator table*. Listing 23.3 shows the accelerator table for the example FileApp application. Windows maps a key and key modifiers, such as the Shift and Control keys, to a specific menu ID. AppExpert creates a basic accelerator table for the standard menu items, but you must provide any accelerator entries that are specific to your menu and application.

You can create an accelerator table or an entry using the accelerator table editor. To do this, simply choose Resource, New and choose ACCELERATOR, or double-click the accelerator table entry in the resource window. Another way to add or modify entries in the accelerator table is via the menu editor, which has selections for keys and key modifiers for each menu selection in the application.

Listing 23.3 A Sample Entry for an Accelerator Table

```
// Accelerator table for short-cut to menu commands.
// (include\owl\editfile.rc) MDI_MENU ACCELERATORS
BEGIN
  VK_DELETE, CM_EDITDELETE, VIRTKEY
  VK_DELETE, CM_EDITCUT, VIRTKEY, SHIFT
  VK_INSERT, CM_EDITCOPY, VIRTKEY, CONTROL
  VK_INSERT, CM_EDITPASTE, VIRTKEY, SHIFT
  VK_DELETE, CM_EDITCLEAR, VIRTKEY, CONTROL
  VK_BACK,   CM_EDITUNDO, VIRTKEY, ALT
  VK_F3,     CM_EDITFINDNEXT, VIRTKEY
END
```

Working with Icons

Each application uses an icon to represent itself with the Windows shell, typically Program Manager. The application also normally displays this icon with its About box. Icons can also be used in dialog boxes and other areas of an application. To easily use icons, Windows permits them to be saved as part of the resource file without having to ship individual icon files for each application. To create and edit icons, Resource Workshop provides a graphical icon editor, as shown in figure 23.12.

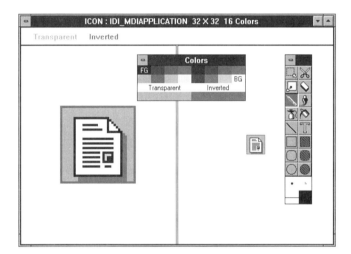

Fig. 23.12
The icon editor.

One thing to remember is that all Windows displays are not created equal. So an icon displayed on an SVGA screen in 256 colors may look very different on a VGA screen in 16 colors. Windows makes provisions for this fact by allowing you to specify different versions of the same icon for different video adapters. Even though an icon file may have different images for these various adapters, the icon is still referenced in the resource script as one entity. Listing 23.4 illustrates a sample icon resource script.

Listing 23.4 A Sample Icon Resource Script

```
// MDI document ICON
IDI_DOC ICON "applsdi.ico"

// Application ICON
IDI_MDIAPPLICATION ICON "applmdi.ico"
```

Working with String Tables

String tables commonly provide a central repository for error messages, prompts, or any other text strings your application uses for informational display to the user. You can define multiple string tables where, generally, each string table contains logical groupings of text for your program. For instance, one table may contain strings specific to file errors while another table may contain strings informing the user of an application's processing or print status.

One of the main reasons for defining strings in string table resources is to allow for easy editing of text without changing your source code. Many times you will display information to the user and, as the application is upgraded or user requirements change, the informational messages will most likely change. Instead of modifying the application's code and having to recompile and relink, you can simply change the message text in the string table resources for the application.

AppExpert generates several string tables for the strings used by OWL applications. Listing 23.5 provides a sample from the FileApp sample program. The string editor presents the strings within a grid that you can select and edit. Windows logically organizes these into groups of 16. The group to which a particular string belongs is a function of its identifier. For example, strings having identifiers falling between 0 and 15 belong to one group, 16 through 31 belong to another, 32 through 47 to yet another. Thus, the values ranging from 0x0 to 0xFFFF identify strings. Figure 23.13 shows the string editor in action.

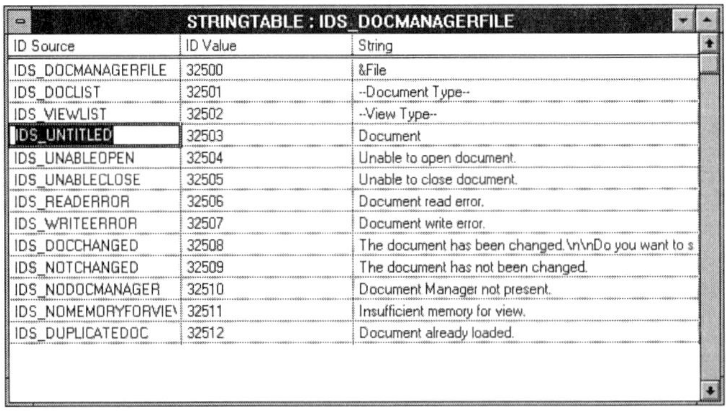

Fig. 23.13
The STRING editor.

ID Source	ID Value	String
IDS_DOCMANAGERFILE	32500	&File
IDS_DOCLIST	32501	--Document Type--
IDS_VIEWLIST	32502	--View Type--
IDS_UNTITLED	32503	Document
IDS_UNABLEOPEN	32504	Unable to open document.
IDS_UNABLECLOSE	32505	Unable to close document.
IDS_READERROR	32506	Document read error.
IDS_WRITEERROR	32507	Document write error.
IDS_DOCCHANGED	32508	The document has been changed.\n\nDo you want to s
IDS_NOTCHANGED	32509	The document has not been changed.
IDS_NODOCMANAGER	32510	Document Manager not present.
IDS_NOMEMORYFORVIE\	32511	Insufficient memory for view.
IDS_DUPLICATEDOC	32512	Document already loaded.

Windows uses the first 12 bits for segment allocation. This orderly grouping of strings facilitates the loading of all related strings at one time. In other words, keep all the prompt strings for one menu option in one segment, all the strings for another option in another, and so on. This allows Windows to fetch all the prompt strings (up to 16) at once—sort of like catching all the fish with one sweep of the net. Where possible, your application will make the table movable and discardable based on the selections made in the Memory Options dialog accessible from the Resource, Memory Options menu selection.

Listing 23.5   String Table Entries

```
// General Window's status bar messages. (include\owl\statusba.rc)
STRINGTABLE
BEGIN
    IDS_MODES                   "EXT¦CAPS¦NUM¦SCRL¦OVR¦REC"
    IDS_MODESOFF                "   ¦    ¦   ¦    ¦   ¦   "
    SC_SIZE,                    "Changes the size of the window"
    SC_MOVE,                    "Moves the window to another
position"
    SC_MINIMIZE,                "Reduces the window to an icon"
    SC_MAXIMIZE,                "Enlarges the window to it maximum
size"
    SC_RESTORE,                 "Restores the window to its previous size"
    SC_CLOSE,                   "Closes the window"
    SC_TASKLIST,                "Opens task list"
    SC_NEXTWINDOW,              "Switches to next window"
END
```

Working with Version Resources

Beginning with Windows 3.1, Microsoft provided version information for resource files. This provides you with a way to detect newer, or older, versions of application and library files (such as DLLs and VBXs). This resource also allows you to display information to the user such as your company name and application copyright information. The version resource also contains useful items to the program, such as the version number of the file, various operating-system-specific information, information pertaining to how and why you created the file, and what languages and character sets the file supports.

AppExpert provides a default version information entry in the application's .rc file. This default version contains all the basic information needed for the application. You can then modify the information to suit your needs.

Listing 23.6 illustrates the version resource from the file example's resource file, fileapp.rc.

Listing 23.6   The Version Information from File .rc

```
// Version info.
//
#if !defined(__DEBUG_)
// Non-Debug VERSIONINFO
1 VERSIONINFO LOADONCALL MOVEABLE
FILEVERSION 1, 0, 0, 0
PRODUCTVERSION 1, 0, 0, 0
FILEFLAGSMASK 0
FILEFLAGS VS_FFI_FILEFLAGSMASK
FILEOS VOS__WINDOWS16
FILETYPE VFT_APP
BEGIN
    BLOCK "StringFileInfo"
    BEGIN
      // Language type = U.S. English (0x0409) and Character Set
      // = Windows, Multilingual(0x04e4)
       BLOCK "040904E4"
      // Matches VarFileInfo Translation hex value.
       BEGIN
          VALUE "CompanyName", "Tristar Systems, Inc\000"
          VALUE "FileDescription", "file for Windows\000"
          VALUE "FileVersion", "1.0\000"
          VALUE "InternalName", "file\000"
          VALUE "LegalCopyright",
         "Copyright © 1995. All Rights Reserved.\000"
          VALUE "LegalTrademarks",
         "Windows (TM) is a trademark of Microsoft Corporation\000"
          VALUE "OriginalFilename", "file.EXE\000"
          VALUE "ProductName", "file\000"
          VALUE "ProductVersion", "1.0\000"
       END
    END

    BLOCK "VarFileInfo"
    BEGIN
       // U.S. English(0x0409) & Windows Multilingual(0x04e4) 1252
       VALUE "Translation", 0x0409, 0x04e4
    END
END
```

Unlike most other resources—except strings—Resource Workshop only allows you to modify version information using the text editor.

From Here...

In this chapter, you learned about Windows resources and the Resource Workshop for creating and editing those resources. Dialog boxes are common windows used to provide information to the user of an application and are easily created in Resource Workshop. To allow access to the functions of an application, menus and accelerators provide a simple means of selecting the functions of an application to execute. Finally, bitmaps, cursors, and icons can be created in Resource Workshop to enhance the aesthetics of your application as well as provide graphical representations of an application's functionality.

For further information, refer to the following :

- Chapter 21, "Using AppExpert," for more information on how to generate a skeletal Windows application without writing a single line of source code.

- Chapter 22, "Using ClassExpert," for information on how to tie resource components to class member functions.

- Appendix C, "Installing a Windows Application," for more information on using the version info resources.

Part V

Advanced Tools and Techniques

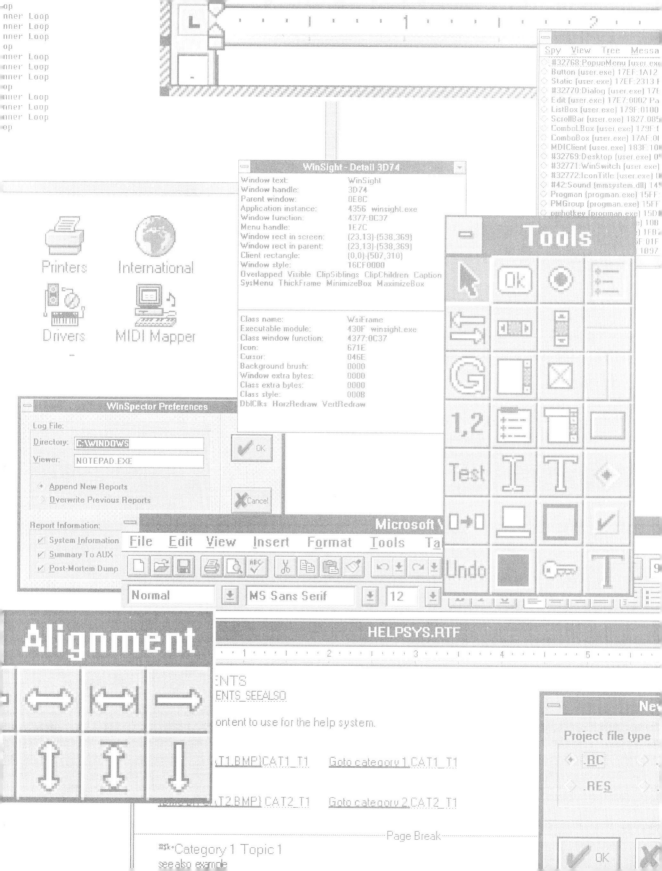

Chapter 24

Windows Programming Basics

Windows programming is both a challenge and a treat. It's a challenge because, unless you've had other experience with event-driven systems, you need to learn a whole new way to think about program development. Windows' event-driven, multitasking architecture forces you to write programs unlike the procedural programs you may have written previously. Windows programming is a treat because the Windows system gives you so much power—power to create applications you could only dream about back in the old DOS days.

The bad news is that learning Windows programming takes a lot of time and dedication. The techniques presented in this chapter only scratch the surface of what you need to know to program under Windows successfully. You may want to invest in a book specifically on programming Windows.

You may be tempted to avoid the straight C++ programming techniques presented in this chapter and instead use Borland's powerful ObjectWindows Library for creating Windows applications. Be forewarned, however: Although ObjectWindows (OWL) helps you create Windows applications quickly, you still should understand how Windows applications work. Such knowledge will go a long way toward helping you understand how OWL handles Windows.

Understanding the Windows System

Before you can start writing Windows programs, you have to know some details about how the Windows system works and how applications interact with that system. Many of the concepts presented in this section may be new to you. If so, be assured that, if this introduction gets a little confusing, the pieces should fall in place as you apply what you learn here to the sample programs that follow.

The topics you need to know about are

- Graphical user interfaces
- Multitasking
- Event-driven programming
- Device independence

In the sections that follow, you'll get a quick introduction to these terms and how they relate to Windows programming.

Graphical User Interfaces

Computers have a bad reputation. This is because, when a novice walks up to one of these strange machines and sees a screenful of mysterious commands, he can't help but feel dumb, incompetent, and maybe even a little nervous. Many people are less intimidated by the cockpit of a 747 than by a glowing computer screen! Computers are so unlike other machines you might find in an office or home. Other machines have labeled knobs and switches that enable people to give them commands. A computer without a graphical user interface, however, responds only to typed commands given by Those Who Know.

In an attempt to make computers more like other machines, computer scientists came up with the *graphical user interface* (GUI, pronounced *gooey*). A GUI is nothing more than an operating system that hides all the mysterious commands from the user, replacing those commands with familiar objects like buttons, sliders, and other controls with which folks are more comfortable. Whether the invention of GUIs has made computing less intimidating is a topic of much heated debate. One thing's for sure: The Windows GUI is a gigantic hit now found on the majority of computers around the world.

Multitasking

Not too long ago, computers could run only a single program at a time. If you needed data from a word processor while working with a spreadsheet program, you had to close down the spreadsheet and start up the word processor. This one-program-only approach to computing made data-handling a clumsy and frustrating process. How much better it would be to have both the word processor and spreadsheet in memory at the same time and instantly switch between them as needed.

This instant switching from one program to another is accomplished by something called *multitasking*. In fact, with multitasking, programs can actually continue running in the background while you work with something else. For example, under a multitasking system like Windows, you can write a fan letter to Eddie Vedder while downloading the latest shareware hit in the background.

This multitasking power doesn't come without a price, of course. The more applications that must share the computer's resources, the slower they run. Particularly under Windows, applications must be written in such a way that they don't steal computing time from other applications that may also be running. Windows incorporates something called *cooperative multitasking*, which means each running application must voluntarily give up the processor. This method is inferior to *pre-emptive multitasking*, in which the operating system, not the applications, decides how to divvy up computing time.

In most cases, you don't have to worry too much about the multitasking aspect of Windows programming. As long as you follow the basic programming rules, your applications will automatically yield to other applications properly. Watch out, however, for functions in your programs that tie up the processor for long periods before exiting. Such functions can bring other Windows applications to a screeching halt.

Event-Driven Programming

Just as it's imperative that you be aware of Windows' multitasking nature, so too must you understand something called *event-driven programming*. Under an event-driven system, your applications receive a constant flow of messages from the operating system. Your application must decide how to handle each message or whether to just ignore the message and pass it back to the operating system.

For example, under Windows (which is an event-driven system), when the user clicks the mouse on your application's window, your application receives a `WM_LBUTTONDOWN` message. This message comes to your application in a little packet containing information about the event. In the case of a `WM_LBUTTONDOWN` message, this packet contains, among other things, the window coordinate at which the mouse pointer was positioned when the user clicked.

In DOS programming, it is your program that tells the operating system what to do. But with Windows programming, Windows is the boss, sending your applications the commands it receives from the user. You could say, in fact, that the user never really uses your application at all. Instead, Windows accepts instructions from the user and passes them on to the appropriate application.

Device Independence

Programming for PC compatibles is a complicated process when one considers that there are literally thousands of different computer configurations on which a program must run. Hundreds of different sound cards, graphics cards, printers, modems, and any number of other add-ons make compatibility problems a pervasive part of this type of computer programming.

To combat compatibility problems, Windows applications are *device independent*. Device independence means that the program itself doesn't need to worry about the details of the hardware on which it's running. The programmer simply creates the application according to Windows' device-independence rules, and Windows takes care of the rest, loading the correct drivers for any devices connected to the user's system.

Unfortunately, device independence creates as much programming work as it saves. Although you can be reasonably assured that your Windows application will run on any correctly configured Windows system, you must create your programs carefully, being sure that you never make unsafe assumptions about any devices the user may be using. (There are a few assumptions you can make about devices. For example, because VGA graphics is now the standard, you can usually assume that the user's screen has a resolution of at least 640×480. But to be perfectly safe, even such "harmless" assumptions should be avoided.)

The fact is that device independence is not a Windows feature that was designed to make life easier for programmers. It was designed to make life easier for users so that they don't have to go through the configuration nightmares that plague DOS systems. If you ever tried to install several different games on a DOS system, you know exactly what I mean.

Your First Windows Application

Now that you know a little about how Windows works, it's time to see how to write a Windows application. Listings 24.1 and 24.2 show the source code for a minimum Windows application. Listing 24.1 is the main program, whereas listing 24.2 is a *module definition file*, a special file that tells Turbo C++'s linker important information about this application. You'll learn more about these files later in the chapter. For now, follow the steps below to compile and run the WINEX1 application:

1. Inside your TCWIN45 directory, create a directory called WINEX1, and copy the WINEX1.CPP and WINEX1.DEF files into this new directory.

2. Start Turbo C++, and select the Project menu's New Project command. You see the New Target dialog box (see fig. 24.1).

Fig. 24.1
The New Target dialog box.

3. Type **C:\TCWIN45\WINEX1\WINEX1.IDE** into the Project Path and Name edit box.

4. Set the Target Type list box to Application [.exe] (and make sure the Platform box is set to Windows 3.x (16), and the Target Model box is set to Large).

5. In the Standard Libraries box, turn off all the checkmarks except for the one next to Runtime. When you're done, the New Target dialog box should look like figure 24.2.

6. Click the OK button, and the application's Project window appears (see fig. 24.3).

7. Click on the WINEX1 [.RC] line in the Project window, and press your keyboard's Delete key to remove this file from the Project window's list.

8. Click the Toolbar's Run button (the button that looks like a lightning bolt) to compile and run the program.

Fig. 24.2
The New Target
dialog box set up
for the WINEX1
application.

Fig. 24.3
The Project
window.

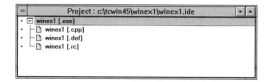

The following are the program listings for the WINEX1 sample application,
for which you created a project in the previous steps.

**Listing 24.1   WINEX1.CPP—The WINEX1 Application's Main
Source Code File**

```cpp
/////////////////////////////////////////////////////////
// WINEX1.CPP: Windows example program 1.
/////////////////////////////////////////////////////////

#include <windows.h>

// Prototype for window procedure.
LRESULT FAR PASCAL _export WndProc(HWND hWnd, UINT message,
    WPARAM wParam, LPARAM lParam);

/////////////////////////////////////////////////////////
// WinMain
/////////////////////////////////////////////////////////
int PASCAL WinMain(HINSTANCE hCurrentInst,
    HINSTANCE hPreviousInst, LPSTR /* lpszCmdLine */,
    int nCmdShow)
{
    WNDCLASS wndClass;
```

```
    HWND hWnd;
    MSG msg;

    // If there's no previous instance of this application,
    // define and register the window class.
    if (hPreviousInst == NULL)
    {
        wndClass.style = CS_HREDRAW | CS_VREDRAW;
        wndClass.lpfnWndProc = WndProc;
        wndClass.cbClsExtra = 0;
        wndClass.cbWndExtra = 0;
        wndClass.hInstance = hCurrentInst;
        wndClass.hIcon = LoadIcon(NULL, IDI_APPLICATION);
        wndClass.hCursor = LoadCursor(NULL, IDC_ARROW);
        wndClass.hbrBackground = GetStockObject(WHITE_BRUSH);
        wndClass.lpszMenuName = NULL;
        wndClass.lpszClassName = "WinEx1";

        RegisterClass(&wndClass);
    }

    // Get the size of the screen.
    UINT width = GetSystemMetrics(SM_CXSCREEN) / 2;
    UINT height = GetSystemMetrics(SM_CYSCREEN) / 2;

    // Create a window of the previously defined class.
    hWnd = CreateWindow(
            "WinEx1",              // Window class's name.
            "WinEx1 Application",  // Title bar text.
            WS_OVERLAPPEDWINDOW,   // The window's style.
            10,                    // X position.
            10,                    // Y position.
            width,                 // Width.
            height,                // Height.
            NULL,                  // Parent window's handle.
            NULL,                  // Menu handle.
            hCurrentInst,          // Instance handle.
            NULL);                 // No additional data.

    // Display the window on the screen.
    ShowWindow(hWnd, nCmdShow);

    // Force the window to repaint itself.
    UpdateWindow(hWnd);

    // Start the message loop.
    while (GetMessage(&msg, NULL, NULL, NULL))
    {
        TranslateMessage(&msg);
        DispatchMessage(&msg);
    }

    return msg.wParam;
}
```

(continues)

V

Tools and Techniques

Listing 24.1 Continued

```
//////////////////////////////////////////////////////////////
// WndProc()
//
// This is the main window procedure, which is called by
// Windows.
//////////////////////////////////////////////////////////////
LRESULT FAR PASCAL _export WndProc(HWND hWnd, UINT message,
    WPARAM wParam, LPARAM lParam)
{
    // Handle the messages to which the application
    // must respond.
    switch(message)
    {
        case WM_DESTROY:
            PostQuitMessage(0);
            return 0;
    }

    // Make sure all messages get returned to Windows.
    return DefWindowProc(hWnd, message, wParam, lParam);
}
```

Listing 24.2 WINEX1.DEF—The WINEX1 Application's Module Definition File

```
;//////////////////////////////////////////////////////////////
;// WINEX1.DEF: Module definition file for WinEx1.
;//////////////////////////////////////////////////////////////

NAME          WINEX1
DESCRIPTION   'Windows example app by Clayton Walnum'
EXETYPE       WINDOWS
STUB          'WINSTUB.EXE'
CODE          PRELOAD MOVEABLE DISCARDABLE
DATA          PRELOAD MOVEABLE MULTIPLE
HEAPSIZE      1024
STACKSIZE     5120
```

Running the WINEX1 Application

When you run WINEX1, you see the window shown in figure 24.4. As you can see, WINEX1 creates a fully functional window that you can resize, minimize, and maximize. In addition, you can double-click the window's Control menu box to exit the program.

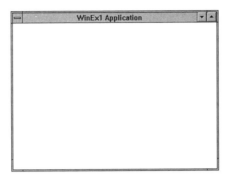

Fig. 24.4
The WINEX1
application.

Although WINEX1 doesn't do anything beyond creating a main window, it is the basic program from which any Windows application can be developed. In later sections in this chapter, you'll see how to do everything from display text in the window to respond to menu commands and display dialog boxes. Now, though, you'll examine WINEX1's source code to see what makes it tick.

Digging Into the WINEX1 Application

Examine listing 24.1 starting from the top. The first line you see (not counting comments) is

```
#include <windows.h>
```

Windows development languages declare a number of standard constants, functions, and data types that Windows programmers need to use. These declarations are found in the WINDOWS.H file, which must be included in every Windows program.

The Window Procedure

Next, you see the prototype for something called a window procedure:

```
LRESULT FAR PASCAL _export WndProc(HWND hWnd, UINT message,
    WPARAM wParam, LPARAM lParam);
```

Remember I said that Windows sends your application a constant stream of messages? You may have wondered how Windows knows where to send these messages. The answer is that Windows communicates with your application through the application's window procedure, whose prototype must look like the above (except you can change the function's name, if you like).

The function's first parameter, hWnd, is a value that identifies the window to which the message is being sent. The h stands for *handle*, which is simply a

V

Tools and Techniques

value that Windows and Windows programs use to identify objects in memory. You'll run into all kinds of handles as you write Windows applications. The second parameter is a value that identifies the message type (such as WM_LBUTTONDOWN or WM_DESTROY). The third and fourth parameters are extra values that may or may not contain additional information about the message being received. The first is a word value, and the second is a long word.

Notice how this function is declared as FAR PASCAL _export. All functions that communicate with Windows must be declared this way.

The *WinMain()* Function

Next in the program, you come across the WinMain() function:

```
int PASCAL WinMain(HINSTANCE hCurrentInst,
    HINSTANCE hPreviousInst, LPSTR /* lpszCmdLine */,
    int nCmdShow)
```

Just as all DOS C and C++ programs begin execution at the main() function, all Windows programs begin execution at the WinMain() function. This function's first parameter is the handle of the current application instance. The second parameter is the handle of the application's previous instance.

What's an instance? Suppose you run Word for Windows. That's the first instance of that application. Now, suppose you run Word for Windows again, without exiting the currently running Word for Windows. The new instance becomes the current instance, and the first one is now the previous instance.

Getting back to WinMain(), the function's third parameter is a pointer to the command line used to run the program. In this case, it's commented out because WINEX1 never accesses it. Finally, the fourth parameter is a value that indicates whether or not the application's window should be shown as an icon rather than a full window.

Inside WinMain(), the program first declares several local variables:

```
WNDCLASS wndClass;
HWND hWnd;
MSG msg;
```

WNDCLASS is a structure that holds details about a window's class. You'll learn more about this structure soon. HWND is a window handle. In this case, hWnd will hold this application's window handle. Finally, MSG is a structure that holds information about a Windows message. You'll see how to use this structure soon.

Defining a Window Class

The first task of a Windows application is to define the application's *window class*. A window class is kind of like a blueprint for a window. Just as a machinist can create many identical gears from a single blueprint, so can your Windows applications create many windows from a single windows class. A window class only needs to be defined once, however, no matter how many instances of an application are running. So WINEX1 first checks whether hPreviousInst contains a valid handle:

```
if (hPreviousInst == NULL)
```

If hPreviousInst is not NULL, there is a previous instance of the application, in which case the application should not redefine the window class. If hPreviousInst is NULL, however, there is no previous instance of the application, and the application must define its window class, which it does like this:

```
wndClass.style = CS_HREDRAW ¦ CS_VREDRAW;
wndClass.lpfnWndProc = WndProc;
wndClass.cbClsExtra = 0;
wndClass.cbWndExtra = 0;
wndClass.hInstance = hCurrentInst;
wndClass.hIcon = LoadIcon(NULL, IDI_APPLICATION);
wndClass.hCursor = LoadCursor(NULL, IDC_ARROW);
wndClass.hbrBackground = GetStockObject(WHITE_BRUSH);
wndClass.lpszMenuName = NULL;
wndClass.lpszClassName = "WinEx1";
```

Here, the style member is set to CS_HREDRAW ¦ CS_VREDRAW, which ensures that the window repaints itself when it's resized. Other class style constants include CS_BYTEALIGNCLIENT, CS_BYTEALIGNWINDOW, CS_CLASSDC, CS_DBLCLKS, CS_GLOBALCLASS, CS_NOCLOSE, CS_OWNDC, CS_PARENTDC, and CS_SAVEBITS. If you want to know more about these styles, look them up in your Turbo C++ documentation. Notice that these constants are ORed together to create bit flags for the complete style.

The second WNDCLASS member, lpfnWndProc, is a pointer to your application's window procedure. This is how Windows knows where to send its messages. The third and fourth members, cbClsExtra and cbWndExtra, are usually set to 0. The fifth member is the application's instance handle, which, in this case, is received by WinMain() as hCurrentInst.

When you minimize a window, it appears as an icon at the bottom of the screen. A handle to this icon is stored in the WNDCLASS structure's sixth member, hIcon. In the previous code segment, this handle is obtained by calling the Windows function LoadIcon() to load the predefined icon identified by the IDI_APPLICATION constant.

V

Tools and Techniques

Every window class has a mouse cursor associated with it. Whenever the user moves the mouse pointer over a window of the class, the mouse pointer changes to the cursor defined for the class. The seventh member of the WNDCLASS structure holds a handle to this cursor. In WINEX1, this handle is obtained by calling the Windows function LoadCursor() to load the pre-defined cursor identified by the IDC_ARROW constant.

Window classes also have a background color associated with them. This color is represented by a brush. (You'll learn about brushes later in this chapter.) Because Windows has several stock brushes that an application can use, WINEX1 calls the Windows function GetStockObject() to obtain a handle to a white brush, which is stored in the WNDCLASS structure's eighth member hbrBackground.

Finally, the last two WNDCLASS members hold the window's menu name and class name. Because WINEX1 doesn't have a menu bar, the lpszMenuName member is set to NULL. The lpszClassName, though, is set to "WinEx1". This name is important because it is the only thing that identifies this window class.

At last, the application's window class has been defined. The next step is to tell Windows about it. This is done by calling the Windows function RegisterClass():

```
RegisterClass(&wndClass);
```

This function's single argument is a pointer to the WNDCLASS structure containing the details of the window's class. After calling RegisterClass(), Windows has created the aforementioned window blueprint from which you can create as many actual windows as you like.

Creating the Window Element

Creating the application's actual main window is WINEX1's next task. But first the program must know the size of the screen. (Device independence, remember?) The Windows function GetSystemMetrics() can provide all sorts of information about the user's system. In WINEX1, it's called like this:

```
UINT width = GetSystemMetrics(SM_CXSCREEN) / 2;
UINT height = GetSystemMetrics(SM_CYSCREEN) / 2;
```

When you call GetSystemMetrics() with the constant SM_CXSCREEN, the function returns the width of the screen. The constant SM_CYSCREEN returns the height of the screen. In the above lines, the program divides these values by two in preparation for creating a window half as wide and half as tall as the screen. Some other constants you can use with GetSystemMetrics() are SM_CXICON, SM_CYICON, SM_CXCURSOR, SM_CYCURSOR, SM_CYMENU, SM_CXFULLSCREEN,

`SM_CYFULLSCREEN`, `SM_CXMIN`, and `SM_CYMIN`. There are many others, too. Look them up in your Turbo C++ documentation.

Now WINEX1's `WinMain()` can create the application's main window:

```
hWnd = CreateWindow(
        "WinEx1",              // Window class's name.
        "WinEx1 Application",  // Title bar text.
        WS_OVERLAPPEDWINDOW,   // The window's style.
        10,                    // X position.
        10,                    // Y position.
        width,                 // Width.
        height,                // Height.
        NULL,                  // Parent window's handle.
        NULL,                  // Menu handle.
        hCurrentInst,          // Instance handle.
        NULL);                 // No additional data.
```

The Windows function `CreateWindow()` creates a window of the given class and returns a handle to the window. The function's eleven arguments are the window class's name, the text to display in the window's title bar, the window's style, the window's x,y position, the window's width and height, a handle to the parent window (in this case `NULL` because there is no parent window), a handle to the window's menu, a handle to the application's instance, and a `NULL`. Make sure that the window class's name is exactly the same as the name you gave the class in the `WNDCLASS` structure's `lpszClassName` member.

Showing a Window

Although the program has now created the window element, the window is not yet visible. It's in memory waiting for the program to decide what to do with it. Usually, the program will next make the window visible, like this:

```
ShowWindow(hWnd, nCmdShow);
```

The Windows function `ShowWindow()` displays a window in various ways. The function's first argument is the window's handle. The second argument indicates how to show the window. Usually, you just give `ShowWindow()` the `nCmdShow` parameter that was passed into `WinMain()`. But you can use a number of other values, represented by the constants `SW_HIDE`, `SW_MINIMIZE`, `SW_RESTORE`, `SW_SHOW`, `SW_SHOWMAXIMIZED`, `SW_SHOWMINIMIZED`, `SW_SHOWMINNOACTIVE`, `SW_SHOWNA`, `SW_SHOWNOACTIVE`, and `SW_SHOWNORMAL`. You can look up these constants in your Turbo C++ documentation.

Now that the window is on the screen (whew!), a call to the Windows function `UpdateWindow()` ensures that the window's client area gets painted:

```
UpdateWindow(hWnd);
```

V

Tools and Techniques

This function's single argument is the handle of the window to update.

Creating a Message Loop

With the window up on the screen, the application can finally start receiving messages from Windows. This is done in a message loop, which almost always looks like

```
while (GetMessage(&msg, NULL, NULL, NULL))
{
    TranslateMessage(&msg);
    DispatchMessage(&msg);
}
```

The above `while` loop iterates continuously until it receives a `WM_QUIT` message. The loop is controlled by the value returned by the Windows function `GetMessage()`, which simply retrieves messages from the application's message queue. `GetMessage()`'s first argument is the address of the `MSG` structure in which to store the message. The other arguments are usually set to `NULL`. The function returns a Boolean value that indicates whether the application has received a `WM_QUIT` message, with a value of `TRUE` indicating that `WM_QUIT` has not yet been received.

Within the loop, the `TranslateMessage()` function facilitates keyboard support, whereas the `DispatchMessage()` function tells Windows to pass the message on to the appropriate window procedure. Notice that none of the messages are actually handled in the loop. The loop really exists for only two reasons: To instruct Windows to pass messages on to the window procedure and to enable Windows' cooperative multitasking to work smoothly. What does the loop have to do with multitasking? When `GetMessage()` finds no further messages for the application, it automatically yields the processor to another application.

Inside the Window Procedure

The messages that Windows sends to the application are actually received by the window procedure defined for the class. Most window procedures do little more than set up a `switch` statement that routes messages to the functions that handle them:

```
switch(message)
```

As you know, the window procedure's `message` parameter contains the current message's ID. All Windows applications must respond at least to the `WM_DESTROY` message, which tells the window that the user is trying to close it:

```
case WM_DESTROY:
```

```
    PostQuitMessage(0);
    return 0;
```

When the window receives the `WM_DESTROY` message, it must call the Windows function `PostQuitMessage()`, which sends the `WM_QUIT` message that ends the message loop. In other programs in this chapter, you'll see how to handle other types of messages as well.

One way or another, every Windows message must be dealt with. Luckily, you don't have to account for all messages in your application. If you don't want to handle a message, you can just send it back to Windows for default processing by calling the Windows function `DefWindowProc()`, with its return value being returned from the window procedure:

```
    return DefWindowProc(hWnd, message, wParam, lParam);
```

`DefWindowProc()`'s arguments are the same as those passed into the window procedure. Keep this in mind: Failure to call `DefWindowProc()` for every message you don't handle in the program will lock Windows up tighter than a teenager's diary!

The Module Definition File

The remaining part of WINEX1's code is found in listing 24.2, the module definition file. As I said previously, the module definition file provides important information about the application to Turbo C++'s linker. In the case of listing 24.2, the first line is the word NAME followed by the module's name. The second line is the word DESCRIPTION followed by any text (within single quotes) you want to include that describes the module. The third line tells the linker that the module will be executable under Windows, while the fourth line tells the linker what to do if the user should try to run the program while not in Windows. The WINSTUB.EXE program displays a brief warning and aborts the application. The CODE, DATA, HEAPSIZE, and STACKSIZE lines provide information about how the module should handle memory.

Because a thorough discussion of module definition files is beyond the scope of this book, look them up in a Windows programming book. However, you can use the module definition file presented here in almost any of your own Windows applications. Just be sure to change the first two lines, giving your application its own name and description.

Displaying Data in a Window

Although the WINEX1 program provides a useful starting point for your Windows applications, it's otherwise useless. To provide the user with some sort of service, an application must at least be able to display data. In the WINEX1 program, you learned how to handle Windows messages. To display data in a window, your program must respond to another message, called WM_PAINT. When your application receives this message, it knows it's time to repaint all or part of its window's client area.

Listings 24.3 and 24.4 show source code for the WINEX2 application, which displays a single line of text in its main window. Compile and run this program to see the WM_PAINT message in action.

Listing 24.3   WINEX2.CPP—The WINEX2 Application's Main Source Code File

```
/////////////////////////////////////////////////////////
// WINEX2.CPP: Windows example program 2.
/////////////////////////////////////////////////////////

#include <windows.h>

// Prototype for window procedure.
LRESULT FAR PASCAL _export WndProc(HWND hWnd, UINT message,
    WPARAM wParam, LPARAM lParam);


/////////////////////////////////////////////////////////
// WinMain
/////////////////////////////////////////////////////////
int PASCAL WinMain(HINSTANCE hCurrentInst,
    HINSTANCE hPreviousInst, LPSTR /* lpszCmdLine */,
    int nCmdShow)
{
    WNDCLASS wndClass;
    HWND hWnd;
    MSG msg;

    // If there's no previous instance of this application,
    // define and register the window class.
    if (hPreviousInst == NULL)
    {
        wndClass.style = CS_HREDRAW | CS_VREDRAW;
        wndClass.lpfnWndProc = WndProc;
        wndClass.cbClsExtra = 0;
        wndClass.cbWndExtra = 0;
        wndClass.hInstance = hCurrentInst;
        wndClass.hIcon = LoadIcon(NULL, IDI_APPLICATION);
        wndClass.hCursor = LoadCursor(NULL, IDC_ARROW);
        wndClass.hbrBackground = GetStockObject(WHITE_BRUSH);
        wndClass.lpszMenuName = NULL;
        wndClass.lpszClassName = "WinEx2";

        RegisterClass(&wndClass);
    }
```

```
    // Get the size of the screen.
    UINT width = GetSystemMetrics(SM_CXSCREEN) / 2;
    UINT height = GetSystemMetrics(SM_CYSCREEN) / 2;

    // Create a window of the previously defined class.
    hWnd = CreateWindow(
                "WinEx2",              // Window class's name.
                "WinEx2 Application",  // Title bar text.
                WS_OVERLAPPEDWINDOW,   // The window's style.
                10,                    // X position.
                10,                    // Y position.
                width,                 // Width.
                height,                // Height.
                NULL,                  // Parent window's handle.
                NULL,                  // Menu handle.
                hCurrentInst,          // Instance handle.
                NULL);                 // No additional data.

    // Display the window on the screen.
    ShowWindow(hWnd, nCmdShow);

    // Force the window to repaint itself.
    UpdateWindow(hWnd);

    // Start the message loop.
    while (GetMessage(&msg, NULL, NULL, NULL))
    {
        TranslateMessage(&msg);
        DispatchMessage(&msg);
    }

    return msg.wParam;
}

//////////////////////////////////////////////////////////
// WndProc()
//
// This is the main window procedure, which is called by
// Windows.
//////////////////////////////////////////////////////////
LRESULT FAR PASCAL _export WndProc(HWND hWnd, UINT message,
    WPARAM wParam, LPARAM lParam)
{
    HDC hDC;
    PAINTSTRUCT paintStruct;

    // Handle the messages to which the application
    // must respond.
    switch(message)
    {
        case WM_PAINT:
            hDC = BeginPaint(hWnd, &paintStruct);
            TextOut(hDC, 10, 10, "This is a test.", 15);
            EndPaint(hWnd, &paintStruct);
            return 0;
```

(continues)

V

Tools and Techniques

Listing 24.3 Continued

```
        case WM_DESTROY:
            PostQuitMessage(0);
            return 0;
    }

    // Make sure all messages get returned to Windows.
    return DefWindowProc(hWnd, message, wParam, lParam);
}
```

Listing 24.4 WINEX2.DEF—The WINEX2 Application's Module Definition File

```
;////////////////////////////////////////////////////////
;// WINEX2.DEF: Module definition file for WinEx2.
;////////////////////////////////////////////////////////

NAME        WINEX2
DESCRIPTION 'Windows example app by Clayton Walnum'
EXETYPE     WINDOWS
STUB        'WINSTUB.EXE'
CODE        PRELOAD MOVEABLE DISCARDABLE
DATA        PRELOAD MOVEABLE MULTIPLE
HEAPSIZE    1024
STACKSIZE   5120
```

When you run the WINEX2 application, you see the window shown in figure 24.5. As you can see, the application's main window now sports the text line This is a test. Although you may think that printing a line of text would be easy, under Windows there are several things you must first know how to handle, including device contexts and the WM_PAINT message.

Fig. 24.5
The WINEX2 application.

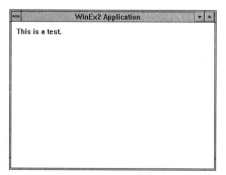

Painting Text in a Window

If you look at WINEX2's window procedure, WndProc(), you'll see that the application responds to two Windows messages, WM_PAINT and WM_DESTROY. You already know that the WM_DESTROY message indicates that the user wants to close the window. The WM_PAINT message is new to you. It indicates that the window's client area needs to be repainted. This may be because you've called UpdateWindow() or InvalidateRect() to force a window repaint or because the user has changed the size of the window or uncovered all or part of the window from beneath another window.

No matter how the WM_PAINT message is generated, your application must respond to it by repainting all or part of the window's client area. The first step in doing this is to call the Windows function BeginPaint(), like this:

```
hDC = BeginPaint(hWnd, &paintStruct);
```

This function call requires as arguments a handle to the window and the address of a PAINTSTRUCT structure. The PAINTSTRUCT structure holds information about the required paint operation and is defined as follows:

```
typedef struct tagPAINTSTRUCT {
    HDC   hdc;
    BOOL  fErase;
    RECT  rcPaint;
    BOOL  fRestore;
    BOOL  fIncUpdate;
    BYTE  rgbReserved[16];
} PAINTSTRUCT;
```

Only the first three members of the structure are useful to a programmer. The first, hdc, is a handle to the device context (DC) that should be used with the paint operation. (A *device context* is simply a set of attributes—such as pen color, brush color, font, and so on—associated with the current graphics operations for the window.) The second member, fErase, is a Boolean value indicating whether the window's background should be erased, and the third member, rcPaint, contains the coordinates of the rectangle in the window that needs to be updated. Because its window-painting process is so simple (displaying only a line of text), the WINEX2 application uses none of the information in the PAINTSTRUCT structure.

The call to the BeginPaint() function fills in the PAINTSTRUCT structure with the appropriate values for the current paint operation. It also returns a handle to the DC that should be used to update the window's contents. This DC handle is the same as the one placed in the PAINTSTRUCT's hdc member by the call to BeginPaint().

After the call to `BeginPaint()`, the application can write to the window's client area, using any of the functions that make up Windows' Graphics Device Interface (GDI), a library of graphics functions for drawing various shapes and objects in a Windows application. One such function is `TextOut()`, which is called in WINEX2 like this:

```
TextOut(hDC, 10, 10, "This is a test.", 15);
```

GDI functions take a handle to a DC as their first argument, as you can see in the call to `TextOut()`. The function's second and third arguments are the coordinates in the window at which to display the text. The fourth argument is the text to display, and the fifth is the number of characters to display.

After the application has finished updating the window's contents, it must call `EndPaint()` to end the paint operations and release the DC. Because Windows has only a limited number of DCs that must be shared by all running applications, your program should control one as briefly as possible, turning it back to Windows as soon as your window painting is complete.

Note that you can draw in a window almost anywhere within your program, not just in response to a `WM_PAINT` message. However, you still must obtain and release a DC. If the text line were being displayed in the window somewhere else in the WINEX2 program, the function calls might look like this:

```
HDC hDC = GetDC(hWnd);
TextOut(hDC, 10, 10, "This is a test.", 15);
ReleaseDC(hWnd, hDC);
```

The Windows function `GetDC()` obtains a DC for the window whose handle is given as the function's single argument. The DC handle returned by `GetDC()` can then be used in whatever GDI calls you need to paint your window's client area. After painting is complete, the program must call the Windows function `ReleaseDC()` to return the DC to Windows. `ReleaseDC()`'s two arguments are the window handle and the handle of the DC to release.

There's more to handling DCs than just obtaining and releasing them, however. In fact, an entire book could probably be written on the use of DCs and the GDI. Although there's no room in this chapter for such comprehensive coverage, in the next section, you'll learn some more DC and GDI basics.

Basics of the Graphics Device Interface

As mentioned previously, Windows features a library of device-independent functions that enable the programmer to more easily draw graphical objects in a window's display (as well as on other devices). This library is called the Graphics Device Interface. To access most of the functions in the GDI, you must first obtain a DC for the device on which you want to draw. When you first obtain a DC, whether by calling `BeginPaint()` or `GetDC()`, the DC contains certain default settings, including a black pen, which is used for drawing lines, and a white brush, which is used for filling shapes. If, for example, you were to call the GDI function `Rectangle()` with the default DC values, you would get a rectangle with a black border and a white interior.

Obviously, if a DC is to be useful, a programmer must be able to modify the attributes associated with the DC. What if you wanted to draw red lines instead of black? What if you wanted shapes filled with red? To do these things, a program must create new GDI objects and select them into (associate them with) the DC. GDI objects include things like pens, brushes, and fonts.

Listings 24.5 and 24.6 are the source code for the WINEX3 program, a Windows application that can display color rectangles in its windows display. WINEX3 demonstrates creating and selecting GDI pens and brushes.

Listing 24.5 WINEX3.CPP—The WINEX3 Application's Main Source Code File

```cpp
//////////////////////////////////////////////////////////////
// WINEX3.CPP: Windows example program 3.
//////////////////////////////////////////////////////////////

#include <windows.h>

// Prototype for window procedure.
LRESULT FAR PASCAL _export WndProc(HWND hWnd, UINT message,
    WPARAM wParam, LPARAM lParam);

// Other function prototypes.
void DrawRects(HDC hDC);
void CreateNextRect(HWND hWnd, LPARAM lParam);

const MAXRECTS = 20;          // Max number of rectangles.

int recs[MAXRECTS][MAXRECTS]; // Array for rectangle coordinates.
int nextRect = -1;            // Number of next rectangle.

//////////////////////////////////////////////////////////////
// WinMain
//////////////////////////////////////////////////////////////
int PASCAL WinMain(HINSTANCE hCurrentInst,
    HINSTANCE hPreviousInst, LPSTR /*lpszCmdLine */,
    int nCmdShow)
{
```

(continues)

V

Tools and Techniques

Listing 24.5 Continued

```
WNDCLASS wndClass;
HWND hWnd;
MSG msg;

// If there's no previous instance of this application,
// define and register the window class.
if (hPreviousInst == NULL)
{
    wndClass.style = CS_HREDRAW | CS_VREDRAW;
    wndClass.lpfnWndProc = WndProc;
    wndClass.cbClsExtra = 0;
    wndClass.cbWndExtra = 0;
    wndClass.hInstance = hCurrentInst;
    wndClass.hIcon = LoadIcon(NULL, IDI_APPLICATION);
    wndClass.hCursor = LoadCursor(NULL, IDC_ARROW);
    wndClass.hbrBackground = GetStockObject(WHITE_BRUSH);
    wndClass.lpszMenuName = NULL;
    wndClass.lpszClassName = "WinEx3";

    RegisterClass(&wndClass);
}

// Get the size of the screen.
UINT width = GetSystemMetrics(SM_CXSCREEN) / 2;
UINT height = GetSystemMetrics(SM_CYSCREEN) / 2;

// Create a window of the previously defined class.
hWnd = CreateWindow(
        "WinEx3",               // Window class's name.
        "WinEx3 Application",   // Title bar text.
        WS_OVERLAPPEDWINDOW,    // The window's style.
        10,                     // X position.
        10,                     // Y position.
        width,                  // Width.
        height,                 // Height.
        NULL,                   // Parent window's handle.
        NULL,                   // Menu handle.
        hCurrentInst,           // Instance handle.
        NULL);                  // No additional data.

// Display the window on the screen.
ShowWindow(hWnd, nCmdShow);

// Force the window to repaint itself.
UpdateWindow(hWnd);

// Start the message loop.
while (GetMessage(&msg, NULL, NULL, NULL))
{
    TranslateMessage(&msg);
    DispatchMessage(&msg);
}

return msg.wParam;
```

```
}

/////////////////////////////////////////////////////////////
// WndProc()
//
// The main window procedure, which is called by Windows.
//
/////////////////////////////////////////////////////////////
LRESULT FAR PASCAL _export WndProc(HWND hWnd, UINT message,
    WPARAM wParam, LPARAM lParam)
{
    HDC hDC;
    PAINTSTRUCT paintStruct;

    // Handle the messages to which the application
    // must respond.
    switch(message)
    {
        case WM_PAINT:
            hDC = BeginPaint(hWnd, &paintStruct);
            DrawRects(hDC);
            EndPaint(hWnd, &paintStruct);
            return 0;

        case WM_LBUTTONDOWN:
            CreateNextRect(hWnd, lParam);
            return 0;

        case WM_DESTROY:
            PostQuitMessage(0);
            return 0;
    }

    // Make sure all unhandled messages get returned to Windows.
    return DefWindowProc(hWnd, message, wParam, lParam);
}

/////////////////////////////////////////////////////////////
// DrawRects()
/////////////////////////////////////////////////////////////
void DrawRects(HDC hDC)
{
    int x;
    HBRUSH hNewBrush, hOldBrush;
    HPEN hNewPen, hOldPen;

    if (nextRect > -1)
    {
        // Create a new brush and select it into the DC.
        hNewBrush = CreateSolidBrush(RGB(0, 255, 0));
        hOldBrush = SelectObject(hDC, hNewBrush);

        // Create a new pen and select it into the DC.
        hNewPen = CreatePen(PS_SOLID, 2, RGB(255, 0, 0));
        hOldPen = SelectObject(hDC, hNewPen);
```

(continues)

V

Tools and Techniques

Listing 24.5 Continued

```
            // Draw all the rectangles.
            for (x=0; x<=nextRect; ++x)
                Rectangle(hDC, recs[x][x], recs[x+1][x],
                    recs[x][x]+20, recs[x+1][x]+20);

            // Restore the old pen and brush.
            SelectObject(hDC, hOldBrush);
            SelectObject(hDC, hOldPen);

            // Delete the new pen and brush.
            DeleteObject(hNewBrush);
            DeleteObject(hNewPen);
    }

}

//////////////////////////////////////////////////////////
// CreateNextRect()
//////////////////////////////////////////////////////////
void CreateNextRect(HWND hWnd, LPARAM lParam)
{
    RECT rect;

    // If there isn't already the maximum number of rectangles...
    if (nextRect < MAXRECTS-1)
    {
        // Increment the rectangle counter.
        ++nextRect;

        // Record the rectangle's position, which is the
        // position of the mouse click.
        recs[nextRect][nextRect] = LOWORD(lParam);
        recs[nextRect+1][nextRect] = HIWORD(lParam);

        // Calculate the position and size of the
        // window's dirty rectangle (the area to redraw).
        rect.left = LOWORD(lParam) - 1;
        rect.top = HIWORD(lParam) - 1;
        rect.right = rect.left + 21;
        rect.bottom = rect.top + 21;

        // Force a portion of the window to be redrawn.
        InvalidateRect(hWnd, &rect, FALSE);
    }
    else
        // Beep if there's no room for another rectangle.
        MessageBeep(0);
}
```

When you run the WINEX3 application, the main window appears. When you click in the window, a color rectangle appears where you clicked. You can place up to twenty rectangles in the window (see fig. 24.6). No matter how you manipulate the window—reducing it, enlarging it, minimizing and maximizing it—it always updates its display correctly, redrawing all the rectangles you placed.

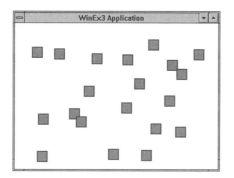

Fig. 24.6
The WINEX3 application.

Listing 24.6   WINEX3.DEF—The WINEX3 Application's Module Definition File

```
;///////////////////////////////////////////////////////////
;// WINEX3.DEF: Module definition file for WinEx3.
;///////////////////////////////////////////////////////////

NAME         WINEX3
DESCRIPTION  'Windows example app by Clayton Walnum'
EXETYPE      WINDOWS
STUB         'WINSTUB.EXE'
CODE         PRELOAD MOVEABLE DISCARDABLE
DATA         PRELOAD MOVEABLE MULTIPLE
HEAPSIZE     1024
STACKSIZE    5120
```

The WINEX3 application not only shows how to create GDI objects and select them into a device context, but it also shows you how to respond to mouse-button clicks. Before digging into the GDI and mouse stuff, though, take a look at the new global data items defined near the top of the program:

```
const MAXRECTS = 20;            // Max number of rectangles.
int recs[MAXRECTS][MAXRECTS];   // Array for rectangle coordinates.
int nextRect = -1;              // Number of next rectangle.
```

MAXRECTS is a constant that controls the maximum number of rectangles the user can place in the window. If you want to see more rectangles, just increase the value assigned to MAXRECTS. The recs[][] array will hold the x,y coordinates for each of the rectangles the user places in the window. Finally, nextRect is used as both a rectangle counter and an index into the recs[][] array.

Dealing with Mouse-Button Messages

If you look at WINEX3's version of WndProc(), you'll see that it responds to three Windows messages: WM_PAINT, WM_LBUTTONDOWN, and WM_DESTROY. The new kid on the block, WM_LBUTTONDOWN, is the message a window receives when the user clicks the left mouse button while the mouse pointer is over the window. In the case of a WM_LBUTTONDOWN message, WndProc()'s lParam parameter contains the mouse pointer's x,y coordinates at the time of the click. The x coordinate is in lParam's low word, and the y coordinate is in lParam's high word. The wParam parameter indicates which virtual keys were pressed at the time of the mouse click. This value can be any combination of MK_CONTROL, MK_MBUTTON, MK_RBUTTON, and MK_SHIFT, which represent the Ctrl key, middle mouse button, right mouse button, and Shift key, respectively.

In WINEX3, when the program receives the WM_LBUTTONDOWN message, it draws a rectangle at the clicked location. The program does this by calling the local function CreateNextRect() in response to the WM_LBUTTONDOWN message, passing as arguments the window's handle and the message's lParam.

Look at CreateNextRect() now. First, the function declares a local variable:

```
RECT rect;
```

A RECT structure looks like this:

```
typedef struct tagRect {
    int left;
    int top;
    int right;
    int bottom;
} RECT;
```

As you can see, the RECT structure holds a rectangle's left, top, right, and bottom screen coordinates.

After defining the RECT variable, the function checks to see whether the user has already placed the maximum number of rectangles:

```
if (nextRect < MAXRECTS-1)
```

If the user hasn't, the program increments the rectangle counter

```
++nextRect;
```

after which it copies the x,y mouse coordinates into the recs[][] array for later use:

```
recs[nextRect][nextRect] = LOWORD(lParam);
recs[nextRect+1][nextRect] = HIWORD(lParam);
```

Notice that the handy LOWORD macro extracts the low word of a long value, whereas the HIWORD macro extracts the high word.

The program then uses the mouse coordinates to determine the smallest rectangular area in the window that must be repainted to keep the window up-to-date:

```
rect.left = LOWORD(lParam) - 1;
rect.top = HIWORD(lParam) - 1;
rect.right = rect.left + 21;
rect.bottom = rect.top + 21;
```

Finally, a call to the Windows function InvalidateRect() forces a WM_PAINT message to be sent to the window:

```
InvalidateRect(hWnd, &rect, FALSE);
```

This function's three arguments are the window's handle, the address of the RECT structure, and a Boolean value indicating whether the window's background must be redrawn.

Painting the Rectangles

After calling the Windows function InvalidateRect(), the program's window procedure receives a WM_PAINT message. As always, the first thing to do is call BeginPaint(), to fill in the PAINTSTRUCT structure and to obtain a DC:

```
hDC = BeginPaint(hWnd, &paintStruct);
```

This time, though, the PAINTSTRUCT's rcPaint member contains the rectangle that we passed to the InvalidateRect() call. This rectangle represents the smallest area of the window that must be repainted. When you use the DC returned by BeginPaint(), Windows will paint nothing outside of this rectangle (called the *clipping rectangle*), thus speeding the window update.

After calling BeginPaint(), WndProc() calls the local function DrawRects() to draw the rectangles in the display:

```
DrawRects(hDC);
```

This function's single argument is the handle to the paint DC. Inside DrawRects(), the function first defines several local variables:

```
int x;
HBRUSH hNewBrush, hOldBrush;
HPEN hNewPen, hOldPen;
```

Here, x will be used as a loop control variable, whereas hNewBrush and hOldBrush are handles to GDI brush objects and hNewPen and hOldPen are handles to GDI pen objects.

To begin the rectangle drawing process, the program checks whether there are any rectangles to be drawn:

```
    if (nextRect > -1)
```

Next, the program calls the Windows function `CreateSolidBrush()` to create a green brush:

```
    hNewBrush = CreateSolidBrush(RGB(0, 255, 0));
```

This function, which returns a handle to the new GDI brush object, takes as its single argument the color of the brush to create. The RGB macro enables you to specify colors as three numbers representing the red, green, and blue color elements, respectively, of the color. These RGB values must be between 0 and 255, with 255 being the brightest. In the above function call, `RGB(0, 255, 0)` represents bright green.

After creating a brush, a program must select the brush into the DC, thus replacing the default brush the DC already contained. This is done by calling the Windows function `SelectObject()`:

```
    hOldBrush = SelectObject(hDC, hNewBrush);
```

This function's two arguments are a handle to the DC and a handle to the GDI object to select into the DC. `SelectObject()` returns a handle to the GDI object that the new object is replacing. The program must save this handle so that it can later restore the DC to its original state.

Now that the program has selected a green pen into the DC, all filled objects drawn in the window will be filled with green rather than white. The next step in WINEX3 is to change the DC's pen. To do this, the program calls the Windows function `CreatePen()`:

```
    hNewPen = CreatePen(PS_SOLID, 2, RGB(255, 0, 0));
```

This function's first parameter is the pen style to create. The constant PS_SOLID creates a pen that draws solid lines. Other constants you can use are PS_DASH, PS_DOT, PS_DASHDOT, PS_DASHDOTDOT, PS_NULL, and PS_INSIDEFRAME. The second argument is the width of the pen, and the third argument is the color of the pen. Here `RGB(255, 0, 0)` represents bright red.

After creating the pen, it must be selected into the DC, just as the new brush was:

```
    hOldPen = SelectObject(hDC, hNewPen);
```

Now that the DC has a red pen and a green brush, the program can draw the rectangles. A for loop controls the number of rectangles to be drawn, iterating from 0 to nextRect:

```
    for (x=0; x<=nextRect; ++x)
```

Inside the `for` loop, the program calls the Windows GDI function `Rectangle()` to actually draw each rectangle:

```
Rectangle(hDC, recs[x][x], recs[x+1][x],
    recs[x][x]+20, recs[x+1][x]+20);
```

This function's five parameters are the DC's handle and the left, top, right, and bottom coordinates of the rectangle to draw. Thanks to the new pen and brush the program created and selected into the DC, these rectangles will be drawn with red borders and green interiors.

After all the drawing is done, the program must restore the DC to its original state, by reselecting the old brush and pen back into the DC:

```
SelectObject(hDC, hOldBrush);
SelectObject(hDC, hOldPen);
```

Restoring the DC releases the new pen and brush so that they may be deleted, which the program does by calling the Windows function `DeleteObject()`. Every GDI object that you create must be deleted. Otherwise, they continue to take up precious memory—even after your application ends. However, you must never delete a GDI object that's still selected into a DC. That's why it's important to restore the old objects to the DC first.

Dealing with Menus

Something almost every Windows application has—and the previous applications in this chapter have been missing—is a menu. A Windows application's menu bar enables the user to easily find the commands he needs to use the program, without having to remember a lot of keystrokes. Programming menus under Windows is a big topic, one that this chapter cannot cover thoroughly. However, in this section, you'll learn the basics. For more information on menus, see Chapter 23, "Using Resource Workshop."

Menus are created as part of an application's resource file. A *resource file* is nothing more than a text script that describes the various objects, such as menus and dialog boxes, that your application must display. You can tell resource files because their file names have the .RC extension.

How do you create a resource file? You could learn the script syntax and then type the resource file in by hand. But an easier way is to use Turbo C++'s Resource Workshop. If you've never used Resource Workshop, you might want to take some time now to read over Chapter 19, "Developing Windows Resources for a User Interface," and Chapter 23, "Using Resource Workshop." Figure 24.7 shows a menu being created with Resource Workshop.

Fig. 24.7
Creating a menu
with Resource
Workshop.

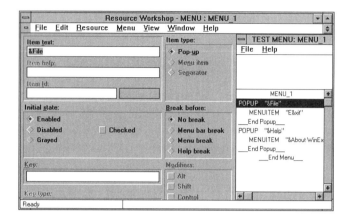

Before you start learning about menus, though, compile and run the WINEX4 program shown in listings 24.7 through 24.9. You compile this program exactly as you compiled the other programs in this chapter, except this time, when you create the application's project, don't delete the .RC file from the project window. (Also, make sure you copy the WINEX4.RC file, as well as WINEX4.CPP and WINEX4.DEF, to the project directory.) Figure 24.8 shows what your Project window should look like for this program.

Fig. 24.8
WINEX4's Project
window.

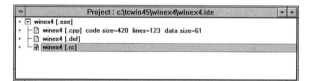

Listing 24.7   WINEX4.CPP—The WINEX4 Application's Main Source Code File

```
/////////////////////////////////////////////////////////
// WINEX4.CPP: Windows example program 4.
/////////////////////////////////////////////////////////

#include <windows.h>
#include "winex4.rc"

// Prototype for window procedure.
LRESULT FAR PASCAL _export WndProc(HWND hWnd, UINT message,
    WPARAM wParam, LPARAM lParam);

// Other function prototypes.
LRESULT PerformMenuCommand(HWND hWnd, WPARAM wParam);
```

```
/////////////////////////////////////////////////////////
// WinMain
/////////////////////////////////////////////////////////
int PASCAL WinMain(HINSTANCE hCurrentInst,
    HINSTANCE hPreviousInst, LPSTR /*lpszCmdLine */,
    int nCmdShow)
{
    WNDCLASS wndClass;
    HWND hWnd;
    MSG msg;

    // If there's no previous instance of this application,
    // define and register the window class.
    if (hPreviousInst == NULL)
    {
        wndClass.style = CS_HREDRAW | CS_VREDRAW;
        wndClass.lpfnWndProc = WndProc;
        wndClass.cbClsExtra = 0;
        wndClass.cbWndExtra = 0;
        wndClass.hInstance = hCurrentInst;
        wndClass.hIcon = LoadIcon(NULL, IDI_APPLICATION);
        wndClass.hCursor = LoadCursor(NULL, IDC_ARROW);
        wndClass.hbrBackground = GetStockObject(WHITE_BRUSH);
        wndClass.lpszMenuName = MAKEINTRESOURCE(MENU_1);
        wndClass.lpszClassName = "WinEx4";

        RegisterClass(&wndClass);
    }

     // Get the size of the screen.
    UINT width = GetSystemMetrics(SM_CXSCREEN) / 2;
    UINT height = GetSystemMetrics(SM_CYSCREEN) / 2;

    // Create a window of the previously defined class.
    hWnd = CreateWindow(
            "WinEx4",              // Window class's name.
            "WinEx4 Application",  // Title bar text.
            WS_OVERLAPPEDWINDOW,   // The window's style.
            10,                    // X position.
            10,                    // Y position.
            width,                 // Width.
            height,                // Height.
            NULL,                  // Parent window's handle.
            NULL,                  // Menu handle.
            hCurrentInst,          // Instance handle.
            NULL);                 // No additional data.

    // Display the window on the screen.
    ShowWindow(hWnd, nCmdShow);

    // Force the window to repaint itself.
    UpdateWindow(hWnd);

    // Start the message loop.
```

(continues)

V

Tools and Techniques

Listing 24.7   Continued

```
        while (GetMessage(&msg, NULL, NULL, NULL))
        {
            TranslateMessage(&msg);
            DispatchMessage(&msg);
        }

        return msg.wParam;
}


//////////////////////////////////////////////////////////
// WndProc()
//
// This is the main window procedure, which is called by
// Windows.
//////////////////////////////////////////////////////////
LRESULT FAR PASCAL _export WndProc(HWND hWnd, UINT message,
    WPARAM wParam, LPARAM lParam)
{
    // Handle the messages to which the application
    // must respond.
    switch(message)
    {
        case WM_COMMAND:
            return PerformMenuCommand(hWnd, wParam);

        case WM_DESTROY:
            PostQuitMessage(0);
            return 0;
    }

    // Make sure all unhandled messages get returned to Windows.
    return DefWindowProc(hWnd, message, wParam, lParam);
}


//////////////////////////////////////////////////////////
// PerformMenuCommand()
//////////////////////////////////////////////////////////
LRESULT PerformMenuCommand(HWND hWnd, WPARAM wParam)
{
    switch(wParam)
    {
        case CM_HELPABOUT:
            MessageBox(hWnd, "WinEx4 Sample Program",
                "About", MB_ICONINFORMATION | MB_OK);
            return 0;

        case CM_FILEEXIT:
            SendMessage(hWnd, WM_CLOSE, 0, 0L);
            return 0;
    }

    return 0;
}
```

Listing 24.8 WINEX4.RC—The WINEX4 Application's Resource File

```
/////////////////////////////////////////////////////////
// WINEX4.RC: WinEx4's resource file.
/////////////////////////////////////////////////////////

#define MENU_1       1
#define CM_HELPABOUT 101
#define CM_FILEEXIT  100

#ifdef RC_INVOKED

MENU_1 MENU
{
 POPUP "&File"
 {
  MENUITEM "E&xit", CM_FILEEXIT
 }

 POPUP "&Help"
 {
  MENUITEM "&About WinEx4...", CM_HELPABOUT
 }

}

#endif
```

Listing 24.9 WINEX4.DEF—The WINEX4 Application's Module Definition File

```
;/////////////////////////////////////////////////////////
;// WINEX4.DEF: Module definition file for WinEx4.
;/////////////////////////////////////////////////////////

NAME         WINEX4
DESCRIPTION  'Windows example app by Clayton Walnum'
EXETYPE      WINDOWS
STUB         'WINSTUB.EXE'
CODE         PRELOAD MOVEABLE DISCARDABLE
DATA         PRELOAD MOVEABLE MULTIPLE
HEAPSIZE     1024
STACKSIZE    5120
```

When you run WINEX4, you see the window shown in figure 24.9. This window features a File menu and a Help menu. The File menu contains the application's Exit command, whereas the Help menu contains an About WinEx4 command. Select the About WinEx4 command, and you'll see the message box shown in figure 24.10.

Fig. 24.9
The WINEX4
application.

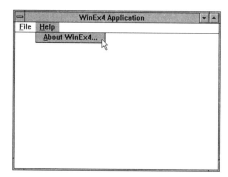

Fig. 24.10
The WINEX4
application's
About message
box.

Examining the Resource File

Before digging into the main program, look at the application's resource file, WINEX4.RC, shown in listing 24.8. This resource file was created by Resource Workshop but also modified by me. (After a resource file is created by Resource Workshop, you can go in and edit it just like any text file.) My first modification is the comment lines at the top of the file:

```
//////////////////////////////////////////////////////////
// WINEX4.RC: WinEx4's resource file.
//////////////////////////////////////////////////////////
```

Comments in a resource file can begin with double slashes just like in a C++ program file.

The next three lines in the file define several constants:

```
#define MENU_1       1
#define CM_HELPABOUT 101
#define CM_FILEEXIT  100
```

These constants represent the resource IDs that are needed by the program to identify its menu and the commands in the menu. These lines were created by Resource Workshop. You'll soon see how these constants are used in the main program.

I added the next line:

```
#ifdef RC_INVOKED
```

This line is a compiler directive that tests whether the `RC_INVOKED` constant has been defined. `RC_INVOKED` is automatically defined by Turbo C++ when the resource compiler is compiling the resource file. See the `#endif` line at the end of the resource file? I added that line, too, which looks like

```
#endif
```

Here's how these compiler directives work. Because the main source code file, WINEX4.CPP includes the WINEX4.RC file near the top of the listing, WINEX4.RC is read in both by the regular Turbo C++ compiler and the resource compiler. When the regular Turbo C++ compiler starts reading the file, it reads in the constant definitions. But when it gets to the `#ifdef RC_INVOKED` line, `RC_INVOKED` is not defined because that constant is defined only when the resource compiler is reading the .RC file. So the Turbo C++ compiler skips over everything up to the `#endif` line, which also happens to be the end of the file. It's a good thing that the Turbo C++ does skip the lines between the `#ifdef` and the `#endif` lines because those lines are not C++ source code and would cause many compiler errors.

When the resource compiler reads in the resource file, it also defines the three constants `MENU_1`, `CM_HELPABOUT`, and `CM_FILEEXIT`. But when it gets to the `#ifdef RC_INVOKED`, it discovers that `RC_INVOKED` is defined, so it continues reading the file, compiling the resource lines between the `#ifdef` and `#endif`. These lines are the resource script that define the application's menus.

In short, the `#ifdef` and `#endif` compiler directives allow the Turbo C++ compiler to include any constants that are defined in the resource file, without getting confused by the actual resource script. The resource compiler, on the other hand, is able to read every line in the file. In this way, the resource IDs defined in the resource file are made available to every file that needs them.

Of course, this isn't the only way to handle resource IDs. Some people like to place all the resource IDs in a separate file, usually with an .RH extension (for resource header). The .RH file can then be included in as many files as you need it. The important thing is that you keep all the resource IDs in one place, so that they are defined consistently from one file to the next.

Adding the Menu to the Window Class

Creating a resource file and including it in your project is the first step towards having a menu bar in your application. The next step is to specify the menu in your window's class. If you look at the definition of WINEX4's `WNDCLASS` structure, you'll see the following line:

```
wndClass.lpszMenuName = MAKEINTRESOURCE(MENU_1);
```

As mentioned previously, the `lpszMenuName` member of a `WNDCLASS` structure holds a pointer to the class's menu name. Unfortunately, in this case, the menu's "name" is actually an integer value represented by the constant `MENU_1`. (Identifying resource objects with integer resource IDs takes up less memory than identifying them with text strings.) As you can see above, that's where the `MAKEINTRESOURCE` macro comes in handy, converting a resource ID to the proper data type for the `lpszMenuName` member. If you wanted, you could have defined the menu's name as a string in the resource file. If you did, the above line would look like

```
wndClass.lpszMenuName = "MENU_1";
```

Adding the menu name to the `WNDCLASS` structure is all you need to do to associate the menu with the application.

Responding to Menu Commands

Now that you've got the menu added to your application's main window, you'd probably like to know how to respond to the user's commands when he selects a menu command. As you may have guessed, selecting a menu command causes Windows to send your application a message—in this case, a `WM_COMMAND` message. This means that you must add the `WM_COMMAND` message to the `switch` statement in the application's window procedure, like this:

```
switch(message)
{
    case WM_COMMAND:
        return PerformMenuCommand(hWnd, wParam);

    case WM_DESTROY:
        PostQuitMessage(0);
        return 0;
}
```

Here, when the application receives a `WM_COMMAND` message, it calls the local function `PerformMenuCommand()`. `PerformMenuCommand()`'s two arguments are the window's handle and the message's `wParam`, which holds the ID of the selected menu command.

An application typically must deal with many different menu commands. This means setting up another `switch` statement that's controlled by the `WM_COMMAND`'s `wParam`, which holds the menu command's ID:

```
switch(wParam)
{
    case CM_HELPABOUT:
        MessageBox(hWnd, "WinEx4 Sample Program",
            "About", MB_ICONINFORMATION ¦ MB_OK);
        return 0;
```

```
        case CM_FILEEXIT:
            SendMessage(hWnd, WM_CLOSE, 0, 0L);
            return 0;
    }
```

The switch statement's case clauses use the menu command IDs that you assigned to the commands in the resource file. For example, in WINEX4's case, when the user selects the Help menu's About WinEx4 command, the application receives a WM_COMMAND message whose wParam equals CM_HELPABOUT. WINEX4 handles this message by calling the Windows function MessageBox(), which displays a message box on the screen.

MessageBox()'s four arguments are the handle of the parent window, the text that appears in the box, the title of the box, and a flag that indicates which message-box elements appear in the box. The MB_ICONINFORMATION flag adds the information icon to the message box, and the MB_OK flag adds an OK button. There are many other constants you can use (by ORing them together as shown above). You should look them up in your Turbo C++ documentation.

The only other menu command that WINEX4 receives is the CM_FILEEXIT command, which indicates that the user has selected the File menu's Exit command. WINEX4 processes this command by calling the Windows function SendMessage() to send a WM_CLOSE message to the application's window. SendMessage()'s four arguments are the window's handle, and the message's ID, wParam, and lParam. No additional information needs to be sent with a WM_CLOSE message, so the last two arguments are zeroes.

Dealing with a Dialog Box

Just as most Windows applications have a menu bar, most also display various dialog boxes at one time or another. Displaying a dialog box is more complicated than displaying a menu, but it's still fairly easy.

As with a menu, the first step is to design your dialog box using Resource Workshop (see fig. 24.11). Please refer to Chapter 19, "Developing Windows Resources for a User Interface," and Chapter 23, "Using Resource Workshop," for more information on how to do this.

Once you have your dialog box designed, the script statements needed to create it are saved in the resource file (see listing 24.11). You can then refer to the dialog box in your application using the dialog box's resource ID. Listings 24.10 through 24.12 are the source code for the WINEX5 application, which displays a dialog box in response to a menu command. Compile and run WINEX5 just as you did WINEX4.

Fig. 24.11

Using Resource
Workshop to
design a dialog
box.

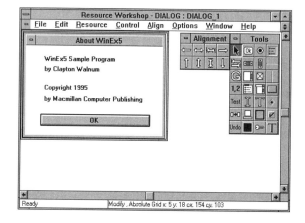

**Listing 24.10   WINEX5.CPP—The WINEX5 Application's Main Source
Code File**

```cpp
///////////////////////////////////////////////////////
// WINEX5.CPP: Windows example program 5.
///////////////////////////////////////////////////////

#include <windows.h>
#include "winex5.rc"

// Prototype for window procedure.
LRESULT FAR PASCAL _export WndProc(HWND hWnd, UINT message,
    WPARAM wParam, LPARAM lParam);

// Other function prototypes.
LRESULT PerformMenuCommand(HWND hWnd, WPARAM wParam);
BOOL FAR PASCAL _export AboutDialogProc(HWND hDlg,
    UINT message, WPARAM wParam, LPARAM lParam);

// Global instance handle.
HINSTANCE hInstance;

///////////////////////////////////////////////////////
// WinMain
///////////////////////////////////////////////////////
int PASCAL WinMain(HINSTANCE hCurrentInst,
    HINSTANCE hPreviousInst, LPSTR /*lpszCmdLine */,
    int nCmdShow)
{
    WNDCLASS wndClass;
    HWND hWnd;
    MSG msg;

    // If there's no previous instance of this application,
    // define and register the window class.
    if (hPreviousInst == NULL)
    {
```

```
        wndClass.style = CS_HREDRAW | CS_VREDRAW;
        wndClass.lpfnWndProc = WndProc;
        wndClass.cbClsExtra = 0;
        wndClass.cbWndExtra = 0;
        wndClass.hInstance = hCurrentInst;
        wndClass.hIcon = LoadIcon(NULL, IDI_APPLICATION);
        wndClass.hCursor = LoadCursor(NULL, IDC_ARROW);
        wndClass.hbrBackground = GetStockObject(WHITE_BRUSH);
        wndClass.lpszMenuName = MAKEINTRESOURCE(MENU_1);
        wndClass.lpszClassName = "WinEx5";

        RegisterClass(&wndClass);
    }

    hInstance = hCurrentInst;

    // Get the size of the screen.
    UINT width = GetSystemMetrics(SM_CXSCREEN) / 2;
    UINT height = GetSystemMetrics(SM_CYSCREEN) / 2;

    // Create a window of the previously defined class.
    hWnd = CreateWindow(
            "WinEx5",                // Window class's name.
            "WinEx5 Application",    // Title bar text.
            WS_OVERLAPPEDWINDOW,     // The window's style.
            10,                      // X position.
            10,                      // Y position.
            width,                   // Width.
            height,                  // Height.
            NULL,                    // Parent window's handle.
            NULL,                    // Menu handle.
            hCurrentInst,            // Instance handle.
            NULL);                   // No additional data.

    // Display the window on the screen.
    ShowWindow(hWnd, nCmdShow);

    // Force the window to repaint itself.
    UpdateWindow(hWnd);

    // Start the message loop.
    while (GetMessage(&msg, NULL, NULL, NULL))
    {
        TranslateMessage(&msg);
        DispatchMessage(&msg);
    }

    return msg.wParam;
}

//////////////////////////////////////////////////////////
// WndProc()
//
// This is the main window procedure, which is called by
```

(continues)

Listing 24.10 Continued

```
    // Windows.
    ////////////////////////////////////////////////////////////
    LRESULT FAR PASCAL _export WndProc(HWND hWnd, UINT message,
        WPARAM wParam, LPARAM lParam)
    {
        // Handle the messages to which the application
        // must respond.
        switch(message)
        {
            case WM_COMMAND:
                return PerformMenuCommand(hWnd, wParam);

            case WM_DESTROY:
                PostQuitMessage(0);
                return 0;
        }

        // Make sure all unhandled messages get returned to Windows.
        return DefWindowProc(hWnd, message, wParam, lParam);
    }


    ////////////////////////////////////////////////////////////
    // PerformMenuCommand()
    ////////////////////////////////////////////////////////////
    LRESULT PerformMenuCommand(HWND hWnd, WPARAM wParam)
    {
        FARPROC lpfnAboutDialogProc;

        switch(wParam)
        {
            case CM_HELPABOUT:
                lpfnAboutDialogProc = MakeProcInstance(
                    (FARPROC)AboutDialogProc, hInstance);
                DialogBox(hInstance, MAKEINTRESOURCE(DIALOG_1),
                    hWnd, lpfnAboutDialogProc);
                FreeProcInstance(lpfnAboutDialogProc);
                return 0;

            case CM_FILEEXIT:
                SendMessage(hWnd, WM_CLOSE, 0, 0L);
                return 0;
        }

        return 0;
    }


    ////////////////////////////////////////////////////////////
    // AboutDialogProc()
    ////////////////////////////////////////////////////////////
    BOOL FAR PASCAL _export AboutDialogProc(HWND hDlg,
        UINT message, WPARAM wParam, LPARAM /* lParam */)
    {
        switch(message)
        {
```

```
        case WM_INITDIALOG:
            return TRUE;

        case WM_COMMAND:
            if (wParam == IDOK)
                EndDialog(hDlg, TRUE);
            return TRUE;
    }

    return FALSE;
}
```

Listing 24.11   WINEX5.RC—The WINEX5 Application's Resource File

```
////////////////////////////////////////////////////////////
// WINEX5.RC: WinEx5's resource file.
////////////////////////////////////////////////////////////

#define DIALOG_1       1
#define MENU_1         1
#define CM_HELPABOUT 101
#define CM_FILEEXIT  100

#ifdef RC_INVOKED

MENU_1 MENU
{
 POPUP "&File"
 {
  MENUITEM "E&xit", CM_FILEEXIT
 }

 POPUP "&Help"
 {
  MENUITEM "&About WinEx5...", CM_HELPABOUT
 }

}

DIALOG_1 DIALOG 6, 15, 154, 103
STYLE DS_MODALFRAME ¦ WS_POPUP ¦ WS_VISIBLE ¦ WS_CAPTION ¦
WS_SYSMENU
CAPTION "About WinEx5"
FONT 8, "MS Sans Serif"
{
 DEFPUSHBUTTON "OK", IDOK, 17, 79, 123, 14
 LTEXT "WinEx5 Sample Program", -1, 21, 11, 97, 8
 LTEXT "by Clayton Walnum", -1, 21, 23, 77, 8
 LTEXT "Copyright 1995", -1, 21, 44, 53, 8
 LTEXT "by Macmillan Computer Publishing", -1, 21, 57, 113, 8
}

#endif
```

Listing 24.12   WINEX5.DEF—The WINEX5 Application's Module Definition File

```
;//////////////////////////////////////////////////////
;// WINEX5.DEF: Module definition file for WinEx5.
;//////////////////////////////////////////////////////

NAME           WINEX5
DESCRIPTION    'Windows example app by Clayton Walnum'
EXETYPE        WINDOWS
STUB           'WINSTUB.EXE'
CODE           PRELOAD MOVEABLE DISCARDABLE
DATA           PRELOAD MOVEABLE MULTIPLE
HEAPSIZE       1024
STACKSIZE      5120
```

When you run WINEX5, you see the window shown in figure 24.12. As you can see, the Help menu contains an About WinEx5 command. Choose this command, and you'll see the dialog box shown in figure 24.13. To dismiss the dialog box, click its OK button.

Fig. 24.12
The WINEX5
application.

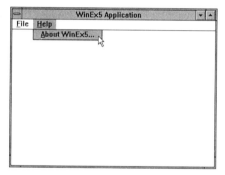

Fig. 24.13
The About WinEx5
dialog box.

Displaying a Dialog Box

Look at WINEX5's main source code listing (refer to listing 24.10). In the local function PerformMenuCommand(), the program first declares a far pointer to a function:

```
FARPROC lpfnAboutDialogProc;
```

Just as a window must have a window procedure that receives messages sent from Windows, a dialog box must have a dialog-box procedure through which Windows communicates with the dialog box. In WINEX5, the `lpfnAboutDialogProc` pointer will hold the address of the About dialog box's dialog-box procedure.

You can see that the program responds to the `CM_HELPABOUT` message by calling three Windows functions, `MakeProcInstance()`, `DialogBox()`, and `FreeProcInstance()`.

The call to `MakeProcInstance()` looks like

```
lpfnAboutDialogProc = MakeProcInstance(
    (FARPROC)AboutDialogProc, hInstance);
```

For reasons too complex to get into here (it has to do with data segments), you must retrieve the pointer to a dialog-box procedure by calling `MakeProcInstance()`. The function's two arguments are the address of the dialog-box procedure and a handle to the application's instance handle.

Once you have the pointer to the dialog-box procedure, you can display the dialog box by calling the Windows function `DialogBox()`:

```
DialogBox(hInstance, MAKEINTRESOURCE(DIALOG_1),
    hWnd, lpfnAboutDialogProc);
```

This function's four arguments are the application's instance handle, the dialog box's resource name, a handle to the parent window, and the pointer to the dialog-box procedure.

After the program calls `DialogBox()`, your dialog box is on the screen, where the user can manipulate it as he sees fit. At this point, messages start arriving in the dialog-box procedure, which you'll examine in a moment. When the user exits the dialog box, program execution returns to the line immediately following the call to `DialogBox()`. A call to `FreeProcInstance()` then releases the dialog-box procedure:

```
FreeProcInstance(lpfnAboutDialogProc);
```

This function's lone argument is the pointer returned by `MakeProcInstance()`.

The Dialog-Box Procedure

Earlier, I compared the dialog-box procedure to a window procedure. In fact, it has almost exactly the same prototype:

```
BOOL FAR PASCAL _export AboutDialogProc(HWND hDlg,
    UINT message, WPARAM wParam, LPARAM /* lParam */)
```

V

Tools and Techniques

The main difference is that the first parameter is the dialog box's handle, rather than the main window's handle. (But because a dialog box *is* a window, maybe this parameter isn't so different after all!) Because the dialog-box procedure is called by Windows, it must be defined as FAR PASCAL _export.

Also just like a window procedure, a dialog-box procedure is usually little more than a switch statement that routes messages received by the dialog box to the code that handles those messages. In AboutDialogProc(), that switch statement looks like the following:

```
switch(message)
{
    case WM_INITDIALOG:
        return TRUE;

    case WM_COMMAND:
        if (wParam == IDOK)
            EndDialog(hDlg, TRUE);
        return TRUE;
}
```

Every dialog box must respond to the WM_INITDIALOG message, which gives the dialog-box procedure a chance to perform whatever initialization it needs to do. In the above case, because the dialog box requires no additional initialization, WINEX5 responds to the WM_INITDIALOG by returning TRUE, something it must do for every message it handles in the dialog-box procedure.

When the user selects the dialog box's OK button, Windows sends a WM_COMMAND message to the dialog-box procedure, just as if the user had selected a menu command. The message's wParam holds the ID of the control that caused the WM_COMMAND message. In the above code segment, the program handles that command by calling the Windows function EndDialog(), which closes the dialog box. EndDialog()'s two arguments are the dialog box's handle and a Boolean value that will be returned to the DialogBox() function that displayed the dialog box. Usually, this argument is TRUE.

Note that the dialog-box procedure must return FALSE for any message it doesn't handle. The last line in AboutDialogProc() handles this task:

```
return FALSE;
```

From Here...

Windows programming is a complicated subject that cannot be covered completely in a short chapter. Once you understand the basics presented here, you should invest in a book or two dedicated to the art of Windows programming.

For more information on building Windows applications with Turbo C++, please refer to these chapters:

- Chapter 19, "Developing Windows Resources for a User Interface." This is an important Windows topic if you want to create user-friendly applications.

- Chapter 23, "Using Resource Workshop," shows you how to create menus, dialog boxes, bitmaps and other resources for your Windows applications.

- Chapter 27, "The ObjectWindows Library," is a general overview of this powerful application framework.

- Chapter 28, "ObjectWindows Applications," shows the fast way to build Windows applications.

- Chapter 29, "Single and Multiple Document Interfaces," provides more information on ObjectWindows.

V

Tools and Techniques

Chapter 25
File I/O

PCs that run DOS and Windows use a directory layout and file storage system. Most applications need to manipulate data within this system at some point. Typical examples include creating files, opening existing files, and reading and writing data into or out of these files.

Reasons for file input/output can vary greatly by application. In a traditional MS-DOS application, file input/output (I/O) is often used for tasks such as the following:

- Database and record storage systems

- Modifying configuration files such as AUTOEXEC.BAT

- Obtaining file header data such as that found in an EXE

- Streaming output for data storage

An application written for Windows commonly uses file I/O for tasks such as those described in the preceding list, as well as the following:

- Manipulating Windows initialization (INI) files

- Creating and deleting temporary files during intermediate processing

- Creating and modifying special Windows files such as MIDI, BMP, and metafiles

The focus of this chapter is primarily on using the functions Windows provides for file I/O. The standard Borland C++ runtime library provides its own version of file I/O functions, as well. The next section, "Standard C Runtime Library Functions," lightly discusses the standard C functions, but only because you will probably stumble across them in your product documentation and may question their use and existence. The emphasis of this chapter is on the file I/O functions provided to you by Windows.

For the sake of simplicity, each code sample in this chapter is written by using EasyWin, which is why I could use the C function `printf()`. For more information on EasyWin, refer to Appendix B, "Working with EasyWin." If you run these samples as part of a standard Windows program, simply replace any references to `printf()` with the Windows API function `MessageBox()`.

The following topics are discussed in this chapter:

- Standard C runtime library functions

- Windows API file I/O functions

- Manipulating Windows initialization files

- A sample application and walk-through

Standard C Runtime Library Functions

MS-DOS provides a handle-based system to manipulate data on the file level. Turbo C++ provides a set of runtime library functions that act as wrappers for these MS-DOS functions. The C RTL functions are as follows:

- `fopen()`, which is used to open or create a file and impose desired attributes such as read-only or append

- `fread()`, which is used to read a specified number of items of a specified length

- `fwrite()`, which is used to write a specified number of items of a specified length

- `fseek()`, which moves a pointer to a location offset by a specified number of bytes

- `fclose()`, which flushes buffered data and closes an open file

You can implement these functions by including the stdio.h header file in your project. There are several more obscure RTL file functions not listed, such as `fdopen()`, which associates a stream with a file handle.

It's okay to implement the C RTL functions in your Windows applications; however, there is a limitation as near pointers are used when the memory model of your C program is small model or medium model. A near pointer provides only the offset portion of the address into memory where the file's data begins. The data won't be retrievable if it's in a segment of memory outside the current segment. If you then try to read the data, it will be invalid. If you try to write data out, it will result in illegal memory overwrite, thus a General Protection Fault will occur. You can find more information about near pointers in Chapter 10, "Pointers." You can get more information about memory models from Chapter 15, "Compiling and Linking." More information about the C RTL file I/O functions is available in the Turbo C++ on-line Help.

Windows API File I/O

The Windows Application Programming Interface (API) defines six primary file I/O functions. You should use these functions for all of your file I/O tasks. They provide you with far pointers for each memory model, and they directly use MS-DOS file handles. These functions have been available, although undocumented, in Windows versions before 3.x. They have been formalized and documented in all versions since.

The primary Windows API file I/O functions are as follows:

- _lcreat()—creates or opens a specified file. If the file does not exist, the function creates a new file and opens it for writing.

- _lopen()—opens an existing file and sets the file pointer to the beginning of the file.

- _lclose()—closes the given file. As a result, the file is no longer available for reading or writing.

- _llseek()—repositions the pointer in a previously opened file.

- _lread()—reads data from the specified file.

- _lwrite()—writes data to the specified file.

Each file I/O function serves a specific purpose: creating or opening files, reading data from files, writing data to files, moving a pointer within a file, or closing an open file. Each function is discussed in more detail throughout this chapter.

V

Tools and Techniques

> **Note**
>
> You'll soon figure out that anytime you use one of the functions, you'll also need one (or more) of the other functions to complete a given task. For example, when a file is opened or created, it must at some point be closed. When you want to move within a file, you must create or open it first, and close it when you're done. You should read this entire chapter before you experiment with file I/O.

The following sections discuss each function in more detail.

Creating a File

This section discusses file manipulation by using the Windows API function _lcreat(). As its name implies, this function can be used to create files.

Caution is essential when using this function, because in addition to creating files, you can also use it to open existing files. Anytime _lcreat() is used with a file name that already exists, Turbo C++ opens the existing file and truncates its length to zero. This proposes a dilemma. Suppose your application uses _lcreat() to create a file named DOC1.TXT. You know that DOC1.TXT does not exist on your hard drive, so you should be okay. What happens, however, if the application is ported to another system that does have a file named DOC1.TXT?

To avoid overwriting data in an existing file, you have three primary options:

- Provide an interface that allows the user to specify the name of the file to create.

- Attempt to create a file with a name you believe is unique.

- Verify that the file to be created does not already exist before using _lcreat().

The first option is fine for interactive applications, but is unacceptable for batch processes. (*Batch processes* are programs that run from start to end without any interaction from the person executing the program.) The second option is fine most of the time, but still leaves room for error.

The third option is the best option. Before using _lcreat(), verify that a file of the same name does not already exist. You can do this by using lopen(), which is described in the next section.

The syntax for _lcreat() is

```
HFILE _lcreat(lpszFilename, fnAttribute)
```

The _lcreat() function takes two parameters. The first is a long pointer to a
NULL-terminated string (LPSTR) or constant character string. The string represents a name to give to the file, and may be optionally preceded by a complete path and even a drive letter. If you choose to include a path along with
the file name, you must double the backslashes. For example

```
_lcreat("c:\\Documents\\DOC1.TXT", 0);
```

The backslashes are doubled because a single backslash has a special meaning
to the compiler. The compiler views a single backslash as a new-line continuation character. What the preceding example would mean to the compiler if
you included only a single backslash in the first parameter is
"c:DocumentsDOC1.TXT." This is invalid and the operation would fail.
When you need an actual backslash, use two backslashes in your code.

The second parameter of _lcreat() is an integer value. When the file is created, it is automatically open and remains open until it is explicitly closed.
The value in the second parameter represents a DOS file attribute that acts as
an instruction as to how to create the file. The possible values are as follows:

Value	Meaning
0	Create and allow both reading and writing
1	Create with the read-only attribute applied
2	Create hidden so that it is not visible in the directory list
3	Create with the system attribute applied; system files are also not visible in the directory list

The Windows API _lcreat() function returns an integer value that is the
MS-DOS handle for the file. The return value must be retained, because it
is used by the other Windows API file I/O functions such as _lclose(),
_lwrite(), and so on. If an error occurs when executing _lcreat(), the return
value will be –1.

Take a look at the following example:

```
{ int iFileHandle;
  char far *lpstrPathFile = "C:\\Document\\DOC1.TXT";

  iFileHandle = _lcreat(lpstrPathFile, 0);
  if ( iFileHandle != -1 )
  { _lwrite(iFileHandle,"Hello World",11);
    _lclose(iFileHandle);
  }
```

V

Tools and Techniques

```
   else
      MessageBeep(0);
}
```

The preceding example declares two variables. The first is an integer called iFileHandle() that will hold the return value from _lcreat(). The second is a char far pointer (or LPSTR), which is initialized to the drive, path, and file name of the file to create. The _lcreat() function is then called with the LPSTR value in the first parameter and a 0 (zero) in the second, specifying that the file should be created with read/write access. The return value is stored in iFileHandle. The iFileHandle variable is then checked to ensure that it is not equal to –1. If it is not, the string "Hello World" is written to the file and the file is closed. If the iFileHandle variable is equal to –1, the Windows API MessageBeep() function is called, which produces a beep.

Opening a File

The Windows API function _lopen() is used to open an existing file. Alternatively, you can use it to verify the existence of a file.

The syntax for _lopen is

```
HFILE _lopen(lpszFilename, fnOpenMode)
```

Like _lcreat(), which was described previously, _lopen() requires two parameters. The first is a long pointer to a NULL-terminated string (LPSTR) or constant character string. The string represents the name of the file to open and may be optionally preceded by a complete path and even a drive letter. If you choose to include a path along with the file name, you must double the backslashes within the string constant. This is explained in the preceding section, "Creating a File."

The second parameter of the _lopen() function is an integer value. The value is used to specify the file access mode. You may choose to open the file as read-only, shared by another application, not shared by other applications, or a combination of the following values:

Value	Result
READ	File is opened as read-only.
WRITE	File is opened allowing only write access.
READWRITE	File is opened as read-rewrite.
OF_SHARE_COMPAT	File is opened allowing access by multiple applications. _lopen() will return –1, using this access mode if the file was previously opened using a different access mode.

Value	Result
OF_SHARE_DENY_NONE	File is opened, allowing access by multiple applications. _lopen() will return –1, using this access mode if the file was previously opened using the OF_SHARE_COMPAT access mode.
OF_SHARE_DENY_READ	File is opened but denies read access by any other application that may request it. If the file was previously opened with read access or using OF_SHARE_COMPAT, _lopen() will return –1.
OF_SHARE_DENY_WRITE	File is opened but denies write access by any other application that may request it. If the file was previously opened with write access or using OF_SHARE_COMPAT, _lopen() will return –1.
OF_SHARE_EXCLUSIVE	File is opened, denying both read and/or write access to the file by another application. If the file was previously opened by another application, _lopen() will return –1.

V

Tools and Techniques

Each of the items shown in the preceding is a constant hexadecimal integer value defined in windows.h. The windows.h file is by default located in the \TCWIN45\INCLUDE directory.

You can use the preceding constants in the second parameter of _lopen() individually or in combination. If a combination is used, the constants must be separated by the ¦ (pipe) symbol. This is the C++ binary OR operator. Observe the following example:

```
iFileHandle = _lopen(lpstrPathFile, WRITE ¦ OF_SHARE_COMPAT);
```

The preceding example uses a combination of the OF_WRITE access mode and the OF_SHARED_COMPAT access mode. Each constant is separated by the pipe symbol (¦). The pipe symbol is an operator used to OR bit patterns into a single value. Using the pipe symbol to OR values together is a very common way in Windows to specify multiple *flags* (values) as a single value or to pass as a single parameter. The result of this combination of access modes is that the file is opened for writing and can be shared by multiple applications that open the file with the same access mode.

The return value of _lopen() is an MS-DOS file handle if the file can be opened according to the specified access mode. If it cannot, _lopen() will return –1.

Because _lopen() will return a –1 if the open operation fails, it is easy to understand how to use _lopen() to determine whether a file exists. This is important if your intention is to use _lcreat() to create a new file. If the file already is on the disk, _lcreat() will truncate it to zero bytes, which can cause problems. Given this, you can use _lopen() to check for the existence of a file before it is created. Take a look at the following example:

```
{ int iFileHandle;
  char far *lpstrPathFile = "C:\\DOC1.TXT";

  iFileHandle = _lopen(lpstrPathFile, OF_READ);
  if ( iFileHandle == -1 )
   { lcreat(lpstrPathFile,0);
     _lwrite(iFileHandle,"Hello World",11);
   }
  else
     MessageBeep(0);
  lclose(iFileHandle);
}
```

The preceding example attempts to open a file by using _lopen(), whose name is stored in the lpstrPathFile variable with an access mode of read-only. The return value of _lopen() is stored in iFileHandle. The iFileHandle variable is checked for a value of –1, which means the file could not be opened. This most likely means that the file does not exist. Because the value is –1, the file is created using _lcreat() with a creation flag of 0, and is then written to with _lwrite(). The function _lcreat() is described in the section "Creating a File." The _lwrite() function is described in the following section, "Writing a File." If the file is successfully opened with _lopen(), program flow drops immediately to the MessageBeep statement, which is a Windows API function that executes a beep. Finally, the file is closed using _lclose(), which is described in the later section "Closing a File."

Writing a File

This section discusses writing an existing file by using the Windows API function _lwrite(). As its name implies, _lwrite() writes data to an open file. The write operation begins at the current location of the file pointer. If the file was just created or opened by using _lopen(), the pointer is at the beginning of the file (BOF). If the file already exists and already contains data, the pointer can be repositioned by using _llseek(). The functions _lcreat() and _lopen() are discussed in previous sections in this chapter. The function _llseek() is described in a later section.

The syntax for _lwrite() is as follows:

```
UINT _lwrite(hf, hpvBuffer, cbBuffer)
```

The _lwrite() function takes three parameters. The first parameter is an integer value. This integer value is an MS-DOS file handle such as that which can be returned using `_lopen()` or `_lcreat()`. Before you enter the value, check it to verify that the handle is valid, and thus not equal to –1.

The second parameter of `_lwrite()` is a long pointer to a NULL-terminated string (LPSTR) or constant character string. The string represents the data to be written to the file.

The third parameter of `_lwrite()` is an integer value. This value specifies the number of bytes contained in the second parameter to write. For example

```
_lwrite(iFileHandle, 'Hello World', 5);
```

would result in only the word Hello being written to the file associated with iFileHandle, because only 5 bytes are specified in the third parameter.

The value returned by `_lwrite()` is the number of bytes actually written to the file, or a –1 if an error occurs. An example of when `_lwrite()` would return a –1 is if you attempt to write to a file that was opened using `_lopen()` and you specified OF_READ for the file access mode.

The following example creates a file called DOC1.TXT and writes two sentences. Sentence one is This is sentence one. Sentence two is on the next line and says This is sentence two.

```
{ int iFileHandle;
  char far *lpstrPathFile = "C:\\DOC1.TXT";
  char far *lpstrBuff = "This is sentence one.\nThis is sentence two.";
  iFileHandle = _lcreat(lpstrPathFile,0);
  if ((int)_lwrite(iFileHandle,lpstrBuff,lstrlen(lpstrOne)) == -1)
     MessageBeep(0);
  _lclose(iFileHandle);
}
```

The preceding code sample begins by declaring three variables. The first is an integer called iFileHandle that will be used to hold the return value from `_lcreat()`. The second variable is a long pointer to a NULL-terminated string called lpstrPathFile and is initialized to "C:\\DOC1.TXT". The reason double backslashes are used is described in the earlier section, "Creating a File." The third variable is also a long pointer to a NULL-terminated string called lpstrBuff. This variable is initialized to the following string:

```
This is sentence one.\nThis is sentence two.
```

The \n provides a special formatting sequence that the compiler recognizes as a new line. The file is then created and opened for read-write using `_lcreat()`. The handle of the newly created file is returned to iFileHandle. The next statement begins an if construct, which tests the return value of `_lwrite()`. If the bytes written (determined by `_lwrite()`'s return value) is equal to –1, an error has occurred. If an error occurs, the system will beep because of the inclusion of the Windows API MessageBeep function.

The _lwrite() function used in the if construct was passed three parameters. The first is the variable iFileHandle, which contains the MS-DOS file handle. The second is lpstrBuff, which is the previously initialized string containing your data. The third is the Windows API function lstrlen(), which returns the length of a given string, thus specifying that the number of bytes to write are equal to the number stored in the lpstrBuff variable.

Reading a File

This section discusses reading an existing file using the Windows API function _lread(). The _lread() function reads the specified number of bytes from the current position of a file pointer into a buffer. File pointers are discussed in the following section, "Moving and Maintaining Your Position within a File."

The syntax for _lread() is

```
UINT _lread(hf, hpvBuffer, cbBuffer)
```

The _lread() function requires three parameters. The first parameter is an integer value. The integer value represents an MS-DOS-level file handle such as that returned by _lcreat() or _lopen(). The functions _lcreat() and _lopen() are discussed in previous sections in this chapter.

The second parameter of _lread() is a long pointer to a buffer. This parameter may be declared as a char far pointer or the Windows-derived data type LPSTR, regardless of which memory model is used for your application. The buffer should have memory allocated to it before it is used with _lread(). Failure to allocate memory to the variable will result in a General Protection Fault error.

The third parameter of _lread() is of type word. This value is used to specify the number of bytes to read from the current position of the file pointer. The file pointer is advanced a number of bytes equal to this value.

The _lread() function returns an integer value that specifies the number of bytes read from the file. If no bytes are read from the file, _lread() returns a value of –1. (See listing 25.1 later in this chapter for an example of using _lread().)

Moving and Maintaining Your Position within a File

This section discusses moving within an open file by using the Windows API function _llseek(). If a file is opened by using _lopen() or _lcreat(), a pointer to a location in the file is positioned at the beginning of the file (BOF). This pointer is internally maintained. You can keep track of the pointer's position and reposition it by using _llseek(). Having the ability to move within a file is very important. You may, for instance, want to move to the end of a file to append data. You may want to move to the first character past the end-of-line to insert data.

The syntax for _llseek() is

```
LONG llseek(hf, lOffset, nOrigin)
```

The first parameter is of type int. The integer is the handle of the open file such as that which is returned by _lopen() and _lcreat().

The second parameter is of type long and will accept a value as large as 2,147,483,646. This value represents the offset in bytes to move the pointer from the current location or from the location specified in _llseek()'s third parameter within the file.

The third parameter is of type int. This value represents the starting position from which to seek within the file. This parameter is also used to specify whether the offset given in the second parameter is to reposition the pointer forward or backward within the file. The possible values for this parameter are as follows:

Value	Meaning
0	Given offset begins from the beginning of the file.
1	Given offset begins from the current position in the file.
2	Given offset begins from the end of file.

Using _llseek(), setting the second parameter to 0 and the third parameter to 0 will reposition the pointer to the beginning of the file. Setting the second parameter to 0 and the third parameter to 2 will reposition the pointer to the end of the file.

The _llseek() function returns a long integer value. The value is the new offset in bytes from the beginning of file (BOF) of the location of the pointer.

V

Tools and Techniques

The following is an example of using _llseek() to move within a file. It makes use of various other Windows API file I/O functions and may require you to review this chapter from the beginning to entirely understand. It also demonstrates the following:

■ Direct movements to BOF and EOF

■ Keeping track of the location of the pointer into the file

■ Use of _llseek() to determine the current location of the pointer into the file without actually moving it

■ How to move backward within a file

```c
{ int    iFileHandle;  // Will store the handle to the file returned
                       // from _lcreat
  long int liByteCount; // Will store return values from  _llseek.
  char far *lpstrPathFile = "C:\\DOC1.TXT"; // Path and name of
                                            // file to create.
  char far *lpstrBuff; // buffer to store data into from _lwrite.
  WORD hGlobalHandle;  // Will store handle to memory block
                       // returned from GlobalAlloc.

  hGlobalHandle = GlobalAlloc( GMEM_FIXED, 12 ); // Allocate 12
                                                 // bytes of global
                                                 // memory.
  lpstrBuff     = GlobalLock( hGlobalHandle ); // Lock the memory
                                               // and return a
                                               // pointer to it.
  iFileHandle   = _lcreat(lpstrPathFile,0); // Create the file
                                            // for normal access.

  if ( iFileHandle != HFILE_ERROR )  // if _lcreat is not equal
                                     // to -1 then ...
  { liByteCount = _lwrite( iFileHandle, "Hello World\0",12 );
// Write NULL terminated string to the file.
    if ( liByteCount != HFILE_ERROR ) // if _lwrite's return
                                      // value is not equal to -1
                                      // then ...
    { printf( "File Pointer after_lwrite: %d\n",liByteCount );
      liByteCount = _llseek( iFileHandle,0,0 ); // Move file
                                                // pointer to BOF.
      printf( "\nFile Pointer set to BOF: %d\n",liByteCount );
// Printout location of file pointer.
      liByteCount = _lread( iFileHandle,lpstrBuff,12 );
// Read 12 bytes from file into buffer.
      if ( liByteCount != HFILE_ERROR ) // If _lread did not
                                        // return -1 then ...
      { printf( "\nFile Pointer after _lread: %d\n",liByteCount );
        printf( "\nData read in from file: %s\n",lpstrBuff );
        // Print out data read in from file.
        liByteCount = _llseek( iFileHandle,0,2 );
```

```
                    // Move file pointer to EOF.
                    printf( "\nFile Pointer after set to EOF: %d\n",liByteCount );
                    liByteCount = _llseek( iFileHandle,-6,2 );
                    // Seek neg 6 bytes back from EOF.
                    printf( "\nFile Pointer after set to -6 offset
                            from EOF: %d\n",liByteCount );
                    liByteCount = _llseek( iFileHandle,0,1 );
                    //  Determine current location.
                    printf( "\nRandom check for current file pointer
                            location: %d\n",liByteCount );
                }
            else
                printf( "No bytes were read from DOC1.TXT" );
            }
            else
                    printf("No bytes were written to DOC1.TXT");
                _ lclose(iFileHandle);
        }
        else
            printf("Could not create DOC1.TXT");
        GlobalUnlock(hGlobalHandle);
        GlobalFree(hGlobalHandle);
    }
```

Although the preceding code sample appears bulky because of the comments, it demonstrates several new elements in addition to those discussed thus far in this chapter.

If you read this chapter from the beginning, by now you may have concluded that the discussed Windows API file I/O functions all return a –1 value if an error occurs. The header file windows.h defines a constant *HFILE_ERROR*, which has a value of –1 that can be used in place of the literal –1. This adds an element of readability to your error trapping. The sample implements error trapping for each operation, checking against HFILE_ERROR. If an error occurs, a message is displayed on-screen. A more robust form of error handling could be implemented by including exceptions and exception handling. See Chapter 14, "Exception Handling," for information on exception handling.

The preceding code sample begins with the declaration of several variables and pointers used throughout the sample. Memory is then allocated to a buffer, which will hold the data from the file that is soon created and read. The Windows API functions GlobalAlloc and GlobalLock are used for the task of the memory allocation. A file is then created with _lcreat() and passed 0 in its second parameter. This causes the file to be created with read/write access. If the file creation is successful, it returns a handle to the file to the iFileHandle variable.

V

Tools and Techniques

Upon successful creation of the file, _lwrite() is used to write a NULL-terminated string to the file. The string is 12 bytes long, including the NULL terminator. If the write operation is successful, it returns the number of bytes written to the file.

Because the file was newly created, the pointer into the file is positioned at the beginning of the file, or position 0. After the write operation, the current file position is 12 because 12 bytes were written. This is reflected by the call to printf immediately following the write operation.

The _llseek() function is then used to position the file pointer back to the beginning of file (BOF). It is passed 0 as the second parameter, representing a 0 offset. It is also passed a 0 as the third parameter to specify that the offset value in parameter 2 is from the beginning of the file (BOF). The value returned is 0, representing the offset from BOF. This is proven by displaying the value with a call to printf.

12 bytes of data are then read into a buffer. The read operation causes the pointer to move forward 12 bytes, thus a 12-byte offset from BOF if the pointer is successfully moved. This is proven by a call to printf, which displays the return value from _lread(). The contents of the buffer are then displayed by using printf.

The _llseek() function, along with subsequent calls to printf, is made three more times. The first time _llseek() is used, an offset of 0 is specified and 2 (EOF) is passed as the third parameter. This causes the pointer into the file to move to EOF. The successful move of the pointer to EOF is validated with a call to printf.

The second time _llseek() is used, an offset of –6 is specified and 2 (EOF) is passed as the third parameter. This causes the pointer into the file to move backward 6 bytes from EOF. The successful move of the pointer backward 6 bytes from EOF is validated with a call to printf.

The third time _llseek() is used, an offset of 0 is specified and 1 (the current location) is passed as the third parameter. This causes _llseek() to return the current location of the pointer into the file without actually moving the file. The successful return of the current pointer position is then validated with a call to printf.

Closing a File

This section discusses closing an open file by using the Windows API function _lclose(). The _lclose() function is by far the simplest to use of all of the Windows API file I/O functions; however, it is possibly the most important for some fairly complicated reasons. This section not only discuss how to use _lclose(), but also provides some information that may help you understand when to use it in your processing.

Whenever a file is opened, it should be closed at the soonest realistic point in your code. Typically, data is buffered, thus it is volatile. If the system crashes before the data is written to disk and the file is not closed, the data will likely be lost. This can occur even if the user of your program reboots, or Windows locks up (which of course never happens) while a file is open. There is even a possibility that just opening a file and failing to close it before terminating your Windows session could cause the file to become corrupt. The final concern is the limited number of file handles available from MS-DOS, which are what the Windows file I/O functions actually use. Each time a file is opened, a handle is used. Failure to close the file results in the file handle remaining allocated.

With these statements, a new design issue arises. For example, if you're writing a program that opens a file and sequentially reads blocks of records into a buffer for a total of ten blocks, you may consider creating a single routine that reads a single block. This would certainly help you avoid repetitive code. You then might call that routine 10 times. So far so good. But where does the file get opened and closed? Ask yourself the following questions:

- Should the file be opened, a single record in a block read, then closed?

- Should the file be opened at the top of the routine that reads in blocks of records, then closed at the end of the routine?

- Should the file be opened, then the routine that reads in blocks of records be called ten times before the file is closed?

Each choice has positive points as well as negative points. If your program constantly opens and closes a file, it will take a performance hit. If your application allows too much processing and processor time between the open and close, there is more of a risk of data loss from an abnormal termination of your program.

The correct method to deal with this issue will vary. Ultimately it is up to you, the programmer. You should consider several factors before you make the decision on how soon to close your file. The primary factor to consider for the preceding example is the number of records in a block and the size of each record. Depending on the hardware, processing 100,000 to 1,000,000 records in the Windows environment could introduce a risk of considerable data loss. If each block is 10 records to 100 or so records, and each record is 256 bytes long, the risk of data loss due to abnormal program termination is less likely.

The grayest area is from 200 records to 100,000 records-plus, and this is where the issue of performance comes into play. If your hardware is fast enough to process a 10,000-record block in a matter of seconds, you may choose to open the file, call the routine that reads blocks of records 10 times, then close the file. If this same operation takes several minutes to complete on your system, it would ultimately be safer to open the file at the beginning of the record block read routine and then close it again at the end of the routine. This will, of course, make an already slow process even slower, because the file would be opened and then closed ten times consecutively. But it's worth it if it maintains the integrity of your data or the data of the person who paid money for your program.

The syntax for _lclose() is as follows:

```
HFILE _lclose(hf)
```

The _lclose() function requires only one parameter of type int. This parameter represents the handle of the file returned from _lopen() or _lcreat(). When this function is called, the handle is discarded, thus making another file handle available. The value of the discarded handle is no longer usable to access the file because the file is now closed.

The return value of _lclose() is 0 if the file is closed successfully and HFILE_ERROR if the close operation fails. HFILE_ERROR is a constant value of –1 and is discussed in the earlier section, "Moving and Maintaining Your Position within a File." The following example uses _lclose():

```
{ int iFileHandle;

  iFileHandle = _lopen("C:\\AUTOEXEC.BAT", READ);

  if (iFileHandle != HFILE_ERROR)
      { iFileHandle = _lclose(iFileHandle);
          if (iFileHandle != HFILE_ERROR)
              printf("File closed successfully.");
          else
              printf("File close failed.");
      }
  else
      printf("File open failed.");
}
```

The preceding example attempts to open the AUTOEXEC.BAT file for read access. If the read operation is successful, the file handle returned from _lopen() is passed to _lclose(). The return value of _lclose() is returned to the variable that initially held the file handle. If _lclose() was successful—thus, not returning HFILE_ERROR—a message is displayed saying it was successful. If it fails, a different message is displayed saying so. If the file could not be opened to begin with, a message is displayed saying so, as well.

Sample Application and Walk-Through

This section provides a small EasyWin application that uses each of the Windows API file I/O functions discussed in this chapter. For more information on EasyWin, see Appendix B. The program in listing 25.1 uses a module main() to execute various processing, including several routines that use the Windows API file I/O functions. The code in this example demonstrates defensive programming techniques with statement-by-statement error trapping. A more efficient form of error handling is creating and using exceptions. See Chapter 14 for information on exceptions.

Listing 25.1   A Sample Application that Backs Up the AUTOEXEC.BAT File and Appends a Statement

```
#include <stdio.h>
#include <windows.h>
#include <string.h>

HFILE CopyFile(LPSTR lpszSourceFile, LPSTR lpszDestFile,
               int iAccess, int iRetFlag);
BOOL AppendStatement(int iFileHandle, LPSTR lpszPath);

//---Begin Main Routine.
void main(void)
{ HFILE iFileHandle;

  iFileHandle = CopyFile("C:\\AUTOEXEC.BAT","C:\\AUTOEXEC.ORG",0,1);

  if (!AppendStatement(iFileHandle,"\nPATH=F:\\MYPATH;%PATH%"))
      printf("Unable to Add Path Statement!");
  else
    printf("Statement Added to file!");

  _lclose(iFileHandle);
}
```

(continues)

V

Tools and Techniques

Listing 25.1 Continued

```
//--- Begin Copy File Routine.
HFILE CopyFile(LPSTR lpszSourceFile, LPSTR lpszDestFile,
               int iAccess, int iRetFlag)

{ HFILE iScrFileHandle, iDestFileHandle;
  long lFileSize, lCtr;
  char cBuff[1];
  int iRetVal = -1;

  iScrFileHandle = _lopen(lpszSourceFile,READ_WRITE);

  if (iScrFileHandle != HFILE_ERROR)
      { iDestFileHandle = _lcreat(lpszDestFile,iAccess);
          if (iDestFileHandle != HFILE_ERROR)
              {     lFileSize = _llseek(iScrFileHandle,0,2);
                    _llseek(iScrFileHandle,0,0);
                    for (lCtr = 1;lCtr <= lFileSize; lCtr++)
                        { _lread(iScrFileHandle,cBuff,1);
                            _lwrite(iDestFileHandle,cBuff,1);
                        }
                    _llseek(iScrFileHandle,0,0);
                    _llseek(iDestFileHandle,0,0);
              }
          if (iRetFlag == 1)
              {   iRetVal = iScrFileHandle;
                  _lclose(iDestFileHandle);
              }
          else
              if (iRetFlag == 2)
                  { iRetVal = iDestFileHandle;
                    _lclose(iScrFileHandle);
                  }
              else
                  iRetVal = HFILE_ERROR;
      }
  return iRetVal;
}

// --- Begin Append Statement Routine.
BOOL AppendStatement(int iFileHandle, LPSTR lpszPath)
{ BOOL bRetFlag = TRUE;

  if (_llseek(iFileHandle,0,2) != HFILE_ERROR)
      { if ((int)_lwrite(iFileHandle,lpszPath,
              strlen(lpszPath)) == HFILE_ERROR)
              bRetFlag = FALSE;
      }
  else
      bRetFlag = FALSE;

  return bRetFlag;
}
```

Listing 25.1 is a small application that opens the file AUTOEXEC.BAT. The contents of the file are read a byte at a time and written to a backup file a byte at a time. The backup file is AUTOEXEC.ORG (the ORG means *original*). The AUTOEXEC.ORG file is then closed. A search path statement is appended to the AUTOEXEC.BAT.

Listing 25.1 begins with the inclusion of several header files necessary for providing constants and function prototypes used in the listing. The preprocessor directive #include is used for this purpose.

Following the #include statements are the prototypes for two functions used in the application. One is for CopyFile(). The other is for AppendStatement(). The prototype is necessary when the implementation of the functions is located below their actual usage. In this listing, the functions follow main(), which uses them.

Following the prototypes is the main() routine. The routine main() begins by declaring the variable iFileHandle. This variable is used to store the return value from the CopyFile() function. The CopyFile() function copies the contents of one file to another and returns the handle of whichever is specified. The return value is stored because it represents a file handle of a file opened in the copy file routine that hasn't been closed yet.

The next statement following the call to CopyFile() is to AppendStatement(). The AppendStatement() function appends a statement to the end of a file. The return value is BOOL (TRUE or FALSE). The call is embedded within an if construct. If the function successfully appends the given statement, a message saying so is displayed. If the function is unsuccessful, a different message saying so is displayed.

Following the call to AppendStatement() is a call to _lclose(). This statement closes the file associated with the file handle passed as its only parameter. The passed value is iFileHandle and is returned from the CopyFile() function if the CopyFile() function is successful. See the section "Closing a File" earlier in this chapter for information on the _lclose() function. This statement ends the main() routine.

Following the main() routine is the CopyFile() function. The CopyFile function accepts four parameters. The first is of type LPSTR and represents the optional path and file name of the file to copy. The second parameter is also of type LPSTR. It is the optional path and file name of the destination file to copy to. The third parameter is of type int and specifies the access mode in which to create the destination file. The program uses a 0, which will open the file for read/write access. The fourth parameter is an integer type and

V

Tools and Techniques

should be a value of 1 or 0. This specifies whether the function should return the handle to the source file or a destination file. The program passes a 1, which represents the source file.

The CopyFile() function begins with the declaration of various variables used within the function. It then makes a call to _lopen(), passing the name of the source file to copy from. If successful, the file is open for read and write and a handle to the file is returned to variable iScrFileHandle.

If the variable iScrFileHandle is not equal to HFILE_ERROR (−1), the destination file is created with a call to _lcreat(). The iAccessMode variable is used to determine how to open the newly created file and the return value of the function is stored in iDestFileHandle.

If the iDestFileHandle variable is not equal to HFILE_ERROR (−1), a call is made to _llseek(). The _llseek() call, in this statement, positions the file pointer to the end-of-file and returns the number of bytes from the beginning of the file to the variable iFileSize. The iFileSize variable is used a few statements later.

Another call to _llseek() is made to reposition the file pointer to the beginning of the file (BOF) before the actual copying begins.

The copying processes in this example take place one byte at a time. If we were dealing with fixed-length data, we could read in a line at a time. Alternatively in this example, we could have created a buffer large enough for the entire file, read the data into the buffer, and written it back out (remember that the file size was obtained with a call to _llseek() two statements earlier).

The copying process is controlled with a for loop construct. For more information on for loops and constructs, see Chapter 9, "Loops and Conditional Statements." The statements in the loop process x times, x being the byte size of the source file that is stored in the variable lFileSize. After the for loop releases control, the copying process is complete.

At the completion of the copying process, the file pointers into the current location of the source and destination files are at EOF. A call is then made to _llseek() for each file to reposition the pointers back to BOF.

The value of iRetFlag is then checked for a 1 or a 0. The iRetFlag variable was passed as the last parameter to the CopyFile function. If it contains a 1 (which it will in this example), the handle of the source file is stored to the iRetVal variable. The destination file is closed using _lcreat(). If the value is 0 (which it won't be in this example), the handle of the destination file is stored to the iRetVal variable. The source file is closed using _lcreat().

The `CopyFile()` function then terminates, returning the value stored in `iRetVal`.

Following the `CopyFile()` function is the `AppendStatement()` function. The function takes two parameters and returns a BOOL (TRUE or FALSE) value. The first parameter is of type `int` and is the valid DOS file handle of an open file. In this application, the value is that which is returned from `CopyFile()` and is passed from the `main()` routine. The second parameter is of type LPSTR. It is the statement that is written to the file represented by the valid handle passed in the first parameter. The value passed in the listing is

```
\nPATH=F:\\MYPATH;%PATH%
```

The `\n` begins the write on the next line following the current location of the pointer into the file. The remainder is what is actually visibly written to the file.

The function begins with the declaration of a BOOL (TRUE or FALSE) variable `bRetFlag` and is initialized to a value of TRUE. The declaration is followed by a call to `_llseek()` to reposition the pointer into the file to EOF. If the return value from `_llseek()` is not `HFILE_ERROR`, the function `_lwrite()` is called. It is passed the buffer `lpszPath`, which contains the string to write to the file. The RTL function `strlen` is used to determine the length of the variable `lpszPath`. If the return value of `_lwrite()` is equal to `HFILE_ERROR`, the `bRetFlag` variable is reinitialized to FALSE. The function then terminates, returning `bRetFlag`.

Manipulation of Windows Initialization Files

If you are new to Windows programming, you may have turned to this chapter to learn file I/O operations for the purpose of implementing Windows initialization files (INI files) into your application.

INI files are used to store initialization information for an application. Perhaps the most recognized INI files used in Windows are the WIN.INI and the SYSTEM.INI files. These files store vital information about how Windows is to operate each time it is started. They remember things such as the colors of the desktop, whether a screen saver is on, the last location of groups or items in a group on the desktop, and so on.

As a Windows programmer, it won't be long before you will find yourself implementing INI files in your applications as well—if, for example, your application is Multiple Document Interface (MDI) and you want to retain the location of the windows for each document that is open. This is one of many types of data that can be stored in an INI file. Another example is if the application you write plays music when the program begins, you may want to have a configurable *on* or *off* setting and store its current configuration in the INI file associated with your application.

If you are not new to C, you may have assumed that the C RTL file I/O functions are how most programmers control the INI files used in their programs. The standard Windows API file I/O functions (discussed previously) are used for these operations more than the C RTL functions. The standard Windows API file I/O functions are, however, not standard when it comes to INI files. The Windows API provides six primary functions designed specifically for INI file manipulation:

- `GetPrivateProfileInt()`

- `GetPrivateProfileString()`

- `GetProfileInt()`

- `GetProfileString()`

- `WritePrivateProfileString()`

- `WriteProfileString()`

Right off you may have noticed the similarities among the names of these functions. Some of them contain the word `PrivateProfile` and some just contain the word `Profile`. Those that contain the word `PrivateProfile` are functions that read or write to an INI file that is specific to an application other than Windows and the WIN.INI file. Those that contain only the word `Profile` are designed for manipulating the WIN.INI file itself. The functions may better be grouped as follows:

WIN.INI file functions

- `WriteProfileString()`

- `GetProfileInt()`

- `GetProfileString()`

Application INI functions

- `WritePrivateProfileString()`

- `GetPrivateProfileInt()`

- `GetPrivateProfileString()`

Specifics of Windows Initialization Files

Windows INI files are stored in text format. They can be opened and read with any text editor, such as Windows Notepad. INI files follow a simple section-and-entry format. Here's an excerpt from a typical WIN.INI file:

```
[Desktop]
Pattern=(None)
Wallpaper=(None)
```

The name of the section is `Desktop`, and you can identify it as a section by the brackets around the word `Desktop`. The entries are the items `Pattern` and `Wallpaper`. You can identify them because they immediately follow the section name, and that they are followed by an = (equal) symbol and then more text. When Windows initializes, it seeks out the section called `Desktop`. Once found, it checks the values to the right of the = symbol for each entry in the section. In the preceding example, Windows would read in the string `(None)` for both the `Pattern` entry as well as the `Wallpaper` entry and would thus not show any pattern or wallpaper on the desktop. The principles of INI files conceptually are simple but very powerful in the way they can make your own applications appear almost intelligent.

You add comments to an INI file by beginning them on their own line starting with a semicolon. For example:

```
;This is the Desktop section
[Desktop]
;This is the Pattern entry
Pattern=(None)
;This is the Wallpaper entry
Wallpaper=(None)
```

Windows API Functions for Manipulating the WIN.INI File

The following sections discuss each of the functions used for reading and writing directly to the WIN.INI file.

Writing a String to the WIN.INI File

The function `WriteProfileString()` is used to write the contents of a buffer to a specific entry of a specific section of the WIN.INI file.

The syntax for `WriteProfileString()` is

```
BOOL WriteProfileString(lpszSection, lpszEntry, lpszString)
```

The function `WriteProfileString()` accepts three parameters and returns a BOOL (TRUE or FALSE) value. The first parameter is an `LPSTR`. It should contain the name of the entry in the WIN.INI file. When writing data to the

WIN.INI about a specific application, the convention for the section name is that of the application.

The second parameter is an LPSTR as well. This value represents the name of the entry next to which the data is to be written. The data is written to the right of the equal symbol. A NULL can be specified in this parameter instead of an entry, which will remove the entire section as well as its entries, excluding any comments.

The third parameter is also an LPSTR. This value is the actual data to be written to the entry. A NULL value can be specified, which will cause the line of the entire entry to be removed.

The interesting thing about this function is how much it does for you. Naturally, it lets you specify the name of the section and the name of the entry into which to append data; what's interesting is that if the section does not already exist, it creates it for you. This is true also if the specified entry does not exist, either. Observe the following example:

```
if (WriteProfileString("LOGGER","USER","ERIC UBER"))
    printf("Data Written");
```

The preceding statements would result in the following being appended to the end of the WIN.INI file:

```
[LOGGER]
USER=ERIC UBER
```

If your application was titled LOGGER and upon installation prompted the user for his name, you could write it out as data in an entry of the WIN.INI file. Obviously, the preceding section and entry did not exist prior to executing the statements in the example and thus were automatically added. The success of the call to WriteProfileString() is proven with the display of the message "Data Written" in the call to printf() (if EasyWin) or MessageBox.

Reading a String from the WIN.INI File

The string data associated with an entry in the WIN.INI file can be retrieved with a call to the Windows API function GetProfileString().

The syntax for GetProfileString() is

```
int GetProfileString(lpszSection, lpszEntry, lpszDefault,
                     lpszReturnBuffer, cbReturnBuffer)
```

The GetProfileString() function takes five parameters and returns an integer value representing the number of bytes read. The first parameter is of type LPSTR and represents the name of the section to find in the INI file.

The second parameter of GetProfileString() is also of type LPSTR. This value is the name of the entry in the WIN.INI file to find. If the passed value is NULL, the data of all of the items in the WIN.INI file following the section specified in the first parameter are copied into a buffer.

The third parameter of GetProfileString() is also of type LPSTR. This is a default value that can be specified to use if the section and/or entry cannot be found. If you don't want to have a default value, you can set this parameter to "".

The fourth parameter is also of type LPSTR. This is a buffer in which the data retrieved from the specified entry of the specified section of the WIN.INI file is stored. The buffer must be at least the size in bytes of the integer value specified in parameter 5 of this function.

The fifth parameter is of type int. This value is used to specify the number of bytes of the retrieved data to copy into the buffer specified in parameter 4 of this function. Take a look at the following:

```
{
  LPSTR lpszDataBuff;
  HANDLE hGlobalHandle;

  hGlobalHandle = GlobalAlloc(GMEM_FIXED,20);
  lpszDataBuff  = GlobalLock(hGlobalHandle);

  if (GetProfileString("Windows","Programs",
      "Default",lpszDataBuff,20) > 0)
      printf("Programs=%s",lpszDataBuff);

  GlobalUnlock(hGlobalHandle);
  GlobalFree(hGlobalHandle);
}
```

The preceding example uses GetProfileString() to retrieve the current program extension assigned to the program entry under the windows section of the WIN.INI file. If the function successfully reads data, a message is displayed showing the value.

The example begins with the declaration of a data buffer named lpszDataBuff. This is the buffer into which the retrieved data will be stored. The next declaration is of a variable called hGlobalHandle that will store the handle of memory allocated for the data buffer as returned from the next statement, which is a call to the Windows API function GlobalAlloc(). The Windows API function GlobalLock() is then used to return a pointer to the memory area.

GetProfileString() is then used to retrieve the data. If the function is successful, a message displaying the value is shown. If the section or entry is not found, the default string "Default" will be displayed instead.

Reading an Integer from the WIN.INI File

Like the function GetProfileString(), Windows makes available a function to retrieve integer data from an entry of a given section in the WIN.INI file. This function is GetProfileInt. Its syntax is as follows:

```
UINT GetProfileInt(lpszSection, lpszEntry, default)
```

GetProfileInt works very similarly to GetProfileString, except it returns numeric data. The return value is of type WORD, which is up to 2 bytes of unsigned data. The function takes only three parameters. The first is of type LPSTR and represents the name of the section in the WIN.INI file. The second parameter is also of type LPSTR and is the name of the entry in the section specified in parameter 1. Like GetProfileString, the GetProfileInt function allows you to specify a default also. This is an integer value placed as the third parameter. Observe the following example:

```
{
 int iBuff;
 iBuff = GetProfileInt("windows","DoubleClickSpeed",0);
 printf("Programs=%d",iBuff);
}
```

The preceding example declares a variable named iBuff, which stores the value returned by GetProfileInt(). GetProfileInt() is passed "windows" in the first parameter, representing the section in the WIN.INI file with this name. The second parameter is the entry "DoubleClickSpeed". The default value to return is 0, as specified in the third parameter. After the function executes, the contents of iBuff are displayed, showing the speed setting that is required between mouse clicks for Windows to register them as a double-click.

Windows API Functions for Manipulating Application INI Files

Windows provides several functions designed to generically read and write to application INI files. Each of these functions is discussed in the following sections. These functions work just like the functions of similar names discussed in the preceding section, "Windows API Functions for Manipulating the WIN.INI File." The only difference is that one more parameter is appended to the end, representing the name of the INI file.

Writing a String into an Application INI File

Windows provides the function `WritePrivateProfileString()` for writing data to an entry of a given section of a specified file. The `WritePrivateProfileString()` function is virtually the same as the `WriteProfileString()` function discussed previously, with the exception of the appending of one more parameter the end of the parameter list. This parameter is of type `LPSTR` and is used to specify the name of the INI file into which the function's data is to be written. The other unique thing about `WritePrivateProfileString()` is that if the file does not exist, it is created. The section, entry, and data will automatically be added to the file.

For example, while the function `WriteProfileString()` would be used as

```
if ( WriteProfileString("SECTION1","ENTRY1","This is the text") ) ...
```

in the WIN.INI file, you would need to use it as

```
if ( WritePrivateProfileString("SECTION1","ENTRY1",
    "This is the text","MYAPP.INI") ) ...
```

in another application's INI file.

Reading a String from an Application INI File

Windows provides the function `GetPrivateProfileString()` for copying data to a buffer from the entry of a given section of a specified file. The `GetPrivateProfileString()` function is virtually the same as the `GetProfileString()` function discussed previously, with the exception of the appending of one more parameter to the end of the parameter list. This parameter is of type `LPSTR` and is used to specify the name of the INI file from which the function's data is to be read.

For example, while the function `GetProfileString()` would be used as

```
iNumBytes = GetProfileString("SECTION1","ENTRY1","Default Text",
                             lpszBuff,13);
```

in the WIN.INI file, you would need to use it as

```
iNumBytes = GetPrivateProfileString("SECTION1","ENTRY1",
    "Default Text",lpszBuff,13,"MYAPP.INI");
```

in another application's INI file.

Reading an Integer from an Application INI File

Windows provides the function `GetPrivateProfileInt()` for retrieving integer data from the entry of a given section of a specified INI file. The

GetPrivateProfileInt() function is virtually the same as the GetProfileInt() function discussed previously, with the exception of the appending of one more parameter to the end of the parameter list. This parameter is of type LPSTR and is used to specify the name of the INI file from which the function's data is to be retrieved.

For example, while the function GetProfileInt() would be used as

```
iIntVal = GetProfileInt("SECTION1","ENTRY2",0);
```

in the WIN.INI file, you would need to use it as

```
iIntVal = GetPrivateProfileInt("SECTION1","ENTRY2",0,"MYAPP.INI");
```

in another application's INI file.

From Here...

This chapter has provided you with lots of variants for your attack on the topic of file I/O. You will find the information useful for even the smallest of applications. Some of the other chapters in this book will act as useful reenforcement for what you have learned:

- Chapter 4, "Data Types, Variables, and Constants," contains information on data types and allocating memory such as those used in the examples in this chapter.

- Chapter 9, "Loops and Conditional Statements," has information on looping constructs such as those that you might use to read data from a file or write data to a file.

- Chapter 14, "Exception Handling," contains information on implementing a better form of error checking.

Chapter 26

Device I/O

Device input and output (I/O) functions within C++ allow you to communicate with the world around the computer. Many applications use the printing functions of the application programming interface (API) to communicate with printers to print financial reports, letters, and memos. Serial communications API functions give applications the capability of communicating with other computers and networks to transfer files and send e-mail and faxes.

This chapter discusses the features and functions of device communications for printing and serial input and output access under Microsoft Windows. This chapter examines the following topics:

- Accessing Windows common dialog boxes

- Printing to a printer

- Accessing communications ports

- Sending and receiving information over a communications port

Performing Print Operations from Windows Applications

By using the Windows API for printing operations, you can perform simple configuration and printing to any type of print device connected to your computer or network. Through the standard Windows API, you have access to a common dialog box in which you can select and configure a printer—just as you do in any standard Windows application. The API also contains functions through which you can send text and graphics to be printed on the printer.

Using Print and Print Setup Dialog Boxes

A Print dialog box contains controls that let a user configure a printer for a particular print job (see fig. 26.1). The user can make such selections about print quality, page range, and the number of copies to print.

Fig. 26.1
The Print dialog box is a common dialog box accessible from within a program, allowing the user to configure a printer and submit a print job.

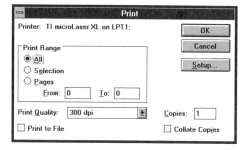

To display a Print dialog box for the default printer, a program must initialize a PRINTDLG structure and then call the PrintDlg() function. Setting the PD_RETURNDC flag of the PRINTDLG structure causes PrintDlg() to display the Print dialog box and return a handle identifying a printer-device context in the hDC member. This device-context handle is passed as the first parameter to all graphics API functions of the *graphics device interface* (GDI) to specify the printer device that will output to the printer.

The sample code in listing 26.1 initializes the members of the PRINTDLG structure and calls the PrintDlg() function prior to printing output.

Listing 26.1 Accessing the Common Print Dialog Box

```
#include <commdlg.h>
#include <mem.h>

PRINTDLG pd;

void main()
{
    //Zero the print dialog structure
    memset(&pd, 0, sizeof(PRINTDLG));

    //Set elements of the print structure
    pd.lStructSize = sizeof(PRINTDLG);
    pd.Flags = PD_RETURNDC;

    //Access the print dialog
    if (PrintDlg(&pd) != 0)
    {
```

```
                //Code to set up and print to the
                //printer
            }
        }
```

The first operation in the program is to clear the Print dialog box structure by using the `memset()` function. Two members of the `pd` variable are set to values to control how the print dialog box behaves when accessed. The `lStructSize` member designates the size of the structure for use in reading the values of the structure by the API functions. The `Flags` member, being set to `PD_RETURNDC`, informs the `PrintfDlg()` function that it should return the device context of the printer.

Device Drivers and the Print Dialog Box

The Print dialog box differs from other common dialog boxes in that one part of its procedure resides in COMMDLG.DLL and the other part in the selected printer driver. The printer driver provides the Print dialog box access to device-specific functions for configuring a printer, converting GDI commands to low-level printer commands, and storing commands for a particular print job in a printer's queue.

A printer driver exports a function called `ExtDeviceMode()`, which displays a dialog box and its controls. In previous versions of Windows, an application called the `LoadLibrary()` function to load a device driver and the `GetProcAddress()` function to obtain the address of the `ExtDeviceMode()` function. This is no longer necessary with the Windows common dialog box interface. Instead of calling `LoadLibrary()` and `GetProcAddress()`, a Windows application can call a single function, `PrintDlg()`, to display the Print dialog box and begin a print job. The code for `PrintDlg()` resides in COMMDLG.DLL.

Printing to the Printer

Once a program has access to the print dialog box and a means of selecting and configuring a printer, the program can send text and graphics to the printer for output. The example program in listing 26.2 uses the print dialog box so that you can select a printer on which to print, and then prints a line of text to the printer.

V

Tools and Techniques

Listing 26.2 Accessing API Calls to Output to a Printer

```
#include <commdlg.h>
#include <mem.h>

PRINTDLG pd;

void main()
{

    //Set all structure members to zero.
    memset(&pd, 0, sizeof(PRINTDLG));

    //Initialize the necessary PRINTDLG structure members.
    pd.lStructSize = sizeof(PRINTDLG);
    pd.Flags = PD_RETURNDC;

    //Print a test page if successful
    if (PrintDlg(&pd) != 0)
    {
        Escape(pd.hDC, STARTDOC, 8, "TC-TEST-PRT", NULL);

        //Print text and rectangle
        TextOut(pd.hDC, 50, 50, "Turbo C++ Test Print Page", 25);
        Rectangle(pd.hDC, 50, 90, 625, 105);

        Escape(pd.hDC, NEWFRAME, 0, NULL, NULL);
        Escape(pd.hDC, ENDDOC, 0, NULL, NULL);

        //Housecleaning operations
        DeleteDC(pd.hDC);
        if (pd.hDevMode != NULL)
            GlobalFree(pd.hDevMode);
        if (pd.hDevNames != NULL)
            GlobalFree(pd.hDevNames);
    }
    else
    {
        //If an error or CANCEL with PrintDlg() then
        //clean house
        if (pd.hDevMode != NULL)
            GlobalFree(pd.hDevMode);
        if (pd.hDevNames != NULL)
            GlobalFree(pd.hDevNames);
    }
}
```

In listing 26.1 you accessed the Print dialog box, while in listing 26.2, code is added to print to the selected printer in the Print dialog box. Immediately following the call to `PrintDlg()`, the call `Escape(pd.hDC, STARTDOC, 8, "TC-TEST-PRT", NULL)` is added to reserve an entry in the Print Manager to ensure that multiple-page documents are not interspersed with other documents.

The call to TextOut(pd.hDC, 50, 50, "Turbo C++ Test Print Page", 25) prints the text "Turbo C++ Test Print Page" to the printer. The first parameter of the function, pd.hDC, is the device-context handle, returned from the call to PrintDlg(), in which you want to print. The second and third parameters are the X and Y start positions of the text in the device-context of the printer. The final two parameters are the text to be printed followed by the number of characters in the string to be printed.

The next call to Rectangle(pd.hDC, 50, 90, 625, 105) prints a rectangle to the printer. You pass the device-context handle of the printer to the function as pd.hDC. The final four parameters are the left, top, right, and bottom coordinates of the rectangle.

The remainder of the program performs housekeeping on the printer and in the program itself. The NEWFRAME escape code tells the printer to issue a form-feed to eject the page that had been printed, while the ENDDOC escape code informs the Print Manager that the document has completed. Cleanup involves the use of DeleteDC() to delete the device context of the printer allocated and returned by PrintDlg(). GlobalFree() deletes the handles used for print-device names and modes allocated for use in the PrintDlg().

Printer Control Functions

In addition to the functions thus far discussed for printers, table 26.1 contains a list of other Windows API functions for printer-specific operations. Many of the control functions listed can be used in place of the Escape() function. For instance, the StartDoc() function makes the STARTDOC printer escape code obsolete, EndPage() makes NEWFRAME obsolete, and EndDoc() makes ENDDOC obsolete. The choice of using the Escape() function with escape codes or explicit function calls remains with the developer.

Table 26.1   The Windows API Functions Available to Control and Print to a Print Device

Function	Description
AbortDoc()	Terminates a print job
DeviceCapabilities()	Retrieves the capabilities of a device
DeviceMode()	Displays a dialog box for the printing modes
EndDoc()	Ends a print job

(continues)

Table 26.1 Continued	
Function	**Description**
EndPage()	Ends a page
Escape()	Allows access to device capabilities
ExtDeviceMode()	Displays a dialog box for the printing modes
GetDeviceCaps()	Retrieves the device capabilities
SetAbortProc()	Sets the abort function for a print job
SpoolFile()	Puts a file in the spooler queue
StartDoc()	Starts a print job
StartPage()	Prepares the printer driver to accept data
QueryAbort()	Queries whether to terminate a print job

Performing Communications Operations under Windows

Communications resources are devices that provide a means of inputting and outputting a single data stream. A serial port is a communications resource that uses a service provider, consisting of a library or driver, which enables applications to access the resource (see fig. 26.2).

Fig. 26.2
A communications service provider provides an interface for access to serial and parallel ports.

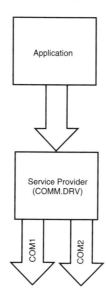

The communication driver (COMM.DRV) is a dynamic-link library containing functions that support opening, reading from, and writing to communications devices. Although the driver exports several functions, Windows-based applications do not directly call these functions. Instead, the applications call functions in the USER module, such as the OpenComm() function, which in turn calls the functions of the communications driver.

The communications driver accesses serial ports COM1, COM2, COM3, and COM4 by using base-address values specified in the BIOS data area of a computer. If the BIOS data area does not specify a value for a physical port, the user can set the base address and IRQ values by using the Control Panel (see fig. 26.3). The Control Panel displays the Advanced Settings dialog box (see fig. 26.4) for each port, which contains selections for base addresses and IRQ settings. The selected values are recorded as COMxBase and COMxIRQ settings in the [386Enh] section of the SYSTEM.INI file.

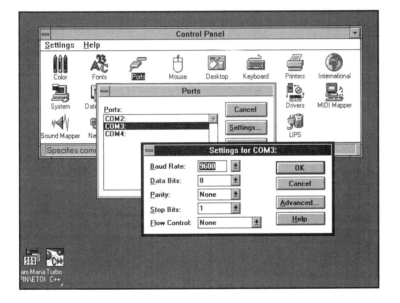

Fig. 26.3

The Control Panel allows you to configure the serial ports of your computer through the Ports applet.

V

Tools and Techniques

Note

The address and IRQ settings of the Ports applet's Advanced Settings dialog box are used for both standard and 386 enhanced-mode operation and override the BIOS data area values. If you are using non-standard ports, you can modify these settings manually to prevent IRQ conflicts for multi-port machines. Such configurations consist of serial ports residing at IRQ3/0x3F8, IRQ4/0x2F8, IRQ5/0x3E8, and IRQ9/0x2E8, which are non-standard port settings and are not specified in the BIOS data area.

Fig. 26.4
In the Ports
applet's Advanced
Settings dialog
box, you can
configure
addresses and
interrupts for each
of your serial
communications
ports.

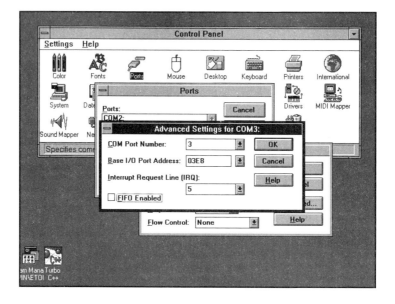

The input and output (I/O) functions of the Windows API provide the basic
interface for opening and closing a communications resource handle and for
performing read and write operations on communications ports. The communications API functions enable applications to perform the following tasks:

- Opening a communications resource and retrieving a handle to that
  resource

- Setting and retrieving configuration information for a serial
  communications resource

- Performing input and output operations on a serial communications
  resource

- Monitoring events that occur for a given serial communications
  resource

- Executing extended functions by sending control commands to the
  communications resource

Opening a Communications Resource

To use a communications resource, a process must call the OpenComm() function to open a handle to a communications resource. Once opened, the program must perform several steps to set the characteristics of the resource.

If the specified resource is being used by another process, OpenComm() fails with a return value less than zero.

Preparing the communications resource uses the BuildCommDCB() function to establish the *device control block* (DCB) information. The DCB contains information regarding the port speed, parity, stop bits, and flow control information. Once the DCB is built, it is passed to the communications resource with a call to SetCommState(). The resource then establishes the characteristics for the port.

The code in listing 26.3 opens a handle to a communications resource, establishes the characteristics of the port, and then closes the port. The call to OpenComm("COM2", 1024, 128) establishes a handle to COM2, setting the input buffer (or *receive buffer*) to 1,024 bytes and the output buffer (or *transmit buffer*) to 128 bytes. The input buffer is where information is stored when the information is received from a remote machine or a modem. The output buffer contains information being sent out by the process. If the call to OpenComm() is successful, the handle to a communications port is returned; otherwise, a value less than zero is returned which represents an error condition (see table 26.2).

Table 26.2 Error Messages Returned by *OpenComm( )* if the Call Is Unsuccessful	
Identifier	**Description**
IE_BADID	The device identifier is invalid or unsupported
IE_BAUDRATE	The device's baud rate is unsupported
IE_BYTESIZE	The specified byte size is invalid
IE_DEFAULT	The default parameters are in error
IE_HARDWARE	The hardware is not available (is locked by another device)
IE_MEMORY	The function cannot allocate the queues
IE_NOPEN	The device is not open
IE_OPEN	The device is already open

V

Tools and Techniques

Listing 26.3 Opening a Port to Establish Communications

```c
#include <windows.h>

int main()
{
    int     iErr, idCommDev;
    DCB     dcb;

    //Open the COM2 communications port setting the
    //receive buffer to 1024 bytes and the output
    //buffer to 128 bytes
    idCommDev = OpenComm("COM2", 1024, 128);
    if (idCommDev < 0)
    {
        MessageBox(NULL,"Error Opening Comm Port",
            "OpenComm",MB_ICONSTOP);
        return 0;
    }

    //Build the DCB setting COM2 to 2400 baud, no parity,
    //8 bits, and 1 stop bit
    iErr = BuildCommDCB("COM2:2400,n,8,1", &dcb);
    if (iErr < 0)
    {
        MessageBox(NULL,"Error Creating DCB",
            "BuildCommDCB",MB_ICONSTOP);
        return 0;
    }

    //Set up the characteristics of the comm port based
    //on the information in the DCB
    iErr = SetCommState(&dcb);
    if (iErr < 0)
    {
        MessageBox(NULL,"Error Setting Comm State",
            "SetCommState",MB_ICONSTOP);
        return 0;
    }

    //Close the comm port
    iErr = CloseComm(idCommDev);
    if (iErr < 0)
    {
        MessageBox(NULL,"Error Closing Comm Port",
            "CloseComm",MB_ICONSTOP);
        return 0;
    }
    return 1;
}
```

The call to BuildCommDCB("COM2:2400,n,8,1", &dcb) builds a communications
DCB to establish the characteristics of a port. The string "COM2:2400,n,8,1"
contains the name of the port, parity, number of bits, and number of stop

bits that are placed into the DCB structure represented by the variable `dcb`. Once the DCB is built, a call to `SetCommState(&dcb)` passes the information in `dcb` to set COM2 to the state specified in the DCB.

Closing the handle to COM2 is performed by calling `CloseComm()` with the parameter to the function being the handle to COM2 returned with `OpenComm()`.

Sending and Receiving Data

Once a handle is retrieved for a communications resource, you can send and receive information through the port represented by the handle returned with `OpenComm()`. Listing 26.4 demonstrates the use of the `TransmitCommChar()` and `ReadComm()` functions to send and receive data over the communications port.

Listing 26.4   Sending and Receiving Information

```
#include <windows.h>
#include <string.h>

int main()
{
    int     iErr, idCommDev, i;
    DCB     dcb;
    char  TransBuff[] = "atdt 555-4567";
    char     RcvBuff[50];

    //Open the COM2 communications port setting the
    //receive buffer to 1024 bytes and the output
    //buffer to 128 bytes
    idCommDev = OpenComm("COM2", 1024, 128);
    if (idCommDev < 0)
    {
        MessageBox(NULL,"Error Opening Comm Port",
            "OpenComm",MB_ICONSTOP);
        return 0;
    }

    //Build the DCB setting COM2 to 2400 baud, no parity,
    //8 bits, and 1 stop bit
    iErr = BuildCommDCB("COM2:2400,n,8,1", &dcb);
    if (iErr < 0)
    {
        MessageBox(NULL,"Error Creating DCB",
            "BuildCommDCB",MB_ICONSTOP);
        return 0;
    }
```

(continues)

Listing 26.4   Continued

```
        //Set up the characteristics of the comm port based
        //on the information in the DCB
        iErr = SetCommState(&dcb);
        if (iErr < 0)
        {
            MessageBox(NULL,"Error Setting Comm State",
                "SetCommState",MB_ICONSTOP);
            return 0;
        }

        //Loop through the TransBuff and output each
        //character to the port
        for(i=0;i<strlen(TransBuff);i++)
        {
            //Send data out the comm port
            iErr = TransmitCommChar(idCommDev, TransBuff[i]);
            if (iErr < 0)
            {
                MessageBox(NULL,"Error Writing to Port",
                    "TransmitCommChar",MB_ICONSTOP);
                return 0;
            }

            //Read data from the comm port
            iErr = ReadComm(idCommDev,RcvBuff,sizeof(RcvBuff)-1);
            if (iErr < 0)
            {
                MessageBox(NULL,"Error Reading Comm Port",
                    "ReadComm",MB_ICONSTOP);
                return 0;
            }
            else
            {
                MessageBox(NULL,RcvBuff,"ReadComm",MB_ICONSTOP);
            }
        }
        //Send a carriage return-line feed to the port
        iErr = TransmitCommChar(idCommDev, 0x0d);
        iErr = TransmitCommChar(idCommDev, 0x0a);

        //Close the comm port
        iErr = CloseComm(idCommDev);
        if (iErr < 0)
        {
            MessageBox(NULL,"Error Closing Comm Port",
                "CloseComm",MB_ICONSTOP);
            return 0;
        }
    return 1;
    }
```

The program in listing 26.4 establishes a `TransBuff` variable used to store the information to be sent out the communications port. This information, for this program, is a dial command (`atdt`) and phone number (`555-4567`) to be dialed by a modem attached to COM2. The program loops through the `TransBuff` character buffer and sends out each character of the buffer by using the `TransmitCommChar(idCommDev, TransBuff[i])` function. The first parameter to the function is the handle returned by the call to `OpenComm()` and the second is the character to be sent out the port.

Each time the program sends a character out the port, the program makes a call to `ReadComm(idCommDev,RcvBuff,sizeof(RcvBuff)-1)` to retrieve responses from the modem attached to the port. For each call to the function, the program passes three parameters. The first is the handle to the port that was retrieved from `OpenComm()`. The second parameter is a buffer, `RcvBuff`, in which to place the received information, while the third is the maximum number of bytes to retrieve from the port for placement in the buffer.

Communications Errors

Communications errors occur on occasion; however, there are ways to catch these errors and correct them. The `GetCommError()` function provides a means of determining an error for a given communications port to allow the program to react to and correct the error.

```
COMSTAT FAR* lpStat;
GetCommError(idComDev, lpStat);
```

When an error occurs for a given API function call, the function returns a value less than zero. When such a condition exists, the program should call the `GetCommError()` function to retrieve the most recent error value and current status for the specified device. When a communications error occurs, Windows locks the communications port until `GetCommError()` clears the error.

The first parameter, `idComDev`, specifies the communications device to be examined. The second parameter, `lpStat`, is a long pointer to the `COMSTAT` structure that is to receive the device status. If this parameter is `NULL`, the function returns only the error values.

The return value specifies the error value for the most recent communications-function call to the specified device if `GetCommError()` is successful. The return value of the function can be a combination of the values in table 26.3.

V

Tools and Techniques

Table 26.3   Error Messages Returned by *GetCommError( )*

Value	Meaning
CE_BREAK	Hardware detected a break condition.
CE_CTSTO	CTS (clear-to-send) timeout. While a character was being transmitted, CTS was low for the duration specified by the fCtsHold member of the COMSTAT structure.
CE_DNS	Parallel device was not selected.
CE_DSRTO	DSR (data-set-ready) timeout. While a character was being transmitted, DSR was low for the duration specified by the fDsrHold member of COMSTAT.
CE_FRAME	Hardware detected a framing error.
CE_IOE	I/O error occurred during an attempt to communicate with a parallel device.
CE_MODE	Requested mode is not supported, or the idComDev parameter is invalid. If set, CE_MODE is the only valid error.
CE_OOP	Parallel device signaled that it is out of paper.
CE_OVERRUN	Character was not read from the hardware before the next character arrived. The character was lost.
CE_PTO	Timeout occurred during an attempt to communicate with a parallel device.
CE_RLSDTO	RLSD (receive-line-signal-detect) timeout. While a character was being transmitted, RLSD was low for the duration specified by the fRlsdHold member of COMSTAT.
CE_RXOVER	Receiving queue overflowed. There was either no room in the input queue or a character was received after the end-of-file character was received.
CE_RXPARITY	Hardware detected a parity error.
CE_TXFULL	Transmission queue was full when a function attempted to queue a character.

Communications Events

To increase the efficiency of an application, the application can monitor a set of events that occur in a communications resource. For example, an application can use event monitoring to determine when the modem detects a ring or when CTS (clear-to-send) and DSR (data-set-ready) signals change state.

To monitor events on a given communications resource, a program can use the SetCommMask() function to create an event mask. To determine the current event mask for a communications resource, a process can use the GetCommMask() function. The values in table 26.4 specify events that can be monitored by a program.

Table 26.4 Events that Can Be Monitored on a Communications Resource	
Value	**Meaning**
EV_BREAK	A break was detected on input.
EV_CTS	The CTS (clear-to-send) signal changed state.
EV_DSR	The DSR (data-set-ready) signal changed state.
EV_ERR	A line-status error occurred. Line-status errors are CE_FRAME, CE_OVERRUN, and CE_RXPARITY.
EV_RING	A ring indicator was detected.
EV_RLSD	The RLSD (receive-line-signal-detect) signal changed state.
EV_RXCHAR	A character was received and placed in the input buffer.
EV_RXFLAG	The event character was received and placed in the input buffer. The event character is specified in the device's DCB structure, which is applied to a serial port by using the SetCommState() function.
EV_TXEMPTY	The last character in the output buffer was sent.

The SetCommEventMask() function allows you to enable or disable event monitoring for a given communications event for a resource. The first parameter of the function call is a handle to the port as returned by the OpenComm() function call. The second parameter is an event to monitor, as specified in table 26.4. Once the desired events are enabled, the program can monitor the device events and perform appropriate event-based operations.

```
SetCommEventMask(idComDev, fuEvtMask);
```

The GetCommEventMask() function retrieves and clears the event word for a communications device. The first parameter, idCommDev, specifies the handle to the communications port to be examined. The second parameter, fnEventClear, specifies which events are to be returned and cleared in the event word.

```
GetCommEventMask(idCommDev, fnEventClear);
```

The return value of the function specifies the current value for the enabled event of the specified communications device. If the call is successful, each bit in the returned-word value specifies whether the specified event has occurred—the return value is set to 1. When one of the events specified in the event mask set by SetCommEventMask() occurs, the program detects this event and performs an operation based on that event.

For example, if the EV_RXCHAR event is specified on a call to SetCommEventMask(), the conditions of the GetCommEventMask() are satisfied if characters have arrived in the driver's input buffer. The sample code in listing 26.5 performs an operation whenever the modem detects a ring event using the EV_RING event mask.

Listing 26.5 Using Event Masks to Perform Event-Based Communications

```c
#include <windows.h>
#include <string.h>

int main()
{
    int iErr, idCommDev, NumOfRings = 0;
    DCB dcb;

    //Open the communications device
    idCommDev = OpenComm("COM2", 1024, 128);
    if (idCommDev < 0)
    {
        MessageBox(NULL,"Error Opening Comm Port",
            "OpenComm",MB_ICONSTOP);
        return 0;
    }

    //Build the device control block
    iErr = BuildCommDCB("COM2:2400,n,8,1", &dcb);
    if (iErr < 0)
    {
        MessageBox(NULL,"Error Creating DCB",
            "BuildCommDCB",MB_ICONSTOP);
        return 0;
    }

    //Set the communications device to the information
    //in the DCB
    iErr = SetCommState(&dcb);
    if (iErr < 0)
    {
        MessageBox(NULL,"Error Setting Comm State",
            "SetCommState",MB_ICONSTOP);
        return 0;
```

```
    }

    //Enable the event mask for EV_RING
    SetCommEventMask(idCommDev,EV_RING);
    for(;;)
    {
        //Monitor and execute operation when the phone
        //rings
        if (GetCommEventMask(idCommDev,EV_RING))
        {
            NumOfRings++;
            MessageBox(NULL,"Riiiiiiiiiiiiiiiiiiing",
                "GetCommEventMask",MB_ICONSTOP);
        }
        if (NumOfRings>2)
            break;
    }

    //Close the communications port
    iErr = CloseComm(idCommDev);
    if (iErr < 0)
    {
        MessageBox(NULL,"Error Closing Comm Port",
            "CloseComm",MB_ICONSTOP);
        return 0;
    }
return 1;
}
```

The code in listing 26.5 opens a communications port and sets up the port characteristics as you have seen in previous listings of this chapter. The primary difference is that you are handling specific communications events for a port.

The function call SetCommEventMask(idCommDev,EV_RING) enables the monitoring of the EV_RING event. This event occurs any time a modem, attached to the port specified by idCommDev, detects that another modem is calling. The program then goes into a loop that calls GetCommEventMask(idCommDev,EV_RING) to see if the represented event, EV_RING, has occurred, thus returning a 1. In the sample program, any time that a ring occurs on the monitored port, the NumOfRings variable is incremented. Once NumOfRings reaches a value of three the program closes the communications port and exits.

Extended Communications Functions

Some communications functions can be called for a device by using the EscapeCommFunction() function. This function sends a code to the device to perform an operation specific to that device. For example, an application can halt the transmission of characters by using the SETBREAK code and resume character transmission with the CLRBREAK code. These particular operations can also be started by calling the SetCommBreak() and ClearCommBreak() functions.

```
EscapeCommFunction(idComDev, nFunction);
```

The first parameter, idComDev, specifies the communications device that will receive the extended function commands. The second parameter, nFunction, specifies the function code of the extended function and can be one of the functions listed in table 26.5.

Table 26.5   Extended Functions that Can Be Sent to a Communications Port to Perform Device-Specific Operations

Value	Meaning
CLRDTR	Clears the DTR (data-terminal-ready) signal.
CLRRTS	Clears the RTS (request-to-send) signal.
GETMAXCOM	Returns the maximum COM port identifier supported by the system. This value ranges from 0x00 to 0x7F, such that 0x00 corresponds to COM1, 0x01 to COM2, 0x02 to COM3, and so on.
GETMAXLPT	Returns the maximum LPT port identifier supported by the system. This value ranges from 0x80 to 0xFF, such that 0x80 corresponds to LPT1, 0x81 to LPT2, 0x82 to LPT3, and so on.
RESETDEV	Resets the printer device if the idComDev parameter specifies an LPT port. No function is performed if idComDev specifies a COM port.
SETDTR	Sends the DTR (data-terminal-ready) signal.
SETRTS	Sends the RTS (request-to-send) signal.
SETXOFF	Causes transmission to act as if an XOFF character has been received.
SETXON	Causes transmission to act as if an XON character has been received.

Communications Functions

In addition to the functions already discussed for communications, table 26.6 contains a list of other Windows API functions for communications resource-specific operations.

Table 26.6 The Windows API Functions Available to Control and Transfer Information to a Communications Port

Function	Description
`BuildCommDCB`	Translates a device-definition string to a DCB
`ClearCommBreak`	Restores character transmission
`CloseComm`	Closes a communications device
`EnableCommNotification`	Enables or disables `WM_COMMNOTIFY` posting
`EscapeCommFunction`	Passes an extended function to a device
`FlushComm`	Flushes a transmission or receiving queue
`GetCommError`	Retrieves the communications-device status
`GetCommEventMask`	Retrieves the device event word
`GetCommState`	Retrieves the DCB
`OpenComm`	Opens a communications device
`ReadComm`	Reads from a communications device
`SetCommBreak`	Suspends character transmission
`SetCommEventMask`	Enables events in a device event word
`SetCommState`	Sets the communications-device state
`TransmitCommChar`	Places a character in the transmission queue
`UngetCommChar`	Puts a character back in the receiving queue
`WriteComm`	Writes to a communications device

V

Tools and Techniques

From Here...

Printing and serial communications are vital parts of many Windows-based applications. The Windows API functions provide a simple mechanism to connect to resources for printer configuration and printing as well as communications resources for the transfer of information such as files and e-mail. In this chapter, you learned about printing and communications and the development of applications to perform each. In the next few chapters, you explore the development of applications by using the ObjectWindows Library, which resides above the standard Windows API.

For further information, see the following:

- Chapter 15, "Compiling and Linking," teaches you about compiling and linking the code in this chapter.

- Chapter 24, "Windows Programming Basics," offers information on Windows API calls.

- Chapter 25, "File I/O," discusses inputting and outputting to disk-based files.

Chapter 27

The ObjectWindows Library

Remember when you bought your first VCR? If you got your VCR back when I got mine, it wasn't much more difficult to operate than a standard audio cassette recorder. The VCR had all the standard controls such as play, fast forward, rewind, and record. And if you were really lucky, it even had freeze-frame.

If you've bought a VCR recently, however, you know that there are so many controls and settings that you need a degree in engineering to figure everything out. Today's VCRs include not only freeze-frame but also slow motion, indexing, multiple-event timers, simulcast recording, multichannel sound, auto repeat, and on-screen clocks. I don't know about you, but to make sure that my recordings come out right, I've resorted to using a checklist to verify that each setting on the VCR is correct.

Programming a computer is a lot like programming a VCR. A few years ago you could sit down in front of your computer with a simple language, such as BASIC, and a slim volume of instructions and write an impressive program— at least it was impressive for those days. Today, however, if you want to write commercial-quality software, you must use sophisticated, object-oriented languages such as C++, and you need enough documentation to cover your desk a foot deep.

Such is progress.

Luckily for today's programmers, while the languages and operating systems are becoming more and more complex, the programming tools are becoming more and more sophisticated. The major Windows compilers today come with code libraries that try to make today's programming tasks quicker and easier. Which brings us, of course, to the ObjectWindows Library (OWL).

ObjectWindows is a C++ code library that simplifies the writing of Windows applications. If you've ever tried to write a Windows program without the help of OWL, you know what an immense task this can be. Using standard C++ programming, you'll need 50 or 60 lines of code just to get an empty window on-screen. A full-fledged Windows application can be immense beyond belief. By using OWL, however, you can get your first window on-screen in six lines or less.

Windows Versus ObjectWindows

Although Windows is complex, it's a veritable workhorse that handles much of your application's activity automatically. Windows applications usually have a main window with a menu bar, scroll bars, sizing buttons, and other controls—all of which are handled to a great extent by Windows. For example, when you create a window with a menu bar, your program doesn't need to control the menu. Windows does this for you, sending your program a message whenever the user selects an item in the menu.

A Windows program can receive hundreds of different messages while it's running. Your application determines whether to respond to these messages or to ignore them. If the user clicks in your window, for example, your program gets a message (WM_LBUTTONDOWN). If the program determines that the user clicked something important, the program can handle the message, performing the function the user requested. On the other hand, the program can simply ignore the message and let Windows take care of it. It's up to you.

All this sounds terrific until you get your first look at a Windows programming manual and see the almost 1,000 function calls included in the application program interface (API). Surely there must be an easier way to program Windows than to plow through thousands of pages of documentation. Isn't there?

Yes and no. No matter what route you take, learning to program Windows—although not especially difficult—takes a lot of time and practice. Before you program your first application, you should be familiar with at least the most-used functions in the API so that you know the tools you have at your disposal.

Borland's ObjectWindows Library goes a long way toward simplifying the process of writing Windows applications, however, by hiding much of the details inside custom window classes. As stated earlier, by using OWL you can create a fully operational window in about six lines of code. Compare this to the more than 50 lines of C++ code required to produce the same window without OWL.

Don't believe it? Take a look at listing 27.1, which is a minimum Windows application written in standard C++. Then compare listing 28.1 to listing 27.2, which is the same program written using OWL. Impressed?

Listing 27.1   MINWIN.CPP: A Minimum C++ Windows Application

```cpp
////////////////////////////////////////////////////////////
// MINWIN.CPP: A minimum C++ Windows application.
////////////////////////////////////////////////////////////

#include <windows.h>

// Prototype for window procedure.
LRESULT FAR PASCAL _export WndProc(HWND hWnd, UINT message,
    WPARAM wParam, LPARAM lParam);

////////////////////////////////////////////////////////////
// WinMain
////////////////////////////////////////////////////////////
int PASCAL WinMain(HINSTANCE hCurrentInst,
    HINSTANCE hPreviousInst, LPSTR lpszCmdLine,
    int nCmdShow)
{
    WNDCLASS wndClass;
    HWND hWnd;
    MSG msg;

    if (hPreviousInst == NULL)
    {
        wndClass.style = CS_HREDRAW | CS_VREDRAW;
        wndClass.lpfnWndProc = WndProc;
        wndClass.cbClsExtra = 0;
        wndClass.cbWndExtra = 0;
        wndClass.hInstance = hCurrentInst;
        wndClass.hIcon = LoadIcon(NULL, IDI_APPLICATION);
        wndClass.hCursor = LoadCursor(NULL, IDC_ARROW);
        wndClass.hbrBackground = GetStockObject(WHITE_BRUSH);
        wndClass.lpszMenuName = NULL;
        wndClass.lpszClassName = "MinWin";

        RegisterClass(&wndClass);
    }

    hWnd = CreateWindow(
            "MinWin",               // Window class's name.
            "MinWin Application",   // Title bar text.
            WS_OVERLAPPEDWINDOW,    // The window's style.
```

(continues)

V

Tools and Techniques

Listing 27.1   Continued

```
                      CW_USEDEFAULT,        // X position.
                      CW_USEDEFAULT,        // Y position.
                      CW_USEDEFAULT,        // Width.
                      CW_USEDEFAULT,        // Height.
                      NULL,                 // Parent window's handle.
                      NULL,                 // Menu handle.
                      hCurrentInst,         // Instance handle.
                      NULL);                // No additional data.

    ShowWindow(hWnd, nCmdShow);
    UpdateWindow(hWnd);

    while (GetMessage(&msg, NULL, NULL, NULL))
    {
        TranslateMessage(&msg);
        DispatchMessage(&msg);
    }

    return msg.wParam;
}


//////////////////////////////////////////////////////////////
// WndProc()
//
// This is the main window procedure, which is called by
// Windows.
//////////////////////////////////////////////////////////////
LRESULT FAR PASCAL _export WndProc(HWND hWnd, UINT message,
    WPARAM wParam, LPARAM lParam)
{
    switch(message)
    {
        case WM_DESTROY:
            PostQuitMessage(0);
            return 0;
    }

    return DefWindowProc(hWnd, message, wParam, lParam);
}
```

Listing 27.2   MINOWL.CPP: The Minimum OWL Application

```
#include <owl\applicat.h>

int OwlMain(int, char*[])
{
    TApplication app("MinOWL App");
    return app.Run();
}
```

Of course, learning to use OWL is no picnic either. OWL has its own set of rules and requirements in addition to those of Windows. This chapter teaches you those rules and requirements.

The ObjectWindows Classes

ObjectWindows includes many classes you can use to write your applications more quickly and easily. These OWL classes represent objects from which a Windows application is created—objects such as windows, dialog boxes, menu bars, window controls, and many more, including some special objects such as status bars and control bars.

Specifically, ObjectWindows 2.5 provides the following main categories of classes:

Applications	Graphics
Windows	Printing
Menus	Validators
Dialog boxes	Documents and views
Controls	Clipboard

In the following sections, you get a brief look at each OWL class category.

The *TApplication* Class

Every ObjectWindows program begins life as an application object. You derive this application object from ObjectWindows' TApplication class, which provides initialization, run-time, and ending services for your Windows program. More specifically, TApplication registers, creates, and shows an application's main window; sets the application's message loop running (so that the application can interact with the user and Windows); and deletes the application when the user is finished.

The TApplication class provides a complete, working Windows program, albeit one that does little more than display a window on-screen. TApplication provides some additional services, such as providing access to the application's command line, allowing you to easily enable Borland's custom controls library or Microsoft's 3-D control library and detecting when the application is idle (has no pending Windows messages).

The Window Classes

When you create a basic OWL application, `TApplication` automatically provides a main window. This main window is fully functional, meaning that it can be sized, moved, maximized, minimized, and closed. Impressive as this may be, such a basic application is more boring than late-night reruns of *Green Acres*. Obviously, OWL must provide a way for you to make your application's main window actually *do* something.

This is where OWL's window classes come in. By forcing your OWL application to create your custom main window rather than its default window, you can add all the functionality you need to your application. To make this task easier for you, OWL features several different types of windows. These windows include the following:

- Generic child windows

- Frame windows

- Decorated frame windows

- MDI windows

- OLE windows

Each type of window is discussed in the sections that follow.

Generic Child Windows

A generic child window is represented in OWL 2.5 by the `TWindow` class. This is a basic window that provides support for menu bars, system menus, scroll bars, control objects, window painting, data transfer, default message processing, and much more. A `TWindow` object can handle just about everything you need a child window to do.

Although you can use `TWindow` to create an application's main window, you should probably reserve `TWindow` for other uses. An application's main window should be a window of the `TFrameWindow` class, which is described in the following section.

Frame Windows

Frame windows, represented by the `TFrameWindow` class, supply all the functionality of the `TWindow` class but also add keyboard-handling and client window support. Frame windows also act as the base class from which decorated, MDI, and OLE windows are derived. Most of a `TFrameWindow`'s capabilities are inherited from its base class `TWindow`, which users of ObjectWindows 1.0 will recognize as the old class for a generic main window. In ObjectWindows 2.5, TFrameWindow takes over as the generic main window class. In fact, the default window constructed by a TApplication object is a frame window.

Decorated Frame Windows

Decorated frame windows—encapsulated in the TDecoratedFrame class and derived from regular frame windows and layout windows—allow you to add decoration objects to your application. These decorations include toolbars, message bars, status bars, and toolboxes, which are represented by the TControlBar, TMessageBar, TStatusBar, and TToolBox classes, respectively. Because OLE applications must support toolbars, their frame windows (represented by the ObjectWindows TOleFrame class) are derived from the TDecoratedFrame class.

When you add decorations to your decorated frame window, the window automatically places the decorations where they belong and keeps them in place as the user moves or resizes the window. Also, you can add an object such as a toolbar or a status bar to your window by constructing the object and using the decorated frame window's Insert() member function. Decorated frame windows also provide member functions for showing and hiding decorations and displaying *hint text* for highlighted menu items. (When the user highlights a menu item, hint text appears and describes the command about to be selected.)

MDI Windows

To support Windows' Multiple Document Interface (MDI), ObjectWindows provides several window classes designed especially for MDI applications. The MDI frame window, encapsulated in the TMDIFrame class, acts as an MDI application's main window. (The OLE version is TOleMDIFrame.) During an application's run, this window contains at least an invisible client window and probably several child windows. The frame window handles the application's menu bar, which includes the special Window pull-down menu. This menu lets the user select windows, as well as cascade, tile, and arrange windows.

The MDI client window, represented by the TMDIClient class, is the window that provides most of an MDI application's functionality. Generally, messages sent to the MDI application are routed to the client window for processing. The client window automatically responds to and handles the four main commands found in an MDI application's Window menu, enabling you to add window tiling, cascading, arranging, and closing to your application with little effort. An MDI client window can also create MDI child windows automatically.

V

Tools and Techniques

All child windows in an MDI application must be MDI child windows, so ObjectWindows provides a special class, TMDIChild, for this type of window. MDI child windows act much like frame windows on the Windows desktop, except their "desktop" is defined by the MDI application's client window. The user can reduce MDI child windows to icons or maximize them to fill the client window.

OLE Windows

As mentioned briefly in the preceding section, OWL also features a set of classes for handling windows in OLE (Object Linking and Embedding) applications. These classes include TOleFrame, TOleMDIFrame, TOleWindow. The TOleFrame class represents an OLE application's main window and provides the basic OLE services for the application, including OLE menu merging and toolbar display. Because this class can trace its ancestry back through the TDecoratedFrame, TFrameWindow, TLayoutWindow, and TWindow classes, it inherits all the functionality of those classes.

The TOleMDIFrame class is derived from TOleFrame, so it shares TOleFrame's ancestry. Because the TOleMDIFrame class also counts TMDIFrame among its ancestors, however, it provides the services needed to create multiple-document OLE applications. Finally, the TOleWindow class, which acts as a TOleFrame's client window, provides the services needed to handle OLE compound documents, which can contain any number of embedded objects. Also, this class responds to drag-and-drop events, creates views for a container application, and allows editing of embedded objects, either through in-place editing or by calling up the object's server application.

Menus

One of a Windows application's distinguishing features is its menu bar. Nearly all Windows applications have a menu bar that follows (or should follow) certain guidelines in menu design. By following these design guidelines, the user can find familiar commands in expected places, regardless of which application he or she happens to be using at the time. For simple menu handling, conventional methods work fine; however, if you need to have more control over your menus, you can use ObjectWindows' handy menu classes: TMenu, TSystemMenu, TPopupMenu, and TMenuDescr.

The TMenu class, which you can use to create and manage an application's main menu, provides member functions for adding items to a menu, modifying menu items, enabling or disabling menu items, showing or hiding menu checkmarks, and even placing bitmaps in a menu. Also, many query member functions supply information about a menu, including the number of items in the menu, the size of the checkmark bitmap, the menu item IDs, the menu's state, and more.

The TSystemMenu class offers extra control over an application's system menu. By using this menu class, you can replace a window's system menu with one of your own. The TPopupMenu class allows you to create pop-up menus that can appear anywhere you like in a window. Finally, the TMenuDescr class handles such tasks as changing among several menu bars, as well as merging menus (such as in OLE applications).

Dialog Boxes

Just as most Windows applications use menu bars to get commands from the user, they also use dialog boxes to get input. Likewise, ObjectWindows features a dialog box class, TDialog. The TDialog class handles all the details of constructing, executing, and closing a dialog box, including built-in responses for the most-used buttons and a mechanism for automatically transferring data to and from the dialog box. Also, your OWL dialog boxes can be modal or modeless, can contain any number of controls, and can even feature a sculpted three-dimensional look provided by Borland's or Microsoft's 3-D custom control DLLs.

OWL also encapsulates into classes Windows' common dialog boxes and other "prefab" dialog boxes. These dialog classes—including TInputDialog, TPrinterAbortDlg, TChooseColorDialog, TFindReplaceDialog, TChooseFontDialog, TPrintDialog, and TOpenSaveDialog—allow the user to input a single line of text, select file names, find text strings, set up a printer, and choose colors and fonts.

Controls

Windows applications are loaded with special controls such as buttons, list boxes, scroll bars, and edit boxes. Because Windows controls are used regularly in Windows applications, OWL encapsulates the controls into classes. For example, the list box control, encapsulated by the TListBox class, includes member functions for adding and deleting strings to and from the list, clearing the list, finding a specific string in the list, finding the number of selected items in the list, retrieving selected strings, setting strings as selected, and much more. The scroll bar class, TScrollBar, provides member functions to get the scroll thumb's position, to set the scroll thumb's position, and set the scroll bar's range—to name just a few.

Besides those mentioned previously, OWL includes classes for buttons (TButton), group boxes (TGroupBox), combo boxes (TComboBox), edit controls (TEdit), check boxes (TCheckBox), radio buttons (TRadioButton), VBX controls (TVbxControl), and static text controls (TStatic). OWL also provides custom control classes that you can use in your applications. For example, the gauge control, represented by the TGauge class, displays a vertical or horizontal bar that indicates how close to completion a process is. The vertical and horizontal slider controls, encapsulated in the THSlider and TVSlider classes, allow a user to select a value from a range of values.

Graphics

Because Windows is a graphical user interface (GUI), all Windows applications depend heavily on various graphical services provided by Windows. These graphical services make up Windows' Graphical Device Interface (GDI). To make the GDI a little easier to use, ObjectWindows provides 10 classes that encapsulate much of the GDI. These include classes for device contexts (TDC), brushes (TBrush), pens (TPen), icons (TIcon), bitmaps (TBitmap), cursors (TCursor), fonts (TFont), palettes (TPalette), device-independent bitmaps (TDib), and regions (TRegion).

The TDC class is the base class for other more specific DC classes. This class encapsulates most of Windows' general GDI functions, such as those for drawing shapes, displaying text, drawing icons and bitmaps, setting the drawing mode, selecting and restoring GDI objects, setting colors, and much more.

The more specific device context classes include window (TWindowDC), client window (TClientDC), paint (TPaintDC), metafile (TMetafileDC), memory (TMemoryDC), and printer (TPrinter) DCs, as well as several others. Each DC class features many member functions that encapsulate Windows' standard function calls related to that specific DC. For example, the TPrintDC class provides functions for starting and stopping a print job, starting and ending a page, setting the number of copies to print, aborting a document, and more.

Printing

Because of Windows' device independence—and thus the great number of printer drivers that can be installed on a user's system—printing documents under Windows has always been a difficult task. But, now, thanks to OWL's new printer classes, you can print any type of document with a minimum of hassle. Specifically, OWL provides two classes for handling print jobs: the TPrinter class, which encapsulates printer functions and the handling of printer drivers, and the TPrintout class, which represents the actual document to be printed. These two classes work together to produce finished hard copy on the currently installed printer.

When you create a printer object, encapsulated by the TPrinter class, your application automatically hooks up with the user's default printer, as found in the user's WIN.INI file. The TPrintout object is equally as powerful, enabling you to print a simple, one-page document by overriding only a single function in the class, in much the same way you override a window's paint function to display the contents of a window. For more complex, multipage documents, TPrintout helps you handle pagination, printer banding, page sizing, and user interaction with the printer dialog box.

Also included in OWL is the TPreviewPage class, which lets you create, with a minimum of programming, a print preview function. With this preview function, the user can display a window containing an image of the data he or she wants to send to the printer.

Validators

Another cumbersome task in Windows programming is validating the contents of a dialog box after the user enters data. Before ObjectWindows 2.5, you had to write your own data-validation functions, which you called before allowing a dialog box to close. OWL now takes over much of this task with its input validator objects. Five specialized validator classes—TFilterValidator, TRangeValidator, TLookupValidator, TStringLookupValidator, and TPXPictureValidator—allow you to check input as the user enters it, validate for acceptable characters, enforce value ranges, check that an entry is in a table of acceptable responses, and apply templates to the user's input.

To use a validator object, you only need to create the object and then associate it with the edit control it must monitor. The edit control then accesses the validator automatically, performing all the validation behind the scenes, with no further programming effort on your part. Of course, you can write your own custom data-validation classes by overriding member functions in the base class TValidator.

V

Tools and Techniques

Documents and Views

Most Windows applications need to handle documents of one form or another. Word processors must handle text files, paint programs must manage graphics files, and sound players must handle sound files. In some cases, an application needs to handle a document in several ways simultaneously. For example, a file editor may handle a file as ASCII text and as binary data displayed in binary or hexadecimal form. To help you manage documents, OWL offers its Doc/View model, which consists of document objects, view objects, and a document manager.

Under OWL, a document object, represented by the TDocument class (TOleDocument in an OLE application), can contain any type of data. The class provides member functions for managing the document and interacting with the document's associated view. For example, you can open and close a document, get or set the directory path of a document, get or set the title of the document, check whether a document has been modified, and notify associated view objects of any changes.

The view object, encapsulated in the TView class (TOleView in an OLE application), acts as a functional layer between a document and the interface being used to manipulate the object (a window or a dialog box, for example). Views allow you to display data in different ways and let the user interact with the data. To make a view useful, you must override a number of the base class's virtual functions, supplying them with appropriate behavior for the type of view you want to create. A single document can be associated with several different view objects.

The Clipboard

One of the many advantages of using Windows is the capability to transfer data between applications. The most common mechanism used for this data transfer is the clipboard. Data from one application can be cut or copied into the clipboard, and then that same data can be pasted from the clipboard into another application's document.

Because the clipboard is used regularly in Windows applications, OWL features a clipboard class, TClipboard, that encapsulates many Windows clipboard functions. Using TClipboard, you can open and close the clipboard, empty the clipboard, check the clipboard's data format, copy data to and paste data from the clipboard, and perform any of the other 14 supported clipboard functions.

OWL also includes a special class, `TClipboardViewer`, which automatically adds or removes itself from Windows' clipboard viewer chain. This class also provides message-response functions for several messages sent by Windows to a clipboard viewer.

The ObjectComponents Library

In an effort to make computers easier to use, Microsoft designed Object Linking and Embedding (OLE), a process by which applications share data in a variety of sophisticated ways. For example, by using OLE, a user can merge into his word processor document a graphical image created by a paint program. Although this merged graphical object is contained in a word processor document, the user can still edit the graphical object. All he or she needs to do is double-click the object, and the object's source application runs so that the user can edit the painting and resave it to the document. If the object's actual graphical data is stored with the document, the object is called an *embedded object*.

Whereas object embedding stores actual data into a document, *object linking* places in the document only a reference to the file in which the object's data is stored. Because of this link, whenever the data contained in the linked object changes, the image of the object in the document also changes. Embedded objects, on the other hand, contain no link to a separate file.

Thanks to OLE, computers are becoming more document-oriented, rather than application-oriented—that is, the user is less concerned with which application creates which type of document than with just creating a document. The capabilities of any OLE-supporting application are available to any other OLE-supporting application, so that the user can create documents that contain almost any type of data, all within a single application. Documents that contain OLE objects (or *Windows objects*) are called *compound documents*.

As you may have guessed, however, OLE-capable applications can be terribly hard to write. Microsoft's *OLE 2 Programmer's Reference*, Volume 1, for example, is more than 900 pages long and reads like the manual for the Apollo spacecraft. (And note that it's only volume 1! Volume 2 is pretty hefty, too.) Moreover, OLE 2 adds hundreds of new function calls and other programming complications to an already complex system—Windows.

V

Tools and Techniques

All told, learning to write OLE-capable applications can take months of research and practice. Luckily, Borland has done most of the dirty work for you by adding its OLE classes to its class libraries and integrating those new classes with the ObjectWindows Library (OWL). Believe it or not, thanks to these new OWL classes, creating a minimal OLE application requires only a few extra lines of code.

Borland's first task in making OLE manageable was to create an OLE engine that isolated the programmer from OLE's intricacies by providing a high-level access to OLE, in much the same way that OWL provides a higher-level access to the Windows API. This OLE engine is shipped with Turbo C++ 4.5 as a dynamic link library (DLL) called BOCOLE.DLL. (BOCOLE stands for Borland ObjectComponents Object Linking and Embedding.) You can access the functions of BOCOLE.DLL through a new set of classes called the ObjectComponents Framework (OCF). You can use OCF directly in conventional C++ programs, or you can take advantage of OWL's new classes, which handle much of OCF for you.

The new OCF classes include TOcApp, TOcDocument, TOcModule, TOcPart, TOcRegistrar, TOcRemView, TOcView, TAppDescriptor, TAutoBase, TAutoProxy, and TOleAllocator. Using OCF, you can create applications that support linking and embedding, drag-and-drop, compound files, clipboard operations, OLE automation, OLE registration, and more. If all this sounds intimidating, you'll be delighted to know that new OWL classes isolate you from many of OCF's dirty details (which in turn isolates you from OLE's dirty details—all of which should give you an idea of what a nightmare programming OLE without Borland's new classes can be).

By using Borland's OWL application framework, you can get started with OLE almost immediately, making only a few changes to existing source code. As you know, these new OWL classes include TOleFrame, TOleMdiFrame, TOleWindow, TStorageDocument, TOleDocument, and TOleView. To modify existing source code to accommodate OLE entails little more than replacing regular window classes with the new OLE window classes (for example, substituting TOleFrame for TFrameWindow) and creating a couple of OCF objects.

From Here...

If you're new to ObjectWindows programming, you may be a bit confused about how this huge class library works, but you can't help but be excited by the possibilities the library offers you, the programmer. To make Windows applications easier to program, Borland has anticipated your needs and provided much of the basic code needed to write just about any type of Windows application. By using OWL, your applications can look and act just like the impressive Windows software found at your local software store.

If you've had experience with OWL version 1.0, you'll be undoubtedly pleased with the extra power offered by ObjectWindows 2.5. With the addition of such classes as `TDecoratedFrame`, `TControlBar`, `TStatusBar`, `TToolBox`, `TValidator`, `TDocument`, `TView`, `TGadget`, and `TPrinter`—not to mention a more complete encapsulation of the Windows API and support for OLE 2— ObjectWindows has metamorphosed into one of the most powerful class libraries available to Windows programmers.

However, learning to use OWL requires writing many OWL programs and experimenting with the classes included in OWL. For more information on using ObjectWindows, see the following chapters:

- Chapter 21, "Using AppExpert." AppExpert creates ObjectWindows applications with a few mouse clicks.

- Chapter 28, "ObjectWindows Applications," gives you the inside scoop on writing Windows applications with ObjectWindows.

- Chapter 29, "Single and Multiple Document Interfaces," discusses writing ObjectWindows applications that can handle one or more document windows.

V

Tools and Techniques

Chapter 28

ObjectWindows Applications

In this chapter, you learn how OWL helps you write a simple Windows application with only a few lines of code. Using ObjectWindows, you can display a fully functional window and even manipulate the window's attributes so that the window looks the way you want and appears at a specific location and a predetermined size. Moreover, using ObjectWindows, your application can respond to Windows messages and menu commands.

ObjectWindows also enables you to quickly incorporate object linking and embedding (OLE), a process by which applications share data in a variety of sophisticated ways, into your applications. Here, you learn about ObjectComponents Framework (OCF), a set of classes that isolates the programmer from many details of OLE 2.0. Moreover, you discover new classes added to ObjectWindows (OWL) that provide easy access to the OCF classes.

When you finish this chapter you will be able to

- Create a basic ObjectWindows application.

- Customize your application's main window.

- Respond to incoming Windows messages.

- Add a menu bar to your application.

- Write an OLE container application.

- Create and manage dynamic menus.

Creating an Application Object

Remember when your mother told you that if something seems too good to be true, it probably is? Well, sometimes something that seems too good to be true really *is* true. Such is the case with creating a basic application with ObjectWindows. In Chapter 27, "The ObjectWindows Library," I said that you can create an OWL application, complete with a working main window, in around six lines of code. Such a claim may have made you think about dear Mom and her sage advice. But, as you'll soon see, this is one of those cases in which reality really does live up to wild claims. As proof, look at the OWL program in listing 28.1.

Listing 28.1   TINIEST.CPP: The Minimum OWL Application

```
#include <owl\applicat.h>

int OwlMain(int, char*[])
{
    TApplication app("Tiny App");
    return app.Run();
}
```

Listing 28.1 is the smallest possible OWL application. As you can see, it comprises only six lines, not including the blank line. By changing the coding style a bit, you could write this application in even fewer lines. When you compile and run this application, the window shown in figure 28.1 appears on-screen. This window is complete with a system menu and all the controls you need to move, resize, minimize, and maximize the window.

Fig. 28.1
The tiniest app.

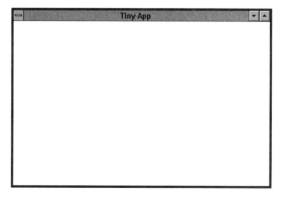

You can see how the program works by looking at listing 28.1. The first line includes the header file for an OWL application object. Most OWL objects have a header file in the TCWIN45\INCLUDE\OWL directory. To use an OWL object, you must include its header file in your program. In listing 28.1, you use only one OWL object—an application object—so there's only one OWL header file included at the top of the listing.

The next line of the listing begins the OwlMain() function, which is where every OWL program starts execution. Besides eliminating the need for a complex WinMain() function, OwlMain() also gives you access to the argc and argv command-line arguments (which aren't used in listing 28.1).

In the body of OwlMain(), you first instantiate your own application object from the OWL base class TApplication. TApplication has two constructors. The first, which is the one used in listing 28.1, accepts only a single argument—the name of the application, which appears in the main window's title bar. This constructor's prototype looks like this:

```
TApplication(const char far *name = 0);
```

Because this constructor's single argument has a default value (a null string), you can actually create your application object with no arguments at all. If you do, however, your main window will have no title.

The other TApplication constructor, which you should use only when you plan to write your own version of WinMain() (something you'll do about as often as you hang upside-down from the ceiling), provides access to the arguments used by WinMain(). This constructor is shown in the following code lines:

```
TApplication(const char far *name, HINSTANCE instance,
    HINSTANCE prevInstance, const char far *cmdLine,
    int cmdShow);
```

In listing 28.1's OwlMain(), you first derive an application object named app. In the next line, you call app's Run() member function, which sets the application into action, initializing the application and getting its message loop running. Run() ends only when the user closes the application.

Understanding an Application's Main Window

Although listing 28.1 creates a fully functional main window for your smallest OWL application, the main window can't respond to the user in any way except through the window's controls, which allow the window to be moved, sized, minimized, and maximized. Not only is such an application as boring as a grass-cutting competition, but it's also mostly useless—unless, of course, the application's purpose is only to show how basic window controls work.

To make your OWL application useful, you must force the application object to create a main window that you've designed, rather than the default window. To do this, you derive your own TApp class from TApplication, then override TApplication's InitMainWindow() virtual member function, as shown in listing 28.2.

Listing 28.2 TINYAPP.CPP: Defines a Custom Main Window

```
//////////////////////////////////////////////////////////
// TINYAPP.CPP: Demonstrates deriving an application
//                class and defining a main window class.
//////////////////////////////////////////////////////////

#include <owl\applicat.h>
#include <owl\framewin.h>

// The application class.
class TApp : public TApplication
{
public:
   TApp(): TApplication() {}
   void InitMainWindow();
};

// The main window class.
class TWndw : public TFrameWindow
{
public:
   TWndw(TWindow *parent, const char far *title):
      TFrameWindow(parent, title) {}
};

//////////////////////////////////////////////////////////
// TApp::InitMainWindow()
//
// This function creates the application's main window.
//////////////////////////////////////////////////////////
void TApp::InitMainWindow()
{
   TFrameWindow *wndw = new TWndw(0, "Tiny App 2");
   SetMainWindow(wndw);
}

//////////////////////////////////////////////////////////
// OwlMain()
//////////////////////////////////////////////////////////
int OwlMain(int, char*[])
{
   return TApp().Run();
}
```

Creating Your Own Customized Window

When you run the program in listing 28.2, you see the window shown in figure 28.2. This window looks and acts exactly like the window produced by listing 28.1, except that it has a different title. But there's a more important difference. Now the main window is a window of your TWndw class and not the default TFrameWindow. Because of this, you can add whatever functions you need to the class to make the window perform as your application requires.

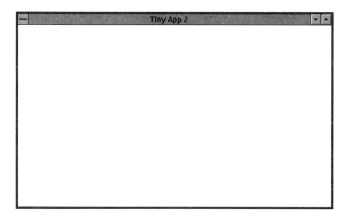

Fig. 28.2
The Tiny App program with a custom window.

To substitute your window class for the default class used by TApplication, you override the application object's InitMainWindow() member function. To do this, first derive your own application class from TApplication. In listing 28.2, this new application class is called TApp. The TApp constructor includes no title string, and instead takes advantage of TApplication's default value for that argument (a null string). You don't need the title string this time; you'll supply it when you define the application's main window. Notice that TApp's constructor calls TApplication's constructor. This allows TApp's base class to perform whatever initialization is necessary for an OWL application. Finally, notice that in the TApp class you've overridden TApplication's InitMainWindow() function. You'll soon see why.

Tip
When overriding a function in OWL, be sure to call the base class's version of the function, if it's necessary.

Deriving a Window from *TFrameWindow*

After declaring the new application class derived from TApplication, you have a complete application not unlike the one you created in listing 28.1; the main difference is that you created your own instance of TApplication. Unfortunately, this still isn't enough to create a useful program. Next, you must declare a main window class for your application. In listing 28.2, this new window class is called TWndw.

The TWndw class is derived from the TFrameWindow class, which is a generic window class. TWndw's constructor takes two arguments—a pointer to a parent window and a window title—that it passes on to the TFrameWindow constructor. (TFrameWindow itself is derived from TWindow.) Remember that because you want to use the TFrameWindow class, you must include its header file, FRAMEWIN.H, in your program.

Constructing the Custom Main Window

Now that you have your window class declared, you must use the new class to create a main window for the application. To do this, you call TWndw's constructor, which you do in TApp's InitMainWindow() function, like this:

```
TFrameWindow *wndw = new TWndw(0, "Tiny App 2");
```

The new operator creates the TWndw object dynamically, returning the necessary TWindow pointer. The TWndw constructor's first argument is 0, because this window has no parent window. The second argument is the title that appears in the window's title bar when the window is created. If you supplied a window title when you created your application object (as in listing 28.1), the title given in the window constructor is the one that appears. This is why listing 28.2 constructs its application object without a title string. It's not used, so why include it?

MainWindow, a pointer to a TWindow, is a data member of the TApplication class, which is TApp's base class (so, of course, TApp inherits its own copy of MainWindow). To set this pointer, you call the application object's SetMainWindow() function, which takes as its single argument a pointer to a TFrameWindow or a window derived from TFrameWindow. That function call looks like this:

```
SetMainWindow(wndw);
```

Your new main window is now on-screen. It looks great but still does nothing useful. What does it take, you ask, to get some life out of OWL? To get things hopping, you need to make your window respond to Windows messages.

Responding to Windows Messages

You may want your application to do many things eventually, but one thing every Windows application must do is respond to Windows messages. The messages sent to your application by Windows are its lifeblood, its connection to not only the outside world (the user) but also to Windows' behind-the-scene workings. When you have Windows on-screen, messages fly between applications like promises between Romeo and Juliet.

You don't have to be too astute to realize that your OWL applications need some mechanism to accept and act on the thousands of messages they will receive from Windows. You do this in an OWL application by creating message-response functions for the messages you want to handle. You then create a response table that matches your message-response functions with the messages they're meant to handle. Listing 28.3 shows how this is done.

Listing 28.3   MSGAPP.CPP: Responding to Windows Messages

```
//////////////////////////////////////////////////////////////
// MSGAPP.CPP: Demonstrates responding to Windows
//             messages.
//////////////////////////////////////////////////////////////

#include <owl\applicat.h>
#include <owl\framewin.h>
#include "msgapp.rc"

// The application class.
class TApp : public TApplication
{
public:
   TApp(): TApplication() {}
   void InitMainWindow();
};

// The main window class.
class TWndw : public TFrameWindow
{
public:
   TWndw(TWindow *parent, const char far *title):
      TFrameWindow(parent, title) {}

protected:
   void EvLButtonDown(UINT, TPoint &point);
   void CmHelpAbout();

   DECLARE_RESPONSE_TABLE(TWndw);
};

DEFINE_RESPONSE_TABLE1(TWndw, TFrameWindow)
   EV_WM_LBUTTONDOWN,
   EV_COMMAND(CM_HELPABOUT, CmHelpAbout),
END_RESPONSE_TABLE;

//////////////////////////////////////////////////////////////
// TWndw::EvLButtonDown()
//
// This function responds to WM_LBUTTONDOWN messages, which
// the application receives when the user clicks the left
// mouse button while the mouse pointer is over the window.
//////////////////////////////////////////////////////////////
```

V

Tools and Techniques

(continues)

Listing 28.3 Continued

```
void TWndw::EvLButtonDown(UINT, TPoint&)
{
    MessageBox("Got the click!", "Message", MB_OK);
}


//////////////////////////////////////////////////////////
// TWndw::CmHelpAbout()
//
// This function responds to CM_HELPABOUT messages, which
// the application receives when the user clicks the Help
// menu's About MsgApp command.
//////////////////////////////////////////////////////////
void TWndw::CmHelpAbout()
{
    MessageBox("MsgApp Sample OWL application",
        "About", MB_OK);
}


//////////////////////////////////////////////////////////
// TApp::InitMainWindow()
//
// This function creates the application's main window.
//////////////////////////////////////////////////////////
void TApp::InitMainWindow()
{
    TFrameWindow *wndw = new TWndw(0, "Message App");
    wndw->AssignMenu(MENU_1);
    SetMainWindow(wndw);
}


//////////////////////////////////////////////////////////
// OwlMain()
//////////////////////////////////////////////////////////
int OwlMain(int, char*[])
{
    return TApp().Run();
}
```

When you run the program in listing 28.3, a window appears on-screen (see fig. 28.3). Click the left mouse button in the window. A message box appears, informing you that the mouse click was received. If you select the Help menu's About MsgApp command, you see a message box telling you about the program. Finally, if you select the File menu's Exit command, the program ends.

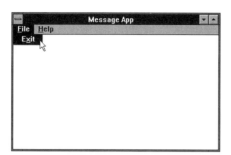

Fig. 28.3
An application
responding to
mouse clicks.

Adding a Response Table to a Window Class

In listing 28.3, the application class TApp remains unchanged. However, the main window class, TWndw, now contains a response table and message-response member functions for left mouse button clicks and the Help menu's About command. Both the response functions and table are declared in the class's declaration.

The programmers at Borland, being the fine people they are, provided in the TWindow class (which is the base class, remember, for TFrameWindow and your own TWndw) predefined response-table macros for all standard Windows messages. As you'll soon see, you use these macros in the response table to automatically match specific message-response functions to the appropriate Windows messages.

EvLButtonDown() is, for example, the response function that matches the WM_LBUTTONDOWN message. The name of this function isn't something your humble author yanked from a hat. You must follow a strict set of naming rules so that Turbo C++ can match the function with the message it's meant to handle.

You determine the necessary function name for a particular Windows message by taking the message's name, replacing the WM_ with Ev, and then spelling the rest of the function name as it appears in the message name, except using uppercase letters for the first letter of each "word" and lowercase letters for the rest. So, WM_LBUTTONDOWN becomes EvLButtonDown, WM_PAINT becomes EvPaint, WM_MOUSEMOVE becomes EvMouseMove, and so on. In the preceding class declaration, you can now see that the member function EvLButtonDown() is meant to respond to WM_LBUTTONDOWN messages.

To declare a response table in a class, you use the DECLARE_RESPONSE_TABLE macro, which requires as its single argument the name of the class for which the table is being declared. That declaration looks like this:

```
DECLARE_RESPONSE_TABLE(TWndw);
```

The table itself is defined outside the class, usually right after the class's declaration:

```
DEFINE_RESPONSE_TABLE1(TWndw, TFrameWindow)
   EV_WM_LBUTTONDOWN,
   EV_COMMAND(CM_HELPABOUT, CmHelpAbout),
END_RESPONSE_TABLE;
```

You start the table with the DEFINE_RESPONSE_TABLE macro. The name of the macro must be followed by the number of immediate base classes from which your class is derived. As is the case with TWndw, this value almost always is 1. The exception is classes derived through multiple inheritance. After the macro name and immediate-base-class count, you provide the name of the class that the table is being defined for, as well as the names of all immediate base classes. The only immediate base class for TWndw is TFrameWindow, so it's the only additional class listed in the macro. The class names are enclosed in parentheses and separated by commas.

As stated a few paragraphs back, Turbo C++ has predefined response-table macros for all standard Windows messages. To enable your window to respond to a particular Windows message, you only need to include its macro in your response table and provide the matching response member function. You can determine a macro's name by taking the Windows message name and adding EV_ to the front. So the response table macro for the WM_LBUTTONDOWN message is EV_WM_LBUTTONDOWN, the macro for WM_PAINT is EV_WM_PAINT, the macro for WM_MOUSEMOVE is EV_WM_MOUSEMOVE, and so on.

In listing 28.3, you've defined a response table that matches the WM_LBUTTONDOWN Windows message to your TWndw member function EvLButtonDown(). By using the response table macro for the WM_LBUTTONDOWN message and carefully naming the response function according to the rules, you don't need to do any more to receive the WM_LBUTTONDOWN message. Turbo C++ generates the necessary code to send WM_LBUTTONDOWN messages to your EvLButtonDown() function. Note that all response table entries must be followed by a comma, even the last.

The EV_COMMAND macro in the response table is used to match up a message-response function to a menu command. In the case of listing 28.3, the menu command is represented by the CM_HELPABOUT constant, and the command's response function is similarly named: CmHelpAbout(). Thanks to the EV_COMMAND entry in listing 28.3's response table, when the program receives a CM_HELPABOUT command, OWL automatically calls the CmHelpAbout() function to handle the message.

Writing Message-Response Functions

Now that you have your class declared and its response table defined, you must define the EvLButtonDown() and CmHelpAbout() response functions. How do you know what types of arguments are returned and received by a particular message-response function? The prototypes for each of the many message-response functions for standard Windows messages are listed in your on-line ObjectWindows reference guide that came with your copy of Turbo C++ 4.5. As you'll see when you look at this list of prototypes, one of the advantages of using Turbo C++'s predefined response-table macros is that the associated Windows message is "cracked" before being passed to your response function. In other words, Turbo C++ automatically extracts the relevant values passed in the wParam and lParam parameters.

> **Note**
>
> To find message-response function prototypes in the on-line help, highlight a message-response function name (such as EvLButtonDown) in your source code and then press F1. When the Search dialog box appears, double-click the function name and then select Standard Windows Messages in the lower list box.

For example, in the case of the WM_LBUTTONDOWN message, Windows encodes a virtual key flag in wParam and the x and y coordinates of the mouse pointer in lParam. But rather than force you to extract this information on your own, Turbo C++ automatically extracts the values and sends them to your EvLButtonDown() function, where the virtual key flag is received as UINT and the mouse's x and y coordinates are in a TPoint object.

In listing 28.3's EvLButtonDown() function, the call to MessageBox() displays a standard Windows message box on-screen whenever the left mouse button is clicked in the window. However, the MessageBox() in this function isn't the same MessageBox() found in the Windows API. This MessageBox() is a member function of the TWindow class. ObjectWindows 2.5 encapsulates as much of the Windows API as possible, making calls to many functions more convenient.

As for functions specified with the EV_COMMAND macro, you can name them whatever you like, although it's standard practice to base the function's name on the name of the message to which the function responds. Such message-response functions don't return values, nor do they have parameters, as you can see by CmHelpAbout()'s declaration:

```
void CmHelpAbout();
```

Adding a Menu

When you run listing 28.3, notice that the main window sports a small but functional menu bar. The menu itself was designed by using Turbo C++'s Resource Workshop. To learn how to use Resource Workshop to design your program's user interface, refer to Chapter 19, "Developing Windows Resources for a User Interface," and Chapter 23, "Using Resource Workshop."

For now, just know that the constants MENU_1 and CM_HELPABOUT used in listing 28.3, as well as the application's menu bar, are defined in the application's resource file, which is created by Resource Workshop (and is often modified by the programmer). Listing 28.3 includes this resource file at the top of the listing.

To add the menu bar to the application's main window, you need to call only the main window's AssignMenu() member function, like this:

```
AssignMenu(MENU_ID);
```

This function's single parameter is the menu's resource ID, which you define when you use Resource Workshop to create the menu. This single function call is all that's needed to attach the menu to your application's main window.

Notice that although the File menu's Exit command works fine, it isn't handled anywhere in listing 28.3. This is because OWL automatically takes care of the Exit command if you give the command the ID value 24310, usually represented by the constant CM_EXIT.

Setting a Window's Attributes

So far you've learned to derive your own application object from TApplication, to derive your own window class from TFrameWindow (and thus from TWindow), and to respond to standard Windows messages. But despite all this OWL power, you still have no control over how your window appears on-screen. Your main window pops up anywhere Windows decides to put it. The window's size, too, is out of your control. Luckily, under ObjectWindows, this situation is easily remedied.

Every window that has TWindow as an ancestor inherits an Attr data member containing the window's attributes. Attr is a TWindowAttr structure that contains the members shown in table 28.1.

Table 28.1	The Members of the *TWindowAttr* Class	
Member Name	**Data Type**	**Description**
Style	DWORD	Window style
ExStyle	DWORD	Extended style
X	int	x coordinate
Y	int	y coordinate
W	int	Width
H	int	Height
Menu	TResId	Menu resource ID
AccelTable	TResId	Accelerator resource ID
Param	char far*	MDI window information

Looking at an Application That Sets a Window's Attributes

To set your main window's attributes, then, you only need to set the appropriate members of Attr in your window's constructor. Listing 28.4 shows you how to do this.

Listing 28.4   WINATTR.CPP: Sets a Window's Attributes

```
//////////////////////////////////////////////////////////
// WINATTR.CPP: Demonstrates setting window attributes.
//////////////////////////////////////////////////////////

#include <owl\applicat.h>
#include <owl\framewin.h>

// The application's class.
class TApp : public TApplication
{
public:
   TApp(): TApplication() {}
   void InitMainWindow();
};

// The main window class.
class TWndw : public TFrameWindow
{
```

(continues)

Listing 28.4 Continued

```
public:
    TWndw(TWindow *parent, const char far *title);
};

//////////////////////////////////////////////////////////
// TWndw::TWndw()
//
// This is the main window's constructor.
//////////////////////////////////////////////////////////
TWndw::TWndw(TWindow *parent, const char far *title):
        TFrameWindow(parent, title)
{
    // Turn off the window's maximize box.
    Attr.Style &= ~WS_MAXIMIZEBOX;

    // Add a vertical scroll bar to the window.
    Attr.Style |= WS_VSCROLL;

    // Position and size the window.
    Attr.X = 100;
    Attr.Y = 100;
    Attr.W = 400;
    Attr.H = 300;
}

//////////////////////////////////////////////////////////
// TApp::InitMainWindow()
//
// This function creates the application's main window.
//////////////////////////////////////////////////////////
void TApp::InitMainWindow()
{
    TFrameWindow *wndw = new TWndw(0, "Attribute App");
    SetMainWindow(wndw);
}

//////////////////////////////////////////////////////////
// OwlMain()
//////////////////////////////////////////////////////////
int OwlMain(int, char*[])
{
    return TApp().Run();
}
```

Examining the WINATTR Application

Listing 28.4 is a bit different from previous programs in this chapter. Its difference is that the main window class's constructor is no longer in-line and has been expanded to include code for setting several of the window's attributes. As always, the constructor first calls its base class's constructors:

```
TWndw::TWndw(TWindow *parent, const char far *title):
        TFrameWindow(parent, title)
```

Then, the first code line in the body of the constructor turns off the window's maximize box:

```
Attr.Style &= ~WS_MAXIMIZEBOX;
```

How did the maximize box get turned on in the first place? A window derived from `TFrameWindow` has a default style of `WS_OVERLAPPEDWINDOW`. A window of this style includes a caption, a system menu, a thick frame, a minimize box, and a maximize box. Therefore, to turn off the maximize box, you must AND the negated `WS_MAXIMIZEBOX` style with `Attr.Style`.

In the constructor's next code line, you can see how to add a style to a window by ORing the new style with `Attr.Style`:

```
Attr.Style |= WS_VSCROLL;
```

In this case, you're adding a vertical scroll bar to the window. Of course, you can completely reset the window's style by using the assignment operator:

```
Attr.Style = WS_POPUP | WS_SYSMENU | WS_CAPTION;
```

The last thing the `TWndw` constructor does is set the window's initial position and size. It does so by setting `Attr`'s X, Y, W, and H members, which represent the window's x (left) coordinate, y (top) coordinate, width, and height, respectively:

```
Attr.X = 100;
Attr.Y = 100;
Attr.W = 400;
Attr.H = 300;
```

In the preceding case, the main window will appear at coordinates 100,100, and will be 400 pixels wide and 300 pixels high. Figure 28.4 shows the window produced by this program.

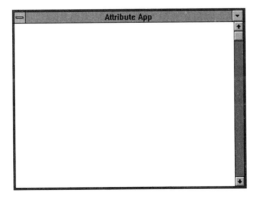

Fig. 28.4
This window's attributes were set in its constructor.

V

Tools and Techniques

Using ObjectWindows with OLE

As you learned in the previous chapter, ObjectWindows provides support for the easy—well, easier, anyway—creation of OLE applications, thanks both to new OWL classes and the ObjectComponents Framework. Although writing OLE applications is a huge topic, in this section you'll get a start on creating your own OLE applications by using OWL.

OLE applications are classified by the types of OLE functionality they provide. For example, an application that allows only OLE objects to be linked or embedded into its documents is a *container application*. It's called a container application because its documents can contain objects created and maintained by other applications.

Those applications that provide OLE objects for a container application are called *server applications* (or, sometimes, *object applications*). Server applications are called on by container applications to create, edit, and maintain objects embedded in the container application's document. Suppose that you're creating a document with Word for Windows, and you want to place a graphical object in the document. You choose Word for Window's Insert Object command and display the dialog box shown in figure 28.5.

Fig. 28.5
The Object
dialog box.

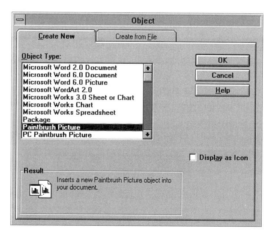

When you select Paintbrush Picture from the list, Windows Paintbrush automatically runs, enabling you to create the picture. When you exit Paintbrush, the newly created picture is embedded into the Word for Windows document. If you want to edit the picture after it's embedded, just double-click it. Paintbrush appears again, enabling you to make whatever changes you need. In this example, Word for Windows acts as the container application and Paintbrush acts as the server application.

Creating OWL Container Applications

There are several ways to create a minimal container application with Turbo C++ 4.5. One way is to use Turbo C++'s AppExpert to generate the source code. The trouble with this method is that, although it saves you some time, unless you know how a container application works, you'll have a hard time completing the code produced by AppExpert. Another way to create a container application is to write a conventional C++ program and draw on the OCF library to make the application OLE-capable. This method, of course, requires a good knowledge of how ObjectComponents Framework works.

Probably the best way to create a container application with Turbo C++ 4.5—one that gives you a chance to learn how everything works without your having to dig too deeply into the complexities of OCF—is to create an OWL OLE container application. This is the method used for the OLECONT program shown in listings 28.5 and 28.6.

To compile this program, first create a new project (select the Project menu's New Project command) using the name OLECONT, being sure to select the OLE 2 and OCF options in the New Target dialog box (see fig. 28.6). Also, select the Large model. After creating the project, select the Project menu's Build All command to create the program's executable file.

Fig. 28.6
The New Target dialog box for an OLE application.

V

Tools and Techniques

Listing 28.5   OLECONT.CPP: An OLE Container Application

```cpp
/////////////////////////////////////////////////////////////
// OLECONT.CPP: Simple OLE container application.
/////////////////////////////////////////////////////////////

#include <owl/applicat.h>
#include <owl/dialog.h>
#include <owl/opensave.h>
#include <owl/controlb.h>
#include <owl/buttonga.h>
#include <owl/statusba.h>
#include <owl/oleframe.h>
#include <owl/olewindo.h>
#include <ocf/ocstorag.h>
#pragma hdrstop
#include "olecont.rc"

// Declare a registrar object.
static TPointer<TOcRegistrar> Registrar;

// Create the application dictionary.
DEFINE_APP_DICTIONARY(AppDictionary);

// Define a buffer for macro expansion.
REGISTRATION_FORMAT_BUFFER(100)

// Create the application's OLE registration structure.
BEGIN_REGISTRATION(AppReg)
    REGDATA(clsid, "{74EC6310-9D6E-101B-9CF6-04021C009402}")
    REGDATA(appname, "Ole Example App")
END_REGISTRATION

// Create the compound document's registration structure.
BEGIN_REGISTRATION(DocReg)
    REGDATA(progid, "OleContn")
    REGDATA(description, "Ole Document")
    REGFORMAT(0, ocrEmbedSource, ocrContent,
        ocrIStorage, ocrGet)
    REGFORMAT(1, ocrMetafilePict, ocrContent,
        ocrMfPict¦ocrStaticMed, ocrGet)
    REGFORMAT(2, ocrBitmap, ocrContent,
        ocrGDI¦ocrStaticMed, ocrGet)
    REGFORMAT(3, ocrDib, ocrContent,
        ocrHGlobal¦ocrStaticMed, ocrGet)
    REGFORMAT(4, ocrLinkSource, ocrContent,
        ocrIStream, ocrGet)
END_REGISTRATION

// Create Link list and add docReg to the list.
TRegLink* regLinkHead = 0;
TRegLink DocLink(DocReg, regLinkHead);

////////////////////////////////////
// The application class.
////////////////////////////////////
```

```
class TApp : public TApplication, public TOcModule
{
public:
    TApp();
    ~TApp();
    TUnknown* CreateOleObject(uint32, TRegLink*);

protected:
    void InitMainWindow();
    void InitInstance();
    void CmFileNew();
    void CmFileOpen();

    DECLARE_RESPONSE_TABLE(TApp);
};

DEFINE_RESPONSE_TABLE(TApp)
    EV_COMMAND(CM_FILENEW, CmFileNew),
    EV_COMMAND(CM_FILEOPEN, CmFileOpen),
END_RESPONSE_TABLE;

///////////////////////////////////
// The frame window class.
///////////////////////////////////
class TWndw : public TOleFrame
{
public:
    TWndw(const char far* title, TWindow* clientWnd,
        bool trackMenuSelection, TModule* module);
    ~TWndw();

protected:
    void CmHelpAbout();
    void CmCommandTest();

    DECLARE_RESPONSE_TABLE(TWndw);
};

DEFINE_RESPONSE_TABLE1(TWndw, TOleFrame)
    EV_COMMAND(CM_HELPABOUT, CmHelpAbout),
    EV_COMMAND(CM_COMMANDTEST, CmCommandTest),
END_RESPONSE_TABLE;

///////////////////////////////////
// Ole container window class.
///////////////////////////////////
class TOleWndw : public TOleWindow
{
protected:
    char fileName[128];
    BOOL gotNewFile;

public:
    TOleWndw(TWindow* parent, char far* fname);
    ~TOleWndw(){}
```

V

Tools and Techniques

(continues)

Listing 28.5 Continued

```
protected:
    void SetupWindow();
    void CmFileSave();
    void CmFileSaveAs();
    void OpenOleFile();
    void SaveOleFile(bool newPath);

    DECLARE_RESPONSE_TABLE(TOleWndw);
};

DEFINE_RESPONSE_TABLE1(TOleWndw, TOleWindow)
    EV_COMMAND(CM_FILESAVE, CmFileSave),
    EV_COMMAND(CM_FILESAVEAS, CmFileSaveAs),
END_RESPONSE_TABLE;

//----------------------------------------------------------
// TWndw's implementation.
//----------------------------------------------------------

////////////////////////////////////////////////////////////
// TWndw::TWndw()
////////////////////////////////////////////////////////////
TWndw::TWndw(const char far* title, TWindow* clientWnd,
    bool trackMenuSelection, TModule* module) :
    TOleFrame(title, clientWnd, trackMenuSelection, module)
{
    TButtonGadget* bg;
    TSeparatorGadget* sg;

    // Create the main menu's menu descriptor.
    TMenuDescr menuDescr(MENU_1);

    // Set the window's menu.
    SetMenuDescr(menuDescr);

    // Create the window's control bar.
    TControlBar* cb = new TControlBar(this);
    bg = new TButtonGadget(NEW_BITMAP, CM_FILENEW,
        TButtonGadget::Command);
    cb->Insert(*bg);
    bg = new TButtonGadget(OPEN_BITMAP, CM_FILEOPEN,
        TButtonGadget::Command);
    cb->Insert(*bg);
    bg = new TButtonGadget(SAVE_BITMAP, CM_FILESAVE,
        TButtonGadget::Command);
    cb->Insert(*bg);
    sg = new TSeparatorGadget;
    cb->Insert(*sg);
    bg = new TButtonGadget(COPY_BITMAP, CM_EDITCOPY,
        TButtonGadget::Command);
    cb->Insert(*bg);
    bg = new TButtonGadget(CUT_BITMAP, CM_EDITCUT,
        TButtonGadget::Command);
```

```
      cb->Insert(*bg);
      bg = new TButtonGadget(PASTE_BITMAP, CM_EDITPASTE,
         TButtonGadget::Command);
      cb->Insert(*bg);
      sg = new TSeparatorGadget;
      cb->Insert(*sg);
      bg = new TButtonGadget(EXIT_BITMAP, CM_EXIT,
         TButtonGadget::Command);
      cb->Insert(*bg);

      // Set the toolbar's ID so that ObjectComponents
      // can find and access it.
      cb->Attr.Id = IDW_TOOLBAR;

      // Add the toolbar to the window.
      Insert(*cb, TDecoratedFrame::Top);

      // Create the window's status bar.
      TStatusBar* sb =
         new TStatusBar(0, TGadget::Recessed,
         TStatusBar::CapsLock | TStatusBar::NumLock |
         TStatusBar::Overtype);

      // Add the status bar to the window.
      Insert(*sb, TDecoratedFrame::Bottom);
}

//////////////////////////////////////////////////////////
// TWndw::~TWndw()
//////////////////////////////////////////////////////////
TWndw::~TWndw()
{
}

//////////////////////////////////////////////////////////
// TWndw::CmHelpAbout()
//////////////////////////////////////////////////////////
void TWndw::CmHelpAbout()
{
    // Display the About dialog box.
    TDialog *dialog = new TDialog(this, DIALOG_1);
    dialog->Execute();
}

//////////////////////////////////////////////////////////
// TWndw::CmCommandTest()
//////////////////////////////////////////////////////////
void TWndw::CmCommandTest()
{
    MessageBox("CM_COMMANDTEST received!", "Command");
}

//--------------------------------------------------------
// TOleWndw's implementation.
//--------------------------------------------------------
```

(continues)

Listing 28.5 Continued

```
///////////////////////////////////////////////////////////
// TOleWndw::TOleWndw()
///////////////////////////////////////////////////////////
TOleWndw::TOleWndw(TWindow* parent, char far* fname) :
    TOleWindow(parent, 0)
{
    // Set new-file flag.
    gotNewFile = TRUE;

    // Initialize the window's file name.
    if (fname)
        strcpy(fileName, fname);
    else
        *fileName = 0;

    // Create an OLE document and view for the window.
    CreateOcView(regLinkHead, false, 0);
}

///////////////////////////////////////////////////////////
// TOleWndw::SetupWindow()
///////////////////////////////////////////////////////////
void TOleWndw::SetupWindow()
{
    // Call base class's SetupWindow().
    TOleWindow::SetupWindow();

    // If there's a file name...
    if (*fileName)
        // ...open the file...
        OpenOleFile();
    else
        // ...or else start an untitled document.
        SetDocTitle("Untitled", 0);
}

///////////////////////////////////////////////////////////
// TOleWndw::CmFileSave()
///////////////////////////////////////////////////////////
void TOleWndw::CmFileSave()
{
    // If the file has never been saved...
    if (gotNewFile)
        // ...do a Save As.
        CmFileSaveAs();
    else
        // ...or else do a normal save.
        SaveOleFile(false);
}

///////////////////////////////////////////////////////////
// TOleWndw::CmFileSaveAs()
///////////////////////////////////////////////////////////
```

```
void TOleWndw::CmFileSaveAs()
{
    // Create a TData object.
    TOpenSaveDialog::TData
        FileData(OFN_HIDEREADONLY¦OFN_FILEMUSTEXIST,
        "Sample Files (*.sam)¦*.sam¦",
        0, "", "sam");
    *FileData.FileName = 0;

    // Construct a File Save dialog box.
    TFileSaveDialog dialog(this, FileData);

    // Display the dialog box and get the user's response.
    int result = dialog.Execute();

    // If the user exited via the OK button, copy
    // the new file name and save the file.
    if ( result == IDOK)
    {
        strcpy(fileName, FileData.FileName);
        SaveOleFile(true);
    }
}

/////////////////////////////////////////////////////////////
// TOleWndw::SaveOleFile()
/////////////////////////////////////////////////////////////
void TOleWndw::SaveOleFile(bool newPath)
{
    // If this file has never been saved...
    if (newPath)
    {
        // Create a storage object and save OLE parts.
        OcDoc->SaveToFile(fileName);

        // Give the document its title and file name.
        SetDocTitle(fileName, 0);
        OcDoc->SetName(fileName);
    }
    else
        // Save linked and embedded objects.
        OcDoc->SaveParts(0, true);

    // Get a pointer to the document's storage object.
    TOcStorage* storage = OcDoc->GetStorage();

    // Create a stream for the storage object.
    TOcStream  stream(*storage, "Sample",
        STGM_SHARE_EXCLUSIVE¦STGM_READWRITE, true);

    // Commit the storage.
    storage->Commit(STGC_DEFAULT);

    // Turn off new-file flag.
    gotNewFile = false;
}
```

(continues)

Listing 28.5 Continued

```
/////////////////////////////////////////////////////////
// TOleWndw::OpenOleFile()
/////////////////////////////////////////////////////////
void TOleWndw::OpenOleFile()
{
    // Assign a storage to the document.
    OcDoc->SetStorage(fileName);

    // Get a pointer to the document's storage.
    TOcStorage* storage = OcDoc->GetStorage();

    // Assign a stream to the storage.
    TOcStream stream(*storage, "Sample",
        STGM_SHARE_EXCLUSIVE¦STGM_READWRITE, false);

    // Set the document's title.
    SetDocTitle(fileName, 0);

    // Load the OLE parts from the storage.
    OcDoc->LoadParts();

    // Update new-file flag and redraw the display.
    gotNewFile = false;
    Invalidate();
}

//-------------------------------------------------------
// TApp's implementation.
//-------------------------------------------------------

/////////////////////////////////////////////////////////
// TApp::TApp()
/////////////////////////////////////////////////////////
TApp::TApp() : TApplication(::AppReg["appname"])
{
}

/////////////////////////////////////////////////////////
// TApp::~TApp()
/////////////////////////////////////////////////////////
TApp::~TApp()
{
}

/////////////////////////////////////////////////////////
// TApp::InitMainWindow()
/////////////////////////////////////////////////////////
void TApp::InitMainWindow()
{
    // Create the application's frame window.
    TOleFrame* frame = new TWndw(GetName(), 0, true, this);
    SetMainWindow(frame);
}
```

```
////////////////////////////////////////////////////////
// TApp::InitInstance()
////////////////////////////////////////////////////////
void TApp::InitInstance()
{
    // Call the base class's InitInstance().
    TApplication::InitInstance();

    // Go create a new client window.
    CmFileNew();
}


////////////////////////////////////////////////////////
// TApp::CmFileNew()
////////////////////////////////////////////////////////
void TApp::CmFileNew()
{
    // Get a pointer to the frame window.
    TOleFrame* mainWindow =
        TYPESAFE_DOWNCAST(GetMainWindow(), TOleFrame);

    // Construct a new client window.
    TWindow* newClient = new TOleWndw(0, 0);

    // Give the frame window its new client window.
    TWindow* oldClient =
        mainWindow->SetClientWindow(newClient);

    // Delete the old client window, if it exists.
    if (oldClient)
    {
        oldClient->Destroy();
        delete oldClient;
    }
}


////////////////////////////////////////////////////////
// TApp::CmFileOpen()
////////////////////////////////////////////////////////
void TApp::CmFileOpen()
{
    // Construct a TData object.
    TOpenSaveDialog::TData
        fileData(OFN_HIDEREADONLY¦OFN_FILEMUSTEXIST,
        "Sample Files (*.sam)¦*.sam¦",
        0, "", "sam");

    // Get a pointer to the frame window.
    TOleFrame* mainWindow =
        TYPESAFE_DOWNCAST(GetMainWindow(), TOleFrame);

    // Construct a File Open dialog box.
    TFileOpenDialog dialog(mainWindow, fileData);
```

(continues)

Tools and Techniques

V

Listing 28.5   Continued

```
                 // Display the File Open dialog box.
                 int result = dialog.Execute();

                 // If the user selects the OK button....
                 if (result == IDOK)
                 {
                     // Create a new client window.
                     TWindow* newClient =
                         new TOleWndw(0, fileData.FileName);

                     // Give the frame window the new client window.
                     TWindow* oldClient =
                         mainWindow->SetClientWindow(newClient);

                     // Delete the old client window.
                     if (oldClient)
                     {
                         oldClient->Destroy();
                         delete oldClient;
                     }
                 }
        }

        ////////////////////////////////////////////////////////
        // TApp::CreateOleObject()
        ////////////////////////////////////////////////////////
        TUnknown* TApp::CreateOleObject(uint32, TRegLink*)
        {
            return 0;
        }

        ////////////////////////////////////////////////////////
        // OwlMain()
        ////////////////////////////////////////////////////////
        int OwlMain(int, char*[])
        {
            Registrar = new TOcRegistrar(AppReg,
                TOleFactory<TApp>(), TApplication::GetCmdLine());
            return Registrar->Run();
        }
```

Listing 28.6   OLECONT.RC: OLECONT's Resource File

```
////////////////////////////////////////////////////////
// OLECONT.RC
////////////////////////////////////////////////////////

#ifndef WORKSHOP_INVOKED
#include <windows.h>
#endif
```

```
#include <owl\editfile.rh>

#define MENU_1          100
#define DIALOG_1        100
#define CM_COMMANDTEST  101
#define CM_HELPABOUT    102
#define NEW_BITMAP      101
#define OPEN_BITMAP     102
#define SAVE_BITMAP     103
#define EXIT_BITMAP     104
#define CUT_BITMAP      105
#define COPY_BITMAP     106
#define PASTE_BITMAP    107


#ifdef RC_INVOKED

#include <owl/except.rc>
#include <owl/oleview.rc>

MENU_1 MENU
{
  POPUP "&File"
  {
    MENUITEM "&New", CM_FILENEW
    MENUITEM "&Open", CM_FILEOPEN
    MENUITEM "&Save", CM_FILESAVE
    MENUITEM "Save &As", CM_FILESAVEAS
    MENUITEM SEPARATOR
    MENUITEM "E&xit", CM_EXIT
  }

  MENUITEM SEPARATOR
  POPUP "&Edit"
  {
    MenuItem   "&Cut", CM_EDITCUT
    MenuItem   "C&opy", CM_EDITCOPY
    MenuItem   "&Paste", CM_EDITPASTE
    MenuItem   "Paste &Special...", CM_EDITPASTESPECIAL
    MenuItem   "Paste &Link", CM_EDITPASTELINK
    MenuItem   "&Delete", CM_EDITDELETE
    MenuItem   Separator
    MenuItem   "Insert &New Object...", CM_EDITINSERTOBJECT
    MenuItem   "&Links...", CM_EDITLINKS
    MenuItem   "&Object", CM_EDITOBJECT
  }

  MENUITEM SEPARATOR
  POPUP "&Commands"
  {
   MENUITEM "&Test Command...", CM_COMMANDTEST
  }

  MENUITEM SEPARATOR
  MENUITEM SEPARATOR
  MENUITEM SEPARATOR
  POPUP "&Help"
```

(continues)

V

Tools and Techniques

Listing 28.6 Continued

```
  {
   MENUITEM "&About...", CM_HELPABOUT
  }
 }

 DIALOG_1 DIALOG 75, 61, 143, 111
 STYLE DS_MODALFRAME ¦ WS_POPUP ¦ WS_VISIBLE ¦
     WS_CAPTION ¦ WS_SYSMENU
 CAPTION "About"
 FONT 8, "MS Sans Serif"
 {
  DEFPUSHBUTTON "OK", IDOK, 46, 84, 50, 14
  LTEXT "OLE CONTAINER EXAMPLE", -1, 16, 13, 103, 8
  LTEXT "by Clayton Walnum", -1, 23, 26, 87, 8
  LTEXT "Copyright (c) 1995", -1, 16, 47, 60, 8
  LTEXT "by Macmillan Computer Publishing",
      -1, 16, 59, 115, 8
 }

 STRINGTABLE LOADONCALL MOVEABLE DISCARDABLE
 {
   CM_EXIT, "Quits the application"
   CM_HELPABOUT, "Displays application information"
   CM_COMMANDTEST, "Sends a test command to the application"
 }

 NEW_BITMAP BITMAP "c:\tcwin45\expert\owl\new.bmp"
 OPEN_BITMAP BITMAP "c:\tcwin45\expert\owl\open.bmp"
 SAVE_BITMAP BITMAP "c:\tcwin45\expert\owl\save.bmp"
 COPY_BITMAP BITMAP "c:\tcwin45\expert\owl\copy.bmp"
 CUT_BITMAP BITMAP "c:\tcwin45\expert\owl\cut.bmp"
 PASTE_BITMAP BITMAP "c:\tcwin45\expert\owl\paste.bmp"
 EXIT_BITMAP BITMAP "exit.bmp"

 #endif
```

Running the OLECONT Application

When you run the OLECONT application, you see the window shown in figure 28.7. The application features commands for opening, saving, and editing documents. When the application begins, you can see by the title bar that the current document is called Untitled. The document receives its real title when you load a document from disk or when you use the Save As command (either from the File menu or from the toolbar).

You have to create a document before you can save or load one, of course. To do so, choose the Edit menu's Insert New Object command and add some text from an OLE-capable text editor. Suppose that you have Word for Windows 6.0 on your system. (Word for Windows 6.0 was used for the examples in this chapter.) Then, the object type Microsoft Word 6.0 Document will be in the Object Type list box. Selecting this type of object will cause Word for Windows to create a new document object for your container application. Because it supports *in-place editing* of objects, Word for Windows merges its menus with those of the container application. Moreover, Word for Windows also places its own tool bars in the container application's window, making the application look more like Word for Windows (see fig. 28.8) than the simple application you started out with.

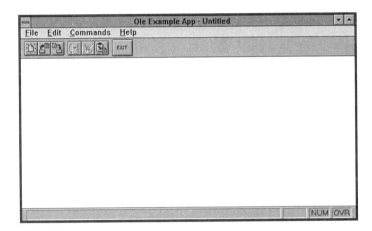

Fig. 28.7
The OLECONT application.

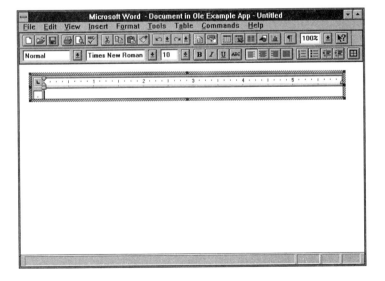

Fig. 28.8
The container application after you create a new Word for Windows document object.

V

Tools and Techniques

> **Note**
>
> If you had inserted a Windows Paintbrush object instead, the Paintbrush application would appear on top of the container window, because Paintbrush doesn't support in-place editing of its objects. Instead, Paintbrush must run, transfer the object to its own window, let the user edit the object in its window, and then transfer the edited data back to the container application.

Continuing with the Word for Windows example, once the new document object appears, you can type and edit text almost exactly as though you were working with Word for Windows itself (see fig. 28.9). After the document object is created, clicking outside the object's borders embeds the object and removes Word for Windows' controls from the container application (see fig. 28.10).

Fig. 28.9
Editing the
new Word
for Windows
document object.

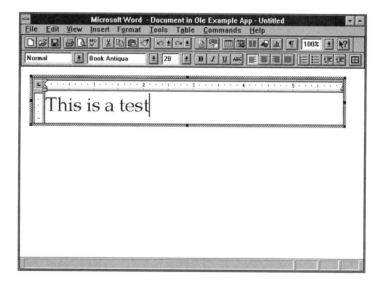

After embedding the Word for Windows document object, you can still edit it at any time just by double-clicking it, which again calls up Word for Windows' menus and toolbars. Also, when you select the object by clicking it once, an outline appears around the object. What's more, the container application's Object command (on the Edit menu) changes to Document Object and provides access to a submenu that displays the selected object's verbs (see fig. 28.11). Object *verbs* are commands that can be applied to the selected object.

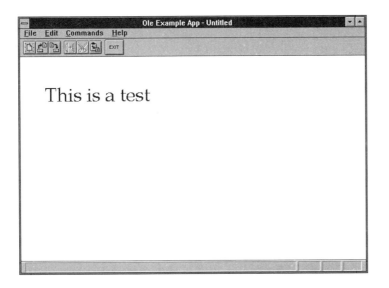

Fig. 28.10
The embedded Word for Windows document object.

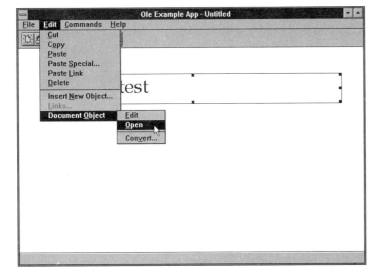

Fig. 28.11
Selecting the object and accessing its verbs.

In the case of the Word for Windows document object, the Edit verb acts just as though you had double-clicked the object, causing Word for Windows to display its menus and toolbars and enabling the user to edit the object in-place. The Open verb actually runs Word for Windows as a separate application and loads the object into the window for editing. The standard Convert selection allows the user to convert some types of objects to others. In the case of Word for Windows (on the system used to run this simple container application), no conversions are available, as shown in figure 28.12, which shows the Convert dialog box. You could, however, select the Display as Icon check box, and thus have the object appear in the container window as an icon rather than as the full document object (see fig. 28.13).

Fig. 28.12
The Convert dialog box.

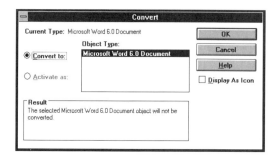

Fig. 28.13
The Word for Windows document object displayed as an icon.

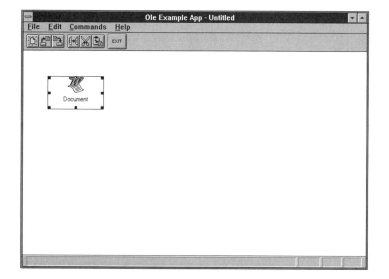

After you add your text object, choose Insert New Object again and add a Windows Paintbrush Picture object. After adding the picture object, move the object so that you can see the text and the picture, as shown in figure 28.14.

Now, to give your new compound document a name, as well as save it to disk, choose the File menu's Save As command (or the toolbar's Save button). The Save As dialog box appears, which lets you give the file a name. Note that the suggested extension for files created with this sample application is SAM. Save the file under the name TEST.SAM. When you do, the application stores the compound document on disk and displays the document's new name in the title bar (see fig. 28.15).

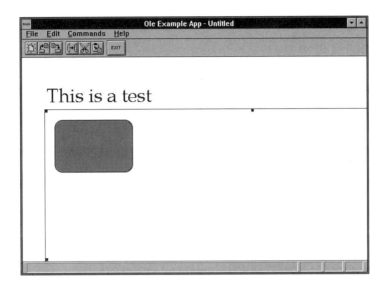

Fig. 28.14
The OLECONT
application
containing two
OLE objects.

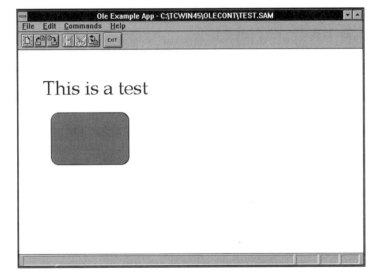

Fig. 28.15
The OLECONT
application, after
the document is
saved.

V

Tools and Techniques

Next, choose <u>N</u>ew from either the <u>F</u>ile menu or the toolbar. The application
closes the TEST.SAM document and presents you with another Untitled document. Finally, to prove that your TEST.SAM compound document was saved
correctly, choose the <u>F</u>ile menu's <u>O</u>pen command (or the toolbar's Open
button) and select the TEST.SAM file from the dialog box that appears. The
application loads the TEST.SAM document and displays its name in the
window's title bar.

OLE compound documents are stored in a special format, using what Microsoft calls the *Structured Storage Model*. When you save data under the Structured Storage Model, the file you create isn't unlike a minidisk with its own directories, nested directories, and files. By using such a storage format, your OLE applications can store and retrieve not only all the OLE objects (embedded and linked) that make up a compound document, but also any native data in your document.

Programming the OLECONT Application

Now that you have some idea of what a container application can do, you'd probably like to know how all this magic works. At the top of listing 28.5, you see the following lines:

```
#include <owl/applicat.h>
#include <owl/dialog.h>
#include <owl/opensave.h>
#include <owl/controlb.h>
#include <owl/buttonga.h>
#include <owl/statusba.h>
#include <owl/oleframe.h>
#include <owl/olewindo.h>
#include <ocf/ocstorag.h>
#pragma hdrstop
#include "olecont.rc"
```

These lines bring into the program the header files for the classes the program uses. If you've done any OWL programming, you should already be familiar with the header files APPLICAT.H, DIALOG.H, STATUSBA.H, CONTROLB.H, OPENSAVE.H, and BUTTONGA.H. They're the header files for the OWL classes TApplication, TDialog, TStatusBar, TControlBar, TOpenSaveDialog, and TButtonGadget, respectively.

The header files OLEFRAME.H and OLEWINDO.H are new to you. These are the OWL OLE classes that the OLECONT application uses directly. OLEFRAME.H declares the TOleFrame class, which represents a frame window in an OWL OLE application. OLEWINDO.H declares the TOleWindow class, which represents the client window of an OWL OLE application. Finally, OCSTORAG.H is the header file for the TOcStorage and TOcStream classes, which handle loading and saving files.

Following the program's include files, you see the following mysterious lines:

```
static TPointer<TOcRegistrar> Registrar;
DEFINE_APP_DICTIONARY(AppDictionary);
```

The first of these lines declares a registrar object, which every OLE application needs in order to handle OLE registration tasks. By using the TPointer<TOcRegistrar> template, you declare a pointer that's automatically deleted when the program shuts down. The actual registrar object will be created in the program's OwlMain() function. The second line is a macro call that creates the program's application dictionary. Turbo C++ OLE programs use an application dictionary to keep track of any client applications now using the program as an OLE server. But you don't need to understand all the details; just copy these two lines verbatim into your OLE programs.

Next, OLECONT creates the application's TRegList structure, which contains information about how to register an OLE application with the system. Every OLE application must perform this registration so that Windows knows how to refer to the application, what OLE functionality it supports, and myriad other data too complex to examine here. (Actually, according to Microsoft's OLE 2.0 guidelines, only servers and containers that allow linking to embedded objects must register themselves in the system registry, but OCF, through the TOcApp object, seems to register all types of OLE applications.)

Because creating a TRegList is a meticulous task, Turbo C++ supplies macros you can use to set up this structure more easily. Listing 28.5 creates its TRegList with the following lines:

```
REGISTRATION_FORMAT_BUFFER(100)

BEGIN_REGISTRATION(AppReg)
    REGDATA(clsid, "{74EC6310-9D6E-101B-9CF6-04021C009402}")
    REGDATA(appname, "Ole Example App")
END_REGISTRATION
```

The uppercase items are the macros needed to create the registration structure. The REGISTRATION_FORMAT_BUFFER macro creates a buffer needed to expand other macros in the table. The BEGIN_REGISTRATION macro begins the table that builds the TRegList structure. Its single parameter is the name of the application's registration list, which is usually AppReg. The REGDATA macros place values into the registration structure. This macro's two parameters are a key and the value for the key. For a simple container application, the only two keys you usually need to define are clsid and appname.

> **Tip**
> Refer to your Turbo C++ 4.5 documentation for other macros you can use to create a TRegList structure.

The application's clsid is a unique number that identifies the application. No two applications can have the same clsid, so it's imperative that you acquire your application's clsid properly. Never use a clsid from another program! One way to acquire a clsid is to contact Microsoft, who will be happy to assign to you a whole block of server IDs that you can use for your OLE applications.

An easier way to obtain a `clsid`, though, is to use Turbo C++'s AppExpert. To do this, first select AppExpert from the IDE's Project menu. When the New AppExpert Project dialog box appears, give the project a name and click OK. When the AppExpert Application Generation Options dialog box appears, open the Applications topic and select OLE 2 Options. The dialog box then displays a new server ID (see fig. 28.16). Copy the ID, and then choose Cancel to avoid creating the project. (Or you can choose Generate to create the application, in which case there's no need to copy the server ID.)

Fig. 28.16
Getting an OLE
server ID.

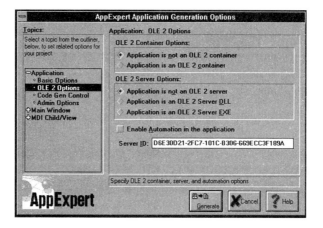

Finally, `appname` is another string, which can be up to 40 characters long. This string appears in the application's title bar and is usually the application's complete name.

The `END_REGISTRATION` macro ends the registration table. For more information on the registration list and its various keys, consult your Turbo C++ 4.5 documentation.

> **Note**
>
> The `REGISTRATION_FORMAT_BUFFER` macro's single argument is the size of the buffer to create. To calculate how big the buffer should be, provide 10 bytes for each `REGFORMAT` item, and then add in the sizes of any string parameters used with the `REGSTATUS`, `REGVERBOPT`, `REGICON`, and `REGFORMAT` macros. Consult your Turbo C++ documentation for more information on these macros.

Next, the application defines its `DocReg` structure:

```
BEGIN_REGISTRATION(DocReg)
    REGDATA(progid, "OleContn")
    REGDATA(description, "Ole Document")
    REGFORMAT(0, ocrEmbedSource, ocrContent,
        ocrIStorage, ocrGet)
    REGFORMAT(1, ocrMetafilePict, ocrContent,
        ocrMfPict¦ocrStaticMed, ocrGet)
    REGFORMAT(2, ocrBitmap, ocrContent,
        ocrGDI¦ocrStaticMed, ocrGet)
    REGFORMAT(3, ocrDib, ocrContent,
        ocrHGlobal¦ocrStaticMed, ocrGet)
    REGFORMAT(4, ocrLinkSource, ocrContent,
        ocrIStream, ocrGet)
END_REGISTRATION
```

Your OLE container application must have such a registration structure for its compound document. In the preceding macro table, the progid and description keys provide the same type of information they do in the application's registration structure. The REGFORMAT macro, however, is new to you. This macro lets you register the types of data that the document can exchange with the clipboard. The ocrEmbedSource, ocrMetafilePict, ocrBitmap, ocrDib, and ocrLinkSource are standard OLE formats. Refer to your Turbo C++ 4.5 documentation for more information on the many values that can be used in the registration structures.

The document's registration structure also requires a clsid, but this value is supplied automatically by OCF. OCF calculates this ID by incrementing the low-order field of the application's clsid. Therefore, be sure to allow for this calculation when determining the next clsid for an application.

Besides defining the DocReg structure, you must add the document structure to the application's document list, as follows:

```
TRegLink* RegLinkHead = 0;
TRegLink DocLink(DocReg, RegLinkHead);
```

Here, a pointer to the head of the list is defined and set to NULL. Then, the list is created by calling the TRegLink class's constructor, passing a reference to the DocReg structure and the pointer to the list.

Declaring the Application Class

Next in listing 28.5 is the application class's declaration:

```
class TApp : public TApplication, public TOcModule
{
public:
    TApp();
    ~TApp();
    TUnknown* CreateOleObject(uint32, TRegLink*);
```

V

Tools and Techniques

```
protected:
    void InitMainWindow();
    void InitInstance();
    void CmFileNew();
    void CmFileOpen();

    DECLARE_RESPONSE_TABLE(TApp);
};

DEFINE_RESPONSE_TABLE(TApp)
    EV_COMMAND(CM_FILENEW, CmFileNew),
    EV_COMMAND(CM_FILEOPEN, CmFileOpen),
END_RESPONSE_TABLE;
```

This application class looks like application classes you've used in other OWL programs. The most important difference is that you derive the class from the TApplication and TOcModule classes. The class must also provide the CreateOleObject() member function, as shown in the preceding code. This function, which is responsible for creating a server document, plays a more important role in server applications. In a container application, CreateOleObject() can simply return a zero.

Besides the CreateOleObject() member function, your application class should provide a constructor and destructor, as well as override the InitMainWindow() and InitInstance() member functions. The constructor can do as little as just call the TApplication constructor, as follows:

```
TApp::TApp() : TApplication(AppReg["appname"])
{
}
```

Notice the reference to AppReg in the constructor's parameter. This is a reference to the application's TRegList structure. The square brackets are an operator defined by the TRegList class. By using these brackets, you can access the value of a particular key. Therefore, the call to TApplication's constructor has as its single parameter the string assigned to the registration structure's appname key, which is the application's name.

Now look at the application class's InitMainWindow() function:

```
void TApp::InitMainWindow()
{
    TOleFrame* frame = new TWndw(GetName(), 0, true, this);
    SetMainWindow(frame);
}
```

Here, the application creates its frame window, which must be derived or instantiated from the TOleFrame OWL window class for OLE applications. In an OWL OLE application, you use the TOleFrame class wherever you would use the TFrameWindow class in a conventional OWL program. The TOleFrame class provides default handlers for a number of OLE-related messages, enabling, for example, the merging of menu bars and tool bars with the frame window, and displaying status messages from the server in the application's status bar.

The `TOleFrame` constructor requires as arguments the window's title, a pointer to its client window (which, at this point, should be 0), a Boolean value indicating whether the frame window should shrink to exactly fit around its client window (usually `TRUE`), and a pointer to a `TModule` object.

After constructing its main window, `InitMainWindow()` calls `SetMainWindow()` to give the application a pointer to its main window.

The last initialization the application object requires happens in its overridden `InitInstance()` function:

```
void TApp::InitInstance()
{
    // Call the base class's InitInstance().
    TApplication::InitInstance();

    // Go create a new client window.
    CmFileNew();
}
```

Here, the program first calls the base class's `InitInstance()` function, after which it constructs the frame window's client window by calling the message-response function `CmFileNew()`, which looks like this:

```
void TApp::CmFileNew()
{
    TOleFrame* mainWindow =
        TYPESAFE_DOWNCAST(GetMainWindow(), TOleFrame);

    TWindow* newClient = new TOleWndw(0, 0);

    TWindow* oldClient =
        mainWindow->SetClientWindow(newClient);

    if (oldClient)
    {
        oldClient->Destroy();
        delete oldClient;
    }
}
```

This function first gets a pointer to the application's frame window. It then constructs a new `TOleWindow` for the new document. This window must be derived or instantiated from the OWL `TOleWindow` class, which not only provides an OWL OLE application with the capability to handle OLE objects within its documents, but also supplies command enabling for menus, various editing services (cut, copy, paste, and so on) for OLE objects, the selection and activation of embedded and linked objects, and more.

Next, the program gives the new window to the frame window by calling the frame window's `SetClientWindow()` member function through the pointer. Because the call to `SetClientWindow()` returns a pointer to the old client window (if one exists), the function checks that return value. If the pointer isn't null, the program destroys and deletes the old client window.

Declaring the Frame Window Class

Now, look at the frame window class's declaration:

```
class TWndw : public TOleFrame
{
public:
    TWndw(const char far* title, TWindow* clientWnd,
        bool trackMenuSelection, TModule* module);
    ~TWndw();

protected:
    void CmHelpAbout();
    void CmCommandTest();

    DECLARE_RESPONSE_TABLE(TWndw);
};

DEFINE_RESPONSE_TABLE1(TWndw, TOleFrame)
    EV_COMMAND(CM_HELPABOUT, CmHelpAbout),
    EV_COMMAND(CM_COMMANDTEST, CmCommandTest),
END_RESPONSE_TABLE;
```

This class, which is derived from OWL's `TOleFrame` class, contains a constructor, a destructor, and two message-response functions. In the frame window's constructor, you supply your OLE application with its toolbar and status bar (`TOleFrame` windows are actually decorated windows derived from `TDecoratedFrame`), as well as a menu descriptor.

In its constructor, the OLECONT program first creates and sets the window's menu:

```
TMenuDescr menuDescr(MENU_1);
SetMenuDescr(menuDescr);
```

Notice that the program doesn't use the usual `AssignMenu()` OWL function to give the window its menu. This is because OLE applications must be able to merge their menus with those of other OLE applications; thus, menu descriptors must be created from specially built menu resources. Later, you'll see how you must create these special menu resources. In the preceding example, the program first creates a `TMenuDescr` object from the menu resource whose

ID is MENU_1. It then gives the window the menu by calling the member function SetMenuDescr(), whose single argument (in this case) is a TMenuDescr object.

Next, the program creates the window's toolbar and inserts a various buttons in the toolbar:

```
TControlBar* cb = new TControlBar(this);
bg = new TButtonGadget(NEW_BITMAP, CM_FILENEW,
    TButtonGadget::Command);
cb->Insert(*bg);
bg = new TButtonGadget(OPEN_BITMAP, CM_FILEOPEN,
    TButtonGadget::Command);
cb->Insert(*bg);
bg = new TButtonGadget(SAVE_BITMAP, CM_FILESAVE,
    TButtonGadget::Command);
cb->Insert(*bg);
sg = new TSeparatorGadget;
cb->Insert(*sg);
bg = new TButtonGadget(COPY_BITMAP, CM_EDITCOPY,
    TButtonGadget::Command);
cb->Insert(*bg);
bg = new TButtonGadget(CUT_BITMAP, CM_EDITCUT,
    TButtonGadget::Command);
cb->Insert(*bg);
bg = new TButtonGadget(PASTE_BITMAP, CM_EDITPASTE,
    TButtonGadget::Command);
cb->Insert(*bg);
sg = new TSeparatorGadget;
cb->Insert(*sg);
bg = new TButtonGadget(EXIT_BITMAP, CM_EXIT,
    TButtonGadget::Command);
cb->Insert(*bg);
```

The program next assigns the window ID IDW_TOOLBAR to the toolbar:

```
cb->Attr.Id = IDW_TOOLBAR;
```

Every OWL OLE application with a toolbar must assign the toolbar an ID of IDW_TOOLBAR. Failure to do this will leave OWL unable to find the toolbar during in-place activation of an OLE object. If OWL can't find your toolbar during in-place activation of an OLE object, it can't remove it to make room for the server application's toolbar.

After the toolbar is constructed and given its ID, the program finally inserts the toolbar in the window:

```
Insert(*cb, TDecoratedFrame::Top);
```

The frame-window constructor's final task is to create and insert the application's status bar, as follows:

```
TStatusBar* sb =
    new TStatusBar(0, TGadget::Recessed,
    TStatusBar::CapsLock ¦ TStatusBar::NumLock ¦
    TStatusBar::Overtype);
Insert(*sb, TDecoratedFrame::Bottom);
```

Unlike the window's toolbar, you don't have to do anything special to get a working status bar in an OWL OLE container application. OWL takes care of all the details for you.

The remaining functions in the TWndw class respond to the CM_HELPABOUT and CM_COMMANDTEST messages. If you're familiar with OWL programming, these functions require no further explanation. If you don't know about OWL programming, read Chapter 27, "The ObjectWindows Library," as well as the first section of this chapter, which describes how to write basic ObjectWindows programs.

Declaring the Client Window Class

Turn your attention now to the client-window class, which, in an OWL OLE application, is derived from the TOleWindow class. Here's the class's declaration:

```
class TOleWndw : public TOleWindow
{
protected:
    char fileName[128];
    BOOL gotNewFile;

public:
    TOleWndw(TWindow* parent, char far* fname);
    ~TOleWndw(){}

protected:
    void SetupWindow();
    void CmFileSave();
    void CmFileSaveAs();
    void OpenOleFile();
    void SaveOleFile(bool newPath);

    DECLARE_RESPONSE_TABLE(TOleWndw);
};

DEFINE_RESPONSE_TABLE1(TOleWndw, TOleWindow)
    EV_COMMAND(CM_FILESAVE, CmFileSave),
    EV_COMMAND(CM_FILESAVEAS, CmFileSaveAs),
END_RESPONSE_TABLE;
```

This class has the usual constructor and destructor, as well as a number of additional member functions. Also, the class overrides the SetupWindow() member function.

As mentioned earlier, you derive the client window in an OWL OLE application from the `TOleWindow` class. The `TOleWindow` class is itself derived from the general `TWindow` class but adds the extra functionality required for an OLE application. The client-window class's constructor has an important task it must complete, which is to create the window's document and view objects:

```
CreateOcView(regLinkHead, false, 0);
```

The call to `CreateOcView()` has as arguments a pointer to the application's document list, a Boolean value indicating whether the view is a remote view (an embedded object), and a pointer to an `IUnknown` object. The `TOleWindow` class has two protected data members called `OcDoc` and `OcView`, which are pointers to the window's `TOcDocument` and `TOcView` objects. The `TOcDocument` class represents the window's compound document, which, if you recall, is a document that comprises embedded or linked OLE objects. The `TOcView` class, on the other hand, is responsible for displaying each embedded or linked object in a compound document.

The `TOleWindow` class also maintains a pointer to the application's `TOcApp` object. The class's `Init()` member function, which is called by its constructor, takes care of initializing this pointer. For this reason, you must never create the client window before you create the frame window. It's from the frame window that `Init()` extracts the `TOcApp` pointer.

Listing 28.5's `TOleWndw` class also overrides the `SetupWindow()` function:

```
void TOleWndw::SetupWindow()
{
    // Call base class's SetupWindow().
    TOleWindow::SetupWindow();

    // If there's a file name...
    if (*fileName)
        // ...open the file...
        OpenOleFile();
    else
        // ...or else start an untitled document.
        SetDocTitle("Untitled", 0);
}
```

After calling the base class's `SetupWindow()`, this function opens a file if necessary and sets the title of the new OLE document. If the new window doesn't load a file, the program sets the document title to Untitled by calling the class's `SetDocTitle()` function. The `SetDocTitle()` function's first argument is the document's title. The second argument is a document-title index, which you can usually leave at 0.

V

Tools and Techniques

Handling the Save or Save As Command

In the OLECONT application, the OLE container window is responsible for responding to all Save commands. If the user is saving a file for the first time, the Save As dialog box appears, whether or not the user actually chose the Save or Save As command.

Programming the common dialog boxes in Windows can be a little tricky if you've never done it before. The first step toward using the Save As or Open dialog boxes is to include the header file OPENSAVE.H in the program's source code:

```
#include <owl\opensave.h>
```

This header file declares the TOpenSaveDialog class, as well as the TFileOpenDialog and TFileSaveDialog classes, which are derived from TOpenSaveDialog. You don't need to include a special resource file for a Windows common dialog box. Those resources are part of COMMDLG.DLL, a dialog box library shipped with Windows.

To prepare to display the Save As dialog box, construct a TOpenSaveDialog::TData object, as follows:

```
TOpenSaveDialog::TData fileData(
    OFN_HIDEREADONLY ¦ OFN_OVERWRITEPROMPT,
    "Sample Files (*.SAM)¦*.sam¦All Files (*.*)¦*.*¦",
    0, 0, "*");
```

TOpenSaveDialog's version of TData has a constructor that requires five arguments. The first is a set of flags that determine how the dialog box looks and acts. Table 28.2 lists the constants that represent these flag values. To create the type of Save As dialog box you want, you OR together the appropriate flags.

Table 28.2 TOpenSaveDialog::TData Flag Constants	
Name	**Description**
OFN_ALLOWMULTISELECT	Allows multiple file selections.
OFN_CREATEPROMPT	Asks whether the user wants to create the file if it doesn't exist.
OFN_EXTENSIONDIFFERENT	Notifies the caller that the selected file has a different extension from the default.
OFN_FILEMUSTEXIST	Disallows the selection of nonexistent files.
OFN_HIDEREADONLY	Prevents the read-only check box from being displayed.

Name	Description
OFN_NOVALIDATE	Doesn't validate a selected file name.
OFN_NOCHANGEDIR	Resets the directory to the current directory at the time the dialog box started.
OFN_NOREADONLYRETURN	Notifies the caller when the selected file isn't read-only and isn't write-protected.
OFN_NOTESTFILECREATE	Forces file creation without first checking for such errors as a full or inaccessible disk.
OFN_OVERWRITEPROMPT	Prompts the user for permission to overwrite an existing file.
OFN_SHAREAWARE	Returns the selected file name, even if a file-sharing conflict exists.
OFN_SHOWHELP	Shows the dialog box's Help button.

The second argument in TOpenSaveDialog::TData's constructor is the list of
file filters that should appear in the dialog box's file filters list box. You can
include as many filters as you need, but each entry must be in the following
form:

```
text¦filter¦
```

in which text is the file filter description that appears in the list box and
filter is the actual DOS filter.

The third argument in TOpenSaveDialog::TData's constructor allows you to
add a pointer to a buffer for storing user-entered custom filters. You almost
always set this buffer to 0 (NULL). The fourth argument is the initial directory
to which the dialog box will open. For the current directory, set this argument to 0. Finally, the fifth argument is the extension that will be added to
any file name the user enters (without a file extension).

After constructing the TData object, the CmFileSaveAs() function sets the
TData object's FileName field to null:

```
*fileData.FileName = 0;
```

When the user closes the Save As dialog box, the file name he or she chose
will be stored in the FileName field.

After constructing a TData object, you construct the Save As dialog box by
calling the TFileSaveDialog class's constructor, which requires as arguments a
pointer to the dialog box's parent window and a reference to the dialog box's
TData object:

V

Tools and Techniques

```
TFileSaveDialog saveDialog(this, fileData);
```

A call to the dialog box's `Execute()` member function then brings up the dialog box and allows the user to use its controls to select a file:

```
int result = saveDialog.Execute();
```

The user can exit the Save As dialog box by choosing either OK or Cancel. By exiting with the OK button, the user has selected a file to save; the file's name is stored in the `TData.FileName` member, where it's easily accessed.

Saving an OLE File

Whether the user is saving a file for the first time or only saving changes to a previously stored file, it's the `TOleWndw` class's `SaveOleFile()` function that does the dirty work. The `SaveOleFile()` function's single parameter, `newPath`, is a Boolean value indicating whether the file is being saved under a new file name or an old one. If the file is getting a new file name, `SaveOleFile()` first calls the `TDocument` object's `SaveToFile()` member function:

```
OcDoc->SaveToFile(fileName);
```

This function call creates the document's storage object and saves any embedded or linked objects to that storage. The single argument is the document's new file name (including the path).

After saving the document to its storage, the program sets the document's title and file name by calling the window's `SetDocTitle()` function and the document's `SetName()` function:

```
SetDocTitle(fileName, 0);
OcDoc->SetName(fileName);
```

If the document has been previously saved, `SaveOleFile()` doesn't need to create the document's storage and set its title and file name. It only needs to call the document object's `SaveParts()` function, to save any embedded or linked objects:

```
OcDoc->SaveParts(0, TRUE);
```

`SaveParts()` requires as arguments a pointer to the document's storage (because the document already has its storage, use 0) and a Boolean value indicating whether the document's file name has changed (`FALSE`) or is the same (`TRUE`).

Whether the file name is new or not, the program finalizes the save by *committing* the changes. This is done by getting a pointer to the document's storage object, creating a `TOcStream` object for the storage, and then calling the storage object's `Commit()` member function. The following code fragment shows this process:

```
TOcStorage* storage = OcDoc->GetStorage();
TOcStream  stream(*storage, "Sample",
    STGM_SHARE_EXCLUSIVE¦STGM_READWRITE, true);
storage->Commit(STGC_DEFAULT);
```

The flags used with the `Commit()` function can be `STGC_DEFAULT` (the most commonly used), `STGC_OVERWRITE` (allows new data to overwrite old data), `STGC_ONLYIFCURRENT` (protects changes made to a file by multiple users), and `STGC_DANGEROUSLYCOMMITMERELYTODISKCACHE` (commits changes, but doesn't save those changes to the disk cache). If the descriptions of these constants boggle your mind, just stick with `STGC_DEFAULT`—or buy a copy of Microsoft's *OLE Programmer's Reference*, Volume 1, and prepare to be further boggled.

Handling the Open Command

In the OLECONT application, the application object handles the opening of existing files and the creation of new ones. In the case of opening files, the `CmFileOpen()` message-response function springs into action, while `CmFileNew()` handles the creation of new files.

In the case of opening an existing file, though, it's the client window's `OpenOleFile()` function that actually opens the file and reads in the data. That function looks like this:

```
void TOleWndw::OpenOleFile()
{
    // Assign a storage to the document.
    OcDoc->SetStorage(fileName);

    // Get a pointer to the document's storage.
    TOcStorage* storage = OcDoc->GetStorage();

    // Assign a stream to the storage.
    TOcStream stream(*storage, "Sample",
        STGM_SHARE_EXCLUSIVE¦STGM_READWRITE, false);

    // Set the document's title.
    SetDocTitle(fileName, 0);

    // Load the OLE parts from the storage.
    OcDoc->LoadParts();

    // Update new-file flag and redraw the display.
    gotNewFile = false;
    Invalidate();
}
```

This function first calls the document object's `SetStorage()` member function to set up the document's storage. Next, the program calls `GetStorage()` to obtain a pointer to the document's storage, after which the program constructs a TOcStream object. Finally, a call to `SetDocTitle()` sets the window's title and a call to `LoadParts()` loads any embedded or linked objects in the file.

Dealing with Dynamic Menus

As you saw when you ran the OLECONT application, a server application often merges its menus and toolbars with those of the container application. When you use OWL to create your OLE container application, you can pass the buck on handling the toolbar by simply giving the toolbar the `IDW_TOOLBAR` window ID. OLE menus, however, are a little more complex. To get a better understanding of what goes on with OLE menus, you should know about something called dynamic menus.

Sophisticated Windows applications often allow the user to perform many types of tasks. In fact, if the application is large enough, it may end up having overly long and complicated menus. To avoid this problem, you can create *dynamic menus* that change their contents according to the user's current needs. For example, an application that has yet to open a window may have only the File and Help menus. When the user opens a document window, the menu bar can expand to incorporate the commands the user now needs to manipulate the window and its data. OWL's dynamic menus are the basis of OLE menus, which allow server applications to merge their menus with those of the container application.

To create dynamic menus, you have to think of each pop-up menu as belonging in one of six groups: File, Edit, Container, Object, Window, and Help. (These groups are very important to OLE applications, as you'll see.) The File group contains file-handling commands, the Edit group contains document-editing commands, the Container group contains nonstandard menus, the Object group provides an area in which OLE embedded objects can merge their own menus, the Window group provides window-handling commands, and the Help group offers access to the application's help system.

Building an OLE Container Application's Menus

Now that you have some background in dynamic menus, you can better understand how to construct menus for your OLE container applications and why those menus must be constructed the way they are. As you know, dynamic menus are separated into six groups: File, Edit, Container, Object, Window, and Help. When you construct your container application's menu resources, you must place menu separators between each group. For example, look at the following menu resource:

```
MENU_1 MENU
{
 POPUP "&File"
 {
  MENUITEM "E&xit", CM_EXIT
 }

 MENUITEM SEPARATOR
 POPUP "&Edit"
 {
  MENUITEM "Insert &New Object...", CM_EDITINSERTOBJECT
  MENUITEM "&Links...", CM_EDITLINKS
  MENUITEM "&Object", CM_EDITOBJECT
 }

 MENUITEM SEPARATOR
 POPUP "&Commands"
 {
  MENUITEM "&Test Command...", CM_COMMANDTEST
 }

 MENUITEM SEPARATOR
 MENUITEM SEPARATOR
 MENUITEM SEPARATOR
 POPUP "&Help"
 {
  MENUITEM "&About...", CM_HELPABOUT
 }

}
```

The menu resource begins with the File menu, which is, of course, in the File group. Because the File group is the first menu group, you don't need to mark its beginning with a menu separator. OWL can find that group easily on its own. Following the File pop-up menu is this line:

```
MENUITEM SEPARATOR
```

This is the menu separator that marks the beginning of the Edit group. This menu separator is followed by the Edit menu, which, in this application, makes up the entire Edit group. You could also place in this group other menus related to editing tasks.

Following the Edit group is another menu separator, which marks the beginning of the Container group. This application provides a menu called Commands for this group. Other menus can be placed in this group, also.

After the Container group menus is the separator marking the beginning of the Object group. There are no menu resources here for the Object group. The menus for the Object group are supplied by any server application that wants to place menus there. Because the Object group contains no menus, it's followed immediately by the menu separator marking the beginning of the

Window group. Because this application isn't a Multiple Document Interface (MDI) application and doesn't require a Window menu, no menu appears in this group either.

The last menu separator marks the beginning of the Help group, which contains the application's Help menu.

All these menu separators in the top-level menu (the menu bar) probably look a little strange to you. However, it's these separators that enable OWL and OCF to place a server application's pop-up menus in the correct groups.

Providing Menu Command Hints

It's often been said that a picture is worth a thousand words, but when it comes to command icons, you know that this old saying falls flat. How often have you tried to figure out what all those strange symbols in an application's toolbar mean? To combat this problem, modern Windows applications use command hints that appear in the application's status bar whenever a menu command or toolbar button is selected. To make your OWL application capable of producing these hints, you must do only three things:

1. Construct your frame window with its `trackMenuSelection` argument set to `TRUE`:

```
TOleFrame* Frame =
    new TWndw(GetName(), 0, TRUE, OcApp);
```

2. Be sure to provide your application with a status bar, which you usually create in the frame window's constructor:

```
TStatusBar* sb =
    new TStatusBar(0, TGadget::Recessed,
    TStatusBar::CapsLock | TStatusBar::NumLock |
    TStatusBar::Overtype);

Insert(*sb, TDecoratedFrame::Bottom);
```

3. You must attach the hint text strings to the appropriate menu commands. You do this by creating in your resource file a string table that contains the hint text. Each string's ID should be the same as the ID of the command for which it is a hint, as shown in the following resource code fragment:

```
STRINGTABLE LOADONCALL MOVEABLE DISCARDABLE
{
  CM_EXIT, "Quits the application"
  CM_HELPABOUT, "Displays application information"
  CM_COMMANDTEST, "Sends a test command to the
application"
  CM_EDITLINKS, "Edit links to the document"
```

```
        CM_EDITINSERTOBJECT, "Insert an object into the
    document"
        CM_EDITOBJECT, "Ask an object to perform an action"

        IDS_EDITOBJECT, "&Object"
        IDS_EDITCONVERT, "Convert..."
    }
```

Note

The IDS_EDITOBJECT and IDS_EDITCONVERT strings in the string table are especially important. Without them, the application's <u>O</u>bject command on the <u>E</u>dit menu will fail to work correctly.

Note

Turbo C++ 4.5 comes with many resource files that you can include in your own resource files so as to avoid having to write string tables and other commonly used resources by hand. Unfortunately, when you include such files in your resource file, you also include many resources you may not use in your application. For this reason, you might want to simply copy the resources you need from Turbo C++'s ready-made files and paste them into your own resource file. You can then edit them however you see fit, without worrying about corrupting the original files and without adding a great deal of extra baggage to your application.

Running an OLE Application

When you look at listing 28.1's OwlMain() function, you see that the program doesn't call the application's Run() function, as is typical with an Object-Windows program. Instead, WinMain() must deal with the application's registrar object, as shown here:

```
    int OwlMain(int, char*[])
    {
        Registrar = new TOcRegistrar(AppReg,
            TOleFactory<TApp>(), TApplication::GetCmdLine());
        return Registrar->Run();
    }
```

In the OwlMain() function of an OLE program, you must first create the application's registrar object. This is done by calling the TOcRegistrar constructor, as shown. The constructor's arguments are a reference to the application registration structure, the factory callback function, and the command line passed to the application. As you can see, you can easily take care of the factory callback function by using the TOleFactory<> template, giving it the name of your application object.

After creating the registrar object, you set the program into action by calling the registrar object's Run() function, rather than TApplication's Run() function.

From Here...

Whether you want to create a quick and dirty, single-window Windows application or a fancy commercial-quality application with full support for OLE, ObjectWindows is there to lend a hand. However, learning ObjectWindows takes time and patience. If you found this chapter difficult to follow, you may want to read or review the following chapters:

- Chapter 21, "Using AppExpert." AppExpert-generated programs are good ObjectWindows example applications.

- Chapter 24, "Windows Programming Basics." Information that will help you better understand what ObjectWindows does for you.

- Chapter 27, "The ObjectWindows Library." A general overview of ObjectWindows.

- Chapter 30, "Object Linking and Embedding." This topic will help you learn more about this complex subject.

- Chapter 29, "Single and Multiple Document Interfaces." This topic is not as complex as OLE applications, so it is easier to understand.

Chapter 29

Single and Multiple Document Interfaces

If there's one thing folks in this ambition-driven world understand, it's that the more you can get going at once, the more you're going to get done. Nothing makes a boss happier than walking into an employee's office and seeing a printer cranking out spreadsheets, a modem gathering the latest stock-market figures, and a fax machine sending out the day's correspondence—all while the employee sits behind the desk going over the notes for an afternoon presentation.

That's one reason Windows is so popular. Using Windows, you can have all sorts of things chugging along at once. Spreadsheets, word processors, databases, and telecommunications programs can all be in memory simultaneously, sharing data and getting multiple jobs done fast.

Two other Windows features also help you get out of the office faster: the single and multiple document interfaces. The *Single Document Interface* (SDI) allows for simple, easy-to-use applications. One window, one task. No juggling needed. Windows *Multiple Document Interface* (MDI), on the other hand, enables you to work with as many documents simultaneously as you like, all within a single application.

In this chapter, you learn:

- ■ The difference between SDI and MDI applications
- ■ How to create a single-document application
- ■ How to create a simple text editor
- ■ How to incorporate command hints into your application

- How to program Windows Open dialog box

- How to create a multiple-document application

- How to create a multiple-document text editor

A Review of the Single Document Interface

Windows Single Document Interface (SDI) enables programmers to create simple, easy-to-use applications. An SDI application loads and displays only a single document at a time, so it's ideal for programs that perform "quickie" tasks. A good example of an SDI application is the Windows Notepad application (see fig. 29.1). Using Notepad, you can work with only one text file at a time. You must close one file before opening another. Although an application like Notepad would never make it as a word processor, it's the perfect program for creating short notes (thus its name).

Fig. 29.1

Notepad is a perfect example of an SDI application.

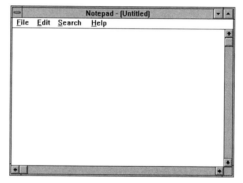

What exactly makes up an SDI application? The following is a list of the most important characteristics:

- An SDI application has a main window that provides a workspace for the display of data. (In an ObjectWindows SDI application, the main window actually holds a client window, which itself holds the application's data.)

- When a new file is opened in an SDI application, the new file replaces any previously opened document. That is, an SDI application can have only one document open simultaneously.

- An SDI main window usually has a menu bar, which often includes at least the File, Edit, and Help menus. (The menus displayed in the application's menu bar depend, of course, on the commands the user needs to control the application.)

- An SDI main window usually has a toolbar that contains buttons for quickly selecting menu commands and a status bar that displays *hint text* for menu items. (Hint text appears on the status bar when the user places his mouse pointer over a menu command or control bar button. The text gives a brief description of the selected command.)

Figure 29.2 shows the main elements of an SDI application. However, the client window is one element that isn't visible in the figure. Remember that, in an ObjectWindows SDI application, the main window (actually a frame window) contains a client window that holds the application's data. You can't actually see the client window because it has no visible controls.

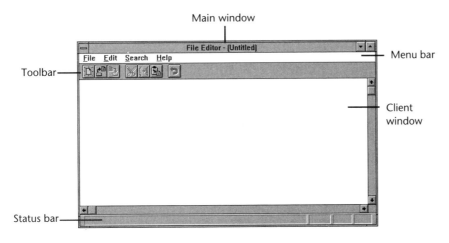

Fig. 29.2
The main elements of an SDI application.

Now that you have a good idea of what an SDI application is, you might want to put together your own. Listings 29.1 through 29.3 show a basic "do-nothing" SDI application.

Listing 29.1   SDIAPP.CPP—A Basic SDI Application

```cpp
///////////////////////////////////////////////////////////
// SDIAPP.CPP: Demonstrates the basic SDI application.
///////////////////////////////////////////////////////////

#include <owl\applicat.h>
#include <owl\framewin.h>
#include "sdiapp.rc"

/////////////////////////////////////////
// The application class.
/////////////////////////////////////////
class TSDIApp : public TApplication
{
public:
   TSDIApp();
   ~TSDIApp();
   void InitMainWindow();
};

/////////////////////////////////////////
// The main window class.
/////////////////////////////////////////
class TWndw : public TFrameWindow
{
public:
   TWndw(TWindow* parent, const char far* title);
   ~TWndw();
};

//-------------------------------------------------------//
// The TWndw class's implementation.
//-------------------------------------------------------//

///////////////////////////////////////////////////////////
// TWndw::TWndw()
//
// This is the frame window's constructor.
///////////////////////////////////////////////////////////
TWndw::TWndw(TWindow* parent, const char far* title) :
   TFrameWindow(parent, title)
{
   // Give the window its menu.
   AssignMenu(MENU_1);

   // Size and position the frame window.
   Attr.X = 50;
   Attr.Y = 50;
   Attr.W = 500;
   Attr.H = 300;

   // Set the frame window's icon.
   SetIcon(GetApplication(), ID_SDIAPP);
}
```

```
///////////////////////////////////////////////////////////
// TWndw::~TWndw()
//
// This is the frame window's destructor.
///////////////////////////////////////////////////////////
TWndw::~TWndw()
{
}


//---------------------------------------------------------//
// The TSDIApp class's implementation.
//---------------------------------------------------------//


///////////////////////////////////////////////////////////
// TSDIApp::TSDIApp()
//
// This is the TSDIApp class's constructor.
///////////////////////////////////////////////////////////
TSDIApp::TSDIApp() : TApplication()
{
}


///////////////////////////////////////////////////////////
// TSDIApp::~TSDIApp()
//
// This is the TSDIApp class's destructor.
///////////////////////////////////////////////////////////
TSDIApp::~TSDIApp()
{
}


///////////////////////////////////////////////////////////
// TSDIApp::InitMainWindow()
//
// This function creates the application's frame window.
///////////////////////////////////////////////////////////
void TSDIApp::InitMainWindow()
{
    // Construct the main frame window.
    TFrameWindow *wndw =
      new TWndw(0, "SDI App");

    // Set the application's MainWindow pointer.
    SetMainWindow(wndw);
}


///////////////////////////////////////////////////////////
// OwlMain()
///////////////////////////////////////////////////////////
int OwlMain(int, char*[])
{
    return TSDIApp().Run();
}
```

Listing 29.2   SDIAPP.RC—SDIAPP's Resource File

```
/////////////////////////////////////////////////////////
// SDIAPP.RC
/////////////////////////////////////////////////////////

#ifndef WORKSHOP_INVOKED
#include "windows.h"
#endif

#include <owl\window.rh>

#define MENU_1    100
#define ID_SDIAPP 101

#ifdef RC_INVOKED

MENU_1 MENU
{
 POPUP "&File"
 {
  MENUITEM "E&xit", CM_EXIT
 }

}

ID_SDIAPP ICON "sdiapp.ico"

#endif
```

Listing 29.3   SDIAPP.DEF—SDIAPP's Module Definition File

```
NAME SDIAPP
DESCRIPTION 'SDI example by Clayton Walnum'
EXETYPE WINDOWS
STUB 'WINSTUB.EXE'
CODE PRELOAD MOVEABLE DISCARDABLE
DATA PRELOAD MOVEABLE MULTIPLE
HEAPSIZE 1024
STACKSIZE 8192
```

When you run this program, you see the window shown in figure 29.3. The window's File menu contains only an Exit command, which you can use to close the application. Although the window doesn't have a toolbar and a status bar (they're not required in an SDI application, but it's suggested that a full application have them), it does contain the client window in which the application's data can appear. You'll add the toolbar, status bar, and other finishing touches in the next version of the program.

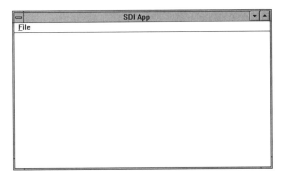

Fig. 29.3
The SDIAPP
application.

Programming the Basic SDI Application

When you have ObjectWindows to help you along, putting together an SDI application is fairly easy. (If you don't know about ObjectWindows, you might want to read Chapter 27, "The ObjectWindows Library.") The first step is to create the application class, which looks like the following in SDIAPP:

```
class TSDIApp : public TApplication
{
public:
    TSDIApp();
    ~TSDIApp();
    void InitMainWindow();
};
```

This class contains the usual constructor and destructor, as well as the `InitMainWindow()` function, which every ObjectWindows application must override to create the application's main window.

In the class's implementation, the constructor does nothing more than call the base class's constructor:

```
TSDIApp::TSDIApp() : TApplication()
{
}
```

It's the `InitMainWindow()` function that sets up the application's main window:

```
void TSDIApp::InitMainWindow()
{
    // Construct the main frame window.
    TFrameWindow *wndw =
        new TWndw(0, "SDI App");
```

```
        // Set the application's MainWindow pointer.
        SetMainWindow(wndw);
}
```

Here the program first constructs a window object of the TWndw class and then calls the application object's SetMainWindow() function to make this new window the application's main window.

This application's main window is represented by the TWndw class, which is derived from ObjectWindow's TFrameWindow:

```
class TWndw : public TFrameWindow
{
public:
    TWndw(TWindow* parent, const char far* title);
    ~TWndw();
};
```

The class's constructor calls the base class's constructor to set up the basic frame window, after which the program makes the changes required for this specific window:

```
TWndw::TWndw(TWindow* parent, const char far* title) :
    TFrameWindow(parent, title)
{
    // Give the window its menu.
    AssignMenu(MENU_1);

    // Size and position the frame window.
    Attr.X = 50;
    Attr.Y = 50;
    Attr.W = 500;
    Attr.H = 300;

    // Set the frame window's icon.
    SetIcon(GetApplication(), ID_SDIAPP);
}
```

First, the program calls AssignMenu() to give the main window its menu bar. The single argument is the resource ID of the menu you want to assign to the window. Next, changing the window's Attr structure gives the window its initial size and position. Finally, the call to SetIcon() assigns the application's icon. This icon appears at the bottom of the screen whenever the application is minimized.

That's about all there is to creating the basic SDI application. Unfortunately, this application doesn't do much. To make an SDI application useful, you must enable it to load, edit, and save files. How you do this depends, of course, on what type of document the application will handle. In the next example, you'll see how to use ObjectWindows to put together a snappy little text editor, not unlike Notepad.

An SDI Text Editor

If I were to demand that you write a text editor by sundown, you would probably have a good laugh. If I were to tell you that I expected not just any text editor, but one that could handle sophisticated editing features such as search and replace, as well as featured block-editing commands, you would stop laughing and move away slowly to call the guys in the white coats. But not only is such a task possible, it's downright easy—as proven in listings 29.4 through 29.6.

Listing 29.4   SDIEDIT.CPP—An SDI Text Editor

```
/////////////////////////////////////////////////////////
// SDIEDIT.CPP: A single-document interface application
//              for editing text files.
/////////////////////////////////////////////////////////

#include <owl\applicat.h>
#include <owl\decframe.h>
#include <owl\editfile.h>
#include <owl\controlb.h>
#include <owl\statusba.h>
#include <owl\buttonga.h>
#include "sdiedit.rc"

////////////////////////////////////////
// The application class.
////////////////////////////////////////
class TSDIApp : public TApplication
{
public:
    TSDIApp();
    ~TSDIApp();
    void InitMainWindow();
};

////////////////////////////////////////
// The main window class.
////////////////////////////////////////
class TWndw : public TDecoratedFrame
{
protected:
    TControlBar *controlBar;

public:
    TWndw(TWindow* parent, const char far* title,
        TWindow* clientWnd, BOOL trackMenuSelection);
    ~TWndw();
```

(continues)

Listing 29.4 Continued

```
protected:
   void CmFileNew();
   void CmFileOpen();
   void CmHelpAbout();

   DECLARE_RESPONSE_TABLE(TWndw);
};

DEFINE_RESPONSE_TABLE1(TWndw, TDecoratedFrame)
  EV_COMMAND(CM_FILENEW, CmFileNew),
  EV_COMMAND(CM_FILEOPEN, CmFileOpen),
  EV_COMMAND(CM_HELPABOUT, CmHelpAbout),
END_RESPONSE_TABLE;

//----------------------------------------------------------//
// The TWndw class's implementation.
//----------------------------------------------------------//

//////////////////////////////////////////////////////////////
// TWndw::TWndw()
//
// This is the frame window's constructor.
//////////////////////////////////////////////////////////////
TWndw::TWndw(TWindow* parent, const char far* title,
    TWindow* clientWnd, BOOL trackMenuSelection) :
    TDecoratedFrame(parent, title, clientWnd,
    trackMenuSelection)
{
   // Give the window its menu.
   AssignMenu(MENU_1);

   // Size and position the frame window.
   Attr.X = 50;
   Attr.Y = 50;
   Attr.W = 500;
   Attr.H = 300;

   // Create the control bar.
   controlBar = new TControlBar(this);
   controlBar->
      Insert(*new TButtonGadget(ID_NEW, CM_FILENEW));
   controlBar->
      Insert(*new TButtonGadget(ID_OPEN, CM_FILEOPEN));
   controlBar->
      Insert(*new TButtonGadget(ID_SAVE, CM_FILESAVE));
   controlBar->
      Insert(*new TSeparatorGadget(10));
   controlBar->
      Insert(*new TButtonGadget(ID_CUT, CM_EDITCUT));
   controlBar->
      Insert(*new TButtonGadget(ID_COPY, CM_EDITCOPY));
   controlBar->
      Insert(*new TButtonGadget(ID_PASTE, CM_EDITPASTE));
```

```
      controlBar->
         Insert(*new TSeparatorGadget(10));
      controlBar->
         Insert(*new TButtonGadget(ID_UNDO, CM_EDITUNDO));

      // Set the hint mode to show hints instantly.
      controlBar->SetHintMode(TGadgetWindow::EnterHints);

      // Insert the control bar into the frame window.
      Insert(*controlBar, TDecoratedFrame::Top);

      // Create the status bar.
      TStatusBar *statusBar = new TStatusBar(this,
         TGadget::Recessed,
         TStatusBar::CapsLock ¦ TStatusBar::NumLock ¦
         TStatusBar::Overtype);

      // Insert the status bar into the frame window.
      Insert(*statusBar, TDecoratedFrame::Bottom);

      // Set the frame window's icon.
      SetIcon(GetApplication(), ID_SDIEDIT);
   }


   /////////////////////////////////////////////////////////
   // TWndw::~TWndw()
   //
   // This is the frame window's destructor.
   /////////////////////////////////////////////////////////
   TWndw::~TWndw()
   {
   }


   /////////////////////////////////////////////////////////
   // TWndw::CmFileNew
   //
   // This function creates a new edit control when the user
   // selects the File menu's New command or when the user
   // selects the New button on the control bar.
   /////////////////////////////////////////////////////////
   void TWndw::CmFileNew()
   {
      // Create a new file-editing control.
      TEditFile *editFile = new TEditFile;

      // Make the edit control into the client window.
      TWindow* oldClient = SetClientWindow(editFile);

      // Delete the old client window.
      if (oldClient)
         delete oldClient;
   }
```

(continues)

Listing 29.4   Continued

```
///////////////////////////////////////////////////////
// TWndw::CmFileOpen
//
// This function creates a new edit control when the user
// selects the File menu's Open command or when the user
// selects the Open button on the control bar.
///////////////////////////////////////////////////////
void TWndw::CmFileOpen()
{
   // Create the dialog box's TData object.
   TOpenSaveDialog::TData fileData(OFN_FILEMUSTEXIST¦
      OFN_HIDEREADONLY¦OFN_PATHMUSTEXIST,
      "All Files (*.*)¦*.*¦Text Files (*.txt)¦*.txt¦",
      0, 0, "*");

   // Start the file name out as an empty string.
   strcpy(fileData.FileName, "");

   // Create the Open dialog box.
   TFileOpenDialog *dialog =
      new TFileOpenDialog(this, fileData);

   // Execute the Open dialog box.
   int result = dialog->Execute();

   // If the user exits via the OK button...
   if (result == IDOK)
   {
      // Create a new file-editing control.
      TEditFile* editFile =
         new TEditFile(0, 0, 0, 0, 0, 0, 0,
         fileData.FileName);

      // Make the edit control into the client window.
      TWindow* oldClient = SetClientWindow(editFile);

      // Delete the old client window.
      if (oldClient)
         delete oldClient;
   }

   // Erase any old hint text.
   controlBar->SetHintCommand(-1);
}


///////////////////////////////////////////////////////
// TWndw::CmHelpAbout()
//
// This function shows the About dialog box when the user
// selects the Help menu's About command.
///////////////////////////////////////////////////////
void TWndw::CmHelpAbout()
{
```

```
      MessageBox("A sample SDI editor", "About");
   }


   //----------------------------------------------------------//
   // The TSDIApp class's implementation.
   //----------------------------------------------------------//


   ///////////////////////////////////////////////////////////
   // TSDIApp::TSDIApp()
   //
   // This is the TSDIApp class's constructor.
   ///////////////////////////////////////////////////////////
   TSDIApp::TSDIApp() : TApplication()
   {
   }


   ///////////////////////////////////////////////////////////
   // TSDIApp::~TSDIApp()
   //
   // This is the TSDIApp class's destructor.
   ///////////////////////////////////////////////////////////
   TSDIApp::~TSDIApp()
   {
   }


   ///////////////////////////////////////////////////////////
   // TSDIApp::InitMainWindow()
   //
   // This function creates the application's main window.
   ///////////////////////////////////////////////////////////
   void TSDIApp::InitMainWindow()
   {
      // Create a new file-editing control.
      TEditFile* editFile = new TEditFile;

      // Create the frame window.
      TDecoratedFrame *frameWnd =
         new TWndw(0, "File Editor", editFile, TRUE);

      // Enable Microsoft's 3-D controls.
      EnableCtl3d(TRUE);

      // Set the application's MainWindow pointer.
      SetMainWindow(frameWnd);
   }

   ///////////////////////////////////////////////////////////
   // OwlMain()
   ///////////////////////////////////////////////////////////
   int OwlMain(int, char*[])
   {
     return TSDIApp().Run();
   }
```

V

Tools and Techniques

Listing 29.5   SDIEDIT.RC—SDIEDIT's Resource File

```
//////////////////////////////////////////////////////////
// SDIEDIT.RC
//////////////////////////////////////////////////////////

#ifndef WORKSHOP_INVOKED
#include "windows.h"
#endif

#include <owl\editfile.rh>

#define ID_SDIEDIT   101
#define MENU_1       100
#define CM_HELPABOUT 101
#define ID_UNDO      CM_EDITUNDO
#define ID_SAVE      CM_FILESAVE
#define ID_PASTE     CM_EDITPASTE
#define ID_OPEN      CM_FILEOPEN
#define ID_NEW       CM_FILENEW
#define ID_CUT       CM_EDITCUT
#define ID_COPY      CM_EDITCOPY

#ifdef RC_INVOKED

#include <owl\except.rc>
#include <owl\statusba.rc>

MENU_1 MENU
{
 POPUP "&File"
 {
  MENUITEM "&New", CM_FILENEW
  MENUITEM "&Open...", CM_FILEOPEN
  MENUITEM "&Save", CM_FILESAVE, GRAYED
  MENUITEM "Save &As...", CM_FILESAVEAS
  MENUITEM SEPARATOR
  MENUITEM "E&xit", CM_EXIT
 }

 POPUP "&Edit"
 {
  MENUITEM "&Undo", CM_EDITUNDO
  MENUITEM SEPARATOR
  MENUITEM "&Cut", CM_EDITCUT
  MENUITEM "C&opy", CM_EDITCOPY
  MENUITEM "&Paste", CM_EDITPASTE
  MENUITEM "&Delete", CM_EDITDELETE
  MENUITEM "C&lear All", CM_EDITCLEAR
 }

 POPUP "&Search"
 {
  MENUITEM "&Find...", CM_EDITFIND
  MENUITEM "&Replace...", CM_EDITREPLACE
```

```
  MENUITEM "&Next", CM_EDITFINDNEXT
  }

  POPUP "&Help"
  {
   MENUITEM "&About...", CM_HELPABOUT
  }

}

STRINGTABLE
{
 CM_FILENEW, "Start a new document"
 CM_FILEOPEN, "Open an existing document"
 CM_FILESAVE, "Save the current document"
 CM_FILESAVEAS, "Save the current document under a new name"
 CM_EXIT, "Quit the editor"
 CM_EDITUNDO, "Undo the most recent operation"
 CM_EDITCOPY, "Copy the selected text into the clipboard"
 CM_EDITCUT, "Cut the selected text into the clipboard"
 CM_EDITPASTE, "Insert the contents of the clipboard"
 CM_EDITCLEAR, "Clear the contents of the current window"
 CM_EDITDELETE, "Delete the selected text"
 CM_EDITREPLACE, "Find and change a string of text"
 CM_EDITFIND, "Find a string of text"
 CM_EDITFINDNEXT, "Find the next matching text"
 IDS_UNTITLEDFILE, "(Untitled)"
 IDS_UNABLEREAD, "Unable to read file %s from disk."
 IDS_UNABLEWRITE, "Unable to write file %s to disk."
 IDS_FILECHANGED, "The text in the %s file has changed.\n\n\
Do you want to save the changes?"
 IDS_CANNOTFIND, "Cannot find ""%s""."
}

ID_UNDO BITMAP "c:\tcwin45\expert\owl\undo.bmp"
ID_CUT BITMAP "c:\tcwin45\expert\owl\cut.bmp"
ID_COPY BITMAP "c:\tcwin45\expert\owl\copy.bmp"
ID_PASTE BITMAP "c:\tcwin45\expert\owl\paste.bmp"
ID_NEW BITMAP "c:\tcwin45\expert\owl\new.bmp"
ID_OPEN BITMAP "c:\tcwin45\expert\owl\open.bmp"
ID_SAVE BITMAP "c:\tcwin45\expert\owl\save.bmp"

ID_SDIEDIT ICON "sdiedit.ico"

#endif
```

V

Tools and Techniques

Listing 29.6   SDIEDIT.DEF—SDIEDIT's Module Definition File

```
NAME SDIEDIT
DESCRIPTION 'SDI Editor example by Clayton Walnum'
EXETYPE WINDOWS
STUB 'WINSTUB.EXE'
CODE PRELOAD MOVEABLE DISCARDABLE
DATA PRELOAD MOVEABLE MULTIPLE
HEAPSIZE 1024
STACKSIZE 8192
```

Run this program, and you will see that you have a full-fledged text editor (see fig. 29.4) that does just about anything except print files. The application has full File, Edit, and Search menus that contain all the commands you expect to find. In addition, you can access several menu commands from the program's control bar. As you move your mouse pointer over any menu command or control button, hint text (which describes the command) appears in the status bar, and the status bar also tracks the status of your keyboard's Num Lock, Caps Lock, and Insert keys. Finally, if you minimize the application, its icon appears at the bottom of your Windows desktop.

Fig. 29.4
The SDIEDIT
application.

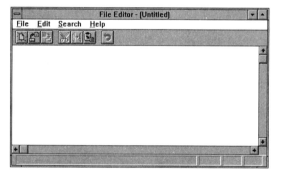

How can such a short program do so much? Mostly, you can thank the ObjectWindows Library (OWL) for its special classes—TFileEdit, TControlBar, and TStatusBar—which encapsulate much of the code necessary to handle the application's many commands.

Begin by examining the main window's class, which looks quite different from the previous version:

```
class TWndw : public TDecoratedFrame
{
protected:
    TControlBar *controlBar;
```

```
public:
  TWndw(TWindow* parent, const char far* title,
    TWindow* clientWnd, BOOL trackMenuSelection);
  ~TWndw();

protected:
  void CmFileNew();
  void CmFileOpen();
  void CmHelpAbout();

  DECLARE_RESPONSE_TABLE(TWndw);
};

DEFINE_RESPONSE_TABLE1(TWndw, TDecoratedFrame)
  EV_COMMAND(CM_FILENEW, CmFileNew),
  EV_COMMAND(CM_FILEOPEN, CmFileOpen),
  EV_COMMAND(CM_HELPABOUT, CmHelpAbout),
END_RESPONSE_TABLE;
```

This class has a `protected` data member, `controlBar`, which points to the application's control bar. This pointer enables the application to access the associated control bar object anywhere within the window's class. The `TWndw` class also has the usual constructor and destructor. However, three `protected` message-response functions—`CmFileNew()`, `CmFileOpen()`, and `CmHelpAbout()`— provide responses for the File menu's New and Open commands and for the Help menu's About command.

Before a window appears on-screen, the `TWndw` class's constructor sets up the main window. First, the constructor assigns the window's menu:

```
AssignMenu(MENU_1);
```

Then it modifies the window's `Attr` structure to size and position the window:

```
Attr.X = 50;
Attr.Y = 50;
Attr.W = 500;
Attr.H = 300;
```

The next task for the constructor is the construction of the application's control bar:

```
controlBar = new TControlBar(this);
controlBar->
  Insert(*new TButtonGadget(IDB_NEW, CM_FILENEW));
controlBar->
  Insert(*new TButtonGadget(IDB_OPEN, CM_FILEOPEN));
controlBar->
  Insert(*new TButtonGadget(IDB_SAVE, CM_FILESAVE));
controlBar->
```

V

Tools and Techniques

```
        Insert(*new TSeparatorGadget(10));
controlBar->
        Insert(*new TButtonGadget(IDB_CUT, CM_EDITCUT));
controlBar->
        Insert(*new TButtonGadget(IDB_COPY, CM_EDITCOPY));
controlBar->
        Insert(*new TButtonGadget(IDB_PASTE, CM_EDITPASTE));
controlBar->
        Insert(*new TSeparatorGadget(10));
controlBar->
        Insert(*new TButtonGadget(IDB_UNDO, CM_EDITUNDO));
```

Here the call to TControlBar's constructor has a single argument, a pointer to the control bar's parent window.

Then the program calls the control-bar class's Insert() function several times to add button and separator gadgets to the control bar. The TButtonGadget constructor takes as parameters the resource ID of the bitmap to use for the button and the resource ID of the menu command that the button should initiate.

A TSeparatorGadget only places an empty space on the control bar. The TSeparatorGadget constructor's single argument is the size of the space in pixels.

After adding buttons to the control bar, the program calls the control bar's SetHintMode() function:

```
controlBar->SetHintMode(TGadgetWindow::EnterHints);
```

SetHintMode() determines how hint text appears in the window's status bar. The setting TGadgetWindow::EnterHints causes the hints to appear whenever the mouse pointer is over a button in the control bar. The two other possible settings are TGadgetWindow::PressHints and TGadgetWindow::NoHints. The first causes hints to appear only when the button is pressed and the second turns off the hints.

After setting up the control bar, the program adds it to the window by calling the Insert() member function:

```
Insert(*controlBar, TDecoratedFrame::Top);
```

The first argument is a reference to the control bar (here, the reference is created by dereferencing the pointer) and the second is the control bar's position, which can be TDecoratedFrame::Top, TDecoratedFrame::Left, TDecoratedFrame::Bottom, or TDecoratedFrame::Right.

With the control bar taken care of, the program next constructs the window's status bar:

```
TStatusBar *statusBar = new TStatusBar(this,
    TGadget::Recessed,
    TStatusBar::CapsLock ¦ TStatusBar::NumLock ¦
    TStatusBar::Overtype);
```

Here the `TStatusBar` constructor takes as arguments a pointer to the parent window, the border style (`TGadget::None`, `TGadget::Plain`, `TGadget::Raised`, `TGadget::Recessed`, or `TGadget::Embossed`), and a mode indicator for the keyboard status (`TStatusBar::ExtendSelection`, `TStatusBar::CapsLock`, `TStatusBar::NumLock`, `TStatusBar::ScrollLock`, `TStatusBar::OverType`, or `TStatusBar::RecordingMacro`, any or all of which can be ORed together).

Another call to the window's `Insert()` member function then places the status bar in the window:

```
Insert(*statusBar, TDecoratedFrame::Bottom);
```

Finally, the program calls `SetIcon()`, which determines the icon that'll appear when the application is minimized:

```
SetIcon(GetApplication(), ID_SDIEDIT);
```

This function's two arguments are a pointer to the application object (supplied by `GetApplication()`) and the resource ID of the icon.

> **Note**
>
> If you're like most programmers, you're very careful to delete any objects that you allocate dynamically (using the new operator). So you may find it mysterious how OWL programmers dynamically allocate child windows (including status bars and toolbars) yet never explicitly delete them. The secret is that OWL keeps a list of all child windows and automatically deletes those child windows when the parent window is deleted.

The Message-Response Functions

The three remaining functions in the `TWndw` class (besides the empty destructor) are the message-response functions. The first is `CmFileNew()`, which responds when the user selects the File menu's New command (or clicks on the New button):

```
void TWndw::CmFileNew()
{
   // Create a new file-editing control.
   TEditFile *editFile = new TEditFile;

   // Make the edit control into the client window.
   TWindow* oldClient = SetClientWindow(editFile);

   // Delete the old client window.
   if (oldClient)
      delete oldClient;
}
```

This function first constructs a new TEditFile control and makes the control the frame window's new client window. Because the SetClientWindow() function returns a pointer to the old client window, the program can examine that pointer to determine whether there's an old edit control that must be deleted (there should be).

The second message-response function, CmFileOpen(), is a bit more complicated:

```
void TWndw::CmFileOpen()
{
   // Create the dialog box's TData object.
   TOpenSaveDialog::TData fileData(OFN_FILEMUSTEXIST¦
      OFN_HIDEREADONLY¦OFN_PATHMUSTEXIST,
      "All Files (*.*)¦*.*¦Text Files (*.txt)¦*.txt¦",
      0, 0, "*");

   // Start the file name out as an empty string.
   strcpy(fileData.FileName, "");

   // Create the Open dialog box.
   TFileOpenDialog *dialog =
      new TFileOpenDialog(this, fileData);

   // Execute the Open dialog box.
   int result = dialog->Execute();

   // If the user exits via the OK button...
   if (result == IDOK)
   {
      // Create a new file-editing control.
      TEditFile* editFile =
         new TEditFile(0, 0, 0, 0, 0, 0, 0,
         fileData.FileName);

      // Make the edit control into the client window.
      TWindow* oldClient = SetClientWindow(editFile);

      // Delete the old client window.
      if (oldClient)
         delete oldClient;
```

```
    }

    // Erase any old hint text.
    controlBar->SetHintCommand(-1);
}
```

Because the user needs to select the file to open, CmFileOpen() must display a Windows Open dialog box. The first step in displaying this dialog box is to construct a TData object. Then because the dialog box will not contain a default file name, the program sets fileData.FileName to an empty string. With the TData object successfully created and initialized, CmFileOpen() constructs a new TFileOpenDialog dialog box and calls its Execute() function to display it.

When the user exits the dialog box, the pressed button appears in result. If result equals IDOK, the user exited by selecting the OK button; therefore, the user must have selected a file name. CmFileOpen() uses the file name, which is stored in fileData.FileName, in a call to the TEditFile constructor.

The TEditFile constructor may take as many as nine arguments, all of which have a default value of zero. The nine arguments are as follows:

- A pointer to the parent window

- A resource ID

- A pointer to the text that should appear in the window

- The edit control's x,y coordinates

- The edit control's width and height

- A pointer to a file name

- A pointer to a TModule object

By constructing a TEditFile object this way, not only is the object created, but the file given in the file-name argument is automatically loaded into the window.

After constructing the TEditFile object, CmFileOpen() calls SetClientWindow() to make the new control (containing the selected file) the new client window, after which the program deletes the old client window (which is the old edit control).

The CmHelpAbout() message-response function, which responds to the Help menu's About command, simply displays a message box containing information about the application.

V

Tools and Techniques

The *InitMainWindow()* Function

The application's `InitMainWindow()` function is the last function in this program that's of any real interest:

```
void TSDIApp::InitMainWindow()
{
   // Create a new file-editing control.
   TEditFile* editFile = new TEditFile;

   // Create the frame window.
   TDecoratedFrame *frameWnd =
       new TWndw(0, "File Editor", editFile, TRUE);

   // Enable Microsoft's 3-D controls.
   EnableCtl3d(TRUE);

   // Set the application's MainWindow pointer.
   SetMainWindow(frameWnd);
}
```

As you know, `InitMainWindow()` is called when the application first starts and is responsible for creating the main window. The first task is to create the initial `TEditFile` control that'll be used as the main window's client window. Then the program calls the `TDecoratedFrame` class's constructor to create the main window. This constructor requires as arguments a pointer to the parent window (in this case, there is no parent window), the window's title, a pointer to the client window, and a Boolean value indicating whether the window displays menu hint text. `TDecoratedFrame` is a special window class that provides support for control bars, status bars, and other types of "decorations."

After constructing the application's main window, `InitMainWindow()` calls `EnableCtl3d()` to turn on Microsoft's 3-D controls and calls `SetMainWindow()` to pass the main window's pointer on to the application.

A Review of the Multiple Document Interface

Windows Multiple Document Interface (MDI) offers programmers a powerful way to control the objects—especially the document windows—that make up an application. An MDI application not only creates a mini-desktop on which the user can organize related windows and icons, but it also provides the programmer with many easy-to-implement functions that automatically handle those windows. MDI applications require a little more effort to program, but their advantages far outweigh any extra labor involved.

MDI applications in Windows are plentiful. The Windows Program Manager and File Manager, for example, are MDI applications. Other MDI applications with which you may be familiar include Microsoft Works for Windows, Quicken for Windows, Windows System Configuration Editor, PageMaker, and Borland's Resource Workshop.

What exactly makes up an MDI application? The following is a list of the most important characteristics:

- An MDI application's main window is called a *frame window*. The frame window doesn't provide a workspace for the display of data (as does a conventional window); rather, it provides a desktop-like surface for the organization of child (document) windows.

- When a new file is opened in an MDI application, it's represented by a document window that appears over the frame window's client area. An MDI application can open any number of document windows simultaneously.

- An MDI frame window always has a menu bar, which includes— but is not limited to—a Window menu for controlling MDI document windows. From this menu, document windows can usually be selected, tiled, and cascaded—among other things.

- MDI document windows have no menu. They receive commands from the application's frame-window menu.

- MDI document windows cannot be moved outside the frame window.

- When an MDI document window is minimized, it's displayed as an icon at the bottom of the frame window.

- When an MDI document window is maximized, it takes over the entire frame window, and its controls merge with those of the frame window.

- An MDI application's frame window is covered by an invisible client window, which acts as a parent to windows and controls that appear over the frame window.

- An MDI frame window usually has a toolbar that contains buttons for quickly selecting menu commands and a status bar that displays hint text for menu items.

Figure 29.5 shows the main elements of an MDI application. The client window is one element that isn't visible in the figure. The *client window* is an invisible window that usually covers the frame window's entire client area. The client window is a child to the frame window, and MDI child windows are children to the client window. The client window controls most of what makes an MDI application work. You might think of it as an invisible container that holds several of the elements—including child windows, scroll bars, and icons—that have to work together in an MDI application.

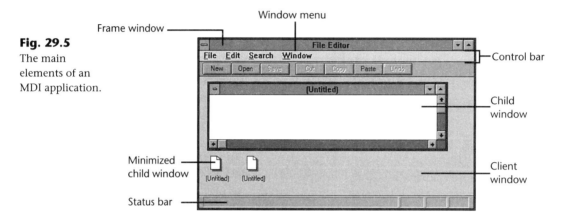

Fig. 29.5
The main elements of an MDI application.

Although the client window may seem mysterious, it's still nothing more exotic than a window. Like any window, you can manipulate it in various ways. For example, you can resize the client window so that it no longer entirely covers the frame window's client area. Consider that MDI child windows have the client window (not the frame window) as their parent and cannot be moved outside the client window. When you reduce the size of the client window, you restrict the area in which the child windows can function. In fact, this characteristic of the client- and child-window relationship makes OWL's TControlBar, TMessageBar, and TStatusBar objects possible. By reducing the size of the client window, OWL can sneak these special windows into the frame window.

If all of this sounds a bit perplexing, you'll be delighted to know that you can leave all this client-window manipulation up to OWL and Windows. As listings 29.7 through 29.9 show, creating a basic MDI application is anything but an overwhelming task.

Listing 29.7 MDIAPP.CPP—A Small MDI Application

```cpp
/////////////////////////////////////////////////////////////
// MDIAPP.CPP: Demonstrates the basics of MDI applications.
/////////////////////////////////////////////////////////////

#include <owl\applicat.h>
#include <owl\mdi.h>
#include <owl\mdichild.h>
#include <stdio.h>
#include "mdiapp.rc"

////////////////////////////////////////
// The application class.
////////////////////////////////////////
class TMDIApp : public TApplication
{
public:
   TMDIApp() : TApplication() {}
   void InitMainWindow();
};

////////////////////////////////////////
// The client window class.
////////////////////////////////////////
class TMDIClientWnd : public TMDIClient
{
protected:
   int childNum;

public:
   TMDIClientWnd();

protected:
   TMDIChild *InitChild();
};

//----------------------------------------------------------//
// The TMDIClientWnd class's implementation.
//----------------------------------------------------------//

/////////////////////////////////////////////////////////////
// TMDIClientWnd::TMDIClientWnd()
//
// This is the client window's constructor.
/////////////////////////////////////////////////////////////
TMDIClientWnd::TMDIClientWnd() : TMDIClient()
{
   childNum = 1;
}

/////////////////////////////////////////////////////////////
// TMDIClientWnd::InitChild()
```

(continues)

Listing 29.7 Continued

```
//
// This function, which overrides a function in the
// TMDIClient class, constructs an MDI child window whose
// parent is the client window.
///////////////////////////////////////////////////////////
TMDIChild* TMDIClientWnd::InitChild()
{
   char s[20];
   sprintf(s, "Child Window #%d", childNum);
   ++childNum;
   return new TMDIChild(*this, s);
}

//----------------------------------------------------------//
// The TMDIApp class's implementation.
//----------------------------------------------------------//

///////////////////////////////////////////////////////////
// TMDIApp::InitMainWindow()
//
// This function creates the application's frame and
// client windows.
///////////////////////////////////////////////////////////
void TMDIApp::InitMainWindow()
{
   // Create the client window.
   TMDIClient *clientWnd = new TMDIClientWnd;

   // Construct the main frame window.
   TMDIFrame *wndw =
      new TMDIFrame("MDI App", MENU_1, *clientWnd);

   // Set the application's MainWindow pointer.
   SetMainWindow(wndw);
}

///////////////////////////////////////////////////////////
// OwlMain()
///////////////////////////////////////////////////////////
int OwlMain(int, char*[])
{
   return TMDIApp().Run();
}
```

Listing 29.8   MDIAPP.RC—MDIAPP's Resource File

```
/////////////////////////////////////////////////////////
// MDIAPP.RC
/////////////////////////////////////////////////////////

#ifndef WORKSHOP_INVOKED
#include "windows.h"
#endif

#include <owl\mdi.rh>
#include <owl\window.rh>

#define MENU_1    100

#ifdef RC_INVOKED

MENU_1 MENU
{
 POPUP "&File"
 {
  MENUITEM "E&xit", CM_EXIT
 }

 POPUP "&Window"
 {
  MENUITEM "C&reate", CM_CREATECHILD
  MENUITEM "&Cascade", CM_CASCADECHILDREN
  MENUITEM "&Tile", CM_TILECHILDREN
  MENUITEM "Arrange &Icons", CM_ARRANGEICONS
  MENUITEM "C&lose All", CM_CLOSECHILDREN
 }

}

 #endif
```

Listing 29.9   MDIAPP.DEF—MDIAPP's Module Definition File

```
NAME MDIAPP
DESCRIPTION 'MDI example by Clayton Walnum'
EXETYPE WINDOWS
STUB 'WINSTUB.EXE'
CODE PRELOAD MOVEABLE DISCARDABLE
DATA PRELOAD MOVEABLE MULTIPLE
HEAPSIZE 1024
STACKSIZE 8192
```

When you run this program, you see the window shown in figure 29.6. The window's File menu contains only an Exit command, but the Window menu contains Create, Cascade, Tile, Arrange Icons, and Close All commands— all the commands you expect to find in an MDI application's Window menu.

Choose the Create command to create a new MDI child window. After you've created several child windows, you can use the Cascade and Tile commands to arrange them in the client window. Reduce the windows to icons, drag the icons around the client window, and then use the Arrange Icons command to line up the icons at the bottom of the client window. Finally, choose Close All to close all child windows simultaneously. (You can use a window's system menu to close only that window.)

Fig. 29.6

MDIAPP's main window.

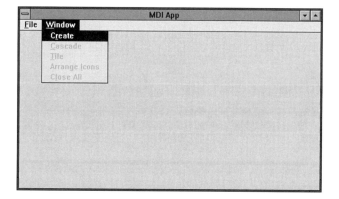

There's a lot going on here for such a short program. Windows and ObjectWindows handle so much of the work that there's not much left for you to do in the program's code—which probably suits you just fine. That's not to say, of course, that you don't need to know a few things before you program your own MDI applications.

First, look at the application's `InitMainWindow()` function:

```
void TMDIApp::InitMainWindow()
{
    // Create the client window.
    TMDIClient *clientWnd = new TMDIClientWnd;

    // Construct the main frame window.
    TMDIFrame *wndw =
        new TMDIFrame("MDI App", MENU_1, *clientWnd);

    // Set the application's MainWindow pointer.
    SetMainWindow(wndw);
}
```

`InitMainWindow()` first constructs the application's client window. Every OWL MDI application must have a client window derived from the `TMDIClient` class, which means you must include the header file `MDICHILD.H`, as well as `MDI.H`, in your program. This program has its own client window class, which is, of course, derived from OWL's `TMDIClient` class. `TMDIClient` is, in turn, derived from `TWindow` and provides message-response functions for the MDI commands in the <u>W</u>indow menu, including `CmCreateChild()`, `CmCloseChildren()`, `CmCascadeChildren()`, and `CmTileChildren()`. `TMDIClient` also features command enablers for the <u>W</u>indow menu, so you don't need to fuss over enabling and disabling items in the <u>W</u>indow menu. (*Command enablers* are special functions that enable, disable, and check mark menu items. For more information, search for "TCommandEnabler" in your on-line Turbo C++ documentation.) Finally, `TMDIClient`'s member functions `GetActiveMDIChild()` and `InitChild()` enable you to get a pointer to the active child window and to create custom MDI child windows.

After constructing the client window, the program constructs the application's main window, which must be of the `TMDIFrame` class (or a class derived from `TMDIFrame`). `TMDIFrame`'s constructor takes as parameters a title string, a menu resource ID, and a reference to a client window. The `TMDIFrame` class is derived from `TFrameWindow` and handles such tasks as finding and storing the position of the application's <u>W</u>indow menu. In addition, this class provides the member functions `GetClientWindow()`, which returns a pointer to the frame window's client window, and `SetMenu()`, which you can call to update the position of the <u>W</u>indow menu after you install a new menu bar.

This program doesn't create just any client window, but rather its own version, `TMDIClientWnd`, derived from `TMDIClient`:

```
class TMDIClientWnd : public TMDIClient
{
protected:
    int childNum;

public:
    TMDIClientWnd();

protected:
    TMDIChild *InitChild();
};
```

This class has a protected data member, `childNum`, that counts the number of child windows the user has opened. This number is used in each child window's caption to distinguish one child window from another. The program initializes `childNum` to 1 in the class's constructor. The `TMDIClientWnd` class overrides `TMDIClient`'s `InitChild()` function in order to create the type of child windows the program needs. When the user selects the <u>W</u>indow menu's C<u>r</u>eate command, OWL calls `InitChild()` to create the child window:

```
TMDIChild* TMDIClientWnd::InitChild()
{
    char s[20];
    sprintf(s, "Child Window #%d", childNum);
    ++childNum;
    return new TMDIChild(*this, s);
}
```

This function first creates the child window's caption string. Then it increments the child window counter, `childNum`, and returns a pointer to a new `TMDIChild` window. All child windows in an MDI application should be of the `TMDIChild` class (or derived from this class). The `TMDIChild` class is itself derived from `TFrameWindow`. Its constructor takes as parameters a reference to the client window and the new child window's caption string.

And that's all there is to the entire program! Although the program does nothing more than show how MDI applications work—that is, you can create child windows, but you can't type text or draw pictures in them—it's still amazing how far you can get with a few lines of code.

There is, however, one trick to getting so much work out of OWL. You must be sure that your menu item IDs are the values defined by OWL for the <u>Win</u>dow menu. The resource header file `MDI.RH`, found with Borland's other include files, defines a set of constants that you can use for this purpose. These constants are `CM_CASCADECHILDREN` (24361), `CM_TILECHILDREN` (24362), `CM_TILECHILDRENHORIZ` (24363), `CM_ARRANGEICONS` (24364), `CM_CLOSECHILDREN` (24365), and `CM_CREATECHILD` (24366). An OWL client window already has message-response functions that respond to these menu item IDs.

Next, you see how to flesh out this MDI shell into a fully functional text file editor.

An MDI Text Editor

Back when I told you you'd be able to create a full-fledged SDI text editor with only a few lines of code, you probably thought I was nuts. Now, you'll discover how to make that SDI editor into an MDI application that lets you edit many different text files simultaneously. Honest! Just look at listings 29.10 through 29.12.

Listing 29.10   MDIEDIT.CPP—An MDI Text Editor

```cpp
/////////////////////////////////////////////////////////
// MDIEDIT.CPP: A multiple-document interface application
//              for editing text files.
/////////////////////////////////////////////////////////

#include <owl\applicat.h>
#include <owl\decmdifr.h>
#include <owl\editfile.h>
#include <owl\mdi.h>
#include <owl\controlb.h>
#include <owl\statusba.h>
#include <owl\buttonga.h>
#include "mdiedit.rc"

///////////////////////////////////////
// The application class.
///////////////////////////////////////
class TMDIApp : public TApplication
{
protected:
   TMDIClient *clientWnd;
   TControlBar *controlBar;

public:
   TMDIApp() : TApplication() {}
   void InitMainWindow();

protected:
   void CmFileNew();
   void CmFileOpen();

   DECLARE_RESPONSE_TABLE(TMDIApp);
};

DEFINE_RESPONSE_TABLE1(TMDIApp, TApplication)
  EV_COMMAND(CM_FILENEW, CmFileNew),
  EV_COMMAND(CM_FILEOPEN, CmFileOpen),
END_RESPONSE_TABLE;

/////////////////////////////////////////////////////////
// TMDIApp::InitMainWindow()
//
// This function creates the application's main window,
// client window, control bar, and status bar.
/////////////////////////////////////////////////////////
void TMDIApp::InitMainWindow()
{
   // Create the client window.
   clientWnd = new TMDIClient;
```

(continues)

V

Tools and Techniques

Listing 29.10 Continued

```
// Create the frame window.
TDecoratedMDIFrame *frameWnd =
    new TDecoratedMDIFrame("File Editor",
    MENU_1, *clientWnd, TRUE);

// Size and position the frame window.
frameWnd->Attr.X = 50;
frameWnd->Attr.Y = 50;
frameWnd->Attr.W = 500;
frameWnd->Attr.H = 300;

// Create the control bar.
controlBar = new TControlBar(frameWnd);
controlBar->
    Insert(*new TButtonGadget(ID_NEW, CM_FILENEW));
controlBar->
    Insert(*new TButtonGadget(ID_OPEN, CM_FILEOPEN));
controlBar->
    Insert(*new TButtonGadget(ID_SAVE, CM_FILESAVE));
controlBar->
    Insert(*new TSeparatorGadget(10));
controlBar->
    Insert(*new TButtonGadget(ID_CUT, CM_EDITCUT));
controlBar->
    Insert(*new TButtonGadget(ID_COPY, CM_EDITCOPY));
controlBar->
    Insert(*new TButtonGadget(ID_PASTE, CM_EDITPASTE));
controlBar->
    Insert(*new TSeparatorGadget(10));
controlBar->
    Insert(*new TButtonGadget(ID_UNDO, CM_EDITUNDO));

// Set the hint mode to show hints instantly.
controlBar->SetHintMode(TGadgetWindow::EnterHints);

// Insert the control bar into the frame window.
frameWnd->Insert(*controlBar, TDecoratedFrame::Top);

// Create the status bar.
TStatusBar *statusBar = new TStatusBar(0,
    TGadget::Recessed,
    TStatusBar::CapsLock | TStatusBar::NumLock |
    TStatusBar::Overtype);

// Insert the status bar into the frame window.
frameWnd->Insert(*statusBar, TDecoratedFrame::Bottom);

// Set the frame window's icon.
frameWnd->SetIcon(this, ID_MDIEDIT);

// Enable Microsoft's 3-D controls.
EnableCtl3d(TRUE);
```

```
      // Set the application's MainWindow pointer.
      SetMainWindow(frameWnd);
}


//////////////////////////////////////////////////////////
// TMDIApp::CmFileNew
//
// This function creates a new window when the user
// chooses the File menu's New command or when the user
// clicks the New button on the control bar.
//////////////////////////////////////////////////////////
void TMDIApp::CmFileNew()
{
      // Create a new file-editing control.
      TEditFile *editFile = new TEditFile;

      // Create a child window for the new file.
      TMDIChild *childWnd =
         new TMDIChild(*clientWnd, "", editFile);

      // Set the window's icon.
      childWnd->SetIcon(this, ID_DOCUMENT);

      // Display the new child window.
      childWnd->Create();
}


//////////////////////////////////////////////////////////
// TMDIApp::CmFileOpen
//
// This function creates a new window when the user
// chooses the File menu's Open command or when the user
// clicks the Open button on the control bar.
//////////////////////////////////////////////////////////
void TMDIApp::CmFileOpen()
{
      // Create the dialog box's TData object.
      TOpenSaveDialog::TData fileData(OFN_FILEMUSTEXIST¦
         OFN_HIDEREADONLY¦OFN_PATHMUSTEXIST,
         "All Files (*.*)¦*.*¦Text Files (*.txt)¦*.txt¦",
         0, 0, "*");

      // Start the file name out as an empty string.
      strcpy(fileData.FileName, "");

      // Create the Open dialog box.
      TFileOpenDialog *dialog =
         new TFileOpenDialog(MainWindow, fileData);

      // Execute the Open dialog box.
      int result = dialog->Execute();

      // If the user exits via the OK button...
      if (result == IDOK)
      {
```

(continues)

Listing 29.10   Continued

```
    // Create a new file-editing control.
      TEditFile *editFile =
        new TEditFile(0, 0, 0, 0, 0, 0, 0,
        fileData.FileName);

      // Create a new child window for the file.
      TMDIChild *childWnd =
        new TMDIChild(*clientWnd, "", editFile);

      // Set the window's icon.
      childWnd->SetIcon(this, ID_DOCUMENT);

      // Display the new child window.
      childWnd->Create();
    }

    // Erase any old hint text.
    controlBar->SetHintCommand(-1);
  }


  ///////////////////////////////////////////////////////////
  // OwlMain()
  ///////////////////////////////////////////////////////////
  int OwlMain(int, char*[])
  {
    return TMDIApp().Run();
  }
```

Listing 29.11   MDIEDIT.RC—MDIEDIT's Resource File

```
  ///////////////////////////////////////////////////////////
  // MDIEDIT.RC
  ///////////////////////////////////////////////////////////

  #ifndef WORKSHOP_INVOKED
  #include "windows.h"
  #endif

  #include <owl\mdi.rh>
  #include <owl\editfile.rh>

  #define ID_MDIEDIT  101
  #define ID_DOCUMENT 100
  #define MENU_1      100
  #define ID_UNDO     CM_EDITUNDO
  #define ID_SAVE     CM_FILESAVE
  #define ID_PASTE    CM_EDITPASTE
  #define ID_OPEN     CM_FILEOPEN
  #define ID_NEW      CM_FILENEW
  #define ID_CUT      CM_EDITCUT
  #define ID_COPY     CM_EDITCOPY
```

```
#ifdef RC_INVOKED

#include <owl\except.rc>
#include <owl\statusba.rc>

MENU_1 MENU
{
 POPUP "&File"
 {
  MENUITEM "&New", CM_FILENEW
  MENUITEM "&Open...", CM_FILEOPEN
  MENUITEM "&Save", CM_FILESAVE, GRAYED
  MENUITEM "Save &As...", CM_FILESAVEAS
  MENUITEM SEPARATOR
  MENUITEM "E&xit", CM_EXIT
 }

 POPUP "&Edit"
 {
  MENUITEM "&Undo", CM_EDITUNDO
  MENUITEM SEPARATOR
  MENUITEM "&Cut", CM_EDITCUT
  MENUITEM "C&opy", CM_EDITCOPY
  MENUITEM "&Paste", CM_EDITPASTE
  MENUITEM "&Delete", CM_EDITDELETE
  MENUITEM "C&lear All", CM_EDITCLEAR
 }

 POPUP "&Search"
 {
  MENUITEM "&Find...", CM_EDITFIND
  MENUITEM "&Replace...", CM_EDITREPLACE
  MENUITEM "&Next", CM_EDITFINDNEXT
 }

 POPUP "&Window"
 {
  MENUITEM "&Cascade", CM_CASCADECHILDREN
  MENUITEM "&Tile", CM_TILECHILDREN
  MENUITEM "Arrange &Icons", CM_ARRANGEICONS
  MENUITEM "C&lose All", CM_CLOSECHILDREN
 }

}

STRINGTABLE
{
 CM_FILENEW, "Start a new document"
 CM_FILEOPEN, "Open an existing document"
 CM_FILESAVE, "Save the current document"
 CM_FILESAVEAS, "Save the current document under a new name"
 CM_EXIT, "Quit the editor"
 CM_EDITUNDO, "Undo the most recent operation"
 CM_EDITCOPY, "Copy the selected text into the clipboard"
 CM_EDITCUT, "Cut the selected text into the clipboard"
```

(continues)

V

Tools and Techniques

Listing 29.11 Continued

```
      CM_EDITPASTE, "Insert the contents of the clipboard"
      CM_EDITCLEAR, "Clear the contents of the current window"
      CM_EDITDELETE, "Delete the selected text"
      CM_EDITREPLACE, "Find and change a string of text"
      CM_EDITFIND, "Find a string of text"
      CM_EDITFINDNEXT, "Find the next matching text"
      CM_CASCADECHILDREN, "Cascade all windows"
      CM_TILECHILDREN, "Tile all windows"
      CM_ARRANGEICONS, "Arrange window icons"
      CM_CLOSECHILDREN, "Close all windows"
      IDS_UNTITLEDFILE, "(Untitled)"
      IDS_UNABLEREAD, "Unable to read file %s from disk."
      IDS_UNABLEWRITE, "Unable to write file %s to disk."
      IDS_FILECHANGED, "The text in the %s file has changed.\n\n\
Do you want to save the changes?"
      IDS_CANNOTFIND, "Cannot find ""%s""."
      }

      ID_UNDO BITMAP "c:\tcwin45\expert\owl\undo.bmp"
      ID_CUT BITMAP "c:\tcwin45\expert\owl\cut.bmp"
      ID_COPY BITMAP "c:\tcwin45\expert\owl\copy.bmp"
      ID_PASTE BITMAP "c:\tcwin45\expert\owl\paste.bmp"
      ID_NEW BITMAP "c:\tcwin45\expert\owl\new.bmp"
      ID_OPEN BITMAP "c:\tcwin45\expert\owl\open.bmp"
      ID_SAVE BITMAP "c:\tcwin45\expert\owl\save.bmp"

      ID_DOCUMENT ICON "doc.ico"
      ID_MDIEDIT ICON "mdiedit.ico"

      #endif
```

Listing 29.12 MDIEDIT.DEF—MDIEDIT's Module Definition File

```
      NAME MDIEDIT
      DESCRIPTION 'MDI Editor example by Clayton Walnum'
      EXETYPE WINDOWS
      STUB 'WINSTUB.EXE'
      CODE PRELOAD MOVEABLE DISCARDABLE
      DATA PRELOAD MOVEABLE MULTIPLE
      HEAPSIZE 1024
      STACKSIZE 8192
```

Run this program, and you will see that you have a full-fledged MDI text editor (see fig. 29.7) that does just about anything except print files. The application has full File, Edit, Search, and Window menus that contain all the commands you expect to find. In addition, you can open as many documents as you want, reduce the documents to icons, and access several menu commands from the program's control bar. As you move your mouse pointer over any menu command or control button, hint text appears in the status bar,

and the status bar also tracks the status of your keyboard's Num Lock, Caps
Lock, and Insert keys. Finally, if you minimize the application, its icon appears at the bottom of your Windows desktop.

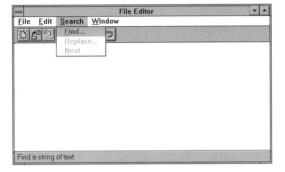

Fig. 29.7
The MDIEDIT
application,
a multiple-
document
text editor.

This program is short, but it sure does a lot. Mostly, this is due to OWL's
special MDI window classes—TMDIFrame, TMDIClient, TMDIChild, and
TDecoratedMDIFrame—which encapsulate much of the code necessary to
handle MDI applications. You can also give a nod to OWL's edit control class,
TEditFile, which encapsulates most of the behavior of a text-editing window.
(TEditFile "inherits" behavior from OWL's TEdit and TEditSearch classes;
their lineage can be traced through TStatic and TControl all the way up to
TWindow.)

Begin by examining the application's class, which looks quite different from
previous application classes used in this chapter:

```
class TMDIApp : public TApplication
{
protected:
   TMDIClient *clientWnd;
   TControlBar *controlBar;

public:
   TMDIApp() : TApplication() {}
   void InitMainWindow();

protected:
   void CmFileNew();
   void CmFileOpen();

   DECLARE_RESPONSE_TABLE(TMDIApp);
};

DEFINE_RESPONSE_TABLE1(TMDIApp, TApplication)
   EV_COMMAND(CM_FILENEW, CmFileNew),
   EV_COMMAND(CM_FILEOPEN, CmFileOpen),
END_RESPONSE_TABLE;
```

This class has two protected data members, `clientWnd` and `controlBar`, which point to the application's client window and control bar, respectively. These pointers enable the application to access the associated client window and control bar objects anywhere within the application class. The application also has the usual constructor and `InitMainWindow()` function. However, two protected message-response functions, `CmFileNew()` and `CmFileOpen()`, provide responses for the File menu's New and Open commands.

In this version of the program, the application class has taken on message-handling tasks. Because messages received by an MDI application pass from the application down to the active child's window, up to the client window, and finally up to the frame window, you can choose to intercept a particular message at a number of points. By handling the file messages in the application object, however, this program avoids deriving new `TDecoratedMDIFrame` and `TMDIClient` classes, and instead simply uses OWL's stock `TDecoratedMDIFrame` and `TMDIClient` classes. Of course, because the application class handles the `CM_FILENEW` and `CM_FILEOPEN` messages, it must also define a response table.

Before a window appears on-screen, much of the work in this program is handled in the application class's `InitMainWindow()` function. First, this function constructs a client window:

```
clientWnd = new TMDIClient;
```

Then because this application features a control bar and status bar, it constructs a `TDecoratedMDIFrame` window rather than a plain `TMDIFrame` window:

```
TDecoratedMDIFrame *frameWnd =
    new TDecoratedMDIFrame("File Editor",
    MENU_1, *clientWnd, TRUE);
```

The `TDecoratedMDIFrame` class is derived from both the `TMDIFrame` and `TDecoratedFrame` classes and is simply an MDI frame window that can handle decorations such as control bars and status bars. Its constructor actually takes the following five parameters, although the last three have default values:

- The window's title string
- A menu resource ID
- A reference to a client window
- A Boolean value indicating whether menu tracking should be enabled
- A `TLibId` object

The first two parameters—the window's title string and a menu resource ID—are required. If you don't supply the client window reference, the constructor automatically constructs a TMDIClient window. The Boolean argument defaults to FALSE, and the TLibId argument defaults to zero. Because this program uses menu tracking to display hint text in the status bar, the preceding TDecoratedMDIFrame constructor call provides a Boolean argument of TRUE. Note that to use the TDecoratedMDIFrame class you must include the header file DECMDIFR.H in your program.

After constructing the frame window, the program uses the frame window's pointer to access the window's Attr structure in order to size and position the window:

```
frameWnd->Attr.X = 50;
frameWnd->Attr.Y = 50;
frameWnd->Attr.W = 500;
frameWnd->Attr.H = 300;
```

The next task for InitMainWindow() is the construction of the application's control bar:

```
controlBar = new TControlBar(frameWnd);
controlBar->
    Insert(*new TButtonGadget(IDB_NEW, CM_FILENEW));
controlBar->
    Insert(*new TButtonGadget(IDB_OPEN, CM_FILEOPEN));
controlBar->
    Insert(*new TButtonGadget(IDB_SAVE, CM_FILESAVE));
controlBar->
    Insert(*new TSeparatorGadget(10));
controlBar->
    Insert(*new TButtonGadget(IDB_CUT, CM_EDITCUT));
controlBar->
    Insert(*new TButtonGadget(IDB_COPY, CM_EDITCOPY));
controlBar->
    Insert(*new TButtonGadget(IDB_PASTE, CM_EDITPASTE));
controlBar->
    Insert(*new TSeparatorGadget(10));
controlBar->
    Insert(*new TButtonGadget(IDB_UNDO, CM_EDITUNDO));
```

This code should look familiar from the SDI version of the editor.

Next InitMainWindow() sets the control bar's hint mode:

```
controlBar->SetHintMode(TGadgetWindow::EnterHints);
```

V

Tools and Techniques

As you already know, the `EnterHints` mode immediately displays hints when the mouse pointer passes over a control object, whereas the `PressHints` mode displays hints only when the associated control object is selected.

Now that the control bar is ready to go; `InitMainWindow()` adds it to the top of the frame window:

```
frameWnd->Insert(*controlBar, TDecoratedFrame::Top);
```

Next the program constructs the status bar:

```
TStatusBar *statusBar = new TStatusBar(0,
    TGadget::Recessed,
    TStatusBar::CapsLock ¦ TStatusBar::NumLock ¦
    TStatusBar::Overtype);
```

After creating the status bar, the program adds it to the bottom of the frame window:

```
frameWnd->Insert(*statusBar, TDecoratedFrame::Bottom);
```

Finally, `InitMainWindow()` assigns an icon to the frame window, enables the Microsoft 3-D control library, and sets the application's `MainWindow` pointer to the frame window:

```
// Set the frame window's icon.
frameWnd->SetIcon(this, ID_MDIEDIT);

// Enable Microsoft's 3-D controls.
EnableCtl3d(TRUE);

// Set the application's MainWindow pointer.
SetMainWindow(frameWnd);
```

After calling the frame window's `SetIcon()` function, the icon with the resource ID `IDI_MDIEDIT` appears on the Windows desktop whenever the application is minimized. This 16-color icon is 32×32 pixels in size and was created in Borland's Resource Workshop (see fig. 29.8). As you soon see, this program uses a similar icon to represent a minimized document in the application's frame window.

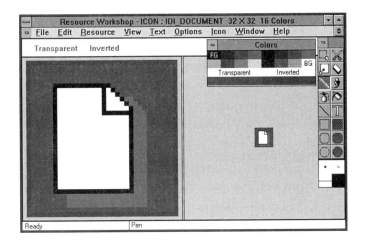

Fig. 29.8
Creating an
icon with
Resource
Workshop.

As you now know, the call to EnableCtl3d() brings Microsoft's 3-D control library into play. This difference results in 3-D dialog boxes such as the one in figure 29.9.

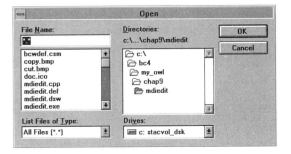

Fig. 29.9
A dialog box created
with Microsoft's 3-D
control library.

Tools and Techniques

V

When the user chooses the File menu's New command, OWL calls
CmFileNew():

```
void TMDIApp::CmFileNew()
{
    // Create a new file-editing control.
    TEditFile *editFile = new TEditFile;
```

```
        // Create a child window for the new file.
        TMDIChild *childWnd =
            new TMDIChild(*clientWnd, "", editFile);

        // Set the window's icon.
        childWnd->SetIcon(this, ID_DOCUMENT);

        // Display the new child window.
        childWnd->Create();
    }
```

This function works almost exactly the same as the one found in the SDIEDIT
application. The main difference is that this version must create an MDI child
window, as well as the new TEditFile object. Because this window is an MDI
child window that may get minimized, the program assigns an icon to the
window. This icon appears at the bottom of the main window whenever the
user minimizes the child window. SetIcon()'s two arguments include a
pointer to the window and the icon's resource ID. Finally, CmFileNew() calls
the child window's Create() member function to display the child window.

At this point, the user has a new fully functional text-editing window. Moreover, because OWL's edit control classes have their own command enablers,
you don't need to provide command enablers for the Edit and Search menus.

When the user chooses the File menu's Open command, program execution
branches to CmFileOpen():

```
    void TMDIApp::CmFileOpen()
    {
        // Create the dialog box's TData object.
        TOpenSaveDialog::TData fileData(OFN_FILEMUSTEXIST|
            OFN_HIDEREADONLY|OFN_PATHMUSTEXIST,
            "All Files (*.*)|*.*|Text Files (*.txt)|*.txt|",
            0, 0, "*");

        // Start the file name out as an empty string.
        strcpy(fileData.FileName, "");

        // Create the Open dialog box.
        TFileOpenDialog *dialog =
            new TFileOpenDialog(MainWindow, fileData);

        // Execute the Open dialog box.
        int result = dialog->Execute();

        // If the user exits via the OK button...
        if (result == IDOK)
        {
            // Create a new file-editing control.
            TEditFile *editFile =
                new TEditFile(0, 0, 0, 0, 0, 0, 0,
                fileData.FileName);
```

```
            // Create a new child window for the file.
            TMDIChild *childWnd =
                new TMDIChild(*clientWnd, "", editFile);

            // Set the window's icon.
            childWnd->SetIcon(this, ID_DOCUMENT);

            // Display the new child window.
            childWnd->Create();
    }

    // Erase any old hint text.
    controlBar->SetHintCommand(-1);
}
```

Again, this function is much like the function of the same name in the previous SDIEDIT application, except this version must create and show an MDI child window, as well as create the new TEditFile object.

There you have it! A multiple-document text editor in less than 100 code lines (counting only actual program lines, not comments, blank lines, and so on). A perfect example of how well Windows and OWL work together.

From Here...

As you've discovered, SDI applications provide a way to create simple, easy-to-use programs. But most Windows users expect to be able to open more than one document window at a time. If your application doesn't give the user this power, the user will likely pass your application over in favor of another. Although handling multiple documents makes programming a little more tricky, Turbo C++ programmers can take advantage of the powerful ObjectWindows library, which does much of the work for them. Using OWL, MDI applications aren't much more difficult to implement than SDI applications.

If you found this chapter difficult to follow, you may want to read or review the following chapters:

- Chapter 27, "The ObjectWindows Library," is a general overview of ObjectWindows.

- Chapter 28, "ObjectWindows Applications," helps you get started writing OWL programs.

Chapter 30

Object Linking and Embedding

OLE, more formally known as object linking and embedding, is fundamentally a technology designed to change the way people use their computers. OLE addresses such a vast range of application development and user interface issues that it has been likened by some to being the equivalent of one-third of an entire operating system. Interapplication communication and integration, data-type transparency, compound documents, and component-based application objects...what does it all mean?

It means that, like it or not, OLE is a powerful and enabling technology that is picking up momentum to be *the* standard programming interface for application integration. This chapter explains what all the fuss is about. It shows you what the various OLE technologies are and then explains how Borland has designed an object-oriented software layer that almost completely hides the very complicated low-level OLE programming interfaces. Finally, a simple OWL-based document/view application is transformed into a fully OLE-enabled program. Even better, you'll get a head start on learning how to accomplish the same feats from within your own programs.

This chapter addresses the following topics:

- Why Microsoft decided to develop the OLE 2.0 technology

- A synopsis of OLE services

- Problems with OLE

- Borland's approach to OLE support

- Writing an OWL-based OLE application

Computing in the Dark Ages

To understand some of the motivating concerns driving Microsoft's development of OLE requires a bit of historical perspective. Don't worry; this historical overview will be brief.

The operating system delivered with the very first IBM personal computer was probably the same operating system that you have loaded on your computer now: DOS. Obviously DOS has evolved substantially over the last decade or so, but the operating system itself really hasn't changed that much. DOS's user-interface (that is, the command-line prompt) remains the same, and despite the addition of a nicety here or there, MS-DOS 6.x is very similar to DOS 1.0.

Amazingly, as ugly and ungainly as DOS was, people were actually able to use their computers to some benefit. New versions of DOS periodically arrived that added just enough new functionality to keep people from openly revolting and defecting *en masse* to a new operating system. Still, although many of the most popular software titles ran under only DOS, it was not uncommon to catch a PC user sneaking envious glances at his neighbor's Macintosh when no one was looking. Then in 1990, Microsoft shipped Windows 3.0 and changed everything.

Earlier versions of Windows had been around for years, but the truth was, they weren't very good. Even though Windows sits on top of DOS and is itself just another DOS program, it provides considerable added value by making it appear as if DOS has been completely replaced. Windows 3.0 was the first graphical environment for DOS that performed reasonably well and took advantage of Intel's 80386 processor. Computers were also becoming significantly faster and being shipped with more memory and hard-disk space. All of these things helped to make Windows a runaway hit.

One of the most useful features of Windows was, ironically, one that the Macintosh had been sporting for years (and which Apple, in turn, had "borrowed" from Xerox's earlier Star microcomputer). The public clipboard allowed data to be shared between applications. Because the Windows clipboard could be used to cut and paste different types of data, the feature proved to be a big time saver. Unfortunately, new computer users often had a difficult time with the cut-and-paste metaphor, and it was common to find applications that did not support popular clipboard formats.

One of the main reasons that it was so easy to find applications that did not support each other's clipboard formats was because the applications themselves had their own internal and completely different data representation schemes. These schemes typically manifested themselves in the form of proprietary document types. Each application had a different document format that other programs could not read and understand.

This sorry state of affairs degenerated to the point where the most sophisticated and popular applications were often those that understood the largest number of popular document formats. A whole new class of utility program sprang into existence whose only purpose was to convert one document format into another.

Microsoft set out to clean up this mess with OLE 2.0. The first version of the specification had been designed primarily as a way to facilitate the construction of compound documents. (If you don't know what compound documents are, don't worry because you will soon enough.) With OLE 2.0, Microsoft wanted to establish a whole new way for applications to share data and services.

> **Note**
>
> As the name implies, OLE 2.0 isn't Microsoft's first compound document effort. It's interesting to note that OLE version 1.0 was not a failure. Version 2.0 reflects an elaboration and maturation of the 1.0 technology, and directly addresses some of the critical problems that were exposed with the first version. OLE 2.0 also introduces a host of services that aren't necessarily concerned with compound documents; this new version expands the focus of the specification to include things such as generalized data transfer, a new object model, and structured files.

So What's the Big Deal about OLE?

Although people generally talk about OLE as if it performs only one function, nothing could be further from the truth. OLE is several different technologies operating together in concert. Most of the OLE services exist at one of three different levels. Some of the services, like the Component Object Model and structured storage, reside deeply in Windows and are never directly seen by the user. Other services, like drag and drop, resemble features that have been previously available to users of certain programs as an application-specific behavior. Finally, services like compound documents and in-place editing profoundly change the way that users directly interact with their software.

V

Tools and Techniques

Compound Documents

If you wanted to produce an invitation that told your friends about your spouse's upcoming surprise birthday party, how would you do it? Chances are you would begin by getting into Windows and starting up the word processor. You would probably click on a toolbar button or make a selection from a menu, and the application would create a new document for you. After designing the invitation you would start another application to select some clip art. You would cut and paste some of the clip art into your invitation document. Then you would print a dozen copies, save the file, and you would be done.

Now how would you go about building a new house? Would you start by driving across town to "Foundations-Are-Us," have the friendly sales staff completely design and build a concrete foundation, and then cart it back to your property strapped to the roof of your mini-van? Of course not. You would hire a contractor to come out to your property and build the foundation there. And yet you would "go" to a graphics program to select your clip art and then cart it all the way back across your Windows desktop to your word processor. Why not bring the tools to you and design your clip art from within your document?

The answer is that until now you couldn't. Perhaps the most compelling feature of OLE is its capability to help programs create compound documents. Take another look at your hypothetical party invitation. It is composed of several different data types. You have text and clip art. If you are really ambitious you may even use a mailing list from a database program to help you print your envelopes. You currently have to rely on a different program to manipulate and manage each one of these data types. If you want to change any part of your document, you need to go back to the original application, edit the appropriate part, and then re-import it into your word processor.

In many ways, a compound document is very similar to an everyday word processing document. It is also composed of different parts, each with its own unique data type. The difference is that each of these parts is explicitly associated with their owner application and can be edited on the fly. For example, although an OLE-enabled word processor may not know how to edit the photograph part embedded in its current document, the OLE subsystem knows which application needs to be activated when the user wants to crop the picture. The word processor in turn understands the OLE protocol and can manipulate various presentation characteristics of the part without caring about the part's content.

Sound like magic? It's not, but as you might imagine, controlling the interactions between applications in a truly generic fashion can get quite complicated. OLE is very powerful, but if you're trying to learn about it from the ground up, it can be rather overwhelming.

The compound document model represents a fundamental shift away from users viewing their interaction with the computer as one where they deal with individual applications that are each responsible for managing their own data. Instead, with compound documents, users are embracing a concept called *document-centric computing*. In document-centric computing, the document provides the central abstraction instead of the application. In the document-centric model, users start with a document and use tools to manipulate aspects of that document as needed. As you learn later on, this is a powerful concept that really does change the way that the user interacts with the computer.

> ### Note
>
> The current software market is replete with large, bloated application programs that have adopted the "I can do everything" manifesto. Word processors are now shipping with built-in equation editors. Database programs are appearing with form construction modules. Spreadsheets are sporting add-on drawing components. Average people use only a fraction of the features offered by their programs, but they pay for them nonetheless.
>
> Compound documents suggest a new model for software construction: component software. With component software, applications get smaller—not larger. Monolithic programs get separated into smaller pieces of distinct functionality. Users have to pay for only the features that they know they are going to use. Entire software companies can dedicate themselves to concentrating on a single set of features and doing them exceptionally well.

Although it is possible to write an entire book simply on using OLE (and Que has just that book, *Using OLE 2.x in Application Development*), the next sections demonstrate how a user interacts with OLE's compound document features.

OLE Containers

To understand the compound document model in more detail, you need to become familiar with the OLE terms *container* and *server*. When you talk about compound documents and OLE compound documents in particular, what you're actually talking about is a specialized variety of application called an OLE container. Containers know virtually nothing about their contents.

Instead, they act as repositories for *parts*. The applications that are responsible for manipulating the contents of the parts are called OLE servers.

Containers interact with their parts in a number of ways. They are usually most concerned with those characteristics that are directly related to where a part is located: placing the part on the screen, setting the part's size, scaling, and things like that. Note, however, that a container is never concerned with what a part looks like or how it is displayed. The only entity that knows about displaying a given part is that part's server.

One of the nice things about the OLE standard is that it provides a set of rules and guidelines that dictate precisely how users are supposed to interact with compound documents. This is valuable because if OLE didn't provide these rules, every container would behave differently and users would have to learn how to use each vendor's interpretation separately.

Take a look at figure 30.1. This screen shot depicts the Circle2 container that you get to know quite intimately later in the section "Creating the OLE Container: Circle2."

Fig. 30.1
The Circle2 OLE container application.

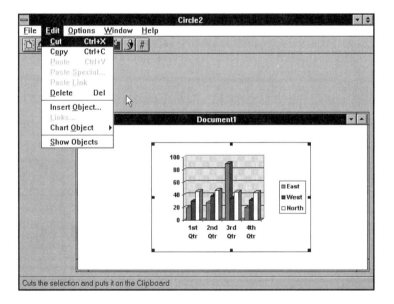

In this figure you can see that the container (that is, Circle2) is holding a single document and that the document has an object embedded within it, denoted by the black square with sizing handles. These handles are used to provide visual cues to the user about how the embedded part can be resized and moved about within the container. By clicking and dragging on these handles, or by clicking and dragging the middle of the embedded object, the part can be managed and manipulated in a manner independent of its content.

The containers you'll be looking at in this chapter have some interesting characteristics. Notice how in figure 30.1 the application's Edit menu is dropped down. There are a number of options on this menu that you may not be familiar with. Specifically, the Paste Special, Paste Link, Insert Object, Links, Object, and Show Objects menu options are all OLE container commands that relate to creating and manipulating parts inside a compound document.

By selecting the Insert Object menu choice, the user is directing the container to insert a new part into their compound document. Figure 30.2 shows the standard OLE Insert Object dialog box.

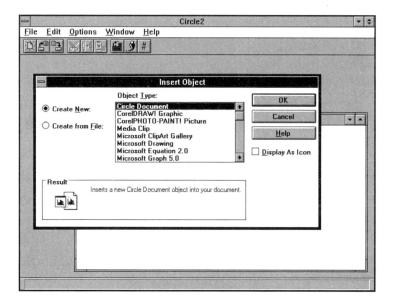

Fig. 30.2
Inserting a new part into a compound document.

V

Tools and Techniques

As you can see, different document types are listed in the Object Type list box. The user can choose to insert a part from a document that already exists. Figure 30.3 shows how the Insert Object dialog box modifies itself when the Create from File option button is selected.

The user at this point selects the type of part to create. The container activates the appropriate server with the intent of adding a new part to the document. The user is free to interact with the server. Figure 30.4 shows the process of creating and embedding a new VISIO part inside the Circle2 document.

Fig. 30.3
Inserting a previously existing part into a compound document.

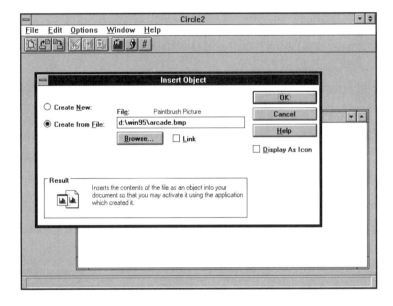

Fig. 30.4
Creating the new part.

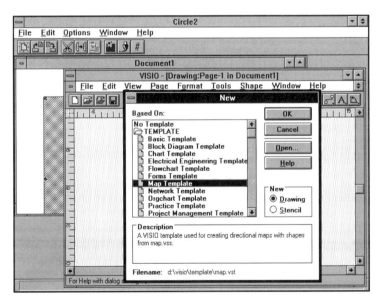

Once embedded in a compound document, the user's interaction with parts is controlled by the container. However, using the mechanisms described in the next section, the user can at any time initiate an editing session with the appropriate OLE server.

OLE Servers

As mentioned previously, an OLE server is the application responsible for actually manipulating the part's data. For example, if a compound document has a graphic embedded in it, the OLE server is the program that allows the user to actually draw lines and squares, and otherwise manipulate the picture.

A server can communicate to a container what actions it supports. These actions are referred to as *verbs*. The container in turn, because it has no knowledge of the part's contents, blindly places these verbs onto the Object cascading menu. The Object cascading menu can be accessed in one of two ways. On the Edit menu there is a command that displays the Object cascading menu. In a similar manner, clicking the right mouse button on an embedded part displays a pop-up menu that allows the user to cut and paste the object. This pop-up menu also contains an option for displaying the Object cascading menu.

When using the Turbo C++ OLE libraries, the default behavior is to have servers expose two verbs: Edit and Open. Of course it is possible for servers to offer other verbs as deemed necessary. Once again, it is important to note that the container is ignorant of what the server verbs actually mean or imply. It simply modifies its menus in a way dictated by OLE and the server.

The first option on the Object cascading menu is referred to as the default verb, and it is the option that is selected whenever the user double-clicks on the embedded part. For Turbo C++ applications, the default verb is Edit. Figure 30.5 shows the Object cascading menu for the embedded VISIO part.

Apart from having to coordinate certain aspects of their behavior with containers, OLE servers are full-fledged application programs that can be as elaborate as you want to make them. Just because your server may have its main output window restricted in size and placement doesn't mean that you can't do things like create modeless dialog boxes and child windows. (Indeed, see figure 30.6, which shows that the VISIO server application uses a variety of elaborate supplementary user interface elements.)

As a final word on containers and servers, notice that an application can be both a container and a server. In fact, the Circle3 sample program discussed later in this chapter is both a container and server.

Fig. 30.5

Displaying an
embedded object's
verbs.

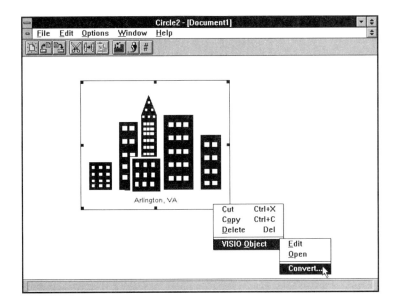

In-Place Editing

When the VISIO part in our example is first being created, the Circle2 container is running in the background and the VISIO server application is running in the foreground (refer to fig. 30.4). While this is quite convenient, it's hardly optimal. As evidenced by the two separate program windows, it's obvious that there are two applications running; the only thing that you've really gained is the automated handoff of control from the container to the server. Enter in-place editing.

In-place editing is really the key to seamlessly integrating applications. It allows a server application to merge its menus and toolbars with the container application. When the user double-clicks on the embedded object (or selects Edit from the Object cascading menu), the container program is "transformed" into the server program. In figure 30.6, you can see the effect that in-place editing has on the Circle2 container. The Circle2 menus have been merged with the VISIO application and the toolbar has been replaced with the VISIO version.

In-place editing epitomizes what document-centric computing is all about. Remember that in document-centric computing the focus point is the document and its data. The applications are ancillary tools that the user uses to manipulate the data. By switching menus and toolbars dynamically, OLE is facilitating a tool-oriented approach to building documents as opposed to an application-oriented approach. That being said, if you really want to (or more likely if your server application doesn't support in-place editing), you can also select Open from the Object cascading menu and start the server application separately.

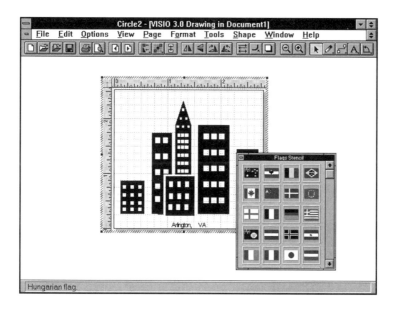

Fig. 30.6
In-place editing of an embedded part.

Embedding Versus Linking

By this point you're probably wondering whatever happened to the "linking" part of object linking and embedding. The previous sections have shown examples of embedding, but where's the linking? If you look closely at figure 30.3, you will notice the rather innocuous Link check box next to the Browse button. Marking this option causes the OLE container to place a link reference into the compound document instead of the entire part. While OLE servers typically display a linked object in exactly the same fashion they do an embedded object, there are a number of important differences.

Why would you ever want to link a part instead of embed it? While embedding a part may be convenient, it can also create very large document files. Imagine, for example, a technical document that is not very long and contains only a couple of paragraphs of text. This same technical document, however, also has six graphic images that together are several megabytes in size. In this case, when saved, the compound document is more than several megabytes in size. In addition, linking allows data within the document to be updated *dynamically*. If the user changes the linked file that is referenced by the compound document, those changes are communicated to the container and updated on the fly. This allows a group of people (on a network, for example) to share a set of linked files and have changes in those links reflected in the individual compound documents.

> **Note**
>
> Servers that support linking and embedding are sometimes referred to as *full servers*, while servers that just support embedding are referred to as *mini-servers*. A mini-server cannot run as a stand-alone application and can be started only by a container that is either creating a new part or editing an existing one.

Application Automation

In previous sections you read about how OLE servers expose verbs to their containers. This provides a crude mechanism for furnishing a generic user interface to server activation. Unfortunately, this level of interaction is limited to setting menu options in a container application. OLE automation, on the other hand, is a more powerful manifestation of a similar, related concept.

Using OLE automation, an object can "publish" a set of interfaces to a generalized audience. Programs that have never heard of your objects can, through standard OLE system calls, query information about what interfaces are available and what arguments various function calls accept.

This feature allows for the creation of generic application scripting capabilities. For example, a Visual Basic program can call into your application objects and drive your program in much the same way that a user can. Now you could accomplish similar effects by having your Visual Basic programs call directly into dynamic link libraries (DLLs) or using dynamic data exchange (DDE). The OLE automation approach, however, is just as flexible with the added advantage of being standardized and considerably more robust. Additionally, Microsoft plans on extending the capabilities of OLE to span across machine boundaries. That means that OLE automation can be extended to support scripting and macro recording on a network basis. Imagine the possibilities of simple user-written scripts and macros that can reach out across the network, manipulate co-workers' applications, and return function results to the home machine in a convenient data structure.

Structured Storage

One of the ironies of OLE 2.0 is that the concept of structured storage is prevalent throughout virtually every aspect of the system and that most users of OLE-enabled applications are blissfully unaware that structured storage even exists.

Structured storage provides an abstract interface for applications to store compound documents. A normal disk file supports operations that support a single compartment-like metaphor. A program opens a file, reads and/or writes to its single storage area, and then closes it. The structured storage model, on the other hand, is based on *streams* and *storages*. Streams are simply the structured storage equivalents of directories; storages are equivalent to files. Structured storage is simply a way of mapping a lightweight file system into a single file. The advantage to this approach is that an application that is responsible for saving compound documents to disk (that is, a container application) can assign each of its parts to a storage within the document file. The part is responsible for saving and loading its data from its assigned storage (or storages) without regard for where in the file the data is located or where in the file data for other parts may be located.

By delegating the responsibility for saving and loading data onto its constituent parts, the container maintains a hands-off attitude that guarantees its independence from the storage details of its parts.

OLE Data Objects

OLE supports a set of services referred to as the *Uniform Data Transfer*. Uniform Data Transfer objects abstract the movement of information into a single interface, regardless of the mechanism being used to accomplish the transfer. The same piece of code, for example, can be used to share information through a clipboard operation, a drag-and-drop action, a DDE conversation, or a standard OLE API call.

The primary emphasis of an OLE data transfer is on the Data Object (the official object name is `IDataObject`). In the course of a data transfer it's actually a data object that is being moved. A data object can contain a chunk of memory. Depending on the flexibility or sophistication of the data object, it may know how to render its memory into a variety of different formats. However, a data object can also refer to a structured storage object—a compound document. This makes the transfer of large objects through the clipboard and through drag and drop more feasible and easier to implement because all of the data being moved doesn't have to all be in memory at once. Instead, a relatively small data object can be used to refer to a document file, and only this small object instance needs to be moved from one application to the other. The target application can then access the document file through the data object without really knowing or caring whether the file is completely contained in memory.

V

Tools and Techniques

Drag and Drop

Limited forms of drag and drop (D&D) have been built into Windows for quite some time now. The operative term here is "limited." Most of the Windows APIs that deal with D&D are concerned with dragging files from the File Manager on to application windows. While there is certainly little doubt that this functionality is useful, it's not nearly flexible enough to support the sort of pervasive D&D operations that you see embodied in the Apple Macintosh, for example.

D&D is also an easier user interface metaphor for novice users to grasp than the clipboard. Instead of having to fool around with the cumbersome "select-cut-switch applications-paste" process, it is much more intuitive to select an item, pick it up, and move it to wherever you want it to be. With D&D the entire data transfer is direct and immediate. Figure 30.7 shows the archetypal D&D example: moving a spreadsheet range from Excel into a Word document.

Fig. 30.7
Drag and drop in action.

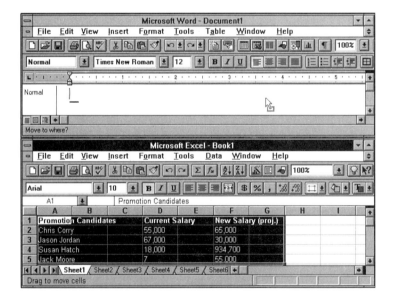

As an added bonus, because OLE uses the same interfaces for clipboard support as it does to implement elements of D&D, programs that are modified to use OLE standard data transfers are already halfway there to supporting drag-and-drop operations.

OLE Problems and Alternatives

From the general overview presented in the previous sections, you may be under the impression that OLE is the greatest thing since sliced bread. There's certainly no doubt that OLE represents an impressive piece of software engineering. The capabilities of OLE, when properly implemented, can be quite stunning and are virtually dripping with potential. However, OLE is not without its flaws.

OLE's Steep Learning Curve

Probably the most frustrating part of writing OLE-enabled applications is that OLE is very difficult to program. The lowest-level APIs are complex and require a thorough understanding of many intricate and interdependent software components. If you are interested in learning how to program OLE from the ground up, prepare yourself for a long and arduous experience.

On the other hand, there is a ray of hope clearly shining out of Borland headquarters. By wrapping OLE in a software layer that provides a simpler and more programmer-friendly interface, Borland has provided you with the tools to get up to speed on OLE programming much faster than normal. If the basic behaviors of the Borland classes don't do what you need, you can always create your own subclasses and write to the lower levels of code. However, in the vast majority of cases, you'll find that the default behaviors to be perfectly acceptable.

Slow-Motion OLE

OLE suffers from other problems, of course, that Borland cannot solve. For example, applications that are OLE-enabled are often criticized for being too slow. The simple fact of the matter is that OLE makes serious demands on the operating system and your computer hardware. When you buy into OLE, remind yourself that you are buying into a software technology that may place your software out of the usable range of some machines. If a computer doesn't have enough computing muscle, memory, or hard-disk space, the OLE system requirements may reflect poorly on your application. This argument, however, will become less of an issue as computers continue to grow more powerful while still experiencing commensurate drops in pricing.

The Development Investment

There is also the larger issue of whether OLE is going to catch on and actually be the great application unifier that Microsoft is billing it as. So far the

V

Tools and Techniques

Microsoft marketing machine has been doing an outstanding job of promoting OLE as the single most qualified standard for the creating of compound documents under Windows. Developers are scrambling left and right to support OLE, so it seems increasingly unlikely that a decision to integrate OLE support into your applications will lead to wasted effort.

Another Option: OpenDoc

There is, however, an alternative to OLE. Component Integration Laboratories (CIL) is a consortium of big-name Microsoft competitors who have developed their own compound document technology called OpenDoc. In many respects OpenDoc is technically superior to OLE. For example, OpenDoc allows parts in containers to utilize non-rectangular shapes and to be arbitrarily nested. OpenDoc also benefits from being an open standard that has had cross-platform support designed into it from its inception. Whereas OLE is predominately a Windows phenomenon (it is available on the Macintosh but developers have been slow to embrace it there), OpenDoc's first commercial release supports Windows (16 and 32 bit), Macintosh, and OS/2; more platforms are to follow.

OpenDoc can also claim technical superiority when talking about issues of object-oriented purism. Unlike OpenDoc, OLE is not a truly object-oriented system. The OLE object model does not, for example, support inheritance. Many argue, however, that while this may be true, the inheritance limitation can be faked in OLE using a design construct called *aggregation*. Aggregation supports "subclasses" by having every child object contain an instance of a parent object. Interface calls that the child does not support can be passed on to the parent instance. It's not elegant but it can work.

The OpenDoc system is also fundamentally based on a distributed object model. This means that while Microsoft is feverishly working at providing support for interactions across a network in some future version of OLE, the first version of OpenDoc fully supports network-aware behaviors. As an example, your OpenDoc container can utilize servers that reside somewhere other than on the machine the container is running.

Finally, the members of CIL insist that OpenDoc is fully compatible with OLE. OpenDoc containers are able to interact with OLE servers and vice versa. This can be seen in two ways: good for Microsoft because developers feel safe knowing that even if the OpenDoc technology wins out, their OLE programming investment will be preserved, and good for CIL because developers feel safe that even if the OLE technology wins out, their OpenDoc programming investment will be preserved. Which of these two viewpoints makes the most sense depends entirely on which of the two technologies you favor.

Microsoft's OLE...Borland-Style

Borland has done an impressive job of wrapping the vast majority of OLE services into a set of C++ interfaces and class libraries. This is an important feat because a lot of the grunt work of interacting with the OLE system is hidden from the programmer. This allows you to concentrate on writing your application instead of learning OLE. That being said, Borland's OLE support is quite comprehensive and has a learning curve of its own. However, the Borland OLE classes are considerably easier to learn than the OLE APIs are.

The Component Object Model

Object linking and embedding rests on a foundation called the Component Object Model (COM). COM is a binary specification for implementing language-independent objects. It describes how an object is laid out in memory and—perhaps more importantly—it dictates how programs should interact with these objects. COM also stipulates how function calls and their parameters are passed across address spaces.

A COM object can be viewed as a black box in memory that has at least one exposed interface. A COM interface is simply a collection of functions that are grouped together because they are semantically related. A database object, for example, may expose an `ITable` interface containing functions like `CreateTable` and `AddColumn`. A calculator object may expose an `IOperator` interface with functions `Add`, `Subtract`, `Multiply`, and `Divide`. By convention, OLE interface names are prefaced with a capital I (for example, `ITable`, `IQuery`, and `IDisplay`).

COM objects can be manipulated only through their interfaces. In C++ parlance an object's interface is the semantic equivalent of its public member functions. There is no support in COM for public data. Instead, interfaces implement functions like `GetData` and `SetData`.

Every COM object implements at least one interface called `IUnknown`. The `IUnknown` interface contains three member functions, `QueryInterface`, `AddRef`, and `Release`. The last two functions are related to reference counting and are irrelevant for the purposes of this discussion, but the first function, `QueryInterface`, provides the mechanism by which programs detect and request non-`IUnknown` interfaces. Using `QueryInterface`, a program can determine whether a particular anonymous object can support various operations. For example, if an application wanted to know if an object supported in-place editing, it would use `QueryInterface` to see if the object supported the `IOleInPlaceObject` interface.

OLE sits on top of COM and relies on the binary object specification for its implementation of OLE system objects. Excluding the additional support for OLE controls and other optional services, the OLE 2.0 system exposes approximately 65 distinct interfaces. Remember that an interface is a group of functions; that's 65 function groups. You should be starting to get a feel for just how large OLE really is.

BOCOLE

The Borland Object Components OLE support (BOCOLE) contains a set of high-level interfaces to prevalent COM objects. Many of the most common and crucial interfaces are encapsulated into new COM interfaces contained in the BOCOLE DLL. In a nutshell, BOCOLE is responsible for simplifying some of the interactions that an OLE application must go through to access and utilize OLE services.

The BOCOLE engine also simplifies some of the COM architecture by bundling multiple interfaces into a single interface. This is accomplished with inheritance, which is one of the advantages to using C++ objects over straight COM objects. The `IBDataConsumer` class, for example, inherits from `IBDataNegotiator`, which in turn inherits from `IUnknown`. To the rest of the OLE world, however, these new interfaces simply appear as the aggregated sum of their subclasses.

With BOCOLE you have access to a bunch of COM objects that further abstract OLE interactions. This only means, however, that you've eased some of the hassles of interacting with the OLE system layer. While BOCOLE helps to simplify aspects of interacting with COM objects, BOCOLE is still COM-based and does little to facilitate seamless OLE interaction with a C++ application.

This discussion of COM objects and interfaces is important because, although they share many of the same behaviors and attributes, an OLE COM object is not a Turbo C++ object. That means that if you want to manipulate OLE and BOCOLE objects in the same way that you manipulate ordinary C++ objects, someone or something has to wrap or connect these COM entities with a corresponding C++ object shell. That something is the Object Components Framework.

The Object Components Framework

Assuming that you are a programmer who doesn't want to go through learning OLE from the ground up, the vast majority of what you want to accomplish can probably be achieved using the Object Components Framework (OCF), with or without OWL. OCF is the class library that contains the real meat of Borland's OLE support.

OCF is responsible for bridging the gap between C++ objects and COM objects. This is accomplished with a set of classes that Borland refers to as connector classes. The connectors present the programmer with class representations of common OLE entities. Connector object method calls are mapped onto COM interface function calls as appropriate. For example, an application that wants to use OLE services creates an instance of a TOcApp class. TOcApp is a connector that implements OLE interfaces that every compound document application needs.

Some of the connector classes in OCF have a one-to-one relationship with existing COM objects. There is, for example, a class in OCF named TUnknown. You probably won't be too shocked to learn that this class is responsible for encapsulating the COM IUnknown interface. Because all COM objects are required to implement the IUnknown interface, all of the classes in the OCF class hierarchy that directly represent COM interfaces are derived from TUnknown. Figure 30.8 depicts the relationship between OCF connector classes and COM objects and interfaces.

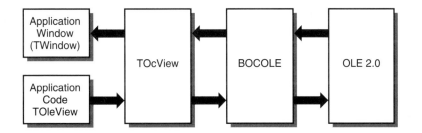

Fig. 30.8
The relationship between connector classes and COM objects.

In an OLE environment, OLE objects often need to call container and server applications. This usually happens when OLE wants to notify the application that an event of some importance has occurred. OCF intercepts these notifications and repackages them into the form of a window message (WM_OCEVENT). If your program is not an OWL program you can intercept and process these messages manually or, if your application does use OWL, you can use the standard OWL response table mechanism to receive these messages.

> **Note**
>
> It is important to stress that OCF and OWL are separate class libraries that are completely distinct. OCF can be used to create OLE-enabled applications that are not OWL-based. In fact, it is even possible to use OCF with compilers from other vendors. For example, although there is little reason to do it, you can build an application using Microsoft's MFC class libraries and then add OLE support with Borland's OCF and BOCOLE systems. More realistically, you can use OCF to OLE-enable applications built with other compilers whose class libraries are not already OLE-aware.

The OCF class library doesn't completely wrap the BOCOLE engine. Some OCF object methods are little more than pass-throughs to standard OLE objects. The nice thing is that your application doesn't care. You can use the standard OCF classes and make progress with little regard for what layers are actually carrying out the implementation details of your application's functionality.

> **Note**
>
> There are a number of COM interfaces that the BOCOLE engine and OCF class libraries do not support. Most notably, OCF knows nothing about OLE control interfaces like IOleControl, IConnectionPoint, and ISpecifyPropertyPages. This is not too surprising when you consider that the OLE control specification was available from Microsoft only in a beta form at the time that the first version of OCF was being developed. You can rest assured that Borland programmers are working at getting OLE control support into the next version of OCF.

OCF is a powerful tool that you can use to vastly simplify your OLE programs. The connector classes employed by an OCF application are robust and comprehensive enough to handle all but the most esoteric OLE applications. But Borland has made OLE even more approachable than its OCF support implies. With some simple extensions to the ObjectWindows libraries, Borland provided a very simple migration path for OWL applications that already employ the document/view model.

OLE Support in OWL

OWL supports the creation of OLE servers and containers through a mere half-dozen new classes. Most of these new OLE classes are derived from common OWL classes and are used in much the same way as their OWL counterparts. For example, as you will see in the sample programs, OWL programs that are OLE-enabled replace references to classes like TWindowView with

`TOleView`. `TOleView` acts just like a `TWindowView` but is OLE aware. Classes like `TOleView`, `TOleDocument`, and `TOleWindow` help to make the process of migrating your existing OWL code to OLE virtually painless. You'll get to see exactly how these classes are used when we go over the sample programs in upcoming sections.

Figure 30.9 shows the overall structure of Borland's support for OLE 2.0. Borland provides a lot of insulation between your application and the barebones OLE system. Although this may seem a little scary at first—BOCOLE, OCF, and OWL certainly seem to be taking on a lot of responsibility—the best part is that it all works.

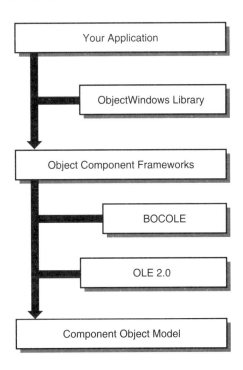

Fig. 30.9
Borland's OLE support systems (that is, BOCOLE, OCF, and OWL).

V

Tools and Techniques

Getting Down to Brass Tacks

The rest of this chapter will briefly discuss some of the issues inherent in OLE-enabling an existing OWL application. In the first step, you see how easy it is to enable the sample application to support OLE containers; the second step modifies the program even further to create a fully functional OLE server. OLE automation, however, is not tackled in these examples.

The program that is discussed in the next few sections is called Circle. The Circle program is a simple OWL application that is based on the document/view model and utilizes OWL's built-in support for the multiple document interface (MDI). Turbo C++ also allows you to add OLE support to OWL programs that do not conform to the document/view model or that use the single document interface (SDI) instead of MDI. These types of application migrations are not discussed in this chapter, although the steps you take are similar.

The document/view model is the fundamental mechanism that OWL uses to abstract the presentation of data from the data itself. An OWL application will typically write one or more classes derived from a view class (for example, TWindowView) and at least one class derived from a partnered document class (for example, TFileDocument).

Caution

The upcoming sample programs demonstrate how easy it is to integrate OLE support into MDI applications that rely on the OWL document/view model. If you are not familiar with OWL, the document/view model, or OWL's support for MDI, you are strongly urged to read the chapters in this book that deal with these issues first. Although Borland has done a great job of integrating OLE support into OWL, you still need to have a good understanding of how classes like TApplication, TView, and TDocument are expected to interact with each other. If you don't have a solid understanding of these basic OWL concepts, you're liable to find some of these sample programs rather tough to follow.

Chapter 28, "ObjectWindows Applications," provides you with an introduction to the ObjectWindows Library, while Chapter 29, "Single and Multiple Document Interfaces," discusses SDI and MDI. If you're interested in learning more about OWL, you might want to check out *Object-Oriented Programming with Borland C++ 4*, also from Que. Additionally, the on-line documentation that is provided with Turbo C++ includes a comprehensive OWL tutorial.

The Circle program creates, appropriately enough, circle documents. A circle document is not a particularly interesting (or useful) entity, although a given circle document can be rather pretty. These types of documents are generated by selecting a command from a menu or toolbar. When a circle document is generated, the program draws a random display of circles into the document window. Although the sizes, colors, and fill characteristics of the circles are randomly determined, the program does let the user specify the number of circles to draw. The user can also set the background color of the document.

The initial version of the Circle program (that is, Circle1) is generated using the AppExpert feature of Turbo C++ 4.5. This initial version was generated as a simple MDI application, with no initial OLE support provided. (To brush up on AppExpert, and how you can use it to jump-start the development of your OWL programs, see Chapter 21, "Using AppExpert.") One of the big disappointments of AppExpert is that it is only a one shot deal; once you've created an AppExpert project you cannot regenerate the program utilizing different feature sets without starting over from scratch.

You may want to follow the action depicted in these sections by actually building the Circle2 and Circle3 programs. In moving from Circle1 to Circle2 and from Circle2 to Circle3, you have to generate your project with AppExpert and then cut and paste code from the previous version into the new shell. You may find it more convenient to simply refer to the code and project files supplied on the accompanying source code disk.

The Starting Point: Circle1

The Circle1 application is depicted in figure 30.10. It is a straightforward OWL implementation that shares many features with the OWL tutorial example. If you are familiar with the tutorial, you are right at home with the Circle1 program.

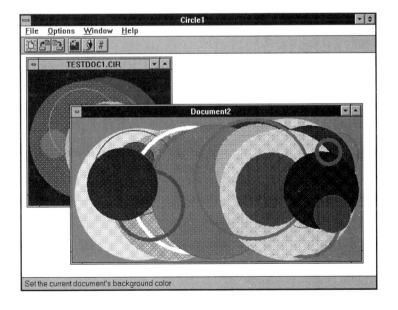

Fig. 30.10
The Circle1 program.

Circle1 is broken down into five source files, each with an accompanying header file describing the classes contained within the .cpp file. Table 30.1

shows the breakdown of the Circle1 classes and indicates which classes are contained within what source files. The Circle2 and Circle3 programs that you investigate contain a similar structure, although class names may differ slightly from program to program. Any changes to source file names and class names are also indicated in table 30.1.

Table 30.1 The CircleX Source Files and Classes	
File	**Contains Class(es)...**
aboutdlg.cpp	AboutDlg
circsdlg.cpp	GetNumCircsDlg
circ1app.cpp	CircleApp
circ2app.cpp	CircleApp (for Circle2)
circ3app.cpp	CircleApp (for Circle3)
circledc.cpp	Circle CircleDoc (for Circle1) CircleOleDoc (for Circle2 and 3)
circlevw.cpp	CircleView (for Circle1) CircleOleView (for Circle2 and 3)

For the sake of brevity, both the AboutDlg and GetNumCircsDlg classes are not shown in any of these examples. The AboutDlg class is a virtually unchanged version of the AboutDlg class created by AppExpert and is therefore of only peripheral interest.

The GetNumCircsDlg class is invoked by the CircleView (or CircleOleView class in later versions of the program) when the user indicates that he wants to change the number of circles in the current document. GetNumCircsDlg is a straightforward TDialog-derived class and is of little technical interest from an OLE standpoint.

> **Note**
>
> Notice that by default the AppExpert generates intermediary MDI client and child classes. This is done to allow you to override specific MDI behaviors that may be inappropriate for your application. In the case of the Circle programs, however, the TMDIClient and TMDIChild classes are perfectly adequate, so the excess classes have been removed.

Listing 30.1 shows the circ1app.h header file; listing 30.2 shows the circ1app.cpp source file. These two files are responsible for implementing the central application class, CircleApp.

Listing 30.1   The circ1app.h Header File

```
#if !defined(__Circ1App_h)
#define __Circ1App_h

/*   Project Circle1
     Using Turbo C++ 4.5, Special Edition
     Copyright ® 1995 Que Publishing. All Rights Reserved.

     SUBSYSTEM:     circle1.exe Application
     FILE:          Circ1App.h
     AUTHOR:        Chris Corry


     OVERVIEW
     ========
     Class definition for CircleApp (TApplication).
*/

#include <owl\owlpch.h>
#pragma hdrstop

#include "Circ1App.rh"              // Definition of all resources.


//{{TApplication = CircleApp}}
class CircleApp : public TApplication {

public:

        // Constructors and destructors
        CircleApp ();
        virtual ~CircleApp ();

        // Public methods
        void CreateGadgets (TControlBar *cb, BOOL server = FALSE);

        // Public member variables
        TMDIClient   *mdiClient;

private:

        // Private methods
        void SetupSpeedBar (TDecoratedMDIFrame *frame);

// Overridden virtual methods
//{{CircleAppVIRTUAL_BEGIN}}
```

(continues)

Listing 30.1 Continued

```
public:
     virtual void InitMainWindow ();
//{{CircleAppVIRTUAL_END}}

// Response table methods
//{{CircleAppRSP_TBL_BEGIN}}
protected:
     void EvNewView (TView& view);
     void EvCloseView (TView& view);
     void CmHelpAbout ();
     void CeOptionsMenu(TCommandEnabler& ce);
//{{CircleAppRSP_TBL_END}}
DECLARE_RESPONSE_TABLE(CircleApp);
};    //{{CircleApp}}

#endif                                        // __Circ1App_h sentry.
```

Listing 30.2 The circ1app.cpp Source File

```
/*  Project Circle1
    Using Turbo C++ 4.5, Special Edition
    Copyright © 1995 Que Publishing. All Rights Reserved.

    SUBSYSTEM:    circle1.exe Application
    FILE:         Circ1App.cpp
    AUTHOR:       Chris Corry


    OVERVIEW
    ========
    Source file for implementation of CircleApp (TApplication).
*/

#include <owl\owlpch.h>
#pragma hdrstop

#include "AboutDlg.h"   // Definition of about dialog box.
#include "Circ1App.h"
#include "CircleVw.h"

//{{CircleApp Implementation}}

//{{DOC_VIEW}}
DEFINE_DOC_TEMPLATE_CLASS(CircleDoc, CircleView, DocType1);
//{{DOC_VIEW_END}}

//{{DOC_MANAGER}}
DocType1 __dvt1("Circle documents (*.cir)", "*.cir", 0, "CIR",
                                        dtAutoDelete    ¦
                                        dtAutoOpen      ¦
```

```
                                         dtSingleView    |
                                         dtHideReadOnly  |
                                         dtUpdateDir);
//{{DOC_MANAGER_END}}


//
// Build a response table for all messages/commands handled
// by the application.
//
DEFINE_RESPONSE_TABLE1(CircleApp, TApplication)
//{{CircleAppRSP_TBL_BEGIN}}
      EV_OWLVIEW(dnCreate, EvNewView),
      EV_OWLVIEW(dnClose,  EvCloseView),
      EV_COMMAND(CM_HELPABOUT, CmHelpAbout),
      EV_COMMAND_ENABLE(CM_OPTREGEN, CeOptionsMenu),
      EV_COMMAND_ENABLE(CM_OPTBKGND, CeOptionsMenu),
      EV_COMMAND_ENABLE(CM_OPTCIRCLES, CeOptionsMenu),
//{{CircleAppRSP_TBL_END}}
END_RESPONSE_TABLE;


////////////////////////////////////////////////////////////
// CircleApp
// =====
//
CircleApp::CircleApp () : TApplication("Circle1")
{
      SetDocManager(new TDocManager(dmMDI, this));
}


CircleApp::~CircleApp ()
{ }

void CircleApp::CreateGadgets (TControlBar *cb, bool server)
{
      if (!server) {
            cb->Insert(*new TButtonGadget(CM_MDIFILENEW,
                                 CM_MDIFILENEW));
            cb->Insert(*new TButtonGadget(CM_MDIFILEOPEN,
                                 CM_MDIFILEOPEN));
            cb->Insert(*new TButtonGadget(CM_FILESAVE,
                                 CM_FILESAVE));
            cb->Insert(*new TSeparatorGadget(6));
      }

      cb->Insert(*new TButtonGadget(CM_OPTREGEN, CM_OPTREGEN));
      cb->Insert(*new TButtonGadget(CM_OPTBKGND, CM_OPTBKGND));
      cb->Insert(*new TButtonGadget(CM_OPTCIRCLES, CM_OPTCIRCLES));

      // Add fly-over help hints.
      cb->SetHintMode(TGadgetWindow::EnterHints);
}

void CircleApp::SetupSpeedBar (TDecoratedMDIFrame *frame)
```

V

Tools and Techniques

(continues)

Listing 30.2 Continued

```
{
    //
    // Create default toolbar New and associate toolbar
    // buttons with commands.
    //
    TControlBar* cb = new TControlBar(frame);
    CreateGadgets(cb);

    // Setup the toolbar ID used by OLE 2 for
    // toolbar negotiation.
    cb->Attr.Id = IDW_TOOLBAR;

    frame->Insert(*cb, TDecoratedFrame::Top);
}

/////////////////////////////////////////////////////////
// CircleApp
// =====
// Application initialization.
//
void CircleApp::InitMainWindow ()
{
    if (nCmdShow != SW_HIDE)
        nCmdShow = (nCmdShow != SW_SHOWMINNOACTIVE) ?
                    SW_SHOWNORMAL : nCmdShow;

    mdiClient = new TMDIClient(this);
    TDecoratedMDIFrame* frame = new TDecoratedMDIFrame(Name,
                                        MDI_MENU,
                                        *mdiClient,
                                        true,
                                        this);

    //
    // Assign ICON w/ this application.
    //
    frame->SetIcon(this, IDI_MDIAPPLICATION);

    //
    // Menu associated with window and accelerator table
    // associated with table.
    //
    frame->AssignMenu(MDI_MENU);

    //
    // Associate with the accelerator table.
    //
    frame->Attr.AccelTable = MDI_MENU;

    SetupSpeedBar(frame);

    TStatusBar *sb = new TStatusBar(frame);
```

```
        frame->Insert(*sb, TDecoratedFrame::Bottom);

        SetMainWindow(frame);

        frame->SetMenuDescr(TMenuDescr(MDI_MENU));

        //
        // Borland Windows custom controls.
        //
        EnableBWCC();
}

///////////////////////////////////////////////////////////
// CircleApp
// =====
// Response Table handlers:
//
void CircleApp::EvNewView (TView& view)
{
        TMDIClient *mdiClient =
                TYPESAFE_DOWNCAST(GetMainWindow()->GetClientWindow(),
                TMDIClient);
        if (mdiClient) {
                TMDIChild* child = new TMDIChild(*mdiClient,
                                        0, view.GetWindow());

                // Associate ICON w/ this child window.
                child->SetIcon(this, IDI_DOC);

                child->Create();
        }
}

void CircleApp::EvCloseView (TView&)
{
        // We don't need to do anything in here
}

///////////////////////////////////////////////////////////
// CircleApp
// ===========
// Menu Help About Circle1.exe command
void CircleApp::CmHelpAbout ()
{
        //
        // Show the modal dialog box.
        //
        AboutDlg(GetMainWindow()).Execute();
}

void CircleApp::CeOptionsMenu(TCommandEnabler& ce)
{
        ce.Enable(mdiClient && mdiClient->GetActiveMDIChild());
}
```

(continues)

V

Tools and Techniques

Listing 30.2   Continued

```
int OwlMain (int , char* [])
{
     // Seed the random number generator
     randomize();

     try {
          CircleApp    app;
          return app.Run();
     }
     catch (xmsg& x) {
          ::MessageBox(0, x.why().c_str(), "Exception", MB_OK);
     }

     return -1;
}
```

This code should look familiar if you have had much experience with AppExpert. The `CircleApp` class is basically the same as the standard `TApplication`-derived class generated by AppExpert. As you can tell by the `CircleApp` response table, the only notable addition to `CircleApp` is in the form of a command enabler method, `CeOptionsMenu`. This method is called by OWL whenever it wants to know if certain menu options and toolbar buttons should be enabled or disabled. The Circle1 application supports three operations that are not valid unless there is a currently open document: generate the document, set the document's number of circles, and set the document's background color. The command enabler simply checks to make sure that there is a single `TMDIClient` window in existence. If there is, the application knows that there is at least one open document window and the various command options can be enabled.

Listings 30.3 and 30.4 show the header file and source file for the `CircleView` class. Recall that the view class in the document/view model is responsible for the presentation of data contained by a partnered document class.

Listing 30.3   The circlevw.h Header File for the Circle1 MDI Application

```
#if !defined(__circlevw_h)
#define __circlevw_h

/*  Project Circle1
    Using Turbo C++ 4.5, Special Edition
    Copyright © 1995 Que Publishing. All Rights Reserved.
```

```
      SUBSYSTEM:    circle1.exe Application
        FILE:         circlevw.h
        AUTHOR:       Chris Corry


        OVERVIEW
        ========
        Class definition for CircleView (TWindowView).
*/

#include <owl\owlpch.h>
#pragma hdrstop

#include "Circ1App.rh"            // Definition of all resources.
#include "CircleDc.h"


//{{TWindowView = CircleView}}
class CircleView : public TWindowView {

public:

    // Constructors and destructors
    CircleView (CircleDoc& doc, TWindow* parent = 0);
    virtual ~CircleView ();

    // Public member variables
    CircleDoc* pCircleDoc;

protected:

    // Command handler methods
    virtual void CmRegenerate();
    virtual void CmSetBkgndColor();
    virtual void CmSetNumCircles();

private:

    // Private methods
    void EraseBkgnd(TDC& dc) const;

// Overridden virtual methods
//{{CircleViewVIRTUAL_BEGIN}}
public:
    virtual void Paint (TDC& dc, BOOL erase, TRect& rect);
//{{CircleViewVIRTUAL_END}}

// Response table methods
//{{CircleViewRSP_TBL_BEGIN}}
protected:
    BOOL EvEraseBkgnd (HDC dc);
//{{CircleViewRSP_TBL_END}}
DECLARE_RESPONSE_TABLE(CircleView);
};    //{{CircleView}}

#endif     // __circlevw_h sentry.
```

V

Tools and Techniques

Listing 30.4   The circlevw.cpp Source File for the Circle1 MDI Application

```
/*  Project Circle1
        Using Turbo C++ 4.5, Special Edition
        Copyright ® 1995 Que Publishing. All Rights Reserved.

        SUBSYSTEM:    circle1.exe Application
        FILE:         circlevw.cpp
        AUTHOR:       Chris Corry


        OVERVIEW
        ========
        Source file for implementation of CircleView (TWindowView).
*/

#include <owl\owlpch.h>
#include <stdio.h>
#pragma hdrstop

#include "Circ1App.h"
#include "CircleDc.h"
#include "CircleVw.h"
#include "CircsDlg.h"


//{{CircleView Implementation}}


//
// Build a response table for all messages/commands handled
// by the application.
//
DEFINE_RESPONSE_TABLE1(CircleView, TWindowView)
//{{CircleViewRSP_TBL_BEGIN}}
    EV_WM_ERASEBKGND,
    EV_COMMAND(CM_OPTREGEN, CmRegenerate),
    EV_COMMAND(CM_OPTBKGND, CmSetBkgndColor),
    EV_COMMAND(CM_OPTCIRCLES, CmSetNumCircles),
//{{CircleViewRSP_TBL_END}}
END_RESPONSE_TABLE;


//////////////////////////////////////////////////////////
// CircleView
// ==========
// Construction/Destruction handling.
CircleView::CircleView (CircleDoc& doc, TWindow* parent) :
        TWindowView(doc, parent),
        pCircleDoc(&doc)
{ }

CircleView::~CircleView ()
{ }

// Overridden virtual methods
```

```
void CircleView::Paint (TDC& dc, BOOL, TRect&)
{
    // Is this just a normal paint for an already open document?
    if (pCircleDoc->IsOpen()) {

        // Loop through our circles, asking each one to
        // draw themselves
        USHORT usLoop = pCircleDoc->GetNumCircles();
        for (; usLoop > 0; usLoop--)
            pCircleDoc->GetCircle(usLoop).Draw(dc);
    }
}

// Event handlers

BOOL CircleView::EvEraseBkgnd (HDC hDC)
{
    // Set brush to desired background color
    TDC dc(hDC);
    EraseBkgnd(dc);
    return TRUE;
}

// Command handler methods

void CircleView::CmRegenerate()
{
    // Regenerate the document and redraw the view
    pCircleDoc->RegenerateDoc();
    Invalidate();
}

void CircleView::CmSetBkgndColor()
{
    // Setup the custom colors array
    static TColor clrUserDefines[] =
                    { TColor::LtRed,    TColor::LtMagenta,
                      TColor::LtYellow, TColor::LtGreen,
                      TColor::White,    TColor::LtCyan,
                      TColor::LtBlue,   TColor::LtGray,
                      TColor::Gray,     TColor::Black,
                      TColor::Black,    TColor::Black,
                      TColor::Black,    TColor::Black,
                      TColor::Black,    TColor::Black };

    // Setup the common color dialog box data
    TChooseColorDialog::TData ColorData;
    ColorData.Flags = CC_RGBINIT;
    ColorData.CustColors = clrUserDefines;
    ColorData.Color = pCircleDoc->GetBkgndColor();

    // Activate the dialog box
    TChooseColorDialog *dialog =
                new TChooseColorDialog(this, ColorData);
    int iResult = dialog->Execute();
```

(continues)

V

Tools and Techniques

```
Listing 30.4   Continued
            // If the user selected a color, change the background
            // color, set the document attribute, and redraw the view
            if (iResult == IDOK) {
                pCircleDoc->SetBkgndColor(ColorData.Color);
                Invalidate();
            }
    }

    void CircleView::CmSetNumCircles()
    {
        // Activate the dialog box
        USHORT usCurrNumCircles = pCircleDoc->GetNumCircles();
        if (!usCurrNumCircles)
            usCurrNumCircles = DEFAULT_NUM_CIRCLES;
        GetNumCircsDlg *dialog =
                    new GetNumCircsDlg(this, usCurrNumCircles);
        int iResult = dialog->Execute();

        // If the user entered a new number, set the
        // document attribute and redraw
        if (iResult == IDOK) {
            pCircleDoc->SetNumCircles(dialog->GetNumCircles());
            Invalidate();
        }
    }

    // Private methods

    void CircleView::EraseBkgnd(TDC& dc) const
    {
        dc.SelectObject(TBrush(pCircleDoc->GetBkgndColor()));
        dc.PatBlt(GetClientRect(), PATCOPY);
        dc.RestoreObjects();
    }
```

The CircleView class is a little more interesting. Because the view is responsible for actually displaying the Circle objects, it should come as no surprise that the CircleView class overrides the standard OWL Paint method. The actual painting procedure is quite simple; the view queries the document for each circle and then tells the circle to draw itself using the device context object—dc—passed into this method by OWL.

Although they are a little bit longer, the CmSetBkgndColor and CmSetNumCircles command handler methods are also very straightforward. The CmSetBkgndColor method loads up the Windows color selection common dialog box and, assuming the user selected a color instead of canceling, stores the resulting color value inside the document instance. In a similar fashion, the `CmSetNumCircles` method displays a `GetNumCircsDlg` dialog box and stores the new "number of circles" value in the document.

You might be wondering why the `EraseBkgnd` method has been set off in its own method. For the purpose of the Circle1 application there is little need to do this, but this segregation becomes useful in later versions of Circle. For now the `EraseBkgnd` method simply `PatBlts` the entire client window. `PatBlt` is used because it has a reputation for being incrementally faster than other window painting mechanisms like `Rectangle` or `FillRect`.

The final parts of the Circle1 application, circledc.h and circledc.cpp, are presented in listings 30.5 and 30.6, respectively. These files contain the implementation of `CircleDoc`. This class manages the data representation of the circle document and is responsible for coordinating the loading and saving of document files.

Listing 30.5   The circledc.h Header File for the Circle1 MDI Application

```
#if !defined(__circledc_h)
#define __circledc_h

/*  Project Circle1
    Using Turbo C++ 4.5, Special Edition
    Copyright © 1995 Que Publishing. All Rights Reserved.

    SUBSYSTEM:    circle1.apx Application
    FILE:         circledc.h
    AUTHOR:       Chris Corry


    OVERVIEW
    ========
    Class definition for Circle & CircleDoc (TFileDocument).
*/

#include <owl\owlpch.h>
#pragma hdrstop

#include "Circ1App.rh"          // Definition of all resources.


// Constants
#define       DEFAULT_BACK_COLOR    TColor::White
const USHORT DEFAULT_NUM_CIRCLES = 6;


// Circle structure
struct Circle {
```

V

Tools and Techniques

(continues)

Listing 30.5 Continued

```
    // Public member variables
    BOOL    boolIsFilled;
    TColor  clrCircle;
    USHORT  usLineThickness;
    TPoint  pntOrigin;
    USHORT  usDiameter;

    // Public methods
    void Draw(TDC& dc) const;
};

// Circle-aware operators
istream& operator >>(istream& is, Circle& circle);
ostream& operator <<(ostream& os, const Circle& circle);


//{{TFileDocument = CircleDoc}}
class CircleDoc : public TFileDocument {

public:

    // Constructors and destructors
    CircleDoc (TDocument* parent = 0);
    virtual ~CircleDoc ();

    // Public getters and setters
    const Circle& GetCircle(const USHORT usCircleNum) const;
    TColor        GetBkgndColor() const { return clrBackground; }
    USHORT        GetNumCircles() const { return usNumCircles; }
    TSize         GetDocSize() const { return sizeDoc; }

    void SetBkgndColor(const TColor& clrNewBkgnd);
    void SetNumCircles(const USHORT usNewNumCircs);

    // Other public methods
    void RegenerateDoc();

private:

    // Private member variables
    TColor   clrBackground;
    TSize    sizeDoc;
    USHORT   usNumCircles;
    Circle*  CircleArray;

// Overridden virtual methods
//{{CircleDocVIRTUAL_BEGIN}}
public:
    virtual BOOL Commit (BOOL force=FALSE);
    virtual BOOL IsOpen ();
    virtual BOOL Open (int mode, const char far* path=0);
//{{CircleDocVIRTUAL_END}}
};      //{{CircleDoc}}

#endif  // __circledc_h sentry.
```

Listing 30.6   The circledc.cpp Source File for the Circle1 MDI Application

```
/*  Project Circle1
       Using Turbo C++ 4.5, Special Edition
       Copyright © 1995 Que Publishing. All Rights Reserved.

       SUBSYSTEM:    circle1.apx Application
       FILE:         circledc.cpp
       AUTHOR:       Chris Corry


       OVERVIEW
       ========
       Source file for implementation of Circle &
       CircleDoc (TFileDocument).
*/

#include <owl\owlpch.h>
#include <assert.h>
#pragma hdrstop

#include "CircleDc.h"

//{{Circle Implementation}}

void Circle::Draw(TDC& dc) const
{
    // Declare helper objects
    LOGBRUSH logbrush = { BS_HOLLOW, COLORREF(0), 0 };
    TPen NewPen(clrCircle, usLineThickness, PS_SOLID);
    TBrush* pNewBrush;

    // If this is a filled circle, we don't need
    // to use the LOGBRUSH
    if (boolIsFilled)
        pNewBrush = new TBrush(clrCircle);
    else
        pNewBrush = new TBrush(&logbrush);

    // Load up helpers into the device context
    dc.SelectObject(NewPen);
    dc.SelectObject(*pNewBrush);

    // Draw the circle
    dc.Ellipse(pntOrigin.x, pntOrigin.y,
                   pntOrigin.x + usDiameter,
                   pntOrigin.y + usDiameter);

    // Restore everything to normal and release memory
    dc.RestoreObjects();
    delete pNewBrush;
}
```

V

Tools and Techniques

(continues)

Listing 30.6   Continued

```
// Dump the circle to a stream
istream& operator >>(istream& is, Circle& circle)
{
    COLORREF cfColor;
    is >> circle.boolIsFilled;
    is >> cfColor;
    circle.clrCircle = cfColor;
    if (!circle.boolIsFilled)
        is >> circle.usLineThickness;
    else
        circle.usLineThickness = 0;
    is >> circle.pntOrigin;
    is >> circle.usDiameter;
    return is;
}

// Read in the circle from a stream
ostream& operator <<(ostream& os, const Circle& circle)
{
    os << circle.boolIsFilled << " ";
    os << circle.clrCircle << " ";
    if (!circle.boolIsFilled)
        os << circle.usLineThickness << " ";
    os << circle.pntOrigin << " ";
    os << circle.usDiameter << " ";
    return os;
}

//{{CircleDoc Implementation}}

CircleDoc::CircleDoc (TDocument* parent):
    TFileDocument(parent),
    clrBackground(DEFAULT_BACK_COLOR),
    usNumCircles(0),
    sizeDoc(0, 0),
    CircleArray(NULL)
{ }

CircleDoc::~CircleDoc ()
{
    // If we've allocated any memory, release it
    if (CircleArray)
        delete [] CircleArray;
}

// Overridden virtual methods

BOOL CircleDoc::Commit (BOOL force)
{
    // Don't do any work if we don't have to
    if (!IsDirty() && !force)
        return true;
```

```
    // Get a pointer to our output stream
    TOutStream *os = OutStream(ofWrite);
    if (!os)
        return false;

    // Write the number of circles
    *os << usNumCircles << " ";

    // Loop through the circle array, outputting each one
    USHORT usLoop;
    for (usLoop = 0; usLoop < usNumCircles; usLoop++)
        *os << CircleArray[usLoop];

    // Write the background color
    *os << clrBackground << " ";

    // We're all done here -- release the stream
    delete os;

    // Because we've just saved, we're no longer dirty
    SetDirty(false);

    return true;
}

BOOL CircleDoc::IsOpen ()
{
    return !(CircleArray == NULL);
}

BOOL CircleDoc::Open (int /* mode */, const char far* path)
{
    // If we're being called from a File | Open, set the path
    if (path)
        SetDocPath(path);

    // Are we opening from a file?
    if (GetDocPath()) {

        // Get a pointer to our input stream
        TInStream *is = InStream(ofRead);
        if (!is)
            return false;

        // We are rebuilding the array so delete anything that
        // may be currently in it
        if (CircleArray)
            delete [] CircleArray;

        // Read in the number of circles
        *is >> usNumCircles;

        // Allocate our new array of Circles
        CircleArray = new Circle[usNumCircles];
        if (!CircleArray)
            return false;
```

(continues)

Listing 30.6   Continued

```
            // Loop through the circle array, inputting each one
            USHORT usLoop;
            for (usLoop = 0; usLoop < usNumCircles; usLoop++)
                *is >> CircleArray[usLoop];

            // Read in our background color
            COLORREF cfBackground = (COLORREF) 0;
            *is >> cfBackground;
            clrBackground = cfBackground;

            // We're all done here -- release the stream
            delete is;

            // Because we've just loaded, we're not dirty
            SetDirty(false);
            return true;
        }

        return false;
    }

    // Public methods

    const Circle& CircleDoc::GetCircle(const USHORT usCircleNum) const
    {
        assert(usCircleNum <= usNumCircles);
        return CircleArray[usCircleNum-1];
    }

    void CircleDoc::SetBkgndColor(const TColor& clrNewBkgnd)
    {
        clrBackground = clrNewBkgnd;
        SetDirty(true);
    }

    void CircleDoc::SetNumCircles(const USHORT usNewNumCircles)
    {
        usNumCircles = usNewNumCircles;
        RegenerateDoc();
    }

    void CircleDoc::RegenerateDoc()
    {
        // We are rebuilding the array
        if (CircleArray)
            delete [] CircleArray;

        // Allocate our array...
        if (!usNumCircles)
            usNumCircles = DEFAULT_NUM_CIRCLES;
        CircleArray = new Circle[usNumCircles];
```

```
        // Get our view and determine the size of our drawing area
        TWindowView* pView =
                    TYPESAFE_DOWNCAST(NextView(NULL), TWindowView);
        assert(pView);
        TRect rect = pView->GetClientRect();
        sizeDoc.cx = rect.right - rect.left;
        sizeDoc.cy = rect.bottom - rect.top;

        // And fill each one in
        USHORT usLoop;
        for (usLoop = 0; usLoop < usNumCircles; usLoop++) {

            // Is this circle filled?
            CircleArray[usLoop].boolIsFilled = random(2);

            // If not, how wide should the line be?
            CircleArray[usLoop].usLineThickness =
                        (CircleArray[usLoop].boolIsFilled ?
                        0 : random(7) + 1 );

            // How wide should this circle be?
            CircleArray[usLoop].usDiameter =
                    random(min(sizeDoc.cx, sizeDoc.cy));

            // Where is the center point of this circle?
            CircleArray[usLoop].pntOrigin.x = random(sizeDoc.cx -
                        CircleArray[usLoop].usDiameter);
            CircleArray[usLoop].pntOrigin.y = random(sizeDoc.cy -
                        CircleArray[usLoop].usDiameter);

            // What color is this circle?
            CircleArray[usLoop].clrCircle = RGB(random(255),
                                    random(255),
                                    random(255));
        }

        SetDirty(true);
    }
```

V

Tools and Techniques

These files are home to the Circle class and the CircleDoc class. As you can see, a Circle object is little more than a glorified structure that knows how to draw itself when given a device context. The Circle class can also stream itself in and out of memory. The class contains data for representing a single circle: this includes an origin point, a diameter measurement, a Boolean value indicating whether the circle is filled, a color value, and a line thickness attribute that is used only if the circle is not to be filled.

The CircleDoc class is responsible for managing a collection of Circle object instances. The Commit method dumps the circle data to a stream provided by the TFileDocument class. Similarly, the Open method reads in circles from an input stream also provided by the parent TFileDocument class.

Probably the most interesting method in the `CircleDoc` class is `RegenerateDoc`. This method queries the document's view for the current size of the view's client window. This information is used during the generation of the `Circle` objects to ensure that all of the circles are fully visible. After all, if a user has indicated that she wants to see a dozen circles, drawing some of them somewhere where they cannot be seen doesn't do any good.

And there you have it—Circle1. The application really is quite simple. It's not expected to do much, and it doesn't. In the next section, however, you see how you can turn Circle1 into a fully functional OLE container with barely any changes to the application-specific areas of the code base.

Creating the OLE Container: Circle2

The Circle2 application is very similar to Circle1; it has already appeared in figures earlier in the chapter (if you've forgotten what the application looks like, go back and take a look at figures 30.1 through 30.6). As mentioned previously, the easiest way to make modifications is to generate a new program skeleton using AppExpert. Figure 30.11 shows the AppExpert Settings dialog box that addresses OLE support. To create an application that is functionally similar to the Circle2 program, you want to make sure that the *Application Is an OLE 2 Container* option button setting is selected. Don't worry about the OLE 2 server functionality yet. That is addressed by Circle3.

Fig. 30.11
Setting OLE support options in AppExpert.

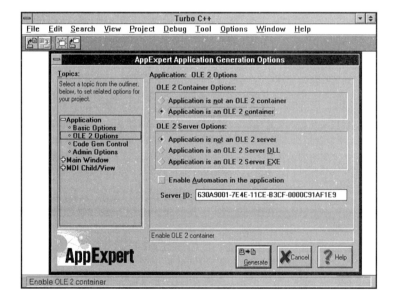

The first thing that you will notice is that circ2app.cpp and circ2app.h are very different from their Circle1 counterparts. Or are they? The Circ2App class is now multiple-derived from both TApplication and TOcModule. Although the structure of the class is still the same, the AppExpert-generated code has made a number of subtle changes to the way that it initializes itself and creates new views. The remarkable thing is that none of the application-specific code needed to change at all.

However, there is one section of the circ2app.cpp source file that bears listing here, although explaining the section thoroughly is beyond the scope of this chapter. Listing 30.7 is an extraction from circ2app.cpp that shows the OLE registration tables for the Circle2 application.

Listing 30.7   The Circle2 Registration Tables from circ2app.cpp

```
      BEGIN_REGISTRATION(ApplicationReg)
          REGDATA(clsid, "{50DE9CE0-30A2-101C-BE11-8EE4E88D5631}")
          REGDATA(appname, "Circle2")
          REGDATA(description, "Circle2 Container Application")
          REGDATA(cmdline, "")
      END_REGISTRATION

      BEGIN_REGISTRATION(__dvReg1)
          REGDATA(progid, "Circle2.Document.1")
          REGDATA(description, "Que Circle Document")
          REGDATA(extension, "CIR")
          REGDATA(docfilter, "*.cir")
          REGDOCFLAGS(dtAutoDelete ¦ dtHideReadOnly ¦ dtUpdateDir ¦
                      dtAutoOpen ¦ dtRegisterExt)
      //  REGDATA(debugger, "TDW")
          REGFORMAT(0, ocrEmbedSource,  ocrContent,  ocrIStorage,
                      ocrGet)
          REGFORMAT(1, ocrMetafilePict, ocrContent,
                      ocrMfPict ¦ ocrStaticMed, ocrGet)
          REGFORMAT(2, ocrBitmap, ocrContent,
                      ocrGDI ¦ ocrStaticMed, ocrGet)
          REGFORMAT(3, ocrDib, ocrContent,
                      ocrHGlobal ¦ ocrStaticMed, ocrGet)
          REGFORMAT(4, ocrLinkSource, ocrContent,  ocrIStream, ocrGet)
      END_REGISTRATION
```

Windows needs someplace to store information that OLE requires to match up document types with servers. Under Windows 3.x, Windows NT, and Windows 95, this information cache is called the *registry* (although the implementations of registries vary widely by operating system). All containers and servers are required to enter information into the registry that uniquely identifies the application and describes its functional capabilities. For Borland OCF applications, this registration information is automatically placed into the system registry when you run your program.

Perhaps the most important information that is entered into the registry for the Circle2 application is that found in listing 30.7's first registration table. Take special notice of the registry key named clsid.

```
REGDATA(clsid, "{50DE9CE0-30A2-101C-BE11-8EE4E88D5631}")
```

An OLE application's class ID is a name that OLE uses to uniquely identify the server or container. It is very important that no two OLE applications installed on the same machine have the same class ID. If this were to happen, the OLE system cannot accurately match parts with their corresponding server, and chaos ensues. Luckily the Turbo C++ AppExpert can generate class IDs automatically for you, and for the most part, you don't have to worry about this issue. Remember though, that if you are cutting and pasting source code between applications and an OCF application registration table is included, you need to have the AppExpert generate a new class ID for the application that the code is intended for. Be sure to use the AppExpert—if you just make up an arbitrary class ID, you are virtually certain to create an illegal one. Play it safe.

The most important thing that has happened to the document class (called CircleOleDoc in Circle2 and Circle3) is that it is now derived from the OLE-aware TOleDocument class. Apart from this singular fact, most of the changes made to CircleOleDoc have been pretty trivial (for example, there's no longer a need for an IsOpen method). Listing 30.8 is a code excerpt taken from Circle2's version of circledc.cpp. Although only minor changes had to be made to the document class, the most important fall inside those methods that are responsible for saving and loading the compound document to and from a stream.

Listing 30.8 The Document Save and Load Methods from Circle2

```
// Overridden virtual methods

BOOL CircleOleDoc::Commit (BOOL force)
{
    // Let the OLE document get a crack at this first
    TOleDocument::Commit(force);

    // Get a pointer to our output stream
    TOutStream *os = OutStream(ofWrite);
    if (!os)
        return false;
```

```
        // Write the number of circles
        *os << usNumCircles << " ";

        // Loop through the circle array, outputing each one
        USHORT usLoop;
        for (usLoop = 0; usLoop < usNumCircles; usLoop++)
            *os << CircleArray[usLoop];

        // Write the background color
        *os << clrBackground << " ";

        // We're all done here -- release the stream
        delete os;

        // Commit the OLE "transaction"
        TOleDocument::CommitTransactedStorage();

        // Because we've just saved, we're no longer dirty
        SetDirty(false);

        return true;
}

bool CircleOleDoc::Open (int mode, const char far* path)
{
        // Let the OLE document get a crack at this first
        TOleDocument::Open(mode, path);

        // Are we opening from a file?
        if (GetDocPath()) {

            // Get a pointer to our input stream
            TInStream *is = InStream(ofRead);
            if (!is)
                return false;

            // We are rebuilding the array so delete anything that
            //   may be currently in it
            if (CircleArray)
                delete [] CircleArray;

            // Read in the number of circles
            *is >> usNumCircles;

            // Allocate our new array of Circles
            CircleArray = new Circle[usNumCircles];
            if (!CircleArray)
                return false;

            // Loop through the circle array, inputting each one
            USHORT usLoop;
            for (usLoop = 0; usLoop < usNumCircles; usLoop++)
                *is >> CircleArray[usLoop];

            // Read in our background color
            COLORREF cfBackground = (COLORREF) 0;
```

(continues)

```
Listing 30.8   Continued

                *is >> cfBackground;
                clrBackground = cfBackground;

                // We're all done here -- release the stream
                delete is;

                // Because we've just loaded, we're not dirty
                SetDirty(false);
        }

        return true;
}
```

In the `Commit` method, which is responsible for saving the document to a stream provided by the parent class, the code has been modified to call the parent class' version of `Commit` first. This allows the `TOleDocument` class to save any embedded or linked parts before Circle2 writes out the circle information. In a similar manner, when the file is opened, the `TOleDocument` class is given first crack at retrieving its embedded parts.

One of the more profound changes in the handling of the `CircleOleDoc` class is completely invisible to the application code. Remember how the `CircleDoc` class in the Circle1 program relied on the parent `TFileDocument` class to provide a stream to save to? Now that the parent class is `TOleDocument` the stream that is being used to load and save our circle information isn't a normal C++ file stream at all; instead, the `TOleDocument` class is using streams that are directly wired into a structured storage compound document. The only clue that something fishy may be happening is the addition of a call at the end of `Commit`.

```
// Commit the OLE "transaction"
TOleDocument::CommitTransactedStorage()
```

Data placed into structured storage can be cached in memory until it is forced to disk by calling `CommitTransactedStorage`. In the `Commit` method, the Circle2 application needs to make this call to ensure that the circle document is stored in its totality.

Look at listing 30.9, which shows part of the `header` file for the `CircleOleView` class (previously known as `CircleView` in the Circle1 application). Apart from the fact that this class is now derived from `TOleView` instead of `TWindowView`, this class is almost completely identical to Circle1's view class. Yet without the benefit of a single line of code, the Circle2 application has gained the ability to coordinate the display and screen management of embedded and linked parts.

Listing 30.9   An Excerpt from Circle2's *CircleOleView* Header File (circlevw.h)

```cpp
class CircleOleView : public TOleView {

public:

    // Constructors and destructors
    CircleOleView (CircleOleDoc& doc, TWindow* parent = 0);
    virtual ~CircleOleView ();

    // Public member variables
    CircleOleDoc* pCircleDoc;

protected:

    // Command handler methods
    virtual void CmRegenerate();
    virtual void CmSetBkgndColor();
    virtual void CmSetNumCircles();

private:

    // Private member variables
    TControlBar *ToolBar;

    // Private methods
    void EraseBkgnd(TDC& dc) const;

public:
    virtual void Paint (TDC& dc, BOOL erase, TRect& rect);

protected:
    BOOL EvOcViewShowTools (TOcToolBarInfo far& tbi);
    BOOL EvEraseBkgnd (HDC dc);
};
```

Apart from the inheritance modification, the only other change worthy of note is the addition of the new EvOcViewShowTools event handler that AppExpert has added to the class. This method is responsible for managing the application's toolbar on a per-document basis.

That pretty much summarizes the changes made to Circle2. Almost none of the application code changed at all. The most profound and significant modifications were made to the Circ2App class, but AppExpert took care of every aspect of those changes. This is definitely one case where, at least for the OLE novice, ignorance is bliss. As you've seen, by simply regenerating an application skeleton and modifying a couple dozen lines of code, you can have a fully functional OLE container. Try doing that with the normal OLE APIs!

Creating the OLE Server: Circle3

The coup de grace is modifying the Circle2 application so that it can also operate as an OLE server. You only have to make four minor modifications to the CircleOleView class, and one of these changes is needed to work around a Borland bug (or documentation omission, depending on your perspective). Listings 30.10 and 30.11 show the modified circlevw.h and circlevw.cpp header and source files.

Listing 30.10 Circle3's Modified *CircleOleView* Class Header File (circlevw.h)

```
#if !defined(__circlevw_h)
#define __circlevw_h

/*  Project Circle3
    Using Turbo C++ 4.5, Special Edition
    Copyright © 1995 Que Publishing. All Rights Reserved.

    SUBSYSTEM:    circle3.exe Application
    FILE:         circlevw.h
    AUTHOR:       Chris Corry


    OVERVIEW
    ========
    Class definition for CircleOleView (TOleView).
*/

#include <owl\owlpch.h>
#pragma hdrstop

#include "Circ3App.rh"          // Definition of all resources.
#include "CircleDc.h"


//{{TOleView = CircleOleView}}
class CircleOleView : public TOleView {

public:

    // Constructors and destructors
    CircleOleView (CircleOleDoc& doc, TWindow* parent = 0);
    virtual ~CircleOleView ();

    // Public member variables
    CircleOleDoc* pCircleDoc;

protected:

    // Command handler methods
    virtual void CmRegenerate();
    virtual void CmSetBkgndColor();
    virtual void CmSetNumCircles();
```

```
private:

    // Private member variables
    TControlBar *ToolBar;

    // Private methods
    void EraseBkgnd(TDC& dc) const;

// Overridden virtual methods
//{{CircleOleViewVIRTUAL_BEGIN}}
public:
    virtual void Paint (TDC& dc, BOOL erase, TRect& rect);
//{{CircleOleViewVIRTUAL_END}}

// Response table methods
//{{CircleOleViewRSP_TBL_BEGIN}}
protected:
    BOOL EvOcViewShowTools (TOcToolBarInfo far& tbi);
    BOOL EvOcViewPartSize(TOcPartSize far& size);
//{{CircleOleViewRSP_TBL_END}}
DECLARE_RESPONSE_TABLE(CircleOleView);
};     //{{CircleOleView}}

#endif  //  __circlevw_h sentry.
```

Listing 30.11   Circle3's Modified *CircleOleView* Class Source File (circlevw.cpp)

```
/*  Project Circle3
        Using Turbo C++ 4.5, Special Edition
        Copyright © 1995 Que Publishing. All Rights Reserved.

        SUBSYSTEM:    circle3.exe Application
        FILE:         circlevw.cpp
        AUTHOR:       Chris Corry


        OVERVIEW
        ========
        Source file for implementation of CircleOleView (TOleView).
*/

#include <owl\owlpch.h>
#include <stdio.h>
#pragma hdrstop

#include "Circ3App.h"
#include "CircleDc.h"
#include "CircleVw.h"
#include "CircsDlg.h"

//{{CircleOleView Implementation}}
```

(continues)

Listing 30.11 Continued

```
//
// Build a response table for all messages/commands handled
// by CircleOleView derived from TOleView.
//
DEFINE_RESPONSE_TABLE1(CircleOleView, TOleView)
//{{CircleOleViewRSP_TBL_BEGIN}}
    EV_OC_VIEWSHOWTOOLS,
    EV_OC_VIEWPARTSIZE,
    EV_COMMAND(CM_OPTREGEN, CmRegenerate),
    EV_COMMAND(CM_OPTBKGND, CmSetBkgndColor),
    EV_COMMAND(CM_OPTCIRCLES, CmSetNumCircles),
//{{CircleOleViewRSP_TBL_END}}
END_RESPONSE_TABLE;

//////////////////////////////////////////////////////////
// CircleOleView
// ==========
// Construction/Destruction handling.
CircleOleView::CircleOleView (CircleOleDoc& doc, TWindow* parent) :
    TOleView(doc, parent),
    pCircleDoc(&doc)
{
    ToolBar = 0;
}

CircleOleView::~CircleOleView ()
{ }

// Overridden virtual methods

void CircleOleView::Paint (TDC& dc, BOOL erase, TRect& rect)
{
    // Make sure we are using the expected mapping mode
    dc.SetMapMode(MM_TEXT);

    // Let the OLE view get first crack at this
    TOleView::Paint(dc, erase, rect);

    // Erase our background
    EraseBkgnd(dc);

    // Loop through our circles, asking each one to
    // draw themselves
    USHORT usLoop = pCircleDoc->GetNumCircles();
    for (; usLoop > 0; usLoop--)
        pCircleDoc->GetCircle(usLoop).Draw(dc);
}

// Event handlers

bool CircleOleView::EvOcViewShowTools (TOcToolBarInfo far& tbi)
{
    // Construct & create a control bar for show,
    // destroy our bar for hide
```

```
          if (tbi.Show) {
               if (!ToolBar) {
                       ToolBar = new TControlBar(this);

                       CircleApp *theApp =
                       TYPESAFE_DOWNCAST(GetApplication(), CircleApp);
                       CHECK(theApp);

                       theApp->CreateGadgets(ToolBar, true);
               }

               ToolBar->Create();
               tbi.HTopTB = (HWND)*ToolBar;
          } else {
               if (ToolBar) {
                       ToolBar->Destroy();
                       delete ToolBar;
                       ToolBar = 0;
               }
          }

          return true;
}

BOOL CircleOleView::EvOcViewPartSize(TOcPartSize far& size)
{
     TSize sizeDoc = pCircleDoc->GetDocSize();
     size.PartRect.top = size.PartRect.left = 0;
     size.PartRect.right = sizeDoc.cx;
     size.PartRect.bottom = sizeDoc.cy;
     return true;
}

// Command handler methods

void CircleOleView::CmRegenerate()
{
     // Regenerate the document and redraw the view
     pCircleDoc->RegenerateDoc();
     Invalidate();
     InvalidatePart(invView);
}

void CircleOleView::CmSetBkgndColor()
{
     // Set up the custom colors array
     static TColor clrUserDefines[] =
                          { TColor::LtRed,     TColor::LtMagenta,
                            TColor::LtYellow,  TColor::LtGreen,
                            TColor::White,     TColor::LtCyan,
                            TColor::LtBlue,    TColor::LtGray,
                            TColor::Gray,      TColor::Black,
                            TColor::Black,     TColor::Black,
                            TColor::Black,     TColor::Black,
                            TColor::Black,     TColor::Black };
```

Tools and Techniques

V

(continues)

```
  Listing 30.11  Continued

        // Setup the common color dialog box data
        TChooseColorDialog::TData ColorData;
        ColorData.Flags = CC_RGBINIT;
        ColorData.CustColors = clrUserDefines;
        ColorData.Color = pCircleDoc->GetBkgndColor();

        // Activate the dialog
        TChooseColorDialog *dialog =
                    new TChooseColorDialog(this, ColorData);
        int iResult = dialog->Execute();

        // If the user selected a color, change the background
        // color, set the document attribute, and redraw the view
        it (iResult == IDOK) {
            pCircleDoc->SetBkgndColor(ColorData.Color);
            Invalidate();
            InvalidatePart(invView);
        }
    }

    void CircleOleView::CmSetNumCircles()
    {
        // Activate the dialog
        USHORT usCurrNumCircles = pCircleDoc->GetNumCircles();
        if (!usCurrNumCircles)
            usCurrNumCircles = DEFAULT_NUM_CIRCLES;
        GetNumCircsDlg *dialog =
                    new GetNumCircsDlg(this, usCurrNumCircles);
        int iResult = dialog->Execute();

        // If the user entered a new number set the
        // document attribute and redraw
        if (iResult == IDOK) {
            pCircleDoc->SetNumCircles(dialog->GetNumCircles());
            Invalidate();
            InvalidatePart(invView);
        }
    }

    // Private methods

    void CircleOleView::EraseBkgnd(TDC& dc) const
    {
        dc.FillRect(GetClientRect(),
                TBrush(pCircleDoc->GetBkgndColor()));
    }
```

If you have approached things correctly (like the Circle programs), turning your program into an OLE server is almost completely transparent to your code. OWL and OCF take care of all of the details for you! With the exception of the four minor modifications described in the following text, there's no need for further analysis and explanation.

Start with the easier changes first. Notice that the painting of the view's background has been moved into the `Paint` method, and that the implementation of the paint has been changed from using `PatBlt` to using `FillRect`.

```
void CircleOleView::Paint (TDC& dc, BOOL erase, TRect& rect)
{
    // Make sure we are using the expected mapping mode
    dc.SetMapMode(MM_TEXT);

    // Let the OLE view get first crack at this
    TOleView::Paint(dc, erase, rect);

    // Erase our background
    EraseBkgnd(dc);

    // Loop through our circles, asking each one to
    // draw themselves
    USHORT usLoop = pCircleDoc->GetNumCircles();
    for (; usLoop > 0; usLoop--)
        pCircleDoc->GetCircle(usLoop).Draw(dc);
}
```

To understand the rationale for this, realize that when a server is finished editing a part, the container asks the server to give the container one last "snapshot" of the part before the server becomes inactive. This snapshot manifests itself in the form of a last, solitary paint message. This time, however, the device context that is given to the server is not a standard GDI window-painting TDC. Instead, the output of the paint routine is channeled into a metafile. A *metafile* is simply a way to record a sequence of window drawing and painting commands into a primitive sort of API macro. Unfortunately there are a few graphics routines that are incompatible with 16-bit Windows metafiles, and `PatBlt` is one of them. Had the decision been made back in Circle1 to always use `FillRect` to cover the background during the window painting message, none of this code would have changed.

The second change is easier to explain. Whenever the document is modified and needs to update its display, the Circle programs are designed to force a repaint of the view's client window. This is accomplished by calling the view's `Invalidate` method. When the application is a server, it also becomes necessary to call the `InvalidatePart` method so that the container's impression of the part is also updated. As you can see from listing 30.7, `InvalidatePart` calls have been added immediately following the `Invalidate` calls in `CmSetNumCircles`, `CmSetBkgndColor`, and `CmRegenerate`.

```
if (iResult == IDOK) {
        pCircleDoc->SetNumCircles(dialog->GetNumCircles());
        Invalidate();
        InvalidatePart(invView);
    }
```

This code shows the actions that the program executes after the user has entered the new number of circles for the document. Note that it doesn't really matter what gets called first, Invalidate() or InvalidatePart(). If you don't call InvalidatePart() at all, however, you will end up having the view of the part inside the container not match the view of the part inside the server (for example, at edit time).

The third modification is to trap the EvOcViewPartSize message that is sent from the container to the server when the container wants to get a feeling for how large (in screen real estate terms) the part is. In this case, the view simply returns the document's size, which is equal to the size of the view the last time that the document was regenerated.

The final modification is a workaround needed to circumvent a bug in the TOleWindow class's SetupDC method. The crux of the problem is that in your server's Paint method, you can never be certain what mapping mode the GDI graphics subsystem is running in. The SetupDC method always sets the mapping mode to MM_ANISOTROPIC and does not reset it to what it was previously, assuming it wasn't MM_ANISOTROPIC to begin with (note that the default mapping mode for an application is MM_TEXT, which partitions the graphic's viewport into pixels). The important thing to understand is that your Paint method must have the call to SetMappingMode(MM_TEXT) to ensure that your view gets updated correctly.

This final version of the Circle program is capable of acting as both an OLE server and container. Figure 30.12 shows a Circle document that has been embedded into a Word for Windows document.

Fig. 30.12

A Circle document part embedded in a Word for Windows document.

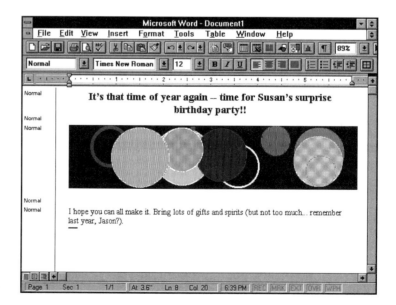

From Here...

I hope this chapter has helped you understand some of the vast potential harbored within OLE 2.0. With the introduction of Borland's Object Components Frameworks coupled with the ease-of-use of the new Turbo C++ for Windows 4.5 product, building sophisticated OLE applications is now easier than it's ever been before. Take advantage of it, and be the first programmer on your block to gain a reputation for being an OLE guru—you won't even have to tell anyone that Borland did most of the work for you.

You might want to investigate some of the other chapters in this book that discuss ObjectWindows programming features and techniques:

- Chapter 12, "Classes and Objects." Both the ObjectWindows Libraries and the Object Components Framework are serious, professional-level class libraries. They require you to have a certain degree of C++ programming sophistication to fully leverage their potential. Use Chapter 12 to review basic C++ concepts.

- Chapter 13, "Object-Oriented Methods." To fully exploit the Borland class libraries, you'll want to investigate ways that you can use inheritance and polymorphism to enhance your programs. Chapter 13 explains these concepts in detail.

- Chapter 27, "The ObjectWindows Library." This chapter gives a basic overview of the services and capabilities of OWL. Be sure to read this chapter if you're looking for ways to improve your programs and give them a more polished look and feel.

- Chapter 28, "ObjectWindows Applications." Look here for more information on the ins and outs of OWL programming.

V

Tools and Techniques

Chapter 31

Dynamic Data Exchange

Many operating systems provide applications with methods to communicate with one another to transfer information for sharing and synchronization. This capability is essential to high-speed functionality and communications between tasks on one machine, as well as tasks residing on different machines. Under Microsoft Windows, *Dynamic Data Exchange (DDE)* is the mechanism that enables two applications to communicate with each other by continuously and automatically exchanging data. This exchange of data provides a means of keeping disparate data consistent. When data linked via DDE changes on one side of a link, it is automatically sent to the task for update at the other end of the link.

One primary use of DDE is automating the manual cutting and pasting of data between applications. This automatic operation provides a much faster means of updating information between applications.

Another use of DDE is sharing information between processes that are performing cooperative functions for an application. An application can, for instance, have one process that operates as a graphical user interface and another that operates as a database manager. The user interface and the database manager communicate to exchange data for display to and entry by a user. Such implementations are quite common and make very heavy use of DDE for information exchange.

This chapter details Dynamic Data Exchange to provide you with a strong foundation for additional development with Turbo C++. In this chapter, you learn:

- The DDE protocol
- Client/server conversations
- DDE messages

■ Transactions

■ The DDE Management Library (DDEML)

■ DDEML in an application

DDE Protocol

Dynamic Data Exchange (DDE) is a method of *interprocess communication (IPC)*, or communications, that provides a means of transferring information between processes. To accomplish this task, applications utilize shared memory to exchange the information and a *protocol* to synchronize the exchange of the information.

In much the same manner as a language, a protocol provides a common set of rules that all communicating applications use to exchange information. When two people communicate, they must speak the same language to properly exchange ideas. DDE conversations use a common protocol when exchanging information so that all applications using DDE can communicate with one another.

DDE conversations occur between two applications—a client and a server. Applications involved in a DDE conversation assume the role of either a client or a server.

As part of a client/server scenario, *client* applications usually initiate DDE conversations with server applications supporting DDE. Once a client application receives an acknowledgment to its initiation request, it proceeds to query services of the server.

The *server* is an application that provides a service to any application making a request. When its services are requested, it maintains communications with the requesting client until the client disengages the DDE link.

Overview of Client/Server Conversation Using DDE Protocol

As shown in figure 31.1, clients and servers pass information by using shared memory while using the DDE communications link to synchronize information transfer.

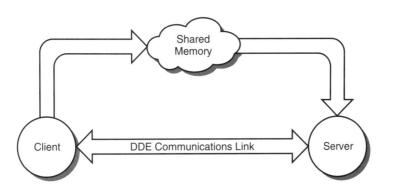

Fig. 31.1
The client and server pass data through shared memory and communicate data availability by way of DDE.

When initiating a conversation, a client makes a request for a particular server's services. The client first makes a request to all servers to locate a server to handle a particular request. In figure 31.2, the client is a word processor in search of a fax application. Once the fax application is located, the word processor receives an acknowledgment of the connection and communications can begin.

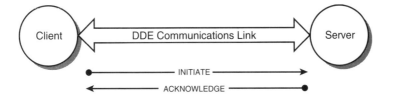

Fig. 31.2
The client application initiates a conversation with the server to have a request serviced.

The client knows that the server that acknowledged can perform the fax service requested. Information regarding the fax operation can now be sent to the server from the client to initiate a fax operation. As shown in figure 31.3, the client places a pointer to the document in shared memory and informs the server that the document is ready. The server retrieves the reference to the document from the global data area and transmits the fax. Once the fax operation is complete, the server responds to the client that the service has been performed.

As shown in figure 31.4, once the client has had its service request tended to by the server, it makes a request to the server to close the DDE link. Once the server receives the disconnect request, it responds with an acknowledgment and closes the DDE link.

V

Tools and Techniques

Fig. 31.3
The client makes a service request to a server over an established DDE link.

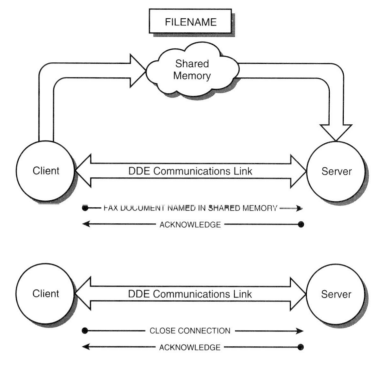

Fig. 31.4
Once the client is satisfied that a request has been serviced, it makes a request to the server to close the DDE link.

Elements of a Conversation

DDE applications maintain a three-tiered information management system through the use of *identifiers*. These identifiers are the application name, *appname*; the topic name, *topic*; and the item name, *item*. Each identifier contains strings that identify a particular piece of information be requested from a server by a client.

When identifiers are created, they are allocated by Windows and stored in shared memory for access by all applications. To access these strings, applications utilize what is known as an *atom*. Each application requiring access to an identifier uses an atom to gain access to the string pointed to by the atom.

The application name identifier names the server application with which the client wishes to communicate. Client applications must request a conversation using a specific server application name when requesting service that is available by that server application. For instance, a client application can make a request to utilize Microsoft Excel by naming EXCEL as the application name.

The topic name identifies a service or object that the client application wishes access to for a named server. For instance, a topic that can be used when communicating with Microsoft Excel is `Sheet1`. In this instance, you want to access a worksheet named Sheet1 of the Microsoft Excel application.

Finally, the item is a particular thread of conversation to be carried on for a given topic. Once again, for Excel, we can request the item `R1C1` in order to retrieve the information stored in row 1, column 1 of Sheet1.

Starting a Conversation

DDE conversations are initiated when a client broadcasts the `WM_DDE_INITIATE` message to all applications windows with the Windows API `SendMessage()` function. This function takes four arguments, as shown in following the code line:

```
SendMessage(HWND hwnd, UINT uMsg, WPARAM wParam, LPARAM lParam)
```

As shown in figure 31.5, the `SendMessage()` function sends the message specified in *uMsg* to one or more windows. When the function is called, it waits until the specified window(s) sends a response and does not return until the window procedure has processed the message.

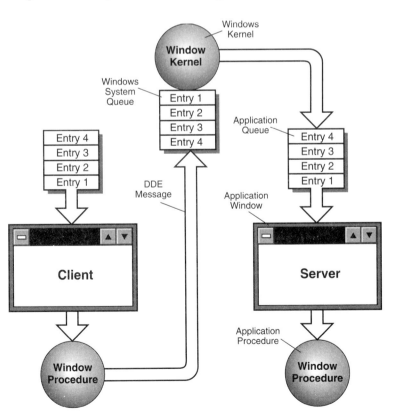

Fig. 31.5

The *SendMessage()* function places a message in a window queue, which is then processed by the window procedure.

V

Tools and Techniques

The *hwnd* parameter identifies the window to which a message, pointed to by *uMsg*, will be sent for processing by that window's message handling procedure. By setting the parameter to HWND_BROADCAST, the message in *uMsg* is sent to all application windows in the operating system including disabled, invisible, overlapped, and pop-up windows. The HWND_BROADCAST identifier is used when the client does not know which server to communicate with to service a request. By sending *uMsg* to the broadcast window handle, the client is essentially searching for a server within the Windows operating system.

The *wParam* (word) and *lParam* (long) parameters contain additional information required for processing specific to the message in *uMsg*. For example, *uMsg* contains WM_DDE_INITIATE, *wParam* contains the handle to the client's window, the low word of *lParam* contains the atom identifying the desired application (appname) with which the client wishes to communicate, and the high word of *lParam* contains the atom identifying the desired topic (topic).

Once a DDE server receives the WM_DDE_INITIATE message, the server processes the message in its main window procedure. The window procedure processes the WM_DDE_INITIATE message by calling GlobalAddAtom() to add atoms for its application name (appname) and topic name (topic). Once the atoms are registered, it verifies that the atoms supplied by the client in *lParam* match the registered atoms.

If the atoms match, the server creates a hidden child window that will handle all subsequent DDE messages for the initiating client in the DDE conversation. The client's window handle, from *wParam*, is then stored in a variable or in the window's extra window memory for the given class. The server then acknowledges the WM_DDE_INITIATE message by sending a WM_DDE_ACK message back to the client's window. In the return message, the *wParam* parameter is the handle of the server's child window for this conversation, while *lParam* contains the atoms identifying the server application name and the topic name.

Figure 31.6 shows the detailed conversation of a DDE link initiation.

Terminating a DDE Conversation

At the other end of the DDE communications spectrum is the termination of a DDE conversation between a client and a server. Termination of a conversation occurs when either party sends a WM_DDE_TERMINATE message. When the receiving party accepts the WM_DDE_TERMINATE message, it responds by sending a WM_DDE_TERMINATE message as an acknowledgment. Upon completion of the WM_DDE_TERMINATE message exchange, the server destroys the child window used in the conversation.

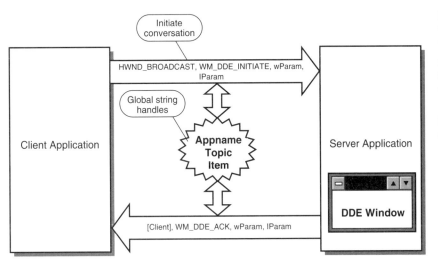

Fig. 31.6
The client sends a
WM_DDE_INITIATE
message to all
servers and waits
until it receives a
WM_DDE_ACK
message before
continuing.

Figure 31.7 demonstrates the termination of a DDE conversation. As is shown
in this figure, the client is terminating the conversation and, in response,
receives a termination message from the server.

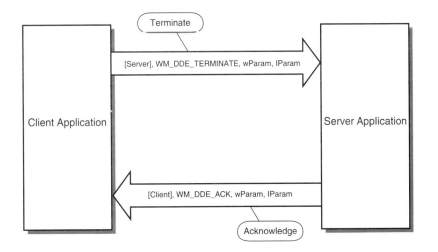

Fig. 31.7
A DDE conversa-
tion can be
terminated by
either involved
party. The
receiving applica-
tion must respond
to the termination
to properly close
the link.

DDE Messages

You have already been introduced to initiating, acknowledging, and terminating messages; however, there are several other messages available to manage conversations between applications. Table 31.1 lists all DDE messages
which are also defined in the dde.h include file.

Table 31.1 DDE Messages Provide the Methodologies for Protocol Management and Communications between Clients and Servers

Message	Description
WM_DDE_ACK	Acknowledges DDE transactions
WM_DDE_ADVISE	Starts an advise loop with a DDE server
WM_DDE_DATA	Passes a data item to a DDE client
WM_DDE_EXECUTE	Passes a command to a DDE server
WM_DDE_INITIATE	Initiates a DDE conversation
WM_DDE_POKE	Sends unsolicited data to a server
WM_DDE_REQUEST	Requests a data item from a DDE server
WM_DDE_TERMINATE	Terminates DDE conversations
WM_DDE_UNADVISE	Ends DDE advise loops

When a client posts a WM_DDE_REQUEST message to a server, the client wants data associated with a particular item (item). When the server services a request it responds with a WM_DDE_DATA message containing either the data or a WM_DDE_ACK message if it is unable to handle the client's request.

The WM_DDE_REQUEST message enables the client to request data when needed; however, what about a means of data transfer that provides report by exception? The WM_DDE_ADVISE message provides a mechanism by which the server can submit information to a client without the client making an originating request for the data. This type of operation can be tricky because the server must recall which items the client requires advice about.

> **Note**
>
> The term *report by exception* defines the submission of information from a server to a client only when the data on the server has changed. This eliminates the need for requesting data from the server as well as streaming a lot of unnecessary data between applications.

Opposite of the WM_DDE_ADVISE message is the WM_DDE_UNADVISE message. This message is sent by a client application to inform the server that the client no longer wants to receive unsolicited input from the server. The server responds with a positive or negative acknowledgment using the WM_DDE_ACK message once the unadvise operation is complete.

Client applications post a WM_DDE_EXECUTE message to a server application to submit a string containing commands for the server application to execute. When the server application processes all of the commands in the command string, it responds to the client with a WM_DDE_ACK message.

A client application submits a WM_DDE_POKE message to a server application to request that the server accept an unsolicited data item (item). This data item is used to update information, or items, within the server such as spreadsheet cells in a Microsoft Excel spreadsheet. Once the server processes the update, it replies with a WM_DDE_ACK message indicating that it has accepted the data item.

DDEML

The basic implementation of DDE is, as you have seen thus far, quite complex. Complications arise when messages are not acknowledged, when unsolicited responses are sent, or when unexpected requests are encountered. These problems bring out the need for a set of functions that belong to the *Dynamic Data Exchange Management Library* (DDEML). DDEML is a dynamic link library that provides a nice application programming interface (API) for the DDE protocol. The API provides a standard method for implementing DDE communications by forming a layer between the user application and the DDE messaging protocol rules.

DDEML is much easier to use than the lower level message-based DDE protocol explained earlier in this chapter. DDEML encapsulates the protocol.

The DDEML functions, as listed in table 31.2 and found in ddeml.h, allow you to implement DDE protocol without having to control all the messages and message responses. When utilizing DDEML, it is not necessary to include dde.h since DDEML encapsulates the functionality of DDE in dde.h. DDEML will take care of the management of the passing of the DDE messages.

Table 31.2 DDEML Functions Encapsulate the DDE Protocol, Making DDE Communications Much Easier to Incorporate into Windows Applications

Function	Description
DdeAbandonTransaction	Abandons an asynchronous transaction
DdeAccessData	Accesses a DDE global memory object
DdeAddData	Adds data to a DDE global memory object
DdeClientTransaction	Begins a DDE data transaction
DdcCmpCtringHandloc	Compares two DDE string handles
DdeConnect	Establishes a conversation with a server application
DdeConnectList	Establishes multiple DDE conversations
DdeCreateDataHandle	Creates a DDE data handle
DdeCreateStringHandle	Creates a DDE string handle
DdeDisconnect	Terminates a DDE conversation
DdeDisconnectList	Destroys a DDE conversation list
DdeEnableCallback	Enables or disables one or more DDE conversations
DdeFreeDataHandle	Frees a global memory object
DdeFreeStringHandle	Frees a DDE string handle
DdeGetData	Copies data from a global memory object to a buffer
DdeGetLastError	Returns an error value set by a DDEML function
DdeInitialize	Registers an application with the DDEML
DdeKeepStringHandle	Increments the usage count for a string handle
DdeNameService	Registers or unregisters a service name
DdePostAdvise	Prompts a server to send advise data to a client
DdeQueryConvInfo	Retrieves information about a DDE conversation
DdeQueryNextServer	Obtains the next handle in a DDE conversation list
DdeQueryString	Copies string-handle text into a buffer
DdeReconnect	Reestablishes a DDE conversation

Function	Description
DdeSetUserHandle	Associates a user-defined handle with a transaction
DdeUnaccessData	Frees a DDE global memory object
DdeUninitialize	Frees DDEML resources associated with an application

As can be seen in table 31.2, the functions provide the same functionality as that of the low-level messages of DDE. Each function is accessible directly from within an application without the need to be concerned about the messages passed with standard DDE.

Initiating and Terminating DDEML Conversations

Since DDEML encapsulates the messages involved, a means is required to transfer the information to the application making use of the library. To pass information from DDE conversations to the application, the application registers a callback function with the library. This callback function is executed every time a message arrives at the application in order to pass the message to the application.

The callback function is registered with DDEML using the DdeInitialize() function, as shown in the following code segment:

```
UINT DdeInitialize(DWORD FAR* PFNCALLBACK lpidInst,
    DWORD pfnCallback, DWORD afCmd, uRes);
```

The *lpidInst* parameter provides the *instance identifier* for the application registering a callback function. When you originally pass this identifier, it must be set to 0. DDEML uses instance identifiers in order to support multiple DDEML instances for some applications. For each DDEML call, each instance of an application must pass its instance identifier.

The *pfnCallback* parameter is a function pointer that points to an instance of the callback function within your application. To create an instance of the function, you must call the lpDdeProc = MakeProcInstance((FARPROC) DdeCallback, hInst) function. The lpDdeProc callback instance variable is passed to the DdeInitialize() function to register the function with DDEML.

The afCmd array filters DDE messages being passed to the application's callback function. These filters, known as *transaction filters*, optimize system performance by informing DDEML which transaction messages are to be filtered out for the application's callback function. Application filters should specify a transaction filter flag for each type of transaction message that is *not* required by the callback function. The flags shown in table 31.3 can be bitwise ORed to combine the flags to establish filtering for the application.

The uRes parameter is currently reserved and must be set to 0 for all calls to the function.

Table 31.3 Filters Provide a Means of Determining which Messages to Allow Passage to the Callback Function

Flag	Description
APPCLASS_MONITOR	Allows the application to monitor DDE activity in the system
APPCLASS_STANDARD	Registers the application as a standard DDEML application
APPCMD_CLIENTONLY	Prevents the application from becoming a server in a DDE conversation and reduces resource consumption by the DDEML by not querying the application during broadcasts
APPCMD_FILTERINITS	Prevents the DDEML from sending XTYP_CONNECT and XTYP_WILDCONNECT transactions to the application until the application has created its string handles and registered its service names
CBF_FAIL_ALLSVRXACTIONS	Prevents the callback function from receiving server transactions
CBF_FAIL_ADVISES	Prevents the callback function from receiving XTYP_ADVSTART and XTYP_ADVSTOP transactions
CBF_FAIL_CONNECTIONS	Prevents the callback function from receiving XTYP_CONNECT and XTYP_WILDCONNECT transactions
CBF_FAIL_EXECUTES	Prevents the callback function from receiving XTYP_EXECUTE transactions
CBF_FAIL_POKES	Prevents the callback function from receiving XTYP_POKE transactions
CBF_FAIL_REQUESTS	Prevents the callback function from receiving XTYP_REQUEST transactions

Flag	Description
`CBF_FAIL_SELFCONNECTIONS`	Prevents the callback function from receiving `XTYP_CONNECT` transactions from the application's own instance, thus preventing an application from establishing a DDE conversation with its current instance
`CBF_SKIP_ALLNOTIFICATIONS`	Prevents the callback function from receiving any notifications
`CBF_SKIP_CONNECT_CONFIRMS`	Prevents the callback function from receiving `XTYP_CONNECT_CONFIRM` notifications
`CBF_SKIP_DISCONNECTS`	Prevents the callback function from receiving `XTYP_DISCONNECT` notifications
`CBF_SKIP_REGISTRATIONS`	Prevents the callback function from receiving `XTYP_REGISTER` notifications
`CBF_SKIP_UNREGISTRATIONS`	Prevents the callback function from receiving `XTYP_UNREGISTER` notifications

Once an application has completed its use of DDEML, it should call `DdeUninitialize(idInst)`. This function forces DDEML to release all resources allocated to the application as well as to terminate any current conversations open for the application. As shown in the following code fragment, the function requires one parameter—the application instance identifier:

```
BOOL DdeUninitialize(DWORD idInst);
```

On some occasions DDEML may encounter difficulty when terminating a conversation. This situation occurs when an application at the other end of a conversation fails to terminate its end of the conversation. In this case, the system enters a modal loop while waiting for any conversations to be terminated. To remedy a possible endless loop situation, a system-defined time-out period is associated with this loop. If the time-out period expires before conversation termination, a message box appears, giving you the choice of waiting for another time-out period, waiting indefinitely, or exiting the loop.

Note

A *modal loop* occurs when the application in which the loop is occurring can perform no other operations. The term modal also applies to modal dialogs where no other window of the application can receive messages until the modal dialog is acknowledged—such as file save dialogs and file print dialogs.

V

Tools and Techniques

Issuing DDEML Transactions

Once an application has registered a callback function for use by DDEML, it can commence issuing transactions. The first transaction that should be initiated is to create a conversation between applications. Once the conversation is initiated, messages may be sent between the client and the server applications. Upon completion of the conversation, the client and the server should disconnect their link to end communications.

Issuing a Connect Request to a Server

Tip
The reason that the application instance identifier is important is so that DDEML will know to which instance of an application messages should be sent. The use of this identifier parallels the postal service and your home address, where letters (messages) are delivered to your home address (instance identifier).

Client applications initiate conversations with servers by calling the DdeConnect() function as shown in the following code segment. This function uses *idInst* to specify the application-instance identifier. This identifier is retrieved by a call to the DdeInitialize() function you saw previously.

```
DdeConnect(DWORD idInst, HSZ hszService, HSZ hszTopic,
  CONVCONTEXT FAR* pCC);
```

The *hszService* parameter specifies the service name (appname) of the server application with which to establish a conversation. This handle is created by a call to the DdeCreateStringHandle() function. If this parameter is NULL, a conversation will be established with any available server (HWND_BROADCAST).

The *hszTopic* parameter identifies the topic (topic) on which a conversation is to be based. This handle is also created by a call to the DdeCreateStringHandle() function. If this parameter is NULL, a conversation on any topic is supported by the selected server.

The *pCC* parameter points to a CONVCONTEXT structure that contains conversation-context information. The information in this structure contains language and context information to allow applications in different languages to communicate using a common method for data sharing. If this parameter is NULL, the server receives the default CONVCONTEXT structure during the XTYP_CONNECT or XTYP_WILDCONNECT transaction.

If no server returns TRUE from the XTYP_CONNECT transaction, the client receives NULL from the DdeConnect() function and no conversation is established. If a server does return TRUE, a conversation is established and the client receives a conversation handle that identifies the conversation. The client proceeds to use this handle in subsequent DDEML calls to communicate with the server.

The code segment in listing 31.1 requests a conversation on the Sample_Topic topic with a server that recognizes the service name Sample_Server. The hszServName and hszSysTopic parameters are string handles created using the

`DdeCreateStringHandle()` function. When executed, the `DdeConnect()` function causes the DDE callback function of the server application's DDE callback function to receive an `XTYP_CONNECT` transaction.

Listing 31.1   The *DdeConnect()* Function Establishes a Connection with a Named Server Application

```
hszService = DdeCreateStringHandle (idInstAPP, "Sample_Server",
                                CP_WINANSI );
hszTopic = DdeCreateStringHandle (idInstAPP, "Sample_Topic",
                                CP_WINANSI );
hszItem = DdeCreateStringHandle (idInstAPP, "Sample_Item",
                                CP_WINANSI );

hConvAPP = DdeConnect (idInstAPP, hszService, hszTopic,
                        (PCONVCONTEXT) NULL );

if (hConv == NULL)
{
    MessageBox(hwndParent, "Sample server is unavailable.",
                (LPSTR) NULL, MB_OK);
    return FALSE;
}
```

Responding to a Connect Request

In listing 31.2, the server responds to the `XTYP_CONNECT` transaction by comparing the topic string handle that the DDEML passed to it with each element in the array of handles the server supports. If the server finds a match, it establishes the conversation.

Listing 31.2   Upon Receipt of an *XTYP_CONNECT* Message a Server Determines if the Topic Presented by the Client Is Supported by the Server

```
#define CTOPICS 5

HSZ hsz1;
HSZ ahszTopics[CTOPICS];
int i;

.
. // Use the switch statement to examine transaction types.
.

case XTYP_CONNECT:
    for (i = 0; i < CTOPICS; i++)
```

(continues)

```
Listing 31.2   Continued
    {
        if (hsz1 == ahszTopics[i])
            return TRUE;    // establish a conversation
    }

    return FALSE; // topic not supported; deny conversation

    .
    . // Process other transaction types.
    .
```

If the server returns TRUE in response to the XTYP_CONNECT transaction, DDEML sends an XTYP_CONNECT_CONFIRM transaction to the server's DDE callback function. The server can obtain the handle for the conversation by processing this transaction.

Wildcard Conversations

Wildcard conversations enable a client to connect to any server that answers to a connect request. A client establishes a wildcard conversation by specifying NULL for the service-name string handle, the topic-name string handle, or both in a call to the DdeConnect() function. When at least one of the string handles is NULL, DDEML sends the XTYP_WILDCONNECT transaction to the callback functions of all DDE applications. Each server application should respond by returning a data handle to a null-terminated array of HSZPAIR structures.

The HSZPAIR array should contain at least one structure for each service and topic that matches the pair specified by the client. The DDEML selects one of the pairs to establish a conversation and returns to the client a handle that identifies the conversation. The DDEML sends the XTYP_CONNECT_CONFIRM transaction to the server. The code in listing 31.3 shows a typical server response to the XTYP_WILDCONNECT transaction.

```
Listing 31.3   A Wildcard Connection Allows You to Connect to
Any Server that Is Listening and Retrieve All Topics Supported by
a Given Server
```

```
#define CTOPICS 2

UINT type;
UINT fmt;
HSZPAIR ahp[(CTOPICS + 1)];
HSZ ahszTopicList[CTOPICS];
```

```
HSZ hszServ, hszTopic;
WORD i, j;

if (type == XTYP_WILDCONNECT) {

    //
    // Scan the topic list, and create array of HSZPAIR
    // structures.
    //

    j = 0;
    for (i = 0; i < CTOPICS; i++)
    {
        if (hszTopic == (HSZ) NULL ||
                hszTopic == ahszTopicList[i])
        {
            ahp[j].hszSvc = hszServ;
            ahp[j++].hszTopic = ahszTopicList[i];
        }
    }

    //
    // End the list with an HSZPAIR structure that contains NULL
    // string handles as its members.
    //

    ahp[j].hszSvc = NULL;
    ahp[j++].hszTopic = NULL;

    //
    // Return a handle to a global memory object containing the
    // HSZPAIR structures.
    //

    return DdeCreateDataHandle(
        idInst,              // instance identifier
        &ahp,                // points to HSZPAIR array
        sizeof(HSZ) * j,     // length of the array
        0,                   // start at the beginning
        NULL,                // no item-name string
        fmt,                 // return the same format
        0);                  // let the system own it
}
```

After a conversation is established, the client application can issue transactions by using the DdeClientTransactions() function. This function should only be called after a conversation has been established, since the function requires the conversation in order to transfer transactions. The DdeClientTransaction() function is shown in the following code segment:

```
HDDEDATA DdeClientTransaction(void FAR* lpvData, DWORD cbData,
    HCONV hConv, HSZ hszItem, UINT uFmt, UINT uType, DWORD uTimeout,
    DWORD FAR* lpuResult);
```

The *lpvData* parameter contains the address of the data to be passed to a server for *uTypes*, in the *uType* parameter, XTYP_EXECUTE or XTYPE_POKE. This transaction enables you to execute commands on the server, poke data into an item on the server, or simply exchange data with the server.

The *cbData* parameter is the length, in bytes, of the data pointed to by the *lpvData* parameter. This parameter should be −1 if *lpvData* is a handle to data and not actually the data itself.

The *hConv* parameter is a handle to the conversation in which this transaction is to be sent. This is the line of communications established between the client and the server.

The *hszItem* is an item handle that identifies the item for which data is being exchanged in the conversation. This handle must be created by a call to the DdeCreateStringHandle() function. This parameter is ignored and should be NULL if the *uType* parameter is XTYP_EXECUTE.

The *uFmt* parameter specifies the clipboard format in which the data item is being submitted or requested (see table 31.4). This format information defines how the data is to be handled within the application.

Table 31.4 Clipboard Format Specifiers Provide Information about the Type of Information Being Transferred in a DDE Conversation	
Format	**Description**
CF_BITMAP	Bitmap handle (HBITMAP)
CF_DIB	A device-independent bitmap
CF_DIF	Software Arts' Data Interchange Format
CF_DSPBITMAP	Bitmap display format associated with a private format
CF_DSPENHMETAFILE	Enhanced metafile display format associated with a private format
CF_DSPMETAFILEPICT	Metafile-picture display format associated with a private format
CF_DSPTEXT	Text display format associated with a private format
CF_ENHMETAFILE	A handle to an enhanced metafile
CF_METAFILEPICT	Handle of a metafile picture format as defined by the METAFILEPICT structure

Format	Description
CF_OEMTEXT	Text format containing characters in the OEM character set
CF_OWNERDISPLAY	Owner-display format where the clipboard owner must display and update the Clipboard Viewer window
CF_PALETTE	Handle of a color palette on which the application data depends
CF_PENDATA	Data for the pen extensions
CF_PRIVATEFIRST through CF_PRIVATELAST	Range of integer values for private clipboard formats
CF_RIFF	Represents audio data more complex than can be represented in a CF_WAVE
CF_SYLK	Microsoft Symbolic Link (SYLK) format
CF_TEXT	Text format where each line ends with a carriage return/linefeed (CR-LF) combination
CF_WAVE	Represents audio data such as 11 KHz or 22 KHz pulse code modulation (PCM)
CF_TIFF	Tagged-image file format
CF_UNICODETEXT	Unicode text format where each line ends with a carriage return/linefeed (CR-LF) combination

The *uType* of the function specifies the transaction type (see tables 31.5 and 31.6).

Table 31.5 The Advise Transaction Handles Unsolicited Data Sent from Server to Client

Type	Description
XTYP_ADVSTART	Begins an advise loop to transfer unsolicited data from the server to the client. This transaction type can be accompanied by the following flags: XTYPF_NODATA instructs the server to send a notification to the client if any data changes; however, the data is not sent to the client XTYPF_ACKREQ instructs the server to wait until the client acknowledges that it received the previous data item before sending the next data item

(continues)

V

Tools and Techniques

Table 31.5 Continued

Type	Description
XTYP_ADVSTOP	Ends an advise loop
XTYP_EXECUTE	Begins an execute transaction to execute commands sent by the client on the server
XTYP_POKE	Begins a poke transaction to set data items on the server with data sent by the client
XTYP_REQUEST	Begins a request transaction to request a data item from the server

The *uTimeout* parameter specifies the maximum number of milliseconds that the client will wait for a response from the server application in a synchronous transaction. For asynchronous transactions, this parameter should be set to TIMEOUT_ASYNC.

The *lpuResult* parameter is a long pointer to a variable that receives the result of the transaction. If you decide not to check the result, you should set this value to NULL. For synchronous transactions, the low word of this variable will contain any flags resulting from the transaction. For asynchronous transactions, this variable is filled with a unique transaction identifier for use with the DdeAbandonTransaction() function and the XTYP_XACT_COMPLETE transaction.

The return value for this function is a data handle to be used by the server to transfer data back to the client. If a conversation does not involve data transfer, the function returns TRUE for successful asynchronous transactions or FALSE for all unsuccessful transactions.

Table 31.6 Additional Transaction Types Allow Applications to Transfer Data and Provide Communications Synchronization and Handshaking

Transaction	Description
XTYP_ADVDATA	Passes advise data to a client
XTYP_ADVREQ	Prompts a server to send advise data to a client
XTYP_ADVSTOP	Ends an advise loop
XTYP_ADVSTART	Requests an advise loop
XTYP_CONNECT	Requests a DDE conversation

Transaction	Description
XTYP_CONNECT_CONFIRM	Confirms a DDE conversation
XTYP_DISCONNECT	Terminates a DDE conversation
XTYP_ERROR	Notifies a DDEML application of a critical error
XTYP_EXECUTE	Executes a server command
XTYP_MONITOR	Informs a DDE monitor application of a DDE event
XTYP_POKE	Sends unsolicited data to a server
XTYP_REGISTER	Registers a service name
XTYP_REQUEST	Requests data from a server
XTYP_UNREGISTER	Unregisters a service name
XTYP_WILDCONNECT	Requests multiple DDE conversatio
XTYP_XACT_COMPLETE	Confirms completion of an asynchronous transaction
XTYP_ADVSTART	Begins an advise loop. Any number of distinct advise loops can exist within a conversation. An application can alter the advise loop type by combining the XTYP_ADVSTART transaction type with one or more of the following flags: XTYPF_NODATA instructs the server to notify the client of any data changes without actually sending thedata. This flag gives the client the option of ignoring the notification or requesting the changed data from the server. This is the means to set up a warm link XTYPF_ACKREQ instructs the server to wait until the client acknowledges that it received the previous data item before sending the next data item. This flag prevents a fast server from sending data faster than the client can process it
XTYP_ADVSTOP	Ends an advise loop
XTYP_EXECUTE	Begins an execute transaction
XTYP_POKE	Begins a poke transaction
XTYP_REQUEST	Begins a request transaction

Either the client or the server can terminate a conversation at any time by calling the DdeDisconnect() function. This causes the callback function of the partner in the conversation to receive the XTYP_DISCONNECT transaction. Typically, an application responds to the XTYP_DISCONNECT transaction by

V

Tools and Techniques

using the `DdeQueryConvInfo()` function to obtain information about the conversation that terminated. After the callback function returns from processing the `XTYP_DISCONNECT` transaction, the conversation handle is no longer valid. A client application that receives an `XTYP_DISCONNECT` transaction in its callback function can, however, attempt to reestablish the conversation by calling the `DdeReconnect()` function.

Sample DDE Application

The sample application, found on the disk accompanying this book, demonstrates both client and server DDEML functionality. The client portion of the application reads mouse clicks in the application window and sends a notification to the server portion that the mouse has been clicked.

Before you jump into the code, I'll list all of the things that must occur in a DDEML client/server application for appropriate implementation. The following list should help you understand the sequence of events in a DDEML application so that you can better follow the code that you review shortly.

1. At the beginning of any DDEML application you must define a callback function in order to process transactions passed by DDEML. The following is a sample definition for a server's callback function. The callback function must be declared as follows to allow DDEML to properly access and pass the parameters of the function.

```
HDDEDATA EXPENTRY DdeCallback(
        UINT type,              // transaction type
        UINT fmt,               // clipboard data format
        HCONV hConv,            // handle to the conversation
        HSZ hsz1,               // handle to a string
        HSZ hsz2,               // handle to a string
        HDDEDATA hData,         // handle to global memory object
        DWORD dwData1,          // transaction-specific data
        DWORD dwData2)          // transaction-specific data
```

2. The `DdeInitialize()` function must be called to obtain an instance identifier. This must be done before calling any DDEML functions.

3. String handles must be created for application, topic, and item strings using the `DdeCreateStringHandle()` function.

4. Servers must notify all DDEML applications that a new server is available. This server registration is accomplished by calling the `DdeNameService()` function.

5. Clients initiate a conversation with a server by calling the `DdeConnect()` function.

6. Clients establish hot links with a server by specifying `XTYP_ADVSTART` in a call to the `DdeClientTransaction()` function. When a hot link exists, servers send a data handle to the client application whenever the value of the specified data item changes.

   Conversely, a warm link forces the server to notify the client when data has changed; however, the data is not sent. Manual links are specified by a client with the `XTYP_ADVSTART ¦ XTYPF_NODATA` flags in the call to `DdeClientTransaction()`.

7. Whenever the values of data items change, the server application calls the `DdePostAdvise()` function to notify the client application that data is available.

   The `DdePostAdvise()` function submits a `XTYP_ADVREQ` transaction to the server application's callback function. The server processes the `XTYP_ADVREQ` transaction by returning a handle to the data. DDEML then informs the client of the data by sending an `XTYP_ADVDATA` transaction to the client `hData` set to the data handle of the server application.

   Upon receipt of the `XTYP_ADVDATA` transaction, the client may call the `DdeGetData()` function to copy the data item from the global memory object to a local buffer and return the `DDE_FACK` value. The client may also call the `DdeAccessData()` function to obtain a pointer to the data object and then call the `DdeUnaccessData()` function to release the pointer.

8. Client applications end an advise loop (a hot link) by specifying `XTYP_ADVSTOP` in a call to the `DdeClientTransaction()` function.

9. Either application involved in a conversation may call `DdeDisconnect()` to terminate the conversation at any time.

10. Servers should call `DdeNameService()` to unregister its service name just before terminating.

11. All string handles, created by the `DdeCreateStringHandle()` function, must be freed before termination of the application.

12. All DDEML applications should call `DdeUnitialize()` to free the DDEML resources allocated for the application.

V

Tools and Techniques

13. If a a DDEML function fails, the application should call the
DdeGetLastError() function to receive information about the failure.

Initialization

All DDEML applications should perform initialization to register themselves
with the Windows system and to provide a means of interfacing with other
DDEML applications. Initialization of the application window is found in the
code of listing 31.4.

When the application first initializes, it creates a window class for use with
the client portion of the application. This window is used to provide a means
of accepting input from the user. To begin the registration operation, a window class variable, W, is created and the members of the structure are assigned
values to describe the class.

Each of the values assigned to W provides characteristics for the class.
The primary members to be aware of are the lpfnWndProc and the hInstance
members. The lpfnWndProc member is a function pointer that points to the
callback for the window. The hInstance member is a word that contains the
instance identifier for the application as provided by Windows on startup.
The remaining members merely provide default cursors, default icons, and a
pointer to a menu located in the resource file (RC) of the application.

**Listing 31.4 The *WinMain()* Function of the Application Performs
the Creation of the Main Window and Cleanup Once the Message
Loop Exits**

```
int PASCAL WinMain(HINSTANCE hCurrInstance,HINSTANCE hPrevInstance,
                LPSTR lpCmdLine, int nCmdShow)
{
    HWND hwndParent = NULL;// The first window has no Parent
    int returnvalue;       // Check Returnvalue of Functions
    MSG msg;               // Message Structure from GetMessage
    WNDCLASS W;            // Window Class Structure
    HWND hwnd;             // Window handle from CreateWindow
    DWORD style;           // Hold the makeup style of the Window

    // Set up and register a window
    memset(&W,0,sizeof(WNDCLASS));

    W.style           =    CS_HREDRAW ¦ CS_VREDRAW;
    W.lpfnWndProc     =    wndprc;
    W.cbClsExtra      =    0;
    W.cbWndExtra      =    0;
    W.hInstance       =    hCurrInstance;
    W.hIcon           =    LoadIcon(NULL,IDI_APPLICATION);
```

```
W.hCursor           =     LoadCursor(NULL,IDC_UPARROW);
W.hbrBackground     =     (HBRUSH) GetStockObject(WHITE_BRUSH);
W.lpszMenuName      =     NULL;
W.lpszClassName     =     lpszwindowname;

RegisterClass(&W);

style = WS_OVERLAPPEDWINDOW ¦ WS_CAPTION ¦ WS_SYSMENU ¦
        WS_THICKFRAME ¦ WS_MINIMIZEBOX ¦ WS_MAXIMIZEBOX;

hwnd = CreateWindow(W.lpszClassName,lpszwindowname,style,
                    10,10,300,200,hwndParent,NULL,
                    hCurrInstance,NULL);
 if ( !hwnd )
     return ( FALSE );

ShowWindow(hwnd,nCmdShow);      // Make window visible
UpdateWindow(hwnd);             // Paints window, Not needed?

if (hPrevInstance)
{
    MessageBox(hwnd,"Only one copy allowed","Note",MB_OK);
    return(FALSE);
}

// The Main Windows Message Loop
while (GetMessage(&msg, (HWND) NULL, 0, 0))
                                // Take out casting  = 0
{
        TranslateMessage(&msg);   // Convert keystrokes
        DispatchMessage(&msg);    // Call Window Procedure
}

DdeUninitialize(idInstAPP);
DdeUninitialize(idInstSERVER);

MessageBeep(MB_OK);      // Beep the speaker
returnvalue = 0;
return(returnvalue);    // Return value is not used,
                        // but it is good practice and is
                        // useful in debugging

}
```

The RegisterClass(&W) function will register the window class defined in W for subsequent calls by the CreateWindow() function. The CreateWindow() function creates an instance of a window with characteristics defined in the registered class. This window then uses the wndproc window callback function to handle all messages for the window.

Once created, the window is displayed with the ShowWindow() function. This function call sets the visibility of the window within the application. Visibility options include hidden, minimized, maximized, and normal. Once visible, the window is updated with the UpdateWindow() function. This function updates the client area of the given window by sending a WM_PAINT message to the window if the update region for the window is not empty. The function sends a WM_PAINT message to the window procedure, wndproc, bypassing the application queue.

The application then enters the GetMessage() loop to retrieve messages from the application queue and send them to the window callback function. Any message, from mouse or keyboard, intercepted by the window is handed to the window procedure and processed based on the event.

When the application is informed that it is exiting, it leaves the GetMessage() loop, allowing each of the DdeUninitialize() functions to be called. DdeUninitialize() deinitializes the DDEML for the server and the client portions of the application, thus freeing resources allocated for the application.

Window Callback Function

A window callback function is a function attached to a window that processes window messages. This function, wndproc in listing 31.5, is named in the lpfnWndProc of the window class registered with the RegisterClass() function involved in window initialization.

Listing 31.5   The Window Callback Function Performs Processing for Information Specific to the Main Window

```
case WM_RBUTTONDOWN : // Connects and Disconnects Server
{
    if ( hConvAPP == NULL )
    {
        hszService = DdeCreateStringHandle (
            idInstAPP, "Sample_Server", CP_WINANSI );
        hszTopic = DdeCreateStringHandle (
            idInstAPP, "Sample_Topic", CP_WINANSI );
        hszItem = DdeCreateStringHandle (
            idInstAPP, "Sample_Item", CP_WINANSI );
        hConvAPP = DdeConnect (
            idInstAPP, hszService, hszTopic,
            (PCONVCONTEXT) NULL );
        uError = DdeGetLastError(idInstAPP);
        if ( hConvAPP == NULL )
            MessageBox(hwnd,"Server Not Available.","Status:",
                        MB_OK);
        else
            MessageBox(hwnd,"Connected to Server.","Status:",
                        MB_OK);
    }
    else
```

```
            {
                 DdeDisconnect ( hConvAPP );
                 hConvAPP = NULL;
                 MessageBox(hwnd,"Disconnected from Server.","Status:", MB_OK);
            }
            break;
      }

      case WM_LBUTTONDOWN : // Sends A Message
      {
            if ( hConvAPP != NULL )
            {
                 strcpy(szDDEString,"Client to Server Message");
                 #if defined(__WIN32__)
                 hData = DdeCreateDataHandle ( idInstAPP,
                                                (LPBYTE) szDDEString,
                 #else
                 hData = DdeCreateDataHandle ( idInstAPP, szDDEString, #endif
                                 sizeof ( szDDEString ), 0L, hszItem, wFmt, 0 );

                 if ( hData != NULL )
                 {
                      hData = DdeClientTransaction ( (LPBYTE)hData, -1,
                      hConvAPP, hszItem, wFmt, XTYP_POKE, 1000,
                      &dwResult );
                      MessageBox(hwnd,"Transaction sent to Server.",
                      "Status:", MB_OK);
                 }
                 else
                 MessageBox(hwnd,"Unable to create data Handle.",    .
                      "Status:", MB_OK);
            }
            else
                 MessageBox(hwnd,"Connect to Server.","Status:",MB_OK);
            break;
      }

      case WM_LBUTTONUP : // Receives a Message
      {
            if ( hConvAPP != NULL )
            {
                 hData = DdeClientTransaction ( NULL, 0, hConvAPP,
                 hszItem, wFmt, XTYP_REQUEST, 1000, &dwResult );

                 if ( dwResult == DDE_FNOTPROCESSED )
                      MessageBox(hwnd,"No data Available:","Status", MB_OK);
                 else
                 {
                      DdeGetData ( hData, (LPBYTE) szDDEData, 80L, 0L );
                      if ( szDDEData != NULL )
                           MessageBox(hwnd,"SZddeData:","Status", MB_OK);
                      else
                           MessageBox(hwnd,"Message from Server is NULL.",
                           "Status",MB_OK);
                 }
```

(continues)

Tools and Techniques

V

Listing 31.5   Continued

```
        }
        else
            MessageBox(hwnd,"No connection to Server established.",
                        "Status",MB_OK);
        break;
    }

    case WM_CREATE:
    {
        lpDdeProc = MakeProcInstance((FARPROC) DDECallback,
            hInstSERVER);
        returncode =  DdeInitialize( (LPDWORD) &idInstSERVER,
            (PFNCALLBACK)lpDdeProc,APPCLASS_STANDARD,  0L) ;
        lpDdeProc - MakeProcInstance((FARPROC) DDECallback, hInstAPP);
        returncode =  DdeInitialize( (LPDWORD) &idInstAPP,
            (PFNCALLBACK)lpDdeProc,APPCLASS_STANDARD,  0L) ;

        switch (returncode)
        {
            case DMLERR_DLL_USAGE     :
                MessageBox(hwnd,
                "Client Callback Registration Failed: DLL_USAGE",
                "Status:",MB_OK);
                break;
            case DMLERR_INVALIDPARAMETER     :
                MessageBox(hwnd,
                "Client Callback Registration Failed: INVALIDPARAMETER",
                "Status:",MB_OK);
                break;
            case DMLERR_NO_ERROR      :
                MessageBox(hwnd,
                "Callback Registration Successful",
                "Status:",MB_OK);
                break;
            case DMLERR_SYS_ERROR                :
                MessageBox(hwnd,
                "Client Callback Registration Failed:SYS_ERROR",
                "Status:",MB_OK);
                break;
            default     :
                MessageBox(hwnd,
                "Client Callback Registration Failed: Unknown Error",
                "Status:",MB_OK);
                break;
        }

        hszService        = DdeCreateStringHandle ( idInstAPP,
                    "Sample_Server", CP_WINANSI );
        hszTopic          = DdeCreateStringHandle ( idInstAPP,
                    "Sample_Topic", CP_WINANSI );
        hszItem           = DdeCreateStringHandle ( idInstAPP,
                    "Sample_Item", CP_WINANSI );
```

```
        DdeNameService ( idInstSERVER, hszService, (HSZ) NULL,
                    DNS_REGISTER );
        uError = DdeGetLastError(idInstSERVER);
        MessageBox(hwnd,"Registered a Server With Windows.","Status:",
                MB_OK);
        hConvAPP = DdeConnect ( idInstAPP, hszService, hszTopic,
                (PCONVCONTEXT) NULL );
        uError = DdeGetLastError(idInstAPP);
        break;
    }

    case WM_DESTROY:
    {
        if ( hConvAPP != NULL )
        {
            DdeDisconnect ( hConvAPP );
            hConvAPP = NULL;
        }

        DdeFreeStringHandle ( idInstAPP, hszService );
        DdeFreeStringHandle ( idInstAPP, hszTopic );
        DdeFreeStringHandle ( idInstAPP, hszItem );

        FreeProcInstance ( lpDdeProc );

        PostQuitMessage ( 0 );
        break;
    }

    default:
        return ( DefWindowProc ( hwnd, message, wparam, lparam ) );
```

The messages passed to the callback function are processed by way of a
switch()...case statement. As is shown in listing 31.5, each message is listed
in the statement to perform operations based on events intercepted by the
window.

In this application, the WM_RBUTTONDOWN message is received when the mouse is
positioned within the main window and the right mouse button is pressed.
When this message is received, the application checks to see if a conversation
is currently engaged with hConv==NULL. If the conversation handle, hConv, is
NULL, then the application registers its application, topic, and item strings. If
successful, the application calls the DdeConnect() function, passing the string
handles, in order to create a conversation with the server.

Conversely, if hConv is not NULL, the application prepares to disconnect from
the server. This operation is handled with the DdeDisconnect() passing the
conversation handle, hConv, to inform DDEML which conversation to close.

The next message, WM_LBUTTONDOWN, is passed to the callback function whenever the mouse is over the window and the left mouse button is pressed. For this message, if a conversation exists, hConv!=NULL, then the application creates a handle to data with DdeCreateDataHandle() for submission to the server. The application then makes a call to DdeClientTransaction() with the XTYP_POKE flag. This call places the value of the data into the item represented by the hszItem string handle.

When the left mouse button is released, the WM_LBUTTONUP message is sent to the window function. This message is processed by calling the DdeClientTransaction() message with XTYP_REQUEST. This transaction makes a request for the data item named in hszItem from the server. If the request for information was successful, the application calls the DdeGetData() function to copy the information pointed to by the global hData handle into the buffer variable szDDEData.

The WM_CREATE message is passed to the callback function when the window is first created by the CreateWindow() function. The callback function receives this message immediately after the window is created but before it becomes visible. This message is processed by creating procedure instances for the DDE callback function DDECallback(). The new procedure instances are assigned to application instances with the DdeInitialize() function. Return values passed back by the DdeInitialize() function are processed by the switch(returncode)...case block in order to perform processing based on any possible errors.

The WM_CREATE message is then processed further by creating string handles for the server portion of the application. These string handles are used to register the server's service with the DdeNameService(). The application then initiates a connection from the client, represented by the idInstAPP identifier, with the DdeConnect() function.

DDEML Callback Function

The DDEML callback function, listing 31.6, provides the mechanism for handling transactions within the application. The function declaration in the listing is standard for the callback function parameters and provides consistency for use by DDEML.

```
HDDEDATA EXPENTRY _export DDECallback ( WORD wType, WORD wFmt,
          HCONV hConvSERVER, HSZ hsz1,
          HSZ hsz2, HDDEDATA hData, DWORD dwData1,
          DWORD dwData2 )
{
    switch ( wType )
    {
        case XTYP_CONNECT:
        {
            if ( hsz2 == hszService )
            {
                MessageBox(0,"Server Connected to Client.",
                        "Status:",MB_OK);
                return ( (HDDEDATA) TRUE );
            }
            else
            {
                MessageBox(0,"Server Not Connected to Client.",
                        "Status:",MB_OK);
                return ( (HDDEDATA) FALSE );
            }
        }

        case XTYP_DISCONNECT:
        {
            hConvSERVER = NULL;
            MessageBox(0,"Disconnected by Server.",
                    "Status:",MB_OK);
            return ( (HDDEDATA) NULL );
        }

        case XTYP_ERROR:
            break;

        case XTYP_XACT_COMPLETE:
            break;
    }

    return ( (HDDEDATA) NULL );
}
```

V

Tools and Techniques

The XTYP_CONNECT transaction provides a means of handling connect requests to the server when the client calls the DdeConnect() function. If the hsz2 parameter contains the string registered with the hszService string handle, the application displays a dialog box containing a confirmation message for the user. If hsz2 does not contain the appropriate string, a negative confirmation is displayed.

The XTYP_DISCONNECT transaction provides a means of handling the disconnect request generated by the opposing application's call to DdeDisconnect(). Notice that we do not check the hsz2 parameter for the service name in this message. The reason is that the two communicating applications, client and server, converse via a common conversation handle. Issuing a disconnect to the server issues a disconnect for the current session in which the transaction occurred.

Any application that handles transactions through a DDE callback function is formatted in the same manner as that in listing 31.6. Additional messages can be added for processing in order to handle requests and advise loops, as well as execute commands and poke data into items.

From Here...

DDE is a method provided under Windows for interprocess communications; however, its protocol can be quite complicated. To remedy this complication, the DDE Management Library (DDEML) is made available. This library provides a simple means of managing the DDE protocol as a series of transactions that occur between applications. In this chapter you learned about DDE and its base implementation as well as how it fits into the DDEML scheme. You were also exposed to the procedure for setting up a DDEML application and learned how to connect applications and have them converse with one another.

For further information, see the following:

- For information on compiling and linking the code in this chapter, refer to Chapter 15, "Compiling and Linking."

- For information on OLE and ObjectWindows refer to Chapter 28, "ObjectWindows Applications."

- To examine the next level of interprocess communications under Windows, refer to Chapter 30, "Object Linking and Embedding."

Part VI

Appendixes

A   Help for the Turbo C++ for Windows Developer

B   Working with EasyWin

C   Installing a Windows Application

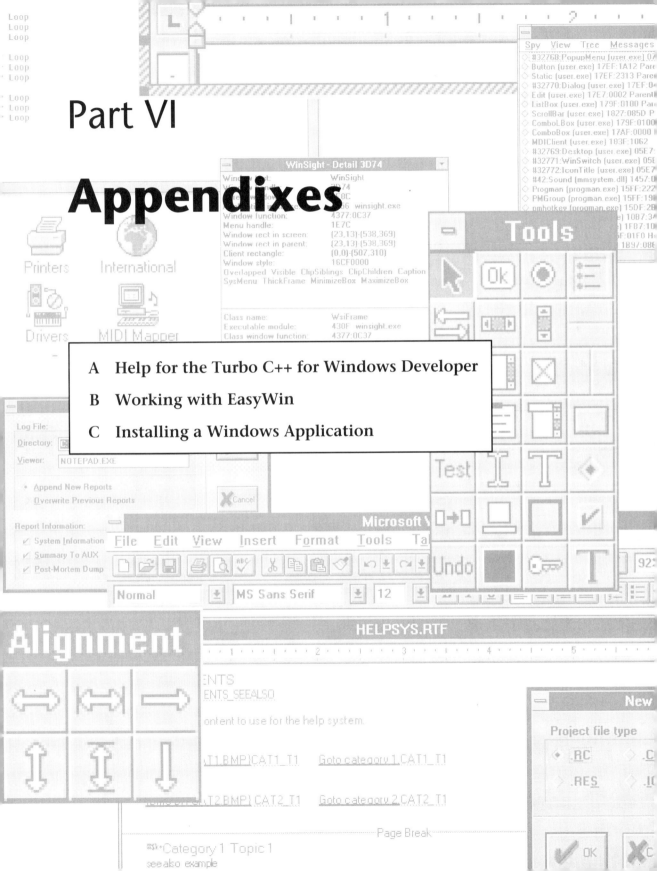

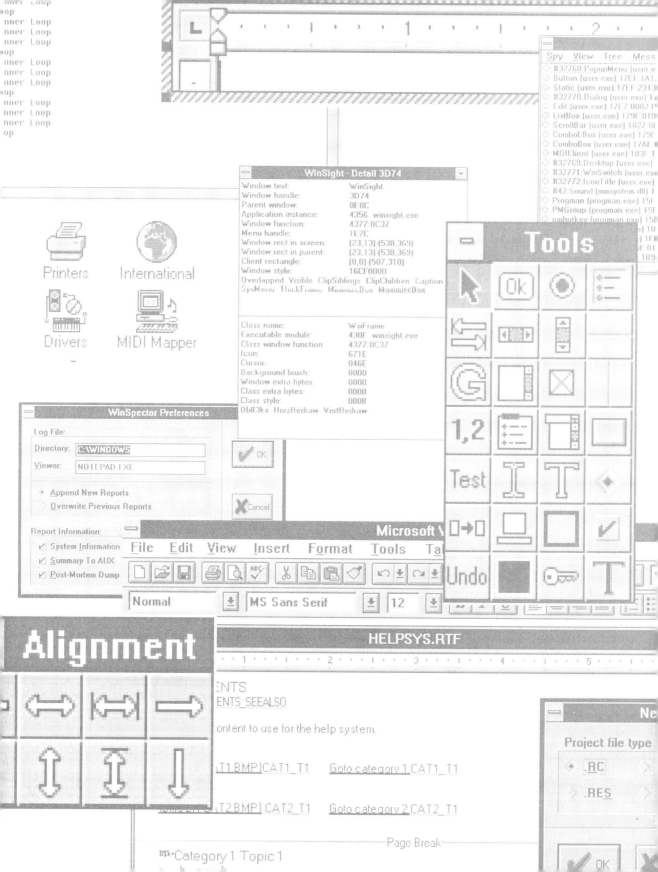

Help for the Turbo C++ for Windows Developer

Developing applications with Turbo C++ for Windows is not an easy task with its vast number of API calls with their many parameters. Windows applications also generate and respond to hundreds of different messages with which a developer must be familiar. Keeping such a large amount of information within one's memory is not possible for most developers, but fortunately Borland and other vendors provide plenty of resources designed to help the Windows developer. This appendix provides a brief overview of various resources available to any developer who is building Turbo C++ for Windows applications. In particular, you'll look at the following:

- Technical support
- Windows Help files
- Sample code
- Resources available via on-line services

VI

Note

This appendix does not indicate an endorsement by the authors or publisher for any of the products or services mentioned. Neither should one consider the non-inclusion of a product or service a lack of endorsement—there are too many services to list them all.

Appendixes

Borland Support

Borland, like many programming tools manufacturers, provides myriad products and services for technical support. Even on the installation CD-ROM, Borland provides several Windows Help files containing the entire Turbo C++ for Windows documentation set. Help files are provided also for the various SDKs and APIs supported by Turbo C++. Borland maintains a presence on many on-line services, including the Internet. Borland provides tech support via support engineers available through on-line services, as well as via direct phone calls. Finally, support is provided via fax and bulletin board services. The following sections provide more detail about help that comes directly from Borland.

WinHelp Files

Borland provides extensive on-line help for its Integrated Development Environment (IDE), the Windows API function calls, the various tools used to develop Windows applications, and other topics such as Borland Custom Controls, OWL, and OLE. Table A.1 contains a brief description of several Help files Borland provides the developer.

Table A.1 Help Files	
Help File	**Description**
OWL.HLP	Borland's ObjectWindows Library
WIN31WH.HLP	Windows 3.1 APIs
OLE.HLP	OLE 2.0 (Object Linking and Embedding)
BCW.HLP	Help for Turbo C++ for Windows
RSL.HLP	Resource Workshop
BWCC.HLP	Custom Controls
CLASSLIB.HLP	Borland's Class Library, containers, queues, and so on
OCF.HLP	OLE Controls
WINSPCTR.HLP	The WinSpector tool
WINSIGHT.HLP	The WinSight tool
CTL3D.HLP	Help for using CTL3D.DLL with Turbo C++
OPENHELP.HLP	Help on using Borland's OpenHelp tool

OpenHelp

Borland provides a tool that transforms the normal Windows 3.1 Help engine into a practical tool for searching multiple Help files (such as those listed in table A.1). With OpenHelp, Borland allows a topic search through multiple Help files, including Help files created by the developer. A search can encompass all Help files specified to the tool, or the search can be limited to a selected range of Help files. Figure A.1 shows the OpenHelp application.

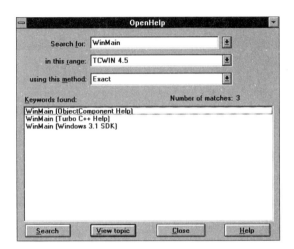

Fig. A.1
The OpenHelp
Windows
Help tool.

Sample Programs

Turbo C++ for Windows 4.5 provides plenty of sample programs, which illustrate myriad programming topics. These files are located in the \examples directory created during installation. Although the general idea is to build and study each program, Borland does not provide an overall listing of each sample program with the distribution. There is, however, a Windows Help file describing each sample program provided. Access the Borland Download BBS (described later in this appendix) and download the file bc40exam.zip. This file provides a description of the samples for the flagship Borland C++ product, but many of those samples are included also with Turbo C++ for Windows. Following is a list of the sample programs that are included with Turbo C++ for Windows, most of which are covered by the Help file.

AUTOCALC	TUTORIAL	REGTEST
LOCALIZE	ARRAYS	ASSOCS
BAGS	BINTREES	DEQUES
LISTS	QUEUES	SETS

STACKS	STREAMS	DATES
HASHTBLS	VECTORS	IDEHOOK
DELIVER	FILTER	MULTITRG
SRCPOOL	STYLESHT	LIST
LABELS	LOOKUP	PSTREAM
QUEUETST	REVERSE	STRINGMAX
TESTDIR	TODO	XREF
BUTTON	COLORDLG	COMBOBOX
COMMDLG	DLLHELLO	DOCVIEW
EDIT	EDITSEAR	GAUGE
GROUPBOX	INSTANCE	LAYOUT
LISTBOX	MDI	NOTIFY
OWNERDRA	PALETTE	POPUP
PRINTING	PRNTPREV	SCROLLBA
SCROLLER	SLIDER	STATIC
TRANSFER	VALIDATE	VBXCTL
ACLOCK	APPLAUNC	BMPVIEW
CALC	CURSOR	DIAGXPRT
DRAW	FILEFROW	GDIDEMO
HELLO	INTLDEMO	MDIFILE
OWLCMD	PAINT	PEEPER
SCRNSAVE	SDIFILE	SWAT
OWLTUTORIAL	OLE	DDEML
DRAGDROP	HELP	MCISOUND
TRUETYPE	PROGMAN	SYSINFO
SOUNDER	CHELP	CMDLG

DDLDEMO   FFIND   HDUMP

HELPEX   TSTAPP   VBDIALOG

WHELLO

Telephone Support

Borland provides many support services via the telephone. Some of those services offer real tech support people to listen to your problems and provide solutions, whereas other services provide faxed and recorded messages with solutions to common problems. Some services are free (except for long-distance charges); however, Borland charges a fee for the use of others.

Up and Running

Up and Running support is available without charge to all registered users. Up and Running is a telephone support line that Borland has committed to getting the user and developer started as quickly as possible. The support line provides answers to installation and configuration questions. The Up and Running support service is available from 6:00 a.m. to 5:00 p.m. Pacific time, Monday through Friday. The Up and Running number for Turbo C++ is (408) 461-9133.

Automated Phone Support

Borland's Automated Support Service provides up-to-date technical information 24 hours a day, seven days a week. By using a touch-tone phone or modem, developers and users can access messages regarding product information, usage tips, troubleshooting, and answers to common questions. For voice support, call (800) 524-8420. Modem support is available at (408) 431-5250.

TechFax

Borland's TechFax is a toll-free, 24-hour automated fax-back service that sends free technical information to your fax machine. TechFax contains more than 1,000 documents on Borland's software products and services. These documents provide valuable information for both the developer and general user that can be used over and over again as reference material. The TechFax phone number is (800) 822-4269.

Fee-Based Services

The preceding telephone support options are available free, except for normal long-distance charges for the call. Borland also supplies tech support via 1-900 numbers ($2 per minute) and 1-800 numbers that use credit cards for

VI

Appendixes

payment. The support numbers for Turbo C++ for DOS are (900) 555-1004 and (800) 368-3366. The support numbers for Turbo C++ for Windows are (900) 555-1002 and (800) 782-5558.

On-Line Support

There is another way to use the telephone system to get support—as an on-ramp to the Information Superhighway. Like many other vendors, Borland supplies support via several on-line services, including several bulletin boards (BBSes), CompuServe, and the Internet. Table A.2 lists the on-line services supported by Borland.

Table A.2 On-line Services Supported by Borland	
Service	**Access**
CompuServe	GO BORLAND
BIX	JOIN BORLAND
GEnie	BORLAND
Internet FTP	borland.com
Borland Download BBS	Dial (408) 431-5096 (up to 9600 baud, 8-N-1)
Borland OAS BBS	Dial (408) 431-5250

Using the Borland BBS

Borland provides an elaborate BBS service for both developers and general users of their products. The developer's BBS is accessible at (408) 431-5096. This number connects you with Borland's download BBS service. Any communications package, such as the Windows Terminal program, can access this BBS at speeds ranging from 300 to 9600 baud. Several download protocols are also supported, such as Kermit and XModem.

Once you are connected, the BBS asks for a user name. If you have never logged into the system before, you are asked a series of questions, such as your name and address, and a password so that you can log into the system in the future.

After completing the login procedure, the BBS presents you with a colorful screen of options, among them access to personal mail and searching and downloading found files.

> **Caution**
>
> Borland restricts the amount of time you can remain on-line, and uses your name to track the time spent on-line. Although the time limit is rather generous, downloading large files at slow speeds might cause you to exceed it.

Using CompuServe

CompuServe somewhat resembles the Borland BBS. You can access CompuServe in several ways. Among them are a normal communications package such as Windows Terminal, WinCim, NavCis, and Tapcis. Many of the stand alone applications automate much of the interaction with CompuServe. For more information on joining CompuServe, call (800) 848-8990 in the US. For more information on CompuServe, see Que's *Using CompuServe, Special Edition*. Borland also has forums on other on-line services such as Prodigy, American Online, and GEnie.

Forums

CompuServe forums allow developers to ask and respond to questions about various Borland products. Each forum also contains a series of sections relating to various topics covered by the particular forum. You can direct a question to Borland technical support people, a single person, or to the entire development community. Although most questions are answered as quickly as possible, some difficult ones might not bring a direct answer, but instead a tip on how to solve the problem. If someone knows the answer, you will get a response or a pointer to where you might find the answer. Table A.3 lists the various forums.

Table A.3   Turbo C++/Borland Developer Forums

Forum	Description
Borland C++ for Windows/OS/2	Borland C++ products
Borland C++ for DOS	C++ compilers for DOS only
Borland Connections	Heavy-duty support for developers
Borland Database Products	Paradox, dBase, and so on
Borland DevTools Forum	Development tools other than compilers

VI

Appendixes

Libraries

The various forums also maintain a library for each section. Each library contains plenty of files that developers may find useful. These files include sample programs, real-world applications, and technical notes on various subjects. CompuServe allows the developer to search, browse, and download files just as they can on the Borland BBS.

The Internet

The Internet, often referred to as the Information Superhighway, is a collection of thousands of computer systems connected via other networks, thus forming a vast web of computers. The support services provided via the Internet are very similar to those of other on-line services, except that Borland and the other vendors have little control over the resources, with the exception of those computers controlled by the vendor. The Internet provides access to USENET news, more typically called *newsgroups*. These newsgroups are similar to CompuServe forums. Many organizations, including Borland, also provide archives of files. These archives are typically accessed via FTP (File Transfer Protocol) and thus are called *FTP sites*. Archives are similar to the various libraries found on CompuServe. For more information on using the Internet see Que's *Using the Internet, Special Edition*.

Anyone not familiar with the etiquette of interacting with the Internet is advised to learn and listen before entering this fascinating world.

Newsgroups

USENET newsgroups number in the thousands and cover a variety of subjects, from the mainstream to the outrageous. Included within this series of newsgroups are ones devoted to Windows programming. Although some groups are specific to Borland's other products, none are specific to Borland's development tools (or any other vendors, for that matter). Instead, newsgroups devoted to Windows development tools are found in the `comp.ms-windows.programmer` hierarchy. The following list provides a few of the most interesting of the newsgroups within this hierarchy. Because none is specific to a particular vendor, you should first determine which newsgroup is appropriate for your question, then specify in the subject line that the posting is related to Turbo C++ for Windows. The more specific you are in your question, the more likely it is that you will receive an answer.

```
comp.ms-windows.programmer.drivers

comp.ms-windows.programmer.graphics

comp.ms-windows.programmer.memory
```

```
comp.ms-windows.programmer.misc

comp.ms-windows.programmer.multimedia

comp.ms-windows.programmer.ole

comp.ms-windows.programmer.tools

comp.ms-windows.programmer.win32

comp.ms-windows.programmer.winhelp
```

Archives

Internet archive sites hold vast collections of software, much like forum libraries. Most archives maintain an archive-wide index list, as well as an index for each area within the archive. These areas are actually subdirectories located for the most part on computers running the UNIX operating system. The index file is typically named index 00-index.txt.

Because most machines run UNIX, FTP (File Transfer Protocol) is used to download files. Unfortunately, there's no single place to get everything, so you must go hunting for what you need. There are tools such as Archie, Veronica, Gopher, and Mosaic that can help in this quest. Please see Que's *Using the Internet, Special Edition* for help with searching and downloading files from FTP sites. Some FTP sites of interest to Turbo C++ and Windows developers are shown in the following list:

```
archie.au

borland.com

ftp.hawaii.edu

garbo.uwasa.fi

microsoft.com

msdos.umich.edu

oak.oakland.edu

wuarchive.wustl.edu
```

CD-ROMs

Chances are you installed Turbo C++ for Windows from a CD-ROM. Borland and other vendors also provide plenty of helpful files, tools, and products via CD-ROMs. Borland provides a CD full of information and useful files for many of its products, including Turbo C++ for Windows.

VI

Appendixes

Borland KnowledgeBase CD

Borland provides a CD-ROM called the Borland KnowledgeBase CD. This
product contains thousands of articles, questions and answers, problem reports, and workarounds, all of which are immediately available through a
powerful text-retrieval engine. Borland charges an annual subscription of
$249 per year (four issues). For more information, call (800) 331-0877.

Microsoft Developer's CD

If you are developing Windows programs, you should also check out the
Microsoft Developer's Network product. This program includes a quarterly
CD-ROM full of information on Windows development. Although this product contains plenty of material aimed at Microsoft's products, plenty of the
material is also useful to Windows developers who use other development
tools.

Internet CDs

Alas, not all developers have access to the Internet and the hundreds of files
scattered throughout the world in various FTP sites. And even if a developer
does have access, downloading files can be inconvenient because of slow
connections or lack of access to a site. Fortunately, many companies collect
the files on the various archive sites and place them on CD-ROMs where
developers can have access to the files on an on-demand basis. Such firms
as Walnut Creek and Infomagic maintain CDs full of Windows programs
for both the general public and for developers.

Appendix B

Working with EasyWin

Often, you want to perform some quick programming task under Windows, without having to get bogged down in all the overhead usually associated with a Windows application. Why, for example, get stuck creating and managing a window when all you want to do is write a quickie program that counts the number of words in a file? Turbo C++ for Windows features EasyWin for just this sort of eventuality.

EasyWin is a project target type that you can select with TargetExpert. The EasyWin target type defines a character mode or DOS application that runs under Windows, which allows DOS programs to be compiled under Windows. EasyWin is the IDE's default setting, which is why the "Hello, world!" program presented in Chapter 1, "The Integrated Development Environment," compiles and runs under Windows without your having to add window-handling code. That is, when you first start Turbo C++ for Windows, you can immediately type and run a DOS program.

Creating and Running an EasyWin Program

Listing B.1 is an example of a program that uses DOS functions that are not supported by the Windows environment, but that can be converted by EasyWin so that they work under Windows. This application continuously reads the keystrokes until you press the Escape key. To compile and run the application, follow these steps:

1. Select Turbo C++'s New command, found in the File menu. A new edit window appears.

2. Type the code shown in listing B.1 into the edit window.

3. Click on the toolbar's lightning button. The program compiles, links, and runs.

Figure B.1 shows the program's output.

Listing B.1   EASYWIN.C—A DOS Program That Can Be Run as an EasyWin Application

```c
#include <stdio.h>
#include <conio.h>

int main()
{
   char ch;

   printf("Character Code\t\tDecimal\t\t\tHex\tOctal\n\n");

   while((ch = getch()) != 27)
   {
      printf("Character: %c\t\t%3d\t\t%x\t%o\n",
         ch, ch, ch, ch);
   }

   return 0;
}
```

Fig. B.1
The EASYWIN application in action.

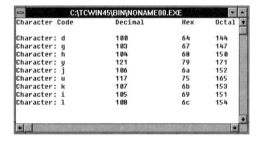

Creating an EasyWin Project

Although you only need to open a text window, type a DOS program, and then select the lightning button in the toolbar to create and run a DOS program, you may, for larger programs, want to create a full EasyWin project. To create a new EasyWin project, follow these steps:

1. Select the Project menu's New Project command. The New Target dialog box appears (see fig. B.2).

2. Type the new project's name and path name into the Project Path and Name edit box. The target name automatically appears in the Target Name edit box.

3. Select EasyWin in the Target Type list box. Turbo C++ sets the rest of the options in the New Target dialog box to their default values.

4. Click the OK button to finalize your choices and create the project.

Using DOS Functions in a Real Windows Application

Despite the many ways Windows provides for displaying information, there may be times when you'd like to use DOS functions in a true Windows application. For example, you might want to debug your Windows program by calling the `printf()` function to display the values of variables. To initiate an EasyWin environment inside a Windows application, insert a call to `_InitEasyWin()`, which generates the code required to use DOS functions in a window.

Listing B.2 is a sample program listing, INITEASY.C. The program is written for the Windows environment, but calls the DOS `printf()` function to perform debugging. The `_InitEasyWin()` call enables the EasyWin environment, which allows the use of `printf()`.

VI

Appendixes

Listing B.2   INITEASY.C—A True Windows Application Using DOS Functions

```c
#include <windows.h>
#include <stdio.h>

// Prototype for window procedure.
LRESULT FAR PASCAL _export WndProc(HWND hWnd, UINT message,
    WPARAM wParam, LPARAM lParam);

int PASCAL WinMain(HINSTANCE hCurrentInst,
    HINSTANCE hPreviousInst, LPSTR /* lpszCmdLine */,
    int nCmdShow)
{
    WNDCLASS wndClass;
    HWND hWnd;
    MSG msg;

    // If there's no previous instance of this application,
    // define and register the window class.
    if (hPreviousInst == NULL)
    {
        wndClass.style = CS_HREDRAW | CS_VREDRAW;
        wndClass.lpfnWndProc = WndProc;
        wndClass.cbClsExtra = 0;
        wndClass.cbWndExtra = 0;
        wndClass.hInstance = hCurrentInst;
        wndClass.hIcon = LoadIcon(NULL, IDI_APPLICATION);
        wndClass.hCursor = LoadCursor(NULL, IDC_ARROW);
        wndClass.hbrBackground = GetStockObject(WHITE_BRUSH);
        wndClass.lpszMenuName = NULL;
        wndClass.lpszClassName = "InitEasy";

        RegisterClass(&wndClass);
    }

    // Get the size of the screen.
    UINT width = GetSystemMetrics(SM_CXSCREEN) / 2;
    UINT height = GetSystemMetrics(SM_CYSCREEN) / 2;

    // Create a window of the previously defined class.
    hWnd = CreateWindow(
            "InitEasy",              // Window class's name.
            "InitEasy Application",  // Title bar text.
            WS_OVERLAPPEDWINDOW,     // The window's style.
            10,                      // X position.
            10,                      // Y position.
            width,                   // Width.
            height,                  // Height.
            NULL,                    // Parent window's handle.
            NULL,                    // Menu handle.
            hCurrentInst,            // Instance handle.
            NULL);                   // No additional data.

    // Enable EasyWin.
```

```
    _InitEasyWin();

    // Display the window on the screen.
    ShowWindow(hWnd, nCmdShow);

    // Force the window to repaint itself.
    UpdateWindow(hWnd);

    // Thanks to EasyWin, the program can now use printf().
    printf("Use printf() as a debugging aid!\n");

    // Start the message loop.
    while (GetMessage(&msg, NULL, NULL, NULL))
    {
        TranslateMessage(&msg);
        DispatchMessage(&msg);
    }

    return msg.wParam;
}

LRESULT FAR PASCAL _export WndProc(HWND hWnd, UINT message,
    WPARAM wParam, LPARAM lParam)
{
    // Handle the messages to which the application
    // must respond.
    switch(message)
    {
      case WM_RBUTTONDOWN :
         printf("Right Button Down\n");
         break;
      case WM_LBUTTONDOWN :
         printf("Left Button Down\n");
         break;
      case WM_DESTROY:
         PostQuitMessage(0);
         return 0;
    }

    // Make sure all messages get returned to Windows.
    return DefWindowProc(hWnd, message, wParam, lParam);
}
```

Figure B.3 shows the running INITEASY Windows program. Notice that the program produces two windows, one for the Windows application and one in which EasyWin displays output from the DOS function printf(). Also notice that, in order to use the _InitEasyWin() function, you must include the STDIO.H header file in your program.

Fig. B.3
The INITEASY
application.

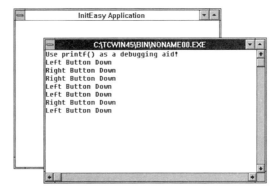

EasyWin-Compatible Functions

The functions listed in Table B.1 are portable to EasyWin programs, but are
not available in Windows 16-bit programs. The functions are provided here
specifically to help you port DOS programs into a Windows 16-bit application running with EasyWin.

Table B.1	EasyWin-Compatible Functions
Function	**Header File**
clreol	conio.h
clrscr	conio.h
fgetchar	stdio.h
getch	stdio.h
getchar	stdio.h
getche	stdio.h
gets	stdio.h
gotoxy	conio.h
kbhit	conio.h
perror	errno.h
printf	stdio.h
putch	conio.h

Function	Header File
putchar	stdio.h
puts	stdio.h
scanf	stdio.h
vprintf	stdio.h
vscanf	stdio.h
wherex	conio.h
wherey	conio.h

Appendix C

Installing a Windows Application

First impressions are important, and your user's first impression will start with how well your application installs. You'll want your program to put its best foot forward then, allowing the user to get up and running with as few distractions as possible. Unfortunately, Borland and most other Windows development vendors do not provide programs to create Setup applications. Instead, the developer must rely on commercial and shareware toolkits. However, as licensed users of the Windows SDK, which is part of Borland's Turbo C++, developers can use the Setup Toolkit provided by Microsoft. This chapter provides a broad overview of the following topics:

- The Setup Toolkit and how to use it
- Invaluable information provided by the sample files for creating installation programs

Microsoft's Toolkit

Microsoft provides a Setup Toolkit that enables you to create a professional-looking, Windows-based, installation program. This Setup Toolkit is part of the Windows 3.1 SDK but is not part of Borland's version of the SDK. You must contact Microsoft to get a copy of these files. See Appendix A, "Help for the Turbo C++ for Windows Developer," for information about how to contact Microsoft. These files are also part of the Microsoft Developer's CD. These files are also available on Microsoft's FTP server at ftp.microsoft.com in the /developer/msdn/jancd/csetup.zip file.

Dealing with Version Information

Chapter 23, "Using Resource Workshop," provided a brief explanation of the VERSIONINFO resource information. This information is useful because Microsoft places a great deal of Windows functionality in DLL files. Thus, you need to distribute only the new DLL file and not the entire system when updates occur. Table C.1 lists the files you, as a developer, can distribute with your application. All of these files are standard with Microsoft Windows and are located in the Windows system directory.

Table C.1 Files You May Distribute	
File	**Description**
COMMDLG.DLL	The Common Dialog Box library
DDEML.DLL	The Dynamic Data Exchange library
LZEXPAND.DLL	The Lemple-Zev file (de)compression library
OLECLI.DLL	Object Linking and Embedding client library
OLESVR.DLL	OLE server library; note: as of this writing, MFC 2.0 supports only OLE 1.0
SHELL.DLL	The Shell application library
STRESS.DLL	Stress testing library
TOOLHELP.DLL	Developer tools library
VER.DLL	Contains the version-checking library
WINMEM32.DLL	32-bit memory support library

In addition, Borland allows developers to distribute the BCWW.DLL custom control library accompanying Turbo C++, which provides the distinct Borland dialog box look and feel. Also, most, if not all, VBX suppliers license you to ship the run-time VBX file with your application. This includes the VBXs Borland supplies in its Visual Solutions Package.

Why check version information? What if you have a new and improved DLL that the user needs to run your application? You would like to detect this and copy the file to the user's system. If the files are the same, you don't want to waste the time copying the file. If your file is older, you probably do not want to copy the file, either.

The Setup Toolkit

The Setup Toolkit uses a script language and dialog boxes that you design.
A run-time version of Microsoft Test interprets this language. Microsoft
provides this program with the Toolkit (MSTEST.EXE). The following paragraphs describe the basic components of the Toolkit.

SETUP.EXE is the bootstrap program that copies needed files to a temporary
directory on the user's hard drive. SETUP.EXE performs the installation. After
installing the system, the program deletes all temp files. The installation kit
requires this file on the first disk, and you must not compress this file.

MSTEST.EXE is a run-time version of Microsoft's Microsoft Test product. This
required program interprets your supplied script file to install your product.
This file should be on your first installation script.

SETUP.LST is a sample file that contains the files SETUP.EXE copies to the
temporary directory. You should create your script file first and then modify
the SETUP.LST file to match your MST file. SETUP.LST has two sections,
[Params] and [Files]. The [Params] section lets you specify various items.
These items include

- The amount of disk space Setup will need for the temporary files

- The title of the window that displays while the program initializes

- The command line with which you invoke _MSTEST.EXE, containing
  the name of the setup script file as well as additional setup parameters

You must not change the last line in the [Params] section that sets the
DrvModName to DSHELL, but you should change the other values to reflect your
installation requirements.

The [Files] section is a list of the files that Setup copies to the temporary
directory. This list should include your script file (MST), your INF file,
SETUPAPI.INC, all DLLs, and _MSTEST.EXE. These files must be on the first
disk. You can compress most of the files except for SETUP.EXE and
SETUP.LST.

The Setup Include Files

INC files contain variables and function declarations needed by your setup
script. Any files you include in your script must be on your first installation
disk, and the SETUPAPI.INC file is required. This file contains the most
commonly used declarations. MSDETECT.INC is required if you use any of

VI

Appendixes

the device auto-detection functions in MSDETSTF.DLL. MSREGDB.INC is required if you intend to use the registration database routines. If you include both this file and the MSSHARED.INC file, you must include the MSREGDB.INC file before the latter. The MSSHARED.INC file contains the declarations for the functions in MSSHLSTF.DLL used to update shared system files.

The Sample Script Files

The Toolkit includes three sample script files, with MST extensions, that illustrate various setup scenarios that you may encounter. You can modify these samples to create your own script files, which must contain an MST extension. Your MST file must be on the first disk. The MST file and all the INC files must be listed in your SETUP.LST file.

Setup's DLLs

The Toolkit includes sample dialog boxes via their resource files and their C implementation files. The kit also provides six DLLs containing useful routines for actions such as detecting the user's current environment, copying files, and modifying INI files. These files are required. The MSUILSTF.DLL contains the user interface library responsible for displaying and manipulating dialog boxes. MSSHLSTF.DLL contains the shell library that manages the frame window. MSINSSTF.DLL contains the install library that handles installing files to the user's hard disk. MSDETSTF.DLL contains the detection library that supplies Setup with information about the user's system. You must create MSCUISTF.DLL. This library provides the routines to manipulate the dialog boxes you create for your installation program. The next DLL file, MSCOMSTF.DLL, contains the supporting routines for the common dialog boxes. The final DLL is VER.DLL. This library is required so that the user can install the application on a Windows 3.0 system.

You can create a set of customized routines not included in MSCUISTF.DLL and place them in a custom DLL. You will need to include this file in your SETUP.LST list. You need to declare the functions in your script file (MST) in the following format:

```
DECLARE FUNCTION function-name LIB "dllname.dll" ( arg1%, arg2%)
    AS VALUE.
```

The *arg1%* and *arg2%* parameters represent arguments that are passed to the function defined by *function-name*. This *function-name* is located in the DLL named by LIB *"dllname.dll"*. The AS VALUE parameter of the declaration defines for Setup that the DLL function returns a value to the caller.

Creating Installation Disks

The DSKLAYT.EXE and DSKLAYT2.EXE programs help you create your installation disks that you ship to your customers.

The MS-DOS program _MSSETUP.EXE allows you to update Windows system files that may be in use when a user tries to install your program. This file reads an MS-DOS batch file, MSSETUP.BAT, that updates the necessary files. The setup function calls ExitWindowsRestart to exit Windows, run MSSETUP.BAT, and then restart Windows. This Windows restart function is available only for Windows 3.1 or higher. If the user is installing to Windows 3.0, you need to tell the user via a message box to shut down Windows and manually execute MSSETUP.BAT to update the system files. If it is needed, _MSSETUP.EXE must be on the first installation disk.

The TESTDRVR.HLP File

This is a Windows Help file for the developer. This file explains the various MSTEST functions demonstrated in the sample setup scripts.

Preparing the Setup Disk

To prepare the distribution kit to properly set up your files, you must perform a series of steps that allow you to determine which files are to be distributed and how. By following each of the steps outlined in this section, you will be able to prepare a robust Setup application with an intuitive user interface for distributing and installing your application.

Step One—Selecting the Files Needed

To create a Setup program, you must first identify the files your application will need. For each file you must decide whether the file is unique or will be shared among a family of applications. Is the file a system file? If so, or if it is a shared file, you will want to check for prior versions before blindly copying the file to the user's hard disk. If the file is currently in use, you may have to use the _MSSETUP.EXE program to complete the installation.

Next you must decide whether the user can choose not to install the file. Perhaps you have sample files that consume large amounts of disk space; if so, you could give the user the choice to load this group of files now or later.

Step Two—Specifying the Directories

The next step is to design the directory structure of the application. You must decide whether all the files will reside in one subdirectory or if some files will reside in a main subdirectory and other files in subordinate directories. An example would be the LIBRARY, INCLUDE, and SAMPLE subdirectories found in the MSVC directory. You will need to place some files, such as an application's INI file or system files like VBXs, in the WINDOWS or WINDOWS\SYSTEM directories.

Step Three—Anticipating Possible User Decisions

The third step is to identify the possible responses you will require from the user. This includes such items as previously mentioned:

- Will the user be allowed to decide which files to install?

- Will you allow the user to enter a company name and user name that you stamp into an application's version resource?

- Will the user be able to decide in which directory to install your application?

All these choices require a dialog box to display information to the user and then retrieve the responses. You may also want to include message boxes along the way. You can use the boxes to suggest that your users send in their registration cards or to alert them that a file is being deleted. These items too will require dialog boxes. This step will give you an idea of which sample script to modify in later steps.

Step Four—Choosing Dialog Boxes

Once you have identified the resources needed, you must then identify the controls you will need. This helps you pick which dialog templates to modify. Table C.2 lists the dialog boxes provided in the DIALOG.RC file.

Table C.2 Dialog Boxes Supplied with the Setup Toolkit	
Dialog Box	**Description**
APPHELP	Displays a help message.
ASKQUIT	Warns the user that the installation is incomplete.
BADPATH	Tells the user that his response is invalid.

Dialog Box	Description
CDALREADYUSED	Warns that this product has been previously installed. This template has two edit fields to place data from the version resource into the dialog box.
CDBADFILE	Same as CDALREADYUSED without the edit fields.
CDBADNAME	Tells the user that a response is required.
CDBADORG	Tells the user that a company name is required.
CDCONFIRMINFO	Displays the company/user name information entered by the user and asks whether the data is correct.
CDGETNAME	Contains an edit field for the user's name.
CDGETNAMEORG	Collects both the user's name and organization.
CDGETORG	Contains an edit field for the user's company name.
CHECK	A simple dialog box with three check boxes.
CUSTINST	Lets the user customize his installation.
DESTPATH	Contains an edit field for the user's destination path choice.
EXITFAILURE	Alerts the user that something bad happened and that the install failed.
EXITQUIT	Similar to the preceding, but this dialog box is displayed in response to the user's wish to exit, instead of a catastrophic failure.
EXITSUCCESS	A dialog box you hope your users always see.
EXTENDEDLIST	Contains a simple multiple column list box.
MODELESS	A sample modeless dialog box for use with the FModelessDlgProc Setup script command. Use these dialog boxes to display messages, such as Now would be a good time to Register, while you are copying files.
MULTILIST	A sample dialog box using a multiple-selection list box.
OPTIONS	A simple option radio button dialog box.
SINGLELIST	Selecting a single item from a list.
TOOBIG	Tells the user that the selected files are too big for their selected drive. You should check for adequate disk space before attempting to install any system.
WELCOME	A dialog box to welcome the user to your installation program.

VI

Appendixes

Each dialog box usually displays your application's icon. Some templates will have from one to four command buttons that allow the user to continue, exit the process, go back to the previous dialog box, or request help.

Using Resource Workshop

You can use Resource Workshop to lay out your dialog boxes, but the Setup Toolkit is an SDK-based product, so you have to make some changes. First, the Toolkit splits the resources into two files, DIALOGS.DLG and DIALOGS.RC. The RC file contains the version information. It also includes the DIALOGS.DLG file as part of the `include` section. To use Resource Workshop, you need to combine the DLG and RC files and then merge the DIALOGS.H files supplied by the Toolkit and created by Resource Workshop.

To customize the procedures for the dialog boxes, you have to modify the DLGPROCS.C file. Chapter 2 of the Setup Toolkit for Windows documentation describes the available functions that are supplied. The Toolkit does not limit you to the specific dialog procedures in DLGPROCS.C because you can add functions as needed to this file, for inclusion into the user interface library. Once all of the procedure modifications are completed, you will have to modify the supplied makefile to reflect the changes made to the various files. This makefile creates a customized user interface library called MSCUISTF.DLL. You can also create user-specific DLLs to perform custom operations for your setup operation.

Step Five—Creating the Setup Scripts

Next you write your setup script file. To help with this process, Microsoft provides three sample script files and their associated information (INF) files. You can modify these files to create your own setup script. We will discuss INF files in more detail later in this appendix.

The first sample script file, SAMPLE1.MST, shows how to set up a simple installation. SAMPLE2.MST illustrates how to set up an application with various options. The final sample, SAMPLE3.MST, details how to set up programs that contain shared files that may require you to shut down Windows and use _MSSETUP to finish your installation process.

Once you've modified the appropriate script file, you need to modify the SETUP.LST file to include your MST file. SETUP.EXE reads this file to determine which files to copy to the user's hard disk.

The Disk Layout Utilities are used to create the INF files for the Setup application. Microsoft suggests that you let these utilities modify the INF files, rather than you trying to do it. The format of an INF file is very strict and may not recover from syntax errors. These INF files state the properties of each application file that is copied to the user's system.

Step Six—Preparing to Create the Disks

Now you need to copy all your files into the directory structure you created. The Disk Layout Utilities then allow you to define each file's special properties. These utilities also create the images you will place on your installation disks. This disk preparation process also creates the INF file for each file of your installing application. These utilities help you specify which files to place on which distribution disk, and which files you can compress to save space.

Step Seven—Testing

Finally, you should test your setup installation by installing the application to a variety of systems under various situations. You can create your distribution disks once you are satisfied with the Setup program.

Creating the Setup Script File

Designing a trouble-free installation process is your primary concern. After the packaging, this is the first impression your users will get of the application. So before you start modifying one of the sample script files, you should ask yourself some questions. You must identify the various parts of the installation process and their associated risks. You can group items of concern into one of two areas: hardware-related or software-related.

Areas of concern include the following:

- Does the user have enough disk space to install your product?

- Will you give the user a choice of which parts to install?

- Does the user need a specific piece of hardware to run your application?

- Will you warn the user or abort the installation if the user's system (hardware or software) is inadequate for the installation?

Other items to be aware of include installing sharable files, installing system files that may require a special exit procedure, and modifying the user's INI files.

VI

Appendixes

Understanding the Setup Script Sections

Once you have a general idea of what your installation program requires, you can write your setup script. You can do it from scratch, but you'll be better off modifying one of the sample scripts included with the Toolkit. Answering the preceding questions will give you a general idea of which sample to modify. Here's a description of each section of a setup script you can modify.

Specifying Include Files

The beginning of each sample contains an INCLUDE section. Here you list the INC files your setup script needs. To specify an INC file, the script line for the Microsoft Test application is as follows:

```
'$INCLUDE 'setupapi.inc'
```

Note the single quotation marks for commands. To mark a line as a comment, you use two single quotes at the beginning of the line:

```
'' This is a comment rather than a command
```

Any string variables used within the script must be enclosed in double quotation marks.

Specifying Constants

You can also specify constants for the resource IDs of each dialog box you intend to use in your program. The constants have the form of CONST *DIALOG* = ID VALUE. For example, the following script line defines a constant called WELCOME that has a value of 1000.

```
CONST WELCOME = 100
```

Initialization and the Symbol Table

In the initialization section, you set the title that appears in the installation window's caption. You can also set the bitmap logo for your program. You initialize any variables you need here, such as strings and integers. To store these variables, the Setup program creates a temporary storage area called a *symbol table*.

Setup automatically creates and initializes three variables when it begins. They are STF_SRCDIR, STF_CWDDIR, and STF_SRCINFPATH. STF_SRCDIR is a string that holds the source directory. STF_CWDDIR holds either the current working directory or the temporary Setup directory. STF_SRCINFPATH holds the path for the INF file. Microsoft recommends you clear all the String Table entries after you use them to conserve memory. The initialization code also reads the INF file to set various variables, as previously described. The code also tells the program which files to copy and whether they need decompressing. The code then sets the needed files' attributes. You can also test prototypes of your DLL functions in this section.

Using Subroutines

After the initialization section of the file, you will find the subroutines to execute your dialog box functions. This section will remind you of a BASIC program. You must preface each procedure with a name followed by a colon, for example, WELCOME :.

The *Install* Subroutine

The Install subroutine, declared in the declaration section as a SUB, is the heart of the install process. In this subroutine you call the various setup script procedures to perform your application's installation. Chapter 5 in the Setup Toolkit for Windows manual details all the setup procedures available to the developer. The samples show you how to add items to the WIN.INI file and how to add groups to Program Manager. You will also see how to add items to program groups. SAMPLE3.MST shows you how to install shared and system files, which can be tricky.

Also make sure you read the supplied README files, because they contain important information left out of the documentation. Especially look over the README.WRI file that contains updates to the Setup Toolkit for Windows manual, detailing the various setup procedures and their parameters.

Specifying Custom Information

One item the samples do not illustrate is how to stamp a program with custom information, such as a company name and user name. The stamping operation allows you to customize version information for the application to be installed. The Knowledge Base article Q92525, "Using the Setup Toolkit Function StampResource()," contains most of this information.

The first step is to include enough empty bytes in your program's resources to hold the strings you plan on adding at install time. The size is up to you, but you must make sure your dialog box limits the users to less than that many characters. Once you have the information, you call the StampResource setup script procedure. The syntax of this command is the following:

```
StampResource szSection$, szKey$, szDst$, wResType%, wResId%,
    szData$, cbData%
```

szSection$ specifies the section in the INF file that contains the description line of the file to be modified, usually your application EXE file. As previously stated, you use the Disk Layout Utilities to create the INF file. The file contains various sections identified by names located between [ ], just like a typical Windows INI file.

The *szKey$* string specifies the reference key to the description line of the file being modified. This is the first item on a line describing the file to be installed. This name is enclosed in quotes. You learn more about the INF file later. The *szDst$* parameter contains the destination directory where the file is currently located—that is, where it has been installed. The *wResType%* specifies the resource identification type. This example uses a String or a resource type, *wResType%*, of 6. Table C.3 lists the possible type values.

Table C.3 Resource ID Types	
wResType%	**Common Resource Name**
1	CURSOR
2	BITMAP
3	ICON
4	MENU
5	DIALOG
6	STRING
7	FONTDIR
8	FONT
9	ACCELERATOR
10	RCDATA
12	GROUP_CURSOR
14	GROUP_ICON
16	VERSION

The *wResId%* parameter specifies the resource ID number and, in the case of string resources, identifies the beginning string table segment. *szData%* contains the data you want to stamp into the resource, and *cbData%* is the size of that data in bytes. If *cbData%* is less than or equal to the original size of the resource segment, StampResource overwrites the data. If *cbData%* is greater than the original size, the function fails.

Specifying Resource Strings

To make life easier, your resource strings should be consecutive in the resource string table. The reason is that StampResource copies bytes and not resources—that is, it does not overwrite a string ID; it overwrites bytes. Also, the resource compiler stores string tables in segments, each containing exactly 16 strings. The resource compiler groups strings with the same upper 12 bits into the same segment. The resource compiler also stores strings with a size value in the first byte followed by the rest of the characters in the string, up to 255 characters.

Not only should your strings be consecutive, but the first string resource ID should be a value where the lower four bits equals 0x00 (for example, 0x4500). This ensures you that it and the following IDs are in the same segment. You usually declare these values in the header file that contains the resource identifiers, but you can also use the Resource Workshop resource editor to place the "modifiable" strings in their own segment. Never place read-only strings in the same segment with modifiable strings.

Stamping the Resource

To write the new strings over the old strings in that segment, fill in *szData$* with the length of each string, followed by the string entered by the user. Make sure to concatenate the strings in the order of their associated IDs. The resulting length of *szData$*, to be placed in *cbData%*, should not exceed the size of the original segment. A piece of sample code is worth a thousand muddled words, so take a look at listing C.1.

VI

Appendixes

Listing C.1   Code to Stamp the Resource

```
// Bound to your application by the resource compiler
IDS_COMPANY_NAME          0x4500    //1st nibble should be 0
IDS_USER_NAME           0x4501    // strings must be consecutive

// Contents of .RC file
STRINGTABLE DISCARDABLE
BEGIN
      // padding! 52
      IDS_COMPANY_NAME       "                              "
      IDS_USER_NAME        "                        "
END
```

(continues)

Listing C.1   Continued

```
// Section of SETUP.MST, Collect strings from user for company
// and name
DEST$ = '' the path to the application's exe.
szUser$ = "Jack Tackett, Jr." ''a value from a dialog box.
szCo$ = "TriStar Systems, Inc." ''usually from a dialog too.
'' build buffer to overwrite the data. remember to place the
'' size of string first.
szBuffer$ = CHR$(LEN(szUser$))+szUser$+CHR$(LEN(szCo$))+szCo$
'' now stamp the resource
'' szSection = "Files", szKey = "gen", szDst = DEST$, wResType = 6,
'' wResId% = &H451
'' H=hex, 45 = 1st 12 bits plus a 1, szData = szbuffer$,
'' cbData= LEN(szbuffer$)
StampResource "Files", "gen", DEST$, 6, &H451, szbuffer$,
      LEN(szbuffer)
```

The Layout Tools

You've heard a lot of talk about the INF file and the layout tools that create it. The INF file describes the files on your installation disks. The format of this file is very rigid, so let the tools create it for you. They will also maintain the INF file throughout your development cycle. Thus, you do not have to create one from scratch every time you add a file or modify a file's attributes. An INF file has a minimum of three sections: Source Media Descriptions, File Descriptions, and Default File Settings.

The Source Media Descriptions section describes each of the disks in your installation set, one line per disk. The File Descriptions section describes each of your files, giving such information as a reference key (the value of the *szKey$* parameter to `StampResource`), file attributes, and whether Setup compressed the file on the disk. If you do not provide default values, the Default File Settings section describes the defaults that Setup uses to install a file. Appendix A of the Setup Toolkit manual describes the layout of the INF file.

The DSKLAYT Disk Layout Tool

You should never have to directly edit the INF file. You use the Windows DSKLAYT program to do this. This program allows you to list the files needed to install your product. This tool also lets you set layout time options, such as where the program can place the file and the file's attributes. You can specify the section and reference key at layout time, too.

DSKLAYT also lets you set install time options. This includes such parameters as indicating whether to back up an existing file before overwriting it.

Once you've created a layout file, you can modify this file later without creating a new one. This allows you to add, delete, or change settings on your installation files. Once you have the files and their properties set, you need to create disk images to copy to disks, and an INF file for your Setup program.

The DSKLAYT2 Disk Layout Tool

Microsoft provides a second program to accomplish the preceding tasks. This program is a DOS-based application that reads the file created by DSKLAYT and creates an image of each disk, which you can copy to floppies for shipment.

From Here...

Projecting a professional image gives your users confidence in your application. Microsoft provides a Toolkit to assist developers in producing robust installation programs. By following the samples provided with the Toolkit and the demo application's Setup program, you can deliver a fantastic first impression to users. Although Borland does not provide a Setup Toolkit of its own, you can use the one provided by Microsoft for Windows developers. Microsoft's Visual Basic also provides a Setup Wizard that is useful to Windows developers, and plenty of commercial and shareware programs create Setup applications.

The Microsoft World Wide Web site at www.microsoft.com provides a generous amount of information for developing professional-looking Windows applications, as well as access to the Microsoft Knowledge Base. You can easily collect information online regarding the Setup Toolkit discussed in this appendix. To access this information, you need to have access to CompuServe and CompuServe's NetLauncher. You can also access the Web through a SLIP service provider.

You can download information from Microsoft, Borland, or other FTP (File Transfer Protocol) sites. FTP access—via CompuServe, America Online, or an Internet service provider—can provide you with information from ftp.microsoft.com.

VI

Appendixes

Index

N

O

P-Q

PLUG YOURSELF INTO...

THE MACMILLAN INFORMATION SUPERLIBRARY™

Free information and vast computer resources from the world's leading computer book publisher—online!

FIND THE BOOKS THAT ARE RIGHT FOR YOU!

A complete online catalog, plus sample chapters and tables of contents give you an in-depth look at *all* of our books, including hard-to-find titles. It's the best way to find the books you need!

● STAY INFORMED with the latest computer industry news through our online newsletter, press releases, and customized Information SuperLibrary Reports.

● GET FAST ANSWERS to your questions about MCP books and software.

● VISIT our online bookstore for the latest information and editions!

● COMMUNICATE with our expert authors through e-mail and conferences.

● DOWNLOAD SOFTWARE from the immense MCP library:
  - Source code and files from MCP books
  - The best shareware, freeware, and demos

● DISCOVER HOT SPOTS on other parts of the Internet.

● WIN BOOKS in ongoing contests and giveaways!

TO PLUG INTO MCP: ➡

GOPHER: gopher.mcp.com

FTP: ftp.mcp.com

WORLD WIDE WEB: **http://www.mcp.com**

How to Install the Disk

The diskette included with *Special Edition Using Turbo C++ 4.5 for Windows* contains the source code for each chapter of the book. You will need at least 3M of free disk space to install the diskette. To install the diskette for this book, just follow these directions:

1. Insert the diskette in your diskette drive (*B*, in this case).

2. Go to the DOS prompt.

3. Type *B:* (where *B* is the letter of your diskette drive).

4. Type **INSTALL** *C:* (where *C* is the letter of your hard drive).

The contents of the diskette will be copied to your hard drive, in the directory C:\SETURBOC.

Licensing Agreement

By opening this package, you are agreeing to be bound by the following:

This software product is copyrighted, and all rights are reserved by the publisher and author. You are licensed to use this software on a single computer. You may copy and/or modify the software as needed to facilitate your use of it on a single computer. Making copies of the software for any other purpose is a violation of the United States copyright laws.

This software is sold *as is* without warranty of any kind, either expressed or implied, including but not limited to the implied warranties of merchantability and fitness for a particular purpose. Neither the publisher nor its dealers or distributors assumes any liability for any alleged or actual damages arising from the use of this program. (Some states do not allow for the exclusion of implied warranties, so the exclusion may not apply to you.)